5/95

9.11 20   3/10

The Romantic Spirit
in German Art
1790–1990

Joseph Beuys
Syringa, 1945
(cat. 226)

The Romantic Spirit
in German Art
1790–1990

Edited by
Keith Hartley
Henry Meyric Hughes, Peter-Klaus Schuster
and William Vaughan

Thames and Hudson

Published on the occasion of the exhibition *The Romantic Spirit in German Art 1790–1990*
at the Royal Scottish Academy and FruitMarket Gallery, Edinburgh, 28 July to 7 September 1994
and at the Hayward Gallery, South Bank Centre, London, 29 September 1994 to 8 January 1995

Translations by David Britt, Michael Robinson and David McLintock

First published in hardcover in Great Britain in 1994 by
Thames and Hudson Ltd, London

First published in hardcover in the United States of America in 1994 by
Thames and Hudson Inc., 500 Fifth Avenue, New York, New York 10110

Text © 1994 National Galleries of Scotland and South Bank Centre
Designed by Herman Lelie
Typeset by Goodfellow & Egan, Cambridge

British Library Cataloguing-in-Publication Data

A catalogue record for this book is available from the British Library

ISBN 0-500-23693-3

Library of Congress Catalog Card Number 94-60293

Printed and bound in Germany

Contents

Art after 1945

Preface

This exhibition has a theme and represents a particular view of German art from the outset. It is addressed to audiences who lack close familiarity with the work of many of the great artists who have been included. In Germany itself, Romanticism is a topic still capable of arousing intense controversy since it has, from the beginning, been tied up with questions of national identity and suffered from the ideological contamination by the Nazis of German idealist philosophy. A number of our close collaborators impressed on us the impossibility of mounting such a project in Germany itself and it is a measure of our temerity, perhaps, and of our dependence on the advice of those same collaborators, that we have been able to press ahead with our plans.

The exhibition presents a sequence of visual arguments, ideas and comparisons, which is intended to be self-sustaining but which is supplemented and amplified by the material in the catalogue. Edinburgh should provide an interesting set of references for the exhibition on the first part of its tour, through the associations with Ossianic myth, northern landscape, yearning for the classical south and medievalising historicism à la Walter Scott. In London, the exhibition will be fully integrated into the South Bank's festival of 'Deutsche Romantik', spanning two hundred years of film, literary, musical and artistic creation and spread between the National Film Theatre, the Royal Festival Hall, the Queen Elizabeth Hall, the Purcell Room and the Hayward Gallery. The setting provided by the third and final venue, at the Haus der Kunst in Munich, will lend piquancy to the theme, since it was here, in the building designed by Ludwig Troost, that the Nazi régime celebrated its short-lived existence at the *Grosse Deutsche Kunstausstellungen*, from 1937–1944; here, too, that Joseph Beuys personally supervised the installation of the largest version of his seminal work, 'The End of the Twentieth Century'.

We are most grateful to the former German Ambassador, His Excellency Baron Hermann von Richthofen and his successor, His Excellency Dr Peter Hartmann, for lending enthusiastic support to Lord Weidenfeld's original concept of a festival and securing the full backing of the German Federal Government in Bonn and the Goethe Institut in Munich, Glasgow and London. Baron von Richthofen was instrumental in facilitating the invaluable link to the Stiftung Preussischer Kulturbesitz in Berlin, and its President, Professor Dr Werner Knopp and Director General, Professor Dr Wolf Dieter Dube, for whose support we should like here to record our warm appreciation.

We were fortunate from the outset to be able to count on the priceless collaboration of the National-galerie in Berlin and, in particular, its Director, Professor Dr Dieter Honisch, and former Chief Curator, Professor Dr Peter-Klaus Schuster, who has now become Director of the Alte Nationalgalerie in Berlin. In addition to the above, we have enjoyed an especially close collaboration with three other cities in Germany, which own particularly rich holdings of work by some of the principal artists in the exhibition: in Dresden, we should like to thank Professor Dr Werner Schmidt, Director General of the Dresden State Art Collections and his colleagues; in Hamburg, Professor Dr Uwe Schneede, Director of the Hamburger Kunsthalle, and his colleagues; and in Munich, Dr Johann Georg Prinz von Hohenzollern, Director General of the Bavarian State Art Collections, Dr Tilman Falk, Director of the State Graphic Collection and Dr Helmut Friedel, Director of the Municipal Art Gallery at the Lenbachhaus, respectively and their colleagues.

The exhibition has been curated jointly by Keith Hartley, Assistant Keeper at the Scottish National Gallery of Modern Art in Edinburgh, whose idea it was to look at the development of Romantic themes through two centuries of German art and who had special responsibility for the twentieth century, and Professor William Vaughan, Professor of History of Art at Birkbeck College, University of London, who had special responsibility for the nineteenth century. In addition, Henry Meyric Hughes and Peter-Klaus Schuster have provided constant advice and assistance. All four formed the editorial board of the catalogue, with Keith Hartley acting as editor-in-chief. We owe a special debt of gratitude to Mr Hartley, for taking the overall lead and editing the catalogue, and to the team in Edinburgh for undertaking the loan and transport negotiations. They have been most ably supported by a large team of helpers and advisors, many of whom have written essays for the catalogue. The names of many of those involved have been listed below, but we should like, in particular, to acknowledge the important advisory role played by the following: Dr Lutz Becker, Richard Calvocoressi, Dr Christoph Heilmann, Dr Wulf Herzogenrath, Professor Dr Werner Hofmann, Dr Wolfgang Holler, Dr Claude Keisch, Dr Roland März, Dr Michael Semff, Dr Angela Schneider, Dr Carla Schulz-Hoffmann, and Professor Dr Jörg Traeger.

Many lenders have made this exhibition possible through their exceptional generosity and we are deeply indebted to them all for allowing us to borrow these works for a considerable period. A full list of institutional and private lenders is given at the back of the catalogue, but we should like to single out for special attention the Stiftung Preußischer Kulturbesitz in Berlin, which has provided a group of key works of early Romanticism from the 'Galerie der Romantik' at Schloss Charlottenburg, for the duration of the exhibition. The State Graphic Collection in Munich has generously lent Edinburgh and London nine each of Franz Marc's precious Drawings from the Front (on view for the first six weeks only of the London showing). Special thanks are due to the collector Heiner Bastian for agreeing to lend a selection of forty drawings by Joseph Beuys.

We are particularly fortunate to have secured the active participation of four contemporary artists – Georg Baselitz, Anselm Kiefer, Sigmar Polke and Gerhard Richter – in the selection of work for this exhibition. Their presence is fundamental to the concept of the exhibition and we should like to thank them for their understanding and collaboration. We should also like to record our warm thanks to Anthony and Anne d'Offay and Helen van der Meij, respectively, for facilitating the loan of works by Anselm Kiefer and Sigmar Polke.

A project of this magnitude would not have been possible without the collaboration of numerous institutions in Germany and scholars and curators, including all those who contributed to the catalogue or in other ways, through their knowledge and experience.

The catalogue with its contributions by 40 authors, two thirds of them of German-speaking origin, bears eloquent testimony to the degree of mutuality involved. We are confident that it will not only elucidate the theme of the exhibition, but make an enduring contribution to scholarship. We should like, therefore, to record our thanks to all the individual authors listed at the back of the catalogue. We should like, in addition, to thank Uwe Kraus and Martina Rudat, of Oktagon Verlag, Stuttgart and the catalogue designer, Herman Lelie, for their patience and determination in seeing this ambitious publication through, from inception to production; David Etheridge, Sarah Bluff and Gordon Theobald at Goodfellow & Egan; also David Britt, who undertook the main burden of translating the texts into English, along with Michael Robinson and Dr David McLintock, and Dr Marion Keiner, who compiled the bibliography and artsts' biographies, as well as editing the German texts.

The Embassy of the Federal Republic of Germany in London has devoted a great deal of energy and resources to the Festival, for which we would like to express our warmest appreciation. In addition to the Ambassadors, past and present, we are grateful to Dr Reinhart Ehni, Head of the Cultural Department, assisted by Herr Stephan Auer, First Secretary; and Herr Friedrich Gröning, Head of the Press Department. We also wish most warmly to thank the Goethe-Institut in London for its enthusiastic support, in particular, its Director, Dr Elmar Brandt; Helga Wilderotter-Ikonomou, Head of the Programme Department and her predecessor, Dr Karin Herrmann. Nicholas Elam, former Head of Cultural Relations at the Foreign and Commonwealth Office, also gave valuable advice.

We are also grateful to the following: Frau van Aalst; Susanne Abegg; Dr Sigrid Achenbach; Colin Bailey; Dr Eduard Beaucamp; Miss Beston (Marlborough Fine Art Ltd, London); Peter Bissegger; Dr Ulrich Bischoff; Dr Eugen Blume; Dr Dieter Bock; Michael Clarke; Professor Gordon A Craig; Robert Dalrymple; Jan Debbaut; Sophie Dord (Lyon); Northild Eger; David Elliott; W. A. Fairhurst & Partners (floor loadings); Anthony Fawcett; Jutta and Wolfgang Fischer; Michaela Giebelhausen;

Detlev Gretenkort; Galerie Gunzenhauser, Munich; Catherine Grout; Dr Joseph Helfenstein; Wolfgang and Ingeborg Henze-Ketterer; Dr Julian Heynen; Dr Hanna Hohl; Dr Wenzel Jacob; Dr Annegret Janda; Dr Jensen; Alan Jones; Erhard Klein; Professor Dr Kaspar König; Walther König; Andrea Krenn (Vienna); Harriet Macandrew; Neil McGregor; Achim Moeller; Dr Paul Müller (Zurich); Wout Nierhoff (Cologne); Andrew Newton; Dr Norbert Nobis; Lorcan O'Neill; Keith Patrick; Rainer Pfefferkorn; Nicole Pohl; Elfreda Powell; Dr Gottfried Riemann; Professor Robert Rosenblum; Dr Martijn Sanders; Dr Gisela Scheffler; Raman Schlemmer; Professor Bernard Schultze; Dr Dieter Schwarz; Dr Hinrich Sieveking; Nikos Stangos; John Sunderland; Robin Vousden; Mr and Mrs Fritz Zapletal; Dr Zimmermann.

On the organisational side, we are grateful, in Edinburgh, to Margaret Mackay, for coordinating the transport and indemnity for the tour and Alice O'Connor, for providing such an efficient and indispensable office back-up; and in London, to Susan May, as the exhibition organiser at the Hayward Gallery with overall responsibility for liaison and coordination at the London end, and to Greg Hilty, Senior Curator at the Hayward Gallery for his help with the installation. The National Galleries of Scotland would like to thank The FruitMarket Gallery (Graeme Murray, Director, Ken Cockburn, Trevor Cromie, Angela Wrapson, Juliet Knight, Sarah Knox and Caroline Neill) and also the Royal Scottish Academy (William Baillie, President, Alan Mathewson, Administrative Secretary, and his predecessor William Meikle) for allowing the exhibition to be held in their galleries.

We should also like to thank all our colleagues and associates in Edinburgh and London who have assisted in one aspect or other of the organisation. In Edinburgh: Janis Adams; Lindsey Callander; Michael Cassin; Jean Denver; Giselle Dye; Patrick Elliott; Peter Fotheringham; Sheila Innes; Victoria Keller; Philip Long; Keith Morrison; Ann Simpson; and Dianne Stein; and in London: Achim Borchardt; Tom Buckley; Tania Butler; Debbi Christophers; Andrew Edwards; Susan Ferleger Brades; Kelly Gerrard; Keith Hardy; Claire Hyde and Nigel Semmens; Mike McCart; Sadie McKinlay; Alison Rowe; Linda Schofield; Graham Sheffield; Kevin Teahan; Jenny Waldman; Jeff Watson; and Penny Wood. In Edinburgh, Lee Boyd Partnership designed the exhibition and Robert Dalrymple was responsible for the exhibition graphics. In London, Paul Williams and Michael Langley, of Stanton Williams Architects, have been responsible for the design of the exhibition, John Johnson and his team for the lighting; and Isabel Ryan for the design of the exhibition graphics.

We should like to thank Nicholas Kenyon and his colleagues, Brian Barfield and Judith Bumpus, for arranging an exciting series of broadcast talks to coincide with the exhibition and the 'Deutsche Romantik' festival in London, on the South Bank. We should also like to thank the British Film Institute, its Director, Wilf Stevenson, and his colleagues, Mark Adams and Ian Christie, for organising a season of film at the time of 'Deutsche Romantik'.

We gratefully acknowledge the help of Kenneth McKenna and Carol Hobley, for securing the indemnification of the exhibition for the Edinburgh showing from the Scottish Office and for the London showing from the Department of National Heritage.

The National Galleries of Scotland wish to express their warm appreciation to the following: their principal sponsors, Beck's (Scottish & Newcastle Breweries); supported by, Morgan Grenfell (Scotland) Ltd., and The European Commission, Edinburgh; with assistance from The Caledonian Hotel, Edinburgh; Craig & Rose plc; Lufthansa; and MoMart.

The South Bank Centre would like to express its warm appreciation to the sponsors of the *Deutsche Romantik* festival: Deutsche Bank, Siemens, Urenco, Daimler Benz, Deminex UK Oil and Gas Ltd, GKN and Lufthansa. We are also grateful to Metallgesellschaft Ltd and Robert Bosch Ltd for their support.

Finally, we wish to express our thanks to Herr Christoph Vitali, the new Director of the Haus der Kunst in Munich, for the enthusiasm with which he accepted our proposal of a third and final showing of this exhibition in Germany, in the handsomely restored east wing of this building.

Timothy Clifford   Henry Meyric Hughes
Director   Director of Exhibitions
National Galleries of Scotland   South Bank Centre

Introduction

The reunification of Germany after four decades of partition in two ideologically opposed countries has had the effect of allowing older questions to rise up the political and intellectual agenda, questions that seemed nugatory not to say taboo in the years before. Above all the often painful merging of two parts of one nation has focused attention on the question of what exactly one means by the German nation, indeed by the term 'German'. Are there unifying characteristics over and above the fact of a common language (which after all is shared with Austria and parts of Switzerland)?

These are questions which have of course been raised before and never so sharply as during the early years of the nineteenth century when Napoleon occupied Germany and when he was eventually defeated in what the Germans call the Wars of Liberation. The tottering structure of the Holy Roman Empire, which had held together a huge number of small states, principalities, and church lands mainly, but not only, in German-speaking Central Europe, had been ended by Napoleon's victories. A new German nation began to evolve, at least in people's hearts and minds, as they looked forward to the end of French occupation and backwards to the Middle Ages and Renaissance when Germany had been united and a powerful indigenous culture had flourished. Patriots took to wearing the *altdeutsch* (old German) coat and floppy hat to indicate their allegiance to a national and cultural cause, as can be seen in the three soldiers pictured in Georg Friedrich Kersting's painting (colour plate, p.248) They saw themselves as German first and foremost, proud of their heritage and of their own individual culture.

Political opposition to France gave an added impetus to such feelings, but in point of fact they go back before 1800 to the *Sturm und Drang* (Storm and Stress) period in the 1770s, when, for example, Johann Wolfgang von Goethe began to admire what he took to be the strong, raw German qualities of Gothic architecture, as exemplified by Strasbourg Cathedral. In opposition to a debased classicism borrowed from the French, Goethe praised a German art that was concerned above all with truth to inner feelings rather than to externally imposed rules about beauty and proportion. Although Goethe was later to change his mind about the relative merits of Gothic and Classical, such polemical writings, together with others by Johann Gottfried Herder and Johann Georg Hamann, ushered in a change of mood in the arts in Germany: this gave pride of place to truth to self, to national characteristics, to Nature and to the divine spirit speaking within. What had been a turbulent movement of protest and rebellion in *Sturm und Drang* became in the Romantic period itself much more complex and multi-faceted, sometimes highly philosophical, sometimes (particularly later on) distinctly populist, sometimes medievalising (seeking its utopias in the Golden Age of Albrecht Dürer), sometimes deeply religious, seeking Salvation by deciphering the Divine presence in Nature. German Romantic art had no unifying style: it drew on both Classical and late Medieval/early Renaissance models; its themes varied from fairy tales, through symbolic or empirically observed landscapes to penetrating portraits. It is perhaps better not to seek one single unifying element that would characterise Romanticism as a whole. Numerous writers in the past have tried and largely failed. Perhaps Arthur Lovejoy got closest when he talked about a series of interlinked Romanticisms rather than a monolithic Romanticism.

When in this exhibition and catalogue we talk about the Romantic Spirit we do so in the knowledge that it is perhaps not unitary and that it is largely undefinable. What we have done instead is to look at a series of themes and concepts that go together to make up the movement as a whole. These go under the main rubrics of Nature, Man and History and deal specifically with ideas such as the divine spirit in Nature, the unity of the cosmos, man's (and more specifically the artist's) ultimate loneliness and subsequent longing for fellowship and community with like-minded individuals, the loss of innocence and consequent longing to regain the wholeness of Paradise, and utopias of the past.

The exhibition is not however simply about the Romantic period itself but about the relevance of German Romanticism for the development of German art over the past two centuries. It seeks to show that many of the roots of what has come to be called Modernism go back to the Romantic period: indeed, that in many respects Modernism could be said to begin around 1800 rather than 1900. This is not a new idea. Many writers and critics have seen the Romantic period as a watershed in Western art: a time when the old forms of patronage by church and crown broke down and forced artists to earn a living in the newly emerging marketplace provided by the middle classes. The old certainties of prescribed subject matter and style gave way to more subtle influences, but ultimately it was now the artist who could decide what and how he was going to paint. This new individuality was strengthened by the Copernican revolution that Kant and subsequent Romantic philosophers brought about in our understanding of the relationship of the self to Nature in general. A new subjectivity ensued that posited the primacy of individual perception and imagination.

The exhibition argues that we are in many ways still living in that same age of subjective individualism, even if the exhilarating sense of freedom and personal discovery around 1800 has turned into today's mixtures of ironic cynicism and almost joyful nihilism. Only rarely, as in the work of Joseph Beuys, do we find a genuine sense of utopian hope and missionary zeal.

Although Romanticism was a thoroughly international movement that had its roots in such diverse writers as Jean-Jacques Rousseau, James Macpherson (the 'translator' of the poetry of Ossian) and Bishop Percy ('Reliques of Ancient English Poetry') and in the spreading popularity of the English Landscape Garden, and although there have been attempts to trace the impact of Romanticism on the development of Modernism as a whole – notably by Robert Rosenblum in his groundbreaking book 'Modern Painting and the Northern Romantic Tradition: Friedrich to Rothko' (1975) – it seemed to the organisers of this exhibition that it was in Germany above all that Romanticism took a particularly deep hold of the popular as well as the artistic imagination; that is was in Germany that twentieth-century artists took such direct inspiration from Romantic art

and ideas, often making specific references in their works and journals. As has been pointed out, it was also in Germany that Romanticism became closely linked to perceptions of national characteristics. This has had both beneficial and disastrous consequences. Beneficial in such a movement as Expressionism, when artists sought to define their own individuality vis-à-vis French art to which they owed so much formal innovation. Disastrous in the Nazi period when Romanticism became part of a narrowly defined and distorted concept of German tradition This link with national characteristics has made Romanticism highly suspect to many postwar artists. It became practically synonymous for them with the unthinking irrationalism of Nazi ideology which placed feeling and intuition above reasoned analysis and moral enlightenment. It is one of Joseph Beuys's great contributions to postwar art that he could help rescue Romanticism from this ideological pigeon-hole and enable other artists to consider its positive aspects: its utopian fervour, its richness of intellectual and emotional resonance, its openendedness.

The exhibition has been divided into five sections which correspond to those periods when Romanticism was a force for positive (or negative) change in German art. The first is devoted to Romanticism itself, including also *Sturm und Drang* and a few late Romantics. However, the emphasis is on its two main elements, namely, the North German (landscape) artists, such as Caspar David Friedrich and Philipp Otto Runge, and the Nazarenes, who were centred on Rome, Munich and Vienna and who concentrated largely on religious or medievalising narrative art. It is in this large section that the main themes and concepts mentioned above and that recur throughout the exhibition are established.

After 1830 Romanticism began to lose much of its initial momentum and clarity of conception. New movements, Realism in particular, came along and led not only to a decline in interest in Romanticism but, in the cases of Friedrich and Runge, to an almost total neglect.

Towards the end of the century, however, there was a renewed interest in Germany in Romantic themes and ideas. In part this was in response to the emergence of the Symbolist movement in France, which in turn owed much to German Romantic theory, but it also grew out of a continuing fascination among German artists with

Italy and the South. These *Deutsch-Römer* (German-Romans), as they became known, continued to deal with such themes as longing, the loss of Paradise or the Golden Age. A small section is therefore devoted to the *Deutsch-Römer* (including Arnold Böcklin, Anselm Feuerbach and Hans von Marees) and Symbolists (such as Ferdinand Holder and Max Klinger). Although two of these artists (Böcklin and Hodler) are Swiss, it was felt that they were such an integral part of the German art world, and seen as such by their contemporaries, that their inclusion would not strain too far what is inevitably an elastic definition of 'German'. However, even though Edvard Munch spent much of his formative and crucial years in Germany, and played a pivotal role in relaying such key Romantic themes as innocence and burgeoning self-awareness to the Expressionist generation – notably the *Brücke* artists – the organisers felt that he always remained an outsider and belonged more to a Northern, Scandinavian tradition, rather than to a specifically German one.

The arrival of Modernism proper in the first three decades of this century owed as much to Romantic notions of cosmic unity, inner necessity and primordial nature as it did to the formal inventions of French Post-Impressionism, Fauvism and Cubism and of Italian Futurism. This rediscovery of Romantic artists and writers was undoubtedly spurred on by the success of Symbolism but it also owed a great deal to the so-called *Jahrhundertausstellung* (Century Exhibition of German Art from 1775 to 1875). Friedrich and Runge had been practically forgotten until the 1890s when such enlightened museum directors as Alfred Lichtwark in Hamburg and Hugo von Tschudi in Berlin began to recognise their signal importance. It was Lichtwark and Tschudi who gave them and other Romantic artists pride of place in the *Jahrhundertausstellung* and thus set in train a rediscovery in the form of books, articles and other exhibitions. It is not coincidental that Romantic writers and philosophers also began to receive proper scholarly attention at that time. This provided a major stimulus to such *Blaue Reiter* artists as Wassily Kandinsky and Franz Marc in their search for spiritual renewal after what they perceived to be the materialistic wasteland of the late nineteenth century. As well as the *Blaue Reiter* and the *Brücke*, the Modernist section also looks at the

Bauhaus and the artists who taught there. It was in the Bauhaus that the concept of a community of artists, pledged to reform art and design, art teaching and, ultimately, society, a utopian ideal which was inspired in part by the Nazarenes and had been present, at least *in nuce*, in both the *Brücke* and *Blaue Reiter* groups, found its fulfilment.

Alongside this utopian strain in Modernist art in Germany went a more sceptical, ironic approach, likewise owing a certain debt to Romanticism, in this case to the Romantic taste for the grotesque, black humour and Romantic irony. Paul Klee's constant use of humour and irony to cut his flights of fancy down to size is here paradigmatic, but it is also present in Schwitters's *MERZ* works, particularly his masterpiece, the Hanover *MERZbau*, alas destroyed in the last war, but since reconstructed and shown in this exhibition.

The impact of the revival of interest in Romantic art in the 1920s is nowhere more clearly to be seen than in the paintings of those artists belonging to the realist movements dubbed at the time Neo-Romanticism and *Neue Sachlichkeit*. Otto Dix, Georg Schrimpf and Franz Radziwill are all represented by important works and in the case of Dix and Radziwill the exhibition also shows works that they made during the Third Reich. They form part of a small section devoted not only to artists whose work was in tune with Nazi ideology and its trivialised and debased concept of Romanticism, but to artists, like Dix and Radziwill, who, while opposed to Nazism, nevertheless had to adapt their style and subject matter – mainly landscapes – so that is was at least not in conflict with it. One can thus see that there is not a strict dividing line between Neo-Romantic and *Neue Sachlichkeit* art on the one hand and some types of Nazi art on the other.

The last section is devoted to the postwar period as a whole. It begins with those abstract artists in the Federal Republic (Wols, Ernst Wilhelm Nay, Fritz Winter, Willi Baumeister, Bernard Schultze) who continued the Romantic tradition of pre-war Modernism, attempting a return to beginnings, both mythical and natural. It also includes the Zero artists (Heinz Mack, Günther Uecker and Otto Piene), whose utopian dreams were built on the *tabula rasa*. In the German Democratic Republic the dominant aesthetic doctrine of Socialist Realism precluded anything more than a superficial engagement with

Romanticism, But artists such as Gerhard Altenbourg and Hermann Glöckner went against the official grain, working for much of the time in lonely isolation. Altenbourg continued the tradition of a deeply personal, poetic fantasy in delicate watercolours and drawings; Glöckner, building on his work of the early 1930s, created abstract panels of simple, often geometrical shapes that emanate a magical significance.

A major break in German postwar art was effected by Joseph Beuys. Not only did his 'extended concept of art' break the bounds of traditional painting and sculpture, blurring the distinctions between art and life, but he was bold enough in his art to treat themes, such as the non-rational side of man's nature, which were central to Romanticism, but which had been tainted by Nazi ideology. Beuys helped re-open German art to this important source of inspiration. He was followed down this path by a number of artists, most notably Anselm Kiefer. By first exploring the myths and realities of an often bloody national history Kiefer has been able to broaden out his focus to encompass the importance of myth to all cultures, of all times.

By the late 1950s much of the abstract art in Germany had become shallow, abitrary and anonymously international. If Beuys helped break its hold by opening up new areas for art to explore and new ways in which to explore them, Georg Baselitz gave a new and urgent impetus to painting. Eschewing both *tachiste* abstraction and literal-minded realism, Baselitz developed a form of aggressive, regressive, 'outsider' painting that was deliberately anti-avant-garde, in the sense that it denied the Modernist utopian notion of progress towards a future goal. Like the Nazarenes and other German Romantic artists it looked back to previous developments as a way forward. It is no coincidence that two of his 'hero paintings', in which he dramatises his own lonely, outsider position as a painter, bear in their titles the names of two German Romantic artists (Franz Pforr and Ludwig Richter).

This return to painting, indeed to a type of painting that made no rigid distinctions between figurative and non-figurative art, was not confined to Baselitz. Gerhard Richter and Sigmar Polke moved in the same direction. Richter painted and continues to paint landscapes, still-lifes and portraits alongside his abstract works. Some of these landscapes (painted after photographs) are conven-

tionally beautiful, derived, as Richter himself admits, from Romantic models. They represent 'a type of yearning for a whole and simple life. A little nostalgic'. Even some of the abstract paintings are evocative of natural phenomena, such as forests. But Richter is no unreconstructed Romantic. While one side of him acknowledges the warm comfort of Romantic nostalgia, another recognises that this is not an option that he can legitimately embrace. The emphasis that he places on the process and materiality of painting, on the means of the paintings' own production, on their openess to multiple interpretation, contains within it an implied criticism of the closed mentality of a backward-looking aesthetic.

Polke makes the discrepancies between different aesthetics and different styles into the very stuff of his paintings. A rich irony pervades the many layers of his paintings; it recalls the continuous fluctuation between self-creation and self-annihilation, 'the clear consciousness of an eternal agility, of an infinitely abundant chaos' of Romantic irony, as defined by Friedrich Schlegel.

This exhibition does not set out to show that Romanticism is a quintessentially German movement, nor that it is a mindset that continually recurs in German art and life, even prior to the historical movement itself. There may be some truth in these positions – they have been asserted often enough in the past – but that is the realm of speculation. Wherever possible the exhibition has preferred to stick to facts, specific references rather than spiritual affinities. By no means all engagements with Romantic ideas have been naively accepting and uncritical. Many modern artists have seen the dangers of an over-reliance on emotion and intuition; they have distrusted mysticism and have shunned links with nationalism. That is why some have been drawn to the grotesque, fantastic elements in Romanticism, why Romantic irony is a major source of inspiration and why other artists have emphasised its constructive, rational and quasi-scientific, observational aspects. In fact, we hope to show that Romanticism is much richer, much more differentiated than its popular image suggests. So rich, indeed, that it is still able to inspire artists today who, for all their apparent dissimilarities of style and approach, share a common engagement with the ideas of the early Romantics.

Keith Hartley

Romanticism
and German Art

Essays

Philipp Otto Runge
Construction of a Cornflower, 1808–09
(cat. 10)

Play and Earnest:
Goethe and the Art of His Day

1.

Johann Wolfgang von Goethe's judgment of the art and artists of his day is not all of a piece. It combines multiple viewpoints: that of the amateur, connoisseur and collector, but also that of the theorist and historian of art. Above all, his judgment springs from a subjective involvement that is possible only for someone who feels himself to be an artist. Its psychological roots lie in the structure of his own creativity. 'The eye, above all, was the organ with which I laid hold of the world,' he recalls in Book 6 of his literary self-portrait, *Dichtung und Wahrheit* ('Poetry and Truth'). A few lines further on, we read: 'Wherever I looked, I saw a picture.' Goethe relied on this eidetic faculty all his life; it was the source both of his metamorphic theory of the *Urpflanze* or archetypal plant – form as variable – and also of his personal *gestalt* concept, based on 'inner necessity': form as definition.

Goethe's visual experiences – if we leave the vast realms of organic and inorganic Nature to one side, and confine ourselves to those that concern art – run through a number of phases. They belong to many 'departments of art', sublime and trivial, present and past. They oscillate between open-minded receptivity and allegiance to preordained norms. So the concrete results of those varied experiences – Goethe's critical verdicts on art, as recorded in essays and reviews – reveal both doctrinaire narrowness and open-minded tolerance, astonishing critical blindness and equally startling insights and prophecies.

It is quite possible that Goethe's more partisan utterances serve to mask his own 'uncertainty of judgment', a condition of which he was well aware. They seem, in any case, to operate on more than one level at a time: they hint, in fact, at the presence of inner conflicts. It is important to recognize this two-way relationship. In later life, he no longer saw the Gothic of Strasbourg cathedral (as he did in 1772, when he wrote his essay 'Von deutscher Baukunst', ['On German Architecture']) as the product of a single sensation, a 'characteristic whole': he had come to see it as the product of the union of 'contradictory elements', namely the sublime and the ingratiating, in which the interaction of these 'two irreconcilable qualities' prevented the 'monstrous' quality of the building from alarming or perplexing the observer.

In 1823 – half a century after the fiery patriotism of his hymn of praise for Strasbourg cathedral – Goethe described how Andrea Mantegna's *Triumph of Caesar* embodies a dichotomy of a different kind: the clash between Nature and the Ideal. He attributed Mantegna's inability 'to achieve a total union of the opposites' to the fact that he was evolving in both directions at once. Goethe saw this 'incompletely resolved opposition' as the 'greatest conflict in which an artist has ever found himself'. Five years later still, in 1828, the aged Goethe referred once more to an artist who combined opposites within himself. This time it was a contemporary, Eugène Delacroix, who had shown the poet his lithographic illustrations to *Faust*. The old gentleman's verdict was couched in laudatory if somewhat convoluted terms: 'Mr Delacroix seems to have felt entirely in his element in a strange amalgam between heaven and earth, possible and impossible, crude and delicate – and between whatever other contrary extremes the imagination might choose to disport itself.'

The value of this judgment was somewhat compromised, not long afterwards, when Goethe mentioned the *Faust* illustrations of one Ludwig Nauwerk in the same breath as those of Delacroix, Peter von Cornelius and Friedrich August Retzsch.

To capture the dichotomy in the art of Mantegna, Goethe added a new word to the German language: *Doppelleben*, 'dual life'. It was a word that expressed something within himself. In *Dichtung und Wahrheit* he described himself as someone 'whose nature constantly tossed him from one extreme to the other'. With this inner chaos evidently in mind, he likened his own work to a Tower of Babel; on another occasion, he presented it as the 'fragments of a great confession': that is to say, not an organic whole, but a patchwork. He described his own purpose in writing *Dichtung und Wahrheit* as that of 'making these fragments complete'. Does not this mean that he cared more for autobiographical truth than for the artistic truth of his work?

Goethe was always finding objective correlatives for his own awareness of his contradictory nature. In the drama *Clavigo* (1774), he appears both as the eponymous, gifted young writer and as Carlos, his opportunistic corrupter; in *Torquato Tasso* (1790), he is both the tormented, self-doubting poet and his antithesis, Chancellor Antonio Montecatino. Finally, Faust lives out the alternative, complementary aspect of his own 'dual life' in and through the figure of Mephistopheles.

This same polarizing dichotomy marked Goethe's analytical approach to works of art. In the process, his systematic habits of thought tended to thwart him and to force his native, eidetic spontaneity into pigeon-holes of speculative thought. Thus, the anti-Newtonian approach of his *Farbenlehre* ('Theory of Colour') derived from premises first stated in the introduction to the periodical *Propyläen* in 1798: 'Perhaps confirmation will be found for the supposition that in Nature the effects of colour – like others, such as those of magnetism and electricity – rest on an reciprocal relationship, a polarity, or whatever one may choose to call the manifestations of duality and even of plurality within a well-defined unity.'

Precisely because his ready intuition gave him insight into a multitude of stylistic possibilities, Goethe felt the impulse to categorize them. He did so most succinctly in the short essay 'Einfache Nachahmung der Natur, Manier, Stil' ('Simple Imitation of Nature; Manner; Style', 1789), using a three-level schema that he was to elaborate ten years later in an epistolary treatise, 'Der Sammler und die Seinigen' ('The Collector and His Friends'). In the 1789 essay, Goethe divided the artist's available expressive options into three levels, each with its own, specific expressive range. Simple Imitation is suited to simple, 'limited objects', and may well produce works of 'eminent perfection'. The artist of Manner does not speak the language of Nature: 'he invents a way for himself, makes a language of his own, in order to express in his own way what he has grasped with his soul.' Manner permits subjective choice; and consequently 'every artist of this kind will see, grasp and reproduce the world differently.' As we shall see, this is

Fig. 1 Johann Wolfgang von Goethe, *The Grave of Theron in Agrigento*, Stiftung Weimarer Klassik

a licence that Goethe is prepared to extend to his own contemporaries, such as Philipp Otto Runge and Caspar David Friedrich. He is at some pains to absolve himself from the suspicion that he regards Manner as something inferior: on the contrary, he means the word to be understood 'in an elevated and respectable sense'. The highest degree of artistic endeavour is that of Style, which is based 'on the deepest foundations of awareness: on the essence of things, insofar as we are permitted to know this through visible and tangible forms'.

The letters that compose 'Der Sammler und die Seinigen' (in *Propyläen*, 1799) elaborate this hierarchical structure, based on the philosophical theory of modes, into something like a taxonomy of artistic characteristics. Goethe invents six categories, each of which is defined by exclusivity and lack of balance. However, these categories do not constitute a catalogue of 'faults': each simply reflects an exclusive concentration on a single mode. 'My six classes', Goethe writes, 'refer to the qualities which, assembled together, would amount to the true artist, and also the true lover of art.' They are as follows: Imitators (*Nachahmer*); Fantasists (*Imaginanten* or *Phantomisten*); Characterists (*Charakteristiker*); Undulists (*Undulisten*, 'those who love the soft, the agreeable, without character or meaning'); Minute Artists (*Kleinkünstler*); and Sketchers (*Skizzisten*).

These categories spring from Goethe's own experience of art and from his practical work as a draughtsman. Beginning as an assiduous Imitator, he then – on the authority of the older works of art in his grandfather's collection – permitted himself the liberties taken by the

Sketchers. Naming no names, he gives vent to his enthusiasm: 'All that had been boldly dashed down, all that was wildly washed in, all that was violent delighted me; I could decipher, and prized excessively, even the hieroglyph of a figure, drawn in a few strokes.'

This reads like a description of his own *Faust* drawings, but it also applies to some of his landscapes (figs. 1 and 2). However, the sketch as a level or mode of discourse satisfied Goethe the collector as little as it did Goethe the draughtsman. He wanted to proceed from brilliant sketch to brilliant execution. But wherever he confined his talent to what he called the 'most definite line', he all too often grew dry and pedantic – as in his own theory of art!

'Der Sammler und die Seinigen' develops a morphology of art through a fictional exchange of letters. In the last letter in the series, the six 'extremes' are linked in three different ways, thus pointing the way to 'True Art'. The six fall into two groups of three, assigned respectively to PLAY and EARNEST. Where all six intersect, the result is STYLE, the sum of the reconciled opposites. Style is thus a product of synthesis; 'dual life' is an intrinsic part of it. Goethe's correspondences may be set out diagrammatically as follows:

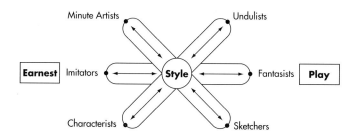

One would like to see Goethe attach artists' names to the possible permutations of this formal topography, but he takes good care to do nothing of the sort. Only one name is mentioned: that of Henry Fuseli (Johann Heinrich Füssli). Fuseli's 'elfin, airy images' are described as strange, witty and wonderful. As they depict a welter of dreams, Fuseli is clearly one of the Fantasists (*Imaginanten*, *Phantomisten*).

Goethe never met Fuseli, but came across his drawings (fig. 3) through Johann Kaspar Lavater. He summarized

Fig. 2 Johann Wolfgang von Goethe, *The Appearance of the Earth Spirit* ('Erdgeist') from *Faust*, Stiftung Weimarer Klassik

his verdict in a note on 9 August 1797: 'Mannered in everything, especially the anatomy, and consequently also the postures.' Fuseli's other salient characteristic, his tendency to juxtapose fantastic, tragic and humorous subjects – his Shakespearean side – did not meet with Goethe's approval. His *alter ego* balked at it, denying the draughtsman the privilege reserved for the poet: that of appealing to the viewer's imagination. Goethe was guilty of a surprising misjudgment of Fuseli's true nature when he contemplated engaging this Anglicized Swiss to design a commemoration of his own second Swiss Journey (1779–80). He wrote to Lavater that his head was full of 'all kinds of ideas and images' for this, and asked that Fuseli should contribute some more out of his own 'immense store'. Fortunately, this hybrid confection – Pelion piled on Ossa – never came to pass.

In Fuseli, Goethe was confronted by the image of his own *Sturm und Drang* period, complete with those wild 'hieroglyphs' of wash that he had long laid aside. True, he still argued (in 'Der Sammler') in favour of Manner, against a spokesman for the Characterists; but inwardly he had already opted for the Norm, euphemistically known as Style. In 1797 he reduced this to a categorical formula: 'From the fine arts one demands explicit, clear, definite representations.' This left no room for the 'intermingling, shifting dreams' of Fuseli. Henceforth Goethe was constantly to fall back on his own anthro-

Fig. 3 Henry Fuseli, *Brunhild Watching Gunther Suspended from the Ceiling*, 1807, Castle Museum, Nottingham (cat. 51)

pocentric position as the guarantee of formal legibility: 'Man is the noblest, indeed the rightful object of fine art,' he wrote in the Introduction to the *Propyläen* (1798).

This periodical was established by Goethe in order to establish teachable principles that would govern German artistic life. The self-styled *Praeceptor Germaniae* was convinced that the latest art stood in greatest need of definite maxims. He accordingly undertook to discipline his own artistic judgment. Where Goethe the draughtsman lived the 'dual life' of an Imitator and a Sketcher, Goethe the theorist sought to transcend this conflict and to take refuge on the secure pedestal of Style. He thus hoped to abandon the uncertainties of subjective taste and set criteria that would apply universally – to the artist, to the patron, to the collector and to the lover of art.

Goethe sought to lend some public authority to his own commitment to Style by organizing, from Weimar, a public art competition intended to curb the rampant growth of subjectivity both in the content and in the form of contemporary art. Goethe and his friends (and

advisers) set the entrants one or two subjects from the *Iliad* and the *Odyssey*. The governing principle, in form as well as in theme, was to be the antique ideal. In his announcement of the competition, Goethe praised that ideal as a world 'to which every true modern artist so gladly transports himself; where all his exemplars, his highest goals are to be found.' The competition was held every year from 1799 until 1805. Measured by its own objectives, it achieved nothing. As a rule, mediocre talents were rewarded, and true originals were rejected on flimsy pretexts. And yet the Weimar undertaking was not entirely blind to the *Zeitgeist*: this is shown by the jury's dealings with Runge and Friedrich.

2.

Philipp Otto Runge (1777–1810) entered the contest in 1801 and chose the theme of *Achilles and the River Gods* (*Iliad* 21). His entry was rejected. The jury condemned his drawing as 'incorrect and mannered', and recommended an 'earnest study of antiquity and of Nature, in the spirit of the ancients'. Stung by this schoolmasterly admonition, Runge reacted with self-confident pride: 'The art exhibition in Weimar, and the whole procedure there, is set on an utterly false path, on which it is impossible to achieve anything good.' Then the lapidary rebuff: 'We are not Greeks any more; we can no longer even feel the sense of wholeness when we see their perfect works of art, far less make such things for ourselves; then why devote our efforts to producing something mediocre?' If Runge owed this perception to the Weimar verdict on his work, then the setback was ultimately a fruitful one.

Runge was disappointed because, favourably impressed by Goethe's introduction to the first issue of *Propyläen*, he had expected to find a similar open-mindedness among the members of the jury. A person – or so Goethe had argued – should seek to absorb whatever is contrary to his own nature: in other words, to live a dual life. 'The lightweight must look for seriousness and severity; the severe must keep before his eyes a being who is light and amenable; the strong must find charm, and the charming, strength. Each will develop his own nature all the more, the more he seems to depart from it.'

This advice embodies the same dual structure of

Fig. 4 Philipp Otto Runge, *The Times of Day* 1805, *Morning*, etching (cat. 9)

Fig. 5 Philipp Otto Runge, *The Times of Day* 1805, *Evening*, etching (cat. 9)

EARNEST and PLAY which appears in Goethe's six-fold 'divisions', and which Runge himself was to incorporate in his *The Times of Day* (figs. 4 and 5). I surmise that these four etchings are an embodiment of the framework defined by Goethe's paired antitheses: the interpenetration of Earnest and Lightness, Severity and Charm, the Tender and the Sublime.

Be that as it may, Goethe himself examined the four prints with 'pleasure', although he added the qualification that he 'did not quite understand them' (letter to Runge, 2 June 1806). The ice was broken. Goethe conceded to Runge: 'Let everyone go as the spirit moves him,' and acknowledged him to be an artist who, in his theory of colour, had 'penetrated these glorious phenomena in his own way' (letter of 22 August 1806). Increasingly fascinated by the 'arabesques' of *The Times of Day*, he referred to their creator (in a review in the *Jenaische Literaturzeitung* in 1807) as 'one of the most brilliant artists of our century'. Discarding his own six 'pigeon-holes', he surrendered to the visual experience that Runge offered to him, with its abundance of 'unprecedented motifs and new combinations'. He went on to announce that he himself intended to make use of Runge's 'theory of colour'.

Runge's death on 2 December 1810 prompted Goethe to revise his overall judgment of the artist. As recently as 1806, he had told Runge that he did not want 'art as a whole to follow the path that you have chosen'; but now, after Runge's untimely death, he uttered the prophetic words: 'The course that he took was not his, but that of the century itself, by whose current contemporaries are willingly or unwillingly swept along' (letter to Runge's brother Daniel, 17 December 1811).

Was Goethe himself one of the willing or one of the unwilling? Either way, his remarks recorded by Sulpiz Boisserée in 1811 show that Runge's inventions had touched him deeply and had led him to the utmost limits of his own understanding of art. Goethe led Boisserée to *The Times of Day*, which hung in his music room: 'What, you haven't seen this? There, just look at that stuff! Something to rave about! Beautiful and mad at the same time.'

Boisserée: 'Yes, like the Beethoven that the man over there is playing. Like our whole age.'

Goethe went on, 'Of course, it's an attempt to embrace everything, and so it's always losing itself in the Elemental – and yet there's such endless beauty in the detail. There, just look, devilish stuff! And here again, the grace and the splendour that the fellow gets out of it! But the poor devil couldn't stand the pace. He's already

Fig. 6 Caspar David Friedrich, *Pilgrimage at Sunrise* 1805, Kunstsammlungen, Weimar

Fig. 7 Caspar David Friedrich, *Summer Landscape with Dead Oak Tree* 1805, Kunstsammlungen, Weimar

gone. It's the only possible way. A man like that, who stands on the very brink – either he dies, or else he goes mad. There's no mercy.'

Runge's formal excellences would have met with Goethe's unqualified approval, if only their central focus had been 'Style', the point at which PLAY is united with EARNEST. But because Runge 'loses' himself in the 'Elemental', Goethe was unable to follow him without reservations, for that was the very chasm into which he himself dreaded to fall. In this, he held himself aloof from the nineteenth-century mainstream, which (as we now know) was to lead ever deeper into the 'Elemental'.

3.

Entrants for the 1805 competition were allowed to make their own selection of a scene from the life of Hercules. This in itself is a sign that the Weimar 'Tribunal' (Cornelius's word for it, in a letter to Goethe in 1804) was loosening the reins. Its verdict on this occasion was a confession of utter bafflement, and Goethe thereupon gave up altogether. One of the entrants, Caspar David Friedrich, ignored the advertised theme and sent in two large sepias, *Pilgrimage at Sunrise* (fig. 6) and *Summer Landscape with Dead Oak Tree* (fig. 7), both unmistakable expressions of his own artistic vision. The jury swallowed this act of defiance and awarded the prize to Friedrich, jointly with the Cologne painter Joseph Hoffmann for his *Cleansing of the Augean Stables*.

With hindsight, this looks like a counsel of despair. How could anyone jointly and equally honour two artists so utterly disparate both in stature and in style? The compromise was an attempt to conceal a widening rift that heralded a historic crisis. This was not simply a clash between two artistic genres – history and landscape – that had hitherto been hierarchically distinct. It was a confrontation between two ways of seeing the world: as history and as Nature. Nature – viewed as a process, *natura naturans* – was the new terrain opened up for nineteenth-century painters by the 'Elemental'. It ranged from J.M.W. Turner's 'cloud service' and 'colour beginnings' to those inconspicuous stirrings of organic life for which Carl Gustav Carus – another who, like Friedrich, exchanged ideas with Goethe – coined the beautiful neologism *Erdlebenbilder*, 'earth-life images'. Goethe, too, was involved in Nature study. His own studies of clouds were based on those of the English meteorologist Luke Howard (to whom he paid tribute in his *Cloud Shape, after Howard*, of 1817); at the same time he turned his attention to 'minute life' (*Kleinleben*) – another neologism, which he used by analogy with 'still life' (*Stilleben*) to express the operation of the gentle, inconspicuous forces of Nature.

Did the jury sense this momentous shift of emphasis, when it meekly accepted Friedrich's intrusion into the sacred preserves of history painting? Monks in prayer now took their places alongside Hercules: meditation alongside action. Goethe must now have seen that his attempt to regulate art had been a failure: he held no more competitions. Later he put the blame on the rise of 'religiosity' (*Frömmelei*).

What initially attracted him to Friedrich is clear from his own six categories. Two of the three levels of discourse assigned to EARNEST were evident in Friedrich's art: the 'Faithful Imitation of Nature' was combined with 'Character'. The third category, that of the 'Minute Artists' (*Kleinkünstler*), was also addressed by Friedrich's interest in what Goethe called *Kleinleben*. (The painter gave this advice: 'Observe form precisely, the least as well as the great; do not separate smallness from bigness, but separate pettiness from wholeness.')

Unable to break free from his own set of pigeon-holes, Goethe relegated Friedrich to the lowest rung of his scale of values, the 'Simple Imitation of Nature'. He thus narrowed Friedrich's art down to the virtues of neatness and industry, without enquiring into its content: 'We do not grasp its [a leafless tree's] significance, even were it to have one.' His admiration was utterly blind to Friedrich's expressive intentions, as can be seen from the following episode. When he visited the painter in his studio in Dresden in 1810, he saw the *Monk by the Sea* (colour plate, p.96) and the *Abbey in the Oakwood*, two paintings now regarded as classic specimens of Friedrich's art. When Goethe saw them, they prompted only a laconic note in his diary: 'To Friedrich. His wonderful landscapes. A foggy churchyard. An open sea.'

Goethe kept his admiration within narrow bounds. He interpreted Friedrich's acknowledged goal of 'faithful imitation' in a narrow and superficial sense: that is to say, without any of its implicit spiritual dimensions. He closed his mind to the whole area of artistic experience known to us since Edmund Burke as the Sublime – a realm that he himself had formerly entered, both in the Ossianic landscapes of *Werther* (1774) and in many of his own landscape drawings of that period. He wrote in retrospect (in Book 6 of *Dichtung und Wahrheit*) that only the young, and uncivilized peoples, are 'suited to the Sublime', which, 'if it is to be aroused in us by outward things, must enfold us – without form, or else fashioned into forms that we cannot encompass – with a grandeur that exceeds our capacity'.

Goethe prefaced these words with an important remark that goes some way to explain his reservations about Friedrich. This concerns the ancestral Teutons and their Nature worship (vestiges of which had survived in the 'hedgerow sermons' of German Protestantism). 'There is', said Goethe, 'no finer worship of God than that which needs no image: that which springs from the dialogue with Nature within our own bosoms!' It was a transgression against this imageless religion to translate 'worship in Nature'– as Friedrich did – into paintings. These might address the 'superior' level of ethical life, but they must fall short of what in Goethe's eyes was the true element of art: the 'supreme' level of sense, which is totally available to visual contemplation.

Under the influence of his artistic mentor, Heinrich Meyer, Goethe gradually came to view Friedrich's work with a critical reserve that occasionally gave way to savage hostility. On 11 September 1815, Sulpiz Boisserée noted in his diary that Goethe had cited Friedrich as an example of the 'perversities' of contemporary art: his pictures '. . . might just as well be looked at upside down. Goethe's fury against such works, as previously expressed by smashing pictures on the table-edge'.

There was accurate observation behind Goethe's anger. At times, Friedrich's landscapes sometimes hover on the brink: they obscure spatial relationships, especially by concentrating on sea and clouds, so that the 'Elemental' undermines the reliable delineation of detail. Goethe was bound to see such instances as crimes against the 'Simple Imitation of Nature'.

Runge had voiced his defiance before he ever came into contact with Goethe; for his part, Friedrich roundly condemned in retrospect 'the perverse procedure of certain gentlemen' who set tasks for artists, handed down precepts, and advertised prize themes: 'Would it not be more in the interests of art if every artist were to set the task for himself?' This was an obvious allusion to Goethe's naïve attempt to supply Friedrich himself with 'cloud commissions', which had prompted the indignant artist to prophesy that 'in future the clouds, light and free as they are, will be forced into these slavish systems' (quoted by Louise Seidler in a letter to Goethe, 8 October 1806).

Could it be that this artist, whom Goethe had assigned to EARNEST and its concomitant categories, was secretly in league with the forces of PLAY? At any rate, Friedrich was no dogmatist: he did not discount all interpretations of his work other than his own. He was a deconstructionist *avant la lettre*, who took the viewer's contribution into account. It was, he said, the artist's task to stimulate the viewer's mind, and to evoke 'thoughts, feelings and sentiments, whether or not they

Fig. 8 Peter von Cornelius, *Faust and Mephisto on the Way to the Brocken* 1811, Städelsches Kunstinstitut, Frankfurt

are his own'. Goethe might have had something similar in mind when he observed, in his notes on his own Mantegna essay, that the viewer must 'surpass the artist's intentions, if he is ever to come near them; for since the artist has already expressed the inexpressible, how is *he* to be expressed in another language, a language of words?' Interpretation as artwork: behind this idea stands Friedrich Schlegel – that is to say, the early Romantic critical awareness of art.

4.

In 1809 Franz Pforr (1788–1812) made a suite of drawings on the theme of Goethe's play *Götz von Berlichingen*, which he sent to the poet in the following year. At that time, Peter von Cornelius (1783–1867) was working on his own *Faust* cycle (fig. 8), of which he was to submit some specimens to Goethe in 1811. The poet's response may be described as one of cautious approval. 'Mr Pforr's drawings achieve much, while promising much.' Goethe was leaving his options open, just in case the promise was not fulfilled. Cornelius, he said, had 'often produced unsurpassably felicitous ideas, and it is therefore probable that he will go *far*, if only he can perceive the steps that still remain to be climbed'.

Goethe entirely applauded the action of both Pforr and Cornelius in taking Albrecht Dürer and the 'Old German' artists as their mentors – as a young man, he had played his own part in this 'back to the Middle Ages' tendency. But, he said, this artistic idiom could never be 'regarded as perfect'. Goethe preferred that of the Italians.

Why then did Goethe publicly disown, some years later, the group of artists who formed the *Lukasbund* in Vienna in 1809, and who later – in Rome, where they were mockingly dubbed the Nazarenes – called for a religious renewal of art? What he mistrusted in Pforr, Friedrich Overbeck and their friends was not only their 'religiosity', their Catholic mysticism and narrowly 'patriotic' horizons, but their neglect of 'universal humanity': their infraction of the dogma of the antique human ideal, which Goethe, as a follower of Johann Joachim Winckelmann, would not allow to be challenged. He failed to notice that the Nazarenes were eclectic artists, fluent in a variety of idioms. Without ever disavowing their archaizing simplicity, they soon turned to the example of the Italian High Renaissance. The frescoes of the *Story of Joseph*, which they began to paint in 1816 for Casa Bartholdy, the house of the Prussian Consul, derive from the mature, not from the early Raphael.

Later, in the 1820s, when Cornelius decorated a museum of antiquities, the Glyptothek in Munich, with mural paintings on themes from the *Iliad*, he demonstrated the truth of Goethe's pronouncement that 'The *Iliad* and the *Odyssey* remain inexhaustible'. This was said in 1830, in an essay in which Goethe reverted to his old fondness for telling artists what to paint. Biblical cycles, he said (perhaps thinking of Casa Bartholdy), had nothing to offer: they 'have been worked over too often for there to be hope of anything new from that quarter. The New Testament in particular, the great value of which lies on the Divine and ethical plane, is unlikely to offer the artist anything new that might satisfy both mind and spirit'.

It was an issue that Goethe had considered long before. He had referred to one answer to the crisis of Christian subject matter in Book 5 of *Dichtung und Wahrheit*, recalling that Lavater had suggested giving emotional immediacy to the myths of the Old Testament by 'putting them in a wholly modern disguise and clothing them … in a garment drawn from contemporary life'.

Goethe himself did just this in the early chapters of *Wilhelm Meisters Wanderjahre* (1807–10, 1st ed. 1822), in which, on his travels, Wilhelm meets a 'Holy Family'. The chapter titles are unequivocal: 'The Flight into Egypt – Saint Joseph the Second – The Visitation'. The setting for this latter-day exercise in typology is a long-since-ruined monastery in a remote valley. What is left of the buildings now serves the ends of the Christianity of good works, which needs no church.

There is something of this same 'modern disguise' in *Seven Scenes from Salzburg and Berchtesgaden, Arranged to Correspond to the Seven Days of the Week*, a cycle of lithographs (1818–22) by Ferdinand Olivier, which combines topographical accuracy with discreet religious metaphors. Everyday activities are Christianized, so that, for instance, a carpenter's family becomes the Holy Family. Olivier had first used this trick of bringing his subjects down to earth in the painting *The Holy Family on a Working Day* – which Goethe, who saw it in the collector Schlosser's house, dismissed with a few sarcastic words.

His annoyance at 'Latter-Day German Religious-Patriotic Art' (the title of the 1817 diatribe by Meyer in which his views were expressed) led him to reflect on the progress of the arts, and inspired a number of historical reflections – which, however, he declined to apply to his own artistic judgments. One of these insights was that, as he casually remarked, 'any progress from a petrified, outworn, artificial state into free, living truth-to-Nature immediately entails a loss'. Ought not this to have made him more tolerant?

Perhaps inspired by Giambattista Vico's cyclical theory of history, Goethe identified the backward-looking tendencies that surrounded him as something unprecedented: 'For the first time in the history of art,' he said to Sulpiz Boisserée on 14 February 1814, 'notable talents [i.e. Cornelius and Overbeck] are taking pleasure in evolving backwards, inaugurating a new era of art by going back to the womb.' His organic metaphor of the womb should have implied rebirth; but any sense of renewal was just what Goethe could not and would not perceive. He saw only the symptoms of an accelerating decline.

By refusing to accept multiple implications – to see 'the plurality within a decided unity' that had dawned on him as he worked towards his theory of colour – Goethe precluded himself from assimilating the 'dual life' of his own age, and from being able to strike a balance of gain against loss. He saw the world as decaying, 'reverting to its elements', as Sulpiz Boisserée reported to his brother Melchior on 6 May 1811.

5.

In Goethe's diagrammatic schema, PLAY and EARNEST engage in an imaginary dialogue, the end and aim of which is Style. If we eliminate this purposive element, the dialogue unfolds within a spectrum of possible metamorphoses and permutations, such as Goethe had in mind when he reflected on the *Urpflanze*. There he needed no reference to Style, or to the antique human ideal. From Naples, on 17 May 1787, he wrote of his discovery to Johann Gottfried Herder: 'With this model [of the *Urpflanze*] and the key to it, it is possible to invent plants ad infinitum, which must be logically consistent: that is to say, even if they do not exist, they could exist; they are not artistic or poetic shadows and appearances, but are endowed with an inner truth and necessity.'

In describing this 'model', Goethe – though an implacable devotee of anthropocentric principles in relation to the art of his own day – pointed to an open-ended artistic project that was to come to fruition only in our own century. It is enough to mention Paul Klee, whose cosmos is founded on the interaction of playful EARNEST with earnest PLAY – albeit freed from the bonds of 'Necessity', whose authority Goethe placed even higher than Freedom.

Werner Hofmann

Translated from the German by David Britt

Faces of Romanticism:

Friedrich, Delacroix, Turner, Constable

A woman stands in the centre of the picture; her figure looms tall against a wide, evening landscape. She has turned to face the setting sun, opening her arms as if to embrace the whole world. Her outstretched arms slot harmoniously into the pattern of sunbeams. The woman knows that she is at one with Creation and can surrender to it unreservedly. She is clad in the 'Old German costume' that was regarded in the German states, in the Restoration period after the Congress of Vienna, as a statement of libertarian views, and of opposition to the arbitrary rule of monarchs. She has her back to the viewer, who is invited to identify with her and to adopt her position within the picture. She offers the possibility of shaking off the oppressive present, and of communing with a Nature in which the power of a distant God is made manifest.

Now the woman turns round and looks us in the face. Once again she occupies the centre of the picture, but this time it is not a peaceful evening landscape. She is standing in the midst of a battlefield. At her feet, the rubble of a shattered building covers a corpse. The woman is dressed in the national costume of her country. Her flowing cloak has fallen open, and her dress is torn. The woman has stretched out her arms. But she has no intention of clasping the world in a loving embrace: she is offering herself as a sacrificial victim. Her outstretched hands recall those of the crucified Christ as He shows the wounds in His hands to the unbelieving disciples. The woman stands for her country. She is ready to die for its liberty; and she will arise from the dead. Soon she will lead the people onto the barricades of the Revolution.

We speak of two famous early nineteenth-century paintings. The first, by Caspar David Friedrich, was painted in Dresden, *c.* 1818, shortly after his marriage to Caroline Bommer. It is entitled *Woman Against the Setting Sun* (fig. 1), and – in spite of its simplified forms, with their suggestion of a monumental scale – it is a painting of very modest dimensions: 22 × 30 cms, less than nine inches high.

The other picture, by contrast, impresses us with its sheer size: 210 × 147 cms, nearly seven feet high. It bears the title *Greece Expiring on the Ruins of Missolonghi* (fig. 2), and dates from just under a decade after Friedrich's *Woman Against the Setting Sun*. Eugène Delacroix painted it in Paris in 1826–27, as a tribute to the English poet Lord Byron, who had lost his life in the Greek War of Independence in 1824.

Both paintings indubitably form part of what we know as Romanticism, and that is how both were seen by their contemporaries (though they still met with a degree of individual incomprehension, not to say hostility). Both possess a symbolic dimension. Both have the same central motif, a standing female figure (in one case resting one knee on a stone slab), who stretches her arms out wide and opens herself to the world. And yet how different they are, both in what they say and in the way in which they say it!

Friedrich's little painting shows us a state of oneness with Nature, which is experienced in pantheistic terms as full of Divine immanence and as the highest destiny of humankind. Delacroix's monumental picture, on the other hand, is a tribute to a courageous people in its fight for liberty. It finds its idealized, transfigured embodiment in the figure of the young woman who offers herself as a victim; and it is idle to debate whether this is a symbol or an allegory. The sensuous presence of the figure elevates her into a symbol; the idea proclaimed in the title puts her into the realm of allegory. Perhaps, too, in devising this figure, Delacroix had Joan of Arc in mind. His message is clear and unmistakable: to die for a just cause is the noblest purpose of human life.

In taking these two outstanding artists of the period, Friedrich and Delacroix, as representatives of German and French Romanticism respectively, and in drawing comparisons to outline the essential differences between their work, we must not forget that their dates of birth (both men lived to the age of sixty-five) were a quarter of a century apart. Friedrich (1774–1840) was a child of early Romanticism; Delacroix (1798–1863) stands for

Fig. 1 Caspar David Friedrich, *Woman Against the Setting Sun* c.1818, Museum Folkwang, Essen

Fig. 2 Eugène Delacroix, *Greece Expiring on the Ruins of Missolonghi* 1826–27, Musée des Beaux-Arts, Bordeaux

the full bloom, and the ultimate exhaustion, of the movement. His death in 1863 marked the end of an epoch. In the same year, Edouard Manet's painting *Le Déjeuner sur l'herbe* was rejected by the Salon jury, and the youthful pioneers of a new art founded a Salon of their own. The dawn of Impressionism was at hand.

In Friedrich and Delacroix, we are comparing not only two different national versions of the Romantic spirit but also two different phases of its evolution: two phases of Romanticism that are also reflected in the work of two short-lived Romantic poets, Novalis (1772–1801) and Lord Byron (1788–1824). What Novalis was to Friedrich, Byron was to Delacroix.

Another distinction requires to be drawn. We can treat Delacroix – and at his side the slightly older Théodore Géricault (1791–1824) – as the representative figures of French Romanticism; but, in a politically fragmented Germany, Friedrich and the slightly younger Philipp Otto Runge (1777–1810) can be regarded as representative only with one highly important qualification. Friedrich, like Runge, stood for the Protestant Romanticism of northern Germany. In the south of the country there was another and very different Romanticism, primarily expressed in the early nineteenth century through the art of the Nazarenes. The Nazarenes' Catholicism had two points of reference:

Rome, to which most of them were irresistibly drawn, and German medieval art (the last representative of which, in their eyes, was a thoroughly Renaissance artist, Albrecht Dürer).

In his controversial book *Modern Painting and the Northern Romantic Tradition*, Robert Rosenblum extends his definition of Romanticism to include the English artists William Blake, Samuel Palmer, Joseph Mallord William Turner and John Constable, and the North Germans Friedrich and Runge – but not the Nazarenes, or Delacroix, or any other French artist. The differences between Friedrich and the Nazarenes would fill a chapter in themselves, analogous in some respects to the contrast between Delacroix and Jean Auguste Dominique Ingres.

At the outset of Romanticism, the artist's gaze is turned inward. To look into an imagined past (often with mythical Gothic echoes) is in itself really to look inward. This is true of Friedrich and – with some reservations – also of Delacroix. It was Friedrich who gave the much-quoted advice, 'Close your bodily eye, that you may see your picture first with the eye of the spirit. Then bring to light what you have seen in the darkness, that its effect may work back on others, from without to within.'

From very early on, Friedrich's landscapes were interpreted as landscapes of the soul, mirrors of the human psyche. The interaction between Nature and psyche had long been established in the consciousness of an educated section of the public – not least through the experience of the English or landscape garden. In his *Garden Terrace*, painted under French rule in 1811, Friedrich takes as his theme the contrast between the rational geometry of the regimented French garden, as a parable of the present day, and the freedom and wide open spaces of a landscape garden, which stands for the utopian vision of a future world that will no longer be regimented or hedged about with prohibitions and commandments.

There is a statement of Delacroix's that echoes Friedrich's injunction to look inward. Delacroix said: 'The theme is oneself . . . . One must look into oneself, not around one . . . . When one entirely surrenders to one's own soul, it totally unfolds before one, and then, in its capricious moods, grants us the supreme happiness of communicating something of it to others, of knowing ourselves, of being able to express ourselves continually in our works.'

In the light of this, we must not regard a work like *The Death of Sardanapalus* as primarily an illustration of a work of literature, or *The Justice of Trajan* as a depiction of a historical event: we must interpret them as the expression of entwined and conflicting forces within the artist's own soul. Again, *The Massacre at Chios* is about the painter's own inner conflicts, just as much as it is a manifesto of Greek independence.

But Delacroix is far too rich and complex a personality to allow his work to be adequately explained as the expression of fiercely contending psychic forces. He does look inward, but he is also fascinated by the alien, the exotic, the 'Orient'. This may spring from the same roots as the gaze into the depths of the self: that is, from the quest for archetypal origins and for a new start. But his obsession with the vivid colours of the Orient simultaneously represents an evolutionary step: a step that defines the move within Romanticism itself, from silent contemplation to spectacular stagecraft. In his maturity, Friedrich Schlegel looked in the same direction, as we know from his often-quoted statement: 'For the acme of Romanticism, we must look to the Orient.'

We know that Caspar David Friedrich never felt the urge to go to Italy, and indeed that he turned down the chance to do so, on the grounds that it would not suit him. What was close at hand, his native landscape, offered him all the contemplative material and all the motifs that he needed; and he censured those artists who made for the South in search of artistic effects and thereby ran the risk of losing themselves.

Not so Delacroix. Only the poor health that plagued him from an early age – and, for many years, sheer lack of funds – frustrated his love of travel. He never saw Italy, which fascinated him all his life; and he never saw, but only 'sought with the soul' (in Goethe's words), the land of Greece. His journey to Morocco (Tangier, Meknès) and Algiers in 1832 was not only the fulfilment of a long-cherished dream but also a decisive turning-point in his work.

The miracle of colour that blazes out in the late work of Delacroix has its origin in three experiences.

At the Paris Salon of 1824 – and on a trip to London in the following year – he studied the way in which John Constable (notably in the painting of a meadow, a sheet of water and the air) dissects a local colour into many closely related chromatic gradations of colour, which create the impression of a shimmering atmosphere. The light of North Africa revealed colour to him in all its richness and fullness, reaching into the deepest shadows; for Delacroix, colour thenceforward meant a source of inexhaustible power. His diary, which he kept regularly on his trip to Morocco and then, after a fifteen-year break, again from 1847 onwards, are full of the most minutely differentiated observations of colour in Nature. The third factor, alongside the experience of Constable and of Nature, was his theoretical study of colour, which led him to notice simultaneous contrasts in the complementary colours of violet, orange and green in Nature, and to introduce into his paintings a dense tissue of interacting coloured reflections that transform surfaces into living textures and link all objects harmoniously together.

Delacroix is an artist of colour. In Friedrich's paintings, on the other hand, all the detail is based on studies drawn from Nature, and the structure of the whole is based on constructional drawings. Draughtsmanship and painting hold each other in balance. It is the drawn framework that supports the painting, though Friedrich uses a multitude of delicate glazes to achieve the most intense colour effects, especially in the darker passages and in the skies. Many of his evening moods possess an irresistible magic of colour.

Where Friedrich constructed his paintings meticulously, Delacroix had faith in spontaneity. Work, for him, was a fever; it was all 'dizziness and intoxication'. He liked to speak of the 'fire of execution'. Where Friedrich sought to eliminate all traces of the painter's hand, Delacroix made his brushstrokes visible. Delacroix drew with the brush. Transparent and opaque areas often alternate in his work. Of all those artists who were not colourists like himself, Delacroix said: 'They don't paint: they just colour-in.'

Both Friedrich and Delacroix felt attracted by the eerie and the macabre, and sought images for the disquiet of the soul. But how different those images were! Friedrich evoked the silence of the deep, as confronted by the *Monk by the Sea* (colour plate, p.96); the cold of the *Sea of Ice* (colour plate, p.97), in which a ship is lost without hope of rescue; the loneliness of the glacier world of *The Watzmann*. The sublime is unapproachable. Terrified by its vastness, we are struck motionless with awe.

In Delacroix, by contrast, terror finds expression in the butchery of innocents (*The Massacre of Chios*); in the tumult that surrounds the dying *Sardanapalus*, who turns his own death into a spectacle as Nero did the blazing city of Rome; in combat with wild beasts, dragons, lions, tigers; in the tumult that surrounds *The Bishop of Liège* as his murderers drag him away to his death; in the execution of *Doge Marino Faliero*, whose corpse tumbles down the steps of the Doges' Palace; in *The Abduction of Rebecca*; in the crime of *Medea*, who in her madness slaughters her own children.

Whereas with Friedrich the individual is isolated in face of an awe-inspiring reality, Delacroix mobilizes masses of figures for a pitched battle against the powers of terror. To internalize his experience of the hostility of Nature, Friedrich is drawn to silent meditation; Delacroix seeks explosive utterance for the passions that rule him.

Friedrich speaks to the heart; Delacroix appeals to the emotions. Friedrich invokes silence and the contemplation of Nature. Delacroix stages a drama. For Friedrich,

what counts is always the landscape; for Delacroix, it is the human being, overwhelmed by his or her own feelings.

Both give us an image of Nature. In Friedrich, the human individual looks into himself or herself as into a mirror; in Delacroix, inner human nature stands revealed in all its passionate and agonized excesses, and tormentors often simultaneously appear as victims.

In Friedrich, an overwhelming Nature threatens to swallow up the human being, who becomes mere staffage within the landscape. Occasionally, by adopting the position of the meditative observer, he or she succeeds in maintaining enough detachment to apprehend Nature from a distance, in all its mysterious immensity. In Delacroix, the relationship between humanity and Nature seems reversed: the landscape is habitually reduced to the status of scenery for a drama. Only exceptionally does landscape play an active role – as in *Ovid among the Scythians*, where it serves to confirm that Ovid is truly an exile, an outlaw in an alien world.

This relationship between humanity and Nature is matched by the painterly technique. Delacroix is interested in the solidity of his figures; he shows them brimful of life. Even in his later and more abstract works, in which dynamic masses of colour confront us as the embodiments of warring forces, and their anecdotal garb becomes largely irrelevant (*The Abduction of Rebecca*, 1846), those masses have an overwhelming solidity.

Friedrich, by contrast, strove for a planar effect. We must not interpret this as a sign of weakness or incapacity. For him, it was a way to articulate a new experience of space. Friedrich set out to present this experience by analysing the space in the painting into a number of discrete planes or strata and stacking these one behind the other. To make this clear, we must imagine that we are looking through two, three or more vertical panes of glass, arranged at intervals: the forms of the foreground are on the nearest pane, and the horizon is on the furthest. Often there is no middleground, and the eye, when it leaves the familiar foreground, is directly confronted with an immeasurable depth into which it has no sense of being able to penetrate.

What is more, even where there are intermediate planes between foreground and horizon, the eye still has to jump from each one to the next. Every spatial layer stands alone, without reference to any other. No diagonal can be struck between them. No field of perspective links them. The spatial continuity is broken. At either side of the picture, the planes of the landscape look as if they go on for ever. There is nowhere for the eye to settle. The human being is subsumed in the Cosmos – or is lost.

What Friedrich found in the religious ideas of his time – those of the clergyman Ludwig Theobul Kosegarten, the poet Novalis, the philosopher Friedrich Emil Daniel Schleiermacher – revealed itself to Delacroix as he plunged into great literature: into the works of Dante Alighieri, William Shakespeare, Byron and Sir Walter Scott. What Friedrich discovered in the contemplation of Nature – the operation of an abiding law behind all change and all transitoriness – Delacroix found reflected in the mirror of history.

This reflection soon led Delacroix on to explore his own period, as we see from works such as *The Massacre at Chios* and *Liberty on the Barricades*. Friedrich, too, was a committed artist, with his own view of the contemporary world. But he always preferred the encoded allusion, the subtle hint, which had the twofold advantage of suiting his own temperament and eluding the censorship. *The Chasseur in the Forest* (1814) is a relatively open statement of the fate of a French soldier in the gloom of the German forests (as in the vast plains of Russia). By contrast, the wayfarer in Old German costume who meditates at *Ulrich von Hutten's Grave* (1823–24, fig. 3) reveals only to the initiated that he is moved by the same libertarian ideals that drive Delacroix's personification of France to mount the barricades with tricolour and fixed bayonet.

If Friedrich and Delacroix represent the twin poles of the Romantic world-view, how are we to define the position of Turner (1775–1851), an almost exact contemporary of Friedrich, whom he survived by eleven years? It would be too simple to say that his position lies somewhere in between. Better: if Friedrich and Delacroix represent the thesis and antithesis of Romantic art, in Turner we find elements of a synthesis.

Like Friedrich (and like Constable, 1776–1837, who was a member of the same generation), Turner was one of the great landscape painters of the age – perhaps, indeed (*pace* Jacob van Ruisdael), the greatest since

Fig. 3 Caspar David Friedrich, *Ulrich von Hutten's Grave* 1823–24, Staatliche Kunstsammlungen, Weimar

Claude Lorrain. All his life, Claude remained his ideal, against whom he felt impelled to measure himself, and whom he constantly tried to surpass. Turner took the myths of landscape, which Claude had begun, and told them through to the end.

David d'Angers, who visited Friedrich in Dresden in 1834, commented that he was the man 'who has discovered the tragedy of landscape'. He said of him: 'Friedrich has a sombre soul. He has understood perfectly that the great crises of Nature can be shown through landscape.'

Much the same might be said of Turner. He too had a 'sombre soul'; and his paintings show – if not the tragedy of landscape – its drama, raised to the utmost pitch of intensity, transported to its climax. To stage that drama, Turner did not need – as Delacroix did – to enlist a large cast of historical and mythological characters, even though on occasion Odysseus or Hannibal may be seen in action on the fringe of some natural spectacle. Turner was satisfied with actors of another kind: the forces of Nature. He reduced his drama to the struggle between light and dark, the clash between the elements, the conflict between fire and water, mist and snow, rain and tempest. In it, human beings seem to be the helpless playthings of natural forces.

The forces of Nature held a magical fascination for Turner. We are told that he had himself lashed to the mast of a ship at sea, in order to feel the whole force of a storm without being swept overboard by the waves; that on his European travels (and he travelled a great deal by any standard, not just by the standard of his time; he was particularly drawn by the Swiss Alps and by the light of Venice) his favourite position, in all weathers, was on the box of a mail coach, next to the driver; that in 1844 he was one of the first passengers on the Great Western Railway to Bristol and Exeter, and thrust his head out of the carriage window in the midst of a violent rainstorm, for a quarter of an hour at a time, to absorb the experience.

Friedrich was another who loved Nature in all weathers. His friend, the philosopher Gotthilf Heinrich von Schubert, described his walks on the island of Rügen:

'The silent wilderness of the chalk mountains and oak forests of the island of Rügen, close to his native shores, were his favourite haunt – in summer, but still more in the stormy times of late autumn and in early spring, when the sea ice broke up along the shore. He mostly stayed at Stubbenkammer, where in those days there was no modern inn; the fisherfolk often feared for his life, when they saw him clambering over and between the sharp mountain spurs and the cliffs that jutted into the sea, for all the world like a man in search of a watery grave. When the gale was at its strongest, and the breakers at their height, there he stood, soaked by the flying spume or by a sudden downpour of rain, watching as if he could never have his fill of those tumultuous joys. Whenever lightning and thunder approached over the sea, he hastened along the rocky coast to meet the storm, as if those powers were his friends; or else he followed them into the oak forest, where the lightning split the hollow tree, and there murmured under his breath, "How great, how mighty, how splendid!"'

What he did not do was to paint any of this. Friedrich is a painter of stillness. He captures the one moment in which the wayfarer pauses, the moment that suggests eternity and infinity. Like all the Romantics, he was fascinated by the drama of Nature; but as a painter he was no dramatist, as Delacroix and Turner were. In his work, contrasts are not seen – as in Delacroix and in Turner – at the instant of maximum tension, but reconciled, brought into harmony with each other. He did not often take as his subject an out-of-the-ordinary phenomenon such as *The Northern Lights*, or the shifting ice floes on the Elbe. In the whole spectacle of Nature, what fascinated him far more than the brief climax of a storm was the slow process of growth and decay, the cycle of flowering and wilting, the recurrence of such events as the rising and setting of the sun and moon. And so all that he painted of a thunderstorm was the rainbow that followed it; and of a rainy night, only the rise of the morning mist. Most of all, he loved the twilight, when light and darkness harmoniously blend.

Turner, by contrast, sought out the orgiastic climaxes of Nature. Friedrich invoked dissolution and transience, the ruined monastery, the dead oak, the vision of the burning Marienkirche in Neubrandenburg; but such reminders of transience did not satisfy Turner: he was positively addicted to the catastrophic and sensational side of Nature. To watch the conflagration that engulfed the Houses of Parliament, on the banks of the Thames in London in 1834; to witness the progress of an avalanche in Grisons; and to see an eruption of Vesuvius, must have been among the cherished moments of his life.

And yet Turner is anything but a reporter. He remains a visionary, even when Nature stages one of her spectacles before his very eyes. When he sets out to consign the spectacle to canvas, he never does so by illusionistic or descriptive means. He looks for suggestion, never for narrative: which is why he transforms a natural event into a painting that is an event in itself. Wherever he can, he exposes himself to experiences that profoundly agitate him. The breaking of a storm, the unleashing of the elements of gale, rain, and snow, make him sense the presence of higher powers. To transform these into pictures that will grip and indeed agitate his viewers, just as the direct experience of Nature has agitated him, is Turner's highest goal. Photographic accuracy has nothing to do with it. Turner's visual memory preserves the total impact of an elemental event, the maelstrom, the undertow, the tumult, the unbridled energies, the dance of particles. Details are unimportant; they blur and dissolve. Whoever is gripped by such elemental experiences – whether in Nature or on the canvas – is in no position to take note of details.

In his late paintings, Turner is always the man at the centre of things, not an outside observer. He is in the thick of it, directly feeling the emotion, the tumult, the chaos; from this viewpoint one no longer perceives any specific objects. One sees nothing that could ever be reproduced in static form. At every moment the world comes to an end and is born anew, arising from the dialectic of the elements. In this chaos, the world's end constantly becomes the world's beginning. Turner drags the eye into this maelstrom of endless transformation. He gives us no point of reference. He puts us into the situation in which he himself has been, and which he recreates in his paintings in swirls of colour.

Turner's technique is entirely in keeping with this intention. First applying broad dashes of the colours that he needs for the action, he then spreads them with brush and spatula, palette knife and sponge; he scratches and wipes; he scrapes with the brush handle, with his thumbnail, with anything that comes to hand – all to the utter horror of his tidy-minded, academically trained contemporaries.

The artist's creative process here takes on a life of its own. The point of departure is the 'Colour Beginnings', abstract colour sketches intended to strike a specific chord and set the basic mood. We might call them colour scores, captured by Turner in watercolour; there were many of them in his studio at his death. Often we cannot tell whether Turner wanted them to be seen as autonomous works, or merely as source material for his paintings. They seem to have performed the same function for him as the semi-automatic techniques used by Max Ernst, such as frottage and grattage: they mobilized his imagination. And at that point it really could not have mattered less whether Turner chose as his subject a real event, like the Parliament fire, or an imagined one, like *The Deluge*. The result always extended into the realm of the fantastic.

Constable was utterly different. He too painted not only landscapes but the weather – as in the *Sea Piece with Rain Clouds* (1824–28). It is all precisely observed, and faithfully translated into painting. The overall impression is convincing, and each detail fits into the

next. It all chimes with our experience, and it works as a painting. But it does not sweep us away, as Turner's storms do.

Friedrich's approach was different again. He was a pedantic, almost an anxious draughtsman. He could stay out for hours, looking at 'his motif' and carefully transferring an old oak tree or a mountain range into his sketchbook. In composing a painting, he combined the most disparate sketches into an imagined whole. First, as a contemporary witness tells us, 'he drew on the neatly stretched canvas, roughly, in chalk and pencil. . . . Then meticulously and completely, with a reed pen and india ink'; then he set about the underpainting. Friedrich, we are told, 'did not begin the picture until it stood, living, before his soul.'

All this sets him fundamentally apart from Turner and his working method. For Turner, the genesis of a painting was a process of continuing inspiration. In every successive phase of his work, the pictorial vision was subject to a constant transformation, and it was only when the inner tension was relaxed – or when Varnishing Day at the Royal Academy came to an end – that Turner stopped; the painting was finished. Friedrich's paintings seem perfect and complete from the first phase onwards, but Turner's remain for ever open.

A lot has been written about the indistinctness of Turner's paintings, and his (alleged) message to a doubtful purchaser has often been quoted: 'Tell the gentleman that imprecision is my forte.' By comparison with the cloudy vagueness of Turner's paintings, those of Friedrich seem precise and clear. But this is only at first sight. If we look at the foregrounds in Friedrich paintings, which are mostly unified by a single dark tone, we are often unable to say what objects are described in them. Are they objects at all? Do not the forms merge into each other? Are they not as vague in close-up as they are on the horizon? Even in detail, Friedrich leaves us unsure more often than he gives us certainty.

The line that has defined an object in the sketchbook continues to define its identity in the painting, draws it into the two-dimensional scheme, emphasizes the outline that serves to set it off against other, remoter layers of space. The line isolates objects and emphasizes contrasts. If these become too harsh, if they threaten to disrupt the coherence of the painting, Friedrich relieves them through colour, bringing them closer to each other by imposing a uniform tonal value. Line separates; colour connects, reconciles, creates transitions. But in Friedrich colour, too, serves to keep phenomena flat on the surface and lends them no solidity. In place of solidity, Friedrich has formal analogies, symmetries, complex correspondences. Any close scrutiny of Friedrich's paintings reveals that there is much to be deciphered.

Take the skyline of a town, visible on the horizon in *Greifswald in the Moonlight* (1816–17). Is it a vision, or is it real? Or is it both? If we imagine it to be close enough to touch, it dissolves like a mirage. If we project it into the distance, it takes on reality.

Constable allows us far more certainty in his *Salisbury Cathedral* (1823), even though he leaves it in a curious state of suspense between near and far, brilliant light and menacing storm. And with Turner, too, when he shows us *The Dogana and Santa Maria della Salute* (1843), we feel that we know where we are. Venice may be a rich source of illusions, but the city itself is no illusion – even though here it is lost in the mist. However hazy the light, whatever the glimmer in the sky, the dome of Santa Maria della Salute will not entirely disappear, for it has long since become part of the light and of the sky, and is as real as they are.

There is more to Romanticism than an inward-turning gaze and a fascination with the Orient: Romanticism is also a minute study of Nature. Many Romantics were interested in the investigation of natural phenomena, and in their different ways Friedrich, Constable and Turner all participated in this. All paid close attention to clouds; and the results show us what they had in common as well as what separated them. In three examples – *Passing Clouds*, by Friedrich (1821), *Cloud Study at Hampstead*, by Constable (also 1821), and *Sunset with Dark Clouds*, by Turner (c. 1826) – the motif is the same throughout; but what a difference!

Of the three painters, Constable is the one whom we can most readily describe as a student of Nature; his eager grasp embraces all that he sees with a tactile immediacy. Turner, for his part, is a student of our means of perception: the vague, imprecise, flowing quality in his paintings is for him the expression of a specific quality of our perception of the world, when we plunge into the midst of events – as the steamer does in *Staffa,*

Fingal's Cave (1832), while we join her in absorbing the rhythm of the sea, the rain, the storm, the waves.

Friedrich is different again. His keen eye seeks to penetrate the clouds; he wants to know what lies beyond, and how it all connects. The *Passing Clouds* in Friedrich's painting are just as much silhouettes as his mountain ranges or clumps of trees – and just as unattainable, as impossible to grasp or to possess. No individual cloud forms can be identified: what we see is an array of banks, fields, walls of cloud, areas of darkness and light. These open to reveal lighter, remoter cloudscapes, and these in turn are torn open, scattered, pulled apart.

Constable tries to paint clouds as they are; Turner, as he perceives them; Friedrich, as he interprets them. Constable investigates their form, Turner their effect, Friedrich their symbolism.

Constable's clouds are precise Nature studies; Turner's clouds are dramatic inventions. Friedrich's are cues for meditation. He is not trying to reproduce typical cloud formations, but to explore celestial space.

Three ways of painting clouds, three ways of seeing the world: all three are characteristic of the Romantic period. Romanticism has many faces.

Wieland Schmied

Translated from the German by David Britt

Map of Europe with today's boundaries, showing the position of some of the cities outside Germany that had strong connections with German Romanticism

Baltic Sea

North Sea

•Lübeck

•Hamburg

•Worpswede

Elbe

Bremen•

Weser

•Berlin

Dessau•

•Göttingen

Düsseldorf•

Kassel•

•Leipzig

Weimar•

Dresden

•Cologne

•Jena

Rhine

Frankfurt-am-Main•

Main

•Nuremberg

•Heidelberg

•Stuttgart

Danube

•Augsburg

•Munich

Murnau•

Map of Germany with today's boundaries, showing the position of some of the cities and towns that were centres of German Romanticism or had strong connections with later artists discussed in this book

Where Did German Romantic Painting Thrive?

To study English or French painting in its broad outlines, we need look no further than London or Paris, respectively. These are true capital cities, where art has evolved through a vigorous exchange of ideas among artists who live close to each other and to their powerful patrons. In Germany – as also in Italy – the situation is very different. The fragmentation of Germany into tiny states, which goes back deep into the past, began to break down in political terms only after the war of 1870–71, and in cultural matters it subsists to this day. It led to the emergence of a multiplicity of centres, all of which lacked the historic grandeur of the great capitals of Europe and were chronically short of resources, both economic and intellectual. The advantages of this system lie not only in its sheer variety – which has a charm of its own – but also in its ability to extract significant individual achievements from often unpromising material conditions.

One outward symptom of the more fluid conditions in Germany has been the scarcity of large-scale works – prestigious decorative schemes for churches and palaces always excepted. Along with a tendency towards smallness of scale, there has been a tendency to favour drawing and printmaking. As a result, an outsider finds German art comparatively difficult to understand. There is a complex historical background to grapple with, not only chronological but intricately geographical. For example, the observer who encounters nineteenth-century German painting in some great collection, housed beneath a single capacious roof, is all too easily misled into overlooking the local peculiarities of Dresden, Munich, Hamburg, Berlin, Frankfurt or Heidelberg. Any attempt to survey German painting on the same lines as its English or French equivalent is doomed to fail. This applies above all to the art of Romanticism, which expressed a striving for national unity, but which, in its search for origins and archetypes – very unlike the aristocratic internationalism of the seventeenth and eighteenth centuries – struck deep local roots. It was a time when the gulf between aspiration and reality yawned particularly wide.

In the years around 1806, when the august if decrepit fabric of the Holy Roman Empire of the German Nation finally collapsed under Napoleonic pressure, its ancient capital city of Vienna was the chosen resort of those German painters who dreamed of restoring the medieval unity of the Reich. Friedrich Overbeck from Lübeck, Franz Pforr from Frankfurt am Main, Philipp Veit from Berlin, the brothers Friedrich and Ferdinand Olivier from Dessau, Julius Schnorr von Carolsfeld from Leipzig, all eagerly made their way to Vienna in the years before the outbreak of the Wars of Liberation; but they found themselves unable to gain a foothold there. The only German artist who succeeded in doing so, Peter Krafft from Hanau, was an inveterate Neoclassicist who even so remained a curiously isolated figure in Vienna.

Johann Adam Klein and Johann Christoph Erhard, who made their way to Vienna in 1816 from the eminently medieval city of Nuremberg, were among those artists who did not stay long. After the Congress of Vienna in 1814–15, Vienna wanted more than ever to be a European capital on its own terms, and in this it succeeded. The Viennese Biedermeier, with Ferdinand Georg Waldmüller as its leading painter, is an art with an unmistakable dialect flavour of its own, entirely devoted to the needs of a specific, cultivated society, and transcending them only in occasional flights of fancy. Neither Emperor Francis I nor the powerful Prince Metternich took much interest in art; and, in the stifling atmosphere of the Restoration period, any breath of fresh air that might be introduced by young, reformist artists served only to arouse suspicion. In 1809, as a gesture of protest against the Viennese Academy and its leading figure, Friedrich Heinrich Füger (from Heilbronn), a number of young painters, led by Overbeck and Pforr, founded the *Lukasbund*, or Brotherhood of St Luke. Significantly, they all left Vienna in the same year to seek their salvation in Rome.

The only significant Viennese Romantics were the sensitive Johann Evangelist Scheffer von Leonardshoff and the rather combative Moritz von Schwind. Scheffer died young in 1822; Schwind left Vienna in 1828. However, Viennese artistic life found a place for the art of Leopold Kupelwieser (from 1825), Joseph Führich (from 1834) and others, who made a patriotic virtue of their Nazarene piety. This Viennese wing of Nazarene painting is marked by a particular closeness to Nature.

The ideas that defined German Romantic art were conceived in Rome. For many, Rome was the seat of a kind of government in exile, which directed artistic developments within Germany from afar. There, artists from different German states met and enjoyed their sense of common identity. True, other nations – notably the French and the English – also maintained a presence there: the French even had an Academy of their own. But in the late eighteenth and early nineteenth centuries the German artistic colony was exceptionally strong, not only in sheer numbers but in relation to the artists who remained at home.

Acclaimed as the renewer of German art, and bathed from early youth in the Promethean aura of genius, Asmus Jakob Carstens (1754–98) believed that he could realize his ideas only in Rome. He lived there from 1792 until his death, and his linear idiom, with its high-flown rhetoric, inspired even the Nazarenes – though Carstens was one of those who hoped to achieve reform through the spirit of antiquity and of Michelangelo rather than that of pre-Reformation Christianity. From the 1790s onwards, Italian art 'before Raphael' was a powerful stimulus, though its main impact was derived from reproductions in line engravings. The whole relationship between Italy and Germany became a theme that interested many Romantic painters: the most celebrated instance is Overbeck's *Italia and Germania*.

The landscape painters Joseph Anton Koch from Tirol, Johann Martin von Rohden from Kassel and Johann Christian Reinhart from Hof – all of whom were to live to a ripe old age – became Romans while yet remaining Germans. Of these, it was Koch who kept in closest touch with the younger Romantics; in 1825–28 he even joined some of the Nazarenes in painting frescoes in the Casino Massimo.

When the French occupied Rome in 1798, most of the German artists fled. As a result, when the *Lukasbrüder* or Brethren of St Luke arrived from Vienna in 1810, they were able to step into a central role. Gottlieb Schick

from Stuttgart – by far the most gifted German artist in Rome after Koch – kept his distance from them, and left the city on grounds of health in 1811. He died in the following year, as did Pforr. The Rhinelander Peter von Cornelius, who arrived in Rome in 1811, joined the *Lukasbrüder* at once; with Pforr dead, he and Overbeck were the acknowledged leaders of the group, and he was soon widely regarded as the greatest German artist of the day. Wilhelm and Rudolf Schadow, a painter and a sculptor respectively, the sons of Johann Gottfried Schadow, arrived from Berlin in 1811. Philipp Veit, another Berliner, moved to Rome in 1815.

The *Lukasbrüder*, who were soon nicknamed Nazarenes, were united by the sense that they were bringing about a renewal of German art both spiritually, by reverting to fundamental religious ideas, and formally, by turning back to the Italian art of the Middle Ages and Renaissance and to Raphael in particular. Most of them came from Protestant backgrounds, but many carried their revulsion against the post-Reformation world – and against the Enlightenment in particular – to the extent of converting to Catholicism.

The defeat of Napoleon, the liberation of Rome from the French and the return of the Pope in 1814 provided a great stimulus to artistic activity, and numbers soon expanded, with the inevitable result that factions appeared. The frescoes of the *Story of Joseph*, painted by Cornelius, Overbeck, Wilhelm Schadow and Veit at Casa Bartholdy in 1815–17, were intended as a beacon for the new age of German art. The memorable exhibitions held in 1819 and 1822 to mark the presence in Rome of Emperor Francis I of Austria and King Frederick William III of Prussia, respectively, afforded opportunities to publicize the artists' ideas, and these were eagerly seized upon. Neither prince had any ambition to achieve fame as a patron of the arts; but one prince who certainly had was the nationalistic Crown Prince Ludwig of Bavaria, who was to become King Ludwig I in 1825. He gave consistent encouragement to German artists resident in Rome, among them a number of landscape painters who followed Koch in pursuing a conception of Nature inspired less by tourist demand than by the *genius loci*. The famous farewell party held at Villa Schultheiß to mark Ludwig's departure from Rome in 1818 was a gesture of thanks for the Crown

Prince's encouragement. In 1819 Ludwig employed Cornelius to paint the frescoes in the Glyptothek in Munich, and in 1825 he appointed him Director of the Munich Academy; in 1827 he secured the services of Schnorr von Carolsfeld.

Overbeck was the only Nazarene who stayed in Rome all his life. Wilhelm Schadow became Director of the Academy in Düsseldorf; Veit became Director of the Städelsches Kunstinstitut in Frankfurt. Both, like almost all the Nazarenes, had difficulty in holding their own in the face of a changing *Zeitgeist*, because the essentially backward-looking Nazarene doctrine allowed only for persistence, not for development. With the extinction of the Romantic movement – here a marked shift is visible in or around 1830 – the importance of Rome and of Italy in German art rapidly declined. The light had been briefly rekindled during Carl Blechen's time in Italy in 1828–29.

The principal centre of art in the south of Germany was Munich. Painting developed strongly there, but not much of it can be called Romantic – if by this we mean an art that hints at ideas behind the visible reality. Romanticism came into existence as a countervailing force to the Enlightenment; but this in itself had never really existed in Bavaria. Catholicism retained its tight hold on all cultural life, and presided over the achievements of the unchallenged tradition that had produced the Bavarian Baroque churches and monasteries. There was no need to go back to the Middle Ages in search of a new piety.

Moritz von Schwind's relationship with Munich exemplifies the city's rather aloof attitude to Romanticism. A born nomad with a marked feeling for poetry and music, Schwind never enjoyed a position commensurate with his great gifts all the time that he lived there, which was from 1828 to 1840 and from 1847 until his death in 1871. He was a solitary figure who looked for archetypal origins, both in external Nature and in the world of heroic legend and fairytale. The artist closest to him, in his strong taste for narrative, was Eugen Napoleon Neureuther.

In Munich, Ludwig I pursued a building policy that radically transformed the old-world appearance of the city. As autocratic as any Baroque despot, he set out to arouse memories of Rome or Florence with spectacular new buildings, regardless of the existing, organic growth of the city. He adorned the walls and ceilings of his new buildings with cycles of paintings that represented an almost systematic coverage of salient areas of his own mental and cultural universe: ancient and modern literature, the history of art, the history of the Wittelsbach dynasty, and religious themes. The landscape and genre painting that emerged from all this was directly inspired by the proximity of the Bavarian mountains. The only painter to give a philosophical dimension to his view of landscape was Carl Rottmann, from Heidelberg. His views of Italy and Greece are far more than mere *vedute*: the Greek landscapes, above all, convey an often painful awareness of the contrast between the present scene and the lost world of antiquity. A cosmic wind strikes an ominous chill through these paintings, far removed from the patron's thirst for prestige, and from his political message.

Rottmann was enabled to see history and Nature in this light because he came from Heidelberg. This was the former seat of the Electors Palatine, where the massive ruin of the Renaissance castle, high above the city, proclaimed the transience of earthly power – and simultaneously cried out against an unjust fate. Heidelberg had not forgotten that its castle had been destroyed by Louis XIV, and the Wars of Liberation led to a new wave of anti-French feeling. The city witnessed an effort to revive the ideals of medieval chivalry; its students formed fraternities – *Burschenschaften* – and cultivated democratic ideas.

Heidelberg, Jena and Göttingen were the major centres of literary Romanticism, but it was only in Heidelberg – with Rottmann, Carl Philipp Fohr and Ernst Fries, all born between 1795 and 1801 – that a significant school of Romantic landscape painting emerged, marked by a cult of genius, an atmosphere of unrest and a tendency towards dark colouring. All three artists had a strong affinity with Blechen; and they and other local painters drew inspiration from the landscapes of the Neckar valley. Jena and Göttingen had no such natural settings, and this was probably why they produced no painting of any note to set beside their literary achievements. The brothers Franz and Johannes Riepenhausen, of Göttingen, were at university there when they discovered their artistic vocation; but the decisive influence on them was that of Dresden Romanticism, and both left for Rome as early as 1805.

The Neckar flows into the Rhine; and the banks of the Rhine are steeped in history like those of no other German river. It is the only river to have had a Romanticism of its own: *Rheinromantik*. In painting, however, this Rhine Romanticism never became associated with specific painters, or with a particular interpretation of the landscape. It encompassed a great deal of work by visiting artists, both German and foreign, for whom the river and its mountains and castles supplied motifs; but it produced little that went beyond mood and atmosphere into the realm of ideas.

Cologne, with its unfinished cathedral, was the largest, oldest and most prestigious city on the Rhine. It acted as a powerful stimulus to Romantic architecture and thought (including art history), but not to Romantic painting. We have comparatively few early nineteenth-century paintings of Cologne subjects, and hardly any of them goes beyond the faithful representation of things seen. What flourished in Heidelberg fell on barren soil here.

There was a decided air of decay, even senility, about Cologne in 1800 or so. The same went for Nuremberg; but there a great native artistic tradition had persisted until as late as the seventeenth century. The Romantics revered the genius of Albrecht Dürer as much as they did that of Raphael, although they did not imitate him to the same extent: Dürer's influence was principally confined to Romantic drawing. In 1828, however, the German artistic community came together *en masse*, at his grave in the Johannesfriedhof in Nuremberg, to commemorate the tercentenary of his death. A number of Romantic artists grew up in Nuremberg under Dürer's influence; but the best of them – Erhard and Klein – did not stay. Bavaria was in the grip of cultural centralizers, who sought to concentrate all the glory in Munich and took good care to prevent Protestant Nuremberg from developing into an independent focus of power.

In Augsburg, the other great bourgeois art centre of southern Germany, the situation was much the same. The city played no part in the history of Romantic painting.

Frankfurt, which owes its central position in German commerce to its tradition of annual fairs, was always open to artistic influences, notably from the Netherlands. Frankfurt enjoyed a historic aura of reverence as the place where, from the Middle Ages until the demise of the Empire, the Holy Roman Emperors were elected and crowned; and until the mid eighteenth century it possessed a vigorous artistic life, of which the benefits spread to the nearby courts of Wiesbaden, Darmstadt and Mainz. Frankfurt painting was markedly bourgeois, with cosmopolitan aspirations. It went into gradual decline in the late eighteenth century.

In such an atmosphere, it was inevitably difficult for Romantic art to gain a foothold. What painting did emerge had a Nazarene look to it. A beneficial influence was exerted by the collector and patron Johann Friedrich Städel and the publisher and bookseller Johann Friedrich Wenner. Pforr, who was born in Frankfurt, had a mind filled with medieval echoes and imperial pageantry; Goethe was another influence, as is shown by Pforr's illustrations to his *Götz von Berlichingen*. But Goethe did not remain in his native city. Cornelius was there in 1809–10, shortly before embarking on his illustrations for Goethe's *Faust*. When Veit arrived in the city in 1830, he was able to attract talents of the order of Alfred Rethel and Edward Steinle, but he felt the resistance of an entrenched, prosaic realism and finally withdrew. Frankfurt nevertheless remained a lively centre of art throughout the nineteenth century. Both Schwind (1844–47) and Hans Thoma (1876–99) felt at home there; but it was there, too, that Gustave Courbet found admirers from an early stage in his career.

Leipzig was analogous to Frankfurt in many ways: as a great bourgeois city, which liked to call itself Little Paris (*Klein-Paris*); as a commercial centre; and also as a publishing town. Its artistic tradition was not quite so brilliant as Frankfurt's, but what it did have was a university that was a centre of Enlightenment culture. To this was added, in 1764, an Academy of Art, independent of Dresden. Its first director was Johann Joachim Winckelmann's friend, Adam Friedrich Oeser; and his successor, between 1800 and 1812, was Johann Friedrich August Tischbein, who with Anton Graff was the leading portrait painter in Germany. There were also some valuable private collections. Leipzig's sober business ethos – fostered, as in Frankfurt, by a trade fair – ensured that artists could make a living; but ideologically this was not Romantic terrain. Schnorr von Carolsfeld was a native of the city, but he left it early in life. The most important field of artistic activity was portraiture.

The situation in Hamburg was very similar. Overseas trade brought wealth and fostered a down-to-earth, civic-minded attitude. Culturally, the city looked to the Netherlands and England. There were also contacts with Denmark, which enjoyed a notable artistic flowering around the end of the eighteenth century. The Danish artist Jens Juël studied in Hamburg for several years.

Philipp Otto Runge, one of the two outstanding painters of early Romanticism, lived in Hamburg from 1804 until his untimely death in 1810 and felt at home in the city's business world – although his exalted ideas were very much out of keeping with local artistic tradition. Born at Wolgast in Pomerania, Runge had been steeped in the experience of the sea and its wide horizons since early childhood, so that there was much in Hamburg that was familiar to him. However, the decisive inspiration for his set of four 'arabesques' on the theme of *The Times of Day* had come to him in Dresden, through his friendship with Ludwig Tieck and through the stimulus of the city's artistic treasures. In Hamburg, Runge added a new dimension to portraiture (generally rather disdained by the Romantics, because of its social dimension) by seeking to evoke the inner kinship between the Soul, which might well be the soul of a child, and the Cosmos. Of other Hamburg painters, the closest to Runge was Erwin Spekter. Wilhelm Tischbein, too, lived in Hamburg from 1801 to 1809 before moving to Eutin; though much older – born in 1751 – he absorbed something of Runge's fantasy into his later pictorial idylls.

Julius Oldach, Carl Julius Milde (who moved to Lübeck in 1838) and Victor Emil Janssen were three Hamburg artists who commanded a style that impressively unites concentrated seriousness with sober intimacy. Kindred spirits included Friedrich Wasmann and Johann August Krafft. The countryside around Hamburg also inspired a strain of landscape painting that was more Biedermeier than Romantic.

It is curious that the other great and wealthy Hanseatic port on the North Sea, Bremen, produced no artistic culture of the same density. Lübeck, with its wealth of medieval buildings, had once supplied the whole Baltic coastline with paintings; it was the birthplace of Overbeck, and it was there that his sense of history and his longing for a new religious feeling in life and art were first aroused. But Lübeck lacked the strength to produce a Romantic school of art with an identity of its own.

After Rome, the most important centre of German Romantic painting was probably Dresden, thanks to the presence of the two greatest early Romantic painters, Caspar David Friedrich (from Greifswald) and Runge. It cannot have been by accident that these two artists, born within thirty kilometres of each other and only three years apart – in 1774 and 1777 respectively – launched their independent careers in the same city, in the same year, 1803, and with works on the theme of the Times of Day. Unlike Runge, Friedrich stayed on in Dresden; but even there it was important to him to remain an outsider, a solitary figure who had his roots in Greifswald. The importance of the *genius loci* to romantic painters is nowhere so precisely identifiable as it is with Friedrich, who – as he himself said – adopted Dresden as his home for the sake of its surrounding countryside and the paintings in its Gemäldegalerie.

The sandstone mountains known as the 'Saxon Switzerland', and the Elbe valley above Dresden, with the gorges of its tributaries, were the most important sources of inspiration for Dresden Romantic landscape painting. The inimitable intensity of Friedrich's vision of landscape, with its sense of Nature as a kind of language, had precedents of a sort in the eighteenth century, in the work of such artists as Adrian Zingg or Johann Christian Klengel. The city of Dresden – which remained, until its destruction in 1945, a uniquely effective, self-contained Baroque creation – never offered the Romantics very much visual stimulus. It dated only from the rise of absolute monarchy in Saxony, and was therefore too recent. Nature far outweighed history, therefore; but the Gemäldegalerie was there to set standards and to act as a spur. There to be worshipped was Raphael's *Sistine Madonna*, the most precious painting in the whole world.

Before the Wars of Liberation, Berliners (beside those in Berlin) regarded the annual exhibitions of the Dresden Academy as the most important in Germany. Nowhere were artistic controversies pursued with such vehemence, as is exemplified by the dispute over Friedrich's *Tetschen Altar* (fig. 1) in 1818; for here the elder generation, which resisted innovation, was particularly influen-

Fig. 1 Caspar David Friedrich, *The Tetschen Altar* 1807–08, Staatliche Kunstsammlungen Dresden, Gemäldegalerie Neue Meister

tial. A lively literary scene added life to the debate, which took on a political tinge after the defeat of Prussia in 1806.

After 1815, Friedrich was joined in Dresden by Carl Gustav Carus, Ernst Ferdinand Oehme and – for a time – the young Ludwig Richter, among others, although he never formed a school. The Norwegian artist Johan Christian Clausen Dahl, who arrived in 1818, became friendly with Friedrich and shared his house; but within the context of Dresden landscape painting the vitality and the brusque immediacy of Dahl's approach to Nature made him, in a sense, Friedrich's polar opposite. Georg Friedrich Kersting, from Güstrow, held a special place within the Dresden scene; in his interiors he used portraits or genre figures as expressions of states of mind.

Because Saxony stayed too long on Napoleon's side in the Wars of Liberation, it ended among the losers and forfeited a large part of its territory; and with this went

much of Dresden's importance as an artistic centre. There were no resources to support a school of monumental painting, such as emerged in Munich. A Nazarene movement, which also existed in Dresden, and which included Carl Vogel von Vogelstein, Carl Peschel, Gustav Heinrich Naeke and Adolf Zimmermann, caused little stir. In 1847 one of the most important Nazarenes, Schnorr von Carolsfeld, took up a post in Dresden, and he continued to produce outstanding drawings until his death in 1872. Probably the most popular of German nineteenth-century artists was Richter; again mostly through drawings, he extolled the simplicity of rural life, and that of children in particular, as an antidote to the evils of modern urban life. His mildness concealed an insight.

Where Dresden stood for several generations of intensive cultivation of art in the capital of a kingdom, Dessau and Weimar showed what poorer princes might achieve from scratch in a single generation, by dint of sheer enthusiasm and acumen. The 'garden kingdom' that Prince Leopold Friedrich Franz of Anhalt-Dessau had created at Wörlitz from 1776 onwards, and the philanthropic institutions that he set up in his country, had their roots in the Enlightenment, but they led over without a break into Romanticism. The etcher Karl Wilhelm Kolbe the Elder (Eichenkolbe, Oak Kolbe) saw plant life – which commands so much attention only in flat country – as the home of mysterious forces, to which man has no choice but to submit. Before the brothers Ferdinand, Friedrich and Heinrich Olivier left their native countryside, it was in the 'English Garden' at Wörlitz that they learned to read the messages of Nature and history. It was an artistic flowering that ended with the Prince's death in 1817.

In Weimar, by contrast, the will of one minor prince, Duke Carl August of Saxe-Weimar, drew Goethe and the greatest literary figures of German Classicism to a court that came to dominate the literary life of all Germany. Goethe mistrusted Romanticism, and in 1817 he inveighed against modern artistic trends – without knowing very much about them – in his essay *Neudeutsche religiös-patriotische Kunst* ('Latter-Day German Religious-Patriotic Art'); but even his immense influence was not enough to establish a Weimar school of painting in keeping with his own ideas. All efforts in this direction through the prize competitions held by the 'Weimar Friends of Art' from 1799 to 1805, were unsuccessful. The most talented artist born in Weimar, the draughtsman Franz Horny, entirely escaped Goethe's notice.

Academic teaching produced no Romantic art. The Academy founded in Kassel in 1777, with Johann Heinrich Tischbein the Elder at its head, did very successful work, and something like a Kassel school did emerge; but it is significant that the most Romantic artist in Kassel, Ludwig Emil Grimm – the third of the Brothers Grimm – lived rather out of the limelight, although he did become a professor at the Academy in 1832. He painted little, though he drew and etched a great deal; with his unprejudiced and penetrating view of life, and with occasional flashes of humour, he always looked for inner reality and neglected the outward show. One artist worthy to be mentioned in the same breath as Grimm was Ludwig Sigismund Ruhl, who in his youth worked closely with Fohr.

Berlin ranked alongside Dresden as a major location of German Romantic painting. There had long been a rivalry and a dialogue between the capitals of Prussia and Saxony, and this continued to bear fruit in the period around 1800. The Enlightenment had operated with particular intensity in Berlin, and this led to a correspondingly vigorous reaction against it. Wilhelm Heinrich Wackenroder – one of the pioneers of Romanticism in literature, the author of the *Herzensergießungen eines kunstliebenden Klosterbruders* ('Outpourings from the Heart of an Art-Loving Monk'), a friend of Tieck and a man gifted with a particular feeling for visual art – was a Berliner.

Prussia was severely humiliated by Napoleon in 1806, and this produced a correspondingly powerful upsurge of patriotic resistance and reforming zeal, in many fields at once. In art the dominant force was the universal genius of Karl Friedrich Schinkel. After 1815, Schinkel was to work mostly as an architect; but before that date, when there was no money to pay for buildings, he promoted his ideas mainly through drawings, paintings, dioramas and prints. His mentor, Friedrich Gilly, died young in 1800. Schinkel's model of the creative process was the plant-like emergence of an idea from an inner nucleus or germ; and the quality of genius, as he saw it, was action in accordance with Nature.

Very unlike Dresden, which was set in beautiful countryside, Berlin was a place where a painful awareness of the lack of natural beauty stimulated the artist to create his own. Landscape gardening was accordingly very important; and the manmade landscape around Potsdam is perhaps the greatest work of art ever produced by Prussia.

One characteristic feature of the Berlin art of the period was its historical genre painting, in which – stimulated by such writers as Friedrich de la Motte-Fouqué and E.T.A. Hoffmann – artists sought to idealize the life of the Middle Ages. Under Schinkel's influence, they were much inspired by surviving Gothic architecture, such as that of Marienburg (Maebork) in West Prussia. Noteworthy exponents included the painters Karl Wilhelm Kolbe the Younger and Karl Friedrich Hampe. Stage decoration was another field in which Schinkel had a reforming influence, and this carried over into Romantic painting, keeping it in close contact with literature and music. This particularly applies to the work of Blechen, which combines the pensive intensity of Schinkel and Friedrich with the emotional spontaneity of Dahl. For Blechen, Nature is the mirror in which he beholds his own personal, existential problems. There is much more to his work than the evocation of a vague mood.

Mood painting was rather more the province of the Düsseldorf school of painters, founded in 1828 by the Berliner Wilhelm Schadow, initially supported by his pupils and friends Carl Friedrich Lessing, Eduard Bendemann, Julius Hübner, Carl Sohn and Theodor Hildebrandt – all of whom, like Schadow himself, were from the Prussian heartland to the east. In the years that followed, in which it became apparent that Romanticism as such had worn itself out, the Düsseldorf school achieved such success that people looked to it for a new golden age of German painting. The Düsseldorf school was expected to be Prussia's answer to the art of Munich; and, when Bendemann and Hübner went to teach in Dresden in 1837, it was hoped that their appointment would rescue art in that city from its stagnation.

The flagging vitality of Romanticism, which began to be apparent around 1830, went together with a mood of discouragement in the elder artists, who before and during the Wars of Liberation had hoped for a thorough reform of art and a consequent ethical transformation of society. The Düsseldorf school was successful, by contrast, because it gave such elegant expression to a prevalent sense of melancholy, confirming the feelings of contemporaries instead of exhorting them to act and behave differently.

In the 1830s, a reaction set in. This culminated in 1848, promoted by the rift between the Catholic, westward-looking – and thus to some extent democratically minded – Rhineland and the centralized, Protestant Prussian state, ruled from Berlin. The Rhineland had become Prussian only in 1815; it lived in the glow of its glorious past, but present-day aspirations were proving hard to fulfil. King Frederick William IV made an effort to bridge the gulf by promoting the completion of Cologne cathedral as a national monument; he also paid homage to his own historical roots by enlarging the castle of Stolzenfels.

Romantic ideas persisted in the Düsseldorf school well into the second half of the nineteenth century – in the work of Caspar Scheuren, for instance – and were passed down to Anselm Feuerbach and Arnold Böcklin. The city also witnessed a Nazarene revival, carried on by Schadow's former pupils Ernst Deger, Carl Müller and Franz Ittenbach.

It is noticeable that the great cities of Danzig and Breslau (Gdansk and Wrocław), rich though they were in artistic tradition, never again produced painting of any consequence. The reason was that in these far eastern regions of Germany the most talented painters – who included Lessing, Hübner and Hildebrandt – were attracted westwards, first to Berlin and then, in some cases, on to Düsseldorf.

German Romantic painting presents an animated scene, with much local variation. The question why a thing appears in one place and not in another is most often impossible to answer conclusively; but, then, it is always a stimulating question to ask.

Helmut Börsch-Supan

Translated from the German by David Britt

Ludwig I's Munich as a Centre of Artistic Renewal

In the decades following the Napoleonic era, Munich won a reputation as the leading centre for the renewal of the arts in Germany.[1] One of the external reasons and a precondition for this was the establishment of the kingdom of Bavaria, with Napoleon's blessing, in 1806, and the significant increase in its territory, mainly through the incorporation of former imperial lands. The first task was to integrate the new territories, some of which were Protestant, into the original Bavaria. In 1818, at the instigation of the Crown Prince, Bavaria acquired a constitution – shortly after the grandduchy of Saxe-Weimar and decades before Prussia. This guaranteed the people substantial powers in the national parliament and redefined the status of the Catholic and Protestant churches. Self-administration in municipalities and rural districts enabled independent local traditions to flourish and ultimately served to unite the different parts of the kingdom. Next, the capital of the former electorate had to be extended and made into a worthy seat for the royal court and above all a cultural centre. According to contemporary thinking this involved a significant role for the arts, among which Kant had given pride of place to painting because of its ability to convey ideas.[2] The Beautiful, as a force for harmony, was thought to have educative value ever since Kant had put it on a par with the 'Morally Good';[3] it must therefore enter into the life and consciousness of the people and make them sensitive to the True, the Beautiful and the Good: the people must be 'spiritualized'.

In a ceremonial speech held at the Bavarian Academy of Science in 1807, one of its members, Friedrich Wilhelm Schelling, went much further (with consequences which can still be felt in our own century).[4] He put the autonomy of creative art at the very heart of *Über das Verhältnis der bildenden Künste zur Natur* (The Relationship between the Fine Arts and Nature), and categorically rejected art of an archaic manner. Schelling opposed the traditional belief that the highest form of beauty existed in imitating Nature with the liberal principle of artistic individuality, which is respon-sible only to God and Nature. Basic ideas of this individual approach to teaching art can be found in the extremely progressive constitution of the Academy of Arts, founded a year later. Schelling's influence can be detected in this, but his ideas were not recognised by the Academy for very long and did not come truly into their own until later when they were taken up by competing institutions, such as the *Kunstverein* (Society of Fine Arts), founded in 1824, and other institutions that aimed to promote the arts.

In the conception and realization of this aim a central role was played by the Crown Prince, who later became King Ludwig I. He initiated and authorized all the projects. At least this was how it seemed to such diverse art experts as the Prussian Franz Kugler or the Munich critic Ernst Frster. Frster, in his *History of German Art*, judges the king's role as a patron and promoter of the arts in the following terms: 'King Ludwig has become the protector of art like hardly any other in the whole of history; this he has become not only because of his innate love of art, which is inseparable from his life, nor because of his sensitive understanding of it, not through the multitude of his creations, but above all through the spirit in which and with which he created them.'[5]

In all this an important part was played by the idea of arousing patriotic sentiment among the people in response to Napoleon's hegemonic claims. As early as the beginning of 1807 the Crown Prince, then only twenty years old, commissioned designs for the Walhalla, which was to be a national shrine in honour of great Germans past and present.[6] Between 1830 and 1842 a Doric temple was built by Leo von Klenze on the cliffs overlooking the Danube near the former imperial town of Regensburg, which went back to Roman times. The admiration it evoked is attested not least by a famous painting by J. M. W. Turner.[7]

Although his contemporaries were far from unanimous in praising Ludwig's service to art, the results of his unflagging efforts for the cultural development of Bavaria have been held in extremely high regard until

Fig.1 Franz Ludwig Catel *Crown Prince Ludwig in the Spanish Wine Tavern* 1824, Bayerische Staatsgemäldesammlungen, Munich

the present day.[8] Hence every discussion of the subject at the same time involves the personal role of the king.

Within the framework of an unprecedented development programme, public buildings of all kinds – for administrative purposes, education, the arts and sciences, health and welfare, and the church – were erected on the basis of an urban development plan (the *Generallinienplan*) devised by Karl von Fischer, and years before Ludwig's accession to the throne in 1825 the face of the city had begun to change completely. Not long afterwards the King said, 'I wish to make Munich into a city that does Germany such honour that no one will know Germany unless he has seen Munich.'[9]

Not only in the capital, but throughout the country, conditions were created for the education and prosperity of the population; in this connection special attention must be drawn to the building of the Main-Danube Canal and the first railway system in Germany. Behind all this lay a comprehensive concept by which the King let himself be guided, even in his artistic policy, which was of particular concern to him, and which soon earned him admiration, even abroad. W. J. Banks Esq., a British MP who had spoken in favour of Peter von Cornelius, a professor at the Munich Academy, in debates over the extension of the Houses of Parliament, said of the artistic achievements set in hand by the Bavarian king, 'What has the King of Bavaria achieved

by founding such a wide-ranging school of art in so short a time? He has neglected no means of establishing an organic association of artists, not only in the higher kinds of art, but in all, without distinction, right down to the lowest...'[10]

During several months spent in Rome in the spring of 1818, on his way back from Sicily, the Crown Prince's understanding of art, which had hitherto centred on antiquity and classicism – based on his classical education[11] and a visit made to Italy twenty years earlier – was permanently opened and broadened to include the Romantic style of the German artists living in Rome, especially the Nazarenes associated with Cornelius and Friedrich Overbeck.

Ludwig had personal dealings with them and was impressed by their frescoes for the Joseph cycle, recently completed for the Prussian consul Salomo Bartholdy, and he now saw the possibility of realizing his idea of popular educative picture programmes in Munich. Enthusiastic, like the Nazarenes themselves, about the effectiveness of the fresco technique, which had been revived under the influence of the old Italian pictorial language, Ludwig was determined to secure the services of the most important painters in order to create monumental wall paintings on historical themes for his building programme, for he was convinced that this would strengthen the national consciousness that had grown out of the wars of liberation and counter the particularist tendencies that had re-emerged since the Congress of Vienna.

Ludwig, who as Crown Prince of Bavaria was wholly taken up with such unifying patriotic ideas, wanted to be known in Rome as a German and therefore made a point of wearing the so-called German coat, which for political reasons he was not allowed to wear in Munich.[12]

On 29 April 1818 the Nazarenes gave a farewell banquet in honour of their future patron at the Villa Schultheiß. This not only expressed the hope that they would soon be able to work in their own country: it also demonstrates, in the picture sequences of monumental banners conceived by Cornelius, the central importance of historical consciousness for the Romantic conception of art.[13] Johann Georg Sulzer, in his *Theorie der Schönen Künste* ('Theory of the Fine Arts') of 1792, had

pointed to the importance of history for the development of patriotic sentiments.[14]

The Crown Prince had equally close contacts in Rome
with the German Protestant painters on the Capitol,
such as Julius Schnorr von Carolsfeld, Markus Theodor
Rebbenitz, Friedrich Olivier and others, and also with
the classically inclined artists associated with Bertel
Thorvaldsen and Joseph Anton Koch. This open and
undogmatic attitude, to which Franz Ludwig Catel's
memorial picture testifies (fig. 1), was to remain with
Ludwig throughout his life. It led to a certain amount of
criticism regarding the plurality of styles that is typical
of Ludovician Munich.[15] However, all artists were
united in the conviction 'that one must be what one
wishes to represent in the picture; that religious and historical or patriotic subjects are most deserving of representation, but that one must be inwardly Christian and
inwardly German ... so that the representations of both
are true.'[16] Such inwardness, which was demanded from
a religious point of view for the *pictor christianus* of
Dürer's time, favoured the Crown Prince's plans for
artistic commissions in Munich. Whereas other capitals
such as Berlin found no use for the German artists working in Rome, despite urgent representations by the
Prussian ambassador Niebuhr, Crown Prince Ludwig
engaged Peter von Cornelius to paint the state rooms of
the Glyptothek in Munich.

Cornelius probably owed his summons to Munich
partly to the design on which he was working for the
ceiling of the Dante Room in the Casino Massimo, for
which commissions had also been granted to Overbeck
in the late summer of 1817 and somewhat later to
Schnorr. His aim, and that of some other Nazarenes,
agreed with that of the Crown Prince: this was to create
monumental works of art *al fresco* and so attract the
attention of the largest possible number of people.[17]
This was advocated by Johann David Passavant, a friend
of Franz Pforr and Overbeck, in his *Ansichten über die
bildenden Künste*, published in 1820, where he cited
parallels in late medieval Italy.[18] In the Munich
Glyptothek, built by Klenze, Cornelius proceeded in
much the same way as he had done in the Casino
Massimo, where he adopted a design concept in which
the Dante frescoes were structured to fit in with the
room's architecture and the literary material was sym-

Fig.2 Peter von Cornelius *Eos Pleads with Zeus for Her Son Memnon to be Given Eternal Youth* 1826. Fresco formerly in the Hall of the Gods of the Glyptothek, Munich. Destroyed.

bolically interpreted to point to Christian themes.[19] In
preparation for the Ancient and Classical sculptures that
were to be displayed, however, he chose themes from
Greek mythology, which were to be understood symbolically as a total complex of relations between the gods
and the human beings who depended on them. The
vestibule between the Hall of the Gods and the Hall of
the Heroes was dedicated to the legend of Prometheus,
as the prototype of the creative artist. The creation of
man, the breathing of life into him, his fall and subsequent rescue by the demigod Hercules admittedly show
clear analogies to Christian doctrine and accorded with
the basic principles of Romanticism, but in the treatment
of the figures and in the painting of the rooms Cornelius
drew upon the mature style of Raphael (fig. 2), thus sat-
isfying the demand for congruence of form and content.

Cornelius did not see the frescoes in the Glyptothek as
a stylistic reversion, but repeatedly stressed that the
meeting with Antiquity was a necessity for the sake of
his own artistic development and historical continuity.
In a detailed description of the designs for the
Glyptothek frescoes, which Cornelius enclosed with a
letter sent to the Crown Prince from Rome on 9
December 1818, he states: 'Antiquity is now, like nature
herself, an inseparable element of our whole culture, but
like the body it must be enclosed within itself, so that
the supernatural element of Christianity can pour forth
in full force...'[20]

Fig.3 Friedrich Overbeck *Italia and Germania* 1828, Bayerische Staatsgemäldesammlungen, Munich

The poetic fusion of Classical and Christian tradition, the investing of past forms with new content, together the whole consciousness of historical continuity, have always been considered special features of Romanticism. The resultant variety of individual views on art was compared by J. N. Ringseis, the Crown Prince's travelling companion and personal physician, with the multiplicity of birds' voices: 'Yes, we shall again see the efflorescence of an age of art... . Timeless pictures speak to us in new tongues from halls and churches, and the tall statues of the Ancients begin to climb down from their columns. But not to be done to death again by mindless, soulless imitation, but free and born again, and with a strange power.'[21]

Franz Kugler, who has already been mentioned, spoke with similar optimism during an extensive visit to Munich in 1835. Asking himself whether the flourishing plurality of artistic styles in Munich would not have harmful consequences for the further development of art, he gave the well-considered and reasoned answer: 'Our age is only now engaged in developing new elements of art, and in this process it is necessary that we should incorporate all our studies. We cannot frivolously throw away what we have learnt. We can reach true self-understanding only on this historical path.' He pleaded for a variety of means as the prerequisite 'for the lively execution of our ideas. ... To have achieved this is King Ludwig's great service to the German art of

our time... . The art of years to come will honour him as one of the most zealous founders.'[22]

Overbeck could not be induced to take part in the great fresco projects in Munich and remained in Rome all his life: he probably realized that the artistic principles of the Nazarenes were not compatible with the strictly run academic regime under Cornelius. In 1825, the year of his accession, Ludwig acquired Overbeck's famous *Portrait of Vittoria Caldoni*, one of the first paintings in his collection of contemporary art. To house this collection Friedrich von Gärtner began to plan a third museum in 1843. This opened ten years later as the Neue Pinakothek, with a collection of paintings from German and foreign schools that had by now grown to about 300. Even more significant for this collection was the acquisition, in 1832, of Overbeck's main work *Italia and Germania* (fig. 3), which expresses a basic idea of the Nazarenes: the two young female figures, turned towards each other like sisters, symbolize the harmonious link between the classic Italian ideal of art represented by Raphael and the traditional German spirit of Drer; from these two should spring the new efflorescence of art in Germany.

With Julius Schnorr von Carolsfeld Ludwig fulfilled his wish to draw to Munich one of the most gifted painters from the Nazarenes circle, in addition to Cornelius. After completing his Ariosto frescoes in the Casino Massimo, he was first commissioned, in 1827, to work on an Odyssean cycle for the new royal residence, built by Klenze. Before leaving for Munich he travelled with the artistic couple Gottlob and Bianca Quandt to Sicily to study the Homeric sites. Meanwhile, however, Ludwig changed the project in favour of the Nibelung frescoes, which are still extant.[23]

Strongly influenced by Cornelius, Schnorr embarked on a highly symbolic programme of compositions in which the divine origin of monarchy was to be illustrated by reference to scripture. Although he was in agreement with Ludwig's dynastic self-image, the King then insisted on a historical and narrative treatment, which strikes one especially in the rooms that were painted later; these were painted according to Schnorr's designs, but entirely by pupils and assistants (fig. 4). Only the more lyrical scenes such as the *Refusal to Greet Kriemhild* remind one of the harmoniously concentrated

Fig.4 Julius Schnorr von Carolsfeld *Hagen Kills Siegfried* 1845, Fresco in the Nibelung Rooms, Residenz, Munich

Ariosto frescoes with their compositional style inspired by Raphael's Stanze.

This break in style can be traced back to a change of design principles that occurred in the 1830s; these were intended to draw attention to a climactic moment in the historical sequence of events, appealing to the viewer's emotions and enabling him to experience what he saw as reality. This was one of the reasons why Cornelius's painting of the Ludwigskirche, completed in 1840,[24] met with incomprehension and disapproval and why there was general enthusiasm for the new monumental paintings of historical themes by the Belgians[25], with their dramatic pictorial composition. Their theatrical depiction of reality, so-called, was then followed in official historical painting until the turn of the century.

The third painter to receive important commissions for frescoes was Heinrich Maria Hess, who went to Rome in 1821 and painted several oil paintings for the Crown Prince: a small landscape with Roman pilgrims, portraits of *Thorvaldsen* and the *Marchesa Fiorenzi*, and the monumental *Parnassus*. In 1826, at Cornelius's suggestion, he was invited to Munich to teach at the Academy and collaborate on the Glyptothek frescoes. Eventually he received important commissions for religious programme painting: the *al fresco* decoration of the court church of All Saints, modelled on the mosaics of the Capella Palatino near Palermo, and the decoration of the five-aisled Basilica St Bonifaz, built in imitation of an early Christian Italian model.

Apart from the more lyrically narrative murals in the royal state rooms, illustrating German Romantic literature and painted by artists of the Cornelius school such as Moritz von Schwind and Wilhelm von Kaulbach, another genre of fresco painting evolved in Munich in the 1830s – the so called 'historic landscapes' of Karl Rottmann. During his first years in Munich Rottmann, had been able to learn from the heroic landscapes of Joseph Anton Koch, a leader of the German classicists, and then became personally acquainted with him in Rome, when Koch had just finished painting the Dante room at the Casino Massimo. After study visits in the field, Rottmann received a royal commission to paint murals of Italian and Greek landscapes for the arcades of the Hofgarten, which were open to the public. Whereas the cycle of Italian landscapes represents the continuity of Classical culture, in accordance with Romantic notions, the Greek landscapes – though commissioned when philhellenism was at its height – show the historically significant sites in all their present devastation (fig. 5).

The ideal depiction of Greece in the period around 1800, expressing the hope of spiritual renewal of the age as in Koch's *Classical Landscape with Rainbow*, had now been affected by an intervening change in historical and philosophical consciousness. Thus the general theme of the cycle is the overwhelming of man and his culture by nature.[26]

As is clear from the frescoes running round the façade of the Neue Pinakothek, executed between 1848 and 1853 after designs by Kaulbach, the end had come for idealist art. Instead of celebrating Ludwig I programmatically as the patron and reviver of a new German art, as the terms of the contract laid down, the pictures contain more or less overt ironic and satirical commentaries on his patronage and the artists he employed. The fact that the programme was approved at the highest level[27] testifies once more to the King's open and pluralistic attitude. With the crisis in historical painting came a crisis in Romantic Christian painting as practised by the Nazarenes. This is confirmed by Friedrich Theodor Vischer, a writer on aesthetics, who said in 1841: 'Our God is an immanent God… his body is only the whole world; his true presence is only the human spirit. To glorify this God is the highest task of art. History, the

Fig.5 Carl Rottmann *Sikyon with Corinth* 1836–38, Bayerische Staatsgemäldesammlungen, Munich

world as the theatre of the Lord; *natural reality in sharp, not romantically vague outlines … that is the field of the modern artist.'*[28]

Christoph Heilmann

Translated from the German by David McLintock

1 For the details see exh. cat. *Wittelsbach und Bayern*, III, 1. *Krone und Verfassung…Beiträge zur Bayerischen Geschichte und Kunst 1799–1825* (Munich, 1986); esp. Hermann Bauer, 'Kunstanschauung und Kunstpflege in Bayern von Carl Theodor bis Ludwig I', 345ff.

2 Immanuel Kant, *Werke in sechs Bänden*, ed. Wilhelm Weihschedel V (Darmstadt, 1968), 434.

3 Immanuel Kant (as note 2), V, 461.

4 Friedrich Wilhelm Schelling, *Über das Verhältnis der bildenden Künste zur Natur* (Munich, 1807), 61. Quoted by Werner Hofmann, *Das Irdische Paradies* (Munich, 1974), 55. Horst Jantzen, 'Die Kunstgelehrten: Schelling', in *Geist und Gestalt* (Munich, 1959), I: 279ff., reprint of the 'Konstitution Schellings' in *Tradition und Widerspruch: 175 Jahre Kunstakademie München* (Munich, 1985), 327 ff.

5 Ernst Förster, *Geschichte der deutschen Kunst*, Teil 5 (Leipzig, 1960), 21.

6 On the meaning of the Walhalla see Jörg Traeger, *Der Weg nach Walhalla. Denkmallandschaft und Bildungsreise im 19. Jahrhundert* (2nd ed. Regensburg, 1991).

7 *The Opening of the Walhalla*, 1842. Tate Gallery, London. See Martin Butlin and Evelyn Joll, *The Paintings of J. M. W. Turner* (London, 1977), no. 401. Exhibited at the Royal Academy, London, Turner's picture, dedicated to King Ludwig with a poem composed by the artist, was exhibited at the International Art Exhibition in Munich in 1845 and returned to London without comment.

8 Most recently Heinz Gollwitzer, *Ludwig I. von Bayern* (Munich, 1986), 113ff.; *'Ihm welcher der Andacht Tempel baut…' Ludwig I. und die Alte Pinakothek. Festschrift zum Jubilumsjahr 1986*, with contributions by Rolf Kultzen, Christoph Heilmann, Cornelia Syre and others (Munich, 1986).

9 R. Kultzen (as note 8), 11.

10 *Schorns Kunstblatt* 11 (1843), 45.

11 Gollwitzer, (as note 8), 116, describes Ludwig as 'without exaggerating one of the most cultured princes of his time'.

12 P. O. A. Alterbone, *Reiseerinnerungen aus Deutschland und Italien* (Berlin, 1867), 183. Cf. the portrait of K. Stieler painted *c.* 1816, exh. cat. *Deutsche Romantiker. Bildthema der Zeit von 1800–1850* (Munich, 1985), no. 13.

13 Frank Büttner, 'Die Kunst, die Künstler und die Mäzene. Die Dekorationen zur römischen Kunsterfassung 1818', *Festschrift für Jens Christian Jensen. Romantik und Gegenwart* (Cologne, 1988), 19ff.

14 Sulzer, II, 623, quoted by Monika Wagner, *Allegorie und Geschichte* (Tübingen, 1989), 38.

15 Gollwitzer (as note 8), 119.

16 E. Ringseis, *Erinnerungen des Dr Johann Nepomuk Ringseis* (Regensburg and Amberg, 1886), 477f.

17 Herbert von Einem, 'Ein unveröffentlichter Brief des Peter Cornelius', *Festschrift für Wilhelm Waetzold* (Berlin, 1941), 308.

18 *Ansichten über die bildenden Knste und Darstellung des Ganges derselben in der Toscana. Zur Bestimmung des Gesichtspunktes aus welchem die neudeutsche Malerschule zu betrachten ist. Von einem deutschen Knstler in Rom* (Heidelberg and Speyer, 1820).

19 Herbert von Einem, 'Die Ausmalung der Festsäle durch Peter Cornelius', exh. cat. *Glyptothek München 1830–1980* (Munich, 1980), 214ff. For further details see Frank Büttner, *Peter Cornelius. Fresken und Freskenprojekte* I, 3 (Wiesbaden 1980), 125–223.

20 Frank Büttner (as note 19), app. 2, 226 (Peder Mjort, 'Beschreibung der Entwürfe…').

21 Ringseis (as note 16), 469.

22 F. Kugler, 'Ein Besuch in München', *Museum* (1835), no. 24 f. Repr. in *Kleine Schriften und Studien zur Kunstgeschichte* III (Stuttgart, 1854), 132f. Cf. Leonore Koschnik, *Franz Kugler (1808–1858) als Kunsthistoriker und Kulturpolitiker* (diss. Berlin, 1985), 43ff.

23 Inken Nowald, *Die Nibelungenfresken von Julius Schnorr von Carolsfeld im Königsbau der Münchner Residenz 1827–1867* (Kiel, 1978) (Schriftenreihe der Kunsthalle Kiel, fasc. 3). The state rooms of the new wing of the residence were open to the public, on payment of an entry fee, on Sundays and holidays. The basic idea for the building and its internal decoration was that it should contain pictures for edification. See H. Bauer (as note 1), 350f.

24 Frank Büttner, 'Unzeitgemässe Grösse. Die Fresken von Peter Cornelius in der Münchner Ludwigskirche und die zeitgenössische Kritik', *Das Münster* (1993), fasc. 4, 293ff.

25 P. Schoch, 'Die belgischen Bilder', Städel Jahrbuch, N.F. 7 (1979), 177 ff; Christoph Heilmann, 'Zur französisch-belgischen Historienmalerei und ihre Abgrenzung zur Münchner Schule', exh. cat. *Die Münchner Schule 1850–1914* (Munich, 1979), 47ff.

26 Barbara Eschenburg, 'Das Verhältnis von Mensch und Natur in Rottmanns Landschaften', Erika Breiham-Rödiger, *Carl Rottmann 1797–1850* (Munich, 1978), 69ff, esp. 78–82.

27 Werner Busch, *Die notwendige Arabeske. Wirklichkeitsaneignung und Stilisierung in der deutschen Kunst des 19. Jahrhunderts* (Berlin 1985), 123.

28 Friedrich Theodor Vischer, *Kritische Gänge* I (Tübingen, 1844), 193ff.

German Romantic Art Abroad:
A British Perspective

Romanticism and Germany

The roots of Romanticism are various and reach back through the histories of many European countries. But it was in Germany that the movement first emerged above the ground. Even after it had spread to other countries in the early nineteenth century, it continued to be seen as a tendency that owed a particular debt to Germany.

The view of German Romanticism from abroad was, for the most part, a syncretic one. It tended to group together 'programmatic' Romantics like Ludwig Tieck and the Schlegel brothers, Friedrich and August Wilhelm, with older contemporaries such as Immanuel Kant, Johann Wolfgang von Goethe and Friedrich Schiller who had little to do with the movement, or even positively opposed it. It concentrated on extremes. There was much of heaven and hell in German Romanticism, according to this view, but very little of the world between. The 'heaven' tended to be seen as the achievements of Kantian philosophy – revising the insights offered by metaphysics and giving new penetrative powers to the human mind.

'Criticism has assumed a new form in Germany;' wrote the Scottish sage Thomas Carlyle in 1827, 'it proceeds on other principles and proposes to itself a higher aim … it is no study of the hour; for it springs from the depth of thought, and remotely or immediately connects itself with the subtlest problems of all philosophy.'[1]

Carlyle then went on to elaborate how the critical writings of Schiller and others had established the independence of aesthetic beauty, and how it was now possible to analyse and interpret great cultural achievements in a fundamental and objective manner. Never before, it seemed, had it been possible to gauge the true benefit of the arts to mankind, or to produce works that concentrated so exclusively upon this mission. Carlyle was thinking mainly about literature. But the principle remained the same for the other arts – including the visual. German painting – particularly that of the Nazarenes and fellow revivalists – seemed to be infused by a similar analytical principle. When the British Magazine the *Art Union* proclaimed in 1839 that German artists were 'the first in Europe', it justified its claim principally on intellectual grounds, saying 'they alone can give a reason for the treatment of every work of art.'[2]

But while the huge moral and intellectual claims for cultural products might represent the 'heaven' of German Romanticism, the 'hell' was also seen as a product of the same speculative tendency. In this case it led to subjectivity and excess. This strain had already been identified as German before the movement proper had got under way. It had been Goethe's early *Sturm und Drang* (Storm and Stress) novel, *Werther* (1774) that had set the tone. The story of a young man who had literally killed himself for love seemed to epitomize this morbid capitulation to emotion. There were stories of young men throughout Europe following this nihilistic example. German culture was frequently characterized at that time in terms of excess. In Jane Austen's *Mansfield Park* (1814), for example, the foolish young people who take over the household while the master is away demonstrate their proclivities by preparing to perform a play by the sensationalist German author August von Kotzebue.[3] At much the same time one finds complaints about the dangerous physical encounters sanctioned by that new Germanic dance, the waltz. In 1816 a correspondent to the *Gentleman's Magazine* quoted Mme de Staël's remark 'In Germany, love is a religion, a romantic religion, which too easily tolerates every thing that sensibility is willing to excuse,' and then went on to designate the waltz 'the first step in seduction'.[4] None of this had anything to do with Romanticism proper, but it set an expectation that seemed to be confirmed when the wilder flights of fancy of authors like Novalis, Tieck and E.T.A. Hoffmann began to appear.

The Visual Arts

Relatively little was known about contemporary German art abroad in the early nineteenth century, but that little tended to be seen in terms of the polarities set up for the interpretation of literature and philosophy. As has already been mentioned, the Nazarenes were talked about the most. They were thought to have returned to 'first principles', to the pure source of *quattrocento* art and have reinstated the dignity and spirituality of an earlier age. There was as well an interest in the more expressive 'Northern' side of the revival, in particular the emulation of the vigorous draughtsmanship of Albrecht Dürer and other masters of the sixteenth century. On the other hand, there was virtually no interest at the time in German landscape painting. The 'transcendental' symbolic landscapes of Philipp Otto Runge and Caspar David Friedrich were hardly known at all. On the few occasions when it was discussed, German landscape painting was usually censured for its lack of atmospheric effect. In her much respected study of German life and culture, *Visits and Sketches at Home and Abroad* (1834), Mrs Anna Jameson complained: 'Not only have they no landscape painters who can compare with Callcott and Turner, but they do not appear to have *imagined* the kind of excellence achieved by these wonderful artists. I should say, generally, that their most beautiful landscapes want atmosphere. I used to feel while looking at them as if I were in the exhausted receiver of an air-pump.'[5] It was only in the later twentieth century that this censorious view of German landscape painting of the early nineteenth century began to change.

When praising the visual art associated with German Romanticism, commentators of the day were conscious of promoting an alternative, one that ran counter to the norm. For the visual arts – far more than music and literature – were seen as being rooted in the perceptual traditions of the south, in the apprehension of classic form. The speculative and expressive practices of the north offered exciting possibilities. But they could never completely take over. In the subsequent history of the response to German Romantic art one finds sporadic moments of enthusiasm rather than a continuous tradition. At particular moments, it would seem, it becomes attractive to assert the 'alternative' practice, and use it as a means of chastising those who have become too enfeebled by materialism or a slavish imitation of the current norm. British reactions have largely followed the pattern found in France, and latterly in America. Thus, after the initial enthusiasm, one finds knowledge of German Romantic art waning until the period of the Symbolists. Then there is a hiatus again until the Surrealists. After this interest receded again, until the major critique of modernism got under way in the 1970s. It is these moments that will be looked at in this essay.

Revivalism and the 'Mind of Art'

The fact that the Nazarenes were talked about so much more than other German artists in the early nineteenth century was to some extent due to a physical circumstance. In 1810 this group had moved their principle centre of activity from Vienna – where they had established themselves as the Brotherhood of St Luke in 1808 – to Rome. By practising in a multinational artistic community, they were in a prime position to receive international attention. It was here in fact that they gained their nickname, being designated '*Nazareni*' on account of their long hair and loose-flowing, quasi-medieval costumes. In 1815 they were commissioned by the Prussian Consul, Salomo Bartholdy, to paint a series of frescoes on the Story of Joseph for his reception room. These became the talk of Rome, and were soon being reported on in countries ranging from the United States to Russia. The Nazarenes' startling physical appearance certainly helped their reputation. But they also profited from the fact that their art seemed to gain intellectual status from their association with German criticism and philosophy. Their medievalism – which was so extreme and thorough – was not seen as wilful personal eccentricity, but as a reasoned and constructive critique of modern times and modern art. Even those artists who found their anti-naturalism unacceptable respected them for their intellectual position. 'The English have the matter, and the Germans have the mind of art' concluded the English painter Charles Eastlake when writing of the Bartholdy frescoes in the *London Magazine* in 1820.[6] He summed up the dilemma of those who admired the Nazarenes' position without

Fig.1 Peter von Cornelius, Frescoes (1825–26) in the Hall of the Gods, Glyptothek, Munich. Destroyed.

being able to follow it themselves. Perhaps even more revealingly he added, 'they have dignified their art by depriving the spectator of the power of criticizing its execution.' This is not what the Nazarenes themselves had in mind. But it is typical of their wider reception. In reputation at least they can be counted as the first conceptual artists, being admired essentially for the idea of what they were doing.

The Nazarene ideal did not just appeal to connoisseurs. It also recommended itself to religious and political revivalists, and to those who were seeking to undo the 'damage' of revolution and materialism. They were much patronized by conservative monarchies in Germany – notably by Ludwig 1 of Bavaria in Munich. The large public frescoes that they executed – such as those in the Munich Glyptothek by Peter von Cornelius (fig. 1) – seemed to emphasize how effectively these artists could provide a clear, public, didactic art – one

that could gather people together in reverent obedience as religious paintings were thought to have done in the Middle Ages. During the middle years of the century there were official art projects going on throughout Europe by artists emulating the Nazarenes. In France even Ingres took some note of their style in his religious paintings, while muralists like Hippolyte Flandrin and Ary Scheffer became whole-hearted supporters.[7] In Britain in the 1840s, their example was used to encourage the move to decorate the new Houses of Parliament with large nationalistic murals.[8] Their medievalizing style was supported by the Gothic Revivalists in architecture. The pioneer A.W. Pugin referred to them in his polemical book *Contrasts*, which made a series of onslaughts on modern institutions by contrasting them with their counterparts from the fifteenth century. Speaking of one of the leaders of the Nazarenes, Johann Friedrich Overbeck, he wrote: 'the great Overbeck, that prince of Christian painters, has raised up a school of mystical and religious artists, who are fast putting to shame the natural and sensual school of art.'[9]

The 1840s was probably the only time in the history of British art when contemporary German art was imitated in a wholesale manner. Almost the whole community of historical artists – from leaders of the profession like William Dyce and Daniel Maclise down to young hopefuls like Ford Madox Brown and John Everett Millais – tried their hand at a didactic, medievalizing style. The 'German Manner', as it came to be known, did not on the whole lead directly to much distinguished painting. Certainly the resultant murals in the Houses of Parliament can hardly be regarded as a high point in the history of British art. But they did have some significant repercussions. Probably the most important of these was the Pre-Raphaelite Brotherhood. This group, set up by William Holman Hunt, Dante Gabriel Rossetti, Millais and other dissident Academy students in 1848, bore many resemblances to the Brotherhood of St Luke inaugurated in Vienna forty years previously. The English Pre-Raphaelites shared much of the medievalism and high-mindedness of the German Nazarenes. Yet they combined this with a more contemporary concern for realism and sensation, for the pictorial avant-garde of their time. Max Nordau was perhaps right when he claimed in 1889 that

'Pre-Raphaelitism is the grandson of German and a son of French Romanticism.'[10]

The relation between the English Pre-Raphaelites and the German Nazarenes can be taken as an illustration of the point that opposition and rivalry are more likely to produce positive results than uncritical admiration. Often, too, the most fruitful engagements take place in the most unpredictable places. It may well be that one of the most striking responses to Nazarene art can be found in the landscapes of Turner. Turner made his first visit to Italy in 1819. He was in Rome when the Bartholdy frescoes were the talk of the town, and may well have had direct contact with their painters through his friend Charles Eastlake. John Gage has speculated that the sight of the Nazarenes' use of simple, primary colours in their frescoes may have encouraged him in his development towards a more primitive and radical use of colour in his own work.[11] Equally intriguing is the thought that accounts of the Nazarenes may have encouraged the revivalist group of landscape painters who gathered around Samuel Palmer at Shoreham between 1824 and 1830. These young enthusiasts styled themselves the 'Primitives' and took to wearing medievalizing costumes. They were also great admirers of Northern art. Their knowledge of both modern and medieval examples of this came largely through engravings, such as those of Dürer and Lucas van Leyden amongst the ancients, or Cornelius and Friedrich August Retzsch amongst the moderns.[12] In their art one can find an ebullient intensity, an enthusiastic and eccentric Gothicism closer to the early private manifestations of medievalism amongst the Brotherhood of St Luke, than the measured public style of the Nazarenes' later productions.

Prints and Pen Line

Prints were the means by which most German artists of the nineteenth century outside the Nazarene circle became known abroad. Even that great German master of naturalistic painting, Adolph Menzel, was celebrated primarily on account of his lithographs and the wood engravings made from his designs. Both these reproductive techniques had particular association with

Fig.2 Johann Nepomuk Strixner, Page from *Albrecht Dürer's Prayer Book for the Emperor Maximilian* 1808, lithograph

Germany. Lithography was an invention of the Bavarian Alois Senefelder, and its early success abroad was associated with productions from Munich, notably the publication by Johann Nepomuk Strixner of Dürer's prayer book for the Emperor Maximilian in 1808 (fig. 2 and cat. 91). Wood engraving had affinities with the earlier woodcut process which had been used with such success by German masters of the sixteenth century. Many German illustrated books of the period – such as the lavishly produced edition of the *Nibelungenlied* of 1840 – based their style on this earlier work and had a great influence abroad. Above all it was the clarity and power of the line used by the Germans that commanded respect. Even John Ruskin – who was scathing about the Nazarenes on account of their lack of naturalism (he once talked of the 'headless serpent of Teutonic art [ending in German Philosophy constrictor powers – with no eyes]'[13]) could admire the simplifying power of the designs for wood engraving by Adrian Ludwig Richter and Alfred Rethel. Indeed, he recommended them to be studied from this point of view in his *Elements of Drawing*.[14] This interest in the virtue of simplifying line in illustra-

Fig.3 Alfred Rethel, Plate 2 of *Another Dance of Death* 1849, wood-engraving

tion was part of the revival of interest in medievalism and folk culture. The great popularity of German *Märchen* – either in the traditional form as collected by the brothers Jakob and Wilhelm Grimm, or in the modern 'art' form of writers like Adelbert von Chamisso and Friedrich de la Motte Fouqué – helped to seal the success of 'folksy' illustrations by artists like Moritz von Schwind and Richter. As such it had a particular attraction for the Pre-Raphaelites. Most influential of all was the revived woodcut style of Alfred Rethel – particularly when he was using this for large didactic prints in support of traditionalism (fig. 3 and cat. 73). When first turning his mind to the issue of designing medievalizing work for wood engraving Edward Burne-Jones wrote of Rethel's 'perfect outline, as correct as can be without effort, and, still more essentially, neat – and a due amount of quaintness.' He himself wished to produce '100,000 woodcuts as big as *Death the Friend* or bigger'.[15]

While these features were admired in medievalizing work, it was also recognized that the clarity and exactitude of penmanship that lay behind such simplifications could also produce feats of naturalistic effect – as it did in the work of Adolph Menzel. Menzel first reached an international audience through the designs for wood engravings that he made for Franz Kugler's *Life of Frederick the Great* (1840). He set standards of precision for the wood engravers of this work that had a profound effect upon the practice of the medium for the next half century. This is clear in the products of the 'golden age' of Victorian wood engraving: that time when the Pre-Raphaelites and illustrators like Frederick

Sandys and Charles Samuel Keene were working for the medium. Even when wood engraving began to be replaced by photo-mechanical processes at the end of the century, the taste for clear line that had been established seems to have had its advantages. For the early mechanical line blocks were only able to reproduce clear line effectively, and therefore required much the same graphic rigour as the wood engraving. The simplified style of Aubrey Beardsley's pen designs in the 1890s was seen by some commentators as being the descendant of the German graphic revolution of the 1840s. As late as 1924 one historian of that era could write: 'This is the period of the pen line design which commenced with Menzel and ended with Aubrey Beardsley, in whose sensitive hands the linear texture of design was changed from Menzel's solid web of fact to an airy filigree of fancy ....'[16]

Aestheticism and Degeneracy

Beardsley's designs might only seem to connect with German art on the technical point of linear mastery and even here of course this contact is mediated by a myriad of other relationships – notably that of the Japanese woodcut. But there was another link in the minds of many contemporaries in the 'degenerate' aestheticism of his art: the provocative treatment of deviant, amoral or even pornographic themes with exquisite elegance. Such wilfulness related to the darker side of German Romanticism, the 'hell' of subjectivity. By the time that it emerged in Beardsley's art this influence was arriving in Britain largely via the intermediary of France. But the roots of the tendency were not forgotten. John Ruskin – an early opponent of German Idealism – squarely blamed it for the later flourishing of amoral aestheticism.[17] In the 1890s the charge was reiterated by that *fin-de-siècle* Jeremiah, Max Nordau, in his study *Entartung* ('Degeneration').[18] There was little in aestheticism that drew directly on German Romantic visual art. Charles Baudelaire, the guiding light of the movement had, it is true, expressed enthusiasm for the morbidity of Rethel's woodcuts. But this interest was soon overwhelmed by other concerns. The strands of German Romanticism that formed a matrix for the related movements of aestheticism, Symbolism and degeneracy were philosophical and musical rather than visual. It was Richard Wagner rather than Friedrich or the Nazarenes that gave them their leitmotif. The story of how so many key concepts of German Romantic thought – the autonomy of art, synaesthesia, the *Gesamtkunstwerk*, the paradigm of music – re-emerged at this time has frequently been told.[19] German Romantic visual art had a negligible role in all of this. Yet, on the other hand, the very movements that flowered with this reawakening created the environment that enabled German Romantic art to be re-assessed in its own country.

The Rebirth of Romantic Landscape

It was in the 1890s, in fact, that a new interest in the art of the Romantic period began to emerge in Germany. While Max Nordau railed against the Neo-Romantic degeneracy of Symbolism, other critics were finding positive reasons for a close and detailed reassessment. Ricarda Huch's pioneering *Blütezeit der Romantik* ('The Flowering of Romanticism') (1899) provided this in a most impressive way. Huch was largely concerned with literature. But she did consider the visual arts, and made some telling observations. She was one of the first to see them as constituting a kind of uncomplicated project. The fantasies and dreams expressed in the writings of the period were only dimly adumbrated in the pictures. It was one of her contentions that the Symbolists of her own day were in fact bringing that project to fruition. This was particularly so in the case of Arnold Böcklin. In her chapter on symbolic landscape she asks, after having quoted one of the ecstatic visual fantasies in Ludwig Tieck's novel about a young apprentice of Dürer, *Franz Sternbalds Wanderungen*: 'Who can read these fantasies about painting without the name of Böcklin springing constantly to his lips?'

She then went on to hail Böcklin as the realizer of Romantic dreams. 'Then, a hundred years ago, these dreams of art tinged the dawning sky of the new century; the turn of our own century is adorned by the wondrous reality, the fulfilment. Here, too, Böcklin is the very artist whom the Romantics desired and foretold ....'[20]

Huch also represented the new view of German Romantic painting that emphasized landscape at the expense of other genres. For she saw landscape painting as being the one area in the visual arts where the artists had been involved in a subjective response to nature in a manner comparable to the writers of the period.

'And why landscape? Perhaps because it leaves such wide scope, as [August] Wilhelm Schlegel said, for the pure phenomenon: the painter lends the light-filled air a body, and breathes his soul into it.'[21]

This shift towards looking at landscape as the one area in the visual arts where there was an intimation of the more challenging sides of the Romantic experience followed the beginnings of a scholarly revival of interest in landscape painting. At the time that Huch was writing, the resurrection of the works of Friedrich and Runge had already begun. It was a process aided by the advocacy of powerful museum directors, such as Alfred Lichtwark in Hamburg and Hugo von Tschudi in Berlin, and by the publications of a small number of scholars. Foremost amongst these was the Norwegian Andreas Aubert, whose article on Friedrich in the *Kunstchronik* in 1895 (itself an extract from his monograph in Norwegian on Johan Christian Dahl[22]) represented a turning point in the revival. It may well be that Aubert's fellow Norwegian Edvard Munch was stimulated by this enthusiasm. Munch was living in Berlin at the time, and it is certainly striking that his symbolic psychodramas in a landscape setting often bear an interesting formal resemblance to the work of Friedrich at the time. Many of Munch's aphorisms have a distinctly Friedrichian ring about them. His remark that 'Nature is not only what is visible to the eye – it also shows the inner images of the soul – the images on the reverse side of the eyes'[23] seems close to Friedrich's celebrated observation: 'The artist should not only paint what he sees before him, but also what he sees within him.'[24] Aubert quoted a number of such aphorisms in his article on Friedrich.

Be this as it may, it is clear that the revised interest in Romantic landscape painting within Germany and Northern Europe did not have much repercussion elsewhere. Perhaps this is partly because the interest in symbolic landscape became overlaid by a desire to celebrate examples of early naturalism in Germany. This was a response to the growing success of French Impressionist painting. As in Britain, Germans were keen to demonstrate that the artists of their own country had developed a lively naturalism prior to being influenced by the French. The momentous *Jahrhundertausstellung* (Centenary Exhibition of German Art from 1775 to 1875), held in Berlin in 1906, certainly emphasized this dimension. The show was a landmark for the rediscovery of the art of the early nineteenth century in Germany. Outside interest and reporting was sporadic. In Britain it received a notice in *The Burlington Magazine*. The reviewer here mentioned Friedrich as a figure long overdue for re-assessment. But he says nothing of Friedrich's symbolic method and gives the impression that the artist should be appreciated largely for his study of Nature. The same reviewer preferred on the whole to concentrate on the latter part of the nineteenth century. His conclusion was that the one truly great German painter of the nineteenth century was the idealist *Deutsch-Römer* (German-Roman) Anselm Feuerbach. He felt that Feuerbach was the only German painter of the nineteenth century who had shown a real sensibility for paint.[25]

It is perhaps not surprising that German art, let alone German Romanticism, was little attended to in Britain and France at this time. This was, after all, the age of French ascendancy in visual culture, when 'abroad' to most British painters meant Paris or Dieppe. While artists like the *Blaue Reiter* (Blue Rider) group in Munich may have been making their own treaties with a German past, the visible side abroad was that of their engagement with an essentially French modernism. Added to this, of course, was the growing move away from German culture in general in the lead up to the First World War. Such response as existed to German artists at this time, tended to be individual rather than generic.

It is not until the 1920s that one finds the beginning of a more positive response to German Romanticism amongst artists and critics abroad. A key reason for this change lay in the sympathetic treatment of German Romanticism in the Surrealist movement. André Breton, the 'magus' of the movement, was intrigued by the exploration of the irrational by such writers as Novalis and Hoffmann, and was further attracted to the claims of metaphysical philosophy. Once again the visual arts played a relatively low part in this relationship. It could, however, be argued that there was a genealogical rela-

Fig.4 Carl Wilhelm Kolbe, *Dead Oak c.*1830, etching

tion between Surrealist painting and the Romantics via the great impact of the paintings of Giorgio de Chirico. For de Chirico – who studied as an art student in Munich before going to Paris where his 'metaphysical' style developed – had been profoundly impressed by Böcklin's works.[26] A more direct link occurred through the presence of Max Ernst in the movement. Ernst – who began his career as a Dadaist in Germany – drew heavily on the cultural experiences of his childhood and youth in the construction of his pictures. He used his own Rhineland memories as inspiration and was also fascinated with the more expressive and bizarre sides of German symbolic landscape. Amongst the most important sources for him were the wild etchings of struggling trees by Carl Wilhelm Kolbe (fig. 4 and cat. 42) and the silhouettes of trees and moons that occur in the works of Friedrich.[27] Indeed, at a time when in Germany the adulation of Friedrich was taking on an increasingly nationalist dimension, it is interesting to see how the Surrealists promoted an international view of him that emphasized above all his psychological dimensions. His troubling landscapes played their part, too, in the formation of the work of Salvador Dalí and René Magritte. Friedrich eventually received full critical appreciation in the Surrealist camp when an article on him was published in 1939 in *Minotaure* by Madeleine Landsberg.[28]

The Surrealist interest in the psychological landscape set the mood for a wider appreciation of Romantic symbolic landscape. Such interests had stimulated the scholarly and artistic exploration of the British Romantics in the 1930s, in particular Samuel Palmer. It is perhaps

Fig.5 Caspar David Friedrich, *Sea of Ice* c.1823–4, Hamburger Kunsthalle

Fig.6 Paul Nash, *Totes Meer* 1940–41, Tate Gallery, London

significant that the first article on Friedrich in Britain should appear at this time. This was the appreciation by H. Beenken that appeared in *The Burlington Magazine* in 1938. Beenken began by outlining the status of Friedrich in Germany: 'Of late years it has been gradually dawning on people's minds in Germany that the name of Caspar David Friedrich should be added to those of the really great masters of the nineteenth century. For the world outside Germany this will not be easily understandable because original works by this artist are to be found almost exclusively in German collections.'[29]

In his article – which reproduced five paintings by Friedrich, including the *Cross in the Mountain* and the *Abbey in the Oakwood* – Beenken provided a broad characterization, in which he emphasized the poetic side of Friedrich, relating this to Romantic subjectivity and making a few analogies across to Turner and John Crome.

Both the *Minotaure* article – which reproduced amongst others *Das Eismeer* ('Sea of Ice' – then called the 'Wreck of the Hope'; fig. 5 and colour plate, p.97) in 1939[30] – and this *Burlington Magazine* article might have been sufficient to bring Friedrich to the attention of one British landscape painter involved with both Surrealism and the Romantic Revival: Paul Nash. This possibility has intrigued art historians in Britain for some time. When reviewing the Friedrich exhibition at the Tate Gallery in 1972 in the *Times Literary Supplement*, Keith Andrews – that major scholar of German art – remarked on the affinity between the *Eismeer* and Nash's *Totes Meer* (fig. 6). The latter is the picture of crashed German planes in a dump at Cowley,

Oxford. It was painted by Nash as part of his work as an Official War Artist. In this context it might seem highly appropriate that he should depict the fallen might of the *Luftwaffe* by making ironic reference to a German Romantic painting of abandoned hope.

This association has been followed up in greater detail by Andrew Causey in his study of Nash.[31] Causey also notes that while Nash may have responded to Friedrich in terms of design and symbolic intention, he does not imitate the German master's pictorial style. Nash remained faithful to the painterly tradition that was, for his generation, the inalienable sign of modernity in art. Indeed, it seems to have been the lack of 'painterliness' in Friedrich's manner that prevented enthusiasts for Romantic landscape in Britain at the time from acknowledging his importance.

Postwar Responses

This point can be seen in the glancing treatment that Friedrich received in Kenneth Clark's authoritative study of landscape painting, *Landscape into Art* of 1949. Clark's survey did not reach into the twentieth century. But it was strongly influenced by the viewpoints of those British artists who were trying to maintain a place for the representation of Nature in contemporary art practice. Clark was a skilful advocate of the claim that landscape had been central to the development of modern painting. A key issue in the book is the role played by the Romantics in this history. Constable and Turner could easily be accommodated on account of their innovative painterliness. But symbolic landscape was more of a problem. Symbolism smacked of literariness, and might lead to the accusation that such art was merely illustrating ideas. Clark deals with this issue in some detail when considering the art of Samuel Palmer. Ultimately it is Palmer's moments of linear vigour and painterly excess that save him from the charge, and secures him a place as one of the forefathers of modern art. To emphasize this achievement, Clark uses Friedrich as a foil, as an example of an artist who did not pass the test. After his praise for Palmer's pictorial qualities – which he sees as presaging Van Gogh – Clark adds: '. . . in this way he surpasses that other romantic landscape painter whose brooding on nature is in many respects similar to his, Caspar David Friedrich. For Friedrich, for all the intensity of his imagination, worked in the frigid technique of his time, which could hardly inspire a school of modern painting.'[32]

When Clark came to reissue this book twenty-seven years later, in 1976, he made some significant modifications. He dropped the claim that Friedrich could not inspire a school of modern painting. And while he retained the reference to the German artist's 'frigid technique' he added: 'But although he is not so acceptable to English taste, I think we must concede that Friedrich was the greater artist, with a far more extended range than Palmer. No one has expressed more poignantly the gloom of solitude and the sadness of unfulfilled expectations.'[33]

In this later edition Friedrich is also granted an illustration: that of *Woman in the Morning Sun*.[34]

These shifts in commentary and evaluation are interesting as a sign of what had changed in the intervening years. By 1976, the Modernist project was already in trouble, and Clark could no longer justify the relevance of landscape for modernity principally in terms of painterliness. More than that, however, there had been a positive reconsideration of the 'other tradition', which had brought with it a renewed interest in German Romanticism. A harbinger of this in the visual arts had been the great Council of Europe Romantic exhibition of 1959 at the Tate Gallery. This had made clear to certain British critics and scholars how distinct the German contribution to the Romantic movement had been in the

visual arts. Following that momentous show there had been growing scholarly interest – marked, for example, by the publication of Keith Andrews's important study on the *Nazarenes* in 1964. This was the first English language study of the group to have appeared since the mid-Victorian period. The Friedrich exhibition at the Tate Gallery in 1972 was probably more directly relevant for Clark's shift of position. While not much of a critical success, the show did spark off something of a cult in those artistic circles where there was a desire to pursue alternatives to the Modernist norm. Further major showings – the Friedrich bicentenary shows in Germany, the German Romantic exhibition in Paris in 1977, and a series of important exhibitions in America – augmented this tendency. Robert Rosenblum's challenging book *Modern Painting and the Northern Romantic Tradition: Friedrich to Rothko* (1975), reflected the growing mood in the way that it offered a revisionist reading of the development of modern art, weaving a sinuous thread from the Romantics in Germany around 1800 across space and time, through figures like Palmer, Van Gogh, Munch and Ferdinand Hodler to the Abstract Expressionists of New York in the 1950s.

This new look at German Romanticism was complemented by what appeared to be the rebirth of an 'alternative tradition' in artistic practice. The events and installations of Joseph Beuys in the 1970s, and the work of painters like Gerhard Richter and Anselm Kiefer a little later on, have interested an international audience in reflective and ironic forms of artistic discourse that draw a significant part of their resource from the Romantic tradition. We are now at a moment when it is possible to look again at Romanticism and its progeny. Perhaps, indeed, it is necessary to do so. For if we do not, the positive and productive sides of the movement may well become occluded – as they have done at times in the past – by reactionary and retrogressive interests. A serious look at the continuities between German Romantic art and the present will hopefully help to keep the more valuable contributions of the movement alive.

William Vaughan

1 'The State of German Literature', *Edinburgh Review* (1827: Carlyle Centenary Edn), XXVI, 51 ff.

2 *Art Union*, 1839, 136.

3 The play was *Das Kind der Liebe* (Child of Love), which was first performed in England in 1798. See Jane Austen, *Mansfield Park* ed. Tony Tanner (Harmondsworth (1966), 460, 15.

4 *The Gentleman's Magazine* (March 1816), 226.

5 Anna Jameson, *Visits and Sketches at Home and Abroad* (1834), I, 139.

6 *London Magazine*, (1820), 42.

7 For a discussion of the French response to the Nazarenes see Henri Dorra, 'Die französischen "Nazarener"', in *Die Nazarener* (exh. cat.) (Frankfurt, 1977), 337–54.

8 See *The Houses of Parliament*, ed. M.H. Port (London, 1976) and *Works of Art in the House of Lords,* ed. M. Bond (London, 1980), esp. 18–43.

9 A.W. Pugin, *Contrasts* (2nd ed., 1841), 18.

10 Max Nordau, *Degeneration* (London, 1895 translated from the German *Entartung* (Paris, 1889; 2nd edn)), 71.

11 J. Gage, *Colour in Turner* (London, 1969), 101.

12 Cf. W. Vaughan, *The German Manner in English Art* (New Haven and London, 1979), pp. 20–2.

13 John Ruskin, *Preface to the Economy of Xenophon* (London, 1877, Library ed.), XXXI, 23.

14 John Ruskin, *Elements of Drawing* (London, Library ed.), XV, 80.

15 G. Burne-Jones, *Memorials of Edward Burne-Jones* (London, 1906), I, 255.

16 Herbert Furze, *The Modern Woodcut* (London, 1924), 72.

17 John Ruskin, *Modern Painters*, III (London, Library ed.), V, 330.

18 Max Nordau (as note 10).

19 These connections were already described in Nordau's book. The first scholarly treatment of the German sources for aestheticism was probably R.F. Egan, 'The Genesis of the Theory of "Art for Art's Sake" in Germany and England', *Smith College Studies in Modern Languages* II, no. 4 (1921), 11 ff.

20 Ricarda Huch, *Blütezeit der Romantik* (1899, here 3rd ed.,1908), I, 337–8.

21 As note 20: 341.

22 *Den nordiske Naturfølelse og Johan Christian Dahl* (Christiania, 1894). Aubert's article 'Der Landschaftsmaler Friedrich' appeared in *Kunstchronik* NF VII (1895–6), 283-93.

23 Quoted in J.H. Langaard and R. Revold, *Edvard Munch* (Oslo, 1963), 62.

24 C.F. Carus, *Friedrich der Landschaftsmaler* (Dresden, 1841). Reprinted in S. Hinz, *Caspar David Friedrich in Briefen und Bekenntnissen* (Berlin, 1968), 128.

25 *The Burlington Magazine* (1906).

26 See M.F. dell'Arco 'De Chirico in Paris, 1911–1915' in *De Chirico*, ed. W. Rubin (New York, 1982), 11–12.

27 For Max Ernst's involvement with German Romantic imagery see H. Leppien, *Max Ernst. Der Grosse Wald* (Stuttgart, 1967), 18–20.

28 Madeleine Landsberg, 'Caspar David Friedrich, peintre de l'angoisse romantique', *Minotaure*,12–13 (3 May 1939), 25-8.

29 H. Beenken, 'Caspar David Friedrich', *The Burlington Magazine*, LXXII (1938), 171.

30 As note 28. The article reproduces *L'Espoir Échoué*, as well as the *Cross in the Mountains* and the *Monk by the Sea*.

31 A. Causey, *Paul Nash* (Oxford, 1980), 315.

32 K. Clark, *Landscape into Art* (London, 1949), 72.

33 K. Clark, *Landscape into Art* (Revised ed., London, 1976), 143.

34 Now in Folkwang Museum, Essen.

In Search of Paradise Lost
Runge – Marc – Beuys

1. Paradises from Inner Necessity

Of all the serious games in Romanticism, the most earnest and at the same time the most light-hearted is the quest for Paradise Lost. It concentrates the Romantic essence for us, as in a burning-glass. It is the longing for something lost; it is the sorrowful remembrance of primal origins, and of the unity, harmony, happiness and contentment that were present in a distant past but can now be evoked only in imagination, in dreams and fairy-tales or through irony – or rather through the poetic-philosophical exegesis of fragments. In a state of longing, the imagination recreates a lost Whole out of the fragments of past happiness: that is what Romanticism demands of the arts, in defiance of the Enlightenment and all its calculating rationality. Reason stems from the Tree of Knowledge: it was brought to humankind by the Fall, and in gaining it we lost Paradise.

Among the Romantic writers, none more decisively made Paradise Lost into the theme of his life's work than Clemens Brentano. In his fairytale *Gockel, Hinkel, Gakeleia* (first published in 1838), he draws from it an aesthetic manifesto that is the founding document of Modernism in Germany. Here the author himself appears in the guise of a child. In his initial dedication, the poet-child explains to his grandmother how, through this tale, with its blend of jest and earnest, he has created a new Paradise in his imagination. This Paradise Regained is shown on the title-page of the story (fig. 1): it is a playful conglomeration of children, animals, birds and plants, assembled with no regard for scale, and presided over by two beautiful princesses. It was inspired, says the child storyteller, by his grandmother's gallery of scraps or cut-out pictures, by the bridal and ball gowns and jewellery in her attic, and by the other paraphernalia in that 'store of treasure and art'.[1]

The reality of such artificial paradises of leftovers and *objets trouvés* – which Brentano himself illustrates by making virtually proto-Surrealist collages of motifs from

Hieronymus Bosch, Albrecht Dürer and Philipp Otto Runge (figs. 1–3)[2] – is stoutly defended against conventional ideas of reality and of rational education. 'Don't let them confuse you,' Goethe's mother reassures the child narrator, when he worries over his own imaginary Paradise, which he locates in Liechtenstein; 'believe me, your Vaduz is yours and is not on any map .... It is wherever your mind, your heart finds its pasture:

'Where your heaven is, there is your Vaduz,
To you, a country on earth is no use.'[3]

Ironically enough, therefore, in Brentano's tale it is Goethe's mother – as literary adviser to Romanticism – who bestows on the quest for Paradise Lost the same unequivocal endorsement that Brentano himself had put into a long, confessional letter to Runge in 1810. Regardless of any external reality, Runge's art —and the cycle *The Times of Day* in particular (colour plates, pp. 212–13 and cat. 9) – seemed to Brentano to be a Paradise Regained entirely from inner necessity. 'From your endeavours,' he wrote from Berlin to Runge, a stranger, in Hamburg, 'I see that the life of art is truly lost; for the artist must look around within himself to construct Paradise Lost from its own necessity.'[4]

This definition of Runge's art makes him the artistic peer and precursor of Brentano's own poet-child – as becomes directly evident at the end of the tale (fig. 2), where Brentano the illustrator shows the poet-child curled up with his finished work, asleep at the feet of Runge's *Night*. Brentano's paradisal tale thus reaches its consummation in the bosom, as it were, of Runge's invention.

2. Runge

Enlightenment as Fall, and the Renewal of Landscape
Brentano's formula – Paradise Lost, reconstructed from inner necessity – is central to the art of Runge. This is apparent from the letters to family and friends in which Runge thinks hard about the artist's calling and

Fig.1 Clemens Brentano Title-page of *Gockel,
Hinkel, Gakeleia* before 1838, lithograph

Fig.2 Clemens Brentano Final illustration of *Gockel,
Hinkel, Gakeleia* before 1838, lithograph

Fig.3 Clemens Brentano *Gakeleia in the Mouse Kingdom,* illustration for *Gockel,
Hinkel, Gakeleia* before 1838, lithograph

recognizes 'the ancient longing for childhood, for ourselves, for Paradise, for God'.[5] Through the Original Sin of science, 'body and soul have been separated' (HS 2:209). He feels a corresponding contempt for the educational efforts of the Enlightenment. Its frigid, soulless, rule-bound teaching in schools and academies is profoundly damaging: 'It would be a cause worth giving one's life to,' wrote Runge to his mother in 1802, 'if only one could rescue people from the fear inflicted on them by all that accursed art and science' (HS 2:1983).

To this end, he called for a return to 'the prime inwardness of feeling'; for 'We must become children, if we want to attain the best.'[6] Only by turning back to our own early life – 'just as a child lives in Paradise and is blissful without knowing it' (HS 2:209) – only thus can we become conscious of our kinship with Creation and with its Creator, and thus of the likeness to God that we were given in Paradise. 'The image of God', Runge wrote to his brother Daniel in November 1802, 'is simply the noblest and highest that each person has ever been ... To seek out and develop this within us: this we must call the ideal of this art – this flowering of humanity, this land we call Paradise, which lies within us, which we discover, and which alone should delight us, whenever we come upon it' (HS 1:22).

Brentano's formula of reconstructing Paradise Lost from inner necessity thus constitutes the self-imposed, religious mission of Runge's art. 'We stand on the edge of all religions' (HS 1:7) was Runge's clairvoyant diagnosis (in 1802) of the historical moment between French Revolution and Napoleonic conquest. At this turning point in history, when the old orders and values had been destroyed, it was, he said, the mission of art to supply human beings with credible and consoling images by which to reorient themselves. The Neoclassicism favoured by Goethe and his artist friends in Weimar – with its mythological subjects – was inert and outworn. Freshness and life were to be found, said Runge, only in a branch of art hitherto virtually ignored in academic circles: 'Everything pushes towards landscape' (HS 1:7).

Through this advancement of a genre previously considered beneath scholarly notice; through motifs from Nature and natural life, such as flowers, springs, children and mothers; through the rendering of light and of its chromatic refractions; through all those motifs that

Fig.4 Title-plate in Jacob Böhme *Alle de Theosophische of Godwijze Werken*, Amsterdam 1686

Fig.5 Philipp Otto Runge Illustration in Ludwig Tieck's *Minnelieder*, copperplate engraving, 1803

he considered closest to the paradisal dawn of time and its divine origins; through landscape, conceived as a 'work of paradisal totality' (Jörg Traeger) beyond all distinctions of genre, Runge sought to lead the beholder back to the bliss of a former unity with Creation and its Creator.

The Paradise of the Times

Runge accomplished this 'work of paradisal totality' to greatest effect in his cycle of four copper engravings, published in more than 250 copies, *The Times of Day*. Initially devised as a scheme of interior decoration late in 1802, this cycle (to which he simply referred as the *Times*) evolved through a long succession of drawings into a profound configuration of 'arabesques' that — deliberately – invites multiple interpretations.

Formally – hence the admiration of an artist so well versed in collage as Brentano – Runge's *Times* are a calculatedly phantasmagorical combination of disparate pictorial traditions. Neoclassical decorative motifs mingle with playful Renaissance grotesques; hermetic hieroglyphics elucidate arcane images of alchemical and mystical wisdom. One particularly important source of

Runge's artistic edifice, with its combination of plant forms, mathematical symmetry and metaphysics of light, lay in the plates of the 1682 Amsterdam edition of the writings of Jacob Böhme (fig. 4). Runge's own illustrations to Ludwig Tieck's *Minnelieder*, done in 1803 (fig. 5), and the *First Figure of Creation* that he sent to Tieck at the same time (fig. 7), reveal him as supremely at home in all the rich store of mystical imagery that lies between abstraction and reality, between geometrical construction and the playful earnest of the poetic imagination.

Complex in structure though the *Times* are, their meaning cannot have been lost on any contemporary of Runge's who was schooled in allegory. Such an observer will have seen quite clearly that in the four central images Runge associates the Times of Day with the Seasons, and that in the Christian border motifs he links them with the four Ages of Man and the human quest for redemption (see the detailed descriptions by Jörg Traeger).[7]

In turn, this linkage between natural process and human allegory points especially clearly to the idea of

Paradise Lost and Paradise Regained, when seen in the light of the traditional theory of four temperaments. In Eden – according to the traditional belief reflected in Dürer's *Adam* and *Eve* engraving (fig. 6) – our first parents enjoyed a temperament-free *status perfectus*, best expressed through the youthful vigour of the happiest temperament of the four, the sanguine. The temperaments as such – sanguine, choleric, melancholy and phlegmatic – emerged only after this *status perfectus* was corrupted by the Fall. Dürer shows them in the form of the four beasts at Adam and Eve's feet.[8] Runge was familiar with this idea; he wrote to Tieck in 1803: 'Through the Fall, good and evil came into the world, and from their commingling came the passions, inwardly good and outwardly evil' (HS 1:40).

This is visibly reflected in Runge's *Times*. In *Morning*, the children who embrace and make music on the lily of light clearly express the euphoria of the sanguine temperament, proper to early youth. The choleric temperament, which marks the second age of life, is shown in the following image, *Day* – notably in the wrathful angel with the sword in the lower border, who drives humankind out of Paradise after the Fall. The central image here shows the loss of paradisal unity through the separation of the sexes, as embodied in the children who take leave of each other to right and left. The great thorn-branches behind the children, and the noonday heat suggested by the shady arbour, point to the theme of labour – best endured by the choleric temperament. Hot-blooded and combative, a choleric disposition has the virtue of energetically shouldering life's burdens.

Day, which stands for the prime of life, is followed by *Evening*, with its reference to contemplative old age and the melancholy temperament. This is most clearly reflected in the children, faces sombrely cupped in hands, who flank the cross, crown of thorns and chalice in the lower margin; they show that by imitating the Passion of Christ we can transcend this world. In the following image, *Night*, sleep is an emblem of the phlegmatic temperament, always associated with the last age of life. Runge evokes the traditional parallel between sleep and death through the smoking urn in the lower border, a reference to mortality. For the true Christian, who has risen above this world through the imitation of Christ, death also means resurrection into the world

Fig.6 Albrecht Dürer *Adam and Eve* 1504, copperplate engraving

beyond. In the upper border of *Night*, Runge evokes this theme in the butterfly-winged souls that fly over the clouds, rapt in adoration, straight into the beams of light that emanate from the dove of the Holy Spirit.

Every *Night* is succeeded by a new *Morning*; every death – or so the Christian doctrine of redemption has it – is succeeded by the felicity of new and eternal life. Runge shows this in the upper border of *Morning*. Here a glory made up of angelic faces – crowding in contemplation of the divine, around a resplendent disc inscribed with the name of Jehovah – stands for the lasting bliss of the heavenly Paradise, in which the resurrected participate after their earthly death in *Night*. For Runge, *Morning* evidently has its place in the sequence of *Times* before the Fall represented in *Day*; it thus signifies Paradise both Lost and Regained.

In the central image of *Morning*, with its happy children on the lily of light, Runge evokes Paradise Lost through the short-lived earthly Paradise of dawn, springtime and early youth. Paradise Regained is represented by the glory of angels around the divine light in the upper border. The eternal contemplation of divine splendour is the fulfilment of the human aspiration towards redemption that begins all over again, in the lower margin of *Morning*, with the birth of new human souls out of the serpent-ring of eternity. The souls who enter the world anew in the earthly paradise of *Morning* must now pass through the phases set out in the borders of the succeeding *Times*. At the end of their pursuit of redemption, after the death of *Night*, they too will ascend on the following *Morning* as justified souls to Paradise Regained.

In *Morning*, by visually conjoining the earthly and the heavenly Paradise, Runge connects the beginning of the Times with their end. As a representation of the sanguine temperament, the joyous image of *Morning* gives the only possible earthly manifestation of the idea of Paradise. Like Dürer, Runge thus singles out the sanguine temperament for its closeness to our paradisal origins. In earthly terms, meanwhile, the sanguine *Morning* inescapably marks the beginning of a sequence of the four temperaments, and of the times of day and of life that correspond to them. In the light of this twofold vision, Runge had this to say concerning the end and the beginning of his Times, and of the human life for which they stand:

'Like the times of day, the year in its four successive states – blossoming, producing, bearing and destroying – so constantly rushes through my mind that my one longing for this everlasting miracle is for ever regenerating itself; and in artistic terms the last ought always to be the spring, the time of blossom, which is salvaged from the time of destruction, and which, in earthly terms, then produces other times in its turn ....' (HS 1: 66)

In his own 'artistic' terms, when Runge came to interpret his *Times* in painting he confined himself to the single, paradisal image of *Morning* (colour plate, p.94), concentrating on the point of convergence between earth and heaven, Paradise Lost and Paradise Regained.

The Hidden God in the Temple of Total Art

It is therefore not true that Runge's *Times* are – as has been suggested – a vicious circle: that they reduce the Christian doctrine of salvation and redemption to an endless natural cycle.[9] In the quest for Paradise Lost,

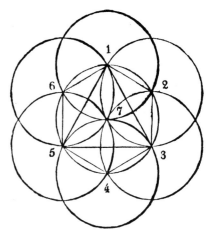

Fig.7 Philipp Otto Runge *First Figure of Creation* 1803

Runge's *Morning* marks both the starting-point and the destination; in it, eschatological finality is visibly reconciled with the cycle of Nature. Runge is not a pantheist: he does not subsume the Creator into his Creation. He accepts the Christian mystics' view of the relationship between microcosm and macrocosm, whereby all Creation partakes of the nature of its divine Creator, but God himself remains inaccessible to man in this world: 'God is not to be grasped by human reason and mind, or rendered by any work of art' (HS 1:21). God appears only in the optical analogy of the point of intersection, in Runge's *First Figure of Creation* (fig. 7), or – as in *Morning* and in the Tieck illustration – in the Hebrew word 'Jehovah' that blazes in the heavens. Runge's Protestant God is a hidden God, who dwells in the infinite.

In manifest terms, God's Creation partakes of infinity through its endless succession of *Times*. Anyone who falls wholly beneath the sway of that Creation can know no rest: 'In this world none comes to repose except in death' (HS 1:42). As Runge knows, and as the borders of his *Times* unmistakably show, 'redemption from this world' occurs only when the world is transcended through the Passion of Christ, 'through Jesus Christ our Lord' (HS 1:290). Brentano understood Runge very well, as he showed when he made his poet-child go to sleep beneath Runge's *Night* and beside an open grave surmounted by a cross. The quest for Paradise Lost comes to its permanent conclusion not in this world but only through death, with the Christian's resurrection on a higher *Morning* into a heavenly Paradise. 'Eternal and

Fig.8 Albrecht Dürer *The Four Apostles* 1526, Alte Pinakothek, Munich

supreme life' is accessible to man, says Runge, only 'in annihilation and remaining in eternal Being' (HS 1:162).

This does not by any means negate the value of Creation. Inasmuch as Creation partakes of divinity, it is – for Runge, as a Christian Neo-Platonist – an allusion and a sign that points the way. In the light-filled joy of the sanguine *Morning*, this Creation retains some of the imagery of Paradise. A further manifestation of Paradise in earthly life is the harmony of all four temperaments, as displayed in Runge's *Times*. Dürer, once again, provides a model of an ideal combination of the four temperaments in his *Four Apostles* (fig. 8), which may have been intended as companion pieces to *Adam* and *Eve*.[10] The biblical quotations that Dürer appends to the *Apostles* show them to be an exhortation to a Christian change of heart, and thus to tolerance in an age of strife and confusion. In this ideal harmony of opposing temperaments, the effects of the Fall seem already compensated for.

The same goes for Runge's *Times*. Runge imagined them as monumental paintings, larger even than Dürer's *Four Apostles*, set up in a specially designed, centrally planned building, its forms modelled on those of the vegetable kingdom. This painted cosmology was to be solemnly contemplated to the accompaniment of music and poetry. The result would be a *Gesamtkunstwerk*, a total artwork or synthesis of the arts, uniting all the

forms of Nature and art; it would thus be a tangible anticipation of Paradise Regained. Reduced to chaos by the Fall, the world would be restored to harmony in the four-part schema of the constantly regenerating *Times* and in the interaction of the arts. Through syncretism and synaesthesia, the language of art and form presented here constitutes a tangible image of Paradise.

In Runge's view, a sacred building of this kind would serve the ends of aesthetic and religious education in many ways. Like his own earlier *Temple of Contentment* (executed in the form of a silhouette, fig. 9), but now with an added, deep cosmological and religious significance, this temple of all-embracing harmony would provide the ideal place of worship for an egalitarian, bourgeois society: one in which persons of differing temperaments might commune and cooperate with each other in peace and mutual pleasure. Alongside the quest for Paradise Lost, this complementary theme of mutual pleasure in human society runs through Runge's work from the subsidiary scenes in the early *Temple of Contentment* through to the last designs for the *Times* —as it does in his numerous portraits of his own parents, siblings, friends and friends' children. The edifice of the *Times*, if it could have been built, would thus have been a place in which people might be educated for civil society. In terms of the model of Nature and Creation portrayed in it by Runge, it would have made the world a better place.

Making the world a better place was part of Runge's view of the purpose of his art. He wanted his art to build visible bridges to the Paradise Lost of his visions. 'We seek to make the way there truly passable,' he wrote to Tieck on 1 December 1802, when he was working on drawings for the *Times*. For the world was not good, 'and we want a better one' (HS 1:26). In pursuit of his scheme of world-improvement, Runge also developed entirely practical forms of aesthetic education. The projected temple of the *Times* might have been a show house, as it were, for the school of art that Runge wanted to set up in Hamburg. The decorative programme of the *Times* – itself originally planned as a scheme of interior decoration – was to provide a point of departure for a general improvement and elevation of taste; through the school, employment would be given to artists across a wide spectrum, abstract designers as well

Fig.9 Philipp Otto Runge *The Temple of Contentment* c.1789, paper cut-out, Hamburger Kunsthalle

as practical executants (HS 1:28ff.) In terms entirely typical of his artistic religion, Runge spoke of Christ's Apostles as the prototypes of a family circle of the arts (HS 1:5), which would forgather in the artists' commune of his school of total art and from there extend its influence into life outside.[11]

In one final dimension of meaning, Runge's paradisal *Gesamtkunstwerk* of the *Times* points to the demise of art. 'I wish,' he said, 'there were no need for me to practise art; for we must transcend art, and in Eternity it will be unknown' (HS 2:223). To evoke the longing for eternity – for the heavenly Paradise – in an image of the earthly Paradise is the point of convergence of Runge's *Times* images and of the sacred motifs in their borders. Runge's aesthetic temple of Nature and humanity – and of the 'unbounded' and 'imperishable' existence of God, which exists within them and transcends them – has as its undoubted, supreme object the evocation of longing for the heavenly Paradise. Runge's theology of art aims at the self-regeneration of Man as the Image of God, and thus at the recovery of Paradise Lost in the individual and in society – which would mean the end of art. His programme of aesthetic education, which leads back to Paradise through art, finds its fulfilment in eternity; and there, as Runge well knows, art 'will be unknown'.

Runge's art derives its necessity from an imperfect world, whose perfection it foreshadows in a utopian spirit. By the very nature of a work that aims for the infinity of God, this utopia must necessarily be unachieved. This arises not only from Runge's early

death but also from the revolutionary and élitist nature of his highly private conception of art as a 'work of paradisal totality': a work that sought (as Goethe admiringly complained) 'to embrace everything' – and which, in characteristically Modernist fashion, was unsupported by any public beyond the artist's immediate circle of family and friends.

3. Marc

The Purity of Animals

Writing in 1923 on 'Runge and the Present', Paul Ferdinand Schmidt described Franz Marc, a few years after his untimely death in battle, as the artist who had carried Runge's work to its conclusion.[12] Schmidt saw the short-lived Marc as the incarnation of a rich artistic impulse that – as with Runge – was compelled to bury its fairest hopes. By the time he was killed on the Verdun salient in 1916, at the age of thirty-six, Marc had nevertheless succeeded – in an intensely concentrated artistic career that spanned less than a decade, from 1905 to the outbreak of war – in translating into Modernist formal terms the utopian Romantic conception of art as the recovery of Paradise Lost. To Marc, who had originally meant to become a clergyman, art extended – as it did for Runge – into the religious realm. He saw his paintings of animals as symbols fit for the 'altars of the coming spiritual religion'.[13]

A comparison between Franz Marc's *Tower of Blue Horses* (1913; colour plate, p. 103) and Runge's painting of *Morning* (1808; colour plate, p. 94) readily reveals what Marc meant by 'altars of the coming spiritual religion'. In Runge's *Morning*, the landscape is elevated into an altarpiece, and the whole of Nature regains its part in the Godhead by turning towards the heavenly light. Similarly, in *Tower of Blue Horses*, Marc develops animal painting into a religious utopia, in which animals grow heavenward as purified and spiritualized beings within a blue, crystalline architecture. To Runge, paradisal origins resided in flowers, children and springs of water; to Marc, there was an archetypal purity in animals. 'The profane human creature all around me (the male, above all) left me unmoved,' wrote Marc to his wife from the battlefield; 'but the animal's intact sense of

Fig.10 Anselm Feuerbach *Iphigenia* 1871 (cat. 120)

Fig.11 Franz Marc *The White Dog (Dog in Front of the World)* 1912, private collection

life set all that was good resonating within me. ... Very early on, I felt man to be "ugly"; animals seemed to me more beautiful, purer.'[14]

By thus sanctifying animal painting, Marc set a new and vastly higher value on a genre that ranked in the academic hierarchy far below even the landscape, which had been ennobled by Runge. Except in fairytales, animals had no soul. In the Paradise Lost of the fairytale – as Brentano's *Gockel, Hinkel, Gakeleia* showed – animals had always been able to act, talk, think and feel like people. For in Paradise – as on the frontispiece of Brentano's tale (fig. 1) – man and beast are still at one. Marc pursues this idea of paradisal unity by composing his animal paintings in accordance with traditional patterns of figure composition. It has rightly been said, for instance, that his tendency to arrange his animals in threes derives from the ancient formula of the Three Graces.[15] Runge uses the same formula, as an image of paradisal harmony, in the group of three embracing children on the lily of light in *Morning*. Marc uses the Three Graces composition to make his groups of animals circle in a round dance, as if held within their own field of force. This distances them from the viewer, like beings under a spell.

Another feature of Marc's animals that makes them seem like higher and alien beings is the way in which the central animal in a triad often looks away, into the picture; Marc also uses this far-away look to ennoble single animal figures, such as that of his own Siberian sheepdog, Russi (fig. 11). The source here is the Romantic tradition of images of longing, which Marc knew through such works as Anselm Feuerbach's *Iphigenia* (fig. 10 and cat. 120). In Marc's world, the animal takes on the human longing for the Distant and the Other, in a metamorphosis that has been summed up in a striking phrase: 'Iphigenia as dog'.[16]

The object of all this longing in Marc can be more explicitly defined. It is the entirely Romantic nostalgia for a primal unity between God and world, between heaven and earth. As Marc described it in 1914, this is 'the longing for indivisible Being, for release from the sensory illusions of our ephemeral life'.[17] It is a longing that can be stilled, he wrote, only 'by my transferring the meaning of my existence into the spiritual: the spiritual, independent of the body; that is, the "abstract"'.[18] These ideas form the theme of a number of Marc's early drawings, which are illustrations to favourite Symbolist poems. One of them (done between 1904 and 1908, and posthumously published in a facsimile volume in 1917) shows a man and an animal marooned on the earth, and above them, inaccessible in the stars, their heavenly homeland (fig. 12). In other drawings in this poetry

Fig.12 Franz Marc *Over There a Star Fell* 1905/08

Fig.13 Franz Marc Title-page of *Stella Peregrina*
1906/08

series, human beings in ideal nakedness – strikingly rem-
iniscent of the children who emerge from flowers in
Runge's *Times* – can be seen turning back towards
Heaven (fig. 13).

This same Christian-Platonist tradition of the soul's
longing to return to its home in the world beyond – the
purification of the earthly into the spiritual – may legitimately be detected in Marc's animal paintings. In tranquil
enjoyment of their animality, resting, playing, gazing
into the distance or looking up to heaven, Marc's animals
form a pictorial cosmos steeped in the longing for Paradise
Lost. This sense of longing is deliberately reinforced by
the way in which Marc's animals, in their purity, seem
far closer to the longed-for goal than the beholder has
any reason to suppose himself or herself to be.

Abstract Worlds
Marc's art can be said to take from Modernism just so
much as serves Marc's own basic and ever-more-radical
purpose: to restore archetypal, paradisal unity. In his
early, naturalistic phase, *c.*1905–06, Marc approached
the idea of primal unity through a deliberate choice of
plain, rustic subjects and an unassuming, tonal palette.
Then, from 1907 onwards, he gave his allegiance to the
two great Modernist outsiders, Vincent van Gogh and
Paul Gauguin, whose artful primitivism held out a
promise of sincerity and primal authenticity. By follow-

ing their example, Marc believed that he could render
Arcadia in a fabulous but earthly vision of pure, strong
colours, peopled by mostly female nudes in familiar converse with animals. He was able to spiritualize this natural idyll to some extent by borrowing the ethereal,
swinging curves of Jugendstil and Art Nouveau; these
continued to influence his animal paintings until 1911
and dominated the mural of *Paradise*, painted in
October 1912 by Marc and August Macke.[19]

From 1912 onwards, grappling with the innovations
of Cubism, Orphism and Futurism, Marc transported
his Arcadias of primal unity out of this colourful and
relatively down-to-earth fairytale world and into the
crystalline immateriality of an increasingly abstract pictorial organization. In the course of Marc's incessant
quest for the new, the original, the pure, his most
momentous discovery was the work of the French artist
Robert Delaunay, five years his junior, which he saw at
the first *Der Blaue Reiter* exhibition at the end of 1911
and then at the *Erstes Deutsches Herbstsalon* in Berlin
in 1913.[20] The fascination that Delaunay exerted, not
only on Marc but also (among the artists of *Der Blaue
Reiter*) on Macke and Paul Klee, derives from his combination of Cubism with chromaticism. Delaunay's rationality of form and pure, glowing colours, together with
the almost total elimination of the object in his
'autonomous paintings' (the name given by Klee to his

Windows of 1911), now supplanted the exotic dream world of Gauguin and the ornamental swirls of Art Nouveau and became the defining pattern of Marc's last animal paintings.

A comparison between Delaunay's *Simultaneous Window on the City* (1912, Hamburger Kunsthalle), probably the finest of his *Window* paintings, and Marc's *Tower of Blue Horses* (1913) reveals the affinity, and also the metamorphosis that took place. Delaunay's view from a window across the vast shimmer of Paris is transformed by Marc into a prismatic structure of colour that strips the animals of all that is earthly and transforms them into a chromatic, glowing, crystalline architecture of basic geometric forms.

Marc's horses, towering into the sky in a crystalline blue radiance, hark back not only to Delaunay's *Window* paintings but also to the same artist's slightly earlier Cubist paraphrases on the Gothic apse of Saint-Séverin. Delaunay treated these Gothic paraphrases – which were shown in the first exhibition of *Der Blaue Reiter* in Munich – as a strict formal experiment, part of his systematic confrontation with Paul Cézanne and with Picasso's Cubism; but to many German artists, the blatant abolition of centralized perspective in these works, and their strong blue cast, made them into symbols of a purely spiritual state, of a transcendental aspiration. The same goes for another leitmotif of Delaunay's, his *Eiffel Towers*, which cascade heavenward like flames. Conceived by Delaunay as signals of metropolitan dynamism, these *Eiffel Towers* transform themselves in German art – right through to Lyonel Feininger's Bauhaus *Cathedral* – into emblems of aspiration and transcendence and, ultimately, into celestial architecture. In his *Tower of Blue Horses*, Marc thus combines three inventions of Delaunay's – his windows, his Gothic visions and his Eiffel Towers – into a wholly immaterial, sanctified, heavenward-bound animal architecture.

What Marc reveals in this structural artistic synthesis, his 'longing for indivisible Being', is also manifest in the rainbow above the Tower of Blue Horses itself. Since time immemorial, the rainbow has been the symbol of reconciliation between God and his Creation. Marc's longing for this paradisal unity is present in the stars and crescent moons on the blue bodies of the animals in his very first sketch for *Tower of Blue Horses*, a New Year's

Fig. 14 Franz Marc *Tower of Blue Horses* 1912–13
Postcard to Else Lasker-Schüler
Staatsgalerie Moderner Kunst, Munich,
Gift of Sofie and Emanuel Fohn

greeting to Else Lasker-Schüler for 1913 (fig. 14). Though still in this world, these are already celestial animals; their earthly beauty points to a beauty in the Beyond. For Marc, as for others, Paradise Regained is not of this world but can be lastingly attained only in the face of eternity. In 1914, Marc formulated the goal of his art in words that read like a paraphrase of Runge's cry of longing for Paradise:

'Death is the beginning of true Being, around which we, the living, swarm restlessly like moths around a flame. The longing for indivisible Being, for release from the sensory illusions of our ephemeral life, is the ground of all art. Its great goal is to dissolve the whole system of our partial sensations; to reveal an unearthly Being that dwells behind all this; to shatter the mirror of life, that we may look into Being.'[21]

Retreat to Arcadia, and the Militant Religion of Art
This same basic idea of Marc's art, the 'longing for indivisible Being', also governed his life, in its polarization between reclusiveness and missionary zeal. In 1909 he deserted the urban art world of Munich for village life in Upper Bavaria, first at Sindelsdorf and then at Ried, near Kochel am See. Marc's enjoyment of time-honoured, rustic patterns of life, amid a Nature still largely intact, was in itself the expression of his longing – as was the restriction of his subject matter (from 1910 onward) to

animals. Alongside the longing, however, there was a proselytizing impulse; and this precluded any escape into total seclusion.

From his Paradise in the Alpine foothills of Bavaria, Marc sent out numerous painted postcards,[22] vivid evocations of the paradisal bliss of wild creatures amid crystalline mountain formations, far from the constraints of urban civilization. His extensive network of contacts made him into the integrative figure of German Modernism, one who carried the message of contemporary art – and of *Der Blaue Reiter* in particular – beyond Munich to Berlin, Cologne and Paris. Far more open to the disparate artistic tendencies of the day than Wassily Kandinsky ever was, Marc was constantly on the move. His was the organizational drive that gave rise to the exhibitions and the Almanac of the group *Der Blaue Reiter*.

Published by Piper of Munich in 1912, this Almanac was nothing less than an encyclopedia of Modernism and its precursors, ranging far and wide through theatre, music and literature and spanning the visual arts from their primitive, folk and popular forms by way of El Greco, Cézanne and Henri Rousseau to Cubism, Orphism and Expressionism. The Almanac became something of a *Gesamtkunstwerk* in its own right, in which the utopian fellowship of European Modernism on the eve of the First World War took on tangible form – and this was Franz Marc's doing, as a practical manifestation of his longing for indivisible Being.

That this international Modernist *Gesamtkunstwerk* took the shape of a book reflects the appeal issued by its joint editors, Kandinsky and Marc, for an immaterial, purely spiritual art. In his own written contributions to the volume, Marc sets out his belief in the spiritualization of art, its cleansing from all paltry material content. He identifies the art of the future with the symbols 'whose place is on the altars of the coming spiritual religion' and writes of 'the mystical and contemplative construction that is the great problem of today's generation'.[23] These aspirations spring directly from Brentano's and Runge's project of constructing Paradise from 'inner necessity'; hence Marc's direct references to Romanticism, and to its renewal of art at the dawn of the nineteenth century. It is, of course, no coincidence that the name 'Blue Rider' (*Der Blaue Reiter*) echoes the 'Blue Flower' of the Romantics.[24]

Fig.15 Robert Delaunay *Circular Forms, Sun, Moon* 1912–13, Stedelijk Museum, Amsterdam

As with the Romantics, there was a sense of involvement in a great adventure, a journey to a promised land of pure spirit whose power Marc believed he could find both in art and in modern everyday life. 'The department store and modern lighting', he wrote, 'positively impose on us the *simultané* of Delaunay. ... Our modern life and thought are Futuristic through and through, from telephone to X-rays.'[25] For Marc, the 'Spiritual in Art' as an expression of longing for Paradise Lost – for paradisal purity and archetypal origins – was no mere retreat into inner life. On the contrary, it was an ambitious effort to shape the whole of modern life on the lines of the Almanac *Der Blaue Reiter*. After Marc's death, this undertaking was to cross over into reality – with firm support from the artists of *Der Blaue Reiter*, as represented by Kandinsky and Klee – in the *Gesamtkunstwerk* known as the Bauhaus.

In Marc's work, from 1912 onwards, the prime consequence of his all-pervading spiritual ideal was an increasing tendency to abstraction. Even in animals – as he was to recall in a letter to his wife from the Front in 1915 – he increasingly found 'so much that was repugnant to my feelings, so much that was ugly, that my images instinctively ... became more and more schematic, more abstract. In that year, trees, flowers, earth, everything showed me more and more ugly, repugnant aspects – until at last the ugliness and impurity of Nature suddenly became clear to me.'[26]

This renewed impulse towards abstraction, rooted in the ancient consciousness of the Fall; this intensified

Fig.16 Franz Marc *Mandrill* 1913, Staatsgalerie Moderner Kunst, Munich, Gift of Sofie and Emanuel Fohn

longing for the Paradise Lost of pure spirit, and for its reconstruction from inner necessity; this (as Marc put it) 'instinctive' espousal of the abstract image was prompted not only by Kandinsky but also, again, by Delaunay. The latter's *Circular Forms* of 1912 (fig. 15) decisively influenced Marc in his progress towards abstraction, as a comparison with the latter's *Mandrill* (1912, fig. 16) and *Fighting Forms* (1914; colour plate, p. 339 and cat. 156) shows.

However, the differences between Marc and Delaunay are just as readily apparent. The simultaneous interplay of colours in Delaunay's *Circular Forms* (identified as sun and moon) is a metaphor of light, seen purely as a phenomenon of this world. Marc, on the other hand, in his *Mandrill* – in which circular forms fragment the shape of the animal and its surroundings – translates Delaunay's prototype into a mysterious dream world that has its vibrant epicentre in the chromatic phenomenon of the mandrill. Animal painting is transformed into a metaphor of Creation, seen as a crystalline world of pure colour forms. The animal itself, which in the *Tower of Blue Horses* was still an expression of elegiac longing, is here ennobled into a world-ordering power: a countervailing energy source, as it were, to those political facts of life – both in Wilhelminian Germany and in her European neighbours – which were so out of tune with Marc's utopia.[27]

The step from *Mandrill* to *Fighting Forms* reveals Marc's progress towards abstraction, and the accompanying radicalization of his attitudes in general. *Fighting Forms* has mostly been interpreted as a philosophical image of conflict between the victorious, expansionary 'spirit' (the red form) and the retreating force of 'matter' (the dark form); but this is clearly disproved by Marc's own use of colour symbolism. In his work, as in the whole Romantic tradition, the spiritual can be represented only by the colour blue; red is the colour of matter.[28] It thus makes far more sense to identify spirit with the dark form on the right, which shades from blue at the edges to black and then to a misty veil of blue in the centre.

The traditional interpretation implies that the dark form shrivels and is utterly destroyed; and this notion too is undermined by a slightly later work of Marc's, *Shattered Forms* (fig. 17). Marc's cycle of four abstract paintings – beginning with *Cheerful Forms* and continuing with *Playing Forms*, *Fighting Forms* and finally *Shattered Forms* – represents a process, but not one that ends in catastrophe. The *Shattered Forms*, in their airy, aspiring structure of red, blue and black shapes against a background filled with colour and light, do not present a scene of devastation but of construction: a new and auspicious start, arising from the synthesis of previously fighting forms.

In these four abstract paintings, painted between April 1914 and the outbreak of war on 1 August of that year, Marc – like Runge in his *Times* – has presented a cyclical process of constant metamorphosis and renewal of form. As with Runge, this is a four-part process, an interplay of earnest and playful forces, in which the end transforms itself into a new beginning. Its circling geometry, a metaphor of the cosmos, echoes Runge's *First Figure of Creation* (fig. 7); the rainbow colour has precedents not only in Delaunay but in the chromatic solids of Runge's *Colour Sphere*.[29] In Marc, the geometrical diagrams of Runge's aesthetico-mystical speculation become the root images of a purely spiritual art. Accompanied, as in Runge, by wide-ranging speculations on the theme of the *Gesamtkunstwerk*, Marc's abstract cycle aims to make visible a better world – a world purified by the artistic process of abstraction. With Marc, too, this constantly self-renewing continuum of glowing colours and forms evokes the idea of a paradisal unity that springs from a contradictory multiplicity.

Marc's longing for undivided Being can fulfil itself only in the beyond; his quest for Paradise Lost, like

Fig.17 Franz Marc *Shattered Forms* 1914, The Solomon R. Guggenheim Museum, New York

Runge's, therefore ends not here on earth but – in accordance with Christian tradition – in a kingdom that is not of this world. For Marc, the ultimate aim of art – as shown by Runge in the upper border of his paradisal *Morning* – is 'to shatter the mirror of life, that we may see Being'.[30] This commitment to transcendence, the goal of Marc's paradisal longings, becomes directly visible in the upward floating shapes of *Shattered Forms* (fig. 17), the concluding image of the cycle.

Against a contemporary background in which much talk of the 'End of Time' alternated with hopes of a 'New Start',[31] Marc meant what he said when he enjoined art 'to shatter the mirror of life'. In August 1914, while Marc was working on his abstract cycle, Germany mobilized for war, and he was immediately posted to an artillery unit. Marc saw the war as a necessary purification, entirely in keeping with the ideas implicit in his paintings. In aphorisms and essays written in the months that followed, he sought to find a higher justification for the war as a purifying 'blood sacrifice', offered up on behalf of a Europe yet to come. Two

months into the war, he wrote from the Front to Kandinsky in Switzerland: 'I live in this war. I see it as the salutary though cruel process that leads to our objectives: it will not cast humanity back but will purify Europe, make it "ready".'[32]

Marc's call for a 'great blood sacrifice' to this end was utterly alien to Kandinsky. He answered early in November: 'This is not how I imagined the clearing of the ground for the building of the future. This clearance takes place at an appalling cost.'[33]

Marc was unrepentant. He answered eight days later: 'My heart is not angry with the war, but deeply thankful; there is no other way through to the Age of the Spirit. The Augean stable, the old Europe, could be cleansed in no other way – or is there one single person who wishes that this war had not happened?'[34]

And Marc, a Nietzschean who shared his master's heroic pessimism, was still glad, after a spell in a military hospital, 'to be drawn back into the vortex of this crazy war'; for to him the old Europe was so corrupt that the 'purgatory' of war was needed to cleanse it.[35]

'Purgatory', 'blood sacrifice' and 'conflagration' – Marc's recurrent war metaphors – can be related to the red form on the left in his *Fighting Forms*, painted a few weeks before the outbreak of war. There have been repeated attempts to interpret this as the stylized outline of a swooping eagle – an association that seems entirely legitimate, for in his wartime essays Marc wrote several times that he would like to draw the German eagle as it showed its warlike talons. For him, as for many contemporary intellectuals, this war was a national duty; for the Germans had taken upon themselves the sacrifice of purging the old Europe through war. Their achievement would be the advent not of a new Reich but – as Marc always stressed – of a new Europe. Himself a Francophile (and of French descent through his mother), Marc insisted that the only purpose of defeating France was that after the purification of war – after the German sacrifice – the new Europe might arise in full flower from the culture of France.[36]

In view of these utterances of Marc's, which translate his creativity into terms of contemporary warfare and elevate war into a continuation of his art, it is fair to view *Fighting Forms* in terms of his aspiration – now partly a political one – towards indivisible Being. Marc's

Fighting Forms thus stands revealed as an allegory of the longed-for dawn of a new age, an artistic premonition of a long-foreshadowed conflict. In this work, abstract formal events become a pictorial metaphor for the First World War, and for the roles assigned by Marc to the German and French nations in the common struggle for a future rebirth of Europe. Marc himself, in his letters from the Front, interpreted his recent paintings as premonitions of the redemption of the world through the purifying apocalypse of war.

In the *Sketchbook from the Field* (1915), there is a drawing entitled *Conflict* (cat. 157) that is a reinterpretation of *Fighting Forms*. As in the earlier work, warfare is shown as a battle between two abstract forms, albeit now with the benefit of direct experience of shellfire. In the same year, 1915, Marc described war as the salutary and necessary school of abstraction: 'This alone was the thunderous reality that wrenched our impassioned thoughts away from the familiar path of known sensory experiences and into an alien Beyond – into a possibility higher and more spiritual than this impossible present.'[37]

Here, Marc's artistic journey through animal painting to abstraction ends in a metaphysics of death. A little later, amid the senseless inhumanity of the trenches, Marc parted with all his illusions. To him, the war was now 'deeply shaming' and 'disgraceful', and he hoped to survive it.[38] The stylized shellfire in his drawings is no longer a purification leading to spirituality – as he had once hoped – but a deadly reality.

In Germany, Marc's error had been shared by the best of his generation (see also the essay by Carla Schulz-Hoffmann in this volume).[39] His voluntary acceptance of death as a higher duty is not to be separated from the religious understanding of Modernity as a purifying and spiritualizing power in the world, which had so recently emerged in the attitudes of *Der Blaue Reiter* both to art and to life. Marc's progression from the theme of animal life to that of death was in tune with the inner necessity that gradually radicalized his paradisal art. Arcadian and abstract in its beauty, it aimed ultimately to embrace the whole of life and all the arts in its longing for a better future, a spiritualized *Gesamtkunstwerk* of life, and – in the beyond – a Paradise Regained. In this world, the militant radicalization of this art of paradise brought Marc up against the end of art itself.

4. Beuys

The End of Time

Runge's exhortation, uttered at the end of the Enlightenment, 'we must become children, if we wish to attain the best', was appropriately reformulated a century later by Marc, thus: We must become animals, to enter the Kingdom of God. At the end of Modernism, both these demands still held good for Joseph Beuys, though art in his time offered a far wider scope for the quest to regain Paradise through strategies of 'primitivism'. From Runge through Marc to Beuys, the longing for Paradise has remained one – and possibly the one – central motif of German art, which thus stands defined as a missionary and universal art. Its tendency to reach out for the Whole – its hankering for the *Gesamtkunstwerk* – lends it a playful earnestness. The aim of art is to transform everything into spiritual substance. However, as Marc's example shows, this earnest play does nothing to obviate the danger that the missionary impulse may be pursued to the point of self-immolation.

By *The End of the Twentieth Century* – to quote the title of his great work of 1983 (colour plate, p. 104 and cat. 261) – Beuys had behind him a long Modernist tradition, both of positive achievement and of error. Out of the multitude of contradictory possibilities available to him, he had developed a charismatic and versatile artistic persona. With positively Franciscan humility and cryptic humour, he bestowed artistic attention on the most banal objects.

Like Runge's vindication of landscape and Marc's humanization of animals, this limitless extension of the material of art was already present in the Romantic fairytale. Brentano's poet-child creates his own artificial Paradises out of anything and everything, the odds and ends of jewel-cases and cluttered boxrooms. In Brentano's illustration *Gakeleia in the Mouse Kingdom* (fig. 3), which is directly based on Runge's paradisal *Morning* (colour plate, p. 94), the child Gakeleia lies in the grass, surrounded by animals that act – like those of Marc – in highly human ways: a procession of mice on the left, and an assembly of cats on the right. In this animal realm, the royal castle and the church are made of discarded everyday objects: baskets, chip boxes, saddles, animal skulls, pumpkins, Dutch cheeses. In the

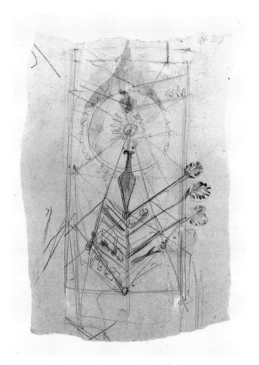

Fig.18 Joseph Beuys *Flower and Sun* 1947, drawing, van der Grinten Collection, Museum Schloß Moyland

context of the tale – the Paradise Regained of Romantic childhood – all these objects come equally alive; and all question of the hierarchy of artistic genres becomes null and void. Landscape; then the inferior *genre animalier*; and on the lowest step of all the still-life of inanimate objects: these (in academic terms) progressively less acceptable levels of subject matter enable the Romantic fairytale to articulate its own longing for Paradise Lost by reference to the totality of all conceivable realities – beautiful and ugly, precious and banal.

The art of Beuys stands in this tradition of universality. Beuys himself, like Runge and Marc before him, escaped into art from bourgeois values and a bourgeois career. Runge was meant to go into trade; Marc was destined for the Church; and Beuys wanted to be a scientist. In all his discontent with the bourgeois world, Beuys – like Runge and Marc before him – never discarded its cultural standards, its notions of universality, or its critical approach to the status quo. Runge felt himself to stand at the end of all religions; to Marc, the materialism of his own time signified the end of all spiritual values; Beuys stood, as it were, at the end of those ends. Religion, philosophy and science had lost their virtue as guides to living, because every area of life had simultaneously been rationalized. Technological perfection and rational administration had reduced the world

to a wilderness and its inhabitants to misery. To quote Edmund Husserl's verdict, late in his career, on the intellectual and spiritual history of the twentieth century: 'In our hour of need, this science has nothing to say to us.'[40]

In the light of this critique, Beuys may be seen as a pioneer drop-out: one who turned his back on our civilization before postwar reconstruction in Germany ever got under way. From 1958 onwards, rejecting science and technology as means to human self-realization (not to say self-obliteration), Beuys devoted himself entirely to the salvation of humanity through art. In defiance of the dictatorship of reason, which came into the world through the Fall, he took the view that only art could bring human beings to life through the totality of their senses. In all his artistic acts of creation and provocation, Beuys aimed to reactivate human creativity, so long submerged by the constant use of reason. Thus creatively revived, the new human being would, Beuys hoped, no longer rest content with a specialized existence disciplined and confined by acquired skills, but would regard himself or herself as a creative portion of an organic Whole; or, in terms of the mystical Christian view of Nature, as the microcosm of a universal macrocosm.

Commentators have repeatedly stressed the influence on Beuys of this microcosm-macrocosm idea, which runs from antiquity through the Renaissance to the holistic natural philosophy of Goethe and the Romantics – and which notably features in the Anthroposophism of Rudolf Steiner.[41] Equally, they have shown how close Beuys came, in his conversion from scientist to artist, to the ideas of Runge on Nature. The leaves affixed to Beuys's early drawings (see colour plates, pp. 18–19) recall the playful virtuosity of Runge's plant silhouettes (see colour plates, pp. 218–19), with their ideal Platonic outlines of vegetable form. Even the complex architecture of plant growth in Runge's *Times* reappears, intact, in the way Beuys's blossoms turn towards the light (fig. 18).[42] Runge's leitmotif – plant life, the feminine, light – all recur in Beuys as central emblems of the renewal of life.

Like Marc, too, in countless drawings of roe-deer, stags and elks (fig. 19), Beuys proclaims his commitment to animals as creatures still largely unalienated and at one with Creation. In this connection, some of the striking analogies with Marc in Beuys's work stem from the

Fig.19 Joseph Beuys *Sheep* 1947, pencil and watercolour, private collection

Fig.20 Joseph Beuys *Elk with Sun* 1957, pencil, Froehlich Collection, Stuttgart

influence of his teacher at the Academy in Düsseldorf, the animal sculptor Ewald Mataré.[43]

In Beuys's animistic cosmos, as in Marc's, the prime intention is to render visible the power for good that lies in animals. To this end – unexpectedly for a sculptor – he dematerializes the animal, as did Marc when he metamorphosed his animals (on the analogy of the recent discovery of X-rays) into translucent, crystalline structures. Beuys's X-ray vision goes deeper, to the point of skinning his creatures alive and making visible, through the structure of their bones and the circulation of their blood, the field of forces within an animal organism (fig. 20). From this it is only a step to the self-orienting scrawl of a child's drawing, in one direction, and to an abstract diagram of philosophical constructs, in the other. In a comprehensive longing for renewal, which embraced both vitalism and pure spirituality, Beuys pursued deliberate primitiveness alongside abstraction. For ultimately – as Runge and Marc both demonstrate – these two options of return to Paradise Lost are inseparable.

Both primitivism and abstraction are therefore present in the encyclopaedic work that Beuys began in London in 1974 and completed in Berlin in 1977: *Directional Forces* (*Richtkräfte*, fig. 21 and 22). To give visual form to the social renewal to which he aspired —classified on Steinerian lines in terms of 'Cultural Life', 'Legal Issues' and 'Economic Issues' – Beuys devised an overview of the microcosm and the macrocosm (as Runge had done in a circular geometric diagram based on the mysticism of Jacob Böhme (see fig. 1, p. 275 and fig. 7, p. 66), and as Marc had done in the elevated imagery of a purely spiritual art (see colour plate, p. 339 and fig. 17, p. 74). Entirely within the mystical-Romantic tradition of

abstract cosmograms, Beuys's *Directional Forces* uses a hundred blackboards, covered with words, scribbles and geometrical diagrams, to present his vision of a world-order governed by Liberty, Equality and Fraternity: a new Paradise created from inner necessity. This blackboard vision of a better world is constantly illuminated by the transparent image of a hare, the 'symbol of the incarnation'. For the hare, in Beuys's words, 'does in reality what the human being can only do in thought'.[44]

There is, of course, something dotty about this schematic image of a better world on blackboards, this plan for a world in white chalk on black wood. The bizarreness of this highly abstract work is reinforced by its disconcerting physical reality. Spilling over a dais, the whole thing looks like the storm-tossed raft of an encyclopedic world-order. Strewn across the floor apparently at random, the blackboards directly convey the process of their writing and thus the genesis of the work. Here, quite clearly, abstraction – the schematic rendering of a cosmos of spiritual forces – has been converted into a solid object that bears every sign of poverty and impermanence. A mental survey of the universe itself, a vision of a better world-order, culminates in a landslide of blackboards.

The idea of the Whole – which Runge was still able to incorporate within the cosmic schema of his four (admittedly syncretic and composite) *Times* – opens out in Marc's abstract cycle into four utterly disparate pictorial formats that coalesce only in the mind's eye. With Beuys, this idea of the Whole as a discordant concord gives way to the wide-open pictorial form of the fragment. The random composition of *Directional Forces* bears witness to an artistic process that incorporates

Fig.21 Joseph Beuys *Directional Forces* 1974–77, Staatliche Museen zu Berlin Preußischer Kulturbesitz, Nationalgalerie

imperfection as part of its truth. 'Show your wound' is written on one of the blackboards. And by this Beuys means: 'Show your mistakes! – Don't wait for the perfect formulation.'[45]

Random, open and fragmentary, *Directional Forces* reflects all those experiences in postwar German art that Beuys was able to absorb and, with a touch of irony, to transmute. The inclusion of found, everyday objects within the work smacks of the Neo-Dadaism of Pop, with its revival of the Readymade. The throwaway action with the inscribed blackboards is a joke at the expense of Tachism and Action Painting. The repetition of rectangular supports is a riposte to Constructivism and Minimal Art. As the outcome of a public demonstration by an artist, *Directional Forces* belongs to the international Fluxus movement, with its Happenings. This work opened the way for Beuys to move from sculpture into performance and – through his association with theatre, music, words and film – towards the ultimate, synaesthetic *Gesamtkunstwerk*.

By contrast with the abstract blueprint for Paradise that is *Directional Forces*, other works by Beuys such as *Hare's Grave*, *Earth Telephone* and *Alarm I* seem saturated with sympathetic magic. Like the contents of Brentano's paradisal lumber-room, they look at first like the merest accumulated detritus. Like Brentano, Beuys relies on stirring and provoking the imagination. The point of the confrontation with poor (often animal) materials, such as felt, fat and honey – their salutary shock effect, significantly reinforced by juxtaposition with such simple utilitarian objects as sleds, bathtubs, mortuary trolleys, batteries, loudspeakers and telephones – the point of all this calculated Anti-Art is to sensitize its beholders both to themselves and to their surroundings. In all this, Beuys embarks on an open-ended project of expanding art into life, for the sole purpose of reawakening life itself through its humblest constituents. Within Beuys's expanded concept of art, even the dingiest scraps, the most revolting detritus – like the bones and chip boxes in Brentano's story – emerge as suitable transmitters of messages, if only the human creature can be fully reactivated as a mental, spiritual and emotional being. The artist's demiurgic power is all the more necessary in a technological and scientific age, says Beuys, because at the century's end the whole of Creation, human and natural, threatens to waste away.

An impressive reminder of this terminal state is provided by Beuys's work *The End of the Twentieth Century* (colour plate, p. 104). The large version of the piece in Munich consists of forty-four basalt stelae. At one end of each stone a cone has been cut out, and each cone has been polished, re-inserted and fixed in its previous position with felt and clay. All the stones look as if they have been given a telescopically protruding eye, or rather a sensory organ with which they can, as it were, both transmit and receive.

The stones thus appear startlingly alive, and the viewer's detachment turns to shock. For these living stones remind us of petrified human beings. Thoughts of a graveyard; memories of ancient tribes, long since vanished from the face of the earth; or of the débris of a battlefield; or of calcined or petrified corpses: there is no end to the horrific associations that arise from this work, which Beuys intended as the writing on the wall for the century's end.

The Renaissance emblem-book tradition used the image of stones scattered on the ground as an example of divine judgment on the human hubris that wilfully violates the natural order.[46] A bleak expanse of rocks becomes the emblem of Nature deprived of the grace of God, and thus of the loss of Paradise. Beuys's expanse of stones has quite rightly been likened to Caspar David Friedrich's painting *Sea of Ice* (colour plate, p. 97);[47] even closer, perhaps – in view of the germs of life that they embody – is the analogy between Beuys's basalt eye-stones and the stony ground underfoot in Runge's *Night*. The cold and rigidity of night and death are visible in Runge's crystalline expanse of rock, but so is the hope of new life in the architecture of plant forms that grows out of the rocks towards the stars. This polarity of rigidity and renewal reappears in the use of basalt rocks to protect the saplings in Beuys's action *7000 Oaks*. Runge's *Times* and Beuys's *The End of the Twentieth Century* embody the same theme of death and life: the total loss of the gifts of Paradise, and their recovery through the vital forces that – even in the petrified rigidity of the world we live in – Nature and consequently humankind have not entirely lost.

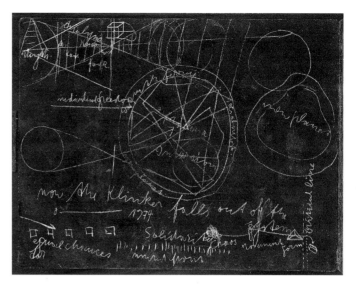

Fig.22 Joseph Beuys One of the blackboards from *Directional Forces* 1974–77, Nationalgalerie, Berlin

Every Human Being an Artist

At the end of the twentieth century – a time of fear, both of ultimate war and of the irrevocable destruction of Nature – Beuys offers a motto for the recovery of Paradise Lost, in the shape of a reminder of individual human artistic potential. 'Every human being an artist':[48] that is Beuys's credo, which he dramatizes in a photographic self-presentation under the title of *La Rivoluzione siamo Noi* (1971, fig. 23). We are the Revolution: this echo of the 1968 slogan 'All Power to the Imagination' means that power for change lies in the creativity of every individual. In the photograph, Beuys faces us as the prototype of the artistic role that every one of us can play. Art will revolutionize the world —in order, Beuys has said, 'that human beings may make use of their power as individuals, as free, creative human beings; that is the basic principle'.[49]

In Beuys's hands, the leitmotif of Romanticism – Paradise Lost, longingly reconstructed from inner necessity – becomes the artistic task of every human being. In the photograph, Beuys sets the example. Grandly, like the risen Redeemer, he turns his back on the closed door, the frame of which surrounds him like a nimbus. Fully accoutred, in gangster's hat and airman's vest, the artist passes serenely on his way with one fist clenched, like something between the Poor Sower and an itinerant preacher. His quasi-Christian message is the renewal of

humanity through art. As we see from the message *Hauptstrom* (Mainstream) and the sign of the cross, stamped beneath his feet, Beuys is a transmitter with a decidedly messianic awareness of his mission.

The Imitation of Christ, which according to Runge's *Times* is the only way to regain Paradise, defines itself for Beuys as the path to human creativity; the restoration of the original divine nature of humankind. For him, as for the Christian humanist tradition, all arts and sciences have their foundation in Christ, the Wisdom of God.[50] Now that science and technology have declined into a purely superficial, materialistic pursuit of progress, Beuys calls upon art to sustain this Christ-impulse within human history, and to liberate human beings once more from reified, one-sidedly rational ways of thought. The self-dramatization of *La Rivoluzione siamo Noi* is clearly meant as one more act of provocation through art – through an apparently artless, poverty-stricken, at times downright pathetic art, made from mostly extra-artistic and often ugly materials, which Beuys charges, in an initiatory process, with ultimate metaphysical meanings. The point of this provocation is to awaken in human beings the therapeutic, creative forces that will free them from the idolatry of mere technological rationalism.

Fig.23 Joseph Beuys *La Rivoluzione siamo Noi* 1971

Through the irrational appeal of art, said Beuys, people can once more comprehend themselves as spiritual, autonomous beings within the total organism of Creation – beings who will then decisively transform their own science and their own social behaviour. 'I am convinced,' he explained in the interview that accompanied *La Rivoluzione siamo Noi*, 'that in our day art alone can be revolutionary. This is achieved, in particular, when the concept of art is freed from all traditional technical assumptions – art leading over into the realm of Anti-Art, art transformed into gestures and actions to make it available to everyone.' It follows ' ... that art is identical with life and, furthermore, that art and man are to be equated. The only means to revolution is a global concept of art.'[51]

Within this global concept of art, the Romantic idea of the *Gesamtkunstwerk* was transformed into the new idea of Social Sculpture. With the vision of the founder of a new university, Beuys set about launching his idea of 'The *Gesamtkunstwerk* of the Future Society'.[52] The aim of this – which goes far beyond the universalistic design aspirations of the old Bauhaus – is to liberate society by remaking the individual, and thereby to restore harmony to the world-order as a whole. The objective is formulated metaphorically as 'the transformation of the earth into the sun': the production of an organic Whole, in which human beings may once more commune in peace with animals, plants, angels and spirits.[53] This harmony to which Beuys aspires is no less than Paradise Regained: a world which is to be created in the future, and which also becomes a reality through death. 'If you look at it as a Mystery,' said Beuys, 'then it is none other than the repetition of the Mystery of Golgotha.'[54]

With Beuys, as with Runge and Marc, faith in the Resurrection – the return of what once was present – is linked with a Paradise Lost that can be regained only through art. In German art from the Romantics to Beuys, the construction of Paradise from inner necessity has led to a succession of all-embracing projects that lend themselves to interpretation as doctrines of redemption. Well knowing how little art can do in its own age – yet also how badly the age needs art – Beuys still plays those earnest games that Brentano's child, under the tutelage of Goethe's mother, once hoped to use to gain deliverance from the tormenting realities of his life. From Runge by way of Marc to Beuys, the Romantic longing for redemption through art has lost none of its power.

Peter-Klaus Schuster

Translated from the German by David Britt

1 Clemens Brentano, *Gockel Hinkel Gackeleia* (Frankfurt am Main, 1973), 13. See Wolfgang Frühwald, 'Das verlorene Paradies. Zur Deutung von Clemens Brentanos "Herzlicher Zueignung" des Märchens "Gockel, Hinkel und Gakeleia" (1838)', *Literaturwissenschaftliches Jahrbuch*, n.s., 3 (1962): 113ff. (Editor's note: The spelling of Ga(c)keleia varies, even within the first edition. According to Friedhelm Kemp the grandmother addressed in the dedication is not Brentano's own.)

2 See Peter-Klaus Schuster, 'Bildzitate bei Brentano', in *Clemens Brentano: Beiträge des Kolloquiums im Freien Deutschen Hochstift* (Tübingen, 1978), 334ff.

3 Brentano (as note 1), 18. (Editor's note: Brentano got to know Goethe when he was a student in Jena. His mother had also been a friend of Goethe in her youth.)

4 Clemens Brentano and Philipp Otto Runge, *Briefwechsel*, ed. Konrad Feilchenfeldt (Frankfurt am Main, 1974), 21—22.

5 Philipp Otto Runge, *Hinterlassene Schriften* (Hamburg, 1840—49; facsimile reprint, Göttingen, 1965), 2:209. Cited hereinafter as HS. On the notion of Paradise in Runge, see Jörg Traeger, *Philipp Otto Runge und sein Werk* (Munich, 1975), 122ff.; Werner Hofmann, 'Runges Versuch, das verlorene Paradies aus seiner Notwendigkeit zu rekonstruieren', in exh. cat. *Runge in seiner Zeit* (Hamburg: Hamburger Kunsthalle, 1977), 31ff.

6 Runge (as note 5), HS 1:7. On the value set on childhood in German Romanticism, see Traeger (as note 5), 128—29; Gerhard Schaub, *Le Génie enfant: Die Kategorie des Kindlichen bei Clemens Brentano* (Berlin and New York, 1973); Jörg Traeger, *Philipp Otto Runge: Die Hülsenbeckschen Kinder. Von der Reflexion des Naiven im Kunstwerk der Romantik* (Frankfurt am Main, 1987); Robert Rosenblum, *The Romantic Child: From Runge to Sendak* (London, 1988).

7 Traeger (as note 5), 131.

8 See Peter-Klaus Schuster and Konrad Feilchenfeldt, 'Philipp Otto Runges "Vier Zeiten" und die Temperamentenlehre', in *Romantik in Deutschland. Ein interdisziplinäres Symposium*, ed. Richard Brinckmann (Stuttgart, 1978), 652ff.

9 This proposition, espoused by Traeger (as note 5), 52, 45, has already been contested by Schuster and Feilchenfeldt (as note 8), 660—61, and by Hanna Hohl, in exh. cat. *Runge in seiner Zeit* (as note 5), 191—92.

10 See Erwin Panofsky, *Albrecht Dürer*, 3rd ed. (Cambridge, Mass., 1948), 1:234—35; Schuster and Feilchenfeldt (as note 8), 659—60.

11 See Traeger (as note 5), 131.

12 Paul Ferdinand Schmidt, 'Runge und die Gegenwart', *Der Cicerone* 15 (1923): 464. For more detail on what follows, see Peter-Klaus Schuster, 'Vom Tier zum Tod. Zur Ideologie des Geistigen bei Franz Marc', in exh. cat. *Franz Marc. Kräfte der Natur. Werke 1912–1915* (Munich and Münster, 1993), 168–69.

13 Franz Marc, 'Die "Wilden" Deutschlands', in *Der Blaue Reiter*, ed. Wassily Kandinsky and Franz Marc (Munich, 1912; ed. Klaus Lankheit, Munich, 1984), 31. (Trans. as *The Blaue Reiter Almanac*, London and New York, 1974.) See also Carla Schulz-Hoffmann, '"Die mystisch-innerliche Konstruktion, die das große Problem der heutigen Generation ist": Anmerkungen zur Frage der Religiosität im Blauen Reiter', in exh. cat. *München leuchtete. Karl Caspar und die Erneuerung christlicher Kunst in München um 1900* (Munich: Staatsgalerie moderner Kunst, 1984), 44ff.

14 Franz Marc, *Briefe aus dem Feld*, ed. Klaus Lankheit and Uwe Steffen (Munich, 1985), 65. On the Christian humanist tradition behind Marc's commendation of animals, see Klaus Lankheit, *Franz Marc. Sein Leben und seine Kunst* (Cologne, 1976), 136ff.; Frederick S. Levine, *The Apocalyptic Vision: The Art of Franz Marc as German Expressionism* (New York, 1979), 104ff.

15 Johannes Langner, 'Iphigenie als Hund: Figurenbild im Tierbild bei Franz Marc', in exh. cat. *Franz Marc* (Munich, 1980), 50ff.

16 See Langner (as note 15), 50.

17 Franz Marc, *Schriften*, ed. Klaus Lankheit (Cologne, 1978), 118.

18 Marc (as note 14), 118.

19 See Ursula Heiderich, 'Sehnsucht nach dem unteilbaren Sein. Zum Wandbild "Paradies" von Franz Marc und August Macke', in exh. cat. *Franz Marc* (as note 12), 94ff.

20 On what follows, see Peter-Klaus Schuster, 'Delaunay und Deutschland', and Johannes Langner, 'Turm und Täufer: Delaunay, Kandinsky und Marc', in exh. cat. *Delaunay und Deutschland* (Munich, 1985), 71 ff, 208ff.

21 Marc (as note 17), 118.

22 See Franz Marc and Else Lasker-Schüler, '*Der Blaue Reiter präsentiert Eurer Hoheit sein Blaues Pferd': Karten und Briefe*, ed. Peter-Klaus Schuster (Munich, 1988). (Abridged English trans. in Franz Marc, *Postcards to Prince Jussuf*, Munich, 1988.) See also Peter-Klaus Schuster, 'Nachrichten von den Tieren. Zu den Postkarten von Franz Marc', in exh. cat. *Die Künstlerpostkarte von den Anfängen bis zur Gegenwart* (Hamburg: Altonaer Museum, 1992), 19ff.

23 Marc and Kandinsky (as note 13), 23, 31.

24 See Carla Schulz-Hoffmann, 'Franz Marc und die Romantik: Zur Bedeutung romantischer Denkvorstellungen in seinen Schriften', in exh. cat. *Franz Marc* (as note 15), 95ff.; Carla Schulz-Hoffmann, 'Utopie und Abstraktion – Franz Marc und die Bedeutung romantischer Denkvorstellungen für die Kunst der Moderne', in exh. cat. *Franz Marc* (as note 12), 153ff.

25 Marc (as note 17), 119.

26 Marc (as note 14), 65.

27 See Peter-Klaus Schuster, 'Franz Marc und Else Lasker-Schüler', in Marc and Lasker-Schüler (as note 22), 126ff.; Marc's *Mandrill* as a characterization of Lasker-Schüler, *ibid.*, 130. See also a recent contribution by Andreas Hüneke, 'Das Jahr 1913: lauter ganz verschiedene Bilder', in exh. cat. *Franz Marc* (as note 12), 153ff.

28 See Marc's letter to Macke, December 1910: 'Blue is the male principle, stark and spiritual. Yellow the female principle, gentle, light-hearted and sensual. Red is matter, brutal and heavy, and always the colour that must be fought and defeated by the other two.' Quoted from Lankheit (as note 13), 58. See also Hüneke (as note 27), 109, and Schuster (as note 12), 181—82.

29 On this see Traeger (as note 5), 194ff. On the cycles of abstract paintings painted by Marc in 1914, see Lankheit (as note 13), 130.

30 Marc (as note 17), 118.

31 See Armin Zweite, 'Die Linie zum inneren Klang befreien. Kandinskys Kunsterneuerung vor dem Horizont der Zeit', in exh. cat. *Wassily Kandinsky, Kleine Freuden. Aquarelle und Zeichnungen*, ed. Vivian Endicott Barnett and Armin Zweite (Munich, 1992), especially 15ff. (Trans. as 'Free the Line for the Inner Sound', in *Kandinsky: Watercolors and Drawings*, ed. Barnett and Zweite, Munich, 1992.)

32 Wassily Kandinsky and Franz Marc, *Briefwechsel*, ed. Klaus Lankheit (Munich, 1993), 263ff.

33 Kandinsky and Marc (as note 32), 265.

34 Kandinsky and Marc (as note 32), 266.

35 Marc (as note 17), 192.

36 Marc (as note 17), 161—62.

37 Marc (as note 17), 201.

38 Marc (as note 14), 148.

39 See Lankheit (as note 13), 139ff.

40 See Peter-Klaus Schuster, 'Der Mensch als sein eigener Schöpfer. Dürer und Beuys – oder: das Bekenntnis zur Kreativität', *Süddeutsche Zeitung*, 22 June 1985.

41 See Armin Zweite, 'Visionär in einer beschädigten Welt. Die romantische Existenz des Joseph Beuys', *Frankfurter Allgemeine Zeitung*, 12 May 1981; Theodora Vischer, *Beuys und die Romantik —individuelle Ikonographie, individuelle Mythologie?* (Cologne, 1983); Laura Arici, 'Joseph Beuys als Esoteriker. Zum Weltbild des deutschen Künstlers', *Anzeiger des Germanischen Nationalmuseums* 1991:303ff.

42 On Beuys and Runge see Vischer (as note 41); Christa Lichtenstein, *Zur Morphologie der Urpflanze von Goethe bis Beuys* (Weinheim, 1990).

43 See Lothar Romain, 'Franz Marc und Joseph Beuys. Zur Wiederkehr des Romantischen in der deutschen Moderne', in *Romantik und Gegenwart: Festschrift für Jens Christian Jensen zum 60. Geburtstag*, ed. Ulrich Bischoff (Cologne, 1988), 197ff.

44 See Christos M. Joachimides, *Joseph Beuys: Richtkräfte* (Berlin: Nationalgalerie, 1977), 10.

45 Quoted in English in Joachimides (as note 44), 11.

46 See Peter-Klaus Schuster, '"Das Ende des 20. Jahrhunderts" —Beuys, Düsseldorf und Deutschland', in exh. cat. *Deutsche Kunst seit 1960. Aus der Sammlung Prinz Franz von Bayern* (Munich, 1985), 39—40, fig. 2.

47 The comparison drawn by Armin Zweite in exh. cat. *Joseph Beuys: Natur, Materie, Form* (Düsseldorf, 1991), 44.

48 See Joseph Beuys, *Jeder Mensch ein Künstler. Gespräche auf der documenta 5, 1972* (Frankfurt am Main, 1975).

49 Quoted from Götz Adriani, Winfried Konnertz and Karin Thomas, *Joseph Beuys, Leben und Werk* (Cologne, 1981), 269.

50 On this see Franz Josef van der Grinten and Friedrich Menekes, *Menschenbild – Christusbild* (Stuttgart, 1984), 103ff.

51 Achille Bonito Oliva, *Partitura di Joseph Beuys: La Rivoluzione siamo Noi* (Naples, 1971).

52 See Joseph Beuys, 'Ich durchsuche Feldcharakter', in Joachimides (as note 44), 14; Volker Harlan, Rainer Rappmann and Peter Schata, *Soziale Plastik. Materialien zu Joseph Beuys* (Achberg, 1976), 10ff.

53 Quoted from Vischer (as note 41), 92.

54 Quoted from Vischer (as note 41), 94.

Romantic-Idealistic Paraphrases in Twentieth-Century Art

'Then I received a command from higher beings:
Not a bunch of flowers! Paint flamingos!'

In his *Vitrinenstück* (Showcase Piece) of 1966 Sigmar Polke combines a picture painted with childlike naïveté in the style of the 1950s with a medley of banal objects, a portrait photo and a panel of writing (fig. 1)[1]. Plastic letters stuck on a felt cloth inform us about the origin of this curious work: 'I was standing in front of the canvas, about to paint a bunch of flowers. Then I received a command from higher beings: Not a bunch of flowers! Paint flamingos! At first I wanted to go on painting, but then I realized that they meant it seriously.' Sweet, kitschy flamingos to symbolize bourgeois German longings in an age of corpulent economic affluence, draped as a wall-covering between the kidney-shaped table and the goldfish-bowl, are inserted as evidence of divine mediation. Thus Polke, with a wink, ironizes the claim to individual creativity. In the same breath he accepts – apparently with amusement – a sacrosanct relation of dependency: the artist is once again confirmed in his function as a medium in the service of higher beings. Thus, in his dadaistically confused memoirs, full of bizarre highways and byways, Polke recalls the 'Palmin-Album', the illustrated dreamworld of childhood, which belongs to the 'bad times', long before economic growth, the throwaway society and media hype – a period that seemed to the boy a distant cockaigne full of palmtrees, coconuts, fat and warmth (figs. 2 and 3). The metamorphosis he hoped for – 'to be a palmtree among palmtrees' – did not materialize; instead – 'I finally fell from the nut and remained what I am called: Polke.'[2] However, the belief in a fated link between 'palm' and 'Polke' remained, to be suddenly revealed in an Egyptian wall-painting. What the name conceals in dry letters clearly emerges here: Polke – so we learn from the translation of these Egyptian hieroglyphs – was the man who once wielded a stick, knocked the coconuts off the palm and was cursed by it when he hid them in a basket and

brought them to men ...[3] With a logic befitting this touching nonsense, which shamelessly manipulates the dubious Egyptian text, there follows from the biographical construct the quasi-divine mediation that validates the artist's fantastic inventions as 'commissioned art'. With subversive jokiness Polke associates himself with a concept of art that derives from idealist philosophy and is increasingly invoked in the twentieth century as a legitimation of artistic endeavour. In a society geared to the amazing triumphs of technology, in which in principle anything and everything can be made and which has developed an inane dynamism of its own, attempts to find fresh justifications for the artist's existence are almost part of the artistic medium itself.

The claim is formulated with far greater pathos by the Italian Enzo Cucchi: 'It is said that, in order to mitigate storms, disasters and earthquakes, the painters, the seafarers, will one day create symbols to determine a route.'[4] In a mixture of pathos and naïveté that is typical not only of Enzo Cucchi, but of much modern art besides, a vision is invoked that makes the artist the missionary saviour in a present that is both meaningless and under threat. This notion derives from a view of reality that depends more on the power of primitive mythical images than on that of the transient events, moods and experiences of the present.

Conceived in more formal terms, this idea marks a tendency in European art since Cézanne, which relies on the exclusive image-worthiness of strict basic forms, freed from all inessentials, and thereby seeks to convey the notion of permanence. For Cucchi, however, the form is meaningful only in relation to its content: the need for a particular form is indissolubly linked with what it expresses. It is thus not a question of the rightness of a form as such: there are no ideal forms, only ideal pictures. Hence, the individual motifs are never *beautiful* or *right* when compared with their natural prototype: rather, their appropriateness depends solely on the statement they make. Cucchi thus places himself

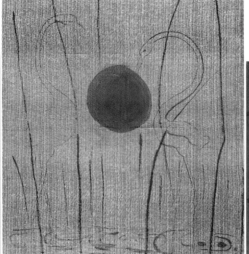

Fig.1 Sigmar Polke, *Showcase Piece* 1966, Wittelsbacher Ausgleichsfonds, Collection of Prince Franz of Bavaria, Munich

within a northern European tradition that was formu-lated especially in German idealism and found its way into various avant-garde movements in art, not least through the agency of Kandinsky and Marc. Especially in the German and Italian art of recent decades this claim has been asserted with a radicalism that, in spite of any accompanying irony, amounts to a desperate act of self-assertion, a statement of identity in a hostile and rootless world. What Kandinsky and Marc could still formulate as utopia – 'creating symbols that belong on the altars of the coming spiritual religion ...'[5] – is asserted as reality. Art as a cure for ills, but also as a refuge in an alien world – this idea, variously refracted, informs wide areas of artistic activity.

It is taken to the extreme in the works of, say, Anselm Kiefer, which grapple with Germany's National Socialist past. Monumental interiors, an architectural mix of Walhalla and the Brown House, as well as the 'House of German Art', supply a setting for an apotheosis of paint-ing (fig. 4): at the centre of a gigantic Fascist shrine, a tiny palette is seen as an object of worship, set upon an altar and dedicated to the 'Unknown Painter'. The mys-terious nocturnal atmosphere reinforces the character of the enigmatic and incomprehensible, to which one must surrender totally if one wishes to believe. Painting becomes something mystical and ecstatic, hence a matter

of faith to which history must submit – even where it was transformed into hideous reality in the notion of a thousand-year Reich! Many contemporary artists, for a variety of motives, propagate a world-view that was rep-resented, with modifications, by some avant-garde movements of the early twentieth century.[6] Significantly, they were not concerned primarily with a new aesthetic programme, but with a fundamental human attitude that could contribute to the harmonious linking of art and life. This conception became the real motor of artis-tic activity, a phenomenon that gave expression to the disappointment resulting from the degradation of art to the status of decoration in the late nineteenth century and its exclusion from any social context. Since the Enlightenment and the development of bourgeois soci-ety, the social position of the artist had gradually shifted. In earlier times his wide-ranging activity on behalf of Church and State had largely guaranteed him security and social recognition, but now he became an increasingly marginal figure with no official artistic tasks to perform. Accordingly the artist, now free to pursue his creative activity without obligations, had to find a new meaning, a new legitimation, for his work; this became a dire necessity towards the end of the nine-teenth century, thanks to the rapid development of pho-tography. The artist was no longer the main communi-

Fig.2 Illustration from a book on Egyptian Art

Fig.3 Reworking of the illustration by Sigmar Polke

cator of visible reality: the photograph could do this much better! This partly explains why avant-garde artists, shortly after the turn of the century, tried to find a new justification for art, based on formal or stylistic criteria (as in the case of the *Fauves* and the Cubists) or on content (as in the case of the existing artists of the Blue Rider). At the same time, however, a new generation clung to the optimistic belief that it could usher in new and better times in opposition to the prevailing materialism. The Wilhelminian era seemed to be played out; hence many young artists welcomed the First World War as a chance to destroy a corrupt social order and begin afresh – an idea that we now find hard to follow.

In many ways art became a substitute for religion, a new and meaningful force in a late bourgeois phase of purely utilitarian thinking. Such a concept of art promised to enhance the artist's position. Although these ideas played an important role in the work of Ernst Ludwig Kirchner and other artists of the *Brücke*, as well as in Max Beckmann's, the artistic consequence of the spiritualization of reality underwent a more rigorous transformation in those branches of Modernism that tended to abstraction. This applies in exemplary fashion to the artists of the Blue Rider, especially Franz Marc,

who was able to revert, in part directly, to Romantic notions. There are three central ideas: the artist's understanding of himself, his definition of nature, and therefore of reality in the widest sense, and – as a substratum deriving from both – the justification of the particular work. The new interest in Romanticism, discernible in Franz Marc and many of his contemporaries, was due to a number of factors. These became significant in the *Deutsche Jahrhundertausstellung* (Centenary Exhibition of German Art) of 1906, organized by Hugo von Tschudi in the National Gallery, Berlin, and the associated revaluation of Romantic art as 'true' and 'genuine' art. This re-orientation came at a time when Wilhelminian society was increasingly criticized for its lack of tradition and there was a growing interest in the national elements in German culture. As evidence of the latter we may cite the incipient movement in favour of *Heimatkunst* (homeland art), reflected for instance in the periodical *Heimat*, which began to appear in 1900, the founding of the *Bund Heimatschutz* (League for the defence of the homeland) in 1904, and the study of folklore. The contradiction between national unity, preached and documented since the foundation of the German Empire in 1870, and the actual variety within it, the contrast

Fig.4 Anselm Kiefer *Monument to an Unknown Painter* 1983, Collection of Céline and Heiner Bastian

between the vertiginous speed of industrialization on the one hand (linked with increased profits for the few) and a general cultural backwardness on the other, encouraged a trend that focused on national values and on aspects of German history to which nationalistic ideas might be oriented.

Interest in Romanticism was determined partly by the factors already mentioned; at the same time it reflected a mood of retrospection. German Romanticism, as a historical phenomenon lying wholly in the past, became more and more a specifically German utopia, in which one could see realized all those features that were to become goals for the future and only occasionally matched the revolutionary claim of Romanticism.

To this extent the dialogue with Romanticism in the work of Franz Marc is not an isolated phenomenon, but an expression and a product of a period that was prompted by the most varied interests to exploit this past epoch in promoting its own ideals.

In Marc's case, however, various points combine to make him the prototype of the 'Neo-romantic' avant-garde artist – what Arnold Schoenberg called the 'conservative revolutionary'.[7] He illustrates perfectly the

positive possibilities, as well as the dangers, that could arise from this revaluation of Romantic traditions.

Like Marc, the early Romantics believed that they stood at the end of a tradition and – as Friedrich Schlegel put it – they 'recognized and knew the character of the golden age that was to come'.[8] In his work *Die Christenheit oder Europa* ('Christendom or Europe'), which tells us much about the Romantics' understanding of history, Novalis writes: 'In Germany, however, one can point with utter certainty to the traces of a new world ... . There are still only hints, ... but to the historical view they reveal a universal individuality, a new history, a new humanity ... a new golden age.'[9] The emergence of a different and better world seemed to guarantee, not a further development of existing conditions, but a truly new beginning. Although Marc and the early Romantics had quite different motives for criticizing their own age, they agreed almost entirely in their views as to the structure of the new age and the function of the individual within it.

Marc's counterpoise to his own 'materialistic age' is based on the criteria of the 'spiritual' and the 'religious', which ultimately mean the same thing. Using

Kandinsky's formulation, he invokes a 'spiritual epoch' in which the concepts of 'God, art and religion will return' and 'new symbols and legends will enter our shattered hearts', in which 'science and applied science' will be demoted to the status of inessentials, because 'spiritual goods will be traded.'[10] Similarly the Romantics justified the new age by a return to spiritual values, for, according to Novalis, 'where there are no gods, ghosts hold sway'.[11] If we also consider the fact that both equated *knowledge* with *self-knowledge*, it becomes clear that religion too means a form of spiritual meditation. It has nothing to do with an institutionalized church, but involves 'religious thinking' in the widest sense, independent of ecclesiastical ties.

The spiritual age that is longed for can logically be conceived and prepared for only by a person who bases his life on the principles of the spiritual and the religious. Here both Marc and the early Romantics recognize the supreme importance of the creative individual, who, to quote Novalis again, becomes the 'transcendental physician' and 'priest',[12] thus filling a gap that can no longer be filled by the church as an institution.

Yet what opportunities has the individual of approaching this somewhat inhuman condition of serene reflection and meditation?

In this connection such concepts as purity, feeling and originality are invoked again and again; there is also talk of the need to free oneself from all things material and so return to the original purity and innocence that is still echoed in the child.

However, since this must remain a dream and can be conceived only as an ideal, longing itself becomes the real motive of artistic endeavour. Moreover, this leads to a serious consequence: the original paradisiac condition that one longs for can be restored only by death, which dissolves all ties with things material – an idea that Philipp Otto Runge expressed in the words: 'Longing would have been hopeless had death not entered the world.'[13]

The longing for death also explains the curious definition of war as 'catharsis', as a process of purification (see pp. 197–205). Even the recurrent mention of the positive meaning of feeling begins to make sense. 'Feeling' does not mean sensual feeling, directed towards a concrete and palpable object – love for a person, for instance. 'Feeling' means 'inwardness', in which there is

no thought of an object – a condition of pure meditation. All these elements are combined in the concept of 'true nature', which of course cannot be found in the reality around us. This was a central concept for both Marc and the early Romantics. True, it took Marc some time to arrive at a consistent separation of the two planes and to resolve the contradiction we find in his early work. At first he still believed he could find an approximation to the original condition in 'external' nature, in a rural and comparatively unspoilt idyll; nature in this sense becomes the opposite pole to the 'urban', in which all the negative phenomena of the age are concentrated. The enthusiasm for a seemingly untainted rustic existence, in which the individual is perceived as being at one with nature, had a practical consequence for the artists of the Blue Rider and others: they moved into village communities. This is to be seen in connection with 'middle-class flight movements' that began around the turn of the century, taking the most disparate forms and to some extent following contrary patterns. The idealization of 'external' nature had no parallel in early nineteenth-century Germany, which was still a largely agrarian society. It may be presumed that the early Romantics enjoyed a more or less intact affinity to nature. In the course of the nineteenth century, however, thanks to industrialization, technology, and the problems that came in their wake – urbanization and alienation from the natural world – 'nature' became a counter-image, positive or negative according to one's point of view.

For Marc this led to the conviction that the concept of 'nature' could mean only an original state, apprehended in pure reflection. For the Romantics the sense and scope of this idea were formulated by Novalis with incomparable clarity. The certainty that knowledge was possible only in the realm of reflection underlies not only all his work, but is also to some extent an article of Romantic faith, what Walter Benjamin called a 'metaphysical credo'.[14] There can be no knowledge without self-knowledge. It follows that knowledge of nature is likewise possible only by way of self-knowledge. The claim to exclusivity urged on behalf of pure, objectless feeling and the rejection of any extraneous norm meant that there could be neither a binding style nor a binding subject. Rather, the individual created pictures that corresponded to his feeling (i.e. to an inner necessity) and sought a concrete pictorial subject that was appropriate only to himself. It follows that faults in the formal execution of a work are of secondary importance. For Marc the essential element was, he said, 'only the content (life-content) ... the "how" was a matter of complete indifference or, to be more precise, the outcome of the content (feeling).'[15] This is based on a definition of beauty formulated by Schlegel and basic to Romanticism. Schlegel distinguished between the 'beautiful' and the 'interesting'. The criterion is no longer beauty as a timeless ideal, which derives from Classical Antiquity, but the idea of a truth that can reveal itself in various forms. Beauty as a timeless ideal belongs to the past, but the interesting is something modern, which belongs to the present and is therefore valid. This view was crucial for Marc when he equated beauty and truth and asked: 'Why should we not speak of true and untrue pictures? You choose to say pure and impure, but you mean the same thing.'[16]

The parallels extend even to colour symbolism. One need only recall Kandinsky's and Marc's choice of the name 'The Blue Rider', which, to judge by other statements of both artists, probably had more than a superficial link with the meaning that attached to this colour in the Romantic period. The 'blue flower' as a symbol of unfulfillable longing in Novalis's *Heinrich von Ofterdingen*, which became the quintessence of the Romantic world-view, can be cited here along with Runge's code of colour symbolism, in which blue is attributed among other things to the day, to God the Father and to the will, hence to spiritual knowledge generally.[17] Something similar finds expression in Marc, who calls blue 'the male principle, austere and spiritual', which must always come to the aid of green 'in order to force the material into silence', and attributes it to the sky as the symbol of the spiritual and thus the goal of human longing.[18]

These ideas, which became fundamental tenets for wide sections of the avant-garde (and still are) were perfectly summarized by Kandinsky: 'If the artist is the priest of the "beautiful", then beauty too must be sought through the same principle of *inner value* that we have found everywhere. The "beautiful" can be measured only by the yardstick of *inner* greatness and *necessity* which has so far always served us well. *The beautiful is what springs from an inner psychic necessity.*'[19] This insistence on the exclusive authority of 'inner values', on a truth that does not conform with visible reality, but usually conflicts with it, had of course various consequences. On the one hand it led to a justification for cutting oneself off from the exigencies of life; on the other hand this was seen to prove that any positive development must begin as a dialogue between the individual and himself.

In artistic discussions in Germany after 1945 the dilemma of course became a good deal more complex. The ambivalent position of abstract art in this historical situation, determined as it is by the desperate search for a new and unspent identity, can be understood only against the background of German history: the oppressive mechanisms of National Socialist cultural policy, the painful experiences of the Second World War, and also the recognition of one's own complicity. Quite logically, those trends in modern art that the Nazis denounced as 'degenerate' and were thus unencumbered by Nazi ideology – and at the same time seemed to afford a refuge from a reality under threat – could be invoked as models. It was not fortuitous that the foundation programme of the Zen 49 group, which contributed significantly to the rehabilitation of outlawed modernism and to the linking of German abstract art to international standards, should have referred to the Blue Rider. With the Blue Rider as intermediary, it was almost inevitable that there should be a reversion to the German idealistic tradition, of which we find evidence in the work of Fritz Winter, one of its chief protagonists (fig. 5). One idealist maxim, the concept of the religious intention of all true art and its consequent interpretation as a spiritual refuge in an irreligious and immoral world, pointed the way for Fritz Winter too. 'Art is religious',[20] 'art as the agent of decision before God',[21] 'filled with the desire to serve God more than ourselves'[22] – such formulations by the artist link him closely with Romantic ideas. In terms of content Fritz Winter combined two basic ideas that were familiar both to the early Romantics and wide areas of the Blue Rider. On the one hand he was undoubtedly conscious of standing at a turning point, able to take a hand in shaping a new future; on the other hand he did not believe that this future could be realized as a livable present. He was

Fig.5 Fritz Winter, *Motive Forces of the Earth*
1944, Collection of Etta and Otto Stangl, Munich

more concerned with an ideal, a spiritual metaphor, though this involved intellectual shifts determined by the specific historical situation. For instance, Fritz Winter did not share the apodeictic attitude of Franz Marc, for recent history had taught him about the individual's complicity in the wrongs of the age; he was therefore much more conscious of the obligation to find an alternative in the world of today. It would accordingly be wrong to construe his pictures as 'symbols for the altars of a future spiritual religion'[23]; rather, they represent positive alternative worlds in a negative age. From this fundamental conviction Winter, like Marc, drew the pictorial concept for his work, which was bound to lead to consistent abstraction, for only in abstraction could the idea of pure spirituality be expressed. This conviction was always advanced as the legitimation for non-representational art, but interpreted by critics as indicating a wish to switch off from reality.

It was against this danger that Joseph Beuys pitted himself so resolutely. Others might assert the lasting quality of a given work that guaranteed the survival of spiritual values, but he adopted a position that related much more to the here and now. Just as the destruction of the individual and the spiritual basis of his life results from wrongful human behaviour, so a regeneration can come only from the individual himself. This basic idea of his plastic theory, which lays responsibility on every indi-

vidual, places Beuys within the German idealistic tradition: he too sees the individual's dialogue with himself as affording the only chance for the revival of spiritual values and so for 'education' in the true sense of the word. The famous cry *La Revoluzione siamo Noi* points to this obligation to work on oneself as the only means of effecting positive change in society and averting disaster.

In the installation, *The End of the Twentieth Century* (fig. 6), which Beuys fundamentally redesigned in 1984 for the Staatsgalerie moderner Kunst in Munich (temporarily housed in the former Haus der deutschen Kunst until the completion of a new building) these ideas become transparent. At the first exhibition at the Galerie Schmela in Düsseldorf, a field of ruins, the site of a past battle, was represented by forty-four basalt blocks. Here, in this new and politically charged location, there is a possible escape. Not that Beuys disguises the historical dimension; on the contrary, he deliberately includes it in all its harshness and simultaneously demands a dialogue. The former *Haus der deutschen Kunst*, built by Adolf Hitler for the officially approved art of Nazi Germany, becomes a setting for reflection on how to deal critically, at the end of the twentieth century, with a history that is specifically German, and at the same time calls for a dialogue involving a possible future perspective. Yet why does Beuys formulate this allegorical picture of a future so near at hand with almost archaic materials and forms that are unlikely to be met with in real life? On the surface at least none of the ciphers and clichés are discernible that might provide a purchase for the concept of an immediate present. Yet it is precisely by this means that he transfers the theme to a more general plane. What occurs in the day-to-day life of an excessively technologized civilization, is still indebted, in its basic structure, to archetypal patterns, no matter how modern the appearances may be. Hence this warning at the end of the century also points to the relativity of individual action, compared with what outlasts millennia. We are being told, it seems, that our responsibility consists in substituting spiritual values for faith in material facts, so that the end of the twentieth century will not turn out to be an absolute end-point. At the same time we must understand that whatever survives has nothing to do with the subjective reality of the individual. 'The End of the Twentieth Century' – where could it

Fig.6 Joseph Beuys, *The End of the Twentieth Century* 1983–84, Staatsgalerie Moderner Kunst, Munich

have greater significance than in a place that originated in an ideology which mocked all the values that Beuys tried to revitalize with his 'social theory'? Where could Beuys demonstrate more clearly his commitment to idealistic thinking than in a historical context that sought to exploit and distort such thinking in the cause of its own ideology? Beuys once again draws attention to what was always crucial to the twentieth-century recycling of Romantic ideas. It was a balancing act: the progressive forces of Romanticism must not be allowed to topple over into the kind of one-sided irrationalism that produced such hideous consequences under National Socialism. Rather, what was positive in Romanticism – the insistence on spiritual values and moral categories – must become the yardstick of thought and action.

This conception, which classical Modernism still believed to be a real utopia and which Joseph Beuys propagated as the only escape from a dilemma we had created for ourselves, carries less conviction with artists of the younger generation, though they are reluctant to discard it. With a mixture of presumption and defiance,

pathos and irony, artists like Polke or Lüpertz defend themselves against both past and present – a stance that naturally presupposes a switch-off from political reality and admits responsibility only to oneself. Lüpertz formulates this position for his own generation: 'Don't die with the problems of your age – the time is ripe – we are the new centre … . At last an elite is developing, an aristocracy of painters – not for everybody – not for the street – not for handling … . Art is proud to be at the disposal of whoever loves it, but does not ingratiate itself. It wants to be courted, not used. Painting shows no consideration and constantly enriches itself with the outstanding achievements of its willing and gifted servants – a monk in the cathedral of art.'[24]

Running parallel to this claim that painting is a quasi-religious icon to be worshipped in purity is a consistent lack of content and socio-political commitment, the product of an insight that is as realistic as it is dispiriting for the artist's self-image. With cynical asperity Lüpertz asserts the ineffectuality of art in a mass society that is geared to the maximization of profit. 'Life is understood

Fig.7 Markus Lüpertz, *Black-Red-Gold, Dithyrambic* 1974,
Galerie Michael Werner, Cologne

Fig.8 Markus Lüpertz, *Spring* 1985, Staatsgalerie Moderner Kunst, Munich

as a job in which one survives with greater or lesser skill
… . Eternity is ruled out; any striving for eternal values
is ludicrous, superfluous, as it is uncommercial, unexpe-
rienceable and unmarketable … . Our whole social
structure sees art only as a therapy, a playground, a
leisure activity on a par with a coffee morning … . In
this age of decadence the artist has to rely on himself to
motivate his vitality, aggression and the compulsive
necessity of his existence. This implies a total renunciation of understanding, appreciation and affection.
Appreciation is impossible in the century he lives in. His
commercial situation is explained by his ability and skill
in manipulating and fascinating the world around him.
Any charlatanry is permissible, necessary and – if witty –
to be welcomed.'[25]

Profound despair that allows *carte blanche* for anything that yields a profit? Or is this too just witty charlatanry? Both are equally probable and merely confirm the
usefulness of a smooth routine, behind which Lüpertz
vanishes as a person. It is characteristic of this way of
thinking that the same value is set on everything, turning
the idea of 'inner necessity', which in the Blue Rider subordinated stylistic norms to the artistic statement, into
something completely arbitrary. Lüpertz behaves like the
shameless consumption fetichist in the supermarket of

art. Everything is allowed, everything is possible. No
style, no artist owns a copyright that can protect him
from exploitation. All subjects theoretically mean the
same and are raised to the status of a pictorial theme at
the whim of the artist. All the props become protagonists in a stage show, and Lüpertz, the director, assigns
them their places. All that counts is being 'clued up': this
alone ensures survival. This too is ultimately a rewrite of
the artist's role as the authority who confers meaning.
Lüpertz of course refuses to allow his pictorial figures to
convey any message or content that points beyond themselves, but by being made into a theme they become the
message: The medium is the message! Hence, brainless
germanomania, the ideology of blood and soil and martial grandiloquence (fig. 7) can be placed on the same
level as silent beauty and harmony (fig. 8), not because
Lüpertz cannot distinguish between them in terms of
content, but because he does not wish to.

Georg Baselitz attempts something similar; he too
wants a new kind of picture that is freed from the ballast
of thematic differentiation but indirectly adopts a clear
position. Take for instance the early group 'Heroes' or
'New Types' (fig. 9). These are well set-up young men,
often with outsize hands; their heads, by contrast, are
small and often pressed close to the upper edge of the

picture. They stand against an almost monochrome background or in ruined landscapes containing fragments of nature or remnants of a devastated civilization. The colours are strong, often aggressive. Despite the strong colours and the robust, 'energetic' appearance of the figures there is no action, no representation of scenes or anecdotes. These 'types', whose stature seems to predestine them to activity, maintain an oddly ambivalent, passive posture that precludes any possibility of action or liberation. Their vulnerability is emphasized by the fact that their trousers are often open. In the display of the stigmata, which testify to earlier traumas, lies a lethargically static accusation that cannot be translated into action and so precludes any possible rescue. By association one is reminded of the 'youth' as a specifically Romantic figure, and this observation is underlined by the art-historical references in the titles of the pictures (e.g. *Ludwig Richter on his Way to Work*, *Portrait of Franz Pforr* or *Bonjour, Monsieur Courbet*). The 'hero' as a symbolic figure is thus deliberately subverted. He becomes the counter-image of the vacuous activist and thus indirectly an emphatically political figure – the silent refusenik, who at the height of the Cold War switched off from political reality in order to build an alternative world. It is hard to resist the impression that Baselitz is protesting against a profoundly unstable and fragile world and using painting as the only medium through which he can create the stability and strength that is proof against factual reality. Yet he differs from the Romantics, the artists of the Blue Rider, and even from Joseph Beuys, in that he offers no vision that can be realized, even theoretically, in the real world: the work remains a deliberately subjective statement.

Whether the cynical parasite of our consumer society or the bringer of salvation wins out remains an open question. What we see is an individual tight-rope act that remains equivocal even in Polke's pictorial and biographical formulations. Yet more pointedly than most others of his generation, and with a certain kindred being because it treats him as a spiritual being and demands of him only the rarest autonomous action. This higher self relates to the human being as the latter relates to nature or the wise man to the child. The human being longs to become like it ... .[26] Despite all his verbal attempts to distance himself, even Polke uses similar arguments when

Fig.9 Georg Baselitz, *Ludwig Richter on His Way to Work* 1965, private collection (ex. cat.)

he surveys the vast complex of concepts, symbols, pictorial motives etc., – in other words everything he perceives as fragments of reality – and relates them to himself as the medium through which higher beings communicate. But this no longer produces normative pictures of the world: binding themes and motives are inconceivable. Nothing is possible but subjective statements about beauty and the dangers threatening it, about feelings, moods and injuries, and these can make use of any form. Is this a cheap envoi to the moral integrity and monkish rigour so dear to Franz Marc, which made any one work the quintessence of a positive utopia? Or is it rather an honest insight into the fundamental meaninglessness of artistic activity in a concrete social context? Both assumptions are correct, for both are symptoms and reflections of their age, our age, which, like hardly any other, mistrusts its own standards.

Carla Schulz-Hoffmann

Translated from the German by David McLintock

1 The illustration shows only an approximation to the installation, which was frequently modified before it was purchased and can hardly be reproduced in its entirety. The various items in the showcase include peas, saucers, matches without heads, picture fragments, and a 'documenta' catalogue.
2 Autobiography, in 'Sigmar Polke – frühe Einflüsse, späte Folgen oder: Wie kamen die Affen in mein Schaffen? und andere ikono-biographische Fragen',

exh. cat. *Sigmar Polke, Bilder-Tücher-Objekte, Werkauswahl 1962–1971*, (Tübingen, 1976), 128.

3 As note 2, 129f.

4 'Dentro il mondo, giorno dopo giorno, per piacere le tempeste, catastrofi, terremoti, si dice che un temo i pittore ... navigatori, versassereo immagini ... perstabilire una rotta.' Enzo Cucchi, 'Albergo', exh. cat. *Enzo Cucchi, Giulio Roma* (Amsterdam/ Basel, 1983/84), appendix without pagination.

5 Franz Marc, *Schriften*, ed. Klaus Lankheit (Cologne, 1978), 143.

6 The first comprehensive study of this thematic complex, which deals with the influence of Romantic traditions in modern art, was produced by Robert Rosenblum, *Modern Painting and the Northern Romantic Tradition – Friedrich to Rothko* (London, 1975). Rosenblum is concerned with an extensive and classified collection of material, which for the first time stakes out the terrain and shows the connections between the various developments. His ambitious aim was to set up an alternative to the exclusive insistence on the French influence on modern painting.

7 Arnold Schoenberg, quoted by Werner Hofmann, 'Antiker und christlicher Mythos – Natursymbolik – Kinder – Familie – Familie und Freunde', Werner Hofmann (ed.), exh. cat. *Runge in seiner Zeit* (Hamburg, 1977), 278ff.

8 Friedrich Schlegel, in Paul Kluckhohn (ed.), *Kunstanschauung der Frühromantik, Deutsche Literatur, Reihe Romantik*, vol 3 (Darmstadt, 1966), 189ff.

9 Novalis, *Monolog, Die Lehrlinge zu Saïs, Die Christenheit oder Europa, Hymnen an die Nacht, Geistliche Lieder, Heinrich von Ofterdingen* (Hamburg, 1963), 47.

10 Franz Marc (as note 5), 111.

11 Novalis (as note 9), 48.

12 Novalis (as note 9), 220, 225.

13 Philipp Otto Runge, in Ernst Forsthoff (ed.), *Schriften, Fragmente, Briefe* (Berlin, 1928), 56.

14 Walter Benjamin, *Der Begriff der Kunstkritik in der deutschen Romantik* (repr. Frankfurt am Main, 1973), 50.

15 Franz Marc, *Briefe aus dem Feld* (Berlin, 1950), 51ff.

16 Franz Marc (as note 5), 178.

17 Runge (as note 13), 18.

18 Franz Marc in a letter to August Macke of 12.12.1910 in Wolfgang Macke (ed.), *August Macke, Franz Marc, Briefwechsel* (Cologne, 1964), 27–30.

19 Wassily Kandinsky, *Über das Geistige in der Kunst* (9th ed. with an introduction by Max Bill (Berne, 1970)), 136f (manuscript completed in 1910).

20 Fritz Winter, quoted by Gabriele Lohberg, *Fritz Winter, Leben und Werk* (Munich, 1986), 348.

21 Winter (as note 20), 349.

22 Marc (as note 5), 152.

23 Marc (as note 5), 143.

24 Markus Lüpertz, in exh. cat. *Markus Lüpertz* (Galerie Rudolf Zwirner, Cologne, 1976), no pagination.

25 Markus Lüpertz, 'Über den Schaden sozialer Parolen in der bildenden Kunst', speech given in London, in exh. cat. *Markus Lüpertz, Bilder 1970–1983* (Hanover, 1983), 19–22.

26 Novalis, *Werke*, ed. with commentary by Gerhard Schulz (Munich, 1969), 377.

Romanticism
and German Art

Colour Plates

Philipp Otto Runge
Morning (small version), 1808
Hamburger Kunsthalle

Philipp Otto Runge
Morning (large version), 1809
Hamburger Kunsthalle

Caspar David Friedrich
Monk by the Sea, 1809–10
Staatliche Museen zu Berlin Preußischer Kulturbesitz, Nationalgalerie

Caspar David Friedrich
Sea of Ice, c.1823–24
Hamburger Kunsthalle

Franz Pforr
Sulamith and Maria, 1811
Schäfer Collection, Schweinfurt

Friedrich Overbeck
Italia and Germania, 1828
Bayerische Staatsgemäldesammlungen, Munich

Arnold Böcklin
Island of the Dead III, 1883
Staatliche Museen zu Berlin Preußischer Kulturbesitz, Nationalgalerie

Hans von Marées
The Golden Age I, 1879/85
Bayerische Staatsgemäldesammlungen, Munich

Wassily Kandinsky
Romantic Landscape, 1911
Städtische Galerie im Lenbachhaus, Munich

Franz Marc
Tower of Blue Horses, 1913
Formerly Nationalgalerie, Berlin
Missing since the end of the Second World War

Joseph Beuys
The End of the Twentieth Century, 1983–84
Staatsgalerie Moderner Kunst, Munich

Themes
and Topics

Essays

'We Draw No Strength from the People'
Artist, Solitude, Community

Surely, solitude and community are constants of the artist's life: first the conceiving of the work – thinking it through in self-imposed, jealously guarded solitude – and then the plunge into stimulating fellowship, the exchange of workshop hints. Artists' bars and cafés are as central to the traditional image of bohemian life as are shared studios – whether shared for reasons of economy or of artistic affinity or both. Artists traditionally relaxed in studio soirées, often with music, where they met kindred spirits in the world of literature and criticism.

There were also alliances of a closer kind. To pursue common ends, painters from a variety of backgrounds gathered in Brittany under the leadership of Paul Gauguin; and, speaking of Gauguin, we should also remember that Vincent van Gogh, that loner *par excellence*, tried desperately hard to enlist his reluctant fellow-artist for his own chimerical *Ecole du Midi* which would be a working fellowship in the south, entirely attuned to light and colour.

Such groupings became common at the beginning of our own century, when artists began to transform their position on the fringes of society into a base from which to conquer the centre. They saw themselves as critics of an outworn social order, and as the pioneers – if not the arbiters – of a future society. This happened in Russia, Italy, Austria, Germany – and England, where the Vorticists launched their onslaught on the post-Victorian Establishment under the leadership of Ezra Pound and Wyndham Lewis. There, an earlier shift in public attitudes to art had been marked back in the mid nineteenth century by the Pre-Raphaelite Brotherhood – itself a metropolitan, sophisticated, up-to-the-minute version of the *Lukasbund* of German artists in Rome, forty years before. With a touch of admiring mockery, the Romans had dubbed those long-haired and rustically shod youths *i Nazareni*. Their objective had been nothing less than the renewal of contemporary art in the pure, plain spirit of early Italian painting.

This kind of return *ad fontes* – to the Roman foun-tainhead – seems to have remained a recurrent feature of German painting, until the days of the 'German Romans': Arnold Böcklin, Hans von Marées, Hans Thoma and Adolf von Hildebrand. Its origins might lie in Johann Joachim Winckelmann's much-misinterpreted ideal of 'noble simplicity and still grandeur' – or indeed in the rarefied aesthetics of Immanuel Kant or of Arthur Schopenhauer, with their emphasis on Form and Idea at the expense of flesh and blood; but other contributory factors had been the lack of a single metropolitan centre in Germany itself, the absence of a binding social web.

By the late nineteenth and early twentieth centuries, the artistic capital of Germany was Paris. The most gifted artists went there: Anselm Feuerbach, Wilhelm Leibl, Adolf von Menzel, Paula Modersohn-Becker, Hans Purrmann, Wassily Kandinsky, Paul Klee, Oskar Kokoschka, Wilhelm Lehmbruck and Max Beckmann, to name but a few. Dispersed across the many regions of Germany, artists longed for a metropolis where they could find their bearings and a consensus with like-minded people. In the event, their pursuit of this fantasy of a supranational community mostly left them more acutely isolated than ever; but it had the advantage of sharpening their artistic self-awareness. For in Paris the first thing that struck them was invariably the sheer otherness of French culture. In France, *la peinture* – a term defined in a formal, aesthetic sense – remains a form of rebellion only so long as it takes for the painter to stretch the canons of the ruling bourgeoisie far enough to include himself. This process can be traced through the Impressionists and the Nabis, by way of the Fauves, to the Cubists. Only Surrealism proved impossible to assimilate, and as a result it was generally dismissed as a frivolous intellectual pastime.

German art, by contrast, often manifests something of a sense of mission in which – though ignored by the public at large – it is supported by a few dynamic individuals in influential museum positions. Many works bypass society as it really is, to address themselves to an imaginary community: a kingdom of the mind, held together by the affinities between artists. This may well partly account for the difference in the evolution of artists' colonies in the two countries. Barbizon and its outposts stood primarily for healthy rural surroundings, inexpensive living and working, mutual support and an exchange of ideas, far from the distractions of the capital. In Germany, there was often much more at stake: nothing less, in fact, than the reform of the whole of life.

This was the case at Hellerau, near Dresden, before 1914; and again at Worpswede, near Bremen, which Heinrich Vogeler turned into a centre of social ferment in the years after Germany's defeat in the First World War. In 1927–28 Vogeler's frescoes at Barkenhoff and his *Komplexbilder* impressed Diego Rivera – who saw them on his way to or from Moscow – enough to influence his revolutionary mural paintings.[1] Political aims were by now part and parcel of the artistic utopia and figured in all the short-lived alliances that were formed in the turbulent period after 1918, among them the Action Committee of Revolutionary Artists (*Aktionsausschuß revolutionärer Künstler*) in Munich, the November Group (*Novembergruppe*) in Berlin, and Dada activities in a number of cities.

With their pursuit of immediate political aims, such groups made a sharp contrast with the utopias of pre-war years, when artists dreamed of a communal life that would be 'natural' and, as it were, pre-industrial. In the *Blauer Reiter* circle in Munich, these dreams took on a cosmic dimension, with an admixture of theosophy. Lulled by colours and sounds, the human being was to be caught up in a spiritual eurhythmy created by the sum total of all forms of artistic utterance. In Paris in 1936 Kandinsky wrote an article for *Cahiers d'art* in which he evoked the memory of Franz Marc – killed in battle twenty years before – and of the almanac *Der Blaue Reiter* which the two men had edited together in 1912: 'At the time I was contemplating a "synthetic" book, which was to eradicate superstitions, "demolish the walls" that existed between one art and another, between official and rejected art, and finally prove that the question of art is not that of form, but that of artistic content. The separation of the arts, their isolated existence inside small "boxes" with high, rigid and opaque walls, was to my mind one of the unfortunate and dangerous consequences of the "analytic" method, which

was suppressing the "synthetic" method in science, and was starting to do the same in art. The consequences were rigidity, narrow viewpoint and feeling, loss of the freedom of feeling, perhaps even its ultimate death. My idea then was to point out by means of examples that the difference between "official" and "ethnographic" art had no reason to exist; that the pernicious habit of not seeing the organic inner root of art beneath outwardly different forms could, in general, result in total loss of reciprocal action between art and the life of mankind.'[2]

Even if we discount for a moment the Munich Expressionist mentality, with its idealistic belief in a new age of integration of the arts, there is something very attractive in this resolve not to separate art from life or banish it to the museums. Art has to do with the whole breadth of life.

Dresden was different. There, the painters of the *Brücke* group meant to find their utopia not over the horizon but here and now – as *la vie immédiate* – in the untroubled nakedness of happy summer days by the Moritzburg Lakes and the Baltic Sea, and in the casual promiscuity of the studio. Primeval nature, strong outlines, glowing colours: over and above exotic influences and the examples of Henri Matisse and the Fauves, this all pointed to a deliberate echo of Jean-Jacques Rousseau. In expectation of the Earthly Paradise, these artists lived a communal life that abolished the constraints of civilization.

In the context of its time all this was inevitably short-lived. The artists soon turned to Berlin and its intoxicating metropolitan atmosphere, and the war brought a final parting of the ways. What followed, in the case of Ernst Ludwig Kirchner, was isolation, illness and despair in the Swiss mountains; in that of Erich Heckel it was the revival of the theme of community on a higher plane in the murals of the Angermuseum in Erfurt.

We have hitherto considered examples mainly from the period between 1910 and 1930. This was the time when the whole issue of solitude and community seems to have crystallized in exemplary fashion. While bearing in mind the overall context of art since the Enlightenment – which was when the artist first found himself a free agent – I shall discuss the issue through a number of examples that belong to this narrower period of two decades.

'*Uns trägt kein Volk*' (We draw no strength from the people), as Klee famously said. He himself had previously used very different language: 'All my artistic powers are at the disposal of the Action Committee of Revolutionary Artists. That I adhere to it goes without saying: for several years before the war I was already producing work of the kind that is now to be set on a wider, public basis. My work and all my other artistic power and insight are available to the Committee.'

Klee wrote these words to the painter Fritz Schaefler on 12 April 1919. Ten days later his application for membership was accepted, and he was appointed one of the seven directors of the Painting Section of the Art Commissariat.

The thoroughbred individualist in the service of the Republic of Workers' Soviets? The contradiction is only an apparent one. On 7 November 1918, even before the official end of the First World War, the Socialist politician Kurt Eisner had proclaimed the People's Free State of Bavaria, and the Wittelsbach monarchy had abdicated. Eisner's proclamation was preceded by a revolutionary march through Munich, and the marchers included the writers Friedrich Burschell and Oskar Maria Graf and the painter Georg Schrimpf. Progressive opinion in Germany expected much of Bavaria. Its leader, Eisner, regarded himself as a writer and believed in artistic creation as a means of altering the consciousness of society. Since the short-lived pan-German assembly in the Paulskirche in Frankfurt in 1848, no German parliament had heard – nor would any hear again – such ideas as he proclaimed to the Provisional National Assembly early in 1919:

'It is one of the peculiarities of German life that politics is kept entirely separate, and that government is an activity for lawyers. I think it was Bismarck who said that governing was an art; and for my own part I think that governing is just as much an art – politics is just as much an art – as the painting of pictures or the composition of string quartets. The object of this political art, the material on which this political art has to prove itself, is society, the state, human beings. There is, I would like to think, no one to whom a true statesman – a true government – should feel closer than to the artists, his fellow professionals. I have not the slightest doubt that any German statesman who is suspected of being able to write a poem will stand under strong suspicion of not knowing the first thing about politics. But then this is a German prerogative, which stems from the fact that since the days of the departed [Wilhelm] von Humboldt no artistic individual has ever been in government – if we make a possible exception for the reactionary artistic gifts of Otto Bismarck.

'And now to the question, what can the state do for art, and what can it do for the artist? If the relationship between state and art is as I have indicated, then the state – by which I mean the government of the state – has the duty, above all, of embodying in itself the totality of the civilization of the age. A government that embodies civilization, if only in this sense, thereby in itself promotes the cause of art. The higher the mental stature of the state's achievement, the higher the level of art will be. I therefore see no opposition, but only the most intimate relationship, between state and art.'[3]

At last, it seemed, the isolated artist had become useful – even needed by the community. Leading artists converged on Munich. In the first six months after the Armistice, the Bavarian capital witnessed a cultural flowering that has never until now received adequate study.[4] In Munich artists were not part of the opposition – as they were in Berlin – but found themselves in sympathy with official cultural policy which had been inspired and in part formulated by a number of distinguished writers, including Ernst Toller, Gustav Landauer and Erich Mühsam.

The visual art scene was a markedly pluralistic one, including abstract as well as figurative painters. The most oddly assorted alliances sprang up, uniting abstraction, Expressionism and Futurism. Those members of the *Blauer Reiter* group who were still in Munich – Klee and Heinrich Campendonck – joined the Action Committee in 1919. Its other members included Schrimpf, Schaefler, Theodor Caspar Pilartz, Stanisław Stückgold, Aloys Wach and Walt Laurent. Its chairman was the Dadaist Hans Richter, a recent arrival from Zürich, who intended to appoint his friends Marcel Janco and Viking Eggeling to teaching posts at the reformed Kunsthochschule.

All of them found great scope for creativity in the Munich system of workers' councils or soviets. Artists of a constructive bent – Klee, Campendonck, Richter,

Eggeling – devised works to serve as models for the structure of the future society. A late version of Expressionism was charged with political and social messages which the woodcuts of Wach and Schaefler carried into the daily press. Numerous portraits, notably those by Schrimpf and Heinrich Maria Davringhausen, depicted those intellectuals who were gaining confidence from the new-found openness of their situation and reflecting on the parts that they would play in the society of the future – utopian though their vision of that society was. There is a great deal in the work of Campendonck, Schrimpf, Schaefler, Carlo Mense – even Klee – that has more to do with reformed lifestyles, nature myths and vegetarian nudism (à la Monte Verità) than with the harsh realities of postwar life.

One artist who came somewhat closer to those realities was Heinrich Ehmsen who made a stark record of the destruction of the workers' state by the irregular troops of the *Freikorps* – among them the later Nazi leaders Rudolf Hess and Ernst Röhm – and of the repression that followed. Artistic as well as political plans were shattered before ever the new, community-minded forms of artistic training could be set in place.

It was Klee, again, who – in a celebrated letter to Alfred Kubin – anatomized their shattered hopes. Landauer, in charge of education, had called for a rapprochement between pure and applied art and had declared himself in favour of amalgamating the Academy with the School of Arts and Crafts. This same idea recurs in Klee's letter, where it is deepened into a fundamental reflection on the role of the 'independent' artist:

'Ephemeral though this Communist republic seemed from the outset, it did afford an opportunity to assess one's prospects of survival in such a commonwealth. It was not without its positive consequences. Of course any extreme, individualistic art is not suited for general consumption: it is a capitalistic luxury. But surely we are something more than curiosities for rich snobs. Somehow, beyond all that, there is something within us that aspires to eternity: and this the Communist commonwealth would be all the more likely to foster. Trickling through altered channels, our example would carry its fructifying effect much further afield. As an experimental laboratory for ideas, we should not be training up new inventors (who would of course not be inventors at all but masqueraders, like those academicians who take after their teachers as children take after their parents). We should be able to convey the results of our inventive activity to the mass of the people. This new art could then spread into the crafts and bring forth a great flowering. For there would be no more academies, only art schools for craftspeople. And so the workers' republic has taught us a great deal. As for the practical application, that is now more than ever unthinkable.'[5]

Or was it? In the very next year, 1920, Klee accepted an appointment at the Bauhaus in Weimar, which had been set up by Walter Gropius with very much the same ideas in mind as those pursued in Munich. The élitist, not to say the 'youth-league' side of Bauhaus training and Bauhaus life eventually transformed the place out of all recognition and led it into a kind of 'splendid isolation'[6] that lasted until Gropius's successor Hannes Meyer radically changed course. Socially committed and keenly aware of the contemporary crisis, Meyer saw the Bauhaus as a centre for social, industrial and housing design, rather than for the aesthetic education of an élite. The Bauhaus painters found themselves marginalized and sought new fields of activity – a development exemplified in the late 1920s by Oskar Schlemmer.

Murals for Essen

In March 1928 the Museum Folkwang in Essen asked Schlemmer to submit cartoons for the decoration of its rotunda.[7] This was a relatively small circular space that linked the vestibule with the gallery and meeting hall. In the centre stood a fountain surrounded by five rapt, kneeling figures of boys, made originally for Hagen by the Belgian sculptor Georges Minne. Light entered from above through a lantern above a dome. The topic of the paintings was laid down by the director of the museum, Ernst Gosebruch: 'young men in motion (play and sport)'.

This idea was very much in the air: the 1920s were the great age of naturism, expressive and nude dance, gymnastics and mass sporting activities. The *Bündische Jugend*, the *Wandervögel*, the *Reformbewegung*, the

Fig.1 View of the third version of Oskar Schlemmer's murals (1931) in the Museum Folkwang, Essen

Landbewegung: there was a fashion for joining youth leagues bound by an initiatory oath, movements with – initially unconscious and later overt – political implications. A cult of *mens sana in corpore sano*, based on the rediscovery of the natural beauty of the human body, can be traced internationally through the whole of sculpture and painting. As choreographer and director of the theatre at the Bauhaus (and in his classroom teaching), Schlemmer was an exponent of this new group dynamic, with its fondness for training people in precise, disciplined collective movement; and this is reflected in his painted nude groups and other multi-figure paintings of the late 1920s.

Behind all this was the need – soon to be exploited by the Nazis – for unity and community in a 'chilly, alienated present'. The artist, as Schlemmer stressed in 1932, was no longer supported 'by any class beyond an isolated few' – the very complaint voiced by Klee. In his own work at least, said Schlemmer, he was attempting to 'show the way out of chaos'. And his statement 'On my Murals for the Museum Folkwang in Essen' (1931) ends as follows: 'We contemporaries, who lack the great symbols and the modes of vision that the ancients had, because we live in an age of decadence, upheaval and – it is to be hoped – renewal: what can we now do but be simple, be plain in the way we show things, be open to all that gathers within us, whether conscious or unconscious, that it may gradually become form.'[8]

This was to happen through restraint and measure, through law and 'strict regularity'. To justify this 'scien-

tific element' in his art, Schlemmer appealed to the Egyptians, to Albrecht Dürer, to Philipp Otto Runge and to the 'precision of the formal elements in music'.

The figures of naked boys on the fountain were to be echoed in the murals. These were divided by the three entrance doors into one group of five paintings and two of two each. Schlemmer felt his way into this difficult commission by stages. He certainly had in mind the arcadian scenes painted by Marées in the 1880s, such as *The Golden Age* (colour plate, p.101) and the *Hesperides* frieze; more generally, also, such mural schemes as those of Pierre Puvis de Chavannes, Ferdinand Hodler and Edvard Munch.

Schlemmer's first design for Essen was dominated by the group idea and by the rhythmic sequence, juxtaposition and opposition of simplified, manikin-like heads and figures. The figures were grouped like schoolboys under the authority of teachers or mentors; and three of the panels bore the explicit title of *Instruction*. There were also a number of athletically built single figures, and a *Fallen Figure with Column*. In view of the rather forced appearance of the groups of scholars, this Icarus figure may have expressed Schlemmer's regret at the loss of universally accepted myths and signs – especially as it was intended to appear opposite the main entrance, where the visitor would see it on arrival.

Early in 1930 Schlemmer produced new designs, much less solidly material in form, drawn in pastel over charcoal on tracing paper. In these the close-knit groups gave way to isolated, timelessly beautiful youths – modern *kouroi* – who seemed to emerge from a void; singly or in clusters, they arranged themselves in weightless harmony along stairways or landings.

Schlemmer then visited Essen, and it was decided to execute one of these paintings as a trial. But instead Schlemmer pulled together the lessons of his first two sets of cartoons and produced a third set (fig. 1). The execution in casein colours, sprayed on canvas and applied to plywood sheets, is in keeping with the cool, geometrically based composition; the figures are lathe-turned manikins, which lack not only the grace and balletic quality of the second version but any trace of human appeal. They are 'architectural and figurative diagrams' (Jan Ulatowski), which duck the confrontation with the naked boys on the fountain while at the same time rather undermining the idea of community.

'I wanted to respond to the simple gesture of Minne's figures on the fountain by presenting the simple existence of figures, without emotive rhetoric, without dramatic movement, and without telling stories.' Schlemmer's words appear in the script of an interview broadcast by Radio Breslau on its 'Silesian Hour' on 3 November 1930 – probably the first radio interview ever broadcast about art, and thus a further attempt on the artist's part to extend his activity into the public sphere. In answer to the very first question, he refers to the still-unrealized medium of television as the ideal place for such encounters: 'Then we too can address the mass of the people.'

Erich Heckel and the Stefan George Circle

The murals by Heckel in the Angermuseum in Erfurt belong to the same context. They constitute the one and only surviving German Expressionist monumental cycle.[9] Heckel was a founder member of the *Brücke* group in Dresden; he represented its moderate wing, in opposition to the eccentric and split-minded Kirchner. A great reader – Friedrich Nietzsche, Fyodor Dostoievsky, August Strindberg, Rainer Maria Rilke and Friedrich Hölderlin were his constant companions – Heckel drew sustenance from literature in his efforts to achieve harmony, a holistic vision of nature and a sense of community. In his painting, the stark, prismatic Expressionist style increasingly receded.

The First World War, in which Heckel served as a medical orderly in Flanders, accelerated this development. In the face of the self-destruction of the old world, he pinned his hopes on a union of like-minded intellectuals and artists. In Ostend, in the medical corps, he met a number of kindred spirits, including Max Beckmann. His section leader was the art historian Walter Kaesbach, a research assistant to Ludwig Justi, who created Germany's first ever public collection of modern art at the Kronprinzenpalais in Berlin. Equally momentous was his friendship with Ernst Morwitz, a close confidant of the poet Stefan George, whose work Heckel already knew. Heckel himself now became attracted to the poet's circle. In Dresden and later in Berlin, the strongest

Fig.2 View of Erich Heckel's murals (1922–23), in the Angermuseum, Erfurt

influence in his work had been his affinity with the *Brücke* artists; now he was captivated by ideas of spiritual renewal, as proclaimed by George and his all-male fellowship. He himself was never accepted as a member, because the Master was a formalist and purist who loathed Expressionism in general and Heckel's paintings in particular.

This did not deter Heckel from depicting George as the central figure in the murals in Erfurt (fig. 2). After the war Kaesbach had become director of the Angermuseum, then a relatively new foundation, and he was building up a contemporary collection dominated by the work of Lyonel Feininger, the Expressionists, the Bauhaus artists and Heckel himself. Heckel was entrusted with the decoration of a small, trapezoidal space adjacent to the pillared ground-floor hall that contained the museum's Late Gothic panel paintings. The work was financed by the Erfurt shoe manufacturer Alfred Hess, a committed collector and patron whose house was frequented until 1933 by the artists, composers, writers and museum people of the Weimar Republic.

What Heckel devised to adorn this tall, narrow, oblique room was a generalized account of his own development, under the title of *Stages of Life*, on an orange-red ground and in muted tones: green, white, brown and flesh-tints. The numerous, mainly male nudes dimly reflect the paradisal nudity of past summers spent painting on the Baltic and at Moritzburg. But the figures are elongated and unsensual, and they are fitted into a kind of universal eurhythmy of nature, with a Neoclassical echo of Runge and Marées; the goal, as with Marées, is an ideal community of mind and spirit.

Against the background of a craggy Alpine glacier stand three hieratic groups. In the centre, in priestly vestments, the white-haired George points with the gesture of John the Baptist towards a naked youth. This radiant figure is Maximilian ('Maximin') Kronberger, from Munich. Kronberger, who died young, was hailed by the pedagogic Eros of Stefan George as the embodiment of the new era.

On the left stand three disciples: the lawyer and poet Morwitz, the art historian Wilhelm Stein and the Hellenist Josef Liegle – all members of George's Berlin circle, as was the figure on the right, who is the sculptor Ludwig Thormaehlen, an associate of Justi's. Outside the group we glimpse a striding figure with the unmistakable, patrician head of Justi himself. As in *The Magic Flute*, we have before us the rites of an esoteric community, with aspirants at different stages of initiation.

Elsewhere in the cycle, in *Mourning*, we see the youthful victims of the war; other scenes refer to Heckel's own life and work. In *Connection* he is seen with his wife Sidi – who, in stylized form, plays almost all the female roles in the composition. Opposite them is *Separation* in which we see the tormented figure of the artist's friend and enemy, Kirchner – an allusion to the daemonic Roquairol in Jean Paul's novel *Titan* – on whom Life, in the form of a woman, turns her back.

Salvation thus does not lie in self-obsessed isolation but in intercourse with a fellowship of minds – not an intimate artistic grouping, like those of the pre-war period, but a community with strict rules and hierarchies. These go far beyond the role assumed, for instance, by Kandinsky as 'first among equals' in the *Blauer Reiter* group. Generally speaking – and this applies to sporting and youth movements and to

Fig.3 Max Ernst, *Au rendez-vous des amis* 1922, Museum Ludwig, Cologne

alliances of all kinds – the need to be organized within a structured group was stronger than it had been before 1914: one more reflection of the general quest for orientation.

Max Ernst and his Friendship Pictures

Klaus Lankheit has given us an account of the form and significance of the friendship picture in Romanticism.[10] What is less well known is the brief but important revival that the genre experienced in Surrealism, and specifically in the work of Max Ernst.[11]

Ernst was an artist who had never been to art school but instead had studied art history – in Bonn, under Paul Clemen among others – and so he was familiar with this type of picture. It was a type that lent itself to subversive use in the very different cultural setting of Paris. The Surrealists in general were fond of mocking bourgeois rituals by standing outworn forms on their heads. There was an element of schoolboy and student humour in all this – as can be seen, for example, in the letters exchanged by Luis Buñuel and Vicomte Charles de Noailles during the making of the film *L'Age d'or*:[12] the roots of the film itself lie in the Madrid student hostel where Buñuel first met Federico García Lorca and Salvador Dalí in the early 1920s.

In Ernst's case, too, jest, satire and irony play an important part. But so ambitiously coded a painting as *Au rendez-vous des amis* (1922, fig. 3) has a deeper meaning, as a record of the taboo-breaking Paris group and their intellectual context. This 'group portrait with lady' was anticipated and accompanied by a number of variations on the theme of the friendship picture as an emblem of spiritual affinity. There were, for instance, the collages made by Ernst and Hans Arp together in Cologne, under the collective title of *FATAGAGA* (*FAbrication de TAbleaux GArantis GAzométriques*, Manufacture of Guaranteed Gasometric Pictures). There was also the painting *Oiseau, poisson-serpent* (Bird, Fish-Serpent, 1921), an encoded double portrait of Ernst and Paul Eluard; and there was *Castor et Pollution* (1923). The mythical Dioscuri in this work are clearly the poets Benjamin Péret and Robert Desnos who form a triad with the painter. In rejecting the Cartesian tradition, Surrealism felt a special bond with German Romanticism and its tradition of community – as André Breton himself emphasized.

Let us remain with the friendship picture for a moment. The *Two Sculptures for a Room by Palermo* (fig. 4) were made by Gerhard Richter for a joint exhibition with his friend Palermo at the Galerie Heiner Friedrich in Cologne in 1971. He had first met Palermo, and also Sigmar Polke, in Düsseldorf ten years before, immediately after his move from East Germany to the West, and Palermo had been with him on his first trip to New York in 1970. The room contained monochrome mural paintings by Palermo, and the sculptures were plaster casts of the heads of both artists, which Richter had painted a neutral grey.

Clearly, the subject of this collaborative work is the crisis that has overtaken such traditional artistic genres as monumental painting and sculpture, portraiture in general, and the bust in particular; but the effect is ambivalent, and it is easy to misread the room (as reconstructed in the Lenbachhaus in Munich) as virtually straight self-advertisement on the two young artists' part – especially as their heads face each other frontally. At the same time, however, the Romantic theme of the friendship picture is once more present, as the germ of all artistic fellowships and as a protection against individual loneliness – an isolation deepened in our age by the loss of representational certainties, and by the randomness of the available choice of artistic devices.

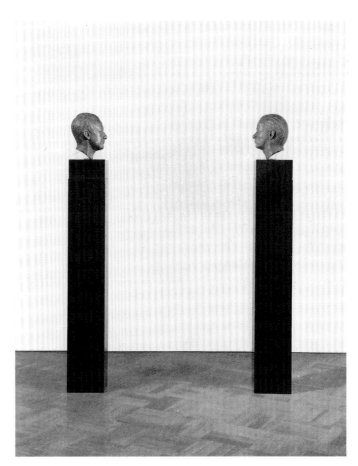

Fig.4 Gerhard Richter and Blinky Palermo, *Two Sculptures for a Room by Palermo* 1971, Städtische Galerie im Lenbachhaus, Munich

Social Sculpture: Joseph Beuys and Rudolf Steiner

In the present context, Joseph Beuys might claim a whole investigation to himself. His work seems to oscillate between an intensely personal basic situation and its social corroboration. Initially reclusive, he gradually turned himself into a public figure, and at one point founded a political party to promote 'direct democracy'. His teaching at the Düsseldorf Academy can be seen as the creation of a group of like-minded students, rescued from their isolation by Beuys. His fundamental concepts – the theory of warmth, the idea of circulation in its various guises, 'social sculpture' – all point beyond the formal domain of art into society at large. Liberating everyone to become creative ultimately means making everyone into an artist. Beuys's utopia goes far beyond the ideas of John Ruskin or the Bauhaus.

Fig. 5 Joseph Beuys during his action *Three Pots for the Poorhouse*, Edinburgh 1974

1 Heinrich Wiegand Petzet, *Von Worpswede nach Moskau: Heinrich Vogeler – ein Künstler zwischen den Zeiten* (Cologne, 1972), 153–54.
2 Wassily Kandinsky, 'Franz Marc' (1936), in Kandinsky, *Complete Writings on Art*, ed. and trans. Kenneth C. Lindsay and Peter Vergo (New York and London, 1982), 796.
3 Kurt Eisner, 'Die Stellung der revolutionären Regierung zur Kunst und zu den Künstlern' (1919), in *Neue Zeitung: Unabhängiges sozialistisches Organ*, no. 3 (Munich, 8 November 1993), 4.
4 Justin Hoffmann, ed., exh. cat. *Süddeutsche Freiheit: Kunst der Revolution in München 1919* (Munich: Lenbachhaus, 1993).
5 Paul Klee, letter to Alfred Kubin, Wiessee am Tegernsee, 12 May 1919 (extract), in exh. cat. *Paul Klee: Das Frühwerk 1883–1922* (Munich: Städtische Galerie im Lenbachhaus, 1979), 93.
6 Konrad Wünsche, *Bauhaus: Versuche, das Leben zu ordnen* (Berlin, 1989).
7 Karin von Maur, ed., exh. cat. *Oskar Schlemmer: Der Folkwang-Zyklus. Malerei um 1930* (Stuttgart: Staatsgalerie Stuttgart, 1993).
8 Oskar Schlemmer, 'Zu meinen Wandbildern für das Museum Folkwang in Essen', *Museum der Gegenwart*, ed. Ludwig Justi, 1, no. 4 (1931), 147–53. For text of Radio Breslau interview with Professor Frank Landenberger on 3 November 1930, see Maur (as note 7), vol. 1, 204.
9 Mechthild Lucke and Andreas Hüneke, *Erich Heckel: Lebensstufen. Die Wandbilder im Angermuseum zu Erfurt* (Dresden, 1992).
10 Klaus Lankheit, *Das Freundschaftsbild der Romantik*, Heidelberger Kunstgeschichtliche Abhandlungen, n.s., no. 1 (Heidelberg, 1952).
11 See Ludger Derenthal, 'Max Ernst: trois tableaux d'amitié', *Les Cahiers du Musée national d'art moderne*, no. 31 (Paris, spring 1990), 72–110.
12 'L'Age d'or: correspondance Luis Buñuel – Charles de Noailles, lettres et documents (1929–76)', *Les Cahiers du Musée national d'art moderne* (Paris, 1993).
13 Exh. cat. *Gerhard Richter* (Paris: Musée d'Art moderne de la Ville de Paris, 1993).
14 Elisabeth Jappe, *Performance Ritual Prozeß: Handbuch der Aktionskunst in Europa* (Munich and New York, 1993).
15 Patrick Beurard, 'Joseph Beuys et Rudolf Steiner: pour en finir avec un tabou', *Opus International*, no. 132 (1993), 8–21.
16 Rudolf Steiner, *Wann die Erde Mond wird: Wandtafelzeichnungen 1919–24*, ed. Walter Kugler (Cologne, 1992).
17 Wolfgang Pehnt, *Rudolf Steiner: Goetheanum Dornach*, photographed by Thomas Dix (Berlin, 1991).

Significantly, in his celebrated performances Beuys created for himself the image of an introverted, indeed almost autistic artist. Performance art in general depends on a slightly voyeuristic confrontation between one individual and the amorphous mass of the audience that he lures into identifying (temporarily) with himself. What made Beuys's performances different from others was their symbolic weight which far transcended the individual occasion. Invariably they addressed contemporary issues on which Beuys then expatiated in lengthy discussion sessions. It might be said that the common denominator of all his art – in a variety of media – was language (fig. 5).

In this there is a parallel with Rudolf Steiner[15] to whose doctrine of Anthroposophy Beuys professed allegiance. We know from eye-witness accounts that Steiner's lectures, which he illustrated by drawing on a blackboard,[16] came over to his hearers as a kind of performance art. Steiner dabbled in the arts and crafts himself, and made a visionary contribution of his own to Expressionist architecture;[17] here he seems directly to have anticipated the 'social sculpture' to which Beuys aspired. Ultimately, of course, Beuys wanted the impossible: no less than to abolish the rift between individual and community that had existed since Romanticism.

Günter Metken

Translated from the German by David Britt

Origin and Archetype:
The Dream of a New Start

And so – said I, a trifle distractedly – ought we
to eat once more from the Tree of Knowledge,
that we may fall back into the state of innocence?
Of course, he replied; that is the last chapter
in the history of the world.[1]

Heinrich von Kleist

The path back to the future, which Kleist describes in
the passage quoted above – and, even more clearly, in
his wonderful image of the locked and barred paradise
to which we can never return except, perhaps, from
behind, after a laborious journey around the world[2] –
that path was discovered and explored by the German
Romantics themselves.

In many of the sayings of those years, Romanticism is
described as a 'yearning for the infinite'; but it is a
yearning whose starting-point and ultimate goal lie in
Ursprünglichkeit: in origin and archetype. In all its subsequent manifestations, too, Romanticism has set out to
renew and widen human horizons through making contact with an original state.

The symbol of this *Ursprünglichkeit*, whether direct
or mediated, is the 'child': the early years of an individual, of a nation or of humanity itself; a time of spontaneous response to experience, when countless possibilities still lie open. Intuitively, Friedrich Schiller wrote of
children: 'They are what we were; they are what we
must again become.'[3]

More than a hundred years later, Carl Gustav Jung
elaborated on this from a theoretical viewpoint in his
account of the archetype of the child.[4] Here, too, childhood is not considered as a particular phase of human
life but as a fundamental human principle. In the course
of his essay – to which the present article owes some
important suggestions – Jung distinguishes the archetype
as a past state from its functions and from its character
as something in the future. For him, too, the child marks
both the beginning and the end of a long evolutionary
process. This archetype has the function of correcting

imbalances in consciousness. For, according to Jung, the
modern, differentiated consciousness is in constant danger of finding itself uprooted; to compensate, it needs the
surviving inner state of childhood. The appearance of
the child image, though it may initially seem retrospective, commonly denotes the opening up of new possibilities. The child appears when there is a contradiction
between the present and the starting-point: 'A man's
present state may have come into conflict with his childhood state ... he has thus become unchildlike and artificial, and lost his roots. All this presents a favourable
opportunity for an equally vehement confrontation with
original truth.'[5]

This process overtakes individuals as it does whole
cultures – which often, at crises in their history, find a
way into the future by looking back to assure themselves of their own origins. 'The historian', wrote
Friedrich Schlegel in the *Athenäum*, 'is a prophet turned
backward.'[6]

The artistic expressions of this longing for renewal are
many: not only the motif of the child itself but also all
seemingly childlike or 'primitive' figures; the whole quest
for 'naturalness', 'truth' and 'wholeness'; the reversion
to past cultural forms. Often these patterns coexist inter-
changeably. Almost always, we encounter the sense of
living in a society in terminal crisis, together with the
longing to make a new start in the company of a group
of like-minded people. Such art is always marked by an
awkward, unpolished anti-academicism. Its products,
widely though they may differ among themselves, thus
reveal that their origins essentially lie in one and the
same longing for renewal.

'We must become children, if we wish to attain the Best' (Philipp Otto Runge)[7]

Philipp Otto Runge's painting *The Mother at the Spring*
(1804, fig. 1) shows a child at the mysterious moment of
beginning, which is also the start of a new world.[8]

Fig.1 Philipp Otto Runge, *The Mother at the Spring* 1804, formerly Hamburger Kunsthalle. Destroyed.

Tightly held by his mother, and reflected in the waters of the spring, the babe-in-arms is still unable to distinguish between self and world, or between feeling and knowing. He does not yet know himself, and so he perceives the world as his own double. For Runge, this is the paradisal state. If the child once touches the surface of the water, he will experience nature as something distinct from himself. Once he becomes aware of his own reflection, that will be the end – for the present – of his stay in the garden of Eden.

Accounts of paradise as an inner place occur several times in Runge's writings.[9] In his lengthy, speculative letters, Runge also speaks of the 'living spirit' that man must put into things, in order to create them truly for himself and thus to regain a portion of paradise: 'Flowers, trees and figures will then be subsumed in us.'[10] Novalis, in the fifth of his 'Hymns to the Night', looks back to a time when 'Rivers, trees, flowers and animals had a human mind.'[11]

The 'living spirit', of which the child is the symbol, is the capacity for intense, unprejudiced seeing and for visionary awareness. It is always both the starting-point and the goal of artistic activity. Runge wrote to his brother Daniel on 9 March 1802: 'We cannot regain the coherence within ourselves until we have returned to the initial inwardness of feeling – or until we have become children again. Everyone passes through this cycle, and at some stage of it one always becomes dead. The more

often it is experienced, the deeper and more inward the feeling surely becomes.'[12]

The motif of wholeness, a 'treasure hard to attain', may appear in many utterly dissimilar forms, including a jewel, a pearl, a flower, or a circle or globe.[13] For Runge, with his strongly symbolic cast of mind, the child is closely associated with the flower, and the two motifs are often interchangeable. Like the baby in Runge's painting, the blue flower of Romanticism (in Novalis's *Heinrich von Ofterdingen*) appears beside a spring.

In his letters, Runge writes of his own age as a turning point in history – the third, after the end of Antiquity and the end of the Middle Ages. In words charged with a powerful sense of mission, he proclaims that it is the task of art to anticipate the coming of a new civilization. In Runge's view of Western history, these times of change are always periods of high artistic achievement, and their art always marks new departures.[14] He told his brother Daniel: 'Art as it is, and as it has hitherto been, is a warped and learned thing – if we look upon it as it is nowadays looked upon. But if human beings would only see the world as children see it, art would be a lovely language.'[15]

Runge longed to see this new, living art thriving in the collective work of a group of kindred spirits. As he worked with the poet Ludwig Tieck and the composer Ludwig Berger towards a *Gesamtkunstwerk* – a synaesthetic work of art – based on his cycle of *The Times of Day*, he evolved the model (never to be realized) of a workshop community.[16]

'Truth': The Nazarene Community of Artists

In 1808, Franz Pforr, Friedrich Overbeck and a number of their fellow-students at the Vienna Academy set up the *Lukasbund*, the first Secession movement in the history of art. It was directed against the mechanical, external, soulless way in which art was practised at the institution they all attended; they were convinced that this not only missed the essence of things but buried all vestiges of genuine feeling. Pforr said: 'We saw a single prevailing mannerism on every side; it might show itself in different ways in this artist or that, but as a whole it is always an aberration, a deviation from nature.'[17]

Fig.2 Friedrich Overbeck, *Portrait of the Artist Franz Pforr* c.1810/65, Staatliche Museen zu Berlin Preußischer Kulturbesitz, Nationalgalerie

Nature, here, was synonymous with 'truth' – which was the motto of the group. Moral and artistic truth may be attained by renouncing all that is facile and sketchy in the practice of art. As an antidote to mere imitation, the Nazarenes advocated following in the footsteps of the great artists of the past. They hailed the German art of the fifteenth and sixteenth centuries – the second of the historical crises and artistic flowerings listed by Runge – as the resplendent dawn of the modern age, a period of youthful ascent that culminated in the supreme masterpieces of Raphael and of Albrecht Dürer. This was the point from which they wanted to start, in order to open up new evolutionary possibilities for their own day. In that past time, or so they believed, the nations of Europe, and the continent as a whole, had been united by a strong bond of religious feeling. This was the goal of their somewhat contradictory yearning for a simply ordered commonwealth that would involve and include artists: a holistic vision of society, utterly unattainable in an age of increasing individualism.

The same historic models had already been proclaimed in early Romantic literature – as, for example, in Wilhelm Heinrich Wackenroder's widely read *Herzensergießungen eines kunstliebenden Klosterbruders*

(Outpourings from the Heart of an Art-Loving Monk), which appeared in 1797. Even more distinctly, Novalis, in his essay *Die Christenheit oder Europa* (Christendom or Europe), had emphasized the patriotic, social impetus behind the Romantic appeal to the past. For Novalis, the Christian Middle Ages were a time when Europe still possessed 'the lovely bloom of its youth, faith and love' – later succeeded by 'the grosser fruits of knowledge and property'.[18] In this, the future utopia of a better past, the Nazarenes sought to ground their 'Latter-Day German Religious-Patriotic Art'.

The portrait that Overbeck painted of his friend Pforr in 1810 (fig. 2) is a first testimony to the kind of artistic beauty to which they aspired; it also displays the Nazarene ideal of the artist. It is delicately and clearly executed, in clear colours and firm outlines; its new forms are simultaneously a social protest and an ethical assertion. The sitter, Pforr, was convinced 'that, in order to be great, the painter must be not just a painter but a man ... that the way to become a truly great painter is identical with the path of virtue'.[19] In this portrait, virtue and ethos are couched in clearly defined form; its relation to its honoured historic prototypes is clarified down to the tiniest detail.

'Nature': The *Brücke* Community of Artists

One hundred years later, in Dresden in 1905, four young students of architecture founded an artistic community under the name of *Brücke* (Bridge). Their aim, once again, was to renew art while living and creating in common, and to rid themselves of cramping conventions and established ways of seeing. Once more, their renewal of art was to extend to the whole of life. Erich Heckel said later: 'We knew what to get away from; but where we were going to was less certain ... [Karl] Schmidt-Rottluff said we might call it *Brücke* – it was a word with plenty of levels of meaning, so that it would not amount to a programme, but would somehow lead across from one shore to the other.'[20]

The group grew rapidly, and remained without a clear defining idea. Its mottoes were naturalness and spontaneity. It sought the wellsprings of the new art in the 'unconscious' and the 'unwilled'. In 1906 there came a

Fig.3 Otto Mueller, *Nudes in a Reed-lined Dyke*, Staatliche Museen zu Berlin Preußischer Kulturbesitz, Nationalgalerie

clarion call, in the form of a woodcut by Ernst Ludwig Kirchner:

'With faith in evolution and in a new generation of creators and enjoyers, we call upon youth to unite. And as youth, as the bearers of the future, we will wrest our freedom of action and of life from the entrenched elder forces. Anyone who gives direct and unfalsified utterance to the impulse that drives him to create is one of us.'[21]

The friends spent the summer of 1910 at the Moritzburg Lakes, near Dresden; there, as in their later sojourns in the country, they strove to discover the true harmony between humanity and nature in a paradisal, unconstrained life outside civilization. One meaning of nature is 'that which exists before culture': and all that civilization has distorted and forgotten, nature can help restore to its evolutionary truth.

The two young daughters of an entertainer's widow, Fränzi and Marcella, modelled for the *Brücke* artists at Moritzburg. The female nude in the landscape, simplified into a sign, became the principal motif of their work. Appropriately so: for this, better than any other theme, expressed their quest for an almost animal, primeval state of harmony between body, mind and Nature. The childlike looks of the two girls reinforced this message, as did the exoticism of the Romany figures

later painted by Otto Mueller, who joined the group in 1910. The motif of the 'alien child' was one that had been important to the early Romantics; it remains a powerful symbol of the forgotten origin.

Precedents from ancient and exotic cultures formed part of the same quest for origins and archetypes. The *Brücke* artists drew inspiration from medieval woodcuts, and from the expressive sculptures of distant nations. Kirchner had discovered Far Eastern art for himself. For his part, Mueller was to write to Paul Cassirer in 1919: 'What I am striving for, most of all, is to express the feeling of landscape and man, as simply as possible. My prototype – for its sheer craftsmanship, among other things – is and has long been the art of the ancient Egyptians.'[22] Mueller, whose work (fig. 3) has a dream-like, lyrical sweep that often startlingly recalls early Romanticism, was to remain faithful to this theme until the end of his life.

References to alien cultural forms – it did not greatly matter what they were – helped to achieve immediacy through unfamiliarity of form. But new expressive forms also required new techniques. Many of the *Brücke* artists used oil paint thinned with turpentine; Mueller developed a special form of size colour, with which he could dash down his ideas spontaneously and definitively in the heat of the moment (exactly what the Nazarenes had condemned). The *Brücke* artists also wanted to deprive paintings of their elegant surface gloss, to make them seem refractory and awkward. The use of coarse burlap as a support often added unevenness of structure.

A certain awkwardness in expression or in form is part of any art that is seeking to rediscover its beginnings. It serves the necessary purpose of marking a distinction from established art and emphasizing the individual freedom of the artist. At the same time, the unprepossessing signs of 'insignificance … show how precarious is the psychic possibility of wholeness, that is, the enormous difficulties to be met with in attaining this "highest good"'.[23]

Fig.4 Paul Klee, *The Tightrope Walker* 1923,
Paul-Klee-Stiftung, Kunstmuseum Berne

Seemingly Naïve and Childlike Form: Paul Klee

The symbol of the bridge recurs in Paul Klee's depictions of acrobats on the high wire. The added element here is that the skilled walk along the wire is clearly dangerous in itself. Nietzsche's Zarathustra (Klee read the book several times) says of a tightrope walker: 'Man is a tightrope, strung between beast and superman – a tightrope over an abyss. It is perilous to cross over, perilous to stand still, perilous to shudder and stop. What is great in man is that he is a bridge, and not a goal: what can be loved in man is that he is a crossing, and a fall.'[24]

In wartime, in 1915, Klee noted: 'One leaves the scene on this side and compensates by building across into a scene on the other side, which is free to be all Yes. Abstraction. The cool Romanticism of this unemotive style is unprecedented. The more frightful this world is (as it is today, above all), the more abstract art becomes; a happy world produces a this-worldly art. Today is the crossing point between what is past and what is contemporary.'[25]

The *Tightrope Walker* of 1923 (fig. 4), with his long balancing-pole, is also a reference to Klee's work at the Weimar Bauhaus. At the beginning of his lecture on 12 December 1921, Klee described this figure as 'the utmost realization of the symbol of equilibrium of forces'.[26]

Beneath the tightrope is the face of Oskar Schlemmer's Constructivist logo for the Bauhaus; the cross in the background comes from a drawing by Johannes Itten, with a text from the cult of Mazdaznan to which Itten belonged.

The tension between opposing tendencies within the Bauhaus – the pursuit of rational design on one side and that of intuition on the other – was also the dominant theoretical and artistic issue in Klee's long career. His art, like Runge's, is a mental and spiritual one: an art of signs, accompanied by a markedly rational edifice of ideas. Both painters tried their hands at a theory of colour; both took a keen interest in theoretical issues, in number, in mathematics, and in schematic diagrams of their own devising. The resulting works tend to emphasize the poetry of the logical and rational side of life, but presumably serve as a necessary compensation and counterbalance to each artist's true thoughts.

Like the early Romantics, Klee assigned a place to the creative human being in his scheme of the cosmos. In a diagram drawn in 1923 (cat. 165), Klee shows him between earthly roots and cosmic awareness, between outward seeing and inward vision.[27] To express these complex ideas, Klee, like Runge, devised a language of signs, ciphers for the undepictable that could give form to the forgotten and to the merely surmised; for 'Art does not reproduce the visible but makes visible.' He hoped to see 'symbols console the spirit, show it that its potential extends beyond the various possible intensifications of the earthly'.[28]

He found formal precedents for this in the unreflective drawings of children, in the psychograms of mental patients and in the magic signs of primeval societies. These, in his view, were among the primordial origins of art: 'All this has to be taken very seriously – more seriously than all the art museums – if the present is to be reformed.'[29]

The goal is expansion, the gaining of space – an important concept for Jung, who uses it to stand for the individuation process. In a lecture at Jena museum in 1924, Klee said: 'Our beating heart drives us down, deep down to the primal depths. What then grows out of this impulse, call it what we may – dream, idea, imagination – is to be taken seriously only when it unites with the appropriate artistic means into significant form. Then

Fig.5 Joseph Beuys, *Manresa Action* 1966

those curiosities become realities: realities of art, which expand life into something wider than it normally seems.'[30]

Chaos and Intuition: Joseph Beuys

Expansion – in the tension between reason and intuition, nature and mind or spirit – was a vital objective to Joseph Beuys. His art, too, was a reaction to a profound crisis in society. Thinking was reduced to rationally verified knowledge, learning was confined to narrow and unconnected specializations, the pattern of life itself was cramped, and uniformity was imposed on thought, action, and feeling. To counter this, he sought to mobilize spiritual traditions, far-off rites, and all the neglected powers of emotional awareness. Beuys in 1958–59: 'I had no interest in continuing to concentrate exclusively on logic: what I wanted was for all the subconscious residues to be broken open and churned into utter tur-

bulence, in the form of a chaotically liberating process; for a new start always takes place in chaos.'[31]

Frequently ritualistic in character, Beuys's 'actions' united elements of ancient symbolism into a private mythology, intended to provoke deeper insights and intuitions. With their vast ambitions, embracing an implicit message of redemption, they harked back to the origins of art. Beuys expanded the definition of art itself, both in content and in form, to cover great swathes of the terrain of life: 'I declare that the creative is the artistic; and that is my working definition of art.'[32]

This definition of art included science, insofar as science could accommodate pre-rational relationships with nature and cosmos. In this way, Beuys hoped, the whole of being might once more become accessible to experience. This same ambition, as Theodora Fischer has pointed out, was shared by the early German Romantics.[33]

The polarity between rationality and intuition, cognition and awareness, was the subject of Beuys's action, *Manresa*, which took place in the Galerie Schmela, Düsseldorf, in December 1966 (fig. 5). The title refers to the Catalan village where, in 1523, St Ignatius of Loyola drafted his *Spiritual Exercises*: a layer of meaning recently explored by Friedhelm Mennekes.[34] The two principal objects involved were a felt half-cross (Element 1, Reason), symbolizing logical, abstract, 'crystalline-rigid' thought, and an electrical induction apparatus (Element 2, Intuition), which symbolically charged the missing half of the cross with energy and thus expanded thought by adding the realm of feeling and spirit, which to Beuys was the organic principle. A plate, held in front of the cross, later took over the function of a mandala. The action was accompanied by a repeated spoken refrain:

Now Element 2 has climbed up to Element 1
Now Element 1 has climbed down to Element 2

At regular intervals, a voice enquired after Element 3: the future whole.[35]

More complex than would appear from this description, this action – like all actions and happenings – was not intended as the vehicle of any succinctly definable meaning. It was a device to disrupt the settled and the defined, through inspiration and reflection, performance and play. Beuys was most at home in the subversive role of the shaman, celebrating rites of his own devising: he was the heretic in the art world. 'The other good starting-point', he said, 'would be the age of German Idealism; the conception that I now have came up then. You find it in the Romantics, in Novalis ...'[36]

The early Romantics spoke up for intuition quite emphatically. As a pre-rational source of awareness, it had an important place in, for instance, the philosophy of Friedrich Wilhelm Joseph von Schelling. Their thinking was open-ended, often subversive; they were critical of absolute truths. A firm decision in favour of subjectivity might yet retrieve what had been lost. Novalis: 'Stories, with no coherence, and yet with associations, like dreams. Poems, simply euphonious and full of beautiful words, but again with no meaning or coherence at all – at most, one strophe comprehensible here or there – like so many fragments from the different things. True poetry can have, at most, an allegorical, general meaning and an indirect effect – like music, etc. Nature is therefore purely poetic: it is an enchanter's or a physicist's cell, a nursery, a rumpus room, a lumber room.'[37]

Angelika Wesenberg

Translated from the German by David Britt

1 Heinrich von Kleist, 'Über das Marionettentheater', in Kleist, *Sämtliche Werke und Briefe*, ed. H. Sembdner, 3rd ed., 2 (Munich, 1970), 345.

2 Kleist (as note 1), vol. 2, 342.

3 Friedrich von Schiller, 'Über naive und sentimentalische Dichtung' (1795–96), in Schiller, *Philosophische Schriften*, vol. 20 of *Werke* (Weimar, 1962), 413–14.

4 Carl Gustav Jung, 'The Psychology of the Child-Archetype' (1941), in Jung and Carl Kerényi, *Introduction to a Science of Mythology*, trans. R. F. C. Hull (London, 1951), 97–138.

5 Jung (as note 4), 112.

6 Friedrich Schlegel, Fragment no. 80, in Schlegel, *Kritische Ausgabe seiner Schriften* (Munich, Paderborn and Vienna, 1958–), 2 (1967): 176.

7 Philipp Otto Runge, *Hinterlassene Schriften*, 2 vols. (Hamburg, 1840), 1, 7.

8 Formerly at the Hamburger Kunsthalle; burnt in 1931 in the Glaspalast, Munich. See Jörg Traeger, *Philipp Otto Runge und sein Werk* (Munich, 1975), 122–24, 367–68 (cat. no. 298). See also Kurt Grützmacher, *Novalis und Philipp Otto Runge. Drei Zentralmotive und ihre Bedeutungssphäre: Die Blume – Das Kind – Das Licht* (Munich, 1964), 49–65.

9 Runge (as note 7), vol. 1, 16, 22, 24, 44.

10 Runge (as note 7), vol. 1, 17.

11 Novalis, 'Hymnen an die Nacht', no. 5, in Novalis, *Werke in einem Band* (Berlin and Weimar, 1984), 8.

12 Runge (as note 7), vol. 1, 11.

13 Jung (as note 4), 109.

14 Runge (as note 7), vol. 1, 7, 8–9.

15 Runge (as note 7), vol. 2, 223.

16 Runge (as note 7), vol. 1, 179.

17 Fritz Herbert Lehr, *Die Blütezeit romantischer Bildkunst: Franz Pforr, der Meister des Lukasbundes* (Marburg, 1924), 39.

18 Novalis (as note 11), 330.

19 Lehr (as note 17), 70–71.

20 Hans Kentel, 'Aus einem Gespräch mit Erich Heckel', *Das Kunstwerk* 12, no. 3 (1958), 24, quoted from exh. cat. *Expressionisten: Die Avantgarde in Deutschland 1905–1920* (Berlin, 1986), 28.

21 Exh. cat. Expressionisten (as note 20), 8 (ill. of woodcut), 78 (ill. of printed programme).

22 Lothar-Günther Buchheim, *Die Künstlergemeinschaft Brücke* (Dresden, 1957), 270.

23 Jung (as note 4), 117–18.

24 Friedrich Nietzsche, *Also sprach Zarathustra* (Stuttgart, 1921), 16.

25 Paul Klee, *Tagebücher 1898–1918* (Leipzig and Weimar, 1980), 270, 271 (facsimile).

26 Paul Klee, 'Beiträge zur bildnerischen Formenlehre: Vorträge im Wintersemester 1921/22', in Klee, *Kunst-Lehre* (Leipzig, 1987), 120. On what follows, see also Wolfgang Kersten, *Paul Klee: Übermut, Kunststück Nr. 3959* (Frankfurt am Main, 1990), 24–31.

27 Paul Klee, 'Wege des Naturstudiums', in Klee (as note 26), 69.

28 Paul Klee, 'Schöpferische Konfession', no. 7 (1920), in Klee (as note 26), 60, 65.

29 Paul Klee, journal for 1912, no. 905, in Klee (as note 25), 230.

30 Paul Klee, 'Über die moderne Kunst' (Jena, January 1924), in Klee (as note 26), 83–84.

31 Götz Adriani, Winfried Konnertz and Karin Thomas, *Joseph Beuys* (New York, 1979; Cologne, 1981), 83–84.

32 Christos M. Joachimides, exh. cat. *Joseph Beuys: Richtkräfte* (Berlin, Nationalgalerie, 1977), 5.

33 Theodora Vischer, *Beuys und die Romantik* (Cologne, 1983). See also Lothar Romain, 'Franz Marc und Joseph Beuys: Zur Wiederkehr des Romantischen in der deutschen Moderne', in *Romantik und Gegenwart: Festschrift für Jens Christian Jensen* (Cologne, 1988), 197–207.

34 Friedhelm Mennekes, *Joseph Beuys: Manresa, eine Aktion als geistliche Übung zu Ignatius von Loyola* (Frankfurt am Main, 1992).

35 Götz Adriani, Winfried Konnertz and Karin Thomas, *Joseph Beuys* (Cologne, 1973), 87–90; Uwe M. Schneede, *Joseph Beuys: Die Aktionen* (Stuttgart, 1994), 146–65.

36 Vischer (as note 33), 10.

37 Novalis, *Schriften*, ed. J. Minor, 4 vols. (Jena, 1907), vol. 2, 308.

Mood Indigo

From the Blue Flower to the Blue Rider

1.

... Price question:

1. Anna Blossom has wheels.
2. Anna Blossom is red.
3. What colour are the wheels?
   Blue is the colour of thy yellow hair.
   Red is the whirl of thy green wheels.
   Thou simple maiden in everyday-dress,
   Thou dear green animal,
   I love thine...

Kurt Schwitters, 'Anna Blossom has wheels' (1942)[1]

Kurt Schwitters's paradoxical handling of colour in his best-known poem, originally published in German in 1922, where the contraries are elided into a syncretic conception of love, may stand as a sign of one of the most durable features of German attitudes to colour from the Romantics to the Modern Movement. Despite the central importance of that most *anschaulich*, as well as most comprehensive of colour-handbooks, Goethe's *Farbenlehre* ('Theory of Colour') (1810), German approaches to colour continued to be far more abstract and symbolic than perceptual. Where French theorists from Philippe de la Hire (*Dissertation sur les differens accidens de la Vuë* ['Dissertation on Various Occurrences in Vision'], 1685) to Auguste Rosenstiehl (*Traité de la couleur au point de vue physique, physiologique et esthétique* ['Treatise on the Physical, Physiological and Aesthetic Aspects of Colour'], 1913), and French painters from Chardin to Matisse, wrestled with colour-relationships as presented to and processed by the human vision, Germans were more concerned with the ideal relationships articulated by the burgeoning colour-order systems of the eighteenth and nineteenth centuries. It was the schematic logic rather than the empirical richness of Goethe's theory that most impressed his sympathetic contemporaries, and it was the German physicist and physiologist Hermann von Helmholtz who persuaded the French most decisively in the second half of the nineteenth century that to opt for a radical perceptual realism was to misunderstand the nature of visual experience.[2]

Schwitters showed himself to be sufficiently up to date in his knowledge of colour systems to make blue the contrary of its complementary, yellow (in Goethe's day the complementary of blue had usually been seen as orange, the product of the mixture of the two remaining primaries, yellow and red); but it seems clear that his oxymoronic play with colours was simply because they are opposites: we need to look no further than the words on the page. Indeed, his idea may have a literary rather than a scientific background, and in this essay I want to look at the way in which some of his Expressionist contemporaries took up and revalued the approaches to colour first articulated so vividly in German Romanticism. To do so I shall focus on that supremely Romantic colour, blue.

Blue established its central place in the Romantic imagination chiefly through the work of the geologist, poet and novelist, Friedrich von Hardenberg, who wrote under the name of Novalis. Novalis's novel, *Heinrich von Ofterdingen* (1800) opens with the sleepless hero yearning to see the blue flower of which he has heard from a stranger. He falls asleep and dreams of setting out on a quest for the flower, which takes him to a remote cave in a wild country, filled with bluish light reflected from a fountain. Later he finds himself in a meadow surrounded by dark blue rocks under a dark blue sky, where he discovers the tall light-blue flower in whose centre he sees a face.[3] This face turns out to be that of his beloved who, when Heinrich meets and dances with her, is revealed to have light sky-blue eyes and blue veins on her neck. One of Heinrich's chief helpers in this quest is the shepherd-girl Cyane, whose name derives from the Greek term for 'blue', and who, in the uncompleted continuation of the novel, picks the blue flower for him. Cyane claims to be the daughter of Mary, Mother of God.

The identification of colours and flowers was a central

theme of German Romanticism. The Hamburg painter Philipp Otto Runge used the expressive imagery of flowers in all his *The Times of Day* (colour plates, pp. 212–3, cat. 9) which themselves had their own characteristic colours; and the theorist of Romanticism, Wilhelm Heinrich Wackenroder, wrote in an essay on colours edited by Runge's friend Ludwig Tieck, who was also close to Novalis, that: 'In nature, even a single flower, a single isolated petal, can enchant us. It is no surprise that we express our pleasure simply in its colour. The various spirits of nature speak to us through the individual colours, just as the spirits of the heavens speak through the various sounds of musical instruments. We can hardly express how moved and touched we are by every colour, for the colours themselves speak to us in a gentler accent…'[4]

Similarly, in an essay on the meaning of colour in nature appended to Runge's *Farben-Kugel* (Colour Sphere, cat. 13) of 1810, the Danish scientist Henrik Steffens, who like Novalis was interested in minerals, speculated that the colour of flowers was, like their perfume, a function of their powers of attraction, an idea he may well have drawn from that early botanical classic, C.K. Sprengel's *Das entdeckte Geheimniss der Natur im Bau und in der Befruchtung der Blumen* ('The secret of Nature revealed in the structure and fertilisation of flowers', 1793), which argued for the importance of colour in attracting pollinating insects, and pointed, for example, to the powerful yellow-blue contrast of the forget-me-not (*Myosotis palustris*) and the blue iris.[5] Goethe, in the Didactic Part of his *Farbenlehre*[6] also pointed to the relative rarity of one of his primary colours, blue, among the flora, and argued that yellow was far more common.

Modern commentators on *Heinrich von Ofterdingen* have debated the identity of the blue flower with little agreement; some have concluded that Novalis had no specific flower in mind. One suggestion has been that since, like Ludwig Tieck, Johann Gottfried Herder and Jean-Paul Richter, he showed some interest in the newly available literature of India, the very name 'Indigo' (*Indigblau*) i.e. 'Indian', may have been uppermost in his mind.[7] But certainly the colour seems to have come before the flower: as Novalis wrote in a notebook,[8] 'The character of colours: everything is blue in my book'.

Novalis was probably introduced to colour systems by his teacher and friend, the geologist A.G. Werner who, like many natural scientists in the eighteenth century, had introduced colour into his own taxonomical scheme.[9] Novalis was probably also familiar with the early theory of Goethe, whom he had met in 1798. A note on coloured shadows in blue and yellow[10] seems to point to the older poet,[11] and it is likely to have been important for the scheme of polarities blue-yellow and red-green, which interested Novalis, as it interested so many exponents of *Naturphilosophie* in his day.[12] The polarity of colour was one of its characteristics which, as we shall see, continued to fascinate German artists and theorists well into the twentieth century, for it could readily be understood in terms of either a physiological or a psychic dynamism.

The contrasting dynamics of blue and yellow seem hardly to have concerned Novalis, but in a dream-sequence in a novel by his contemporary Jean-Paul Richter, which may well have given some stimulus to the introduction of the blue flower in *Heinrich von Ofterdingen*, the hero is sucked like a dewdrop into a blue flower, and lifted up into a lofty room within reach of the mysterious sister of his own genius-figure. As in Novalis's novel, the blue and the feminine share an active power of attraction.[13] Goethe was soon to write in his *Farbenlehre* (Didactic Part § 781): 'As we readily follow an agreeable object that flies from us, so we love to contemplate blue, not because it advances to us, but because it draws us after it.'[14]

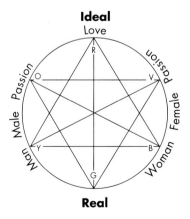

This gendering of blue was also felt by Runge who, in a diagram of about 1809 (fig. 1 directly above, translated into English) conceived of the warm (yellow-orange) side of the colour-circle as male, and the cool

Fig.2 Philipp Otto Runge, *Morning* (small version) 1808, Hamburger Kunsthalle

(blue-violet) as female. Runge may have been responding to the chemical ideas of Steffens who, in his essay of 1810, argued for red as a symptom of the contractive, oxygenizing effect in metals, and blue as the sign of the more expansive effect of hydrogen on them.[15] Goethe, in a similar vein, included the affinity with acid and affinity with alkalis among the characteristics of his polar blue and yellow.[16] But in a much earlier statement about the natural meaning of the primary colours, which may be linked to the first versions of *The Times of Day*, Runge had characterized blue as emblematic of God the Father and red of God the Son; in the painted *Morning* (small version) of 1808 (fig. 2 and colour plate, p. 94), red is clearly linked to the female figure of Aurora, as well as with the small baby beneath her.[17] Here Runge may have taken his cue from J.G. Herder's aesthetic treatise *Kalligone*, in which that precocious anthropologist argued, unfortunately without giving details, that because of their supreme beauty (after white), 'several nations' called blue and red the 'beautiful colours', attributing them to man and woman: 'firm blue to the

man, soft red to the woman.'[18] This common belief in the polar structure of colour-space was to be characteristic of German thought throughout our period, although, as usual, there was no consensus about the meaning of specific colours.

2.

Herder's appeal to popular 'national' usage proved very congenial to German artists in the Romantic period, and especially to painters of the figure. The two young painters Friedrich Overbeck and Franz Pforr, who moved from Vienna to Rome in 1810 to found the *Lukasbund*, had already shared a belief that the colours of dress were, and should be, represented in pictures as expressive of character. These notions would be most appropriate for depicting women, since men's clothing, they thought, was largely determined by profession; and yet there was a remarkable uniformity in female dress. Black hair, said Pforr, went best with combinations of black and violet, black and blue, or white and violet; brown hair with green and violet, white and blue, yellow-green and violet, and so on; blond suited quiet colours, such as blue and grey, grey and crimson, reddish-brown with a crimson cast, violet-grey and black. Black hair, he thought, was expressive of a proud and cool personality or, on the other hand, of cheerfulness and happiness; brown of happiness and good temper, innocent roguishness, naïveté and cheerfulness; blond of solitariness, modesty, good-heartedness and calm, more passive than active. Pforr added that he did not need to spell out the meaning of red hair, 'with an appropriate face', probably an allusion to the legendary red hair of Judas and the Jews.[19] Yet in Pforr's *Sulamith and Maria* of 1811 (fig. 3 and colour plate, p. 98), the allegorical figure of the South, the brown-haired Sulamith, wears white, green and red, and the blond northerner Maria wears a bright red dress with a white apron.[20] Overbeck, who dressed his later *Italia and Germania* (1828, colour plate, p. 99) in red, blue and white, and pink, green and white, respectively, had argued to his father in 1808 precisely that blond hair with grey and crimson was expressive of 'feminine gentleness and amiability or rather true femininity'.[21] The move to Rome may well have worked a powerful change in the

Fig.3 Franz Pforr, *Sulamith and Maria* 1811, Schäfer Collection, Schweinfurt

Nazarenes' colour perceptions. As that veteran grand tourist Goethe wrote in these years, when he was in touch with, if not entirely sympathetically disposed towards, their art: 'The inhabitants of the south of Europe make use of very brilliant colours for their dresses. The circumstances of their procuring silk stuffs at a cheap rate is favourable to this propensity. The women, especially, with their bright-coloured bodices and ribbons, are always in harmony with the scenery, since they cannot possibly surpass the splendour of the sky and landscape.'[22]

Perhaps, too, for Pforr and Overbeck this iconography of colour had to yield in practice to more private, aesthetic considerations: Pforr's detailed account of his *Sulamith and Maria* mentioned Maria's red dress, 'just as we have so often spoken about it', and even then not all his details of the colouring were followed exactly in the painting.[23]

Goethe was also happy to muse, in anthropological vein, on colour preferences in clothing in Europe and beyond, in north and south, male and female: 'The female sex in youth is attached to rose-colour and sea-green, in age to violet and dark green. The fair-haired prefer violet, as opposed to light yellow, the brunettes blue, as opposed to yellow-red, and all on good grounds …'[24]

It might well have been expected that Goethe's *Farbenlehre*, shaped as it was by the poet's experience of art, and bearing his vast international reputation with it, would have been taken up at once by painters, as it was by philosophers such as Hegel and Schopenhauer.[25] Yet this was hardly the case. The Frankfurt painter and art-historian Johann David Passavant, to whom Pforr had confided his views on colour in 1808, studied Goethe's treatise while he was a pupil of David's in Paris somewhat later; and the book seems to have been in great demand among German artists in Rome as early as 1811.[26] But there is little sign that they were prepared to make use of its somewhat hermetic principles, and indeed, Wilhelm Schadow, a collaborator with Overbeck, and one of the several Nazarenes to leave Rome and take up academic positions in Germany, was still maintaining in an essay on the training of artists in the late 1820s the traditional view that colour was essentially unteachable.[27] By the middle of the century, however, teachers at the academies of Berlin and Dresden, as well as German artists in Rome, were looking more closely at Goethe's *Farbenlehre*, and supporting a new wave of detailed attempts to vindicate its arguments against Newtonian optics.[28]

3.

As we might expect, however, German painting in the nineteenth century was not immune from the perceptualism or the emphasis on the material qualities of pigments which were so highly developed in France. If German Romantic painting, with its particular closeness to watercolour, often presented rather abstract painterly surfaces, so that even Schadow, the most 'painterly' of the Nazarenes, could argue that it was immaterial from the point of view of colour what support or medium – fresco, oil, wax or watercolour – was used,[29] Germany was also the home of a school of plein-air painters which there, as elsewhere, gave a good deal of attention to vigorous impasto and brushwork. This was a tendency which was sometimes hostile to theory; Max Liebermann, for example, deliberately rejected the Neo-Impressionist divided touch in the interest of his 'simple' browns and greys.[30] The increasing attention to qualities of materials and surface, so familiar in French painting, was also marked among German artists in the later nineteenth century. The Basel Symbolist Arnold Böcklin, for example, made a profound and practical study of the history of techniques, and it was in Munich that one of the earliest painters' groups to test the properties of the proliferating new synthetic materials, the Deutsche Gesellschaft zur Beförderung rationeller Malverfahren, was established in 1886.[31] This was an emphasis on the materiality of materials which was to pass, via Henry van de Velde, to the Bauhaus, and beyond, to Joseph Beuys and Anselm Kiefer.

Böcklin was also engaged in a detailed examination of the perceptual qualities of colour contrast, which had been put high on the nineteenth-century painterly agenda by Michel Eugène Chevreul in the first half of the century, but which had been given a far more extensive and nuanced treatment in the 1870s by Wilhelm von Bezold, a Munich meteorologist who frequented a circle of artists in that city, and was personally known to Böcklin. Some of Böcklin's particular colour interests, for example his wide-ranging concern for simultaneous and complementary contrasts, and his close attention to controlling the colour effects of his paintings by working on them in their frames, can be related to Bezold's ideas.[32] Von Bezold's treatise of 1874 seems to have been closely studied in Munich: his unusually extended discussion of the spatial effect of 'warm' and 'cool' colours became a central interest for Böcklin's younger Symbolist contemporary Franz von Stuck, among whose pupils in Munich were not only Wassily Kandinsky and Paul Klee but also Josef Albers, whose *Interaction of Color* (1963) cites Bezold on colour-spread ('The Bezold-Effect'), and also uses Bezold's striking device of overlaid cut-out colour planes to demonstrate vividly the contrast and relativity of colours.[33]

Yet these more perceptually oriented tendencies remained the exception in German colour theory for artists who, in the tradition of Goethe's moral and symbolic values for colours, developed elaborate schemes of symbolic correspondences during the nineteenth century and early modern period. Böcklin had studied Goethe's *Farbenlehre* in depth, but he devised his own set of moral associations: to him black, green and white in combination suggested seriousness, red-yellow and blue cheerfulness, blue restfulness, and so on.[34] Stuck simi-

larly exploited the connotations of his colours in painting: red for passion, sulphur-yellow for danger, green for hope, and blue for mystery, eternity, intellectuality and poetic worth.[35] Such attitudes to colour were much stimulated during the second half of the century by the developing – and largely German – science of experimental psychology, from G.T. Fechner's *Vorschule der Aesthetik* ('Primer of Aesthetics') (1876) to the important work on colour-affects and preferences emanating chiefly from the Leipzig laboratory of Wilhelm Wundt around 1900. Thus the great interest in the dynamics of colour which, with the late-Romantic Bähr (*Der dynamische Kreis* – The Dynamic Circle), had been expressed in terms of light and chemistry, so that Bähr's blue, for example (in contrast to Steffens's), represented oxygen, was now directed inwards, and was nourished by experimental work with many human subjects. Colour was now largely a matter of psychology.

4.

Before the prestige of the Vienna School focused attention on psychiatry and psycho-analysis, it was experimental psychology which provided the concepts shaping public awareness of the problems of mind. Thus the politician and critic Friedrich Naumann could, in a periodical review of a Munch exhibition in Berlin in 1906, appeal quite naturally to Wundt for an explanation of the Norwegian painter's divided touch.[36] It was in Wundt's laboratory that the most sustained experimentation on the non-associative effects of colour was carried out in the twenty years up to the First World War. In a study of fourteen young, professional and mainly German subjects in the early 1890s, Jonas Cohn found a surprising love of contrasts of highly saturated colours, and he concluded that there was a common, basic, sensual instinct for strong colour which was only later modified by culture.[37] A later researcher in the same laboratory, F. Stefănescu-Goangă, reinforced Cohn's conclusions, emphasizing 'the individual consciousness and above all individual experience'.[38] Stefănescu-Goangă found that blue was experienced as calming, depressing, peaceful, quiet and serious, nostalgic (*sehnsüchtig*), melancholy, cool and calm, or dreamy. Several of his subjects followed Goethe in feeling that this colour drew

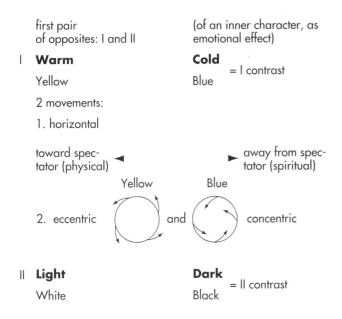

first pair
of opposites: I and II

(of an inner character, as
emotional effect)

I **Warm**   **Cold**
                                        = I contrast
Yellow   Blue

2 movements:

1. horizontal

toward spec-   ◄   ► away from spectator (physical)   tator (spiritual)

        Yellow   Blue

2. eccentric   and   concentric

II **Light**   **Dark**
                                        = II contrast
White   Black

2 movements:

1. The movement of resistance

Eternal resistance   complete lack of

and yet possibility   **White Black**   resistance and no

(birth)   possibility (death)

2. Eccentric and concentric, as in the case of yellow and blue,
    but in petrified form.

Fig.4 Wassily Kandinsky, *Table 1, On the Spiritual in Art* (original German edition, Munich 1912)

them after it, and others described it as a 'mysterious' colour.[39] All this seemed to reinforce the attitudes of recent researchers into synaesthesia and chromotherapy, that colour was primarily a matter of immediate feeling rather than of intellectual judgment, and it was thus of the greatest importance to artists engaged in developing a non-representational art. As the critic Karl Scheffler wrote, in an article which may have introduced Kandinsky to both synaesthesia and chromotherapy, 'never before was the sense of colour such a matter of nerves'.[40]

Kandinsky had a particular liking for blue. 'The inclination of blue towards depth', he wrote in *On the Spiritual in Art* (1911–12): 'is so great that it becomes more intense the darker the tone, and has a more characteristic inner effect. The deeper the blue becomes, the more strongly it calls man towards the infinite, awakening in him a desire for the pure and, finally, for the supernatural … Blue is the typically heavenly colour. Blue unfolds in its lowest depths the element of tranquil-

ity. As it deepens towards black, it assumes overtones of a superhuman sorrow. It becomes like an infinite self-absorption into that profound state of seriousness which has, and can have, no end. As it tends towards the bright [tones], to which blue is, however less suited, it takes on a more indifferent character and appears to the spectator remote and impersonal, like the high, pale-blue sky. The brighter it becomes, the more it loses its sound, until it turns into silent stillness and becomes white. Represented in musical terms, light blue resembles the flute, dark blue the 'cello, darker still and the wonderful sound of the double bass; while in a deep, solemn form the sound of blue can be compared to that of the deep tones of the organ.'[41]

This passage is crucial to understanding Kandinsky's approach to colour because it is informed by a whole range of reading which the painter had made his own. The traditional spirituality of blue had been intensified at the beginning of the century by the theosophical movement, to which Kandinsky was sympathetic, although he was never a member. In *Thought Forms* (1901) which had been translated into German in 1908, Annie Besant had argued that: 'The different shades of blue all indicate religious feeling, and range through all hues from the dark brown-blue of selfish devotion, or the pallid grey-blue of fetish-worship tinged with fear, up to the rich deep clear colour of heartfelt adoration, and the beautiful pale azure of that highest form which implies self-renunciation and union with the divine. … '[42]

Kandinsky's musical analogies are particularly striking, since the 'cello was his own instrument, whereas the flute, on the other hand, had been widely characterized as light blue in the technical literature of synaesthesia from the 1870s onwards.[43] So his responses to blue were both personal and potentially universal. Certainly we should not take as exhaustive Kandinsky's late and rather off-hand story of the origins of the title, *The Blue Rider*, for the almanac which he and Franz Marc decided to edit in 1911, and which was to gather together examples of artistic creativity widely separated in time and space. 'We both loved blue, Marc horses; I riders. So the name invented itself.'[44]

Marc was indeed enthusiastic about blue horses (see his 1911 painting in the Staatsgalerie Stuttgart), but he was no less convinced than Kandinsky of the masculine spiritualilty of blue. In a letter of 1910 to his friend, the painter August Macke, he had revived the Romantic aspiration of Runge to divide the colour-circle according to gender; '*Blue* is the *male* principle, sharp and spiritual, *yellow*, the female principle, soft, cheerful and sensual, *red* the *material* and ever the colour which must be resisted and overcome by the other two!'[45]

Here too, although the agenda may seem to have been a specifically Romantic one, contemporary psychology was uncovering similar attitudes among a range of subjects; Stefǎnescu-Goangǎ, for example, reported that among those he interviewed in 1910–11, 'some characterized [yellow] as feminine and soft, in contradistinction to red, which had a masculine, serious cast'.[46]

What links the Blue Rider group most clearly to the Romantic tradition of colour theory is the belief in polarity, in contrast, which informs all their thinking, and which often seems to be related specifically to Goethe. Kandinsky's table of polarity between blue and yellow (fig. 4) is perhaps the most succinct illustration of this, but Macke, too, in response to a questionnaire from the art magazine *Kunst und Künstler* in 1914, also argued that the supremely modern means of pictorial organization was the strong overall contrast created by individual areas of contrast in the painting; and he cited especially the work of Robert Delaunay.[47] In the early years of the century Goethe's *Farbenlehre* underwent a wide-ranging revaluation among German artists, from the apparently academic circle around the scientist Arnold Brass in Munich to the Expressionist E.L. Kirchner in Dresden.[48] It was probably under the stimulus of Goethe that Marc in the winter of 1910–11 began to look through a prism at the snowy landscape and his dog Russi, and to attempt on the canvas to match the brilliance of the coloured fringes he saw at the junctions of light and dark. Goethe had described his own experience of brilliant and delicate coloured shadows on the snow during a journey in the Harz mountains, although on that occasion he had not used a prism.[49] Marc told Macke of the 'amazing coloured fringes' he saw around his dog, a Siberian Shepherd, and of how he completed the painting as a study of the contrasts between yellow, white and blue.[50] This fascination with the prism and this enthusiasm for the powerful effects of colour contrast it revealed also became attractive to a number of

Fig.5 Wassily Kandinsky, *Yellow-Red-Blue* 1925, Musée national d'art moderne, Paris

artists and critics close to Herwath Walden's Sturm Gallery in Berlin during and after the war. In 1916 S. Friedländer (later Friedländer-Mynona) published in the gallery's journal *Der Sturm* an article in which he argued that colour-polarity was Goethe's distinctive discovery, and the following year he amplified this in a discussion of Goethe's prismatic experiments.[51] Arthur Segal, a painter who had exhibited with *Der Sturm* during the war, began to experiment with Goethe's prismatic fringes in paintings of the early 1920s in order to find a way of reconciling the equal demands of colour and form: 'The polar interaction of light and darkness', he wrote, 'is manifested in the optical effect of things, thus in forms and colours.'[52]

Goethe's theory was an abiding presence among German modernist painters; Kandinsky began to engage with it in a more thoroughgoing way as a teacher at the Bauhaus in the 1920s, and in *Yellow-Red-Blue* of 1925 (fig. 5) he developed an unusually sophisticated visualization of the creation of red from the augmentation (*Steigerung*) of yellow and blue, as described in Goethe's *Farbenlehre*.[53] Extracts from a later section of the book which also treats of this process appear among the lecture-notes for Kandinsky's Bauhaus courses, but he amplifies them with his own myth of the sun (yellow) and the moon (blue) which link on the edges of night and day as red sunrise or sunset.[54] It was perhaps in the context of this new agenda that Kandinsky reversed the theosophical and Blue Rider concept of the masculine spirituality of blue, and suggested that blue represented the feminine, for in many cultures the moon was conceived of as female, although not, of course, in Germany (*der* Mond), so that Kandinsky was drawn to its Latin title, 'Luna'.[55] At the Dessau Bauhaus, with its more decisively modern and technological orientation, he was now taking a more detached view of 'the theosophists', and made much more reference to the ideas of Wilhelm Ostwald, the best-known of German scientific colour theorists, to Wundt and to the more recent school of Gestalt psychology. But in an institution where the systems of Runge and Ostwald were given equal attention, Kandinsky was also investing the abstract categories of German Romantic colour with new vitality.[56]

John Gage

1 K. Schwitters, *Das Literarische Werk*, ed. F. Lach, I, (Cologne, 1973), 150. The first German version, *Die Blume Anna (Der Sturm*, XIII/2 March 1922 176, in *ibid.* I, 292) runs:
 '... Preisfrage:
 1. Anna Blume hat ein Vogel.
 2. Anna Blume ist rot.
 3. Welche Farbe hat der Vogel?
 Blau ist die Farbe seines gelben Haares.
 Rot ist das Girren deines grünen Vogels.
 Du schlichtes Mädchen im Alltagskleid, du
 liebes grünes Tier, ich liebe dir...'
2 I have traced some of the French developments in *Colour and Culture: Practice and Meaning from Antiquity to Abstraction*, (London 1993), pp. 191–201, 209–12, 222; for Goethe's immediate supporters, 202–3.
3 Novalis, *Schriften*, ed. P. Kluckhohn and R. Samuel, I, (Stuttgart, 1960), 195–7. Subsequent references in the text and notes are to this edition.
4 W. Wackenroder, 'Die Farben', in *Phantasien über die Kunst*, ed. L. Tieck (1799), repr. W.H. Wackenroder, *Werke und Briefe*, ed. F. von der Leyen (Berlin, 1967), 195f.
5 H. Steffens, 'Über die Bedeutung der Farben in der Natur', in P.O. Runge, *Farben-Kugel* (Hamburg, 1810; repr. 1977), 59. C.K. Sprengel, *Das entdeckte Geheimniss der Natur*, ed. P. Knuth (Leipzig, 1894) I: 9 (Myosotis): 89 (Iris).
6 Johann Wolfgang von Goethe, *Farbenlehre* (1810) § 626.
7 A. Leslie Willson, 'The *Blaue Blume*: a new dimension', *Germanic Review*, 34 (1959), 57. Willson's article reviews the earlier identifications of the blue flower. For a well-illustrated historical study of indigo, see the catalogue of the exhibition, *Sublime Indigo*, Musée de Marseille, 1987.
8 Novalis (as note 3), III, 676.
9 Novalis refers to Werner's system of classification in a note of 1799/1800 (as note 3) III, 259. The Wernerian terminology was introduced in *Von den äusserlichen Kennzeichen der Fossilien* (1774; English translation, Dublin 1805), 36–72. Werner noted that flowers were a good example of standard colours, and the majority of his blues, the rarest colour among minerals, had pigment or flower names (1805, 49ff.). Novalis's notes on colour from Werner are as note 3, III: 147–56.
10 Novalis (as note 3) III, 295.
11 Goethe's unpublished essay on coloured shadows had been composed in 1793 (*Leopoldina Ausgabe der Schriften zur Naturwissenschaft*, I Abt. 3, ed. R. Matthaei (Weimar, 1951) 66). A reference to Goethe's optical work in a letter from Caroline and A.W. Schlegel to Novalis of February 1799, in *Schriften*, IV (1975) 523, suggests that the young writer was familiar with these researches.
12 For Novalis's scheme of opposites (as note 3) III, 150, and for another note on colour-polarity, III, 148.
13 Jean-Paul Richter, *The Secret Society (Die unsichtbare Loge)*, 1793, I Theil, 20 Sektor, in *Sämtliche Werke*, ed. E. Berend, I/2 (Weimar, 1927), 165–6. Novalis had read the novel by the end of 1795 (as note 3) IV, 406.
14 J.W. Goethe (as note 6) Didactic Part § 781.
15 Steffens (as note 5) 48f. For Steffens and Runge, J. Gage, 'Runge, *Goethe and the Farbenkugel*', in Hamburger Kunsthalle, *Runge Fragen und Antworten* (Munich, 1979), 62–5.
16 J.W. von Goethe (as note 3) Didactic Part, § 696.
17 Gage (as note 15), 64.
18 J.G. Herder, *Kalligone* (1800), ed. H. Begenau, (Weimar, 1955), 32.
19 F.H. Lehr, *Die Blütezeit romantischer Bildkunst: Franz Pforr, der meister des Lukasbundes* (Marburg, 1924), 275–7. See also the discussion in B. Rehfus-Dechêne, *Farbengebung und Farbenlehre in der deutschen Malerei um 1800*, (Munich, 1982), 108. For the red hair of the Jews, R. Mellinkoff, 'Judas' red hair and the Jews', *Journal of Jewish Art*, IX, (1983), 31–46.
20 Colour plate in K. Andrews, *The Nazarenes* (Oxford, 1964), pl. 2.
21 K. Andrews (as note 20), pl. 3. The letter is published in A. Kuhn, *Peter Cornelius und die geistigen Strömungen seiner Zeit* (Berlin, 1921), 98–9.
22 J.W. von Goethe (as note 6) § 836. For Goethe and the Nazarenes, C. Lenz, 'Goethe und die Nazarener' in Frankfurt, Städel, *Die Nazarener* (Frankfurt am Main, 1977), 295–315.
23 For the description, Lehr (as note 19), 286–92. Lehr points out the changes of mind.
24 J.W. von Goethe (as note 6), § 840.
25 See now P.F.H. Lauxtermann, 'Hegel and Schopenhauer as partisans of Goethe's Theory of Color', *Journal of the History of Ideas*, (1990), 51.
26 A. Cornill, *Johann David Passavant*, I (Frankfurt am Main, 1864), 56; O. Dammann, 'Goethe und C.F. Schlosser', *Jahrbuch der Goethe-Gesellschaft*, 16, (Weimar, 1930), 54f. For Schlosser's close contact with Overbeck and Pforr in Rome, M. Howitt, *Friedrich Overbeck: Sein Leben und Schaffen*, I (Freiburg, 1886, repr. 1971), 189–90, 219, 228–9.
27 W. Schadow, 'Meine Gedanken über eine folgerichtige Ausbildung des Malers', *Berliner Kunstblatt*, I (1828), 266, 270. I am much indebted to Robin Middleton and W. O'Malley for access to this rare periodical. For Schadow's career, K. Gallwitz (ed.) *Die Nazarener in Rom: ein deutscher Künstlerbund der Romantik* (Munich, 1981), 220–6. For the unteachability of colour, J. Gage, *Colour in Turner: Poetry and Truth*, (London, 1969), 11–12, and for Goethe's own reluctance to include colour in art-school teaching, Gage (as note 2), 202–3.
28 J.K. Bähr, *Der dynamische Kreis*, (Dresden, 1860), 6f. 228. Bähr, who had been in touch with the Nazarenes in Rome in the 1820s, and was now teaching at the Dresden Academy, also published *Vorträge über Newton und Goethes Farbenlehre*, (Dresden, 1863). He tells us that Karl Beckmann, Professor of Architecture and Perspective at the Berlin Academy, was an enthusiastic follower of Goethe and that other artists welcomed the most substantial new attempt to vindicate his ideas: F. Grävell, *Goethe im Recht gegen Newton* (Berlin, 1857).
29 Schadow (as note 27), 271. The abstractness of the pictorial surface around 1800 was noted by T. Hetzer and by W. Schöne: W. Schöne, *Über das Licht in der Malerei* (Berlin, 3rd ed. 1979), 214 n. 391.
30 M. Bunge, *Max Liebermann als Künstler der Farbe* (1990), 52–5. Impasto outdoor painting goes back of course in Germany to Georg von Dillis, J.C.C. Dahl and Adolf Menzel among others in the early part of the century.
31 H.G. Müller, 'Künstlerfarbenmanufakturen im 19. Jahrhundert' in H. Althöfer (ed.), *Das 19. Jahrhundert in der Restaurierung* (1987), 231–2. For Böcklin, H. Kühn, 'Technische Studien zur Malerei Böcklins' in R. Andree, *Arnold Böcklin: Die Gemälde* (Basel and Munich, 1977), 106–127.
32 For simultaneous and complementary contrasts, Kühn (as note 31), 108; H. Rebsamen, 'Farbe im Sinnbild: Arnold Böcklins "Heimkehr" 1887', in M. Hering-Mitgau et al. (eds.) *Von Farbe und Farben: Albert Knoepfli zum 70. Geburtstag*, (Zurich, 1980), 360; H. Althöfer, 'Arnold Böcklin – Maltechniker und Kolorist', in Althöfer (ed.) (as note 31), 196–7. W. von Bezold, *Die Farbenlehre im Hinblick auf Kunst und Kunstgewerbe* (1874; American ed. *The Theory of Color in its relation to Art and Art-Industry*, Boston, 1876), esp. ch. IV. For gold frames, Althöfer (as note 31); Bezold 1876, 43. Böcklin's

contact with Bezold is documented by E. Berger (ed.), *Böcklins Technik* (1906) Sammlung Maltechnischer Schriften I, 103f.

33 For Stuck on the spatial effect of 'warm' and 'cool' colours, J. Albers in H. Voss, *Franz von Stuck 1863–1928: Werkkatalog der Gemälde mit einer Einführung in seinen Symbolismus* (Munich, 1973), 66, 89 n. 288. Cf. Bezold (as note 32), 113, 197–8, 231. Albers gives a brief account of the 'Bezold-effect' in *Interaction of Color* (German ed. 1970; New Haven, paperback ed. 1979), XIII.

34 For Böcklin and the *Farbenlehre*, Rebsamen, (as note 32). For his colour-equivalents, A. Reinle and J. Gantner, *Kunstgeschichte der Schweiz*, IV (Frauenfeld, 1962), 217.

35 Voss as note 33, p. 59.

36 F. Naumann, 'Experimentelle Malerei', *Hilfe*, 12 (1906), in *Werke*, ed. H. Ladendorf, VI, (Cologne, 1969), 57.

37 J. Cohn, 'Experimentelle Untersuchungen über die Gefühlsbetonung der Farbhelligkeiten und ihrer Combinationen', *Philosophische Studien*, X (1894), 601.

38 F. Stefănescu-Goangă, 'Experimentelle Untersuchungen zur Gefühlsbetonung der Farben', *Psychologische Studien*, VII (1912), 287f.

39 F. Stefănescu-Goangă 309. For association as a secondary colour effect, *ibid.* and p. 332.

40 K. Scheffler, 'Notizen über die Farbe' *Dekorative Kunst*, IV, II Heft (1901), 190. On chromotherapy and *audition colorée*, 187, Scheffler saw Böcklin as the greatest modern colourist. Kandinsky mentioned his article in a note to Ch. VI of *On the Spiritual in Art* (1912). For his interest in chromotherapy, synaesthesia and the non-associative effects of colour, *ibid*, Ch. V. One of the most outspoken arguments for the idea that the affects of colour, even in chromotherapy, were largely associative came from an art historian turned psychologist: R. Müller-Freienfels, 'Zur Theorie der Gefühlstöne der Farbenempfindungen', *Zeitschrift für Psychologie*, 46 (1907), 241–74.

41 W. Kandinsky, *Complete Writings on Art*, ed. K.C. Lindsay and P. Vergo, I (London, 1982), 181–2.

42 A. Besant and C.W. Leadbeater, *Thought Forms* (London, 6th repr. 1961), 21.

43 See references gathered in Gage (as note 2) 298 n. 89 (Germ ed. 302 n. 89).

44 Kandinsky (as note 41) II: 747; see also W. Kandinsky and F. Marc (eds.) *Der Blaue Reiter* (Dokumentarische Neuausgabe von K. Lankheit) (Munich, 3 Aufl. 1979), 263.

45 Gage (as note 2) 207 (both eds.) Marc may have been stimulated by Runge, although of course his gender scheme is opposite to Runge's, since the Romantic artist had been included in the 1906 Deutsche *Jahrhundert-Ausstellung* in Berlin and his approach to colour, at once mystical and scientific, had been celebrated in the catalogue by Hugo von Tschudi, who became close to the Blue Rider group in Munich, and to whom they dedicated the almanac. See *Ausstellung deutscher Kunst aus der Zeit von 1775–1875* (Berlin 1906), I, xix repr. in H. von Tschudi, *Gesammelte Schriften zur neueren Kunst*, ed. E. Schwedeler-Meyer (Munich, 1912), 191.

46 Stefănescu-Goangă (as note 38), 320.

47 D. Schmidt, *Manifeste Manifeste, 1905–33*, I (Dresden, 1964), 82.

48 For Brass, Gage (as note 2) 207. For Kirchner, see esp. Groninger Museum, *Goethe, Kirchner, Wiegers. De Invloed van Goethe's Kleurenleer*, (2nd printing 1985).

49 J.W. von Goethe (as note 6) Didactic Part § 75.

50 F. Marc, letter of 14 February 1911 in W. Macke (ed.), *August Macke – Franz Marc Briefwechsel* (Cologne, 1964). Marc's painting, *Liegender Hund im Schnee* now in the Städelsches Kunstinstitut in Frankfurt, is in K. Lankheit, *Franz Marc: Katalog der Werke* (Cologne, 1970), no. 133.

51 S. Friedländer, 'Nochmals Polarität', *Der Sturm* (1916) VI, 88; 'Das Prisma und Goethes Farbenlehre', *Der Sturm*, VIII (1917–8), 141–2.

52 A. Segal, 'Das Lichtproblem in der Malerei', in A. Segal and N. Braun, *Lichtprobleme der bildenden Kunst* (Berlin, 1925), n.p. The essay is dedicated to Friedländer-Mynona, who also contributed an article, 'Goethes Farbenlehre und die moderne Malerei' to the catalogue, *Sammlung Gabrielson Götheborg, 1922–3*, which included two works by Segal. The only recent discussions of Segal seems to be N. Lynton, 'Arthur Segal and German Cubism', *Studio International*, July/August 1969, pp. 22–4, F. Whitford, 'Arthur Segal and German Expressionism', in 'Arthur Segal: Woodcuts', Ashmolean Museum, Oxford 1977 and N. Lynton, 'Introduction' to 'Arthur Segal 1875–1944',

Fischer Fine Art, London 1978; and perhaps the only readily accessible colour-reproductions are in Sotheby's catalogue, *Twenty-Five Works by Arthur Segal* (London, 16 April 1970), esp. lots 7, 11.

53 J.W. von Goethe (as note 6), Didactic Part, § 517–23.

54 W. Kandinsky, *Cours du Bauhaus*, ed. P. Sers (Paris, 1984), 46–7, from Goethe (as note 6) § 765–94; cf. also 65. These notes have still to be published in their original German and in an annotated edition. For *Yellow-Red-Blue* C. Derouet and J. Boissel, *Oeuvres de Vassily Kandinsky (1866–1944)* (Paris, 1984), no. 331 (repr. in colour). See also C.V. Poling, *Kandinsky Unterricht am Bauhaus* (Weingarten, 1982) 58f. (English ed. 1987).

55 Kandinsky (as note 54), 53, and for 'Luna', 65.

56 For Runge's great reputation as a colour-theorist at the Bauhaus, J. Traeger, *Philipp Otto Runge und sein Werk* (Munich, 1975), 195–7; H. Matile, *Die Farbenlehre Philipp Otto Runges* (Mittenwald, 2nd ed. 1977), 281–99. For Ostwald at the Bauhaus, Gage (as note 2), 259–262 (both eds.).

Music and the Visual Arts

One striking feature of German Romanticism is the seemingly unbounded, and almost universal, admiration for music. Inasmuch as specific analogies were drawn between music and the visual arts, these were usually intended to demonstrate the imagined superiority of the former;[1] indeed, by comparison with all other forms of art, music was widely thought to possess a number of quite definite advantages of which two, in particular, were emphasized. The first was its non-material aspect: Goethe, for example, extolled music because it had, in his words, 'no material that need be discounted'.[2] By material (*Stoff*) he meant on the one hand substance, the fact that music is not 'weighed down' by any material embodiment, on the other hand subject-matter or narrative. With the gradually diminishing importance of the narrative or didactic subject in painting, music's freedom from a ponderous repertory of moral or heroic or generally edifying subjects was something artists especially admired. The second was its direct appeal to the emotions. The writer Wilhelm Heinse, author of *Ardinghello*, observed that no other art 'affected the soul as directly as does music; as if it and the soul are one and the same nature, so immediately and completely are they united. Painting, sculpture and architecture are lifeless by comparison … .'[3] Similar arguments concerning the essentially 'spiritual' or 'emotive' character of music were advanced by numerous writers on art from the late eighteenth century onwards.[4]

A generation later, music's claim to superiority was given new authority by the philosopher Arthur Schopenhauer. In places Schopenhauer is reliant on an older tradition of discourse, as when he points to the 'mathematical' aspect of music, by which he means its apparently God-given orderliness, its instrinsic principles of harmony and proportion.[5] But he also places music in an entirely different category from other art forms for metaphysical as well as physical reasons, seeing it as analogous to the Platonic ideas which, in his eyes, were the true objects of art. His writings were extraordinarily influential, not least on account of the beauty and lucidity of his style. His reflection on the unique role of the composer, for example, who 'reveals the innermost essence of the world, expressing the profoundest wisdom in a language our reason is incapable of understanding, like a galvanized sleepwalker offering an insight into things of which, waking, reason has no conception'[6] presages Wagner's description of the incomparable power of 'purely musical expression' which 'affects the listener's innermost being … must appear to us like a revelation from a completely different world; in truth reveals to us relationships between the phenomena of existence utterly foreign to those of everyday logic – connections which undeniably impress themselves upon us with such overwhelming conviction, and which give such definite form to our emotions, that logical reasoning is thereby entirely bemused and disarmed.'[7] And almost a century later, the composer Arnold Schoenberg, who was at the same time a dedicated (even if self-taught) painter, was to reproduce verbatim the above-quoted passage from Schopenhauer in his article 'The Relationship to the Text' published in that famous 'synthetic' publication, the *Blue Rider Almanac* of 1912[8] – evidence of the continuing influence of the philosopher's ideas among artists of the Expressionist generation.

Echoes of Schopenhauer and of Goethe, of German Idealist philosophy generally, pervade much of German Romantic writing about music and art. E.T.A. Hoffmann virtually paraphrases Goethe when he writes that 'no other art proceeds so directly from the inner, spiritual nature of man, no other art is so exclusively reliant on purely spiritual, ethereal means'.[9] Not infrequently, comparisons or analogies between music and other art forms are exaggerated almost to the point of caricature. Gottfried Keller has the principal character of his *Bildungsroman, Der Grüne Heinrich*, recite, not without irony, passages from an (imaginary?) review of a symphony in which the critic describes the 'warmth of colour, division of light and shade, the shadows of the lower notes, blurred horizon of the accompaniment, transparent chiaroscuro of the inner parts, the bold contours of the finale ... .'[10] But perhaps the most remarkable passage of writing of this kind is to be found in Adalbert Stifter's essay of 1842 in which he describes an eclipse of the sun, an experience which he set down in what we, ahistorically, might be tempted to describe as purely synaesthetic terms: ' ... this inexpressibly tragic music composed of colours and lights, which pervaded the entire sky – a requiem, a *dies irae* such as to break one's heart ... might one not imagine a music for the eye, created out of the simultaneous or successive juxtaposition of lights and colours, in just the same way that sounds create music for the ear ... should it not be possible for harmony and melody of light to provoke a total effect as powerful and moving as that created by sound? I, at least, could think of no symphony, oratorio or the like composed of such noble music as those few minutes of light and colour in the sky.'[11]

Interestingly, this call for a new art of coloured light which might appeal to the eye as hitherto music had appealed to the ear was to be answered – though not for another fifty years. Not until nearly the end of the nineteenth century did the invention of electricity make possible the artificial equivalent of the phenomenon Stifter had witnessed: colour-light performances, which consisted of projecting coloured lights on to a screen or the walls of an auditorium by means of powerful lenses and even more powerful lamps, often to the accompaniment of music – manifestations which, for a time, vied in popularity with the early cinema.[12]

By contrast with the exalted tone and exaggerated metaphors of much of German Romantic writing about music and art, nineteenth-century experiments at creating 'musical paintings' or incorporating musical principles into painting often seem hesitant or inconclusive. The painter Moritz von Schwind, in his youth a close friend of Franz Schubert in Vienna, executed a painting entitled *Symphony*, which he referred to as 'my musical picture', based not only on the supposed 'narrative' of Beethoven's *Choral Fantasia* but also on its musical structure: 'the overall composition is more complex still, falling into four parts analogous to the movements of a symphony.'[13] He also projected a cycle of wall paintings (unrealized) for a room in which works by Schubert were to be performed, each wall devoted to the principal poets who had provided the texts for the composer's

Fig.1 Max Klinger *Accord*, plate 1 of *Brahms-Phantasie*, Opus XII, 1894, engraving

songs: Mayrhofer, Goethe, Schiller and the German Romantics. Though these attempts at 'musical painting' remain, in the end, somewhat pedestrian, Schwind's scheme for a 'Schubert room' has an important precedent in Philipp Otto Runge's likewise unrealized project for a cycle of pictures, *The Times of Day*, which he dreamed of installing in a Gothic temple-like structure in which the paintings were to be viewed to the accompaniment of music.[14] These projected paintings, which Runge, too, described as having been composed 'like a symphony',[15] are remarkable in that the artist clearly envisaged an interaction of different kinds of aesthetic experience, 'an abstract, pictorial musical fantasy of a poem with choruses, a composition for all three arts together, and architecture should contribute a special building in which to house it'.[16] On the one hand, this notion of a coming-together or synthesis of different forms of art foreshadows Richard Wagner's ambition to reunite the different arts, long separated (as he saw it) from one another, in the service of a new art form, soon to become known as 'music drama'.[17] On the other, Runge's idea of a group of related paintings all 'responding' to one another or 'in tune' with one another provides the starting point for a long tradition of 'cyclical' works inspired by music such as Max Klinger's graphic cycle *Brahms-Phantasie* (fig. 1).

Any attempt to assess adequately Wagner's significance for the later Romantic movement would far exceed the limits of this short essay. Quite apart from the impact of his musical and dramatic innovations, his ideas – long-winded though his writing may seem to us – exerted an extraordinary influence on subsequent generations (though it must be said that a number of artists – Schwind, Anselm Feuerbach and Arnold Böcklin among them – were stubbornly hostile to Wagner and everything he stood for). He was an important link in the chain by which Schopenhauerian notions were communicated to the later nineteenth century. Many artists who probably never read Schopenhauer in the original can be shown to have read Wagner's celebrated essay on Beethoven of 1870, which consists partly of an extended and elegant paraphrase of the philosopher's ideas. Wagner's conception of the operatic stage as a forum or meeting place for the different arts, his notion of the *Gesamtkunstwerk* or 'total work of art' – one art form reinforcing the impact of another (and hence of the drama overall, drama rather than music being seen as the highest form of art)[18] – also encouraged artists to try their hand at a variety of media, rather than limiting themselves to a single art form. The stage experiments of Kandinsky, Kokoschka and Schoenberg were all, in their various ways, answers to the Wagnerian call for a new form of 'synthetic' art for which the theatre provided both the vehicle and the showcase. Kandinsky, who rarely acknowledged his intellectual sources, devotes considerable space to a discussion of Wagner's ideas in his essay 'On Stage Composition', published in the *Blue Rider Almanac* as a preface to his play *Yellow Sound*[19] – though he takes issue with Wagner on a number of specific points, not least what Kandinsky sees as the 'materialistic' character of the Wagnerian leitmotif.

By the end of the nineteenth century, there existed growing numbers of works of visual art which sought to 'illustrate' musical themes, or to evoke particular emotional states, as music was thought to do, or even claimed to be a kind of visual paraphrase or translation of specific works of music. Mention has already been made of Klinger's *Brahms-Phantasie* which, in the end, does little more than juxtapose startlingly literal images, some (though by no means all) relating to music and musical performance, with almost surreal landscape visions.[20] More specific in its attempt to devise a visual equivalent for a particular piece of music is the frieze which Klimt created for the fourteenth exhibition of the Vienna Secession (1902),[21] an exhibition which had as its centrepiece Klinger's recently completed polychrome

Fig.2 Gustav Klimt, *Beethoven Frieze* 1902, view of final section ('Diesen Kuß der ganzen Welt'), Österreichische Galerie, Vienna

sculpture of Beethoven. While the exhibition itself was undoubtedly conceived as a 'total work of art',[22] Klimt's *Beethoven Frieze* takes as its starting point the composer's Ninth Symphony – indeed, even more specifically, its final movement, which includes a choral setting of Schiller's 'Ode to Joy'. The progression of the desires and aspirations of 'weak humanity' as described in the catalogue,[23] symbolized by the 'floating forms' which occupy the upper part of the frieze, may well have been intended to mirror the progress of the 'joy' theme in the finale of the Choral Symphony, the musical transformations which it undergoes and the interruptions it suffers before returning in jubilant apotheosis in the last bars of the movement (fig. 2).

Despite its underlying 'musical' programme, Klimt's *Beethoven Frieze* is still couched (as is Klinger's *Brahms-Phantasie*) in surprisingly representational language, given that there existed by the early 1900s a considerable body of theory which pointed to the possibility of an abstract, expressive vocabulary of line and form which might parallel the 'abstract', evocative power of music. The *Jugendstil* theorist and designer August Endell, in a statement which appears to foretell many of Kandinsky's later utterances, wrote of his vision of an art which would 'mean nothing and depict nothing and recall nothing, and yet affect our souls as deeply, as powerfully as only the tones of music are capable of doing'.[24] This notion is repeated again and again not only by designers but also by *Jugendstil*-influenced artists such as Adolf Hoelzel and his pupil Johannes Itten, both of whom made significant experiments with abstraction. It is, however, worth remarking that Endell's 'prophecy' relates specifically to an abstract art of *ornament* (which, in any case, already existed); whereas Kandinsky, who was concerned with the possibility of abstract *painting*, was apprehensive about what he termed the 'danger of ornamental form', fearing that a kind of painting bereft of objects or any form of representation might degenerate into mere pattern-making, 'like a tie or a carpet'.[25] Though he may well have been interested in, and even influenced by, the theories of the Munich *Jugendstil* designers, their ideas could not offer an adequate justification for a wholly non-representational art,[26] and he also turned to the nineteenth-century tradition in German philosophy for an answer to the question which tormented him for so many years: 'what is to replace the missing object?'[27]

In the *Blue Rider Almanac*, Kandinsky reproduces Goethe's aphorism to the effect that 'painting lacked any knowledge of the 'ground base' (*Generalbass*), of any accepted, approved theory such has long since existed in the case of music'.[28] The choice of quotation is telling. Goethe is here pointing, not to the abstract character of music, but to its inherent orderliness, its recourse to system: a matter of some importance to Kandinsky, clearly concerned that painting without objects might lay itself open to the charge of incoherence. It was this concern which led him to take a lively interest in the new music of Schoenberg and his pupils, likewise published (in musical facsimile) in the *Blue Rider Almanac*, and especially in the principles underlying such unconventional methods of composition. In his treatise *On the Spiritual in Art*, he cites – not without envy – Schoenberg's conviction that there existed 'certain conditions that govern whether I choose this or that dissonance', even if these were incapable of being defined at present.[29] Moreover, despite a somewhat shaky grasp of musical theory, Kandinsky set himself to study and indeed translate (into Russian) passages from Schoenberg's *Treatise on Harmony* of 1911, no doubt in the hope that the composer's justifications for the abandonment of the tonal principle might offer a model after which a similar justification for the abandonment of representation in painting might be formulated.[30]

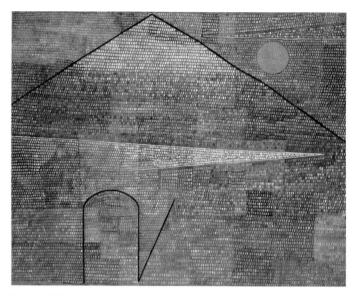

Fig.3 Paul Klee, *Ad Parnassum* 1932, Paul-Klee-Stiftung, Kunstmuseum Berne

Kandinsky was the only one of the Blue Rider artists in Munich prior to the First World War to pursue abstraction consistently as a clearly defined, even if distant and problematic goal. He was also the only member of the group to attempt the creation of a 'synthetic' art in the form of his stage compositions: not only *Yellow Sound*, but also *Black and White, Green Sound, Violet*, all of which are partly rooted (as their titles suggest) in his own preoccupation with synaesthetic experience.[31] The remaining members, on the other hand, though they did little more than experiment in a somewhat desultory fashion with abstraction, were for the most part greatly interested in music and the possibility of applying musical principles to painting. Both Franz Marc and August Macke were much occupied with the underlying systematic character of music. Marc, describing in a letter to Macke the famous concert of Schoenberg's music held in Munich in January 1911 and which the Blue Rider artists (including Kandinsky) all attended, attempted to apply Schoenberg's notion of 'unresolved dissonance' to his own use of complementary and non-complementary colours.[32] Macke, in a letter of 1907 to his fiancée, wrote of the 'undreamed of power one would possess, if only one could organize colours into a system, like notes';[33] he also created 'fugal' paintings, or paintings intended specifically as a homage to Bach – abstract colour compositions whose starting point shows clearly his preoccupation with music's principles of formal organization.[34]

Of the artists associated with the Blue Rider group in Munich at this time it was, however, Paul Klee who over a number of years developed perhaps the most sophisticated and detailed analogies between visual art and music,[35] drawing extensively on musical theory in the context of his teaching at the Bauhaus during the 1920s, and creating a considerable number of 'musical' paintings of quite different kinds. Some, like his famous *Ad Parnassum* (1932) (fig. 3), are concerned with translating the contrapuntal structures of eighteenth-century music into visual terms (as its title, an allusion to Johann Josef Fux's treatise on counterpoint *Gradus ad Parnassum* of 1725, implies). Others make specific allusion to particular pieces of music – scenes from named operas, for example – or depict musicians or instruments, often metamorphosed into humorous or grotesque form. Yet others take as their starting point music's graphic aspect, incorporating notational symbols such as the treble clef or the *fermata*[36] or even mimicking the layout of notes and stave as they appear in the written score. Of these, one of the most interesting and complex is his 'two-part' *Einst dem Grau der Nacht enttaucht* (Once Surfaced from the Grey of Night) (fig. 4) which, it has been pointed out, 'sets' the text of a poem to colour, rather as a composer 'sets' the words of a song to music,[37] but which is at the same time a translation into visual terms of the way in which two voices – for example, of a fugue or canon – might be laid out on the page, based quite possibly on a two-part invention by Bach – a composer whom Klee greatly admired and whose work he often took as a starting point for his graphic deliberations.

Klee also sought visual equivalents for rhythm and measure and, like Adolf Hoelzel, Josef Albers and many other painters, created 'fugue' paintings,[38] of which the best known is his *Fugue in Red* of 1921.[39] He showed, on the other hand, as little interest as Marc or Macke in seeking some pictorial equivalent for the purely evocative aspect of music, its capacity to conjure up particular emotions or dream-like states. Nor did he give much credence to the notion of the *Gesamtkunstwerk*, or attempt to create 'synthetic' stage works, as Kandinsky had done. None the less, he shared with Kandinsky the profound conviction that the burden of the relationship between visual art and music lay, not in attempting to

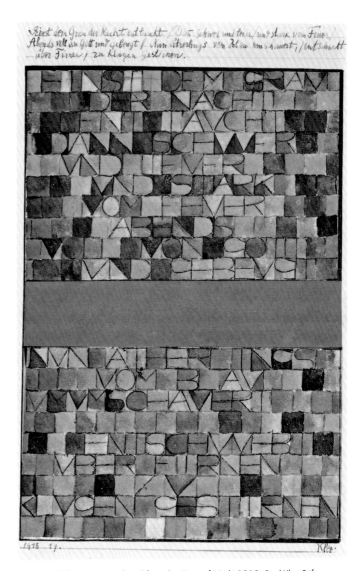

Fig.4 Paul Klee, *Once Surfaced from the Grey of Night* 1918, Paul-Klee-Stiftung, Kunstmuseum Berne

find some system of equivalence between colours and musical tones, but in the fact that both colour and music were capable, as Goethe had insisted, of being 'referred back to a universal formula ... both are derivable, though each from itself, from this higher law'.[40]

Klee's experiments seem in retrospect to unite in a quite remarkable way several of the most important 'musical' tendencies in modern art. Many twentieth-century artists displayed a fascination with the music of Bach, seeing in his works the epitome of those principles of organization and order which, for them, music symbolized. Some went so far as to create specific 'representations' or 'depictions' of Bach's music, as in the case of Heinrich Neugeboren's monumental sculpture entitled

Plastic Representation of Bars 52–55 of the Fugue in E-flat by J.S. Bach (model, 1928).[41] Others, among them artists such as John Cage or Sigmar Polke, like Klee exploited the graphic aspect of music by transforming notes or staves into visual representations,[42] bearing little if any relation to actual performance. Cage, on the other hand, who repeatedly acknowledged Klee's 'inspiration', as a composer and performer in his own right also provides a link between the development of German Expressionism (of which Klee might be regarded as a somewhat belated – even if distant and uncommitted – representative) and those later artists who occupied themselves more with the performance aspect of music, and with staged 'events' of various kinds. Of these, the most notable manifestations were the celebrated Fluxus-concerts and 'happenings' of the mid-1960s – a tradition which draws, in the end, more on Futurism than on Expressionism or on the example of artists working in Germany in the earlier part of this century.

Peter Vergo

1 There is an extensive literature on earlier forms of comparison between music and the visual arts, for example R. Wittkower, *Architectural Principles in the Age of Humanism* (3rd ed. London, 1962); E. Winternitz, 'Leonardo and music', in L. Reti (ed.), *The Unknown Leonardo* (New York, 1974); J. Onians, 'On how to listen to High Renaissance art', *Art History* (1984), vii, 410–37; A. Alfassa, 'L'origine de la lettre de Poussin sur les modes ...', *Bulletin de la Société de l'Histoire de l'Art français* (1933), 125–43; J. Bialostocki, 'Das Modusproblem in den bildenden Künsten' *Zeitschrift für Kunstgeschichte* (1961) xxiv, 128–41. See also R.W. Lee, *Ut pictura poesis: the humanistic theory of painting* (New York, 1967); T. Puttfarken, *Roger de Piles' theory of art* (New Haven/London, 1985).

2 Jutta Hecker (ed.), *J.W. von Goethe. Maximen und Reflexionen* (Leipzig, 1941), no. 486.

3 Letter to Jacobi, 22 November 1780, quoted after Franzsepp Würtenberger, *Malerei und Musik. Die Geschichte des Verhaltens zweier Künste zueinander* (Frankfurt a.M./Bern/Las Vegas, 1979), 13.

4 Compare, for example, F. Schlegel, who described music as 'far more elevated than the visual arts', or Wackenroder, who in his *Herzensergiessungen eines kunstliebenden Klosterbruders* ascribed to music 'first place, alongside theology, amongst all the human arts and sciences'; quoted in M. Lingner, 'Der Ursprung des Gesamtkunstwerkes aus der Unmöglichkeit "Absoluter Kunst"', in the catalogue *Der Hang zum Gesamtkunstwerk*, ed. H. Szeemann (Zurich, 1983), 52 f. Wackenroder, in his essay *'Die Wunder der Tonkunst'*, also extols music's unique capacity to translate the spirit directly: 'Language counts and names and describes its transformation in an alien medium; music pours out to us the thing itself'; quoted in H.R. Rookmaker, *Gauguin & 19th Century Art Theory* (Amsterdam, 1972), 212.

5 In this context, Schopenhauer writes that music derives a 'kind of certitude from the fact that its forms can be referred back to quite definite laws, expressible in mathematical terms, from which it can never depart without altogether ceasing to be music.' He also quotes Leibniz's famous definition of music as a 'secret exercise in mathematics performed by a mind unaware of

the fact that it is counting' [*exercitium mathematicae occultum nescientis se numerare animi*]: see Arthur Schopenhauer, *Die Welt als Wille und Vorstellung* (1818 and subsequent editions), III, para 52.

6 Schopenhauer (as note 5).

7 R. Wagner, 'Zukunftsmusik' (1860), quoted in W. Golther (ed.), *Richard Wagner, Gesammelte Schriften und Dichtungen*, VII (Berlin/Leipzig, n.d.), 110.

8 Arnold Schoenberg, 'Das Verhältnis zum Text', in W. Kandinsky and Franz Marc (eds.), *Der Blaue Reiter* (Munich, 1912), 28.

9 'Alte und moderne Kirchenmusik' (1814), quoted in Würtenberger (as note 3), 17.

10 Gottfried Keller, 'Der Grüne Heinrich', III, ch. 11, quoted in Otto Stelzer, *Die Vorgeschichte der abstrakten Kunst. Denkmodelle und Vorbilder* (Munich, 1964), 54.

11 'Die Sonnenfinsternis am 8. Juli 1842', in Adalbert Stifter, *Wien/Die Sonnenfinsternis* (Stuttgart, 1963), 79, 81.

12 They were also taken very seriously by writers on art. One of the most influential early surveys of avant-garde painting devoted a whole chapter to the art of 'colour music': see Arthur J. Eddy, *Cubists and Post-Impressionism* (Chicago, 1915); also A. Wallace Rimington, *Colour Music. The Art of Mobile Colour* (London, 1912); A.B. Klein, *Colour Music. The Art of Light* (London, 1926). The relationship between colour-light performances and the early evolution of film is discussed by Sara Selwood, 'Farblichtmusik und abstrakter Film', in Karin von Maur (ed.), *Vom Klang der Bilder. Musik in der Kunst des 20. Jahrhunderts* (Munich, 1985), 414–21.

13 O. Stoessl, *Moritz von Schwind. Briefe* (Leipzig, n.d.), 250 (letter of 24 November 1849); quoted in Würtenberger (as note 3).

14 See William Vaughan, *German Romantic Painting* (New Haven/London, 1980), 49 f; also J. Traeger, *Philipp Otto Runge und sein Werk. Monographie und kritischer Katalog* (Munich, 1975).

15 Runge, letter to his brother Daniel, 30 January 1803, quoted in Hannelore Gärtner (ed.), *Philipp Otto Runge: Die Begier nach der Möglichkeit neuer Bilder. Briefwechsel und Schriften zur bildenden Kunst* (Leipzig, 1978), 130 f.

16 Runge, letter dated 22 February 1803; quoted in Ulrich Finke, *German Painting from Romanticism to Expressionism* (London, 1974), 20.

17 For a detailed comparison between Runge and Wagner, see the essay by M. Linger (as note 4).

18 R. Wagner, 'Das Kunstwerk der Zukunft' (1850), in W. Golther (ed.) (as note 7) III, 162. On the origins of Wagner's notion of the *Gesamtkunstwerk*, and the subsequent misunderstandings and misinterpretations to which this term was subjected, see the introduction by H. Szeemann to the catalogue *Der Hang zum Gesamtkunstwerk* (Zurich, 1983); also P. Vergo, 'The Origins of Expressionism and the notion of the *Gesamtkunstwerk*', in S. Behr, D. Fanning, D. Jarman (eds), *Expressionism Reassessed* (Manchester, 1993), 11–19.

19 *Der Blaue Reiter*, 103 f.

20 On Klinger's relationship with music in general, and with Brahms in particular, see Hellmuth Christian Wolff, 'Max Klingers Verhältnis zur Musik', in the catalogue *Max Klinger. Wege zum Gesamtkunstwerk* (Mainz a.R., 1984), 81–90.

21 See Marian Bizanz-Prakken, *Gustav Klimt. Der Beethovenfries: Geschichte, Funktion und Bedeutung* (Salzburg, 1977); also P. Vergo, *Art in Vienna. Klimt, Kokoschka, Schiele and their contemporaries* (3rd ed. London, 1993), 67f.

22 On the 14th Secession exhibition as *Gesamtkunstwerk* see Ekkehard Mai, *Expositionen. Geschichte und Kritik des Ausstellungswesens* (Munich/Berlin, 1986), 41 f.

23 The catalogue description is reprinted in P. Vergo (as note 21), 70.

24 August Endell, 'Formenschönheit und dekorative Kunst', *Dekorative Kunst* I, no. 1, (1898), 75.

25 Wassily Kandinsky, *Über das Geistige in der Kunst* (1912), trans. in Kenneth C. Lindsay and Peter Vergo (eds.), *Kandinsky. Complete Writings on Art* (Boston/London, 1982), 197.

26 It has been argued that much of Kandinsky's aesthetic theory, as well as his artistic practice, was indebted to the ideas of Munich *Jugendstil*: see Peg Weiss, 'Kandinsky and the "Jugendstil" Arts and Crafts Movement', *Burlington Magazine* CXVII, no. 866, (1975), 270–9, also the same author's

Kandinsky in Munich. The Formative Jugendstil Years (Princeton, 1979). For critical reactions to Weiss's thesis, see Jelena Hahl-Koch, *Kandinsky* (London, 1993), 53, 386.

27 Wassily Kandinsky, 'Rückblicke' (1913), trans. in Lindsay and Vergo (eds) (as note 25), 370.

28 *Der Blaue Reiter*, 42.

29 Lindsay and Vergo (eds) (as note 25), 149.

30 Kandinsky's translation appeared in the catalogue of the exhibition *Salon 2 ...* (Odessa, 1910–11); see Lindsay and Vergo (eds) (as note 25), 91 f.

31 On Kandinsky's stage works, see the article by Jessica Boissel, '"Ces choses-là ont leur propre destin" – Kandinsky et le théâtre expérimental', in the catalogue *Le Cavalier Bleu* (Berne, 1986), 240 f; also Shulamith Behr, 'Deciphering Kandinsky's *Violet*: activist Expressionism and the Russian Slavonic milieu', in Behr Fanning and Jarman (eds) (as note 18), 174–86.

32 W. Macke (ed.), *August Macke – Franz Marc, Briefwechsel* (Cologne, 1964), 40; see also Jelena Hahl-Koch (ed.), *Arnold Schoenberg, Wassily Kandinsky, letters, pictures, and documents* (London, 1984), 135 f.

33 August Macke to Elisabeth Erdmann, letter dated 14.7.1907, quoted in the catalogue *Der Blaue Reiter: Sammlungskatalog 1* (Munich, 2nd ed. 1966), 89.

34 August Macke, *Farbige Komposition I (Hommage à J.S. Bach)*, 1912 (Wilhelm-Hack-Museum, Ludwigshafen).

35 On Klee's relationship with music see the fundamental study by Andrew Kagan, *Paul Klee, art and music* (Ithaca/London, 1983); also Richard Verdi, 'Musical influences on the art of Paul Klee', in *Museum Studies* no. 3, (Chicago, 1968) 81–105; Christian Geelhaar, 'Moderne Malerei und Musik der Klassik – eine Parallele', in the catalogue *Paul Klee. Das Werk der Jahre 1919–1933* (Cologne, 1979), 31–44; Marcel Franciscono, 'La place de la musique dans l'art de Klee: une remise en cause', in the catalogue *Klee et la musique* (Paris, 1985), 19–32.

36 For example Klee's pen and ink drawing *With the fermata* (1918/209); Kunstmuseum, Berne, Paul Klee-Stiftung).

37 Kagan (as note 35), 63.

38 Adolf Hoelzel, *Fuge über ein Auferstehungsthema*, 1916 (Landesmuseum für Kunst- und Kulturgeschichte, Oldenburg); Josef Albers, *Fuge*, 1925 (Kunstmuseum, Basel).

39 1921/69; formerly collection Felix Klee, Berne.

40 See in particular the chapter 'Klee, Goethe, Mozart', in Kagan (as note 35), 145 f; also 38–9.

41 Reproduced in Karin von Maur (ed.) (as note 12), 36, which also includes numerous further examples of 20th-century paintings inspired by Bach; see also the essay by Friedrich Teja Bach, 'Johann Sebastian Bach in der klassichen Moderne', in *ibid*, 328–335.

42 For example Cage's *Score Without Parts*, 1978 (Staatsgalerie Stuttgart, Graphische Sammlung).

The Sublime

Writing in 1970 the literary critic Ronald Taylor insisted that: 'In German culture one may ... legitimately talk of a Romantic tradition which has a central position in the unfolding of the modern German spiritual, intellectual and political life and in the constitution of the national German psyche.' Taylor added: 'It is a complex tradition, drawn from a complex pattern of historical impulses, the reality of whose existence is not disproven by difficulties of definition.'[1] Among the myriad complexities, the aesthetic and emotional engagement with the intangible, the unrepresentable and the unknowable is a recurring element in German painting after 1800 and one which can be identified as a central, even defining element in German painting, not only during the Romantic period but over the last two centuries. From the Alpine landscapes of the 1800s to the figurative painting of the *Junge Wilden* in the 1970s and 1980s, a recurring preoccupation in German painting has been the attempt to capture or portray on canvas ideas or visions that transcend our powers of imagination. Central to this tradition, both chronologically and emotionally, are the visionary images of German Expressionism, produced in the first two decades of the twentieth century.

The fears and pleasures of the unknown and the unimaginable point to the aesthetic concept of the sublime, a notion which itself defies accurate definition. The simplest characterization can be derived from the customary contrast of the sublime and the beautiful. While our delight in the beautiful stems from the recognition of a perceptible totality arranged according to the dictates of measure, proportion and harmony, our delight in the sublime derives from the absence of these very qualities.

In Joseph Anton Koch's painting of the *Schmadribach Falls* of 1811 (fig. 1) a tiny figure in the foreground takes a pot-shot at a duck, while towering in the distance above him are gargantuan waterfalls and Alpine peaks. The artist's delight in the disproportionate physical scale of man and nature, and the air of menace generated by the brooding masses of the mountains as they roll away into infinity link Koch's painting to the early Alpine views produced by Caspar Wolf in the 1770s, and to the *Sturm und Drang* enthusiasms of the same decade. High among these enthusiasms was the Ossian cult[2] which set the imagery of the wild and untamed nature to be found at the northern periphery of Europe against the measured delight of the Mediterranean south. Ossianism was closely linked to eighteenth-century British speculation on the sublime which was further developed by German aestheticians towards the end of the century. Symptomatic of this connection is the rhetorical question posed by Friedrich Schiller in an essay on the sublime written in the early 1790s: 'Who would not rather ... feast his eyes on Scotland's wild cataracts and misty mountains – Ossian's great realm of nature – than on the sour victory of patience over the most obstinate of the elements in the dead-straight Dutch countryside.'[3]

With Koch's painting and Schiller's observations in mind, one might turn to Joseph Addison's celebrated articles on 'The Pleasures of the Imagination' published in the *Spectator* in 1712. Differentiating between Greatness, Novelty, and Beauty as sources of aesthetic delight, Addison offers 'huge heaps of mountains, high rocks and precipices, or a wide expanse of water' as appropriate stimuli. Confronted with such natural phenomena, 'we are flung into a pleasing astonishment at such unbounded views, and feel a delightful stillness and amazement in the soul at the apprehension of them.'[4] Later in the century Edmund Burke added the emotion of terror to Addison's delight in limitless nature, prompting a taste for the morbid – for graveyards, ruins, and natural disasters – that provided early Romantic art with a rich vein of literary and pictorial motifs.[5] Apocalyptic expectations derived from medieval theology lay behind the supernatural terrors of the charnel-house and the graveyard. As Burke explained: 'Whatever is fitted in any sort to excite the ideas of pain, and danger, that is to say, whatever is in any sort terrible, or is conversant about terrible objects, or operates in a manner analogous to terror, is a source of the *sublime*;

Fig.1 Joseph Anton Koch, *The Schmadribach Falls* 1811, Museum der Bildenden Künste, Leipzig

that is, it is productive of the strongest emotion which the mind is capable of feeling … . When danger and pain press too nearly, they are incapable of any delight, and are simply terrible; but at certain distances, and with certain modifications, they may be, and they are delightful, as we every day experience.'[6] Viewed from below, with our feet planted firmly by Koch in the green pastures, the icy Alps take on an aspect of fearsome delight that closer proximity would destroy.

Both Addison's joy in escaping the confines of daily life and Burke's *frisson* at contemplating objects and situations of fear from a safe distance represent very simple models of sublimity. Addison, however, did point the way forward in a subsequent article in which the pleasure of the sublime was ascribed to a dissonance between our powers of reason and of imagination. 'The understanding, indeed, opens an infinite space on every side of us, but the imagination, after a few faint efforts, is immediately at a stand, and finds herself swallowed up in the immensity of the void that surrounds it: Our

reason can pursue a particle of matter through an infinite variety of divisions, but the fancy soon loses sight of it, and feels in itself a kind of chasm, that wants to be filled with matter of a more sensible bulk. We can neither widen, nor contract the faculty to the dimensions of either extreme. The object is too big for our capacity, when we would comprehend the circumference of the world, and dwindles into nothing, when we endeavour after the idea of an atom.'[7]

Developed by Immanuel Kant as the *Grenze der Einbildungskraft* (The Limit of our Powers of Imagination), this gap between the realms of reason and imagination has the potential to engender both fear and creativity. When confronted by the enormity or the minuteness of the object and the void of incomprehension, the observer experiences fear, which is then superseded by pleasure as new rational criteria are summoned to explain and contain that which had previously been beyond comprehension. In the process, the power of imagination is stretched and extended to encompass new conceptions of space and time, and the power of reason generates visions of the world that extend to the limits of fiction.

As Kant makes clear, the sublime exists not in the observed object itself but in the response of the observer. Nevertheless, certain phenomena are more likely to provoke sublime reactions than others, and Kant himself offers a list of likely candidates: 'Bold, overhanging, and, as it were, threatening rocks, thunderclouds piled up the vault of heaven, borne along with flashes and peals, volcanoes in all their violence of destruction, hurricanes leaving desolation in their track, the boundless ocean rising with rebellious force, the high waterfall of some mighty river, and the like, make our power of resistance of trifling moment in comparison with their might. But provided our position is secure, their aspect is all the more attractive for its fearfulness; and we readily call these objects sublime, because they raise the forces of the soul above the heights of the vulgar commonplace, and discover within us a power of resistance of quite another kind, which gives us courage to be able to measure ourselves against the seeming omnipotence of nature.'[8] The sublime resides in our reaction to the abyss or the raging torrent and the attempt to master our fear through the redefinition of our rational perspectives. Aesthetic judgment is thus akin to moral

Fig.2 Caspar David Friedrich, *Wanderer above the Sea of Fog* c.1818, Hamburger Kunsthalle

judgment, and the chaos of creation given order by the intervention of free, rational man.

To the early Romantic mind nature in her most extreme manifestations offered moral and metaphysical insights into the human spirit. Creative engagement with the magnitude and power of natural phenomena offered the chance to link the individual soul and the universal spirit. The negative condition held equally true, and current theorizing on the sublime linked the disorder of the natural landscape with the uncertain anarchy of the world of morality. While both natural and moral chaos provoked an initial response of fear and distaste, both were susceptible to rational control, and fear could be superseded by the certainty of a transcendant order. Novalis makes this point perfectly in one of his *Blütenstaub* Fragments, written in 1798: 'Fantasy sets the coming world either in the heights or in the depths, or in metempsychosis to ourselves. We dream of journeys through the cosmos; but is the cosmos not in us? We do not know the depths of our soul. The secret path leads inwards. Eternity, with its worlds of past and future, exists either within ourselves or not at all.'[9] The

sublime response to the chaos and menace of nature offers us a way out of the world of purely sensuous knowledge, and reveals the existence within us of an absolute moral capacity. This capacity exists independently of the world of natural phenomena, yet is triggered by the sublime response to the natural world. The negative or dialectical response to the real world of appearances makes possible a world of the spirit.

The landscapes of Caspar David Friedrich invite a reading in these terms. We can only speculate what the traveller is thinking when he looks across the fog-shrouded peaks in the painting created around 1818 (fig 2). Death, transcience and human mortality are often suggested by Friedrich's own observation: 'To live one day eternally, one must give oneself over many times to death.'[10] In his *catalogue raisonné* on Friedrich, Helmut Börsch-Supan notes that 'the observer of nature does not appear here submissively moved but in a thoughtful pose', adding that this is only understandable if the figure represents someone who is already dead.[11] Yet the logic of the sublime suggests a more positive reading, and one that works equally convincingly for comparable compositions by Friedrich, such as *Two Men Contemplating the Moon* of 1819 (fig. 3 and colour plate, p. 221). In confronting and overcoming the abyss of incomprehension, the observer gains a heightened understanding of human potential and of the power of human rationality to overcome the chaos of creation and the intractability of nature.

In these two examples we are concerned with what Kant dubbed the 'mathematical' sublime, which is concerned with the effect of physical size and magnitude on the imagination. The second Kantian variant is the 'dynamic sublime', which relates to the effect of power. In the pre-industrial world the two qualities often worked in unison. The Schmadribach Falls, for example, offer images of vastness both in scale and power. With the emergence of industrial production and urban concentration in the nineteenth century, however, the inventions of man rather than nature offered a new focus for sublime contemplation. As Paul Crowther has noted in his recent study of the Kantian sublime: 'The structures of capitalism and the conflicts it engenders provide immediate and inescapable images that overwhelm our perceptual or imaginative powers, yet make the scope

Fig.3 Caspar David Friedrich, *Two Men Contemplating the Moon* 1819, Staatliche Kunstsammlungen Dresden, Gemäldegalerie Neue Meister

Fig.4 Carl Blechen, *Ravine near Amalfi* 1831, Staatliche Museen zu Berlin Preußischer Kulturbesitz, Nationalgalerie

of rational comprehension or human artifice and contrivance all the more vivid.'[12] In the nineteenth century industrial production, the speed and power of steam technology and the burgeoning metropolis or industrial city stimulated the sensations of awe, terror and exaltation previously associated with such natural phenomena as cliffs, waterfalls and deserts. Carl Blechen's painting *Ravine near Amalfi*, painted in 1831 (fig. 4), offers a telling image of this realignment of sublime sentiment. With a steam hammer set above a roaring torrent, a symbol of mechanical power and danger is contrasted with the same forces in nature.

In the context of the Victorian cities of Britain, Nicholas Taylor lists among the sublime delights of the new century 'the haranguing of the Evangelical preacher; the ecstasy of the Anglo-Catholic Mass; the scientific wonders of panoramas and exhibition halls; the traveller's thrill in catching trains and climbing mountains; the capitalist's pride in the hum of mass production and hubbub of the market.'[13] The city of brick and stone, driven by the limitless technological power of steam and iron, with its vast and ever-expanding scale and its bru-

tal contrasts of splendour and deprivation, replaced the menacing mountains, crags and cliffs of the eighteenth century. The conquest of the Alps and the conquest of the industrial city demanded similar qualities and provoked parallel aesthetic responses. The sublime dimension of the response to the burgeoning German cities at the beginning of the twentieth century offers a valuable insight into the workings of German Expressionism and further supports the initial contention of a Romantic tradition that links the nineteenth and twentieth centuries.

The metaphor of the city as an endless sea of stone recurs frequently in the literature of German Expressionism, written in the first two decades of the twentieth century. In Gerrit Engelke's poem *Stadt* (City), for example, the city appears as a man-made mountain, bristling with energy and menace:

Ten thousand staring, rigid blocks are built in
  the valley,
Stone piled high upon stone on wood and iron frames;
And block upon block pressed into a mountain,
Spanned by steam-pipe, tower and railway,

By wire spinning net over net.
The mountain, cleft deep by many fissures:
This is the great labyrinth
Through which human destiny washes.[14]

In similar vein, Alfred Wolfenstein saw in the city the
ravines and cliffs of the sublime mountainscape:

Shyness looms and the blind parting!
Still we stand in stony disguise,
Escaped the chaos – are still in flight.
Before us the city gapes in crag and chasm.[15]

And just as the chaotic forces of nature exceed our power
of comprehension and threaten us with destruction, so the
great cities of the late nineteenth century were invested
with entropic qualities. Like an overheated boiler, these
massive concentrations of energy carried in their very fabric the potential for self-destruction. The legacy of apocalyptic expectation passed down from medieval theology
to the eighteenth-century theories of the sublime found a
new resonance in early twentieth-century theories of
urban degeneration and collapse. The city of stone would
crush its inhabitants as surely as an avalanche. This is the
message of Ludwig Meidner's celebrated series of apocalyptic landscapes, created in 1913 (fig. 5).

The response of the Expressionist writers, painters,
and architects to the nineteenth century city was double-
edged. As critics their starting point was rooted in the
sublime response of incomprehension and fear: incomprehension at the physical scale of the city and of the
exploding population. This failure of the imagination to
comprehend the extent of the city was reinforced on the
human scale by disbelief at the overcrowded tomb-like
conditions endured by the urban poor. At the micro-
scopic scale, recent advances in bacteriology drew attention to further hidden yet terrifying dangers such as
cholera and tuberculosis, which lurked in the insanitary
city streets.[16] As creative spirits, however, the same
artists and intellectuals turned to the devices of the sublime to produce emotionally laden images intended to
stimulate a rational re-evaluation of how industrial
society should progress.

The comparable use of sublime imagery in nineteenth-
century Romanticism and twentieth-century Expressionism

Fig.5 Ludwig Meidner, *Apocalyptic Landscape* 1913, Los Angeles County Museum of Art, Gift of Clifford Odets

should not be ascribed to conscious imitation: the
Expressionist visionaries and utopians did not keep Kant
under their drawing-boards. There was, however, in the
first decade of this century a climate of ideas that was
sympathetic to the aesthetic concerns and artistic
production of Romanticism. Caspar David Friedrich,
for example, emerged as the undisputed star of the
Deutsche Jahrhundertasstellung (Centenary Exhibition
of German Art) held in Berlin in 1906, which launched a
reappraisal of Romantic painting. Similarly, the Neo-
Kantian movement that had originated in the 1860s
blossomed around 1910. While it is highly unlikely that
the artists or architects would have read the Kantian
studies of Natorp, Windelband, or the young Ernst
Cassirer, the wider intellectual climate in the early years
of this century was clearly receptive to Kantian echoes.
As the painter Franz Marc wrote in 1915: 'Kant looked
far ahead, beyond the nineteenth century into the new
age.'[17]

Among the many visions of a new age produced
during the Expressionist decades, some of the most powerful were architectural. Crystal cathedrals set high in the
Alps and cosmic constructions of coloured glass speeding
through the eternal night were conceived both as a
protest against the insanity of the First World War and
as a pointer to a better society which would devote its
energies to peace and understanding rather than self-

destruction. An important influence on the architects was the writer Paul Scheerbart who published a long succession of fantasy novels, articles and poems between 1889 and his death in 1915, in which he insisted that the universe is far too rich and complex to be comprehended by mechanical reason alone. Only naïve wonder – the basis of the sublime – could promote the development of higher forms of understanding. This position, of course, also had implications for artistic production – as one of the characters explained in his novel *Das Paradies, die Heimat der Kunst* ('Paradise, Home of Art'): 'The concept of art is broadened here; the main issue is no longer representation but rather the invention of things that might be represented … . Our task is not the representation of comprehended perception, but a reorientation of comprehended perceptions. In this way we want to make it possible to comprehend new perceptions. You could call this the preparatory work for the artists who come later.'[18] Rather than depict in minute and squalid detail the poverty and misery of the real world in the manner of Naturalist writers like Gerhart Hauptmann, Arno Holz, and Johannes Schlaf, who dominated German literature in the 1890s, Scheerbart described fantastic astral journeys and despatched his readers to exotic locations on earth, where utopian existences were led under the beneficent shelter of a new architecture of colour and transparency. The transparent envelope was intended to promote self-transcendence by allowing thought to move from the sensuous level to the universal through the medium of endless space. The moral implications of such a sequence had already been noted by Kant in a key passage in *The Critique of Judgment*: 'The spontaneity in the play of the cognitive faculties whose harmonious accord contains the ground of this pleasure, makes the concept in question [the concept of the finality of nature] in its consequences, a suitable mediating link connecting the concept of nature with that of the concept of freedom, as this accord at the same time promotes the sensibility of the mind for moral feeling.'[19] As in nineteenth-century German Romanticism, moral and metaphysical insights were to be derived from excess in nature.

This was the message that linked Scheerbart's writing to the visions of Bruno Taut, the driving spirit behind Expressionist architecture. The first contact between the two men was made in 1912 through the circle of artists and intellectuals that gathered around Herwarth Walden's journal *Der Sturm*. In February 1914 Taut published an article entitled 'Eine Notwendigkeit' ('A Necessity') in *Der Sturm* which called for collaborative work on a great new building of glass, steel and concrete, in which constructional virtuosity and the arts of painting and sculpture would be reunited, as they were in the Gothic cathedrals. The building was to have no function beyond self-transcendence.

Nothing came of this project, and a glass pavilion designed by Taut for an exhibition in Cologne was dismantled following the outbreak of war in August 1914. The senseless butchery on the Western Front, the German defeat, and the abdication of the Kaiser created a climate in which social and political change was deemed essential, without any firm idea or consensus over what form such change might take. Great, ill-defined ideas were in the air, visions of a world without war or nationalism, visions of universal brotherhood. Ideas like this are exactly what Kant pointed to in defining the aesthetic idea as 'that representation of the imagination which induces much thought, yet without the possibility of any definite thought whatever, i.e. concept being adequate to it, and which language, consequently, can never get quite on level terms with or render completely intelligible.'[20] The 'brotherhood of man' is just such a notion that defies complete and convincing representation. Yet some image had to be found as a stimulus for the transformation of the world that was felt to be imminent, and for the change in morality that was necessary for this transformation. As already noted, the aesthetic of the sublime offers a link between such strong human emtions as fear and the longing for self-transcendence and the moral goal of a free, rational man.

In *Alpine Architektur* – a cycle of drawings produced during the war and published in 1919 (fig. 6) – Bruno Taut created a series of gigantomanic visions that embodied almost all those qualities that Edmund Burke had linked to the sublime responses of 'astonishment … admiration, reverence and respect'.[21] High above the wartime trenches, technology and mechanical power over the material world is transformed into a constructive rather than destructive force, with airships, aeroplanes, and unspecified technological wonders employed to build glass temples on the Alpine peaks and launch

SCHNEE
GLETSCHER
GLAS

Fig.6 Bruno Taut, *Alpine Architektur*, no.17 ('The area set aside for building seen from Monte Generosa')

glass satellites into space. Social progress was to be achieved through sublime inspiration, through engagement on a task of almost incomprehensible dimension: 'The execution will involve incredible difficulties and sacrifices, but will not be impossible. "The impossible is so rarely demanded of Man." (Goethe) … But higher knowledge! The greatest work is nothing without the sublime. We must always recognize and strive for the unattainable if we are to achieve the attainable.'[22] Taut's pleas for the transcendental sublime carries unmistakable echoes of Friedrich Nietzsche's demand for man to replace the deist god of Nature: 'We want to suffuse nature with humanity and free it from godly mummery. We want to extract what we need from nature in order to dream *beyond* man. Something should yet emerge that is *more magnificent* than storm, mountain, and ocean – but as the progeny of man!'[23]

Late in 1918, while working on *Alpine Architektur*, Taut also pursued direct political power in the government of Workers' and Soldiers' Councils in Berlin and also entertained brief hopes of a ministerial position in the revolutionary government in Bavaria.[24] This nexus

of sublime vision and concrete political ambition is entirely consistent with the logic of the sublime. As the instrument that makes possible the victory of reason over nature or chaos, the sublime has always had extra-aesthetic dimensions – social and political – which carry with them both the prospect of new perspectives and the dangers of authoritarianism. While Kant's 'mathematical' sublime refers to the faculty of cognition, the 'dynamic sublime' points to the realm of human ambition and desire. David Hume had already made this connection in his *Treatise Concerning Human Understanding* in which he noted that: 'In collecting our force to overcome the opposition, we invigorate the soul, and give it an elevation with which otherwise it would never have been acquainted.'[25] Writing in the mid-nineteenth century, the German aesthetician Theodor Vischer offered a more muscular account of the same insight: 'We feel ourselves elevated because we identify ourselves with the powers of nature, ascribing their vast impact to ourselves, because our fantasy rests on the wings of the storm as we roar into the heights and wander into the depths of infinity. Thus we ourselves expand into a boundless natural power.'[26] With the sublime response so closely linked to perceptions of power and achievement, it is little wonder that the guardians of National Socialist aesthetics looked benignly on this aesthetic mechanism.

An example from the early years of the new regime can be found in Martin Heidegger's exegesis of the Hölderlin poems, written around 1800, in which the poet wrestles with mortal man's attempts to portray the workings of the gods. In *Wie wenn am Feiertag*, for example, Hölderlin offers this dynamically sublime vision of the workings of poetry:

> Yet, fellow poets, us it behoves to stand
> Bare-headed beneath God's thunderstorms,
> To grasp the father's rays, no less, with our own
>   two hands
> And, wrapping in song the heavenly gift,
> To offer it to the people.[27]

The conclusions that Heidegger draws from this half-stanza are entirely compatible with the National Socialist ideology: 'Thunder and lightning are the

Fig.7 Albert Speer, *Große Halle*, Berlin, photograph of model, 1940

language of the gods, and the one whose purpose it is to bear this language without equivocation and place it in the being [*Dasein*] of the people is the poet.'[28]

In painting, too, the aesthetics of the sublime enjoyed a certain pre-eminence under the dictatorship. Just as Friedrich had enjoyed a revival at the beginning of the Expressionist epoch, so another followed during the years of National Socialism. As a German critic claimed in 1940: 'It is no accident that his rediscovery coincides with the beginning of this martial saeculum, and that the pinnacle of his influence coincides with the outbreak of the World War. No accident, too, that since 1933 Caspar David Friedrich's effect has begun to grow.'[29] Symptomatic of this growing interest was the Koch exhibition held at the Nationalgalerie in Berlin early in 1939. To mark this event, a full-page colour illustration of Koch's *Schmadribach Falls* was published in the official art journal *Die Kunst im Dritten Reich*, with an accompanying text noting in Koch's painting the sublime conflict between imagination and reason. 'A rigorous architectural structure articulates the mountainscape, with the natural forms split into individual layers. But

against this wilfully architectonic structure stands the desire to portray the invincible power and dynamism of the forces of nature.'[30] Linking the endless mountainscape and the notion of architectural control is a mutual medium, namely stone, and National Socialist architecture echoes to the exhortation to create 'the word in stone'.[31]

In his attempts to show – rather inconsistently – that even finite objects can produce sublime responses in the observer, Kant offered an architectural example, suggesting that when a visitor enters St Peter's in Rome, 'a feeling comes home to him of the inadequacy of his imagination for presenting the idea of a whole within which that imagination attains its maximum, and, in its fruitless efforts to extend this limit, recoils upon itself, but in doing so succumbs to an emotional delight.'[32] In the context of National Socialist architecture, a similarly sublime response – feeding off the tension between what is perceptually overwhelming yet still known to be artifice – would have awaited the visitor to Albert Speer's projected 'Große Halle' (fig. 7), a giant domed structure set as the terminal feature of an axis that would have cut through Berlin like a surgeon's scalpel.

Speer was also the architect of the Reichskanzlei building, Hitler's seat of power in Berlin, completed in 1939 on the corner of Voss-Strasse and Wilhelmstrasse. In his painting of vast and empty Neoclassical interiors Anselm Kiefer subverts the image of National Socialist architecture to point to the dangers of the dynamic sublime with its authoritarian resonances. This subversion is implicit in a Speer-like interior painted in 1983, and explicit in the title: *To the Supreme Being* (fig. 8). In this and similar works Kiefer adopts the rhetoric of the architectural sublime as a means of addressing the National Socialist experience. The silent terror generated by these images is very potent: more potent in their damnation of the regime than a highly rhetorical account of Nazi criminality. In pointing to the negative potential of the sublime, Kiefer illuminates Schiller's perception that 'the beautiful is valuable only with reference to the human being, but the sublime with reference to the pure daemon in him.'[33] Schiller's observation, in turn, helps explain the continuing importance of the sublime to the present day. As the French philosopher Jean-François Lyotard has noted, the sublime response is

Fig.8 Anselm Kiefer, *To the Supreme Being* 1983, Musée national d'art moderne, Paris

experienced 'when the imagination fails to present an object which might, in principle, come to match a concept.... We can conceive the infinitely great, the infinitely powerful, but every presentation of an object destined to "make visible" this absolute greatness or power appears to us painfully inadequate.' In the attempt to understand the phenomena and events of the twentieth century that go beyond our powers of imagination, the sublime has proved an essential key. As Lyotard suggests: 'It is in the aesthetic of the sublime that modern art (including literature) finds its impetus and the logic of the avant-garde finds its axioms.'[34]

Iain Boyd Whyte

1 Ronald Taylor, *The Romantic Tradition in Germany* (London, 1970), xi.

2 Johann Gottfried Herder, 'Auszug aus einem Briefwechsel über Ossian und die Lieder alter Völker' in Herder, Goethe, Frisi, Moser, *Von deutscher Art und Kunst* (1773, reprint Stuttgart, 1977), 7–62.

3 Friedrich Schiller, 'Über das Erhabene', *Sämtliche Werke* vol. 5, (Munich, 1967), 802.

4 Joseph Addison, *The Spectator*, no. 412 (23 June 1712).

5 Edmund Burke, *A Philosophical Enquiry into the Origin of our Ideas of the Sublime and Beautiful* (London, 1757).

6 Edmund Burke (as note 5), 39–40.

7 Joseph Addison, *The Spectator*, no. 420 (2 July 1712).

8 Immanuel Kant, *The Critique of Judgment*, trans. J.C. Meredith (Oxford, 1973), 109–110.

9 Novalis, 'Blütenstaub', Fragment 16, *Werke und Briefe* (Munich, 1962), 342.

10 Sigrid Hinz, *Caspar David Friedrich in Briefen und Bekenntnissen* (Berlin, 1968), 89. Quoted: William Vaughan, *German Romantic Painting* (London and New Haven, 1980), 76.

11 Helmut Börsch-Supan, Karl Wilhelm Jähnig, *Caspar David Friedrich: Gemälde, Druckgraphik und bildmäßige Zeichnungen* (Munich, 1973), 349.

12 Paul Crowther, *The Kantian Sublime*, (Oxford, 1989), 164–165.

13 Nicholas Taylor, 'The Awful Sublimity of the Victorian City', in H.J. Dyos and Michael Wolff, *The Victorian City: Images and Realities*, (London, 1973), 434.

14 Gerrit Engelke, 'Stadt', in *Rythmus des Neuen Europa* (Jena, 1921) Reprinted in *Deutsche Großstadtlyrik vom Naturalismus bis zur Gegenwart*, ed. Wolfgang Rothe (Stuttgart, 1973), 185–186.

15 Alfred Wolfenstein, 'Neue Stadt' in *Menschlicher Kämpfer* (Berlin, 1919). Reprinted in: Wolfgang Rothe (as note 14), 194.

16 It was in Berlin that Robert Koch identified the tuberculosis germ in 1882 and the cholera bacillus in 1883.

17 *Franz Marc: Schriften*, ed. Klaus Lankheit (Cologne, 1978), 194.

18 Paul Scheerbart. *Das Paradies, die Heimat der Kunst* (1889; 2nd edition, Berlin, 1893), 170.

19 Immanuel Kant, (as note 8), 39.

20 Immanuel Kant, (as note 8), 175.

21 Edmund Burke, *A Philosophical Enquiry into the Origin of our Ideas of the Sublime and Beautiful* (London, 1958), 57.

22 Bruno Taut, *Alpine Architektur* (Hagen, 1919), plates 10 and 21.

23 Friedrich Nietzsche, 'Nachgelassene Fragmente, Sommer 1883', no. 13 (1) in *Kritische Gesamtausgabe*, 7, pt. 1 (Berlin, 1980), 450.

24 See Iain Boyd Whyte, *Bruno Taut and the Architecture of Activism* (Cambridge, 1982), 117–19.

25 David Hume, quoted in Walter John Hipple, *The Beautiful, the Sublime, and the Picturesque in Eighteenth-Century British Aesthetic Theory* (Carbondale, Ill., 1957), 43.

26 Friedrich Theodor Vischer, *Über das Erhabene und Komische und andere Texte zur Ästhetik* (Frankfurt am Main, 1967), 155.

27 Friedrich Hölderlin, 'Wie wenn am Feiertage...', trans. Michael Hamburger, in Hölderlin, *Poems and Fragments* (London, 1966), 375–77.

29 Martin Heidegger, quoted in Karl Heinz Bohrer, 'Am Ende des Erhabenen', *Merkur*, 43 no. 9/10, (September/October 1989), 746.

29 Quoted in Joseph Leo Koerner, *Caspar David Friedrich and the Subject of Landscape* (London, 1990), 65.

30 H. Weber, 'Joseph Anton Koch: Zur Gedächtnisausstellung des Künstlers in der Nationalgalerie in Berlin', *Die Kunst im Dritten Reich*, 3 no. 3 (March 1939), 78–79.

31 For a fascinating essay on the sublimity of stone, see: Hartmut Böhme, 'Das Steinerne: Anmerkungen zur Theorie des Erhabenen aus dem Blick des Menschenfremdesten,' in *Das Erhabene: Zwischen Grenzerfahrung und Größenwahn*, ed. Christine Pries (Weinheim, 1989), 119–42.

32 Immanuel Kant, (as note 8), 100.

33 Friedrich Schiller, 'Über das Erhabene' (as note 3), 806.

34 Jean-François Lyotard, 'What is Postmodernism', in Lyotard, *The Postmodern Condition: A Report on Knowledge* (Manchester, 1986), 77–78.

Arabesque, Cipher, Hieroglyph:
Between Unending Interpretation and Loss of Meaning

Signatures

Romanticism shares with traditional natural philosophy the conviction that conspicuous natural patterns are the signs of deeply hidden qualities and affinities. When Paracelsus and Jacob Böhme speak of 'signatures', or when Johann Georg Hamann and Novalis speak of 'ciphers', they mean visible signs that point to the invisible. Always doubtful in interpretation, simultaneously revelatory and enigmatic, these patterns and figures are reminiscent of hieroglyphs. The human face and figure are also hieroglyphs, and it is the task of the science of physiognomy to interpret them. Physiognomy and the doctrine of signatures thus share a faith in a divine and cosmic semiotics and a certainty that knowledge springs only from the analogies revealed by signatures, rather than from chains of cause and effect.[1]

In visual art, this kind of thinking found a notable early manifestation in Philipp Otto Runge's cycle *The Times of Day* (colour plates, pp. 212–13 and cat. 9) and expanded its scope only in the twentieth century. This is art that pursues neither the illusion of concrete reality nor the lucid plasticity and autonomy of forms governed by law and type. It springs from a kind of pictorial thinking that concentrates on the sympathies between kindred qualities, the visual affinities between structures: metaphorical, abstract, not to say speculative in tendency, this is a cast of mind that is eternally discontented, even when it boldly wields the compasses to construct the basic figures of existence. The resulting restlessly metaphorical forms have no core, no centre: their chief characteristic is the perpetual open-endedness which they share with everything outlandish and fantastic – and which, by long-established usage, must be called Romantic.

Arabesques as Hieroglyphs

Wilhelm Heinrich Wackenroder called art a 'hiero-glyphic script':[2] comprehensible in detail, but in general as inexplicable as Nature. Ludwig Tieck projected this view onto the existing, traditional decorative form of the arabesque – and invented a new art form. In it, he says, the 'strangest' content, 'in a baffling, almost incomprehensible combination', will create an 'entirely unheard-of' effect.[3]

Very soon translated into reality by Runge in his first illustrations, this new pictorial form came under the critical scrutiny of Friedrich Schlegel: '*Hieroglyphs*, veritable emblems, but capriciously assembled from images and views or intimations of Nature, rather than as in the ancient world.'[4] This audacious experiment, he said, must remain an exception. The one sure way was to renew the tradition of Old German painting.

The first writer to speak of Runge's 'mystic arabesques' with total approval was Christian August Semler, in his book of 'Ideas for Allegorical Room Decorations' (1806).[5] And in 1808 Joseph Görres wrote a lengthy review of Runge's set of four prints, *The Times of Day*, in which he waxed lyrical in his praise of the new art form. Rather than 'arabesques', he preferred to call these forms the '*hieroglyphics* of art'. 'Many, many voices are heard' within *The Times of Day*, carrying the mind from the literal times of day to the life of 'all things';[6] a vast and proliferating network of references opens vistas of infinite riches. For Clemens Brentano, too, Runge shows 'that the arabesque is a hieroglyph, and its links are a language of imagery as rich, in the mute poetry of images, as the work of poetry itself is meant to be in speech'.[7] Visual imagery inspired by the doctrine of signatures remains close to writing, above all because it too employs discrete units, which interact to generate the meaning.

Multiple Correspondences

The sources of the Romantic arabesque and hieroglyph, which lay in the doctrine of signatures and in analogical

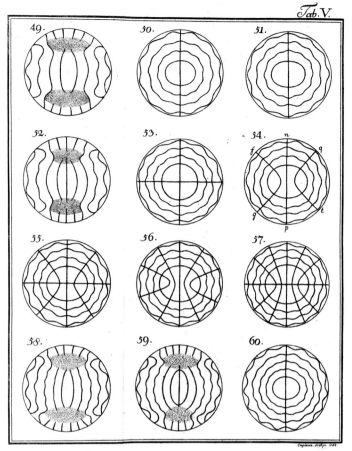

Fig. 1 Ernst Florens Friedrich Chladni, *Acoustic Figures*, table 5 from *Entdeckungen über die Theorie des Klanges* ('Exposition of the Theory of Sound'), Leipzig 1787

thinking, and their goal, which was the opening of an indefinite space of intuitive surmise, were encapsulated by Novalis in a single sentence of the following passage:

'Many are the paths that human beings travel. Whoever traces and compares them will see strange figures taking shape: figures that seem to belong to that great cipher that we see everywhere, on wings and on eggshells, in clouds, in snow, in crystals and rock formations, on water as it freezes, in the inward and outward forms of mountains, plants, animals, human beings, in the lights of heaven, on sheets of pitch or glass when touched or stroked, in iron filings around a magnet, in the oddities of coincidence. We surmise that these figures contain the key, the philology of this wondrous script; but the surmise will never fall into hard and fast forms, and seems to resist becoming a higher key.'[8]

This was the quest for formal correspondences, as pointers to the divine geometry, that had inspired Johannes Kepler two centuries earlier, in his little treatise *Strena seu de nive sexangula* ('The Gift, or Hexagonal Snow', 1611), to link the invariably six-sided

form of snow crystals with hexagonal honeycomb cells, pomegranate seeds and crystalline minerals, and even with the six-petalled structure of lilies. At the same time, Novalis was alluding to more recent discoveries: Georg Christoph Lichtenberg's figures of electrical discharges, and the acoustic figures of Ernst Florens Friedrich Chladni (fig. 1).

He was also taking issue with Immanuel Kant. In his *Critique of Judgment* (1790), Kant had dealt at length with the 'cipher … through which Nature speaks figuratively to us in her beautiful forms',[9] though with the sobering rider that the structures and patterns of snow and mineral crystals, flowers, feathers and shells are the result of a blind natural causality. This philosophical realism – which divorces aesthetic fascination from the numinous, ecstatic Nature worship of the doctrine of signatures – was exactly what Novalis was trying to counter.

Along with the manifold patterns of Nature, the regular forms of geometry also stimulated philosophical and aesthetic speculation. It was clear to the young August Wilhelm Schlegel that these figures invite a 'mystical application', because in them 'seeing is identical with conceiving, and the latter entirely exhausts the former'.[10] These are the most general of all forms: all consideration of structure ultimately leads to them, and their meanings have long been convincingly established: 'The circle will always stand for eternity and for self-contained perfection.'[11]

Even where multiple meanings cluster around the basic figures, and where these figures are pressed into the service of a subjectively defined symbolism, this must still be done with an eye to the most general definitions. When the mathematician Jacob Bernoulli of Basel discovered in 1691 that any portion of a logarithmic spiral need only be enlarged or diminished to make it congruent with any other portion, this consistency so impressed him that he felt impelled to regard it as a threefold symbol: for the emergence of the Redeemer from God, *ut lumen a lumine emanans* (like light emanating from light); for constancy and strength in the vicissitudes of life; and finally for the certainty of the Resurrection. On his tombstone, Bernoulli wanted a figure of this spiral with the motto *Eadem mutata resurgo* (I arise again the same, though changed).[12]

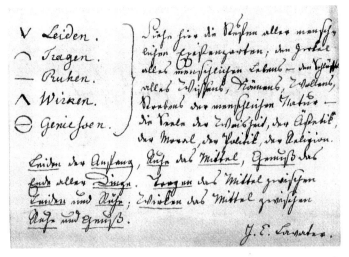

All these instances reveal the same experimental, speculative concern with natural patterns and geometrical figures that underlies Runge's four images of *The Times of Day*. In the metaphorical correspondences between flowers, stars and children, and also in the formal harmonies (chords), especially in the musical variations of compositional structure from one image to the next, it is visual analogies that establish the meaning and extend it, step by step, onto a universal plane – a progression that is deeply involving, not least because it overcomes the most extreme difficulties, allowing a miraculously direct interplay between organic and geometric form. The formal law of the Romantic arabesque points to a meaning that far transcends the traditional playful form itself.

Fig.2 Johann Caspar Lavater, *Keepsake for Luise Countess of Stolberg-Wernigerode* c.1800, private collection, Zurich

(Suffering. Enduring. Resting. Acting. Enjoying. These are the levels of all types of human experience, the circle of all human life – the key to all the knowledge, dreams, wishes and struggles of human nature – the soul of wisdom, aesthetics, morals, politics and religion.
Suffering is the *beginning*, *Rest* is the *middle*, *Enjoyment* is the end of all *things*.
Endurance is the way from *suffering* to *rest*, *action* is the way from *rest* to *enjoyment*.
J.C. Lavater)

Universal Physiognomy

Like the doctrine of signatures, physiognomy regarded itself as a universal theory of expression. In 1768 Antoine-Joseph Pernety declared that whoever studied human physiognomy would acquire knowledge 'that refers to the whole universe'. Everything, he said, bears 'on its outside a distinguishing sign, a hieroglyphic image, through which a beholder may readily discern the hidden forces and qualities within'.[13] In the context of such ideas as this, physiognomy set out to evolve a theory of the expressive value of abstract forms. Even Johann Caspar Lavater, that lover of the concrete and the empirical, was once moved to symbolize human characteristics in abstract terms, in accordance with the principle 'as with lines, so with men'.[14] And in 1791 Johann Christian August Grohmann argued the expressive power of forms and colours, divorced from all objective connotations.[15]

The best evidence of these connections is the *Keepsake* (*Gedenkblatt*, *c*. 1800; fig 2), which Lavater drew in the last year of his life for Countess Luise zu Stolberg-Wernigerode, and which was rediscovered as recently as 1991 by a descendant of his, the graphic artist Warja Lavater.[16] This shows five abstract signs for basic human activities and states, relying on the intuitive comprehension of signs postulated by physiognomy, but carrying their articulation a stage further. Once fitted together into a code, the individual meanings bring

themselves and each other into sharper focus. Suffering (Passivity) and Operation (Activity) are expressed by contrasting signs, with Repose as the neutral centre. Again, the difference between the acute angle of Action and the arc of Bearing is readily comprehensible, as is the relationship between Bearing and Enjoyment. It is only in the lower curve of Enjoyment that the system breaks down, so that one is tempted to round off the system by detaching this part to form a sixth 'activity', perhaps that of Reception or Assimilation.

In the early nineteenth century, such ideas were not at all influential. Like the Romantic arabesque, with its quest for the 'rhythm of the highest life',[17] they were far ahead of their time. One hundred years later, in the early twentieth century, they were to supply the most important arguments for the revival of this very form of art.

Unending Interpretation

According to August Wilhelm Schlegel, the visual art that limits itself to hints and allusions approximates to the state of the hieroglyph. Its identity as a sign constitutes a challenge to the imagination 'to receive the stimulus and to go on in its own way'.[18] In saying this,

Schlegel was following those eighteenth-century connoisseurs who prized the 'art of abbreviation' in Old Master drawings; he was also preparing the way for a freer acceptance of the 'open' pictorial forms of Romanticism.

It was Semler, above all, who recognized that the value of arabesques lay in their suggestive capacity to evoke possible meanings. Through 'Allegorical Room Decorations' (of a kind that Runge, too, had projected), it was possible, said Semler, to express 'highly involved, composite sequences of ideas, far more readily, clearly and unforcedly than through allegorical pictures of any other kind'.[19] In an essay printed in April 1807, Semler went one step further and proposed 'to transform arabesques into hieroglyphs full of sense and significance'. Such a 'poetry of hieroglyphs' might 'allude even to the Divine, and arouse – through its mysterious, mystic ciphers – those dim surmises that dawn upon us as we contemplate the Great Whole'.[20]

Here, as in Tieck's *Franz Sternbald*, the hieroglyph stands for the universal Whole, which is not accessible to reason. Here, Kant's reduction of the categories of understanding to empirical experience made it easy for Semler, as a Kantian, to agree with the Romantics. In another context, he even did some of their work for them. As early as 1800, taking Kant's 'Aesthetic Idea' as his point of departure, Semler had hit upon the concept of 'reverie', and had declared this tentative, many-sided process of surmise and signification to be the noblest aspiration of Romantic landscape painting.[21] Now he was able to extend the concept of reverie to the arabesque, the cipher, the hieroglyph. The continuum of response to which Semler aspired was never fully explored and expounded until Görres; but the framework was already in place. After hearing Görres lecture on 'Runge's 4 heavenly engravings', the young Joseph von Eichendorff noted in his journal: 'Arabesques. Unending interpretation.'[22]

Critique and Crisis

The tentative nature of the new semiotics made it easy for the Neoclassicists to misconstrue Runge's hieroglyphs as classical arabesques. The result, of course, was a studied appreciation of their decorative charm that

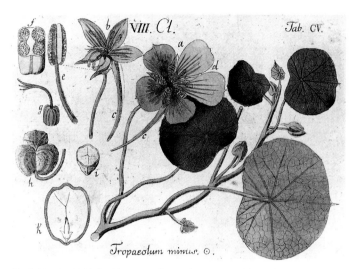

Fig.3 Christian Schkuhr, *Nasturtium* (Tripaeolum minus), table CV from *Botanisches Handbuch*, vol.1 of plates, Leipzig 1808

entirely obscured the underlying spiritual focus. In itself, Johann Heinrich Meyer's somewhat laboured verdict that Runge's engravings 'are not only pleasing to the eye but at the same time are well suited to stimulate the inner sense' reveals that the Weimar Friends of Art had no intention of giving way to any such stimulus: it was enough to state matter-of-factly that the meaning passed 'through the allegorical into the mystical'.[23]

Less diplomatic is the previously overlooked literary skit on Runge and Görres by Alois Schreiber, published in Cotta's *Morgenblatt* in 1810. These 'Ideas for Engravings for the Tingaling Almanac' reduce the hieroglyph to a kaleidoscopic welter of allusions in which the key words and motifs of Romanticism tumble over each other and generate nothing but nonsense. The open-ended, connotative power of the arabesque, highly suspect to the Neoclassical mind, leads into a nightmare imbroglio of Indian myth: 'To the strains of voices and instruments, a chorus of celestial bayadères floats on the clouds and celebrates the great moment; and from the depths a few whales look out, their motions expressive of the whole yearning of the human soul for deliverance. In the middle distance is a shark, devouring a Brahmin, to symbolize the lowest stage of the creature's union with the universe. The scene is illuminated by a comet, which trails a long cow's tail.'[24]

The message of this parody had been delivered *en clair* by Heinrich Voss the Younger, in a letter to Charlotte Schiller in 1807: Görres, he said, was an 'arabesque

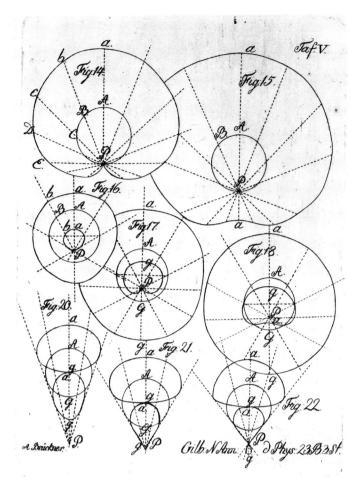

Fig.4 Gerhard Anton Ulrich Vieth, *Geometrical Construction of Leaf Forms: Nasturtium* from *Annalen der Physik*, vol.53, Leipzig 1816

writer', who preached to his Heidelberg readers 'Rungian arabesques, of mystic import . . . His unbridled imagination will have him back in the madhouse one of these days.'[25]

Romantic uses of the arabesque could be ironic, self-mocking, and much closer to the spirit of such criticism than one is liable to suppose. Along with the earlier *quodlibet*, the Romantic arabesque was the most important early pictorial device whereby disparate motifs could be pictorially combined. Görres's own *Musical Landscape*, in the *Zeitung für Einsiedler* ('Hermits' Journal', 1808), is a thoroughly proto-Dadaist composition,[26] as is the plate, 'wrought somewhat in the Early Egyptian style',[27] appended to Brentano's satire, *Der Philister vor, in und nach der Geschichte* ('The Philistine in Prehistory, History und Posthistory', 1811).

The early Romantic initiatives soon petered out in discouragement. In the revised edition of Friedrich

Schlegel's *Gemäldebriefe* ('Letters on Painting', 1823), Runge's art has sunk to the level of a false start, a byway that shows 'what it leads to, when one sets out to paint mere hieroglyphs of Nature, severed from historic, consecrated tradition; to the artist, tradition is the solid mother earth from which he can never depart without peril, and without irreparable damage to himself'.[28] And in 1834 Tieck ruled that Runge had more than once 'fallen into the over-arbitrary denotation, the hieroglyph'.[29] And so the arabesque, once the symbol of the escape of the imagination from hard-and-fast meanings, was forced to become a neutral vehicle of representation, suited to carrying off a random combination of motifs with a certain lightness.

Very soon, the Romantic philosophy of Nature, too, had had its day. The programme represented by Runge's cornflower construction did not come to fruition for more than a century, when D'Arcy Wentworth Thompson published *On Growth and Form* (1917). And it was only when Benoît Mandelbrot discovered fractal geometry in 1975 that new insights became available into the surprising affinities between natural structures. In 1816, when Gerhard Anton Ulrich Vieth published his 'Attempt at a Geometric Construction of the Forms of Organic Natural Bodies',[30] and took some pride in deriving the outline of the nasturtium leaf from the 'shell line of Nicomedes', as developed by him (figs. 3 and 4), even Lorenz Oken's *Isis*, the leading journal of natural philosophy, opined that this was a case of misplaced mathematical ingenuity.[31] All faith in the metaphysical meaning of archetypal patterns had been lost. Georg Büchner, who was Oken's protégé in Zürich, has his Woyzeck say: 'Have you seen what shapes the mushrooms make on the ground? If only someone could read 'em.'[32]

The Connoisseurs' Hieroglyph

With Runge dead, the hieroglyph no longer stood for the secret of the universe; but until well into the twentieth century it continued to stand for the mystery of art, as exemplified in that basic sign or form which underlies all personal style, and whose economy of material and downright non-mimetic primitivism (especially in

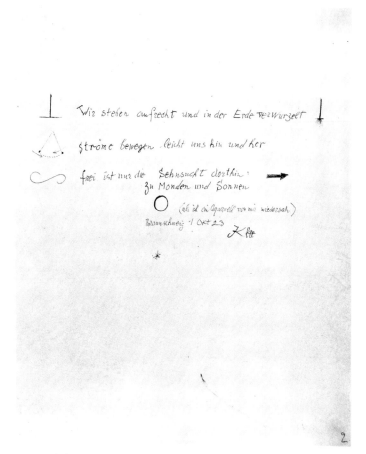

Fig.5 Paul Klee's entry in the visitor's book of the collector
Otto Ralf, 1923, Städtisches Museum, Braunschweig

(We stand upright and rooted in the earth Currents move us backwards and forwards
with ease unrestrained is but the longing thither: to moons and suns
(on seeing one of my watercolours again) Braunschweig 1 Oct 23 Klee)

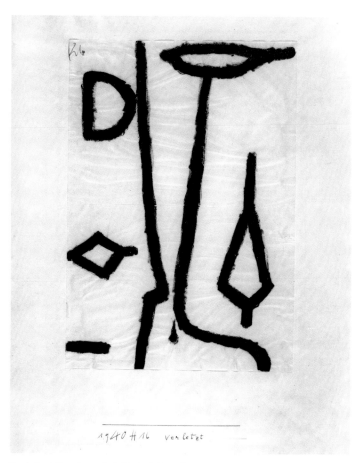

Fig.6 Paul Klee, *Injured* 1940, Paul-Klee-Stiftung,
Kunstmuseum Berne

vigorous, 'wild' sketches) make such a conspicuous contrast with its great expressive power. In this vein,
Schorn's *Kunstblatt* declared in 1837 that Salvator Rosa
seemed often to be exploring 'how far the power of the
idea would go, and how it could make clear and comprehensible even the simplest and most defective hieroglyph of line and form'.[33] As a term of connoisseurship,
this usage stemmed from the eighteenth century; it
enabled Goethe, for example, to speak of the 'hieroglyph
of a figure'.[34]

The term still retained its wealth of meaning in the
mind of Max Liebermann, when he defended
Impressionism against the charge of inartistic vapidity.
First and foremost, he demanded, the painter's imagination must assert itself through the form that it creates
itself, a 'hieroglyph' of its own.[35] And even Ernst
Ludwig Kirchner took up the idea of this 'perfect new
form' when, in the person of his *alter ego*, Louis de
Marsalle, he said of himself: 'With freedom and immediacy, Kirchner forms new hieroglyphs.'[36]

Cosmic Rhythm and Tragic Fragment

The Romantic theory of ciphers had to wait until the
twentieth century to unfold its full artistic potential. For
fin-de-siècle artists, it became the paradigm of painting
as a parable of the Creation. In 1896 Oskar A. H.
Schmitz was fascinated by 'colours and lines, of which
events are no more than possible interpretations': the
goal, in Nature and in art, was the 'profoundly alive',
the quality shared by the 'whispering of the treetops'
and the 'rushing of the water'.[37] And Novalis is an
unmistakable presence behind the passage of enumera-
tion in which Anton Lindner, in 1900, associates the
emotional suggestiveness of abstract form and colour
with an all-pervading, cosmic rhythm:

'Motion, that's it! What stirs up inward motion,
triples it, spiritualizes it, begets growth and warmth –
begets life and the courage to live. The rustling and the
warbling that is stirred up by pollen, in the roots and
leaves – or in our own senses by torrents, summer

nights, high winds; by sunsets, surf and lightning; by moonlight, music, wine or any creative thought what-ever – echoes the rustling and warbling within the inter-play of *lines* and *colours*, which stirs the soul to baccha-nalian rapture or compels it to harken in tranquillity.'[38]

Echoing Lavater, this directly visual semiotics of sig-natures evokes the rhythms of life and growth with even greater freedom than Runge's traditional, metaphorical imagery.

The one artist above all who satisfied these expecta-tions was Paul Klee; he was followed by Fritz Kuhr and Fritz Winter, whose endeavours Ernst Kállai, the friend of the Bauhaus painters, interpreted (in a profound study published in 1933) as 'Bioromanticism'.[39] This inner life preoccupied Klee from very early on, though, like the Romantics, he realized that it could only ever be a surmise: 'I am looking for a remote, archetypal point in Creation, where I sense that there is a kind of formula for man, beast, plant, earth, fire, water, air and all the circling forces at once.'[40]

Klee's painting is the first to rely wholly on the phys-iognomic language of patterns and structures. Klee's ele-mental signs for human existence are far removed from the static system proposed by Lavater, who still believed himself to hold the key that Novalis was never able to find (fig. 5). Their movement is one that knows itself to be unending: from roots to moons and suns, and to an unattainable space of freedom. That the 'archetypal … circling forces' are also free forces is made clear by the transparency of his constructions. His loose grids and swooping swarms of curves combine to form revelatory hieroglyphs. Dissonances are episodes that happily dis-solve in the totality of the image. Only with the experi-ence of illness, in Klee's last years, does this structure of relations cease to suffice. The signs become isolated (fig. 6); enigmatic hieroglyphs convey the artist's mortal predicament. The confident restlessness of 'unending interpretation' gives way to a single, fearful question, the question of humanity.

Hilmar Frank

Translated from the German by David Britt

1 On the connection between signatures and analogies in Nature mysticism see Michel Foucault, *Die Ordnung der Dinge* (Frankfurt am Main, 1991), 46–77; Hans Blumenberg, *Die Lesbarkeit der Welt* (Frankfurt am Main, 1986), especially 233–66.

2 Wilhelm Heinrich Wackenroder, *Dichtung, Schriften, Briefe*, ed. Gerda Heinrich (Berlin, 1984), 192.

3 Ludwig Tieck, *Franz Sternbalds Wanderungen*, ed. Alfred Anger (Stuttgart, 1988), 315.

4 Friedrich Schlegel, 'Dritter Nachtrag alter Gemälde', in Schlegel, *Ansichten und Ideen von der christlichen Kunst*, ed. Hans Eichner (Munich, 1959), 151.

5 Christian August Semler, *Ideen zu allegorischen Zimmerverzierungen* (Leipzig, 1806), v.

6 Joseph Görres, '"Die Zeiten": Vier Blätter, nach Zeichnungen von Ph. O. Runge', *Heidelbergische Jahrbücher der Literatur* 1 (1808), 273, 264, 265.

7 Clemens Brentano, 'Andenken eines trefflichen deutschen Mannes und tiefsinnigen Künstlers', in Brentano, *Werke*, ed. Friedhelm Kemp, 2 (Munich, 1963), 1039.

8 Novalis, '*Die Lehrlinge zu Sais*', in Novalis, *Werke in einem Band*, ed. Hans-Dietrich Dahnke and Rudolf Walbiner (Berlin and Weimar, 1984), 73.

9 Immanuel Kant, *Critique of Judgment* (*Kritik der Urteilskraft*), §42.

10 August Wilhelm Schlegel, 'Ueber Zeichnungen zu Gedichten und John Flaxman's Umrisse', *Athenäum* 2, no. 2 (1799), 221.

11 August Wilhelm Schlegel (as note 10).

12 Jacob Bernoulli, *Opera omnia*, 1 (Geneva, 1744), 502, 30.

13 Anton (Antoine) Joseph Pernety, *Versuch einer Physiognomik* (Dresden, 1784), 19.

14 Johann Caspar Lavater, *Physiognomische Fragmente*, 2 (Leipzig and Winterthur, 1776), 73.

15 Isa Lohmann-Siems, 'J. C. A. Grohmanns "Ideen zu einer physiognomischen Anthropologie" aus dem Jahre 1791: Eine Vorwegnahme kunsttheoretischer Gedanken des 20. Jahrhunderts', *Jahrbuch der Hamburger Kunstsammlungen* 8 (1963), 67–84, especially 78; Isa Lohmann-Siems, 'Der universale Formbegriff in der Physiognomik des 18. Jahrhunderts: Ein Beitrag zur Geschichte der gegenwärtigen Kunsttheorie', *Jahrbuch der Hamburger Kunstsammlungen* 9 (1964), 49–74.

16 The present writer owes a debt of thanks to Frau Warja Lavater of Zürich for supplying a photograph and a copy of the paper in which she presented the drawing to the conference *The Faces of Physiognomy*, Dartmouth College, Hanover, N.H., in November 1991.

17 Daniel Runge, 'Nachricht von Philipp Otto Runge', *Deutsches Museum*, ed. Friedrich Schlegel, 1, vol. 2 (1812), 93.

18 August Wilhelm Schlegel (as note 10), 205.

19 Semler (as note 5), iv.

20 Christian August Semler, 'Sollten wir nicht die Hieroglyphen wieder einführen?' *Zeitung fur die elegante Welt* 7, nos. 63, 64 (20 and 21 April 1807), col. 497–501, 507–09, especially 500ff.

21 See Hilmar Frank, 'Die mannigfaltigen Wege zur Kunst: Romantische Kunstphilosophie in einem Schema Caspar David Friedrichs', *IDEA: Jahrbuch der Hamburger Kunsthalle* 10 (1991), 165–96, especially 182–92.

22 Joseph von Eichendorff, *Tagebücher*, ed. Wilhelm Kosch (Regensburg, n.d.), 203 (9 July 1807).

23 *Jenaische Allgemeine Literaturzeitung*, 1 January 1807, viii.

24 Julius, 'Ideen zu Kupfern für den Kling-Klingelalmanach. Für romantische Künstler', *Morgenblatt für gebildete Stände* 4 (1810), 253–54. The writer was the Heidelberg aesthetician Alois Schreiber (personal communication from Dr Jochen Meyer, Cotta-Archiv, Schiller-Nationalmuseum, Marbach am Neckar). On the possibility that Runge was influenced by the Indian 'mythical image', see Werner Hofmann, ed., exh. cat. *Runge in seiner Zeit*, (Hamburg, 1977), 33–35. Might Schreiber's hostile eye have been sharper, in this matter, than those of Runge's friends?

25 Ludwig Urlichs, ed., *Charlotte von Schiller und ihre Freunde*, 3 (Stuttgart, 1865), 227 (letter of 28 August 1807).

26 *Zeitung für Einsiedler* (Heidelberg, 1808; reprint, ed. Hans Jessen, Stuttgart, 1962). The engraving and Görres's explanation are on unnumbered pages prefixed to the May issue.

27 Brentano (as note 7), 1005.

28 Friedrich Schlegel (as note 4), 151.

29 Ludwig Tieck, 'Eine Sommerreise', in *Urania: Taschenbuch auf das Jahr 1834* (Leipzig, 1834), 73–237, especially 88.

30 Gerhard Anton Ulrich Vieth, 'Versuch, Gestalten organischer Naturkörper geometrisch zu construiren', in Ludwig Wilhelm Gilbert, ed., *Annalen der Physik* 53, no. 3 (Leipzig, 1816), 225–41; 4 plates.

31 Lorenz Oken, ed., *Isis* 1, no. 24 (1817), col. 186–87.

32 Georg Büchner, *Woyzeck*, ed. and reconstructed by Henri Poschmann (Leipzig, 1984), 19.

33 K. Vogel, 'Salvator Rosa's Skizzenbuch', *Kunst-Blatt* 18, no. 66 (17 August 1837), 274.

34 Johann Wolfgang von Goethe, 'Der Sammler und die Seinigen', quoted from Ludwig Volkmann, 'Die Hieroglyphen der deutschen Romantiker', *Münchner Jahrbuch der bildenden Kunst*, n.s., 3 (1926), 159.

35 Max Liebermann, 'Die Phantasie in der Malerei', in Liebermann, *Die Phantasie in der Malerei: Schriften und Reden* (Berlin, 1983), 54.

36 Louis de Marsalle, 'Über die Schweizer Arbeiten von E. L. Kirchner', in Carl Einstein and Paul Westheim, eds., *Europa-Almanach 1925* (reprint, Leipzig, 1984), 66, 70.

37 Oskar A. H. Schmitz, 'Über das Empfinden der Landschaft', *Wiener Rundschau* 1 (1896), 258–59.

38 Anton Lindner, 'Farbe und Linie: Ein Versuch', *Wiener Rundschau* 4, no. 1 (1900), 2–6; no. 2, 31–36; passage quoted 34.

39 Ernst Kállai, 'Zeichen und Bilder', in Kállai, *Vision und Formgesetz: Aufsätze über Kunst und Künstler 1921–1933*, ed. Tanja Frank (Leipzig and Weimar, 1986), 221.

40 Paul Klee, 'Der eigene Standpunkt', in Klee, *Kunst-Lehre*, ed. Günther Regel (Leipzig, 1987), 59–60.

The Crystalline

1.

Hans Sedlmayr was not the first to ascribe the predominance of elementary geometrical forms in the architecture of the Revolution and the tendency to linear two-dimensionality in the painting of the period around 1800 to a penchant for the inorganic. However, what he saw as a cause of decline was interpreted by the Romantics, starting from similar premises, as the deciding factor in a universal advance. In the various strategies designed to endow the rigid forms of art with the certainty of a solid centre in a living nature pervaded by the Divine, the leitmotif was the organic crystal, symbolizing the 'monism of the cosmos', for which Ernst Haeckel attempted to supply a scientific justification a century later.[1] The idea of the inorganic infused with organic life entered above all into Expressionist notions of a German 'will to art' (*Kunstwollen*).[2]

It is not surprising, then, that this *topos* combined with 'German' Gothic and first took shape in an architectural fantasy that Friedrich Schlegel wove into his description of the unfinished cathedral of Cologne. Imagining what it would look like when completed, he compared towers, pillars and buttresses with a natural growth that shoots upwards, and so took up Goethe's earlier reflections of Gothic architecture. Seen from afar the whole complex resembled a wood, but 'when one moves closer it appears more like an enormous crystalline formation'.[3]

Here Schlegel modifies the credo of his friend Wilhelm Heinrich Wackenroder in order to accommodate it to his programme of German Christian art. Whereas Wackenroder had seen nature and art as 'wonderful languages'[4], existing independently of each other and comprehensible only through feeling, the two now fused in a symbol that combined the crystalline with the vegetable. At least we have the 'impression'[5], says Schlegel, that it is all one whether we are dealing with works of art or with the works of Nature. This fiction, masquerading as perception, anticipates Alois Riegl in differentiating

between a tactile near view and an optical distant view and lends conviction to the 'obscure feelings' that Wackenroder had described as 'the genuine God-sent witnesses of truth'.[6] This was the beginning of the art history of perception; it followed the discovery of a 'new organ' in which the mind and the senses act in unison without having to resort to conceptual thought. Through the modernization of the 'outpourings of the heart' in a Gothic without God – secularized as an 'imitation of nature's abundance'[7] – the restorative tendency of Romantic thought gains ground. The crystalline cathedral bids farewell to the 'new church' of the French Revolution that had earlier been welcomed[8] and inaugurates the path that leads inwards to a 'German form' whose Nordic character is assured by the Gothic and the crystalline, though as yet without any social connotations. The republican notion of universal poetry gives way to a religious apprehension of art; the crystalline, defined by Friedrich Wilhelm Schelling as 'the spiritual within the material',[9] preserves the metaphysical basis of Christian art. Moreover, the new science of crystallography (the teachings of René Just Haüy, its founder, had probably become known in Germany in the early nineteenth century) could be used in support of this idea deriving from natural philosophy and so verify the Platonic bodies, as it were. As 'symbols of mathematics',[10] crystals supplied material evidence of the 'spirit of Nature', though only by way of a generalization from mineralogy. It thus seemed possible to derive the world as a whole from formulas: a technological conception, ultimately dedicated to the artificial reproducibility of existing reality, became the content of salvation.

This restoration of the metaphysical prime cause from the spirit of natural science perpetuated the Classical idea that Nature was raised to a higher plane in art. Just as Wackenroder, in a monk's dream, declared Albrecht Dürer and Raphael to be friends, in order to celebrate the union of Nature and 'heavenly beauty', so too Schlegel's imagination aimed at a reconciliation. The crystalline element in Gothic architecture relates it to the Classical ideal, defined by Winckelmann as 'noble simplicity' and already echoed in connection with the unfinished cathedral.[11] Also evoked by mineralogy is the Classical image of man in ancient sculptures, which could also be found in the earth and were in modern times assigned to the same inorganic sphere.[12] They already occupied a symbolic position between 'the power of Nature to form and the power of man to create',[13] which was now depersonalized, so to speak, and attributed to crystalline Gothic. In its imagined fossil character Schlegel tried to justify once more the necessary link between the external and the internal, form and content, beyond the beautiful. After all the criticism of faith in the age of Enlightenment and the overthrow of clerical authority, it was only in the illusion of sensual certainty – as a phantasmagoria – that the infinite could be directly perceived and represented, as it were, 'even without reference to the ideas and mysteries of Christianity'.[14] The historical end of iconography is contradicted by the feeling for form as a symbol.

The situation in which artistic crystalline Nature is viewed is thus so designed that the aesthetic boundary is not accessible to the eye. The viewer surrenders his real self and immerses himself in the other – aesthetic – reality, which can no more be taken in than the reality of living Nature.[15] In this pseudo-transcendency – the putative reality of art[16] – lies the basis of the idea of the total work of art (*Gesamtkunstwerk*). Self-deception, which is inherent in the modern conception of art, is preserved, though not yet essentially tied to reproducibility. The experience of art as experience of the world is now envisaged as a receptive act that is at the same time productive. The symbolism arises in the moment of contemplation and in the moment of creation.

It is hardly fortuitous that in some of his works Caspar David Friedrich, the most advanced artist of his age, came close to Schlegel's backward-looking utopia, as if to mitigate the radical innovation of his painting. Gothic architecture, as a transparent phenomenon in *Vision of the Christian Church* (Schäfer Collection, Schweinfurt), also implies that the experience of the total work of art is essentially religious. In the formal analogy between fir-trees and the churches in the London *Winter Landscape* (cat. 20) Friedrich symbolizes his art as a 'crystalline growth'; through this allegorization of the abstract compositional figure as spiritual Nature he unintentionally conforms to Friedrich Wilhelm von Ramdohr's criteria. Christian iconography is no longer the primary message, but raises artistic production itself to the status of a cult activity, as in the Wanderer's Prayer. Moreover, Friedrich's practice of transforming existing chruches into ruins or, conversely, 'crystallizing' ruins into idealized cathedrals, has the same effect as Schlegel's change of perspective, in that it gives form to an idea current in the eighteenth century: that the destruction of a building that had a utilitarian purpose could arouse interest in its aesthetic form.[17] Crystalline Gothic embodies, as it were, an architecture that arises from the symbiosis of ruin and Nature and acquires aesthetic form in the depiction. Moreover, when it is said that the 'inner geometry of Nature' underlies the Gothic cathedral in the form of 'the triangle and the square, as well as the sphere (!) and the cross', it is possible to understand the covering of the elementary forms with the 'blossoming fullness of life' as a form of disguise. These forms were probably revealed less by the 'old church style' than by the architects of the Revolution.[18] Schlegel here plans the synthetic style of which not only historicism, but the avant-garde will dream.[19]

2.

Eternal values, formerly personalized in God and the prince, could now re-emerge as bourgeois values in an impersonal and empty whole. The natural cycle, represented by Philipp Otto Runge's *The Times of Day* for instance, acquired the status of a Christian eschatology, though now its sole aim was the aesthetic experience – the total work of art. Crystalline stones are the source of *Night* (cat. 9); inorganic nature brings forth the organic and is in turn the aim of the latter. Utopia lies here in the mythology, the eternal changelessness embodied in the structure of the crystal,[20] The name of God is replaced by the 'effective principle'[21] itself. The demonstration of this principle in the formation of crystals is designed to unite history, Nature and art as manifestations of a single urge and to preserve the Christian notion of creation by transferring it to artistic creativity. In Schelling's view the regularity of organic and inor-

Fig.1 Caspar David Friedrich, *Sea of Ice* c.1823-24, Hamburger Kunsthalle

ganic structures stood not only for 'science, through which Nature works', but also for the 'artistic impulse'.[22] The creative act itself consequently becomes the transcendental goal; the work is transfigured as the symbol of this process, since there is no longer any other transcendency it can relate to. Schlegel was not considering the product of artistic creativity, which was for him only the expression of a universal law of movement. The merging of the work into the universal process through which it comes into being creates a unity between the artistic form and its material content, the loss of which was diagnosed by Georg Wilhelm Friedrich Hegel.[23]

However, the emphasis placed on the processual aspect contained something quite modern: to invoke the infinite variability of natural forms implied a new awareness of the historicity of human society; this awareness also reveals the incipient sense that the sphere of production is the basis of society. In the image of crystallization, however, productivity remains one-dimensional. In promoting the bourgeois notion of development as a linear process, it is conceived as an original renunciation, as the expression of natural laws, and thus adheres to the static constitution of society. The temporal straight line leads to the Romantic notion of Nature and history as cyclic and denies the negative factor that is inherent in Nature too. Movement and cessation of movement become opposing poles. The antithetical categories employed in writings on the history of art took up this non-historical sense of the image of the crystal.

Conversely, the avant-garde element in Romantic art can be seen, by contrast with such a cessation of movement, in the dialectic tension between natural and artistic forms. Friedrich's *Sea of Ice* (fig. 1 and colour plate, p. 97) transforms motionless Nature into a monument of art, without equating the abstract form with Nature or, like Runge's arabesque, establishing a congruence between the two. The threshold position between construct and picture, between congealed movement and the work of art, is the artistic statement, which lies beyond traditional iconography. The mountain range, architecturally constructed out of a pile of snowy blocks, like the ornamental crests of the waves, shows the cessation of movement, a temporal factor that at the same time reveals a constructive potential, which is by no means the productive law of Nature, as Friedrich's motto 'Through death to new life' suggests. The opaque density of the water, which can be observed in many of Friedrich's other sea pieces, causes movement to congeal, so that one can experience the change to another movement, not identical with the previous one. The painting *Chalk Cliffs on Rügen* (Oskar Reinhart Collection, Winterthur) shows the same turning-point in the two male figures, both of which probably represent the artist's self. The citizen's gaze, fixed on the abyss, is not taken up in the longing gaze of the patriot. The distance remains empty; the fossil nature of the cliffs offers no relief from their terrible aspect, such as is promised by the contemplation of visionary Gothic.

3.

More effective was the anti-Enlightenment potential of the symbol of the crystal. It was not by chance that it became widely known through the building of the Crystal Palace, the 'glass monster'[24] that took over the heritage of crystalline Gothic. An 'infinite' perspective, inwardly related to Schlegel's, finally made it possible to pass an artistic judgement on the scandalous nudity of the technical construct – disguised as Nature: 'Here too, as in the case of a crystal, there is no real interior and exterior ... . We are in a piece of the atmosphere that has been cut out,' wrote Richard Lucae.[25] The 'almost nonexistent' boundary between Nature and construct did not refer to the actual transparency of the glass wall; this

Fig.2 Wenzel Hablik, *Crystal Castle in the Sea* 1914, National Gallery, Prague

Fig.3 Illustration from Bruno Taut *Alpine Architektur*, Hagen 1919

only lent credibility to the idea. Rather, the crystal created a symbolic identity between casing and kernel, between frame and ornament, whose divorce in the course of industrial mass production had led to a crisis in the world of arts and crafts and plunged architecture into a serious conflict with engineering technique. Gottfried Semper wished to apply his theory of original social needs and natural 'types' of arts and crafts as a remedy for this crisis and to purify the degenerate stylistic forms by means of aesthetic archetypes. Snow crystals, together with organic structures, illustrate the natural law of 'style in the technical and tectonic arts'[26]. This was an early attempt to justify a 'necessary' ornament in an imaginary society, which, conceived as instinct, natural law or need, anticipates the later theories of form and function that led to the rejection of ornament.

Thus the adoption of the crystal as the leitmotif of the avant-garde had its origin in the Arts and Crafts movement, which set itself the impossible task of replacing the eclecticism of historical stylistic choice by a synthesis of 'artistic endeavour' and practical living. This was of course possible only in the imagination, that is, through

the formula of the nature of the crystal. When Peter Behrens, in the role of artist as prophet, solemnly unveiled a diamond crystal on the Mathildenhöhe in Darmstadt, he held out the promise of an art that would give true expression to the life of the citizen, 'as coaldust, seized by the force of the elements, is transformed into the pure, brilliant and clearly formed diamond crystal ... .'[27]

The social aspect of the new architecture necessarily remained a stage play, linked to the idea of a new theatre building that was to unite the stage and the auditorium as a representation of art and life.[28] In the socially utopian dimension of the crystal fantasy we no doubt have to see the intention of defending autonomous art as an ideal way of life. In Marx's appreciation of the value of the commodity as 'crystallized work' we see the 'common social substance'[29] whose idealistic inversion means utopia. The 'artistic endeavour' of the avant-garde confronts the objectifying of human work as a commodity with the model of an abstract, non-alienated mode of working, which cannot fail to seem somewhat arcane, with its denial of both the producing subject and the produced and appropriated object. When Behrens, in an advertisement for an electric lamp, inscribed the brand name AEG on the facets of a crystal[30], he was visualizing not only electric light, but also the precious crystals as a combination of art and nature in the aesthetic of design.

The representative claim of the crystal as a symbol lies in 'making the invisible visible'. This is an aspect of the Divine, which could no longer be formulated in authoritative terms. Hence, the place formerly occupied by the Divine must have been taken over by the metaphysics of the valuable form (*Wertform*). It is the model for the transformation of material, and this in turn characterizes the way in which classical Modernism saw itself as a force for social renewal. Yet the 'precious crystal', as the container of a new community, must also represent the place of the monarch. Not for the first time in the princely foundation of the colony on the Mathildenhöhe, which predates artistic communities right down to the *Gläserne Kette* (Glass Chain), the aesthetic of existence symbolized by the crystal is seen as expressing the historial reconciliation between the aristocracy and the middle class. The crystal symbolism of Expressionism always points to the supreme authority – whether this reveals itself as a castle (fig. 2), as a 'city crown' or as an 'Alpine Architecture' that reaches to the stars (fig. 3). Here the Alps, like Gothic architecture, are seen in their fossil character, in their symbolic function, which points to a sacred archetype. At the beginning of the eighteenth century, Scheuchzer's Physica sacra had taken the Alps as a proof of Genesis, as remnants of the flood. This notion was adapted to the cult of art in the nineteenth century. Viollet-le-Duc saw in the Alps only the deformation of a regular crystalline 'original form'; the notion can still be discerned in Taut's building project, which is in fact a prayer.[31]

In Expressionism the transformation of coaldust into diamonds – symbolizing the purification of 'raw' life and its transformation into beauty – is often taken over by modern technology. Electric light, which turns into day, acquires a transcendental significance. The building as a lamp or a shining heavenly body is a recurrent motif in the crystalline fantasies of architecture. Wenzel Hablik's flying settlements illustrate the crystalline 'growth' of buildings, their self-motion underlining the Futurist craze for technology. Electrical machines can for

Fig.4 Hans Scharoun, *Principles of Architecture* c.1919, Akademie der Künste, Berlin

instance turn sand into glass, and this, as a self-forming substance, assumes the form of a giant glass house.[32] Hans Scharoun's drawing *Principles of Architecture* (fig. 4) – a crystal plant dynamically shooting up – presents the new architecture as a second nature, sublimated by technology. Just as Schlegel, with his crystalline Gothic, 'experienced' his own construct, so Scharoun's idea of a people's house turns 'I' and 'I' into 'you'.[33] The desired social meaning of modern building, seen as the origin of aesthetic form, is nothing other than the 'inner geometry' of nature, now filled with life.

Bruno Taut's fantasies unintentionally reveal the futility of the underlying historical concept, which always started from the 'pure' form, detached from all syntax, and supposed it possible to invest it with a content. The Expressionist crystal no longer conveys a message. The universal building project of *Alpine Architecture* ends in the *Great Void*; the last picture of *The World Architect*, a cinematogrphic series of 1920, shows the crystalline interior of the new architecture congealing with night and the universe to form an abstract structure of facets. Reduced to cosmic emptiness, the cyclic model of the Romantics still provides Taut with the wherewithal for

Fig.5 Erich Heckel, *Day of Glass* 1913, Staatsgalerie Moderner Kunst, Munich

an affirmative turning-point, for absolute negation can equally well be total affirmation. With the help of Master Eckhart, the void can become a vessel for the Divine.[34] The crystalline form as an expression of the 'many-sidedness' of relations – and here it already refers to serial production – can serve any function; in this sense the emptiness of the 'new apartment' (1924) is propagated as a guarantee of real living. With the 'omnisignificance' of his architecture Taut established a recurrent pattern of interpretation that assigns the function of a universal equivalent to the abstract from spanning the genres.

4.

'We do not display personal experience. We shape the primeval image, hard, bronze, crystalline ... .'[35] Under this motto Wilhelm Worringer's concept of a 'primitive urge to abstraction', oriented to 'regular crystalline composition', was advanced as the metaphysical legitimation for the new abstract painting. The anti-French rejection of the 'subjective oversensitivity' of Impressionism[37] was echoed in the German reception of Cubism. At the same time the concept of an essentially crystalline art found its way into painting too. In Erich Heckel's *Day of Glass* (fig. 5) sky and water crystallize into prismatic structures without affecting the conventional picture space. The Cubist destruction of a space unified by perspective is reinterpreted as a way to make the subject dynamic. Lyonel Feininger began with the same prismatic simplification of pictorial subjects, as shown by *Gelmeroda III* (cat. 158), yet although he went on to a much higher degree of abstraction, he adhered to an objective realization of the aesthetic form in the architectonic elements. Although the picture space undergoes a degree of fragmentation, inspired by Cubism, the fragmentation acquired a symbolic character through the transparency of the surfaces, which always convey a 'literal' impression. In the stylized cathedral on the title-page of the first Bauhaus manifesto, Schlegel's total work of art re-emerges 'as the crystalline symbol of a future faith'.[38]

It was Paul Klee who most vehemently opposed the Cubist deformation of the pictorial subject and was all the more consistent in realizing it artistically. At the start of his abstract phase he developed a creative doctrine in which the pictorial means themselves were credited with vital energy; he was thus able, at least in theory, to ensure the organic status of the picture.[39] The water-colour *Crystal-Gradation* (fig. 6) can be fitted into his doctrine of the 'movement' of colours on the colour circle, which Klee conceived in musical terms as crescendo and diminuendo.[40] But his drawing *Genesis of the Constellations* relates also to the genesis of the work; the interpretation of the spots of colour as constellations – which the title suggests – is thus linked with the ambitions of the star-like glass architecture of Taut. Klee's understanding of movement as the 'proper nature of the work'[41] is reflected in the recurrent motif of the arrow, although the synthetic intention of his theory is subverted by his practice. Only in Klee's Bauhaus doctrine did Schlegel's equation of the perception of art with the perception of nature undergo a thorough systematization, the fantastic nature of which has still hardly been appreciated. The essay on 'Ways of Nature Study', for instance, develops the Romantic model of perception

Fig.6 Paul Klee, *Crystal-Gradation, under the Spell of the Stars* 1921, Kunstmuseum Basel, Kupferstichkabinett

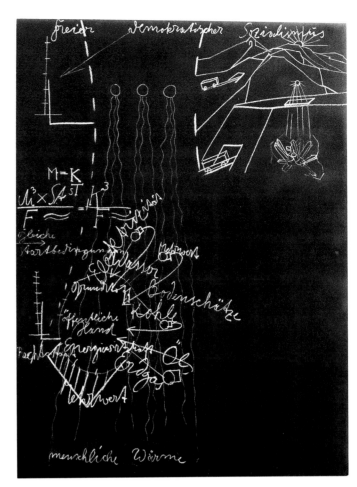

Fig.7 Joseph Beuys, One of the blackboards from *Das Kapital Raum 1970–77*, Hallen für neue Kunst, Schaffhausen. Note the drawing of crystals.

into a 'synthesis of outward seeing and inward contemplation', in order to make the transformation of the artefact into nature and the creation of works credible as a 'simile of the work of God'.[42] The theoretical precondition for the 'total view' of the eye that is visualized here (see cat. 165 *Eye – Centre – You*) is the artist's self-stylization as a 'transcendental subject'. In this way Klee sets himself apart from the 'earth-bound' artists Alfred Kubin and Franz Marc[43] – despite the fact that Marc's view of war as a preliminary to a new spiritual art – of which we find a reflex in the drawing entitled *Conflict* (in the *Sketchbook from the Field*, cat. 157) – was not far removed from Klee's theory of abstraction.[44] His symbolic death in the crystal, evidently dramatized in reference to Worringer in the diary of 1914, defines the abstract 'artistic endeavour' as a kind of self-begetting, which brings back the artist as the creator of a second existence that unified art and life. A parallel is afforded by Dadaist dandyism, whose aesthetic existence culminates in suicide.[45] Schwitters's *MERZbau*, (colour plate,

pp. 360–1), as the first step towards the 'collective shaping of the world, a universal style', updates the subjectless nature of crystalline Gothic.[46]

The advent of Expressionism did not put an end to the crystal boom. The Surrealist idea of an 'automatic' record of the unconscious came into its own. The reference to mineralogy could still prove useful. 'It grows on me like my toe-nails. I have to cut it, but it repeatedly grows back' – this is how Hans Arp described his work as an artist.[47] At the end of the 1930s, as if to complement his organic formal language with inorganic nature, he created a crystal sculpture.[48]

5.

Only postwar art has given up the formal vocabulary of Cubism and Surrealism, which could be united in an organic crystalline whole with its analogue in nature.[49] Informal art developed the process of materialization that began in abstraction and deprived the picture of all

Fig.8 Joseph Beuys, *Das Kapital Raum 1970–77*, Hallen für neue Kunst, Schaffhausen

its linguistic character. The materialization of the artistic object was probably taken farthest by Joseph Beuys, who was nevertheless strongly influenced by the Romantic theory of 'natura artifex'. The growth of crystals on a blackboard of his installation *Das Kapital Raum 1970–1977* (figs.7 and 8) and the early drawing *Lady's Cloak* (1948), which cites Runge's plant studies[50], represent a refraction of the idea of unity deriving from natural philosophy; in other words it is a 'didactic piece' that admits of no immediate emotional approach. Moreover, the title of the installation refers unequivocally to Marx's chief work and thus directly reflects the connection between crystallization and the formation of values. The chalk drawing shows a mine, a traditional symbol of alchemy. Sunlight streams into the mine and so guarantees the formation of crystals, which according to esoteric teachings is the final stage before the extraction of the stone. Tunnels and waggons indicate that the treasures of nature will be appropriated. The chalk drawing – part childishly naïve, part scientific – clearly relates to the diagram on the left, which illustrates the production of energy and expressly leads to 'added value'. Yet no economic model answering to the title 'Free Democratic Socialism' and the aim of 'human warmth' can be discerned as the theme. The 'blackboard pictures' of Beuys defy any attempt to interpret them. The content of the work is not present in the object itself, but lies rather in a temporal factor that can be grasped only in the reflection of the form. The chalk

drawings, like the other objects in the installation, present themselves in a condition that oscillates between *objet d'art* and utilitarian object. The hastiness of the writing, the combination of signs and blackboards, which can hardly be brought into order and related to one another, and the traces of earlier inscriptions that have been obliterated – all these challenge us to see them as fortuitous, invalid, dispensable. The historical element is linked to the present. This also occurs in Friedrich's *Sea of Ice*, though within the subject, in the insoluble contradiction between planes and in the ordering of space. Now it lies solely in the artistic form. Whereas conservative crystal symbolism created a synthesis of movement and non-movement as an eternal process of becoming, and consigned history to the fossil character of the form. Beuys displays the relic as a trace of past action and potential future action. The ruin returns as an image that has been used before and perhaps used up, but whose historicity is not extinguished in the alternative world of crystallized nature. On the contrary, the aesthetic presents itself as the *end* of transcendency; it involves a challenge to destruction, such as we find in the *Fat Corner* and other works. Beuys may show the solid crystal, but only in order to have it melt and revert to liquid form.

Regine Prange

Translated from the German by David McLintock

1 Ernst Haeckel, *Die Lebenswunder. Gemeinverständliche Studien über Biologische Philosophie. Ergänzungsband zu dem Buche über die Welträtsel* (Leipzig, 1906), 16.

2 Above all we should mention Worringer, who defined Nordic artistic endeavour as a 'movement intensified on an inorganic basis': Wilhelm Worringer, *Abstraktion und Einfühlung. Ein Beitrag zur Stilpsychologie* (Munich, 1908, 14th ed. 1987), 151.

3 Friedrich Schlegel, 'Briefe auf einer Reise durch die Niederlande, Rheingegenden, die Schweiz und einen Teil von Frankreich', *Kritische Friedrich-Schlegel-Ausgabe*, vol 4 ('Ansichten und Ideen von der christlichen Kunst'), ed. Hans Behler (Paderborn and Munich, 1959), 178f.

4 Wilhelm Heinrich Wackenroder and Ludwig Tieck, *Herzensergiessungen eines kunstliebenden Klosterbruders*, Berlin, 1797 (Stuttgart, 1979), 64–69.

5 Schlegel (as note 3), 179.

6 Wackenroder (as note 4), 62.

7 Schlegel (as note 3), 180.

8 On Schlegel's justification of the aesthetic in terms of historical philosophy see Karl-Heinz Bohrer, 'Friedrich Schlegels Rede über die Mythologie', id. (ed.), *Mythos und Moderne. Begriff und Bild einer Rekonstruktion* (Frankfurt, 1983), 52–82.

9 F. W. Schelling, 'Über das Verhältnis der bildenden Künste zur Natur' (1807), *Schellings Werke*, ed. Manfred Schröter, 3. Ergänzungsband (Munich, 1959), 388–429. The passage quoted appears on p. 400.

10 Franz von Kobell, *Über Fortschritte der Mineralogie seit Haüy* (Munich, 1832), 6.

11 Schlegel (as note 3), 178.

12 Horst Bredekamp, *Antikensehnsucht und Maschinenglaube. Die Geschichte der Kunstkammer und die Zukunft der Kunstgeschichte* (Berlin, 1993), 19.

13 Bredekamp (as note 12). The synthesis of the rigid crystal of the pyramid with the naturalistic artistic endeavour of the Greeks is envisaged by Worringer too in his vision of Gothic architecture. See Worringer (as note 2), 157f.

14 Schlegel (as note 3), 180. Within the concept of universal poetry ('Athenäum-Fragment 116') infinity was still understood as a category of reflection.

15 Schlegel (as note 3), 179.

16 The continuity of this idea can be seen in Dagobert Frey, 'Der Realitätscharakter des Kunstwerkes' in *Kunstwissenschaftliche Grundlagen. Prolegomena zu einer Kunstphilosophie* (Vienna, 1946; Darmstadt, 1992), 107–49.

17 Cf. Bruno Reudenbach, *G. B. Piranesi. Architektur als Bild. Der Wandel der Architekturauffassung des 18. Jahrhunderts* (Munich, 1979), esp. 92.

18 Schlegel (as note 3), 179.

19 Cf. Schinkel on the ideal form of the religious building, which, since 'art itself is religion', is the 'starting point for the whole definition of architecture' and hence for the new style at which is aimed. 'The whole should give the impression of an infinitely variable nature that constantly seeks to purify itself.' 'Through the substructure the earth should be shown in its crystallization, above which the plant strives towards the sky ... .' Karl Schinkel, *Briefe, Tagebücher, Gedanken*, selected by Hans Mackowsky (Berlin, 1922), 195ff.

20 Cf. Claude Lévi-Strauss, *Strukturale Anthropologie* (Frankfurt, 1967), 253: 'If a daring image is permitted, the myth is a linguistic construct that occupies a similar place in the sphere of spoken language to that of the crystal in the world of physical matter. In relation to language on the one hand and to spoken language on the other, its position would resemble that of the crystal: an object between a statistical aggregate of molecules and the molecular structure itself.'

21 Schelling (as note 9), 399.

22 Schelling (as note 9), 404. This notion from natural philosophy underlies Riegl's term 'artistic intention'.

23 See Werner Busch, *Die notwendige Arabeske. Wirklichkeitsaneignung und Stilisierung in der deutschen Kunst des 19. Jahrhunderts* (Berlin, 1985), 21f.

24 A. Welby Pugin, in an unpublished letter cited by Nicolaus Pevsner, *Wegbereiter moderner Formgebung von Morris bis Gropius* (Cologne, 1983), 13.

25 Richard Lucae, 'Die Macht des Raumes in der Baukunst', excerpt from a special number of the *Zeitschrift für Bauwesen* 19 (1869), quoted by Julius Posener, *Berlin auf dem Wege zu einer neuen Architektur. Das Zeitalter Wilhelms II.* (Munich, 1979), 485f.

26 Gottfried Semper, *Der Stil in den technischen und tektonischen Künsten oder Praktische Ästhetik. Ein Handbuch für Techniker, Künstler und Kunstfreunde, vol. 1:* 'Textile art viewed on its own and in relation to architecture' (Frankfurt am Main, 1960), XXV.

27 Alexander Koch, Grossherzog Ludwig und die Ausstellung der Künstlerkolonie in *Darmstadt vom Mai bis Oktober 1901* (Darmstadt, 1901), 60. The celebratory play for Georg Fuchs was staged in accordance with an idea of Peter Behrens.

28 On the theatrical idea, see Regine Prange, 'Das kristalline Sinnbild' in *Moderne Architektur in Deutschland 1900–1950. Expressionismus und Neue Sachlichkeit* (Frankfurt: Deutsches Architekturmuseum, 1994).

29 Karl Marx, *Das Kapital. Kritik der politischen ökonomie*, vol. l (Hamburg, 1867; Berlin, 1983), 19.

30 Tilmann Buddensieg, *Industriekultur – Peter Behrens und die AEG 1907–1914* (Milan, 1978), 61f.

31 On the tradition of architectural theory, see Werner Oechslin, 'Architecture and Nature. On the origin and convertibility of architecture', *Lotus International* 31 (1981), 4–19. Reproduction of Viollet-le-Duc's scheme of evolution on p. 11, ill. 12.

32 Wenzel August Hablik, 22 July 1920, in Romana Schneider and Iain Boyd Whyte (eds), *Die Briefe der Gläsernen Kette* (Berlin, 1986), 134f.

33 Hablik (as note 32), 4, ill. no. 12.

34 Bruno Taut, 'Das Haus des Himmels', in Ulrich Conrads (ed.), *Bruno Taut. Frühlicht 1920–1922. Eine Folge für die Verwirklichung des neuen Baugedankens* (Berlin and Frankfurt, 1963), 33.

35 Kurt Liebmann, 'Lebt!', *Der Sturm* 13 (1923), 183–86, quotation p. 184.

36 Worringer (as note 2), 79.

37 Wilhelm Hausenstein, *Die Kunst in diesem Augenblick* (Munich, 1920), 2.

38 Walter Gropius, *Programm des staatlichen Bauhauses in Weimar 1919*, quoted from Ulrich Conrads, *Programme und Manifeste zur Architektur des 20. Jahrhunderts* (Berlin and Frankfurt, 1964), 47.

39 Paul Klee, *Beiträge zur bildnerischen Formenlehre*. Facsimile edition of the original manuscript of Paul Klee's first lecture cycle at the Bauhaus in Weimar 1921/ 1922, ed. Jürgen Glaesemer (Basle and Stuttgart, 1979), 5. The genesis of the work 'begins at the point that sets itself in motion'.

40 Paul Klee, *Unendliche Naturgeschichte. Form und Gestaltungslehre*, vol II, ed. Jürg Spiller (Basle and Stuttgart, 1970), 313.

41 Paul Klee, *Pädagogisches Skizzenbuch*, Bauhausbücher 2 (Munich, 1925), 23: 'The work as human action (genesis) is *movement*, as regards both production and reception.'

42 Paul Klee, *Wege des Naturstudiums* (1923), quoted from Christian Geelhaar (ed), *Paul Klee. Schriften, Rezensionen und Aufsätze* (Cologne, 1976), 125f.

43 Paul Klee, *Tagebücher 1898–1918*. New critical edition for the Paul-Klee-Stiftung Kunstmuseum, Berne, by Wolfgang Kersten (Berne, 1988), no. 958: 'Kubin ... longed for the crystalline, but could not free himself from the tough mud of the world of phenomena'. On Klee and Marc, see O. K. Werckmeister, 'Klee im Ersten Weltkrieg' in exh. cat. *Paul Klee. Das Frühwerk 1883–1992* (Munich: Städtische Galerie im Lenbachhaus, 1980), 166–226, esp. 173–88.

44 On this thematic complex, see Regine Prange, 'Hinüberbauen in eine jenseitige Gegend. Paul Klees Lithographie "Der Tod für die Idee" und die Genese der Abstraktion', *Wallraf-Richartz-Jahrbuch* 54 (Cologne, 1994), 281–314.

45 Cf. William S. Rubin, *Dada und Surrealismus* (Stuttgart, s.a.), 13.

46 The spread of the Merz idea. *Merz I Holland Dada* (Hanover, 1923), 9. *Castle and Cathedral with Fountain* appeared as an illustration and with explanatory text in Taut's *Frühlicht* (as note 34), 166. Entirely in the spirit of Taut, Schwitters here designs the transformation of Berlin into a Merz work made up of light and colour.

47 Quoted from Hans Richter, *Dada- Kunst und Antikunst* (Cologne, 1964), 44.

48 Ex. cat. *Arp 1886–1966* (Stuttgart: Württembergischer Kunstverein, 1986), 219 (ill.).

49 'The crystal is the symbol of geometric-abstract art, the pebble the symbol of organic-abstract ... .' (Georg Schmidt, 1938, quoted from Stefanie Poley, 210).

50 Theodora Vischer, 'Beuys und die Romantik', in *7 Vorträge zu Beuys 1986*, publ. by the Museumsverein Mönchengladbach (Mönchengladbach, 1986), 81–106, esp. 98f.

I should like to thank Astrit Schmidt-Burckhardt and Angelika Thiekötter for many valuable suggestions.

The Cathedral of Romanticism
Gothic visions of architecture: Lyonel Feininger and Karl Friedrich Schinkel

Gothic has always lived on the metamorphosis of its idea and form. It is everything within itself, and everything in one: baldacchino, bridge, cathedral, crypt, firmament, forest, grotto, hall, nave, pier, plant, tower. The young Lyonel Feininger saw this at an early stage in the Gothic arch of Brooklyn Bridge and the masts and rigging of the ships on the Hudson River in New York, and then it suddenly flickered before his eyes in the cast-iron 'cathedral stove' in the home of the Clapps, a farming family in Sharon, Connecticut. When the fire of this naïve vision of Gothic architecture went out, a feeling of unsatisfied longing carried Feininger (1871–1956), a young American, back to the land of his fathers in the late nineteenth-century, back to the wellsprings of Gothic architecture and medieval city-building in Europe. It was not the 'spirit of the Gothic',[1] but the feeling of an 'element of longing'[2] for the places of the past that made Feininger into a modern Romantic.[3] While the 'tramp' Auguste Rodin pursued the origins of Gothic in the 'cathédrales de France',[4] Lyonel Feininger was discovering Gothic[5] in the unassuming village churches of Thuringia, and on the Baltic: 'There are church towers in god-forsaken little places that are among the most mystical things I know by so-called cultured man.'[6] The village church in Gelmeroda near Weimar (colour plate on p. 349) with its pointed spire became the leitmotif of Feininger's cathedral vision,[7] which led him from nature-notes to the glassy sounds of his celestial cathedrals and churches in the 1920s.

The ideal nature of the Gothic cathedral was the legacy of early Romanticism, and during his Berlin years (1888–1918) it brought Feininger close to Karl Friedrich Schinkel (1781–1841). Feininger probably saw the visionary Gothic cathedrals Schinkel painted in his 1810–1815 Gothic period and paintings by Caspar David Friedrich in the *Deutsche Jahrhundertausstellung* (Centenary Exhibition of German Art) in Berlin in 1906. He also encountered Schinkel's neo-Gothic church in Friedrichswerder in Berlin. But it is not certain whether Feininger knew Schinkel's artistic utopias in the second

Schinkel Museum, which had only been open to the public since 1931. He never acknowledged Schinkel verbally.[8] And so this was not a declared elective affinity between painter and architect. There are analogies at certain points, but there are differences too, involving spiritual principles, fundamental characteristics of Gothic art (inorganic quality, expression, dynamics, linearity, yearning for the transcendental), and the related situation of a century's social upheaval and change that has always accompanied religious and social utopias.

Gothic cathedral

'Gothic cathedrals, lonely watchers over sunken cities':[9] the poet Adolf Knoblauch used this evocative metaphor in his correspondence with Feininger in the war year 1917. It is reminiscent of Schinkel's painting *Gothic Cathedral by the Water* (fig. 1), painted in 1813. As a constructing Cubist and Expressionist, Feininger made the village church the paradigm of his inner vision;[10] Schinkel, an early Romantic, experienced Gothic in his encounters with the great cathedrals of Prague, Vienna, Milan and Strasburg during his first journey to Italy from 1803 to 1805. The cathedral soars heavenwards over water, medieval city and rising storm, in the light of the setting sun. The building's sublime quality evokes distant memories of the cathedral and St Severi in Erfurt, where Feininger was later to paint. 'Architecture is the continuation of nature in her constructive activity';[11] the sculpted cathedral with its wreath of trees grows out of the hill, an ideal composed from ancient Gothic of various origins, 'easier to understand in cast iron than stone, his cathedral already carries the seminal idea of a historic monument.'[12] Schinkel painted his cathedral by the water as a patriotic symbol[13] and a manifesto for unity in difficult times.

Master builder Schinkel discovered the ancient city of Halle an der Saale on his way to Italy in the summer of 1825: 'One is most uplifted by the picturesque aspect

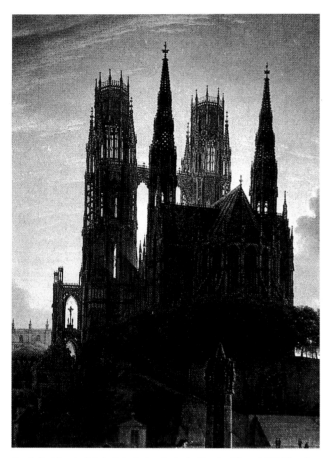

Fig.1 Karl Friedrich Schinkel, *Gothic Cathedral by the Water* 1813 (detail), Bayerische Staatsgemäldesammlungen, Munich

Fig.2 Lyonel Feininger, *Marienkirche with Arrow* 1930, Staatliche Galerie Moritzburg, Halle

of this city's various nooks and crannies; I myself see new and excellent views from points I had not previously known; ... the interior of the market church, executed and preserved most harmoniously in a quite unusual medieval style, with very bold and artful constructions.'[14]

Feininger found his own very personal viewpoints and bold constructions when working on his Halle series[15] in the Moritzburg gatehouse tower. The *Marienkirche with Arrow* (fig. 2) was painted in 1930, from notes made on the spot and photographs. Feininger was particularly fascinated by this early-sixteenth century church with Gothic and Renaissance overlapping in its twin-towered façade, and its bridge. He released the motif from its urban confines by foreshortening the perspective, building up a two-dimensional, woodcut-like structure of triangular elements, with a slight sense of upward movement for the church. In this way the building's night-dark silhouette strives inexorably towards the sky, assisted by the light-coloured arrow. This arrow signals cosmic orientation, but is also a symbol of the future.

The parallel quality of church and arrow symbolizes the 'tragedy of spirituality',[16] as identified by Feininger and Paul Klee at the Bauhaus: a creative conflict between spiritual mobility and earthly confines.

This tragedy of the spirit also haunted Schinkel's Romantic period, and fought its own precarious battle in the Wars of Liberation against Napoleon: being able to dream Gothic, but not to build it. Schinkel's cathedral is all filigree immateriality against a halo of light, but Feininger's Marienkirche is impenetrable matter, rising out of darkness into light. Gothic in its purist form in Schinkel's case and transcendental abstraction in Feininger's, the pictorial canons of Romanticism and Modernism contrasted. But the two paintings are linked by the borderline between evening and night, between being bound and finding release, between past, present and the incalculable future.

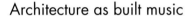

Fig.3 Karl Freidrich Schinkel, *Gothic Church Behind an Oak Grove with Tombs* 1810, lithograph

Fig.4 Lyonel Feininger, *Teltow II* 1918, Staatliche Museen zu Berlin Preußischer Kulturbesitz, Nationalgalerie

Architecture as built music

Friedrich Wilhelm Schelling called architecture a 'frozen music' in his lectures on the 'Philosophy of Art' in 1802–03, and Schinkel added his 'built music'[17] in stone. Typical of this is his commentary below the lithograph *Gothic Church Behind an Oak Grove with Tombs* (fig. 3): 'Attempt to express the peaceful yearning melancholy that fills the heart at the sound of a service coming from a church.' Johann Wolfgang von Goethe once spoke of the 'poetic element of architecture'.[18] This in *Franz Sternbalds Wanderungen*: 'The organ started to play, the hymn began, the church door near Franz was open and the rustle of the trees came into the church, the first notes from the organ swelled up majestically and addressed the listeners like a melodious gale; ... his gaze then left the picture for the green churchyard outside the door and it seemed to him that the trees and shrubs outside were also praying piously and resting in the arms of worship. The soft voices of the departed seemed to sing from their graves and hasten after the organ's solemn tones with ghostly voice.'[19]

Far removed from Schinkel's classical buildings in Berlin, Feininger visited the farming town of Teltow in Brandenburg (fig. 4) from 1910. Its Gothic church of St Andreas had burned down in 1801, and had been rebuilt years later to Schinkel's design. He wrote in 1810: 'For

our building we would be able to agree only on the medieval tower, which so splendidly expresses a striving towards heaven.'[20] The crystalline tower rises in gleaming blue major, and with it the memory of Franz Marc's 'mystic-internal construction'. A rhythmic counterpoint of triangles, in which the tree standing on its head on the left leads down in a dark minor key. Feininger had declared as early as 1913: 'My pictures are coming ever closer to the synthesis of the fugue.'[21] Johann Sebastian Bach and his austere *basso continuo* had recently been rediscovered; the fervent melodies of a composer like Franz Schubert from Schinkel's time had faded away. Bach's *Art of the Fugue* led Feininger to simplify his expressive vocabulary. Feininger's parents were concert musicians, and he had composed several fugues in his years at the Bauhaus between 1921 and 1927, and enjoyed music-making: 'I often sit down at the organ and seek release in Bach's mighty tones. And then a fugue or chorale arises in blissful transport.'[22] The Romantic synaesthesia of painting, architecture and music reached a hitherto unknown degree of polyphonic structure in painting through Feininger's refractions and vibrations, penetrations and intersections, reversals and reflections.

Fig.5 Karl Friedrich Schinkel, *Mausoleum for Queen Luise*, Interior 1810, Staatliche Museen zu Berlin Preußischer Kulturbesitz, Nationalgalerie

Fig.6 Lyonel Feininger, *Bridge I* 1913, Washington University, St. Louis, Missouri

The crystallization of nature

Schinkel saw architecture as a symbol of life: 'Striving, putting forth shoots, crystallization, opening, thrusting, splitting, fitting, driving, soaring, pulling, pressing, bending, bearing, setting, swinging, combining, folding, lying and resting . . .'[23] When Queen Luise of Prussia died in 1810, the architect designed a mausoleum (fig. 5) as a symbol of eternal life. The sarcophagus represents the Queen's death and transfiguration; she is surrounded by winged spirits, and space 'in bright red dawning light' in front of marble walls: the Gothic hall as the forecourt of paradise. In a similar way to J.F.C. Dauthe's Nicolaikirche in Leipzig the interior is constructed as a bright palm grove. The vault ribs rise as branches and the clustered piers as tree-trunks. In this 'church of nature'[24] 'Gothic decoration' serves 'a freely working idea';[25] for Schinkel, Gothic was female by nature. Schelling had just added the 'boundless structure of crystalline nature' to the old idea of the Gothic as a forest. Crystal brought light into the cathedral, and *logos* and mysticism at the same time. Schinkel adopted the idea of crystal in a later mausoleum design, when he placed panes of glass between the Ionic columns in his design for the Orianda Palace in the Crimea in 1838. From crystal to glass and thus to transparent, rhythmic surface design, nature and cosmos in nature's mirror; that thought was also very familiar to an artist like Feininger as well.

So we have 'crystallization' for Schinkel in the Romantic period, and then again in Feininger's work after 1907: 'What is seen must be internally reshaped and crystallized.'[26] In coming to terms with Robert Delaunay's Orphism,[27] Feininger found a way to his own 'prism-ism' in subsequent years, in the form of interpenetrating crystalline rhombuses and surfaces, of internal and external space in his pictures. His *Bridge I* (fig. 6) in Ober-Weimar creates the illusion of a Gothic interior: 'These struts meet and cross like ribs in a Gothic vault in the arches of this bridge. The reflection in the water takes up this sweep and widely spreading arches span across lightly and freshly toned tree silhouettes towards the horizon. A sense of being driven by the surge of forms, or rather a sense of self-abandonment and play.'[28] Feininger's crystalline vision of the New Jerusalem was created from the interpenetration of architecture and nature. Feininger had seen similar things on the Pfaueninsel in Berlin, with its iron bridge amidst Gothic park architecture as an attempt 'to create a boundless space that effectively dissolves in natural space, as the wall stops.'[29] Schinkel also intended his mausoleum to be seen as 'the crystalline as art-symbol'.[30] Both the Gothic cathedral and his design for the funerary chapel were the prelude to the glazed architecture of Bruno Taut and the *Gläserne Kette* (Glass Chain) group. The poet Theodor Däubler celebrated Feininger as the 'Clearest Crystallist' at the beginning of the twentieth century.

Fig.7 Karl Friedrich Schinkel, *Design for a Memorial for the Wars of Liberation* 1815–16, Staatliche Museen zu Berlin Preußischer Kulturbesitz, Kupferstichkabinett

Fig.8 Lyonel Feininger, *Cathedral* (large version) 1919, woodcut

From the cathedral of Liberty to the Cathedral of the Future

'The architect is', wrote Schinkel, 'by definition, an ennobler of all human conditions. His sphere of activity has to include the whole of fine art; for him, in accordance with Man's moral and rational nature, sculpture, painting and the art of spatial relationships melt together into one art.'[31] The idea and practice of the *Gesamtkunstwerk*, the complete work of art,[32] became a patriotic task for Schinkel in the 'fatherland'-Gothic tradition of the medieval stonemasons' lodge when in 1814–15 he dared to tackle a design for a national cathedral as a memorial for the Wars of Liberation.[33] Commissioned by King Friedrich Wilhelm III, the memorial cathedral was intended to 'be a central point for all higher artistic activity in the country'. It was to stand in Leipziger Platz, outside the gates of Berlin. Schinkel's Gothic-style cathedral was intended as a counterpoint to the classicism of Carl Gotthard

Langhans's neighbouring Brandenburg Gate; his design ideas were presented in the Gothic style, as the king had insisted upon the 'stirring style of old German architecture'. Schinkel wrote two memoranda to justify his project as a religious and historic monument that would continue to affect the national consciousness through the ages. He went far beyond the fantasies of Gothic architecture and finally designed a bold pyramid (fig. 7) on three levels: the bottom storey was in the Egyptian style (origin of architecture: 'the earthly kingdom in its crystallization' – battle and death of the freedom-fighter), the central storey was an ancient Greek temple façade (the sublimity of the victorious idea in the sphere of peace), with the pyramid then peaking in a Gothic *tempietto* with a steep spire ('the plant striving towards the sky' – the survival of democratic ideas into the future). All that was realized of this grandiose project's Romantic poetry and architectural utopia was the monument on the Kreuzberg[34] hill in Berlin, designed in 1818 and completed by 1821 in cast iron, modest evidence of conditions in Prussia.

Bruno Taut's glass building[35] for the 1914 Werkbund exhibition in Cologne was the first decisive reply by modern crystalline architecture to the social utopia of Schinkel's unbuilt Cathedral of Liberation. In his book *Die Wiederkehr der Kunst* (The Return of Art), published in 1919, Adolf Behne again confirmed: 'Architectonics is the concealed striving for unity in all art. Architecture is our leader towards unity.'[36] The religiosity and collectivity of the Gothic cathedral emerged again in the euphoria of the November Revolution in 1918; architectural fantasy's finest hour had come, in a 'mixture of Marx and prayer' (Ernst Bloch). Paul Westheim recalled Schinkel's utopias at that time: 'He too was filled with a world of unrealistically large works of architecture that he conjured from his imagination in a virtuoso fashion. He sought refuge in these utopias from the constraints of his times, which were too poor to realize his building ideas on even the most modest scale. His utopias would have held their own against the great buildings of all times, if he had ever been given the opportunity to realize them in stone. Schinkel would have wanted, and, as the true master builder that he was, he would have had the strength to translate these figments of his imagination into stone and iron.'[37] Behne proclaimed effusively: 'The cathedral is itself a people';[38] Walter Gropius drew practical conclusions from idealistic debates in the *Arbeitsrat fur Kunst* (Art Works Council), the *Novembergruppe* and the architects that made up the *Gläserne Kette*: he founded the state Bauhaus in Weimar. The foundation document of April 1919 states: 'Let us, together, wish for, devise, and create the new building of the future, that will be everything *in one*: architecture and sculpture and painting, a building that will at some future time rise into the sky from the workers' million hands, a crystal symbol of a new faith that is to come!'[39] Feininger's title woodcut (fig. 8), enthusiastically celebrated by his contemporaries as a 'cathedral of socialism',[40] a 'cathedral of the future', came to symbolize the Bauhaus programme. The Gothic basilica[41] with its three portals and three towers, surrounded by soaring beams of light and three five-pointed stars, is a crystal structure growing into the cosmos of an imaginary future. The sacred triad of architecture, sculpture and painting has returned in the *Gesamtkunstwerk* known as the Bauhaus.

Early Romanticism provided the bridge: medieval stonemasons' lodge, Schinkel, Taut, Rudolf Belling, Feininger, Gropius, Bauhaus in Weimar and Dessau.

At the end of the Bauhaus's Romantic period, in 1923, the path led from utopia to functionalism, 'from the cathedral of the future to the living-machine.[42] 'Art and technology – a new unity'; Walter Gropius's modern programme was rejected by Feininger and Klee as painters. They stayed with their undramatic Romanticism, committed to Modernism and tradition. For the Nazis both were 'degenerate' artists. After 1933 the pure idea was perverted by the administrators of culture: Feininger's Bauhaus cathedral light-logos was given a new function: as the 'cathedral of light' above the Zeppelin field that was the site of the Nuremberg Rally it was to demonstrate the subjugation of the 'people's society'. It is not without 'Romantic' irony that Adolf Hitler's chief architect Albert Speer of all people had ambitions to become a second super-Schinkel in the 'thousand-year Reich'.

As an émigré, Feininger clung to his Romantic idea of the cathedral, conjured up Gelmeroda in the United States and tried to give metaphysical meaning to the Manhattan skyline's upright architecture by 'abstract dematerialization': ultimately in vain. The pictorial image of the cathedral[43] has long lost its original meaning at the end of this century. Are not today's huge and spectacular skyscrapers[44] the modern cathedrals of the present? A few hundred metres closer to heaven than Schinkel's and Feininger's Gothic cathedrals they are further than ever from the cosmos in spirit and in unfulfilled longing. Utopias seem to have broken down in our post-modern pragmatism, but not to have been destroyed. For utopia – as Ernst Bloch said in his *Prinzip Hoffnung* – is 'something that speaks for itself by remaining silent'.

Roland März

Translated from the German by Michael Robinson

1 Karl Scheffler, *Der Geist der Gotik* (Leipzig, 1917). See also the seminal programmatic book by Wilhelm Worringer: *Formprobleme der Gotik* (Munich, 1911). On this subject: Magadalena Bushart, *Der Geist der Gotik und die expressionistische Kunst: Kunstgeschichte und Kunsttheorie 1911–1925* (Munich, 1990), on Feininger 80, 194 ff., on Schinkel note 57.

2 T. Lux Feininger, 'Mein Vater hat einen Fehler gemacht', in *Du: Die Zeitschrift für Kunst und Kultur*, no. 5, (1986), 65.

3 Andreas Hüneke, Roland März, ed., exh. cat. *Lyonel Feininger und die Romantik*, Lyonel-Feininger-Galerie (Quedlinburg, 1991). Günter Braunsberg, 'Feininger und die Romantik', in exh. cat. *Lyonel Feininger: Städte und Küsten*, Albrecht-Dürer-Gesellschaft, Kunsthalle (Nürnberg 1992), 38–40.

4 Auguste Rodin, *Les Cathédrales de France* (Paris, 1914).

5 Magdalena Bushart, 'Feininger und die Gotik', in exh. cat. Feininger (Nuremberg, 1992), 35–37.

6 Lyonel Feininger to Alfred Kubin, 15.6.1913, in exh. cat. *Lyonel Feininger: Natur-Notizen*, (Kunsthalle in Emden, Museum Ludwig, Cologne, Kunstsammlungen zu Weimar 1994).

7 Peter Krieger, 'Lyonel Feiningers Variationen über das Gelmerodamotiv', in *Zeitschrift des Deutschen Vereins für Kunstwissenschaft* (Berlin, 1967), 89–102. Donat de Chapeaurouge, 'Die "Kathedrale" als modernes Bildthema', in *Jahrbuch der Hamburger Kunstsammlungen* (Hamburg, 1983), vol 18, 155–72. Hans Sedlmayr, *Die Enstehung der Kathedrale* (Freiburg, Basel, Vienna, 1993).

8 There is no direct reference to Schinkel by Feininger is his writings available at the time of writing, but no edition of Feininger's letters and writings has yet been published.

9 'Lyonel Feininger und Adolf Knoblauch: Zwiesprache', in *Der Sturm* (1917), 82–86. Quoted from Lothar Schreyer, *Lyonel Feininger: Dokumente und Visionen* (Munich, 1957), 36.

10 Letter to Paul Westheim, Berlin-Zehlendorf, 14 March 1917, in *Das Kunstblatt* (1931), 216 ff.

11 Quoted from Tilman Osterwold, 'Ichperspektive – Bildperspektive – Weltperspektive: Am Beispiel Caspar David Friedrich und Lyonel Feininger', in Ulrich Bischoff, ed., *Romantik und Gegenwart: Festschrift für Jens Christian Jensen zum 60. Geburtstag* (Cologne, 1988), 182.

12 Rüdiger Becksmann, 'Schinkel und die Gotik: Bemerkungen zur Komposition des viertürmigen Domes von 1813', in *Kunstgeschichtliche Studien für Kurt Bauch zum 70. Geburtstag von seinen Schülern* (Munich, Berlin, 1967), 263–76.

13 Hannelore Gärtner, 'Die Malerei Schinkels im Verhältnis zur patriotischen Romantik', in Hannelore Gärtner (ed.), *Schinkelstudien* (Leipzig, 1984), 185–97.

14 Gottfried Riemann, ed., *Karl Friedrich Schinkel: Reisen nach Italien* (Berlin, 1979), 132. Here see also Schinkel's remarks on Strasbourg cathedral, 145.

15 Exh. cat. *Lyonel Feininger: Die Halle-Bilder*, Staatliche Galerie Moritzburg (Halle, 1991), 28–30, col. pl., 29.

16 Paul Klee, 'Beiträge zur bildnerischen Formenlehre', in Paul Klee, *Kunst-Lehre* (Leipzig, 1987), 234 ff.

17 Harald Szeemann, ed., exh. cat. *Der Hang zum Gesamtkunstwerk: Europäische Utopien seit 1800*, (Zürich: Kunsthaus 1983), 157. Eva Börsch-Supan, 'Die Bedeutung der Musik im Werke Karl Friedrich Schinkels', in *Zeitschrift für Kunstgeschichte* (1971), 257–95.

18 Erik Forssmann, *Karl Friedrich Schinkel: Bauwerke und Baugedanken* (Munich and Zürich, 1981), 37–83.

19 Harald Szeemann (as note 17), 157.

20 In exh. cat., *Karl Friedrich Schinkel 1781–1841*, Staatliche Museen zu Berlin, Altes Museum, (1980–81), 303.

21 Quoted from Hans Hess, *Lyonel Feininger* (Stuttgart, 1959), 56. Laurence Feininger, *Das musikalische Werk Lyonel Feiningers* (Tutzing, 1971). Andreas Hüneke, 'Das Wesen Bachs in der Malerei: Feiningers Bezug zur Musik', in exh. cat. *Lyonel Feininger: Lüneburger Motive 1921–1954*, (Lüneburg: Kulturforum 1991), 16–18.

22 Lyonel Feininger and Adolf Knoblauch (as note 9), 29.

23 Karl Friedrich Schinkel, *Briefe, Tagebücher, Gedanken*, selected, edited and with an introduction by Hans Mackowsky (Berlin, 1922), 193.

24 Jörg Träger, 'Die Kirche der Natur: Kunst und Konfession in der romantischen Epoche', in Christian Beutler, Peter-Klaus Schuster, Martin Warnke, ed., *Kunst um 1800 und die Folgen: Werner Hofmann zu Ehren* (Munich, 1988), 181–99.

25 Schinkel (as note 23), 182. Joachim Gaus, 'Schinkels Entwurf zum Luisen-Mausoleum', in *Festschrift für Wolfgang Krönig: Aachener Kunstblätter* (1971), vol. 41, 254–63.

26 Quoted from Hess (as note 21), 42.

27 Hans Platte, 'Robert Delaunay und Lyonel Feininger', in *Jahrbuch der Hamburger Kunstsammlungen*, (Hamburg, 1958), vol. 3, 39–46. Ulrich Luckhardt, 'Der frühe Feininger und Robert Delaunay', in exh. cat. *Delaunay und Deutschland*, Haus der Kunst (Munich, 1985), 285–97.

28 Paul Westheim, 'Künstlerisches Denken', in *Das Kunstblatt* (1917), vol. 1, 358.

29 Hans-Joachim Kunst, 'Die Vollendung der romantischen Gotik im Expressionismus – die Vollendung des Klassizismus im Funktionalismus', in *Kritische Berichte* no. 1, (1979), 26–30, ill. 5.

30 Regine Prange, *Das Kristalline als Kunstsymbol: Bruno Taut und Paul Klee*, (Hildesheim, Zurich and New York, 1991), on Feininger 169 ff., on Feininger and Klee, 318 ff. Roland März, 'Das Kristallinische im deutschen Expressionismus', in *Bildende Kunst*, no. 3, (1987), 111–13.

31 Harald Szeemann (as note 17), 156.

32 *Ibid*. On our subject, Harald Szeemann names as 'filiations of the *Gesamtkunstwerk*': Schinkel, the *Gläserne Kette*, State Bauhaus, (16). Bazon Brock quotes the Gothic cathedral as one of the 'few things European cultures have in common', (22).

33 Klaus Konrad Weber, 'Denkmal der Freiheitskriege von Schinkel, in *Kaleidoskop: eine Festschrift für Fritz Baumgart zum 75. Geburtstag*, ed. Friedrich Mielke (Berlin, 1977), 169–73.

34 Paul Ortwin Rave, *Karl Friedrich Schinkel*, revised by Eva Börsch-Supan (Berlin, 1981), 57, ill. 2, ill. in text, 21.

35 Prange (as note 30). Exh. cat. *Kristallisationen, Splitterungen – Bruno Tauts Glashaus: Koln 1914*, (Berlin: Werkbund-Archiv, 1993).

36 Adolf Behne, *Die Wiederkehr der Kunst* (Leipzig, 1919), 22.

37 Paul Westheim in *Frankfurter Zeitung*, 30.4.1919. Paul Westheim, 'Schinkel und die Gegenwart', in *Der Baumeister* (1913), no. 4 (supplement), 84.

38 Adolf Behne, 'Die Kathedrale von Reims', in *Sozialistische Monatshefte* (1918), vol. 1, 348. He also says 'that democracy is the true aristocracy; and it is precisely the great cathedrals that prove it' (350).

39 Quoted from Roland März, *Lyonel Feininger* (Berlin, 1981), above pl. 8.

40 The term 'cathedral of socialism' was proverbial as early as 1919. Oskar Schlemmer used it for the programme he wrote for the 1923 Bauhaus exhibition. Cf. Andreas Hüneke, ed., *Oskar Schlemmer, Idealist der Form: Briefe, Tagebücher, Schriften 1912–1933* (Leipzig, 1990), note 77. Schlemmer in his diary, 9 April 1927: 'Did not the majority of the German people want to build the Cathedral of Socialism in 1918? Was not the revolution and the constitution that followed it a declaration of the people's state? And what is a people's state and what does it mean other than socialism? And further: does socialism mean Social-Democratic and Communist Party? Is socialism not a concept, an ethic that is above parties?' (199 ff.).

41 In Tilman Osterwold (see note 11) the pictorial comparison, more compelling in its motif-structure and soaring transfiguration, between Feininger's Bauhaus cathedral and Caspar David Friedrich's painting *Die Kathedrale*, c. 1820, in the Schäfer Collection, Schweinfurt (180, with ill.).

42 Göran Lindahl, 'Von der Zukunftskathedrale bis zur Wohnmaschine: Deutsche Architektur und Architekturdebatte nach dem 1. Weltkrieg', in *Idea and Form: Uppsala Studies in History of Art* vol. 1, (1959), 226.

43 Donat de Chapeaurouge (as note 7), 172. Ludwig Grote wrote as early as 1968: 'Pursuing the cathedral idea would be a task for an arts scholar … ', in exh. cat. *50 Jahre Bauhaus*, (Stuttgart: Württembergischer Kunstverein, 1968), 18. This scholarly study on the subject of 'The Romantic Cathedral' has still not appeared.

44 *Berliner Zeitung*, 8–9 January 1994: 'Tallest skyscraper in the world' (in the form of a Gothic twin-towered façade): 'The American daughter company of the German Philipp Holzmann AG, J.A. Jones Construction Company, is building the tallest skyscraper in the world, 450 metres high, and with 88 storeys, in the Malaysian capital Kuala Lumpur, starting in February of this year. The building is due to be completed in 1996.'

Transparent Painting and the Romantic Spirit:
Experimental Anticipations of Modern Visual Arts

Romantic Metaphors of Light

'Once, and once only, has German art achieved this magic of transformation', writes Emil Waldmann, in the *Caspar David Friedrich Almanac*, of the work that is probably the sole surviving transparency by Friedrich. When the artist placed a lamp behind the picture in a darkened room, the 'wonder lamp' caused 'the mountains of the magical, moonlit night gradually to emerge, and made the universe deeper; as the lamp was moved, evening drew on or night fell; the world became fuller of details; and the whole apparition – now melancholy and gloomy, now softly transfigured – and all the moods of light as it grew weaker and then stronger, evolved against the infinite. It is wholly mysterious and irresistible, like an enchantment.'[1]

It was not until the last years of his career that Friedrich discovered for himself the technique of painting transparencies. Undoubtedly, he was inspired to do so by the popularity of the diorama, which began to increase after 1822. In Europe and elsewhere, the diorama – a product of the genius of the French inventor Louis Jacques Mandé Daguerre – evolved with enormous rapidity into a popular visual medium that was, so to speak, on everyone's lips. Before an astonished public, the diorama displayed unusually large, illuminated, semi-transparent canvases, on which were painted views from all over the world, as well as current events and spectacular natural phenomena of light. The fascination of the illusion was that it came close to reality – indeed suggested the presence of reality. One could become an eye-witness to world events without really being there; one could travel without really travelling.

Alongside this external influence there was an inward impulse that prompted Friedrich to adopt the technique of the transparency. This major Romantic painter was a prophet of light; he was more wedded than any other to metaphors of light and to the symbolism of times of day. The transparency was uniquely suited to these concerns. It offered an entirely new opportunity to create the light effects that Friedrich had customarily captured with oil paint on canvas.

Now images were painted on translucent materials and presented in a darkened room, lit from behind. The viewer was no longer looking at painted light: in the darkness, the real and perceptible light of a moonlit landscape stirred the soul and conveyed Romantic ideas with the greatest possible emotional directness.

Not only for Friedrich but for all the Romantics, philosophers and poets as well as painters, light – as transparency, as moonlight and in other forms – is an essential image. According to the Romantic philosophy of nature, light is the antithesis of matter; it is an 'ideality that dissolves all reality within itself'.[2] The entry of the higher, divine light into the consciousness is the experience of revelation and illumination. And for the artist, closely in touch with his inner life through intuition, feeling and imagination, illumination is identified with inspiration.

For Philipp Otto Runge, transparency, flooded with light, represented the urge to be suffused with the light of the Divine, the longing of all living creatures to rise 'to the light and to the spiritualization of their creaturely nature'.[3] Transparency became a metaphor of the revelation of a spiritual essence behind the material world. Novalis put it perfectly: 'Every transparent body is in a higher state – it seems to have a kind of consciousness.'[4] And Friedrich is said to have told Vasily Andreyevich Zhukovsky that he used the transparency to 'annul the materiality of colour'.[5]

Of all the metaphors of light so beloved of the Romantics, the favourite was the enchantment of a moonlit night. For them, moonlight possessed a magical power to stimulate the imagination. It was their chosen image both of their intellectual awareness of the 'night side of things', which was their answer to the Enlightenment, and of their own poetic emotion. This can be documented in Ludwig Tieck and in Novalis, in Runge and in Friedrich. A landscape lit by the moon was perceived as an encounter with the eternal and the

Fig.1 Caspar David Friedrich, *Mountainous River Landscape in the Morning*, Staatliche Kunstsammlungen, Kassel

Fig.2 Caspar David Friedrich, *Mountainous River Landscape at Night*, Staatliche Kunstsammlungen, Kassel

Divine: an encounter that might change the individual's life. Friedrich was deeply committed to these ideas, and many of his paintings are celebrations of moonlit nights. He wryly remarked that when he died he would surely go to the moon, because he painted nothing but moonshine.[6]

Caspar David Friedrich's Transparencies

It was probably at the instigation of Zhukovsky – Russian poet, privy councillor and imperial tutor – that Friedrich decided in 1830 to execute four transparencies as a commissioned work for the young heir to the throne, Alexander. In a number of letters, Friedrich outlined to Zhukovsky the underlying conception of the pictures, which he planned as a cycle with an elaborate light installation and a musical accompaniment. Musical and allegorical displays, intended for 'a youthful, child-like disposition',[7] were to portray the transformation of the world from its demonic state to its present state, then to the spiritual and finally to the transcendental.

It was not until five years later, in 1835, that Friedrich was able to carry out his project. In a letter dated 14 July 1835, he wrote that the pictures had been 'painted transparently on paper', and that they could be viewed only with a device whereby 'the light falls through a small aperture, and the rest of the room is in darkness'.[8] It was necessary to avoid distracting noise; this could be done by hanging a curtain between the box and the viewers, and by carpeting the room, 'so that music and painting may relate correctly and support each other,

and that all noise whatever may be scrupulously prevented from reaching the hearer and viewer'.[9] Faithful to the Romantic *Zeitgeist*, Friedrich is here unfolding the idea of the *Gesamtkunstwerk*, the synthesis of the arts. The idea of resemblance to Nature was to be countered by the creation of an all-embracing artistic world that would address – or rather captivate – the whole human being.

The four transparencies and the projection apparatus certainly reached St Petersburg, but are since believed lost.[10] Fortunately, however, one transparency painted by Friedrich has survived.[11] Since 1957, the Gemäldegalerie in Kassel has owned the *Mountainous River Landscape* (76 × 130 cm), which was in Friedrich's studio at his death; its date is unknown, but it is probably a late work. It is painted in a mixture of watercolour and tempera on both sides of a sheet of translucent paper, to create two variant versions, day and night (figs. 1–2). In conjunction with suitably placed light sources, Friedrich could use the transparency to present the times of day – with their message of change and impermanence – as a sequence, a process. This use of painting to create a transformation must have fascinated him.

First we see a river valley in daylight, painted in gentle, pastel colours of rose, lilac, olive-green and greyish brown. The wide river flows past a number of islands and between gentle mountain slopes. In the foreground, a solitary boat conveys a loving couple and a boatman.

With the change to back lighting, the daylight view gives way to a nocturnal landscape, dominated by effects of transparency. The wide, cloudy sky is illuminated by the rays of the moon, whose golden light floods across the water. In the distance, against a background of lofty mountain ranges, we see the Gothic spires of a town that was invisible in daylight. The figures in the boat – now seen only as dark shadows – become votaries who have surrendered to the enchantment of the natural scene.

We know from Friedrich's own words that he was concerned to draw a clear distinction between his transparencies and works of mere 'entertainment': 'These are not to be thought of as peepshows.'[12] To him, the painting of transparencies, so fundamentally different from easel painting, was an artistic challenge in which the essential point was experimentation with light – a choice that testifies to his 'artistic wisdom'.[13] He adopted the transparency – as Waldmann says – 'out of the fullness of his idealistic heart', to give visible form to 'the mystery of the moods of nature and the infinite surge of wonders of light, which he inwardly enjoyed with the eye of the soul'.[14]

The Late Eighteenth-Century Origins of the Transparency

The evolution of the transparency began half a century earlier, around 1780. It emerged almost simultaneously, though in most cases independently, in Italy, France, Germany, England and America.

The first thing to appear was the so-called moonlight transparency. This kind of atmospheric view of nature touched a nerve in the late eighteenth century – the 'Age of Sensibility', in which art was often addressed to the feelings. The pioneer was probably Jacob Philipp Hackert, a German painter who lived in Naples. He was regarded as the virtually undisputed inventor of the technique, which was 'still kept secret at that time'.[15] At about the same time Louis Carmontelle, a court artist in pre-Revolutionary Paris, mounted public shows of transparencies.[16] This 'feast for eye and ear' was so popular at court that Carmontelle was known as the 'King of Illusionists'.[17]

In England, in 1781, Thomas Gainsborough invented the so-called Exhibition Box, with the aid of which he showed his one-foot-square transparencies of landscapes, painted on glass. A display of these would be the main attraction at an evening party. Apart from the

entertainment value of these pictorial events, Gainsborough's transparencies were a visual stimulus to his own imagination. They influenced his late landscape painting, in which patterns of lighting play an important role.

Gainsborough's Exhibition Box was inspired by the Eidophusikon of Philip de Loutherbourg, an illusionistic peepshow that was all the rage in London at the time.[18] Loutherbourg's device also inspired the American painter and collector Charles Wilson Peale, founder of the Peale Museum, who opened his 'Exhibition of Perspective Views, with Changeable Effects; or, Nature Delineated, and in Motion' in Philadelphia in 1785. He converted one room in his own museum into a 'Moving Picture Room' for the purpose.

Karl Friedrich Schinkel's Transparent Cathedrals

In the nineteenth century, Romanticism played an essential part in the evolution of the transparency towards the diorama. In Berlin, between 1807 and 1815 – more than twenty years before Friedrich – the young Karl Friedrich Schinkel was already painting transparencies, which he called 'Perspective-Optical Views'.[19] These were extremely popular, especially at Christmas. Schinkel showed moonlit landscapes, views of architecture, and also fantasy scenes and depictions of current events, all with musical accompaniment. One of the favourite and most impressive subjects were views of Gothic cathedrals. For Schinkel, as for the Romantic movement in general, the filigree immateriality and crystalline transparency of these transparent edifices became a visionary symbol of the interpenetration of architecture and nature, which the transparency presented in a preternaturally intensified light. To complete the artistic experience, there was background music, a manifestation of the Romantic synaesthetic impulse.

In 1808 Schinkel showed, among other transparencies, his *Milan Cathedral*, 'the grandest and most beautiful work of Old German and Gothic architecture', as the Berlin architect Ludwig Catel called it: 'Boldly into the air arise countless towers and spires, like devout prayers to the Godhead. Moonlight gently plays about the noble edifice. A solemn torchlight procession entices the eye

Fig.3 Karl Friedrich Schinkel, *Cathedral* 1811, Staatliche Schlösser und Gärten, Berlin

into the illuminated interior of the church and compels the imagination to form its own image of the view inside.'[20]

One year later, in 1809, Schinkel exhibited the interior of Milan Cathedral, and once more he received a full and appreciative press. Among those who came to see the show were members of the royal family and numerous other public figures, including intellectuals and artists. The celebrated Romantic poet Joseph von Eichendorff went along in the company of Clemens Brentano. 'In the evening,' wrote Eichendorff in his journal, 'to the theatre of the talented painter Schinkel. Brentano delighted by the way in which the illuminated announcements snap in from either side. Several displays (the back wall a splendid painted perspective) with church music.'[21]

In February 1811, Schinkel exhibited a *Gothic Cathedral in Morning Light*. 'At very first sight,' reported the *Spenersche Zeitung*, 'the master hand of Schinkel is unmistakable. From a lakeside city on the slopes of a rock, we see a Gothic church with two towers; in front of this is a bridge, built on very tall arches and adorned on every pier with a saint's chapel . . . The scene is illuminated by the rising sun, in whose crimson light the jagged and perforated form of the Gothic towers is all the more clearly discernible. The whole prospect does not represent a landscape that exists in reality but is purely ideal, albeit highly poetic.'[22]

The scene, the writer continued, recalled to mind Schinkel's magnificent exhibitions of previous years,

which had given so much pleasure that it was to be hoped that he would renew them every year. If we follow the detailed description of this vanished work, it reveals a similarity to the oil painting *Cathedral* (fig. 3), painted in the same year, 1811. It is likely enough that Schinkel used the transparency to try out the theme of Gothic architecture suffused with light, and that the success of the exhibition persuaded him to turn it into an oil painting.[23]

The 'True Purpose of Dioramatic Art'

In Dresden, the centre of German Romantic landscape painting, Ernst Ferdinand Oehme and the architectural painter Otto Wagner jointly presented a show of transparencies in the winter of 1832–33. Oehme, who was a pupil of Friedrich, may well have benefited from his master's advice (fig. 4).[24]

The art historian and critic Karl Friedrich Rumohr took the opportunity afforded by the exhibition to reflect on 'dioramatic art', and to define the 'boundaries' and the 'true purpose' of the genre – in which one of the paintings was 'one of the most successful ever achieved'.[25] This showed the interior of a belfry, 'in which a person of fine character and splendid bearing is ringing a tocsin, while another looks out through the open Gothic window, with well-expressed emotions of fear, at a conflagration in the city below. The conception of the painting is to be described as poetic; the economy of means and the stimulus to emotional response, as well as the outward sensory effect, are equally admirable.'[26] Among the remarkably successful effects were 'the frightening truth of the distant fire' and 'the well-expressed softness of its contrast with the open Gothic window tracery and with the cooler and at the same time closer and more distinct light of the lantern that faintly illuminates the depths of the room'. An effect of this kind, said Rumohr, would be 'impossible to achieve without the most skilful assessment of all the advantages of transparency and reflection'; it indicated the elevated nature and true purpose of this artistic genre.[27]

With his strong sense of perspective, Rumohr was shrewd as well as poetic enough to recognize the modernity and topicality of the transparency experiment. He

Fig.4 Ernst Ferdinand Oehme, *The Ruins of Oybin by Moonlight*, Staatliche Galerie Moritzburg, Halle

and sound operated together to create a living artistic experience. Luminous images, previously invisible, came into existence in the presence of an audience, looming out of the darkness to meet an expectant public. These exhibitions were events in themselves, opportunities for social interaction and communication. The real and not painted light that shone through the painting onto the spectator – light as impulse, as energy and as living abstraction – was the essential factor. This experience of light, utterly distinct from traditional modes of experiencing painting, was fundamental to the success of this art of metamorphosis and illusion – and to the continued resonance that it has enjoyed in the twentieth century.

A century and a half after the age of transparent dioramas, they retain a specific historical significance in modern media terms. A wide range of works of contemporary film and visual art expressly allude to the traditions of the nineteenth-century light show, including the transparency. This relationship can only be outlined here.

Such echoes have been pursued to their historical roots in the work of the experimental cinematographer Werner Nekes, of Mülheim an der Ruhr. Nekes's avant-garde films belong to the tradition of 'absolute' film pioneered by Walther Ruttmann, Oskar Fischinger, Viking Eggeling, Hans Richter and others. In varying degrees, all Nekes's films refer to the archaeology of the medium. They make use of optical apparatuses and effects that served the purposes of nineteenth-century science, art and entertainment long before Georges Méliès and the brothers Auguste and Louis-Jean Lumière began to use the movie camera.

It is as an experimenter that Nekes interprets and investigates the art of film through what he calls 'lighter-ature': the creation of form through light. He constantly reflects on processes of genesis and on the perception of filmic information, radically questioning traditional codes and generating an individual poetic aesthetic. Nekes's films, in which painting by cinematic means (which he calls 'light painting') is traced from its origins through a number of distinct artistic periods in the nineteenth and twentieth centuries, include *Diwan* (1973, fig. 5),[29] *Amalgam* (1976) and *Uliisses* (1980–82).

Harking back to such historical precedents as László

sensed its historic significance as a key to the future evolution of art and of the visual media. By 'evoking topographical points and magical effects of nature', the transparency was among those things that provided 'sometimes instruction and a clear vision of distant landscapes or places – and sometimes, at the very least, enjoyable hours': things that 'endow modern life with its distinctive charm'.[28]

Light-Images and Light-Spaces in Twentieth-Century Art

The transparency was an attempt to overcome the limits of painting by painterly means. Structurally – and in terms of the aesthetics of its relation to the public – it bore a clear affinity to film. Before the cinema became a reality, the transparency created illuminated images that anticipated the cinematic vision. Light, space, motion

Fig.5 Werner Nekes, *View of a Landscape with House* (Film-take from *Diwan* 1973)

Fig.6 Ulrich Erben, *Halogen Object* 1972, Museum Folkwang, Essen

Moholy-Nagy's *Light-Space Modulator*, members of the ZERO group, including Günther Uecker, Otto Piene and Heinz Mack, set out to use artworks as catalysts in order to incorporate light as a constituent energy into visual art.[30] At Schloss Morsbroich, Leverkusen, in 1961, Piene presented a *Light Ballet* that dematerialized the walls through a play of reflected light. It was lighting that freed such works as Uecker's nail reliefs from their stasis.

In the exhibition *Szene Rhein-Ruhr '72*, a number of artists experimented with light-rooms, among them Gotthard Graubner, Ulrich Erben and Adolf Luther. In his *Mist Room*, Graubner used projectors reflected by mirrors onto screens in a room five metres square to evoke the impression of mist and involve the viewer physically within the work. In *Halogen Object* (fig. 6), Erben closed off one corner of a room with a translucent screen, lit from both sides by spotlights of different intensities, and suspended a white board between screen and corner. While the screen absorbed the reflection, the corner reflected the light. The result was the impression of a weightless, dematerialized geometric form floating in space. In Luther's *Focusing Space*, stationary and mobile concave mirrors caused the motes of dust in the air of the darkened room, made visible by light, to form into moving cones.

This artistic interest in factual, pure light, freed from illusionistic experiences or mediations, was also the dominant idea of the exhibition *Schattenprojektionen*, at

Schloss Oberhausen in 1993. This audio-visual media art show included the most varied works of 'Light Art', including (among others) the stereoscopic shadow image objects of Ludwig Wilding, the anaglyptic shadow projections of Sibylle Hofter, mirror installations and heliogravures by Markus Raetz, video installations by Alfred Banze, and holograms by Michael Bleyenberg and Dieter Jung. Unusually, and significantly, the organizers produced a catalogue on videotape, in which the work of the twenty-two chosen artists could be presented more authentically than in print.

The importance of light for art has undergone a fundamental change over the course of its history. The nineteenth century witnessed the start of the transition from light as a means of presentation – a vehicle of content – to the pure light-image; and the transparency formed part of this process. As this evolution proceeds, from images using light as a metaphor to self-referential light-images and light-spaces, art itself opens up in media terms, destroying the traditional genres. As frontiers have been crossed, perception has expanded to meet the demands of the present, and to reveal new horizons of physical and mental experience, which – to quote Rumohr again – 'endow modern life with its distinctive charm'.

Birgit Verwiebe

Translated from the German by David Britt

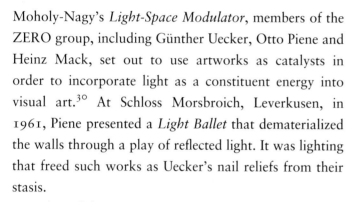

1 Emil Waldmann, *Caspar David Friedrich Almanach*, (Berlin, 1941), 14.

2 Friedrich Wilhelm Joseph Schelling, *Vorlesungen über die Philosophie der Kunst*, part 1, vol. 5, of Schelling, *Sämtliche Werke* (Stuttgart, 1859), 379.

3 Jörg Traeger, *Philipp Otto Runge und sein Werk* (Munich, 1975), 57.

4 Novalis, *Werke und Briefe*, ed. A. Kelletat (Stuttgart, 1975), 450.

5 Werner Sumowski, *Caspar David Friedrich Studien* (Wiesbaden, 1970), 223.

6 Alina Dobrezecki, *Die Bedeutung des Traumes für Caspar David Friedrich: Eine Untersuchung zu den Ideen der Frühromantik*, Beiträge zur deutschen Philologie, no. 55 (Giessen, 1982).

7 Caspar David Friedrich, *Caspar David Friedrich in Briefen und Bekenntnissen*, ed. S. Hinz (Berlin, 1984), 58.

8 Friedrich (as note 7), 67.

9 Friedrich (as note 7), 72–73.

10 Three extant drawings by Friedrich roughly correspond to the descriptions and dimensions that we have of his allegories of 'secular' 'spiritual' and 'celestial' music: the 'Female Lute Player and Guitarist in a Gothic ruin' (private collection), the *Female Harpist* in the Städtische Kunstsammlungen, Chemnitz, and the *Dream of the Singer*, in the Hamburger Kunsthalle. These may well have been preliminary studies for the lost works.

11 Another transparency, whereabouts now unknown, has been recorded in a photograph (Sumowski [as note 5], pl. 152. A *Moonlit Landscape*, watercolour, 23.1 × 36.6 cm); it was last recorded at Zingst, near Stralsund, in 1941, in the possession of one F. Pflugradt, a descendant of Friedrich's sister, Catharina Dorothea Sponholz.

12 Friedrich (as note 7), 67.

13 Waldmann (as note 1), 16.

14 Waldmann (as note 1), 13.

15 Friedrich Johann Lorenz Meyer, *Darstellungen aus Italien* (Berlin, 1792), 304.

16 A transparency 12 or 18 metres long, painted on Chinese paper, was mounted on rollers and unrolled in a box some 50 cm high in front of a burning candle, so that illuminated pictures moved past the spectator.

17 Pierre Francastel, 'Les Transparents de Carmontelle', *L'Illustration* (Paris), 17 August 1929, 159.

18 This peepshow with its mechanical figures also showed painted transparencies. As the name Eidophusikon itself was meant to signify, Loutherbourg was trying to achieve an effective imitation of Nature. The Eidophusikon was a sensational success, renowned all over the world.

19 Sketches and designs for these survive, but no completed originals.

20 Ludwig Catel, 'Darstellungen von merkwürdigen Gegenden und berühmten Bauwerken in der Art der Panoramen', *Spenersche Zeitung* (Berlin), 29 December 1808.

21 Joseph von Eichendorff, *Tagebücher*, vol. 11 of *Sämtliche Werke*, ed. Wilhelm Kotsch and August Sauer vol. 11, (Regensburg, 1908), 257–58.

22 *Spenersche Zeitung* (Berlin), 26 February 1811.

23 In 1830, fifteen years after Schinkel's scenes, his pupil, the stage painter Carl Gropius, presented in his diorama in Berlin (opened in 1827 on the Parisian model) the transparent transformation scene *Gothic Cathedral in Morning Light*, based on the painting of that title by Schinkel (copy by Wilhelm Ahlborn, Nationalgalerie, Berlin): 'In the opening moments, as we contemplate the cathedral in the dim morning light, the clouds, which almost seem to move, alter the scene, and scattered shafts of sunlight illuminate various parts of the town in turn, until a brilliant beam suddenly dispels the lower clouds and reveals the scene itself in the most cheerful daylight.' *Spenersche Zeitung* (Berlin), 20 June 1830.

The most celebrated of all diorama transparencies was another ecclesiastical scene: this was *Midnight Mass in the Church of Saint-Etienne-du-Mont*, first shown in 1834 in Daguerre's diorama in Paris. Over a fifteen-minute cycle, the viewer was taken through twenty-four hours. The view was of the interior of a church, lit from outside. Slowly the twilight fell, and at the same time the lights went on. Gradually, the empty pews filled with worshippers. Then midnight mass was heard, Finally, the lights went out one by one until the church stood dark and empty, as at the beginning, and daybreak approached.

24 In the Staatliche Galerie Moritzburg, Halle, is *The Ruins of Oybin by Moonlight*, which – with the Friedrich in Kassel – is one of the highest-quality transparencies in any German museum. It was long attributed to Friedrich himself, but Marianne Stoelzel, 'Caspar David Friedrich und seine Transparentmalerei mit Musikbegleitung', *Baltische Studien*, n.s., 61 (1975),

76, suggests that it is by his pupil, Oehme.

25 Karl Friedrich Rumohr, 'Über Otto Wagner's und Ernst Oehme's in Dresden aufgestellte Dioramen', in *Beiheft zum Jahrbuch der Preußischen Kunstsammlungen* (Berlin, 1943), 65.

26 Rumohr (as note 25), 66.

27 Rumohr (as note 25), 66.

28 Rumohr (as note 25), 64.

29 In the film sequence *View of a Landscape with House*, from *Hynningen*, Part 5 of his film anthology *Divan*, Nekes for the first time lights the times of day in accordance with the same approach. Here three layers of lighting interpenetrate. In a single location, different time frames blend into each other. The result is a transformation scene with changes of lighting, shifting cloud formations and figures who appear and disappear. Here, Nekes has drawn inspiration from the transformation scenes of the nineteenth-century 'archaeology of the cinema'.

30 These activities by German artists should be viewed in their international context. Since the 1960s, important light/space objects have been made by a number of American artists, including Robert Irwin, James Turrell, Douglas Wheeler, Larry Bell and Eric Orr.

Romantic Irony

'Romantic irony' is a catchy term, whose history may well supply a suitable basis for a discussion of its meaning. The academic question 'What really is Romantic?' – which Arthur Henkel chose as the title of an essay, presumably in allusion to Immanuel Kant's 'Answer to the Question "What is Enlightenment?"'[1] – leads on by analogy to another question: 'What really is Irony?' Henkel's answer to his own question ultimately equates 'Romantic' with 'emancipated', or even possibly with 'enlightened';[2] and in that case irony, whatever it may actually mean, is also its own antithesis, namely non-irony or anti-irony. If, as Kant declares, 'Enlightenment is Man's emergence from a state of tutelage, for which he himself is to blame,'[3] then Friedrich Schlegel's novel fragment *Lucinde*, an early manifestation of Romanticism, is simultaneously a piece of Enlightenment: for it is indebted to the very age and world-view from which it purports to distance itself and its author.

The history of irony, as word and as concept, goes back to the rhetoric of the ancient world. Aristotle in Book 3 of his *Rhetoric* and in his *Ethics*, Cicero in his treatise *On the Orator* and finally Quintilian in Book 9 of his *Education of an Orator* (fig. 1) mostly discuss irony, whether of expression or of formulation, in stylistic terms.[4] This stylistic approach to ironic expression fails to bring out the true distinction between, as Quintilian puts it, 'the irony that is a figure' and the irony 'that is a trope': for, 'in both, what is to be understood is the opposite of what is said'. A critique of rhetorical style thus fails to distinguish adequately between irony as a 'figure' and irony as a 'trope'.

The demarcation line between these different ironies, which Quintilian goes on to define, separates two areas of ironic expression and perception: one that couches the irony in a specific, individual word or words, and one that sees it only in terms of a whole, as process and as context.[5] Quintilian contrasts irony as a rhetorical trope, which, 'although it says something other than what it means, does not pretend to mean that other', with irony as a rhetorical figure, in which 'the whole intention is disguised ... so that there [in the trope] words are contrasted with words, but here the meaning [is contrasted] with the whole language and tone; and sometimes the whole presentation of the case, or even a whole life, seems to be ironic – as it seemed with Socrates, who was called the Ironist because he pretended to be an ignorant man and an admirer of other supposed sages. And so, just as a succession of metaphors forms an allegory, so the *trope* of irony, if sustained, forms the corresponding *figure*.'[6]

This distinction between the irony of a word and the irony of a life, as known to us from the rhetorical tradition of antiquity, elicited no direct response – favourable or unfavourable – in Romantic literature. However, the Romantic interest in the historical figure of Socrates as an 'Ironist' reveals a continuity between the ancient world and German Romanticism, above and beyond the merely verbal resemblance between 'Socratic irony' and 'Romantic irony'. In German Romantic literature the influence of Socrates, as mediated through the dialogues of Plato, can be detected in the poetic dialogues or conversations published by Friedrich Schleiermacher and Friedrich Schlegel. It also manifests itself in the philosophical reinterpretation of rhetorical irony into an aesthetic category that marks the Romantic union of art and life – that central historical achievement that has lent German Romanticism a relevance beyond its own time.

Examples are to be found in plenty in the aphoristic, unsystematic Romantic tradition of the literary fragment. The available material is not hard to interpret, so long as we bear in mind that the fundamental contradiction – the reciprocity – between Nature and Art, between Life and Literature, was the guiding principle of a whole system of thought. 'Novels are the Socratic dialogues of our time. In their liberal form, the wisdom that belongs to life has found a refuge from the wisdom of the schools.'[7] In this *Lyceum* fragment, Friedrich Schlegel (fig. 2) set the novel genre (the historical successor to the dialogue genre) alongside the principle of 'life', as aids to the artistic confrontation with existence.

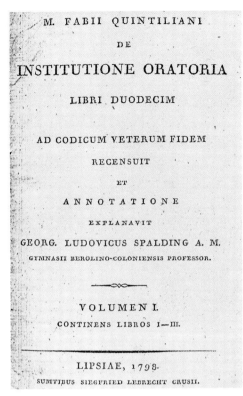

M. FABII QUINTILIANI

DE

INSTITUTIONE ORATORIA

LIBRI DUODECIM

AD CODICUM VETERUM FIDEM

RECENSUIT

ET

ANNOTATIONE

EXPLANAVIT

GEORG. LUDOVICUS SPALDING A. M.
GYMNASII BEROLINO-COLONIENSIS PROFESSOR.

VOLUMEN I.
CONTINENS LIBROS I—III.

LIPSIAE, 1798.
SUMTIBUS SIEGFRIED LEBRECHT CRUSII.

Fig.1 Quintilian, *On the Education of an Orator*. This edition published in Leipzig, 1798

'Philosophy,' wrote Schlegel, 'is the true home of irony, which it is tempting to define as logical beauty; for wherever people philosophize, not systematically but in oral or written conversation, irony must be deployed and encouraged; even the Stoics held urbanity to be a virtue. Of course, there is also such a thing as rhetorical irony, which produces an excellent effect if sparingly used, especially in polemics; but, by comparison with the exalted urbanity of the Socratic muse, this is the brilliance of the most artful oratory as against a tragedy in the high antique style. In this as in other respects, poetry alone can ascend to the heights of philosophy, without relying – as rhetoric does – on individual ironic passages. There are some ancient and modern poems that breathe, throughout and as a whole, the divine afflatus of irony.'[8]

In this *Lyceum* fragment, too, literature and life stand opposed to each other as fundamentally contrary principles – between which, however, connections constantly arise: as in the oral context of conversation, in the 'urbane' context of political debate, and in irony as the medium through which literature and life define each other. Thus, there can be poems that 'breathe', that are alive; whereas 'rhetoric', which follows antique

precedent by using ironic 'passages', is not alive but trapped within its own functional definition.

For Schlegel, then, 'irony' is a shifting term. Traditionally and rhetorically, it denotes a statement that – in terms of verbal usage – means its own opposite; but at the same time it reverses this narrowly rhetorical definition whenever it applies its own rhetorical function, as what Quintilian calls a figure, to a piece of 'whole life'. Irony raises an idea or a statement to a higher power by constantly evoking the opposite of that idea or statement.

'Irony is the form taken by the paradoxical. All that is simultaneously good and great is paradoxical.'[9] Here, in another of the *Lyceum* fragments, Schlegel articulates the underlying contradiction within his own definition of irony – and he does so, appropriately enough, as a paradox, or from its paradoxical side. But, again, such is the contradictory principle of irony that the act of articulation itself casts doubt on the content of the statement. Not only as an oral exchange, but also as a literary genre, dialogue constantly derives new stimulus from the way in which each individual speech in turn is called in question: irony is actually a formative principle of dialogue, and dialogue is the literary form best suited to irony.

Exemplary significance resides in the verbal or written conversation that the author of a work conducts, either with himself as its originator or with someone else, on the subject of himself and his own work. When one is under pressure to give information to another person, or to call oneself to account, irony partly aids communication and partly relieves the strain: it keeps the dialogue going, while simultaneously preventing it from reaching a hard-and-fast conclusion. It allows the author to avoid being pinned down to any specific statement. All he has to do is to confirm it ironically – i.e., contradict it – and then later, still ironically, supplant it with something else.

This idea and its practical consequences form the subject of another *Lyceum* fragment, on the theme of the 'artist' and his work, 'writing', in the course of which Schlegel says:

'So long as the artist is inventing and in a state of enthusiasm, he is in no state to communicate freely. He will want to say everything: which is an erroneous

Fig.2 Johann Gottfried Schadow, *Friedrich Schlegel* 1799

tendency in young geniuses, or else a correct prejudice in old dunces. He consequently underrates the value and dignity of self-restraint, which – for the artist, as for the human being – is the be-all and end-all, the thing most needful and supreme. Most needful: for, wherever one fails to restrain oneself, the world does the restraining, and one becomes a slave. Supreme: for one can restrain oneself only in those matters and in those directions where one's power is infinite – in self-creation and in self-annihilation. Even a friendly conversation that cannot break off at any moment, purely at a whim, has something unfree about it. A writer who cannot and will not stop before he has had his say out – who keeps nothing to himself, but wants to tell all he knows – is much to be pitied.'[10]

In this fragment on writing, Schlegel defines the basics of the artist's condition and, in the process, converts insights drawn from the theoretical debate on literary irony into precepts for life. He draws the analogy between irony as a stylistic device, both in rhetoric and in actual conversation, and those constraints that affect the life of the writer, who – since they are the essential

preconditions of any writing at all – ought to be able to play a part in shaping them for himself. For any utterance made under such constraints, the fragment is the appropriate literary form: hence, logically, the existence of the fragment as a literary genre defined, not as an incomplete scrap of writing, but as a self-contained work in itself. 'A fragment must be like a miniature work of art, entirely cut off from the world around it, and as self-contained as a hedgehog.'[11]

However, if fragments 'must' also simultaneously be conceivable as 'parts of a whole',[12] a contradiction arises: a contradiction that the 'fragment' – meaning something incomplete, as well as a self-contained whole – could never resolve, were it not for irony. When Schlegel elsewhere refers to a 'dialogue' (which by his own theoretical definition is ironic) as 'a garland of fragments',[13] he is making irony into a key defining property of the literary 'fragment'.

There is much more to 'Romantic irony' than the irony 'in theory and form' of the German Romantics, as identified and explained by Ingrid Strohschneider-Kohrs in a study of representative works by a number of leading Romantic writers. Schlegel himself specifically referred to 'Romantic irony' in fragmentary notes made between 1797 and 1801, though these peripheral uses of the term have attracted little attention:[14]

'Shakespeare attained irony in love, in fantasy and in sentiment: so his [irony] is thoroughly Romantic. Ariosto's is not.'[15]

'Petrarch too has Romantic irony.'[16]

'Romantic irony is necessary in all [rhetorical] [dramas]?'[17]

'[Absolute sentiment] and [absolute imagination] may lead [to the Romantic] even without universal poetry; but only with the latter do they lead through dichotomy and opposition to [the absolutely Romantic], or to Romantic irony.'[18]

Taken in conjunction, these few statements in which Schlegel uses the term show that, for him, 'Romantic irony' is a pointer to 'the absolutely Romantic' – and that this in turn is a compound of 'absolute sentiment' and 'absolute imagination'. By confining himself to abstract defining characteristics, he shows that he means his definition of 'Romantic irony' to transcend chronological limitations. For Strohschneider-Kohrs, 'Romantic

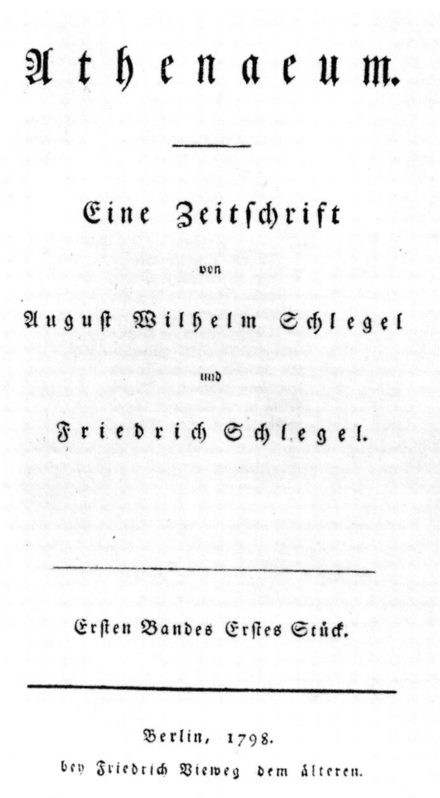
Athenaeum.

Eine Zeitschrift

von

August Wilhelm Schlegel

und

Friedrich Schlegel.

Ersten Bandes Erstes Stück.

Berlin, 1798.

bey Friedrich Vieweg dem älteren.

Fig.3 *Athenäum*. A literary and philosophical magazine edited by the brothers August Wilhelm and Friedrich Schlegel, Berlin, 1798–1800

irony' is a category of aesthetic theory, specific to the period of German Romanticism; but for Schlegel it is a category of literary irony, defined in terms of examples from the past. Shakespeare and Petrarch worked in different genres, but both equally satisfied its criteria; Ariosto, on the other hand, did not.

If Schlegel, speaking as a contemporary of the Romantic movement, was able to detect 'Romantic irony' outside his own period and its label, then this perception may be applicable not only to past ages but equally to developments situated (from Schlegel's viewpoint) in the future. In the twentieth century, Schlegel is not with us to judge at first hand, but it is entirely in keeping with his philosophy of history – and a consequence thereof – that his historical verdict on Shakespeare and Petrarch should have prompted others, both in art and in philosophy, to take up the tradition of Romantic irony. As Schlegel puts it in another of his *Fragments*, 'The historian is a prophet turned backward.'[19]

After Schlegel, and under the direct influence of his *Fragments*, other philosophers took up his attempts at definition in a variety of ways. Carl Wilhelm Ferdinand Solger, Georg Wilhelm Friedrich Hegel, Søren Kierkegaard and Friedrich Nietzsche carried on the debate while altering its premises. As a result, there came to be more interest in a conceptual definition of the theory of irony than in the literary critic's concern with irony as an aesthetic concept.

Modern literary research in Romanticism, insofar as it deals with 'Romantic irony', is therefore of more than specialist interest: its readiness to investigate irony both as a stylistic device – originally rhetorical – and in its effects on form means that in a sense it is a continuation of the debate within Romantic literary theory itself. Strohschneider-Kohrs adduces many examples to illustrate what she calls 'Romantic irony in form', a model of art theory that can be used to confront and ultimately to interpret the dialectic of theory and execution, norm and practice, intention and success, within the individual work: 'seemingly inartistic presentations of reflection bluntly stated, and of overt and conscious self-interpretation and self-effacement – the most manifest denotation and demonstration – all have the power to generate form and coherence'.[20]

Within the field of Romantic studies there is thus a tendency to interpret the whole of Romantic literature and art in terms of 'Romantic irony', as a theoretical category of artistic intention. Similarly, in German literary history at large, there is an established line of enquiry that examines the formal potential of irony, not through the period phenomenon of 'Romantic irony', but through irony as a narrative device, especially in the novel. This is most memorably exemplified in the storytelling of Thomas Mann. His strength as a model lies in the fact that he not only addressed the theme intellectually, writing as a theoretical ironist, but also – in his choice of literary genres and forms, and above all in his letters, journals, essays and stories – cultivated a tradition that might well stem directly (in the case of the *Felix Krull* fragment) from the Romantic aesthetic of irony.[21]

In the early Romantic movement and in its literary productions, 'fragment' and 'irony' are two basic parameters in relation to which the Romantic writer's formal and thematic intentions can interweave and settle into an artistic synthesis of form and theme. Quintilian's

Fig.4 Thomas Mann c.1947. Photographed by George Platt Lynes

definition of irony, whereby 'what is to be understood is the opposite of what is said', denotes a stylistic figure based on a necessary mental reservation – and this reservation is already implicit in the literary genre of the fragment, which by definition conveys only part of a whole and therefore remains an incomplete statement.

Incomplete by definition, a fragment may nevertheless – ironically – lay claim to a global insight and the communicability thereof;[22] and this enhances the value not only of the 'fragment' itself but also of those texts in relation to which the fragment defines itself as fragmentary. Just so long as the fragment does not inherently define itself as the opposite of some abstract whole that is knowable only through this opposition, it will reveal itself as incomplete only within the documentary context of other source material relevant to the same content. If,

in consequence, an artist's or a writer's work cannot speak for itself – if it needs a commentary by its own creator before it can be rightly understood – then the fragmentariness of its utterance can no longer be concealed. The creator or author himself documents the understanding of his work by adding a supplementary text that ought by rights – according to the Romantic theory of irony – to convey the opposite of the original utterance.

In a note written in 1935, under the heading of 'Directions for Use', Ödön von Horváth reflected on the consequences of misleading productions of his plays, which had compelled him to supply a commentary against his will:

'I had always determinedly resisted discussing my plays in any way – the fact is that I was naïve enough to imagine that even without "Directions for Use" people would ... understand my plays. I now freely admit that this was a serious mistake, and that "Directions for Use" are just what I must supply.

'The fault was largely mine: I supposed that many passages that admit of only one interpretation would inevitably be interpreted correctly. They were not. In many cases I have fallen short of the intended perfect synthesis of irony and realism.'

Horváth's 'Directions for Use', a frank confession by a writer who lived many years after the Romantic era, reveals an aesthetic of irony that avowedly seeks its effect not in the comprehensibility of the language or in the classification of the genre but in reality itself. By thus adopting 'life' as his criterion, Horváth assigns blame for the misunderstanding of his plays to himself, to 'those responsible' in the theatre and to the public: all must henceforth exercise greater responsibility.[23]

When Martin Walser placed his 'Frankfurt Lectures' under the overall title of 'Self-Awareness and Irony', he drew the same conclusion from his own experience as Horváth in his 'Directions'. In a work that is complete in itself, the aesthetic of irony is not reflected in the linguistic or stylistic form but only in the relationship to reality. The language is an indicator of this, only if it is ambiguous within the context of the chosen vocabulary.[24]

True to the example of his mentor, Schlegel, Karl August Varnhagen von Ense has left us a collection of

891

mringe über die Zunge, und wenn
zufügt, so glaubt man, daß seine

esteht das Ordal darin, daß der
in Stück Rinde von einem gewiss
ein Gebet hersagen muß, worin
daß ihn der Genuß dieser Rinde
ht unschuldig sey.

Sierra Leona bedient man sich
gleichen Gelegenheiten hinter die
ines Trants, der mit dem Bitter-
ey den Juden im Gebrauch war*),
von den Afrikanern das rothe
Wenn Jemand wegen Diebstahl
wird, so sucht er, im Fall er
ge dadurch zu entkräften, daß er
e Wasser zu trinken. Erst bal-
ne Versammlung, und lassen sich
Vertheidigung vortragen. Wenn
thun, daß die Sache durch eine
schuld entschieden werden müsse,
eine benachbarte Stadt namhaft,
d dem Häuptling seinen Wunsch
othe Wasser zu trinken. Hier-
emeine Berathschlagung gehalten,
iese Bitte zu gewähren sey; wird
ß er eine andere Stadt wählen.
re zufrieden, so bleibt der Ange-
ab verweilt daselbst, ohne sich je-
ten sehen zu lassen, oft zwey bis
Tag anberaumt wird, an welchem
foll. Sobald dieser bestimmt ist,
ten sagen, er solle nach Verlauf
inden, und von seinen Freunden
ihm beliebe.

sser zu bereiten, nimmt man
s, und weicht sie in Wasser, wel-
aft erlangt, daß es als ein star-
en aber als eine Purganz wirkt.
welcher es trant, auf der Stelle
führt natürlich auf die Vermu-
och etwas anderes hineingethan
t absehen läßt, warum schwäch-
davon angegriffen werden sollten,
llen Verdacht zu beseitigen, als
richtig zugehe, wird das rothe
tller möglichen Publicität, unter
Beyseyn einer ungeheuern Menge
e von allen Orten herzueilen, und

p.

worunter besonders viele Frauenspersonen sind, welche nie
unterlassen, sich bey dergleichen Gelegenheiten in ihrem
vollen Glanze zu zeigen.
(Der Beschluß folgt.)

Beyträge zur allgemeinen Geschichte.
(Fortsetzung.)

Finanzen.

Ein Ritter in Jütland, Namens Kalff, fiel von
seinem Lehnsherrn mit zwey Burgen ab, und hielt sich zu
dessen Feinden, die ihm dafür noch eine dritte Burg ga-
ben. Mit diesen dreyen ergab er sich wieder in seines
Herrn Gnade, der mit Lachen sagte: „Das Kalb sey als
ein großer Ochs wieder gekommen."

Abgaben.

Ein polnischer Jude verlor im Handel all sein Geld,
und bald darauf durch den Tod seine Frau. In seiner
Verzweiflung rief er aus: „Hätte nur Gott mir erst die
Frau genommen, mit meinem Geld hätte ich dann leicht
eine andere, reichere gekriegt; dann hätt' er ja nachher
auch mein Geld nehmen können, so hätt' ich eine Frau ge-
habt mit Geld, und er auch."

Fabriken.

Ein reicher Fabrikant prahlte: „Ich nähre über fünfhundert Menschen!" — Im Gegentheil, gab ein Student zur Antwort, Sie werden von fünfhundert Menschen
ernährt.

Industrie.

Ein junger Schriftsteller gab einem Verleger eine
Sammlung vermischter Schriften, die bogenweise bezahlt
wurden. Seine Gedichte bot er dem Manne umsonst an,
aber als dieser nicht wollte, that er sie in das erstere
Buch, und hier mußte der arme Verleger bezahlen, was
er umsonst nicht hatte annehmen wollen.

Luxus.

Wie! haben die nun auch Wagen und Pferde? — Es
wird ja alter Fiaker seyn! — O nein, das ist eine eigene
Kutsche. — Nun so sind doch die Pferde Ackervieh!

Polizey.

Man behauptete, wenn man über eine gewisse Brücke
gehe, müsse man sich wenigstens ein Bein zum Pfand-
geben lassen.

Amtsverwaltung.

Wer da? schrie ein ankommender Student der Schild-
wache am Thor entgegen; diese präsentirte, und antwor-
tete vernehmlich: Stadtsoldat!

Wohlthätigkeit.

Zwey Blinde bettelten. Einer ging vorüber, und sagte:
theilt Euch!

Fig.5 Karl August Varnhagen von Ense. Extract from 'Contributions to Universal History', 1813

ironic reflections, published as 'fragments' under the title of 'Beitrage zur allgemeinen Geschichte' ('Contributions to Universal History') (fig. 5). These all owe their literary point to the writer's confrontation with the reality of life. Varnhagen's preface is exemplary:

'Shaken by the breath of Nature, as if by gales, humankind took shelter in artificial institutions, where those powerful stirrings might be reduced to a gentle breeze. Many tools were devised, ideas sparked, pieces of knowledge acquired, customs practised; Nature herself crept, unremarked and barely changed, into all that was made. In all that is done against her she lies concealed as wit, which abruptly springs to life, to the discomfiture and bafflement of humankind. But no one has yet devised a way for human beings to live together; and so it came to pass, amid fitful lightning flashes, that the days of Europe slid away into the night, from which the following images emerge as a shadow-play, lit by the puny taper that we have hoarded in secret. If the headings often seem to conflict with the content, it should be remembered that the hapless north wind, caught in a winding road and pressed by air from behind, has to follow the bends in the road, and may well be forced round to blow northward again; but he always remains the north wind.'25

Konrad Feilchenfeldt

Translated from the German by David Britt

1 Immanuel Kant, *Werke in sechs Bänden*, ed. Wilhelm Weischedel , vol. 6 (Frankfurt am Main, 1964), 53–61.
2 Arthur Henkel, 'Was ist eigentlich romantisch?', in *Festschrift für Herbert Singer*, ed. Richard Alewyn and Benno von Wiese (Cologne and Graz, 1967), 292–308, especially 297–98.
3 Kant (as note 1), vol. 6, 53.
4 Ernst Behler, *German Romantic Theory* (Cambridge, 1993), 141ff.
5 Marcus Fabius Quintilianus, *Institutionis oratoriae libri duodecim* 9.2. See also Uwe Japp, 'Theorie der Ironie', *Das Abendland*, n.s., no. 15 (Frankfurt am Main, 1983), 171ff.
6 Quintilianus (as note 5), 9.2.45–46.
7 Friedrich Schlegel, *Kritische Friedrich-Schlegel-Ausgabe*, ed. Ernst Behler , vol. 2 (Munich, Paderborn, Vienna and Zurich, 1963–), 149 [26].
8 Schlegel (as note 7), vol. 2, 152 [42].
9 Schlegel (as note 7), vol. 2, 153 [48].
10 Schlegel (as note 7), vol. 2, 151 [37].
11 Schlegel (as note 7), vol. 2, 197 [206].
12 Schlegel (as note 7), vol. 16, 154 [808].
13 Schlegel (as note 7), vol. 2, 176 [77].
14 Ingrid Strohschneider-Kohrs, *Die romantische Ironie in Theorie und Gestaltung*, 2nd ed., Hermaea, n.s., no. 6 (Tübingen, 1977), 7 n. 1.
15 Schlegel (as note 7), vol. 16, 126 [508].
16 Schlegel (as note 7), vol. 16, 145 [709].
17 Schlegel (as note 7), vol. 16, 145 [713].
18 Schlegel (as note 7), vol. 16, 146 [716].
19 Schlegel (as note 7), vol. 2, 176 [80].
20 Strohschneider-Kohrs (as note 14), 427. For a contrary view, see Japp (as note 5), 115–16, n. 16.
21 Hans Eichner, 'Thomas Mann und die deutsche Romantik', in Wolfgang Paulsen, ed., *Das Nachleben der Romantik in der modernen Literatur*, Poesie und Wissenschaft, no. 14 (Heidelberg, 1969), 152–173, especially 158ff. Also Reinhard Baumgart, *Das Ironische und die Ironie in den Werken Thomas Manns: Literatur als Kunst* (Munich, 1964). 72ff.
22 Lucien Dällenbach and Christiaan L. Hart Nibbrig, eds., *Fragment und Totalität*, edition suhrkamp, n.s., no. 107 (Frankfurt am Main, 1984), 107.
23 Ödön von Horváth, 'Gebrauchsanweisung', in Horváth, *Gesammelte Werke in acht Bänden*, ed. Traugott Krischke and Dieter Hildebrandt vol. 8, (Frankfurt am Main, 1972), 659.
24 Martin Walser, *Selbstbewußtsein und Ironie: Frankfurter Vorlesungen*, no. 90 (Frankfurt am Main, 1981).
25 Karl August Varnhagen von Ense, 'Beiträge zur allgemeinen Geschichte', in Varnhagen von Ense, *Werke in fünf Bänden*, ed. Konrad Feilchenfeldt, vol. 4 (Frankfurt am Main, 1987–), 622.

Landscape and the 'Irony of Nature'[1]

'Blechen displays not the gracefulness of the
Italian landscape but rather its irony.'[2]

Romantic Irony and Painting

To talk about the irony of a landscape must strike most
observers these days as an extravagant conceit. Yet
when the above observation was published in 1835, it
was used in an unostentatious manner that suggested
normality. It appeared in the first volume of a standard
work of reference, Nagler's *Künstlerlexikon*, and was a
judgment on the promising young painter Carl Blechen,
who had been puzzling the Berlin art world with his
Italian scenes ever since he had returned from Rome six
years previously. What is even more striking is that this
notion of the irony of a landscape – which Nagler
gleaned from contemporary reviews of Blechen's work –
was applied to works whose treatment now seems
unparadoxical. Their warm tones, bright colours and
spirited handling appear to be symptomatic of that
growing interest in vivid naturalistic effects that can be
found throughout Europe in the 1830s. There seems
little in these attractive scenes to justify such phrases as
'the capriciouness of his conception of nature'.[3]

This problem should not be dismissed lightly. Blechen
might have his place for us amongst the pioneers of
nineteenth-century naturalism, but that should not
obscure the fact that his pictures presented nuances for
his contemporaries of a quite different kind. There were
features in both his subject matter and his manner of
painting for which the term *Ironie* seemed appropriate.

Nagler's use of the word takes on an added significance in view of the striking developments in the concept of *Ironie* that had been taking place in Germany
over the previous three decades. Indeed, the notion of
Ironie had become a key feature in the aesthetic and critical writing of the period. This followed on suggestions
made around 1797–78 by the critic Friedrich Schlegel.
Schlegel went beyond the conventional usage of *Ironie*

as a figure of speech: a straightforward rhetorical device
that consists in saying the opposite to what is meant.
Schlegel's *romantische Ironie* – as he called it – had
deeper implications than this. It implied a recognition by
the artist of the paradoxical nature of his own position.
Art was full of duplicity. It was at the same time all-
meaning and frivolous, deeply revealing yet artificially
constructed. Furthermore such duplicity was not arbitrary. It was a reflection of the paradox of man's existence. It was only by the assumption of a paradoxical
frame of mind, Schlegel argued, that the artist could
achieve works that engaged this duality. As Eichner has
put it: 'He himself must be both detached and involved,
deeply serious about his art and yet capable of treating it
as a mere game, trustful of his deepest impulses and yet
full of critical, conscious awareness.'[4]

This difficult concept started a debate which has still
not terminated. As Feilchenfeldt's essay in this catalogue
shows,[5] it is very much alive today. Yet while *romantische Ironie* has been extensively explored in literary studies, it has been sparingly applied in those of the visual
arts. This seems to be because irony in any form is felt to
be too closely linked to the usages of language to have
effective applications elsewhere.[6]

In his useful general introduction to the notion of
irony D.C. Muecke has observed that 'what makes
music and the graphic arts *less likely* than literature to
be ironical is their greater reliance, implicit in the very
nature of sound, colour, and line, upon a sensuous,
attention-holding surface … what makes it *possible*
for them to be ironical is that they are in a sense
"languages".'[7] Amongst German Romantic writers and
artists the notion of fine art as a language was a
commonplace. It was expressed very directly, for example, in Wilhelm Heinrich Wackenroder's seminal
Herzensergießungen eines kunstliebenden Klosterbruders
('Outpourings of the Heart of an Art-Loving Monk')
(1797). In this Wackenroder states 'art is a language …
It speaks to men through pictures, operating as a kind
of hieroglyphic script …'.[8] Such assumptions laid the

ground for the possibility of seeing the fine arts in terms of irony.

Art may be able to convey irony inasmuch as it is understood to function as a language. But it is a different matter to assume that nature can do so. Muecke asserts that this is impossible, since natural phenomena cannot be considered to operate in any sense as a 'language'. Using an example that is, by chance, highly apposite for the present discussion, he comments '... one cannot paint ironically an Alpine scene, but only, say, a Romantic Alpine scene, that is, an Alpine scene as regarded by others in a certain way. When in the twentieth century, we look at one of Caspar David Friedrich's Romantic landscapes we can easily recognize certain qualities that have become signs of Romanticism or even signs of that particular painter. It is these signs that an ironical painter will work with – and perhaps be abused by some backward art critic for being "literary".'[9]

Certainly the parodying of a recognized style is one of the ways in which a painting can communicate a sense of irony. As it happens, the mimicking of Friedrich's art was one of the devices used by Blechen in the early part of his career.[10] But there is another sense in which landscape could be considered ironic in the early nineteenth century, and which relates more closely to the concept of *romantische Ironie*. This was in the recognition of what Kierkegaard termed, in *The Concept of Irony* (1841), the 'Irony of nature'. In this nature itself seeems to present ironic situations. 'This is not conscious in nature except for one who has an eye for it, for whom it is then as if nature were like a person playing tricks on him, or confiding to him its pain and sorrow.'[11] To have an eye for the 'Irony of nature' it is necessary to behave as though nature does, indeed, communicate in some form of language. This the Germans of the Romantic era were more than ready to do. Wackenroder (to keep to the source already quoted) described the language of nature as that which is spoken only by God but which the man of sensibility to some extent apprehended.[12] In the chapter of *Herzensergießungen* entitled 'Concerning Two Wonderful Languages and their Mystical Power' he brings together God's 'language of nature' and man's 'language of art', seeing in them parallel celebrations of divine creation. For Wackenroder there was no irony in the language of nature. But for those who were less

certain of the presence of a benevolent deity – such as Friedrich Schlegel (in his early years), Heinrich von Kleist, and E.T.A. Hoffmann – the concept could have disconcerting implications.

For landscape – and the painting of it – to be considered capable of irony it was necessary for a very special approach towards nature and the visual arts to be formulated; one which could see both of them in terms of language. This is precisely what happened in Germany around 1800. Elsewhere there was not such explicit formulation – although the notion of nature possessing powers of communication was a commonplace. In England, for example, it can be found readily enough in the poetry of Wordsworth. There were several painters in both England and Germany for whom a 'transcendental' experience before nature was of importance. Of these perhaps only Friedrich and Blechen developed attitudes that can be related explicitly to current concepts of 'Romantic' irony. Turner, however, also comes close to it – particularly in pictures inspired by contemporary poetry. I have explored the significance of ironic strategies for Friedrich and Turner elsewhere.[13] Here I will focus on its significance for Blechen, with some preliminary observations about its presence in the works of Friedrich.

Caspar David Friedrich's 'Serious Game'[14]

One of the most striking features of Friedrich's art is the way it gains intensity and expressive power around 1806. This is partly a thematic change, and partly a formal one. There are more overt references to symbolic affinities between man's life and the cycles of nature, and a greater honing of his imagery to make it more dramatic and powerful.

It is widely accepted that Friedrich received the stimulus to make such alterations through his contact with those 'transcendental' writers and theorists who were so prevalent in Dresden around 1800. Living in Dresden from 1799 Friedrich could hardly have been unaware of such figures as Ludwig Tieck, Novalis and the Schlegel brothers, Friedrich and August Wilhelm. Particularly striking is the relationship between Friedrich's remarks on art and the *Naturphilosophie* of the philosopher

Friedrich Wilhelm Schelling. It seems most likely that Friedrich would have learned of such ideas through K.C.F. Krause and Gotthilf Heinrich Schubert, two pupils of Schelling who were intimate with the artist during the first decade of the nineteenth century. Friedrich understood very well the apparent contradiction that that which is discovered of the outer world is at the same time the outcome of a personal act of conception. 'The artist should not only paint what he sees before him, but also what he sees within him,' he said in a celebrated aphorism.[15]

Friedrich's love of paradox comes out often in his writings. One comment suggests more specifically an acquaintance with current notions about the ironic position of the artist. In a letter to his fellow explorer of 'transcendental' landscape, Philipp Otto Runge, he states, 'Art may be a game, but it is a serious game'.[16]

The idea of art as a game probably derives from the notion of the play-drive (*Spieltrieb*) formulated by Friedrich Schiller in his *Aesthetic Letters on the Education of Mankind* (1794).[17] For Schiller the play-drive was necessary for the exploratory nature of man's cultural activites in which the two contrasting polarities of sense and reason could be brought simultaneously into action. However, the idea of the play element in art soon spread beyond this context, and became widely used amongst German writers of the period. Goethe, for example, in his last letter, referred to his *Faust* as a 'serious jest' (*ernstes Scherz*).[18]

Apart from this serious playfulness, it may be that the paradoxes that lie at the centre of most of Friedrich's pictures – the contrasts between the spiritual and the material, the eternal and the temporal – can be related to current notions of irony. This would be less likely to have come through Tieck or the Schlegels than through Schubert, one of the Schellingian 'nature-philosophers' with whom Friedrich had so much contact in his formative years. Schubert had a positive and highly original concept of irony which showed it to be the inevitable means of expression of the spiritual man. His view on this matter is all the more interesting because he was deeply interested in both the art and personality of Friedrich. He used a version of Friedrich's sepia cycle of the *Times of Year* (*Jahreszeiten*) to illustrate the apprehension of the spiritual through the material of his

Fig.1 Caspar David Friedrich, *Monk by the Sea* 1808–10, Staatliche Museen zu Berlin Preußischer Kulturbesitz, Nationalgalerie

Ansichten von der Nachtseite der Naturwißenschaft ('Views on the Dark Side of the Natural Sciences'), and later pronounced Friedrich to be 'the most extraordinary and original of all my Dresden acquaintances'.[19]

Schubert's notion of irony is unusual, but it was far from being without repercussions. It appears to have been of interest to E.T.A. Hoffmann,[20] and was drawn on by Kierkegaard to illustrate the concept of the 'irony of nature'.[21] Schubert sees irony in the 'contrasts' that occur in nature, such as that which related species provide for each other – as in the case of apes and men. But there is a more profound irony that arises from the contrast that the mysterious region which lies beyond the material inevitably forms with the 'normal' world. Only the spiritually inspired man, the artist or seer (the terms are virtually interchangeable for Schubert) can effect this. It is the 'language of poetry and revelation' that brings this other world to human consciousness and presents an 'ironic' contrast with everyday experience.

Schubert applied such ideas directly to the work of Friedrich when he cited the artist's *Jahreszeiten* cycle as an illustration of the 'relationship ... that exists between a future higher and a present lower existence.'[22]

The paradoxical relationship of the spiritual and the material emerges strongly in Friedrich's most extreme painting, the celebrated *Monk by the Sea* (fig. 1 and colour plate, p. 96). In this the vision of infinity is sharply separated from the foreground shore where the meditative monk stands. Furthermore this vision appears not as an enchanting and delectable distance, but as an oppressive emptiness. Friedrich actually increased this sense of emptiness during the painting of the picture, eliminating two boats that were in the sea.

Contemporary reactions to this picture suggest that it stimulated a strong sense of bewilderment. This can be seen in the famous review published in the *Berliner Abendblätter* that was written by Clemens Brentano and Achim von Arnim and revised by Heinrich von Kleist.[23] In the opening part of the review Brentano complains that the picture fails to provide the fashionable sensation of the pleasure of melancholy, the 'splendid' (*herrlich*) effect of wandering 'in an endless solitude by the side of the sea' and hearing 'the voice of life ... in the roar of the tide, in the buffeting of the wind, in the movement of the clouds ...'. Instead, Brentano encounters nothing but the bareness of the picture. In confusion he abdicates his role as critic and hands over to the public. There follows a series of 'overheard' snatches of conversation in which the Berlin exhibition visitors' reactions to the work are presented as a kind of farce:

'*Man*: Immeasurably deep and sublime!
Woman: You mean the sea. Yes, that must be extraordinarily deep, and the Capuchin is also most sublime.

...

Man: Ossian plucks his harp before this picture (leaves)
(two young ladies enter)
First Lady: Did you hear, Luise, this is Ossian.
Second Lady: No, no ... . You misunderstood him. It is the ocean.'

Brentano's light-hearted dismissal of the work is contrasted by the interpolations that Kleist made in the review. These show a different reaction to the starkness of the picture: 'Nothing can be sadder and more uncomfortable than this position in the world. The single spark of life in the broad realm of death, the lonely centre of a lonely circle.'

Kleist accepted that the picture was meant to be uncomfortable, that the vision of infinity was a frightening one. It did not fit in with delicious sensations on solitary walks in the way that Brentano wanted it to. It was too removed from common experience for this. In no

other picture did Friedrich present so uncompromisingly the conflict between the spiritual and the material worlds. Perhaps he took it to such a degree in this case because, as Börsch-Supan has suggested, the monk is a portrait of Friedrich himself.[24]

The disquieting image of the infinite presented in this picture might be seen in terms of Schubert's notion of irony. However, there is also a sense in which it can suggest the paradoxical position of art described by Friedrich Schlegel in his formulation of 'Romantic' irony. Although the picture is of a broad, open landscape, it seems almost wilfully to destroy any sense of spatial depth. As Brentano complained, the spectator is invited to enter into the picture by the contemplative figure of the monk only to be prevented from doing so by the flat, non-illusionistic treatment of the sea and sky. In recent years this technique has led to the picture being hailed as a first reductive step along the glorious path that led to the triumph of Abstract Expressionism in New York in the 1950s.[25] But it could also be the expression of more contemporary concerns. For it emphasizes that the picture, despite its visionary aspirations, it nevertheless no more than a picture. Even at its most serious, art remains a game.

Blechen's Jests

The notion of irony was never overtly mentioned in the reviews of Friedrich's work – however much it might seem to be there at times by implication. In the case of Carl Blechen, however, the notion did arise – as is suggested by the quotation at the head of this essay. Related to this was the assumption of contemporaries that Blechen's landscapes contained a kind of black humour. Phrases like 'horrible humour' (*schauerlicher Humor*) and 'sarcastic sombreness' (*sarkastisch-Finsternis*) litter the reviews. Indeed, it seems to some extent that Blechen became a victim of such assumptions.

To a large extent the nature of the reception that Blechen's work received was related to the cultural milieu in which his art developed. He was very much a product of Berlin society of the 1820s. After a false start as a banking clerk he entered the Berlin Academy in 1823 at the age of twenty-four. Preferment was rapid after that.

Fig.2 Carl Blechen, *Ruined Gothic Church* 1826, Staatliche Kunstsammlungen
Dresden, Gemäldegalerie Neue Meister

Within a year he had been appointed to the position of
scene painter at the Königstädter Theater, largely due to
the good offices of the architect Karl Friedrich Schinkel.
Blechen had both the versatility and sense of the dramatic to make him eminently successful at this job. But
from the point of view of his development as a landscape
painter it was not altogether beneficial. It encouraged
him to go too easily for showy effects. A visit to Dresden
in 1823 brought him into close contact with the art of
Friedrich and the conventions of 'Northern' landscape.
These he reinterpreted with heightened drama. In subsequent years he exhibited a whole repertoire of ruins,
monks and supernatural phenomena which gained him
widespread notoriety for placing the 'horrible' (*schauerlich*) at the service of landscape.

Blechen's interest in introducing the *schauerlich* into
landscape was widely assumed by his critics to be the
result of his contact with the writing of that master of
the *Schauer-Roman* (horror novel), E.T.A. Hoffmann.
The shadow of Hoffmann – who had died in Berlin in
1822 – loomed large in the cultural life of the Prussian
capital at that time. Blechen probably first took a serious
interest in Hoffmann when working as a scene painter.
By 1826 he was producing works that were being
directly compared with Hoffmann's stories, including a
supposed depiction of 'Pater Medardus', the ill-fated
monk in the macabre *Die Elixiere des Teufels* ('The
Devil's Elixirs').

It is perhaps unlikely that Blechen would have made a
close study of Hoffmann's notions of irony. On the
other hand, his work does seem to pick up the ironic
tone that pervades Hoffmann's work. Hoffmann reinterpreted the idealized notion of irony of the spiritually
minded nature-philosopher Schubert, turning it into a
deadly comedy. Blechen effected a similar revision to the
Friedrichian elements of visionary landscape. In his
Ruined Gothic Church (fig. 2), for example, this can be
seen at work. In Friedrich's pictures Gothic buildings
suggest the spiritual world and provide intimations of
immortality. Only in the abnormality that their appearance suggests can they be said to be ironic. The ironies
in Blechen's pictures are of a different nature. They arise
from a virtual inversion of Friedrich's use of imagery.
The pilgrim in the foreground is not contemplating the
infinite. He is asleep. The building is not viewed as an
aspiring symmetrical structure. It is seen from an angle
and is dank and dark. The reviewer in the *Spenersche
Zeitung* saw in it evidence of 'sarcastic sombreness'
drawing attention to the 'moss and blemishes that are
busily at work undermining what is in existence,
destroying it utterly'.[26] In the distance, on top of one of
the church's walls there is, it is true, a fir tree, one of the
natural phenomena used by Friedrich as a symbol of
hope, but here it is actually part of the vegetation that is
bringing about the destruction of the religious edifice. If
it is a symbol of anything, it is that hope is ill-founded.

In the latter part of his career – particularly after his
visit to Italy – Blechen moved away from the production
of *schauerliche* scenes and inverted 'transcendental'
landscapes to the portrayal of contemporary subjects. At
the same time he showed a new direction in his technique. The experience of Italy – perhaps stimulated by
the sight of Turner's works at his exhibition in Rome in
1828[27] – brought a new sense of light and colour into
his work.

Fig.3 Carl Blechen, *Girls Bathing in the Park at Terni* c.1836, Schäfer Collection, Schweinfurt (cat. 16)

When Blechen started exhibiting Italian scenes on his return to Berlin, his new technique led to bafflement amongst the critics. 'Where did the artist get the red-brown shadows in the background of that gorge from?' asked one reviewer. 'If he has seen such – and we would give much for his vision – then we thank him for drawing our attention to it. However, we cannot recall any such colouration, or discern any circumstance that would give occasion to it.'[28]

Most critics resolved their perplexity by resorting to the Hoffmannesque vocabulary that they had been accustomed to use for Blechen's paintings before his Italian journey. When reviewing some Italian scenes in 1822 *Museum* said that they provided 'the proof that landscape, contrary to what one might have thought, is capable of humour, indeed of terrifying humour.' This reviewer considered the works 'comic, because they stand nature on her head. The light is dark, the shade bright. And despite all this, it is not without a certain truthfulness. It would even be delightful if it were not

the case that it looks ... as though a certain amount of coercion had taken place ... as though nature were actually suffering.[29] It was such reviews that led Nagler to talk in 1835 of Blechen showing the 'irony' of Italian landscape. They did not feel that he was absolutely misrepresenting Italy but they thought he was deliberately emphasizing the most unusual and unexpected side of the country. He seemed to be insisting on the parched land and searing light – sunlight – rather than emulating the noble and poetic vision of green glades and cool mountains dear to the Classicists.

In retrospect there seems nothing perverse about Blechen's insistence that Italy rarely looked like the landscape of Claude Lorrain and Nicholas Poussin. He did, however, often seem to adopt an ironic attitude to the subjects of his scenes. He parodied the staffage of both Classical and Romantic landscapes. This occurs perhaps most strongly in *Girls Bathing in the Park at Terni* (fig. 3 and colour plate, p. 227), a highly popular work that he repeated at least five times. At first glance this picture of girls bathing in a glade seems a perfect idyll. While there are a few hints of the 'scalping' sunlight on the sandy earth and tree-trunks of the foreground, these serve merely to heighten the charm of the main scene. Here the light diffuses amongst the shady foliage, producing a subdued glow on the backs of the maidens. These, together with the reds and whites of their discarded clothes and the deep blue of the stream they are entering, provide a colourful focus for the painting. Yet when the (presumably male) spectator approaches the pictures closely, he encounters not tranquility, but alarm and disapproval as the girls try to conceal themselves from his gaze. They are not the carefree nymphs of Antiquity, but prim modern ladies whose private bathing has been disturbed by the spectator's presence. In this picture Blechen seems less comparable to Hoffmann than to Heinrich Heine. Like that great lyric poet, the painter destroys with a shock the idyll that he is so adept at creating, but of which he is no longer convinced.

Since this picture was exhibited in 1836 it is clear that Blechen continued to play the 'serious games' up to the end of his career. Yet he may not have been altogether happy with this situation or the light that it cast upon his new, more naturalistic manner of painting. In *Girls Bathing in the Park at Terni* the jest of the girls retreating was only introduced into some versions. In others he suggested retreat and seclusion by introducing monks.[30]

By the time he had arrived at this stage, Blechen had already suffered from a nervous collapse. The attacks returned and within two years he was declared incurably insane. Like Hoffmann, his career ended in madness. Many of his friends attributed his illness to lack of public understanding of his work. Bettina von Arnim wrote: 'I am making no error when I ascribe Blechen's derangement to the lack of sympathy and understanding among his contemporaries. When inflamed by the uplifting of his inner being through such bold visions, he was bound on all sides by the stony prison of the world of philistines that surrounded him.'[31]

Yet the prison was to some extent one of his own making. He himself had aroused the expectation of wit and humour in his work. His failure to abandon this habit, furthermore, seems to have been as much a result of his inability to create a viable alternative as of the insensitivity of his audience. He had succumbed, in a way, to his own sense of irony.

William Vaughan

1 The original version of this article was published in *Art History*, 2. no. 4 (1979), 457–73. I am most grateful to Routledge & Kegan Paul for permission to publish this amended and reduced version here.

2 G.K. Nagler, *Neues Allgemeines Künstlerlexikon*, I (1835), 527.

3 Nagler, (as note 2), 527.

4 H. Eichner, *Friedrich Schlegel* (New York, 1970), 70.

5 See pp. 178–83.

6 This is less true today than when this article was originally published. Nowadays it has become a commonplace for art historians to see pictorial practice as a form of linguistic endeavour. This has resulted in a more or less wholesale importation of the strategies of literary and linguistic criticism into their discourses.

7 D.C. Muecke, *Irony* (London, 1970), 6.

8 W.H. Wackenroder, *Werke und Briefe* (Heidelberg, 1967), 69.

9 Muecke (as note 7), 7.

10 See below,

11 S. Kierkegaard, *The Concept of Irony, with Constant Reference to Socrates* (1841). Trans. L.M. Capel (London, 1966), 271.

12 Wackenroder (as note 8), 68.

13 In the original version of this essay, published in *Art History* (see end of note 1).

14 This heading – based on a remark by Friedrich (see below, note 16) – is taken from a paper given by Michael Baxandall at the *Caspar David Friedrich* exhibition at the Tate Gallery, London in October 1972. While not dealing with the subject of Friedrich and irony, the paper was richly suggestive about the artist's mode of perception and practice, and an inspiration to the present writer. Regrettably the paper has never been published.

15 English version from exh. cat. *Caspar David Friedrich* (London, 1972), 103.

16 P.O. Runge, *Hinterlaßene Schriften* (Hamburg, 1940), II, 365.

17 F. Schiller, *On the Aesthetic Education of Mankind*, ed. Wilkinson and Willoughby, (Oxford, 1967), 95–9.

18 J.W. Goethe, *Werke* (Gedenkausgabe, Zurich, 1949), XXI, 1043. See also Werner Hofmann's essay in this volume.

19 S. Hinz, *Caspar David Friedrich in Briefen und Bekenntnissen* (Berlin, 1968), 228.

20 E.T.A. Hoffmann, *Briefwechsel*, ed. H. von Müller, II, (Berlin, 1912), 195.

21 Kierkegaard (as note 11), 271–1.

22 Quoted in H. Börsch-Supan, *Caspar David Friedrich* (Munich, 1975), 70.

23 Hinz (as note 19), 222–6. For an English language translation and commentary see P.B. Miller 'Anxiety and Abstraction: Kleist and Brentano on C.D. Friedrich' in *Quarterly Review of Literature* XVIII, nos 3–4, (1973), 345–54.

24 H. Börsch-Supan, 'Caspar David Friedrich's Landscapes with Self-Portraits' in *Burlington Magazine* CXIV, (1972), 623–4.

25 R. Rosenblum, *Modern Painting and the Northern Romantic Tradition* (London and New York, 1975), 10.

26 Rave, *op. cit.*, p. 6.

27 See W. Vaughan, *German Romantic Painting* (New Haven and London, 1980), pp. 154, 245.

28 Rave (as note 26), 19.

29 Rave (as note 26), 30–1.

30 Rave (as note 26), 1304–10.

31 Rave (as note 26), 47.

Night and Dreams

Nightfall was for the German Romantics an event of singular import. The approach of dusk might strike the prosaic mind as scarcely more than a cue to relax, to sink into pleasurable torpor. Some see nothing at all remarkable in the fact that the sun sets daily at the horizon (though it should be noted that popular myth has already tampered with this 'fact', since in reality it is not the sun that sinks but the earth that rotates). And yet, to poets like Novalis or painters like Caspar David Friedrich, the lengthening of shadows and the fading of daylight were acutely moving experiences which spoke to the spirit and the imagination. As an alluring idea and value, night became the focal point of that inspired swirl of intellectual concepts and affective impulses which constitutes Romantic ideology. A locus of multiple connotations, it served as an unmistakable shorthand for that ultimate apotheosis of poetic, aesthetic and spiritual regeneration to which Romanticism aspired.

As the occasion of literal darkness, night seems a negative prospect. Yet in the face of sensory depletion and constraint, the Romantic may choose to revalorize night, to reconstitute it positively as the radiant domain of dreams, of occult inscriptions, of poetic musing, of bewildering divination, of transcendental revelation. In all spheres of Romantic activity – in poetry, painting, and music, as well as in philosophy and science (which last, within Romanticism, are subsumed under the heading of ['Nature Philosophy'] *Naturphilosophie*) – night represents a dense nexus of associations, a privileged topos, a medium of boundless fecundity. In defiance of the Enlightenment's insistence on equating understanding with lucidity and rationality, in short, the 'wideawake' approach, the Romantics adopted what might be termed the 'nocturnal principle'. A veritable symbol of symbols whose aura radiated their most febrile expectations, night was credited with such an abundance of linked qualities as to speak for every facet of the Romantic project.

The paradox, then, is that night, which common parlance envisages as 'falling', is here seen as *uplifting*.

Rather than accept that dusk should steal the world away from human grasp, the Romantic insists that the world now hovers more closely and intimately. 'I look down', murmurs Novalis, 'into the holy, inexpressible, mysterious Night.' Against commonplace expectations, the literal obscuring of appearances becomes the figurative dawning of their more profound dimensions, the awakening of propensities which lie dormant during daylight.

Dusk is the threshold moment when *something else* excites awareness and refutes a diurnal approach premissed on clear-cut definition. The shift into an alternative register is all the more seductive for being apparently so unsafe: yet it is precisely within the sphere of the shadowy and the undefined that Romanticism will seek to legitimize a new order of certainty, at once enigmatic and strangely persuasive. Within Romantic writings, any mention of night can safely be taken as a coded allusion to the most cherished values. It fell to Novalis, the self-styled Magic Idealist, to achieve the definitive expression of the fixation upon the nocturnal, when in his *Hymns to the Night* (1800), he appealed ecstatically to night as the mythic gateway to a sublimity transcending earthly existence. In his landscape paintings, Friedrich represented the natural world in such a way as to elicit its tacit secondary meanings. Here, the way visible surfaces react to dusk and twilight is offered as a cypher of the sacred, as though to draw a veil over things were a way of pointing to their metaphysical implications.

In a celebrated cycle of public lectures delivered in Dresden in the autumn of 1808 under the title *Aspects of the Night-Side of the Natural Sciences*, the young Nature Philosopher Gotthilf Heinrich von Schubert drew up an agenda for Romantic science, insisting that its understanding of nature could proceed only from the postulate of its being not inert and passive, but wonderfully alive and communicative to man. By virtue of seeing natural phenomena in nocturnal as much as in diurnal terms, physicists like Johann Wilhelm Ritter or doctors like Carl Gustav Carus enhanced observation

Fig.1 Caspar David Friedrich, *Two Men Contemplating the Moon* 1819, Staatliche Kunstsammlungen Dresden, Gemäldegalerie Neue Meister (cat.21)

Fig.2 Caspar David Friedrich, *Morning Mist in the Mountains* c.1808, Staatliche Museen Schloß Heidecksburg, Rudolstadt

with intuition, and formulated their insights in spell-binding images. Schubert invoked nature as 'an embodied dream world', and his vision of a realm of occulted meanings encouraged science to join hands with poetry and philosophy in a multi-disciplinary and essentially synthesizing approach to knowledge.

As a topos for painters, night is an obvious challenge. If it is axiomatic that a truly Romantic artist cannot portray anything dispassionately, it is certainly unthinkable that he should approach a nocturnal scene otherwise than in a state of awe and expectancy. The depiction of darkness is in any case problematic for a medium habituated to rendering aspects of light, and the task of mediating between the visible and the invisible demands fluency not just in material technique but in the rhetoric of symbolism and poetic allusion. In his artistic treatise *Nine Letters on Landscape Painting* (1831), Carl Gustav Carus reserves an entire chapter for the topic of dusk, speaking of it as a metaphor of spiritual change. Friedrich's work is unmistakable in its devotion to twilight and moonlight. One of his best-known devices is that of placing figures in the foreground of a landscape, so that their silhouettes cross the horizon and create a visual link between what is close to and what is remote, between what is palpably real and what lies beyond ordinary perception. Encoded in his diurnal landscapes as the boundary dividing earthly from celestial experience, the skyline becomes, in Friedrich's nocturnal views, an indefinite merging of the two contrasted dimensions.

Some part of the Romantics' eagerness to ascribe such unitary and creative virtue to the 'night-side' of things

may be explained by the fact that, in the early years of the nineteenth century, the common experience of nighttime was one of plenitude, calmness and silence. By night, the physical atmosphere was conducive to impressive effects which then acquired symbolic resonance. To stay awake indoors after nightfall meant sitting by a flickering candle, which at once divide space into zones of clarity and zones of deep, suggestive shadow. To step outside into the open air was to enter a world made enigmatic by shadow, yet often enhanced by moonlight, that perfect agent of 'Romanticization', with its subtleties of silvery discoloration and hesitant outline. Thanks to the uncontaminated atmosphere of a pre-industrial age, the starry sky also regularly offered a spectacle of inspiring brilliance and intricacy. Reworking a classic philosophical passage where Kant links the objective spectacle of the night sky to his personal sense of morality, the mystically inclined Ludwig Görres suggests that the constellations are a pattern of allegories designed for man's spiritual guidance; while Novalis, drawn to archaic beliefs about astrology and the music of the spheres, sees the heavens as a cryptogram to intrigue the poetic mind. Pressing further, Novalis enters a deeper field of analogy pertaining to the illumination of inner space, for 'more divine even than those twinkling stars above appear to us those infinite eyes which Night has opened up within us'.

Given such habits of association, the phenomena of nightfall and moonrise become imbued with a rich spirituality. Again and again, in poems by writers like Joseph Freiherr von Eichendorff or Heinrich Heine, mention of moonrise seems automatically to herald metaphysical or poetic reveries concerning the transfiguration of the terrestrial realm. In his *Nine Letters*, Carus devotes several pages to scenes under moonlight, and himself achieved an uncanny crystallization of the Romantic conception in a painting called *Studio by Moonlight* (1826), where an easel in a dim interior is boldly silhouetted against a window through whose semi-transparent curtain steals a lunar glow. Friedrich once showed Carus how to deal with moonlight, encouraging him to 'put some dark varnish on the palette and, apart from the moon and the most adjacent illuminated areas, to spread it over everything, all the more darkly as I reached the edges of the picture, and then to ascertain the altered effect'. Rarely can a technical recipe have been so steeped in ideology! As faithful partisans of this method, artists like Johan Christian Clausen Dahl and Ernst Ferdinand Oehme would become specialists of the lunar effect in their natural and urban scenes.

Friedrich himself promoted the moon from its classical role as tender and wistful witness to human feeling to a more stark and 'Germanic' embodiment of metaphysical enigma, as witness the picture *Two Men Contemplating the Moon* (1819, fig. 1 and colour plate p. 221), where two figures crane their bodies as though to imbibe an otherworldly numinosity, filtered by gnarled trees and framed by impenetrable shadow. As a cliché of Romantic evocativeness, the moon inspired the vogue of the *transparency*, with which Friedrich experimented in later years – a thrilling, if easily trivalized, medium, whereby a scene painted on paper is lit from behind by a lamp, mimicking moonlight. There exists an interesting letter in which Friedrich describes a set of four such images – since lost – and stipulates that they be viewed in semi-darkness to the music of a glass harp or string instruments. This reminds us that Philipp Otto Runge's cycle of paintings, *The Times of Day*, was also intended to be exhibited with solemn music. Such ideas reflect the Romantic aspiration to the *Gesamtkunstwerk* or multi-media work, an aspiration which may be seen as congruent with the nocturnal principle in so far as the impulse to fuse separate orders of artistic expression has its roots in intuition as much as occult tradition.

Even the many daytime pictures painted by Romantics tend to evince a visionary intensity, enticing the eye into

Fig.3 Caspar David Friedrich, *Wanderer above the Sea of Fog* c.1818, Hamburger Kunsthalle

perspectives of evanescence and dimming. Mindful of Novalis's dictum that 'the external world is the world of shadows', we may see Friedrich's style as one which constantly coaxes visible forms into disclosing the presence – behind and beyond – of an alternative otherworldly light. All his favourite symbols, his skylines, silhouettes, spires, sailing-ships and mountains, may be seen as variant ways of appealing to the same magical latency. His frequent references to fog and mist are further hints at transfiguration: in *Morning Mist in the Mountains* (c. 1808, fig. 2), ostensibly the objective record of a meteorological effect, the artist seems intent on imparting a 'nocturnal' expressivity to the half-smothered trees and rocks. Friedrich once remarked to Carus, 'when a region is cloaked in mist, it appears greater and nobler: it enriches the imagination and intensifies expectancy, like a girl wearing a veil'.

To the symbolic repertoire of forests and opaque mists should be added the motif of the cloud, which already Goethe had addressed as an inspiring example of the organicity of natural processes, and by extension a ready-made receptacle for philosophical or spiritual ideas. In a passage from the *Nine Letters* strongly reminiscent of that paramount Romantic icon, Friedrich's *Wanderer above the Sea of Fog* (c. 1818, fig. 3), Carus exhorts his reader to scale a mountain peak and contemplate the spectacle of nature, allowing the individual ego to merge into the infinite: 'Your whole being experiences a quiet cleansing and purification: your ego dissolves, you are nothing, God is everything.'

Until our century of artificial light, nightfall had always imposed itself on the human psyche as the time for inertia and sleep. Yet for the Romantics, the moment of closing one's eyes and letting consciousness slip away is but the prelude to fresh activity. 'Sleep is the deep reconciliation of the soul with itself,' writes the Nature Philosopher Henrik Steffens. Just as the waking contemplation of the nocturnal world conduces to a decentralization of the self, so does sleep, in its vegetative regression, expose the psyche to a reality kept at bay by waking consciousness. The Romantic mystic Franz von Baader suggests that 'our nervous system is not exclusively our property, but belongs generally to yet other beings'. If night is now to be positively valorized, so sleep must equally be seen as affording access to a mysterious alternative knowledge. Such access is facilitated by two activities dear to the Romantic: dreaming and sleepwalking.

Dreaming is a quintessential Romantic activity. The fluency and volatility of dreams have traditionally supplied the poetic imagination with images, but it was a notable feat of German Romanticism to construct a whole philosophy of creativity upon the oneiric process. Schubert and Carus, as well as the metaphysician Ignaz-Paul-Vitals Troxler and the young Henrik Steffens, devoted serious philosophical works to its study. Schubert's treatise bore the prescient title *Symbolism of the Dream* (1814), and sketches a method for translating dream hieroglyphs. Dozens of writers, from Jean Paul to Eichendorff, and from E.T.A. Hoffmann to Heine, incorporate dream episodes in their stories, not just as decorative interludes, but as seminal passages packed with suggestion. Robert Schumann's earlier collections for piano, such as *Papillon* (1832), *Fantasiestücke* (*Fantasy Pieces*, 1838) and *Nachtstücke* (*Night Pieces*, 1839), contain passages of brooding reverie inspired partly by the literary example of Jean Paul, partly by the pianist's own sense of the subliminal impact of certain phrases and tones. As so often in Romantic art, the music seems to ask us to think twice, to register manifest acoustic shapes while listening for their latent resonance. Literal dream interpretation is but another facet of an approach to knowledge which thrives on the subjective operations of intuition and premonition, as Novalis's hero Heinrich von Offerdingen implies when he insists that even the most garbled dream can enact 'a momentous tearing assunder of that mysterious curtain whose thousand folds tumble down to the depth of our being'.

That dreams occasionally modulate into nightmares may seem only natural, in so far as people do presumably stumble from time to time when advancing in the dark. The nightmare picture of Henry Fuseli, and those Gothic episodes in Hoffmann's fictions where dreaming is overtaken by grotesque hallucination or even insanity (often termed *Umnachtung* – 'nocturnalization'), must qualify our evaluation of the Romantic project. The eccentricities attributed to Hoffmann himself, the psychological depressions of the older Friedrich, Schumann's psychosis, and a considerable list of actual or fictional suicides indicate the prospect of a sinister chasm running along Romanticism's 'night-side'. However, without denying the darker evidence, one should stress that German Romantic nocturnalism is predicated not upon unreason and the abandonment of control but rather upon the positive assumption of dormant powers. When he turns around to follow what Novalis calls 'the mysterious path which leads within' the typical Romantic is intent not to destroy lucidity, but to amplify and perfect it by testing it against the unknown, like pointing a lamp at the darkness.

Somnambulistic or trance states acquire distinction during the Romantic period, and become practically synonymous with poetic insight. Various groups drawn to mystical and occult teachings were established, and Romantic writings include studies of mystics like the nun Katharina Emmerich (whose biography was drawn up by the poet Clemens Brentano) and Friederike Haufe, the seer of Prevorst, whose example inspired Justinus Kerner and his circle to document many instances of clairvoyance, telepathy, telekinesis, spirit apparitions and the like. The entranced state, with its connotations

Fig.4 Georg Friedrich Kersting, *Caspar David Friedrich in his Studio*, c. 1811, Hamburger Kunsthalle

of being transported beyond normal material confines and into an illuminating relation to the cosmos, is valued beyond all else. The plays of Heinrich von Kleist dwell upon the spellbound monologues of protagonists such as the somnambulistic Catherine (in *Das Käthchen von Heilbronn*, 1810), or the prince in *Der Prinz von Homburg* (1821), who thrive on not being fully conscious of their surroundings. In turn, a canvas like Georg Friedrich Kersting's *Caspar David Friedrich in his Studio* (*c.*1811, fig. 4) demands that we equate artistic genius with that 'far-away look' which seems symptomatic of what Novalis defines as 'creative contemplation' (*schaffende Betrachtung*).

Seemingly amorphous states of day-dreaming or *Träumerei* (in turn associated with the innocent intuitionism of children) are thus emblematic of the Romantic mentality, and encourage the positive assessment of wayward fictional figures like Eichendorff's hero, the *Taugenichts* (the good-for-nothing), or of that real-life innocent Kaspar Hauser, an illiterate foundling who enjoyed a brief fame as the embodiment of pristine

naturalness. In Romantic tales, the motif of somnambulism functions not just as a device to negotiate implausible coincidence but as part of a sincere argument about psychic insight. Achim von Arnim's declaration that 'we mortals are sleepwalkers in broad daylight' is a clue to the seriousness of this subliminal commitment. Even in the scientific field, the Romantic prioritized what Johann Wilhelm Ritter calls 'passive consciousness' (*passives Bewusstsein*), a mental technique equivalent to self-induced hypnosis. And, as Friedrich similarly avers, it is not the world of mundane perception that matters so much as the world re-composed by the imagination, it being the painter's task to illuminate this internal image: 'Close your physical eye so that you may first see your picture with the spiritual eye. Then bring to the light of day that which you have seen in the darkness ... .'

Central to Romantic ideology is the precept that qualitative, subjective insights are by definition superior to quantified, objective data: though perceptual facts may suffice to impress the diurnal thinker, poets will always be more enthusiastic about what is gained by presentiment or inspiration. These underdeveloped faculties can only be cultivated at the expense of daytime awarness: it is *by night* that they attain their apotheosis. In this sense, the Romantic programme is nothing less than a proposal to legitimize apparent aberrations like dreaming or clairvoyance as reliable techniques of understanding. Franz von Baader, the philosopher, indeed so insists on the authenticity of perceptions originating *within* the sensibility that he comes close to declaring the supremacy of subjective enthusiasm over external fact. 'It is the internal sense, and not the mere transcription of the external, which illuminates the progress of genius; and every authentic artist, every authentic poet is a seer or a visionary.' Finally, the literary theorist Friedrich Schlegel argues that intellectual progress is inconceivable without intuition, for 'all thought is divination, although man is only just beginning to realize his divinatory powers'.

The fact that experiments in mesmerism (inspired by the example of Anton Mesmer, or by contemporary scientific theories of animal magnetism) were rife during the early Romantic period should be taken as confirmation of a trust in what I have called the 'nocturnal principle', whereby truth is generally seen to lie beyond the limits of an inhibited, ego-bound consciousness. The state of trance attunes the sensibility to its pre-intellectual functions, which in turn connect individual psychic activity to natural impulses in the transpersonal sphere. The Romantic model of the artist is that of a selfless seer whose personal fantasies give shape to inchoate stimuli arising from the universal unconscious, or what the Romantic philosopher Friedrich Wilhelm Schelling will call 'the World Soul'.[1]

Just as slumbering taken to an extreme becomes coma and eventually death, so does the Romantic affinity with the nocturnal conduce to a contemplation of ultimate extinction. Several of Friedrich's paintings undoubtedly traffic in morbid symbols, with trees stricken by lightning or snow-covered graveyards with owls perched on tombstones. Novalis, whose early demise lent his work mythic status as the expression of a death-wish, frequently voices a desire to cross the threshold of contingent life. His *Hymns to the Night* revel in sensuous visions of a journey

Down below into the earth's womb
Out of the realms of light …
Praise be to us the eternal night,
Praise to eternal slumbering.

And yet the bass-note of yearning, inseparable from Romanticism's nocturnal project, is no sign of nihilism. Death is sublime because it means not just the dissolution of individual consciousness, but its transcendence within the higher dimension of universal consciousness. Sleeping, dreaming, dying, these are but preludes to a greater awakening on the far side of the everyday.

Across that internalized night sky that is the Romantic mind, ideas and images seem to float, drift and circulate, tracing wider and wider orbits of implication as they magnetize further and further reaches of analogy. I have argued that night, with its repertoire of shadows, silence, moonlight and stars, becomes synonymous with activities which supersede orthodox mental alertness, namely: dreaming, reverie, trance, intuition. Taken as a total constellation of interlinked meanings, all these highly charged motifs and concepts emerge as a mighty refutation of reasonableness and spell out a visionary programme. Night, it seems, makes everything possible.

The Romantics gamble supremely on the nocturnal principle, and it is always the impulse that comes out of the dark which they will unhesitatingly identify and follow.

Roger Cardinal

1 It is worth recalling that our modern conception of the unconscious predates the work of Freud and Jung, being a crucial element of Romantic psychology almost from the outset. A major antecedent is Carus's *Psyche* (1846), a meditation upon psychic activity below surface consciousness. Equating the unconscious with the vegetative slumbering of organic life, Carus goes on to celebrate it as the realm of reconciliation, imputing to it the power to synthesize through analogy. His further suggestion that this power transcends individuality anticipates Jung's notion of the collective unconscious.

War, Apocalypse and the 'Purification of the World'

'The secret sense of sacrifice is the annihilation of the finite, because it is finite. In order to show that it happens for this reason only, the noblest and most beautiful must be chosen, above all, the human being, the flower of the earth. Human sacrifices are the most natural sacrifices … . The sense of divine creation is first revealed in the enthusiasm for annihilation. Only in the midst of death is the lightning of eternal life ignited.'[1] In this passage, which was probably meant to be understood metaphorically, but certainly gives rise, and has given rise, to misunderstanding, Friedrich Schlegel idealized human sacrifice, annihilation and death as the basis and necessary condition of the eternity we hope for. This thesis was a familiar one in the theory of German idealism. At the beginning of the First World War it inspired many German artists to volunteer for war service. Although the war was emphatically welcomed by many European intellectuals and artists in a way that now seems almost incomprehensible, the justification for this initial euphoria took on a special colouring in Germany. In the sphere of art the difference is revealed precisely by a comparison with Italian Futurism. One of the Futurists' most powerful slogans was directed against any remnant of tradition, which was scorned as 'passatism', and therefore against their entire cultural heritage, whereas anything that seemed even remotely progressive moved to centre-stage, though always – and this is not unimportant – with a view to the future greatness of Italy. The grand gesture, the media spectacle, the anarchistic lifestyle became socially acceptable through Marinetti and his friends, and German artists were fascinated by their provocative slogans, which became familiar at the latest after the first Futurist exhibition, acquired in 1912 by Herwarth Walden for his Sturm-Galerie in Berlin and later shown in Cologne, Munich and Karlsruhe. Almost all the important representatives of the *Brücke*, the *Blue Rider* and Rhenish Expressionism came to grips with the results of an artistic movement that was dominated by an enthusiasm for technology. The fast life of the big city became a central theme both in Germany and Italy, and in the sphere of form German artists found suggestions in Futurism that could be adapted to their own ideas. However, the divergence in content becomes clear when we compare two pictures that are closely linked in theme: Umberto Boccioni's *The Noise of the Street Invades the House* of 1911 and Ludwig Meidner's *Me and the City* of 1913 (fig 1). Superficially Meidner draws substantially on Futurism for his Expressionist formal language: in his case too the houses in the street seem to be collapsing and are to be related, in a centred compositional scheme, to the head of the man anxiously looking out of the picture, though not to unite with him, but to oppress him. The architecture aggressively closes in on him and assails him. Boccioni's picture offers a synthesis, Meidner's a contrast: the latter shows a defenceless individual attacked by the stone of the buildings. Meidner thus embraces a view of the city that inspired the artists of the *Brücke*, especially Kirchner – an interpretation of contemporary life as hectic, destructive and hostile to the individual. Meidner and Boccioni are both concerned to represent movement, but with Meidner it is movement in contrary directions; it reflects a critical and pessimistic view of the world that leaves no one guiltless, in which everyone is implicated – apocalyptic visions of the city that subsequently became reality in Alfred Döblin's celebrated novel of 1929, *Berlin, Alexanderplatz*. Meidner anticipates the vision of an apocalyptic struggle that destroys palpable reality; there is no link with the Futurists' glorification of war, which they saw as a chance to extinguish the past through the achievements of modern technology.

The Futurists took a positive view of the age and clearly focused their attention on their country, despite all their criticism of Italy's overwhelming past. Meidner, Otto Dix, George Grosz and the most notable artists of the *Brücke* started out from an attitude of social criticism, admittedly often highly subjective, which admitted of change in the here and now. On the other hand, the artists associated with the *Blue Rider* tried to confront the crude reality of the age with the hopeful image of a spiritualized reality that was ultimately quite unreal.

Fig.1 Ludwig Meidner, *Me and the City* 1913, Private Collection

Thus Franz Marc drew upon the formal repertoire of the Futurists in order to represent his romantically coloured utopia, a spiritual world belonging to the future. Kurt Schwitters, on the other hand, made use of the Futurist media spectacle – skilfully employed by Carlo Carrà in his highly effective war posters – for his dadaist nonsense (fig. 2). This was the only way he knew of confronting the madness of the age. While Schwitters's ironic, anarchistic paraphrase, inherited from the Romantic notion of irony, was exceptional and little understood, the reactions of the Expressionists – of the most varied provenance – were largely of a piece. The initial thesis at least – the hope of an apocalyptic catharsis through war – was similar, however variously its consequences were envisaged. This ambivalent and in some ways inconsistent attitude towards the possible 'function' of wartime destruction becomes clear when we compare the works of two pairs of artists who, in their way, were typical of their respective generations: Max Beckmann and E. L. Kirchner on the one hand, Paul Klee and Franz Marc on the other. After the outbreak of war Max Beckmann went with a consignment of charity

parcels, organized by Countess von Hagen, to a military hospital in East Prussia. He then volunteered for service as a medical orderly and was posted to Flanders in February 1915; here he worked in a typhus hospital and later in an operating theatre at Courtrai. After the battle of Artois in May and June Beckmann suffered a breakdown and was transferred to the Imperial Hygiene Institute in Strasbourg. In October he was sent on leave, and in 1917, on the recommendation of his new friend from Frankfurt, Major Fritz von Braunbehrens, he was officially discharged.

His war letters, edited in 1916 by Minna Beckmann-Tube and published by Bruno Cassirer[2] present a confused picture, alternating between deep despair on the one hand and fascination with the variety of his experiences and the wealth of different visual impressions on the other. This can be illustrated by some typical passages: '... my will to live is at the moment stronger than ever, although I have been through some dreadful things and died more than once. But the more often one dies, the more intensely one lives. I have done some drawings – this protects me from death and danger' (3.10.1914). 'I myself constantly oscillate between great joy at everything new that I see, depression over the loss of my individuality, and a sense of profound irony towards myself and sometimes the world. After all, it again and again compels my admiration. Its variety is indescribable and its inventiveness boundless' (2.3.1915). '... It was so wonderful out there that even the savagery of mass killing, whose music I heard again and again, could not spoil my deep enjoyment' (28.3.1915). 'I am always accompanied by the round trembling holes in the sky made by the French and Belgian searchlights, like strange transcendental aeroplanes, the nervous, incessant infantry fire and the wonderful apocalyptic sound of the big guns. A rider in the dark at full gallop, and now and then great rats from the muddy roadside ditches, creatures like young cats that now do the useful job of burying the corpses that lie in front of the trenches. It's funny how, with iron logic, the life of peacetime, which we often cursed and groaned over, is now moving up towards paradise' (5.4.1915).

Here Beckmann was never concerned with an abstract vision, but quite pragmatically and soberly with reality, with the human being in all his fascinating variety. It

Fig.2 Kurt Schwitters, *Merzbild 31* 1920, Sprengel Museum, Hanover

would of course be wrong to seek a moral attitude in all this, for in his pictures Beckmann does not deplore wrongful human behaviour or social abuses; he offers no guidelines that could be immediately helpful in the maze of the modern age: he observes and reports, sometimes with an apparently cynical detachment, the oddities and endless entanglements of our existence. The measure of his success in this endeavour is the convincing way in which he transfers his observations into pictures. For my own part I am utterly devoted to 'in-depth painting' (*Raumtiefe Malerei*); in it I try to find my style, which unlike outwardly decorative art, is intended to explore nature and go to the heart of things. I am well aware that many of my feelings were already present. But I also know the feeling that has recently come to me from my world and its spirit. I cannot and will not define this. It is in my pictures.'[3] This statement, which recurs with slight variations in different texts, is an indirect rejection of all the avant-garde developments of his time. His verdict on outwardly decorative art applies not only to Matisse, Gauguin and their successors, but also to Cubism, and particularly to the artists of the Blue Rider.

He also indirectly opposed overt social criticism – pictorial statements that merely drew attention to abuses, such as were produced in the 1920s in the veristic painting of Grosz and Dix. His aim was to translate his experience of reality as precisely as possible into a valid optical form, which, while reflecting the age, created pictures that were independent of it and could appeal to people yesterday, today or tomorrow. In fact he occupies a position that Gottfried Benn described in a radio conversation entitled 'Can poets change the world?', broadcast in 1930. 'Works of art', said Benn, 'are phenomena, historically ineffective, of no practical consequence. This is their greatness.'[4] Later, when asked whether the poet could register the misery of the world dispassionately, he reacted in a way that might at first sight be misunderstood: 'I haven't a moment's hesitation: yes, the poet looks on – not the one who writes about civilization and in the evening supplies intellectual pretexts for the scene-shifts, who sits next to the minister at a banquet, a carnation in the lapel of his tailcoat and five wine-glasses round his place-setting: he signs appeals against the abuses of the age. But the other looks on, knowing that the undeserved misery of the world will never be cured by welfare measures or overcome by material improvements. ... A creation without horror, jungles without bites, nights without nightmares riding their victims – no, the poet looks on, with the undeniable conviction that only he can banish the horror and reconcile the victims. "Go down," he calls to them, "go down, I say", but I could also say "come up".'[5] It is this abstention from a direct reaction to one's age that offers a chance to overcome the restrictions of reality and to banish the deeper existential horror that lies beneath superficial reality.

It is obvious that Beckmann too had to go through a long process of learning and was only gradually able to express what he meant. Hence the few works he produced during the war are studies of exceptional human situations. Some involve extreme compositional arrangements, designed to reflect direct experience. This applies for instance to two etchings of 1914, *The Inspection* (fig. 4) and *The Grenade*, and to *The Mortuary* of 1915 (fig. 3), which represent real human calamities with seemingly unconcerned clarity. Here too we can appreciate Beckmann's dilemma: his experience of war afforded

(Top) Fig.3 Max Beckmann The Mortuary 1915, etching

(Bottom) Fig.4 Max Beckmann The Inspection 1914, etching

him an immense fund of potential pictorial subjects, yet at the same time a frightening vision of the systematic destruction of the individual. The self-portrait in the middle of *The Inspection* (fig. 4) thus becomes comprehensible: it shows Beckmann as the cynical chronicler who merely takes stock of the situation and cloaks his own consternation in order to protect himself. For

Kirchner such sobriety was inconceivable. 'The pressure of the war and the growing superficiality weigh heavier than all else. One feels that a decision is in the air, and all is confused. One feels bloated and hesitates to work, though work is pointless and one is assailed by mediocrity on all sides. One is now like the cocottes I used to paint – here today and gone tomorrow. All the same I am still trying to do what I have to do – to order my thoughts and create a picture of the age out of all the confusion.'[6] Kirchner himself took no part in the bloody carnival. When the war broke out in August 1914 he reported, he said, as an involuntary volunteer and was called up in the spring of 1915. However, 'I wasn't keen on the army. I learnt to ride and look after horses, but I didn't care for the guns. Military service was too much for me, and so I constantly lost weight. ...'[7] Kirchner's psychic instability, which he at first nonchalantly dismissed as unimportant (as on a card sent to Heckel in 1911: '... I am again suffering from severe depressions. To hell with it! Best wishes, Ernst'[8]) led in October 1915 to a nervous breakdown and his discharge from the army. His subsequent sufferings, which can be easily documented, ending with his suicide on 15 June 1938, involve a fruitless and half-hearted attempt to give up drink and pills, a pathological distrust of those around him, various visits to sanatoria, and finally to the Stafelalp near Davos-Frauenkirch. Especially in the years after the outbreak of the war he produced hallucinatorily exaggerated but precise symbols of existential dangers, filtered in the self-portrait of the artist. *The Drinker* of 1915 (fig. 5), originally called *The Absinth Drinker*, transforms Picasso's slightly sentimental transfiguration of a socially marginal figure (in *The Absinth Drinker* of 1901) into the portrait of an artist, an individual who senses the ruined state of the world and in whom the private and the universal combine as in a burning glass. Kirchner, his face rigid and mask-like, with negroid features, sits at a table in his Berlin studio, identifiable by the covers and curtains with applied ornaments known from photos. The perspective of the interior is shifted up towards the picture plane so that the artist sits somewhat insecurely on the sofa. He wears silly stiletto-heeled shoes and a blue housecoat with a blue, yellow and red shawl collar and cuffs; this is draped over the emaciated figure, which seems to have

Fig.5 Ernst Ludwig Kirchner, *The Drinker* 1915, Germanisches Nationalmuseum, Nuremberg

Fig.6 Max Beckmann, *Self-Portrait as Medical Orderly* 1915, Von der Heydt-Museum, Wuppertal

no substance. Kirchner thus presents himself as an individual alienated from reality. In him the attitude of the man of sorrows and the aimless stare combine to create an image of resigned hopelessness, which is nevertheless surrounded by a particular aura. Kirchner sees himself as the victim of a world to which he does not belong. The bright-coloured clothes and pointed shoes are a deliberate costume by means of which the artist detaches himself from reality and rises above, though he cannot free himself from the role of the victim.

It is interesting to see how Beckmann, the critical observer, saw himself in this crisis. In the *Self-Portrait as a Medical Orderly* of 1915 (fig. 6), which Beckmann conceived while still in Strasbourg but probably painted after his return to Frankfurt, the artist presents himself in a role that already belongs to the past. The unstable composition of the half-figure attached only to the edges of the picture is underlined by the expressive ductus of the paint, which departs from the more impressionist pre-

war style. Against the diffuse green and grey ground and in combination with the unmodelled upper body that seems to be hollowed out, the painting hand and the head in particular seem full of volume and precisely worked. Beside Kirchner's *Self-Portrait as a Soldier* of 1915 (fig. 7), Beckmann's vision appears cooler and more detached. Kirchner tries to combine private and universal anxieties in a valid image. Superficially the correctly uniformed soldier with his right hand chopped off reflects the unspeakable horror of war, which leaves the individual physically and psychically crippled and turns him into both a killer and a victim – significant are the mask-like, expressionless face and the cigarette dangling from the corner of the mouth – and that perverts the vital sensuality of human relations into blind killing. The nude, though compositionally related to Kirchner, has no inner relationship with him: the artist with his dark eye-sockets turns away. It is an image of senseless destruction that affects everybody. This general level of interpretation

Fig.7 Ernst Ludwig Kirchner, *Self-Portrait as a Soldier* 1915, Allen Memorial Art Museum, Oberlin College, Oberlin, Ohio

combines with the artist's private anxieties: the arrangement of the scene in the studio, characterized by the nude model and the half-finished canvas, together with the macabre detail of the bleeding arm-stump, point to the threat posed by the war to Kirchner's artistic existence. The physical injury becomes a metaphor for psychic incapacity. The *Self-Portrait as a Soldier* is an expression of Kirchner's agonized sense of no longer being able to capture his world in pictures, in form and colour. For Beckmann, on the other hand, the experience of war seems to have confirmed his surmise that the terrible, yet fantastic variety of life could be seized only in commensurate pictures. This presupposed a sober, unsentimental view of things that made no distinction between self-analysis and analysis of the surrounding world and that combined subjective experience and objective facts with pictures that seem to have no real palpable basis and cannot be rationally decoded. These pictures by Beckmann, together with others on religious themes that he painted shortly afterwards, touched the nerve of the age. This can be seen from a passage by Julius Meier-Graefe, a devotee

of modern, especially French, art and a much-feared critic. As early as 1919 he found unusually powerful words to describe Beckmann's work and its development: 'The pictures are anything but decorative. The approach is much more violent. Such forms are prompted by an almost mystical embitterment: the ecstasy of pain ... . A Grünewald stripped of flesh – of his flesh, but not of his soul. The details are dictated by the painful fervour of our machine age, a fervour that wants to burn out all remaining traces of the baroque.... Any colour that could mitigate the factual detail is eschewed.... What we see is implacably clear. But it still moves. These terrible figures still form an ornament, wish to form an ornament, just as broken limbs wish to grow together.... A powerful sense of superiority has always impelled the rough upstart.... A whole people admits to a sense of superiority; it has sinned immeasurably and it atones immeasurably. Its rotten flesh is burnt away with monstrous instruments of torture so that the spirit can reflect.'[9] In such extreme language Meier-Graefe captures both the form and the content of a picture like *Deposition* (fig. 8), in which the death of Christ is characterized by a numbness that affects all the figures, so that we sense a collective reproach that is almost arrogant in its intransigence. Yet the reproach has no concrete reference; it refers not only to those who were destroyed by the First World War, not only to its savagery and inhumanity: it castigates a universal inadequacy that is bound to no particular time or place. Yet the attitude relates to something real and palpable. In it the individual can rediscover himself and relate it to his own circumstances. Herein lies the essential difference between Beckmann's vision and that of Franz Marc, which related to an unrealizable utopia. This also explains Marc's at first apparently ambivalent statements about the war. His obvious dedication to German idealism led him to see the First World War as a possible 'catharsis', as a process of purification that held out the chance of universal atonement for the wrongs of humanity, which was suffocating in materialism 'because the mendacity of European custom can no longer be endured. Rather blood than everlasting deceit; war is both atonement and a deliberate sacrifice, to which Europe has subjected itself in order to get things straight.'[10] Subjectively the 'dying' involved in war is shifted to the plane of mystic transfiguration, as a longed-for return to

Fig.8 Max Beckmann, *Deposition* 1917, The Museum of Modern Art, New York, Curt Valentin Bequest, 1955

our original state. Significantly Marc speaks of injuries as the real disappointments of war: 'The self awakes, only to find that it has gained nothing: it has merely lost a stupid finger or an arm ... . But the dead are ineffably happy.'[11] In early Romanticism too we find this definition of war and human sacrifice. In our opening quotation Friedrich Schlegel states that the 'secret sense of sacrifice is the annihilation of the finite' and that only 'in the exhilaration of annihilation is the sense of divine creation revealed'.[12] Runge once thought 'of a war that would turn the whole world upside down ... . I saw no other means but the Last Day, when the earth would open and swallow everything up ...'[13]

Paul Klee, by contrast, clearly rejected this grandiose celebration of war and death as something positive. Longing, as understood by the Romantics, was not fundamental to his thinking as a projection into a better future, but a path that led to nowhere in particular. Marc imagined his own utopia as a distant reality and believed in it profoundly: Klee built himself a fantastic dreamworld, spiced with irony, which offered him a

chance to switch off from reality. In entry 941 of his diary for 1914 he noted: 'One leaves the region on this side and builds one on the other side. The cool Romanticism of this style without pathos is unheard-of. The more terrible this world becomes (as it is becoming today), the more abstract art becomes, whereas a happy world produces worldly art.'[14]

The playfulness of a picture like *Full Moon* (fig. 9) endorses this maxim, which conceives of the abstract pictorial world as the positive antithesis of oppressive daily reality. The very year of its composition seems to underline this essential incompatibility of actual and artistic reality. In December 1918 Klee was given leave from war service, then discharged in the following February. In the spring he rented a studio in the small palace of Suresnes in the Werneckstrasse in Munich. On 12 April he joined the Works Council for Art and the Artists' Action Committee. He took part in committees dealing with artistic policy under the Soviet Republic of Bavaria. On 11 June, after the fall of the soviet government, he went to Switzerland for a time.

These facts[15] reveal how intensely Klee was involved in the political events of his time and how clearly and uncompromisingly he saw his artistic thinking as a quite different activity. The simultaneous justification of abstract painting as a pure and unspoilt spiritual world contrasting with the immorality and hopelessness of historical reality links Klee with a kind of thinking that was oriented towards German idealism and Romanticism, a thinking that has since been repeatedly invoked as the theoretical foundation of non-representational art (see also pp. 82–92).

It is interesting that in assessing individual phenomena such as those of war, a way was often chosen that sought to bring the positions of Paul Klee and Franz Marc into synthesis. If we look at the generation of artists whom the Nazis denounced as 'degenerate', it is hard to avoid the rather cynical conclusion that the almost childishly naïve vision that Franz Marc could still entertain without incurring guilt was driven out of them by German political reality. The notable German painters had long since been robbed of their reputation, deprived of their offices and forbidden to paint; they had either emigrated or worked in the so-called 'inner emigration'. An example of the latter group was the abstract

Fig.9 Paul Klee, *Full Moon* 1919, Staatsgalerie Moderner Kunst, Munich

painter Fritz Winter. Five days before the outbreak of the Second World War, on 26 August 1939, he was called up to join the mountain troops and later posted to the Eastern Front. He was taken prisoner by the Russians in May 1945 and released in 1949. During this time he produced several hundred graphite and pencil drawings hardly bigger than the palm of a hand (of which the only extant sheets belong to the period 1939–44).[16] In these we see the artist grappling with the horror of war and destruction and trying to capture it in palpable form (figs. 10 and 11). The cosmic dimensions of a machine designed to annihilate humanity that he seems to have been unable to convey in representational terms are translated into abstract pictorial metaphors. In their modest and unspectacular form they are among the most striking indictments of man's power-madness, pleading for self-determination for the individual, in spite of (or rather because of) the exclusion of individual destinies and their seemingly detached, 'inhuman' orien-

tation to the eternally valid forces of an all-controlling nature. In their formal and technical perfection these little drawings – to some extent a substitute for the oil paintings he could not paint[17] – are executed with extreme care and evince an almost indescribable wealth of nuances in their chiaroscuro values. Executed in cheap sketchbooks on thin paper, they create a rich and mysterious world of light and shadow, of future hope and profound horror – an abstract translation of the experiences of an individual confronted by the chaos of war, a war of unimaginable dimensions, but also by the eternally new and powerful forces of nature. One is struck by the recurrent and continually varied metaphors in which the essence of the theme of 'war' is concentrated, as in a burning glass. Thus the 'wood' becomes an image for emergence and transience, dream and mystery, dark, inexplicable fear, terror that will not yield to rationality.... There are parallels here to the 'dream landscapes' of Max Ernst and indirectly to Freudian psychoanalysis. The cosmic dimensions that Winter found in the 'wood' embrace both the negative and the positive pole. What we have here is a visualization of the energies of nature in the theme of the wood, her opposing forces, and therefore at the same time a metaphor against war. Nature opposes the horrors of war and embraces destruction and renewal; nature is thus 'not only ... but also', both death and life. This is undoubtedly an esoteric vision coloured by Romanticism; it has little connection with harsh reality. Yet in the equation of war with the negative forces of the universe, and despite all its detachment from the suffering of the individual, it offers a much more human view, rooted in the soil, than we find in the reactions of Franz Marc, from the model whom Winter so much admired, to the beginning of the First World War and in his 'Letters from the Field'.[18] Winter could no longer share Marc's conception, which excluded the dead and the wounded, the battles and human sacrifices, from his vision of the future – partly because of the painful experiences of German history. Rather, Winter tries to bring his 'humanity' into harmony with the 'superhuman' demands made on reality. In Winter's work, the divorce between theory and practice that we find in Marc's leads to a synthesis. What is characteristic of him is his profound modesty, which informs all his work and is far

EIN FLUCH WÄLZT SICH ÜBER DIE ERDE

ZERSTÖRUNG

(Top) Fig.10 Fritz Winter, *A Curse Surges over the Earth* 1944, Fritz Winter-Haus, Ahlen, Westphalia

(Bottom) Fig.11 Fritz Winter, *Destruction* 1944, Fritz Winter-Haus, Ahlen, Westphalia

removed from the missionary zeal that inspired so many artists of the early twentieth century. Here is someone who knew the terrors of his own history from immediate experience and could no longer contemplate the world, as Marc could, with the eyes of an 'innocent child'. His artistic statement rests on the moral conviction that

there is something 'that we will have to answer for after we die: the fact that we were there'.[19]

Perhaps artists have become more grown up – but at what a price! And is the frequent *envoi* to any form of critical stocktaking – the cynical view of the artist as a brightly coloured parrot at the centre of an art scene dedicated to entertainment – anything other than the reverse of an unchanging medal?

Carla Schulz-Hoffmann

Translated from the German by David McLintock

1 Friedrich Schlegel, *Fragmente* (Ideen 131), quoted from Paul Kluckhohn (ed.) *Kunstanschauung der Frühromantik*, Deutsche Literatur, Reihe Romantik, vol. 3 (Darmstadt, 1966), 137.

2 Max Beckmann, *Briefe im Kriege, gesammelt von Minna Beckmann-Tube* (Berlin, 1916; repr. Munich, 1955).

3 Max Beckmann, 'Das neue Programm', *Kunst und Künstler*, XII (Berlin, 1914), 301, quoted from Rudolf Pillep (ed.), *Max Beckmann, Die Realität der Träume in den Bildern, Schriften und Gespräche 1911 bis 1950* (Munich, 1990), 17.

4 Gottfried Benn, *Das Hauptwerk*, vol. 3 ('Vermischte Schriften'), ed. Marguerite Schlüter (Wiesbaden and Munich, 1980), 173.

5 ibid., 174f.

6 E. L. Kirchner, letter to Schiefler, 28 March 1916, quoted from Donald E. Gordon, *Ernst Ludwig Kirchner, Mit einem kritischen Katalog sämtlicher Gemälde* (Munich, 1968), 25.

7 E. L. Kirchner, quoted ibid.

8 E. L. Kirchner, quoted from Annemarie Dube-Heynig, *Ernst Ludwig Kirchner, Postkarten und Briefe an Erich Heckel im Altonaer Museum in Hamburg*, ed. Roman Norbert Ketterer in collaboration with Wolfgang Henze (Campione d'Italia, 1984), 176.

9 Julius Meier-Graefe, 1919, in *Blick auf Beckmann, Dokumente und Vorträge* (Munich, 1962), 54f.

10 Franz Marc, *Schriften*, ed. Klaus Lankheit (Cologne, 1978), 58.

11 ibid., 66.

12 As n. 1 above.

13 Philipp Otto Runge, *Hinterlassene Schriften*, ed. by his eldest brother, Part I: facsimile print of the edition of 1940–41 (Göttingen, 1965), 137.

14 Quoted from Paul Klee, *Tagebücher 1898–1918*, new critical edition by the Paul Klee-Stiftung Kunstmuseum, Berne, rev. Wolfgang Kersten (Berne, 1988), 365.

15 See especially the revealing studies of O. K. Werckmeister, *Versuche über Paul Klee* (Frankfurt a.M., 1981); id. *The Making of Paul Klee's Career, 1914–1920* (Chicago and London, 1984).

16 Winter destroyed the drawings done during his Russian captivity before his release; a camp commandant had warned him that they might be suspected of being espionage material.

17 From 1937 Winter was forbidden to paint and was classed as a degenerate artist. Thus even before being called up for service in the Second World War he was unable to do large oil paintings.

18 Franz Marc, *Briefe aus dem Feld* (Berlin, 1940).

19 Fritz Winter, quoted from Werner Haftmann in exhibition catalogue *Fritz Winter* (Berne, 1941), 16.

The Romantic Spirit
in German Art

Romanticism

Romanticism

Romanticism in Germany began as a literary and philosophical movement. But it soon spread to the visual arts. Its impact here was various. In this exhibition we have arranged this variety under three main headings.

The first is NATURE. The new interest in the natural world as a source of emotional and spiritual enlightenment encouraged a profound transformation in landscape painting.

The second is MAN. Already in the *Sturm und Drang* (Storm and Stress) movement there was a recognition of the instinctive forces that affected human behaviour. In the Romantic period this exploration of the intuitive aspect of man continued.

Finally there comes a new sense of history and development, which encouraged a revaluation of the PAST, in particular the Middle Ages. The visual arts played a full role in this tendency, notably in the work of the Nazarenes.

Nature

The first signs of a pictorial response to literary Romanticism occurred in Dresden. It was here, in 1803, that Philipp Otto Runge published the designs for his cycle *The Times of Day*. These four prints were not landscape in the traditional sense. They were symmetrical patterns incorporating flowers, children, musical instruments and symbols relating to Christianity and classical mythology.

Runge died young in 1810, before he was able to complete his elaborate scheme. His career thus embodied another recurring aspect of Romanticism. This was the fragmentary – the sense of incompleteness, indeed of incompletability that Friedrich Schlegel saw as a key feature of Romantic poetry.

By the time of Runge's death another artist working in Dresden, Caspar David Friedrich, had made Romanticism in landscape painting a talking point through his images that combined symbolic forms with vivid atmospheric effects. In 1810, in fact, his key picture of spiritual loneliness, the *Monk by the Sea* had been purchased by the Prussian Crown Prince.

This public honouring of a master of Romantic landscape shows how far the movement had become established by this time. The reasons for this were partly political. Since 1806 much of Germany had been occupied and subdued by the French. Landscapes full of yearning and northern imagery could be seen as a kind of national resistance.

In the following years intense, symbolic landscape painting spread throughout Germany. In Berlin it could be seen in the work of the architect Karl Friedrich Schinkel, in Dresden in that of Carl Gustav Carus and Johan Christian Clausen Dahl. In Vienna it was explored by the Olivier brothers, Friedrich and Ferdinand. Later it was taken up by painters of the Düsseldorf school, such as Karl Friedrich Lessing and Andreas Achenbach. In later decades the forms became more stereotyped, often running the risk of sentimentality – as in the works of Adrian Ludwig Richter. More critical artists invested the genre with a sense of irony – as in the case of the Berlin painter Carl Blechen.

While concerned to convey a sense of the spiritual, Romantic landscape painters were assiduous observers of natural phenomena. Friedrich's pictures are built up from exacting studies of natural forms. Others – such as Carus – were scientists in their own right and related their depictions of scenery to current developments in the earth sciences. Their painted studies and drawings have left an impressive record of the spirit of wonder and enquiry that they brought to their explorations.

Man

In contrast to the rationalists, the Romantics saw man not just as a thinking being, but also as one guided by intuition and emotion. They explored the elemental in man. The pre-Romantic *Sturm und Drang* movement prepared the way for this. Amongst the visual artists affected by this was the Swiss painter Henry Fuseli.

Fuseli's *Nightmare* became a symbol for the age, with its dramatic rendering of the force of the unconscious mind. This view of man as an elemental being also gave a new dimension to portraiture. A striking example of this is the child portraiture of Philipp Otto Runge.

In this new order, the artist took on a heroic, prophetic role. For the artist was seen as having a creative vision that combined both the instinctive and the rational. Many artists adopted heroic postures under the influence of this idea – such as Asmus Jakob Carstens and Joseph Anton Koch. The poet Goethe – who had an ambivalent attitude to Romanticism in general – shared this view of creativity.

This attitude encouraged the view of the artist as social outsider. Yet, while valuing this individuality, the artist often felt a yearning for the security of a community. In Germany this often led to an idealized vision of simple domestic life, as can be seen in some of the charming interiors of Georg Friedrich Kersting.

The Past

The Romantic yearning for nature, for the infinite, for anything, it might seem, that was not here and now, also encouraged an idealization of the past. In the eighteenth century this was focused mainly on classical antiquity, but later more attention was paid to the Middle Ages, to the roots, it seemed, of modern Western societies. In Germany the Middle Ages provided a particular focus. For this was the time when the Holy Roman Empire was at its height and German states seemed to have shared a common culture and political identity. The Napoleonic Wars fostered an intensification of this mood, forming the basis of that nationalist movement that was eventually to culminate in unification in 1870.

In the early nineteenth century many artists were stimulated by this utopian vision of the Middle Ages to depict scenes from that period and to adopt some of the features of the *Altdeutsch* (Old German) style. The most successful group was the *Lukasbund*, a group of students at the Vienna Academy who banded together in 1808 to paint medieval and religious subjects in an archaic manner. After the leaders of this group moved to Rome in 1810 they became known as the Nazarenes.

An important aspect of the medieval revival was its association with folk culture. For the art of the people was seen as a kind of relic from the good old days. In literature it led to the collection of old songs and stories – as in Clemens Brentano's and Ludwig Achim von Arnim's *Des Knaben Wunderhorn* (The Boy's Magic Horn) and the *Kinder- und Hausmärchen* (Children's and Household Stories) of the Brothers Grimm, and to the imitation of these by modern writers. Many visual artists became involved in this through illustration. Artists like Eugen Neureuther and Alfred Rethel appropriately revived the graphic techniques of Dürer and other artists of the sixteenth century to decorate these texts. The tendency also encouraged the depiction of legends and scenes from daily life in a lyrical, folksy manner, notably by Moritz von Schwind and Adrian Ludwig Richter.

At the same time the yearnings for the South – epitomized by the Nazarenes' move to Rome in 1810 – was also coloured by the Utopian vision of the past. Italy and Greece became seen as lands of the past, in which a lost harmony and ideality could be glimpsed. It was a vision that lay behind the depiction of classic lands and legends by generations of German artists, from Koch and Johann Christian Reinhart through Schinkel, Blechen and Carl Rottmann to Anselm Feuerbach and Arnold Böcklin. The later artists – often known as the '*Deutsch-Römer*' (German-Romans) – interpreted the ancient world in a more complex manner under the impact of contemporary classical studies and archaeological finds.

Within Germany, the vision of the past took on a stronger political dimension. In the post-Napoleonic period there was strong official support for fostering cultural identity. One sign of this was the move by Ludwig I of Bavaria to establish a Walhalla at Regensburg, where the heroes of the nation could be honoured, Ludwig was also highly active in supporting the use of the arts to foster cultural identity in his capital city, Munich. Here there were vast building projects, in which museums and art galleries and other cultural and religious institutions were established. Many of these were decorated with large didactic frescoes by the Nazarene Peter von Cornelius and his followers.

William Vaughan

Morning

Day

Philipp Otto Runge
The Times of Day, 1807
(cat. 9)

Evening

Night

Philipp Otto Runge
Lily of Light and Morning Star, 1809
(cat. 12)

Philipp Otto Runge
The Two Right-Hand Angels of Musika, 1809
(cat. 11)

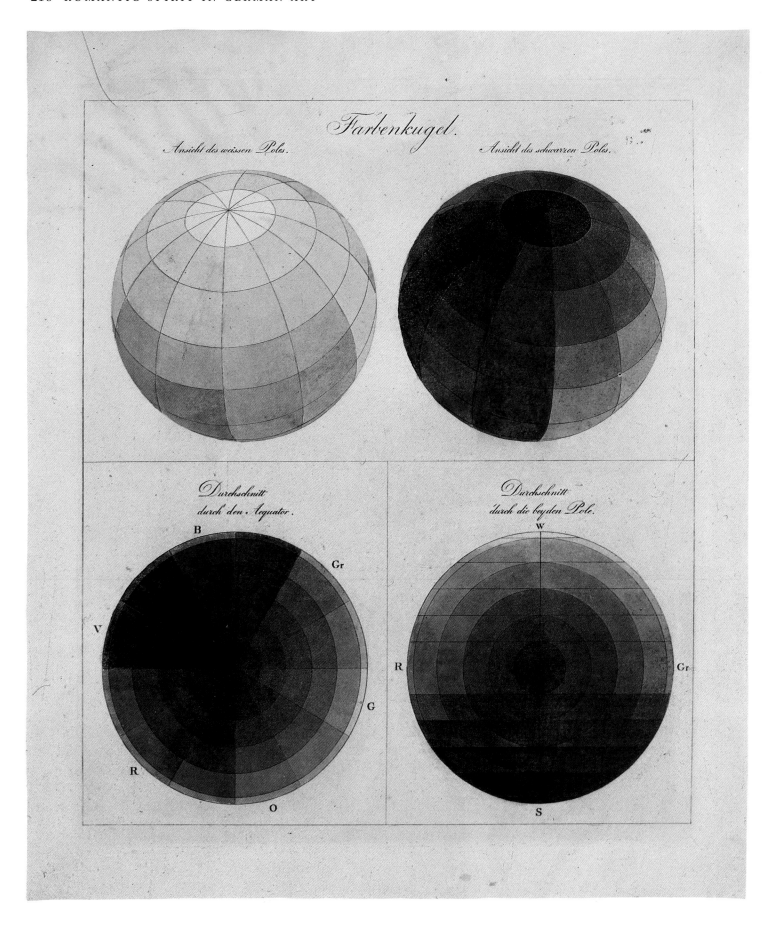

Philipp Otto Runge
Picture Supplement to the 'Colour-Sphere', 1810
(cat. 14)

Philipp Otto Runge
Mother Earth with Her Children, 1803
(cat. 6)

Philipp Otto Runge
Rose Sprig and Thornbush Sprig
(cat. 1)

Philipp Otto Runge
Spray of Leaves with Orange-Lily
(cat. 5)

Caspar David Friedrich
Winter Landscape, 1811
(cat. 20)

Caspar David Friedrich
Two Men Contemplating the Moon, 1819
(cat. 21)

Caspar David Friedrich
Solitary Tree, 1822
(cat. 22)

Caspar David Friedrich
Moonrise on the Seashore, 1822
(cat. 23)

Karl Friedrich Schinkel
Gothic Cathedral by the Water, 1813
(cat. 31)

Karl Friedrich Schinkel
Starry Hall of the Queen of the Night, 1815
(cat. 32)

Carl Blechen
Building the Devil's Bridge, c.1833
(cat. 15)

Carl Blechen
Girls Bathing in the Park at Terni, c.1836
(cat. 16)

Ferdinand Olivier
St Peter's Graveyard in Salzburg, 1818
(cat. 29)

Ferdinand Olivier
On the Frauensteinberg at Mödling, 1823
(cat. 30)

Carl Gustav Carus
Misty Landscape, *c.*1822
(cat. 34)

Caspar David Friedrich
Mist in the Elbe Valley, c.1821
(cat. 41)

Carl Gustav Carus
Evening Clouds over the Riesengebirge, c.1850
(cat. 36)

Johan Christian Clausen Dahl
Study of Drifting Clouds, 1835
(cat. 38)

Johan Christian Clausen Dahl
Cloud Study with Top of Vesuvius, 1820
(cat. 37)

Johann Georg von Dillis
Cloud Study, 1819–24
(cat. 39)

Carl Blechen
Chalk Cliffs on Rügen, 1828
(cat. 33)

Caspar David Friedrich
Old Oak Tree with Stork's Nest, 1806
(cat. 40)

Henry Fuseli
The Nightmare, 1781
(cat. 46)

Henry Fuseli
Thor Battering the Midgard Serpent, 1790
(cat. 49)

Henry Fuseli
Brunhild Watching Gunther Suspended from the Ceiling, 1807
(cat. 51)

Henry Fuseli
Silence, c.1799–1802
(cat. 50)

Henry Fuseli
Self-Portrait, c.1780–90
(cat. 48)

Caspar David Friedrich
Self-Portrait, 1800
(cat. 57)

Victor Emil Janssen
Self-Portrait at the Easel, 1828
(cat. 63)

Philipp Otto Runge
Self-Portrait at the Drawing Board, 1802
(cat. 77)

Peter von Cornelius and Friedrich Overbeck
Double Portrait of Overbeck and Cornelius, 1812
(cat. 56)

Johann Anton Ramboux
The Brothers Eberhard, 1822
(cat. 70)

Georg Friedrich Kersting
Theodor Körner, Friesen and Hartmann on Outpost Duty, 1815
(cat. 65)

Georg Friedrich Kersting
The Wreath Maker, 1815
(cat. 66)

Caspar David Friedrich
Woman with Raven on the Edge of a Chasm, c.1803
(cat. 60)

Caspar David Friedrich
Woman with Spider's Web, 1803
(cat. 59)

Georg Friedrich Kersting
Caspar David Friedrich in his Studio, c.1812
(cat. 64)

Caspar David Friedrich
Woman at a Window, 1822
(cat. 61)

Georg Friedrich Kersting
The Embroideress, 1812
Kunstsammlungen, Weimar

Georg Friedrich Kersting
Before the Mirror, 1827
(cat. 67)

Philipp Otto Runge
Luise Perthes, 1805
(cat. 78)

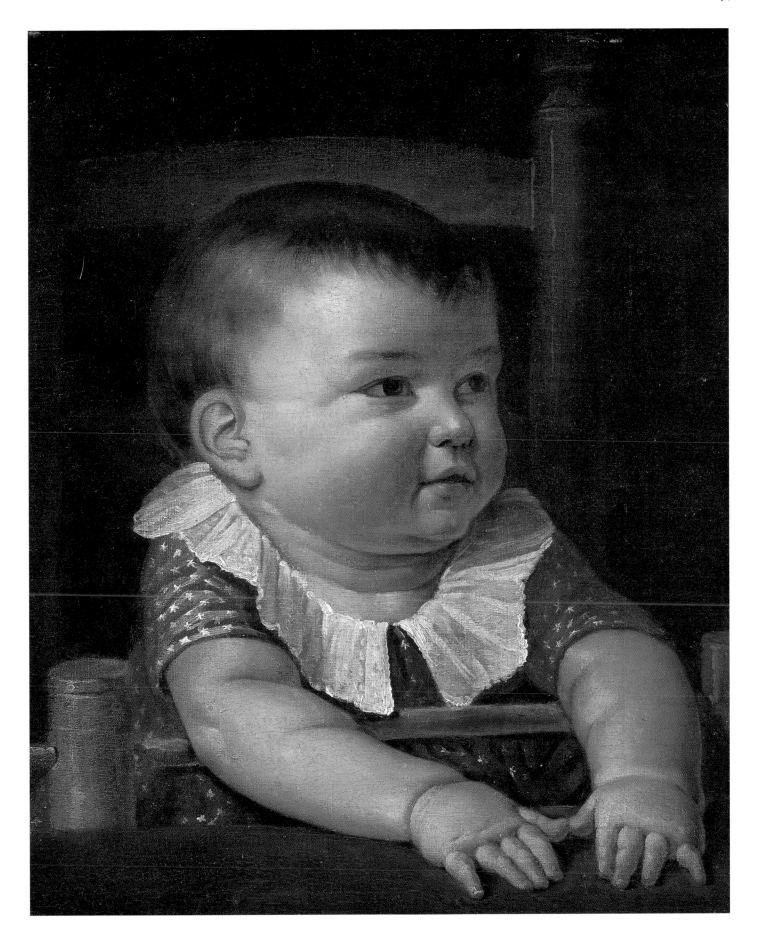

Philipp Otto Runge
Portrait of Otto Sigismund in a Folding Chair, 1805
(cat. 79)

Ferdinand von Rayski
Suicide of the Artist in His Studio, 1837–40
(cat. 71)

Alfred Rethel
Death as Assassin, 1847–48
(cat. 72)

Ferdinand Theodor Hildebrandt
The Warrior and his Child, 1832
(cat. 84)

Heinrich Anton Dähling
Käthchen von Heilbronn
(cat. 83)

Moritz von Schwind
The Captive Princess
(cat. 90)

Moritz von Schwind
Rübezahl, c.1845
(cat. 89)

Peter von Cornelius
Joseph Reveals Himself to His Brothers, 1817
(cat. 92)

Friedrich Overbeck
Sulamith and Maria, 1811–12
(cat. 93)

Julius Schnorr von Carolsfeld
The Vine of the Archpriest in Olevano, 1821
(cat. 97)

Carl Rottmann
Delos, 1837–53
(cat. 95)

Leo von Klenze
Elevation of the Walhalla. Design for a centrally planned building, 1820
(cat. 101)

Leo von Klenze
The Church of St. Salvator and the Walhalla, 1839
(cat. 103)

Peter von Cornelius
Hyacinthus, Clytië und Leucothoë, 1819
(cat. 112)

Philipp Otto Runge: The Times of Day

The Times of Day (cat. 9) – or, better, *The Four Times* – by Philipp Otto Runge is the founding work of Romantic art in Germany. The first sketches were made around Christmas 1802 and the work was completed in July 1803. Each of the four drawings consists of a large central motif with a cosmic significance which derives a Christian interpretation from the surrounding compositional framework. In detail, all of them contain a number of traditional iconographical elements. As a whole, however, they stand right outside conventional norms of pictorial composition.

In the centre of *Morning* a lily rises into space, as an emblem of light, out of the mists above the terrestrial globe. Child musicians represent the music of the spheres. Roses, falling from the lily buds onto the clouds, stand for the ruddy hues of dawn. The pairs of children on the calyx of the lily are embodiments of love. The group of three on the stamens alludes to the Trinity; in formal terms, it recalls the antique group of the Three Graces, but also those three clerics who stand for religious concord in Jacques-Louis David's *Tennis-Court Oath* (1791). Runge may have seen the engraving of David's painting. The morning star, Venus, should thus also be read in an Enlightenment sense. In the border, centrally placed below, are two reversed torches – the Primal Fires of Jacob Böhme (fig. 1) – encircled by a serpent that bites its own tail, the symbol of eternity. Out of the smoke of the spark of life a girl child flies to the right on Psyche's wings, and a boy child flies to the left. Each reaches out to a floating lotus blossom; they stand for the emergence of the male and female souls. Their ascent to the glory of God takes place on either side.

In *Day* the central lily is encircled by a wreath of cornflowers. This may be a reminiscence of the ring of stars in John Flaxman's illustration to Dante Alighieri, *Paradiso* (12.20). Beneath, the Earth Mother sits enthroned beside a pool of water. She is Böhme's 'Matrix', the Mother *tout court*, the earth principle, the Mother of God who brings salvation and redemption after the Fall. In front of her 'the two sexes separate, to work and live apart for the day' (Runge): in the sweat of his brow shall man eat bread. In the border the angel with the flaming sword, with a paradise of flowers behind him, is a reminder of the expulsion of Adam and Eve from Eden. In the corners children plant grain. On either side a child vainly tries to climb an Aaron's rod, which bends under the weight. Above each of them an angel stands on the calyx of a passionflower around which the Serpent twines. Out of the ring of clouds that surrounds the triangle of the Trinity and the rainbow of peace a rose grows towards each angel. *Day*, the zenith of earthly life, marks the farthest point from both the Paradise that is lost and the Paradise that is to come.

In the central motif of *Evening* the lily of light sinks into the clouds. The pairs of children signify love-as-death, the *Liebestod*. On either side are full-blown roses. The children make music, and this, together with the colour suggested by the plants and the sunset, evokes a Romantic synaesthesia. The personified Night spreads out her veil of stars, an image that Karl Friedrich Schinkel was to develop in his stage design for the *Starry Hall of the Queen of the Night* (1815, cat. 32). In the lower border, the Cross with roses and thorns symbolizes the death of the Redeemer. The grieving children with reversed torches, below, and the Lamb of God, above, complete the Christian message that reappears on either side, encoded in the language of plants.

In *Night* a sunflower grows out of stones and crystals, flanked by orange-lilies. The pairs of children in the arbours are asleep. Flowers of many imaginary kinds above which genii spread their wings, embody the bizarre world of dreams. Expressed through plant symbolism, this is the new-found theme of the subconscious which Henry Fuseli in his *Nightmare* (1781) and Francisco Goya in *Capricho 43, The Sleep of Reason Gives Birth to Monsters* (1797–98), had depicted in zoomorphic imagery. The female figure of Night and the genii seated on the poppies – symbols of sleep – are derived from the theme of the *Last Judgment*. In the border below, the flame of peace burns. The owls in the corners, with their

Peter von Cornelius
Apollo in his Chariot, 1819
(cat. 113)

Peter von Cornelius
Apollo and Daphne, 1819
(cat. 114)

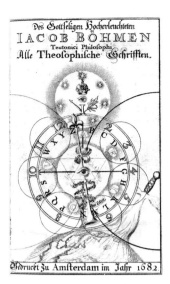

Fig.1 Unknown engraver, *Title-page of the Amsterdam edition of Jacob Böhme's writings* 1682

flower-like eyes, stand for Death. Late in his career Caspar David Friedrich was to hark back to this owl motif. Above, the Dove of the Holy Spirit is adored by three Psyche-winged genii on either side.

In 1807 Runge wrote an account of the meaning of the four drawings: 'Morning is the limitless illumination of the universe. Day is the limitless shaping of the creatures, which fill the universe. Evening is the limitless annihilation of existence into the origin of the universe. Night is the limitless depth of knowledge of unimpaired existence in God. These are the four dimensions of the created Spirit.'

Through the all-embracing significance of the rhythm of the times of day, the artist gives pictorial expression to his own conception of human existence between light and darkness; of history and nature; of infinite being and its renunciation; and of the life of the universe.

The structure of the four drawings is simultaneously religious and revolutionary. The nature imagery of the central composition unfolds between pivotal symbols of Christianity, above and below. As Novalis puts it, the middle world of pantheism has been centred by the mediator of monotheism. The parallels and rhythms that connect the four drawings are based on repetition. This serial element is vital: in it, the image of infinite space connects with that of unending time. At the end of the nineteenth century, these same ideas recur in the imagery of Ferdinand Hodler.

In *The Times of Day*, Runge has given pictorial expression to his celebrated 'Landscape' manifesto of February 1802. By landscape he did not mean the traditional pictorial genre of that name: landscape, for Runge, was an art of the future, replete with meanings in which all genres would be subjectively subsumed into a pictorial structure based on plant growth. Until the end of his short life the artistic elaboration and further development of *The Times of Day* was Runge's central creative concern. However, he managed to turn only one of them into a painting: this was *Morning*, in a small version of 1808 and a larger one of 1809 (colour plates, pp. 94–95). The most important theoretical derivative of *The Times of Day* was Runge's essay *Farben-Kugel* (The Colour Sphere, 1810, cat. 13).

The Romantic writers hailed *The Four Times* as the concrete achievement of their ideals of the arabesque and the hieroglyph. Clemens Brentano was directly inspired by Runge in his illustrations to the fairy tale *Gockel, Hinkel und Gakeleia*. Friedrich and Schinkel, too, were lastingly influenced by the *Times* cycle. But the contemporary public, for its part, regarded Runge's art as not far removed from insanity. The truth is that his artistic conception was far ahead of its time.

For his planned monumental version of the cycle, Runge intended an architectural setting designed on Gothic lines, but based on plant forms, with music provided by a choir – thus anticipating Richard Wagner's ideal of artistic synthesis, the *Gesamtkunstwerk*. His precedent in crossing artistic boundaries was to be followed by the artists of *art nouveau* and *Jugendstil* (notably Max Klinger), and of the Bauhaus (Oskar Schlemmer, among others). The fundamental idea of Romantic synaesthesia reappears in Franz Marc's and Wassily Kandinsky's *Der Blaue Reiter* almanac, and the conception of art as natural growth in Max Ernst (*Sea and Sun*, 1925, cat. 183) and in Paul Klee. Runge's style of painting also influenced the artists of *Neue Sachlichkeit*, and Otto Dix above all – as is most clearly shown by *Nelly in Flowers* (1924) and other paintings of his daughter. Finally, the analogy between nature and history plays its part in the thinking of Joseph Beuys. A work like *The End of the Twentieth Century* (cat. 261) is like a distant echo of the message of *The Times of Day*.

Jörg Traeger

Translated from the German by David Britt

Nature as Language

Conditioned as we are by religion, literature and art, nature evokes so many associations in us that we find it impossible to exclude them entirely when we look at a landscape painting. A painter can, however, try to suppress the connotations of objects as signs. A boat with a sail that forms a precise triangle for compositional reasons is not a suitable emblematic reminder of our voyage through life. Again, the topographical *veduta* seeks to limit the associative response: it registers what is there, and it does not much matter what the viewer is thinking about. Decorative landscapes, intended to impart a cheerful atmosphere to an interior, will also avoid any deep, contemplative dimension. In the Rococo period this was the customary approach to landscape. Medieval manuscript paintings, by contrast, allow no room for doubt that objects, being God's Creation, convey a message. This is shown not only by the relation between image and text but by the way in which the image is set against a background, like a word on a blank sheet of paper.

The actual experience of landscape is different. The sky does sometimes serve as a backcloth to objects on earth, but normally these appear in a profusion that outstrips our perceptual capacity. Individual forms stand out, but most of what we see is experienced only vaguely. Painters who use landscape to convey a message always set out to emphasize those objects that mean something, as against the unmeaning mass of the rest. Now there are some landscapes where the individual, meaningful object is easier to single out than it is elsewhere. In flat country one tree more readily stands out from its surroundings as a sign than it does in the mountains. The whole understanding of nature inevitably differs from one place to another. Thus, Jacob van Ruisdael and other seventeenth-century Dutch painters were able to evolve a form of landscape painting that could – like other kinds of painting – hint at trains of thought.

Later this vision of landscape went into eclipse; but at the end of the eighteenth century it enjoyed a revival in the English landscape garden. Pieces of natural scenery, conceived in pictorial terms, and complete with little buildings, monuments and inscriptions, transformed a stroll in the grounds of a country house into a philosophical or religious lesson based on a temporal sequence of impressions. Literature prepared the sensibility for such an experience, and it is no wonder that – in the wake of the Romantic movement – painting came to rely so heavily on poetry. Landscapes of this kind are often called poetic.

The work of the brothers Ferdinand, Friedrich and Heinrich Olivier from Dessau reveals how the experience of the landscape garden at Wörlitz near their birthplace – the most important 'English garden' in Germany – fostered a view of landscape as a religious message. They used similar landscapes as settings for biblical themes; and their genre scenes, too, were conceived as evocations of the religious life in the midst of Nature – as in Ferdinand Olivier's lithographic series, *Seven Scenes from Salzburg and Berchtesgaden, Arranged to Correspond to the Seven Days of the Week, and Linked by Two Allegorical Scenes* (1823) which was hailed as an important artistic achievement. The didactic Nature of this kind of art, with its implicit dimension of time, prompts the artist to work in series or cycles, or to present images as contrasting pairs – not in the eighteenth-century way, as pendants in decorative symmetry, but in order to point an evolutionary, before-and-after contrast.

Ferdinand and Friedrich Olivier were in Dresden from 1803 until 1807 and were in close touch with Caspar David Friedrich who – like Philipp Otto Runge – had made time and eternity into the central topic of artistic contemplation. From 1794 to 1798, Friedrich had studied at the Copenhagen Academy, and it is noticeable that his few works of that period include several views of landscape gardens there. But it was only after he moved to Dresden in 1798 that Friedrich developed a mode of thought that systematically scrutinized Nature in order to extract anything that might – by serving as a parable for an idea – in a sense do duty for a word. This is the only plausible explanation for his practice of noting down long successions of specific details, such as rocks, spruces, oaks, mountain outlines, ships and other objects, for use in paintings – to the exclusion of other things that he might equally well have observed. Friedrich took from Nature only what he could use to convey meaning; and this gave his painting its essentially linguistic character.

Friedrich was able to differentiate his ideas through the arrangement of signs in the painting, their subtle painterly texture, their colour and other artistic devices. In their austerity, even their sparseness, his works demand of the viewer both a deep absorption and a meditative form of seeing that intuitively thinks in wholes, transcending what is literally shown. They distinguish between the seeing that simply registers things as things and the transcendental seeing that comprehends connections and includes the unseen.

Runge – who wrote in Dresden in February 1802: 'everything thrusts towards landscape, seeks something definite in this indefiniteness, and knows not how to begin' – painted no landscapes in the usual sense of the word. His ideas concerning Nature appear in the backgrounds of his portraits and history paintings, and above all in those arabesque-like compositions that seek to join earthly and heavenly things together in a new way. He, too, aimed to reproduce nature with linguistic precision; but the principal elements in his vocabulary were flowers whose geometry fascinated him as the expression of transcendental law. The geometric organization of a surface mattered more to him than the suggestive power of landscape space. However, he stood even closer to Neoclassicism than Friedrich did, because human beings play so important a part in his paintings. Runge sought to mediate between human and geometrical form.

In Berlin Karl Friedrich Schinkel who had seen works by both Runge and Friedrich, was the champion of the new Romantic landscape. This made its appearance there in connection with the reforms that preceded the Wars of Liberation; its roots, however, stretched further back into the world of the English landscape garden, and of the architecture that went with it. In Schinkel's case this was supplemented by the inspiration of the theatre.

Schinkel, too, interpreted the theme of time through paired antitheses; but he was (in the best sense of the term) a politically minded artist, and to him time meant history above all. It was his central aspiration – which he pursued with a fervour that owed a great deal to the Enlightenment spirit – to bring antiquity and the Middle Ages together in a contemporary synthesis that would lead to a great new flowering of civilization. From the 1820s onwards Schinkel presented his ideas of the evolution of humanity more through figure compositions than through landscape, and to do this he made use of ancient mythology.

To use natural objects as if they were words – words admittedly comprehensible only to the initiated – made particular sense in the period immediately prior to the Wars of Liberation. Nature was seen as the secret language of those opposed to Napoleon; religious and patriotic impulses mingled. In this way art recruited support for the rebirth of Germany.

After the victory of 1815 things changed a great deal. To survive, artists now had to adjust to public taste, instead of educating it; and this brought Romanticism down to earth with a bump. This meant that when Carl Blechen – born in 1798, and thus half a generation younger than the early Romantics – attempted to come to grips with Nature as linguistic communication, he found himself in an entirely new situation. He saw Nature as the mirror of his own inner, psychic state: a ravine, for example, always appears in his work as a metaphor for hopeless entrapment. The visible and painted external world and the felt internal world coincide, and faith in creation as a decipherable message from God has been shaken.

The same shift away from Nature as language can be detected in other painters of the younger generation, such as Carl Rottmann, Ernst Fries or Johann Christoph Erhard. All ultimately succumbed to depression.

Helmut Börsch-Supan

Translated from the German by David Britt

Empirical Studies of Nature

Neither in the Romantic nor in the classical and idealistic view of art can the empirical Nature study be an end in itself. Even when painted in oils, it does not constitute an autonomous work of art. There are several reasons for this. According to classical principles, the mere imitation of Nature is inartistic: the work becomes art only when the natural prototype is purged of contingent individuality, by reference either to an absolute idea that dwells in the artist himself or to an absolute artistic norm sanctified by tradition. Nature study forms part of the artist's training, but from the outset he aspires to leave this transitional stage behind him and to graduate to the highest form of art, the exemplary history piece, defined by ideal form in perfect harmony with the absolute validity of the action shown. For norm and form to coincide, there must be an external point of reference with some claim to objectivity: the monarch, the Church, organized society, or some representative of these interests.

Romantic still incorporated much that was classical; but under the pressure of history the centre of balance had shifted towards fidelity to Nature – whether this appeared in the guise of humility, or of scientific aspirations, or of Nature mysticism, or of all three at once – and also towards the subjective observer, who was enabled to find himself by the presence of Nature. Allegiance to monarch, Church or community was no longer perceived as a norm, and at the same time the hierarchy of genres (with history painting at the head) lost some of its significance. The subjective observer recognized his or her own image, whether in Nature or in history, and reflected on the lesson learned, but no longer expected any direct guidance on how to act in the present.

The intensified Romantic concentration on the phenomena of Nature implied a sense of alienation from Nature, and the desire to make Nature one's own again through visual contemplation. This faculty of contemplative appropriation was – or so the Romantics were firmly persuaded – a particular gift of the artist. For Friedrich Wilhelm Schelling, visual art stands 'as an active bond between the soul and Nature, and can be grasped only in the living middle between the two'. Any one-sided concentration on the 'soul' too easily becomes shallow; conversely, a mere imitation of Nature misses the essence of the thing depicted, producing a dead image. Science, says Schelling, approaches Nature by endless laborious degrees; art can reach its goal at a single bound. Art grasps the essence of Nature by bringing out what is *characteristic*. This can be done neither by beauty of form alone nor by the 'empty shell or demarcation of individuality'. Art discerns the eternal archetype within the individual form, 'and he who has grasped the essence must not fear hardness and rigour: otherwise life could not exist'. The artist descends to minute detail, and does not even shrink from painful form, in the effort to extract the essence of the works of Nature.

These observations, while based in a philosophy of Nature, also have an entirely practical bearing on the artist's work. Hardness and rigour of form; extreme concentration on the individual phenomenon, in order to penetrate to the heart of it; imitation, as a means to possession and knowledge that is scientific but also transcends science: only such an understanding makes it possible to assess the Romantic study of Nature, and to give a meaningful account of the nuances of theory and practice that separate individual artists.

In 1815, when Goethe became acquainted with Luke Howard's terminology of cloud description, it seemed to him that at long last a systematic approach to meteorology had become possible. For Goethe, ever since his second visit to Switzerland in 1779, geology – principally as mediated by Horace Bénédict de Saussure – had been the linchpin of the sciences. But he could make nothing of the Swiss geologist's atmospheric measurements: they seemed to have no correlative in visible phenomena, and he could not meaningfully integrate them into his understanding of the operations of Nature. It was Howard's classification of clouds into stratus, cumulus, cirrus and nimbus that seemed to him to make meteorological sense of the form, formation and transformation of clouds. This was also in harmony with his own ultimately mystical and cabbalistic conception of the workings of the animate earth, the 'Earth Body'. Howard gave him back the sky, which the secular Enlightenment had unpeopled of its heavenly hosts. Now, at last, the sky in all its manifold appearances could once more serve as a linguistic image in Goethe's poetic cosmos. A scientific discovery seemed to have given it back its harmony.

The central importance of this for Goethe's world view is the sole explanation of his special and long-lasting interest in the modest English scientist. It also accounts for his urgent insistence on seeing the new insight reflected in painting. In 1816, on the suggestion of his associate, Johann Heinrich Meyer, he applied to Caspar David Friedrich for some cloud paintings – and was turned down flat. To Friedrich it seemed unthinkable to force the clouds into a system. As he saw it, mechanical observance of the new classification would lead to a revolution in landscape painting: where now the painting, steeped in the sensibility of the artist, gave Nature its soul, a preconceived abstraction would regulate its appearance and squeeze the breath of life out of it.

Friedrich had no idea that Goethe, too, was concerned with the breath of life in Nature, and that to him, natural science was not an end in itself but the equivalent of the exploration of being that Friedrich, after studying Nature in detail, sought to detect within himself and to express in his work. For Friedrich, the essence of things became visible only if brought out – exactly as suggested by Schelling – through the hardness and rigour of the artist's intervention; but hardness and rigour of artistic form emerges, in the Romantic view, only in the moment of self-concentration that permits an intimation of universal connectedness. Moreover, formal hardness and rigour acts as a pointer to the viewer's response to the work. In the act of perception the viewer actualizes the meaning that the artist has placed in the work in a state of potentiality. In Friedrich's view, Howard's system would prevent just this.

Friedrich's *Mist in the Elbe Valley* (c. 1821; colour plate, p. 231) was interpreted as a study of Nature, but also as a Christian allegory in which the foreground stands for this world, with a hint of the world beyond emerging through the mist as the goal of the future eternal life; the bridge was seen as the link between the two spheres. Here, once more, we agree with Schelling who said that every true work of art is 'capable of an infinity of intepretations ... and yet one can never say whether this infinity resided in the artist or whether it simply resides in the work.' More specifically, we would say that this deliberate interpretative openness is specific to the Romantic work of art. Specific, partly because by its very nature – that is, in its whole artistic approach – the Romantic work of art 'delivers an oracle with many meanings'.

The objects in Friedrich's painting – tree in leaf, leafless tree, bridge, smoke from a human habitation, morning mist – may be read as signs; the painting permits this interpretation. But this reading is not the only interpretation of the painting. Rather, the painting demands an approach that opens a range of possible experience and interpretation. It does so by discreetly, but repeatedly and therefore unmistakably, emphasizing the central vertical axis. The position of the sun, as revealed by its rays; the highest point on the hill; and above all the only clear notch or angle in the whole picture, where the corner of the building in the middleground meets the line of the foreground terrain: all these lie precisely on the central axis of the painting. The viewer is thus gently manoeuvred into position in front of the painting. This contains no human action; but smoke and mist blow across it, so it is not frozen into immobility. It depicts a single moment, and yet – as Schelling puts it – it seems to exist outside time: it embodies pure essence, pure being. This is what Schelling means by bringing out the essence of Nature. Only when the painting, through the hardness and rigour of its form, sets the viewer pondering the connectedness of things, does Friedrich regard it as a fully valid work. However, this pondering is not abstract reflection: it takes place in the process of visual contemplation itself – or rather *as* visual contemplation.

It is certainly untrue that there are no pure Nature studies by Friedrich. There certainly are; but they are drawn on principle and for a purpose: trees, rocks, plants and views, architectural or technical details, mostly dated precisely to the day, with details of place and, more rarely, of colour or distance. The trees are shown with all the characteristics of their species, and mostly drawn early in the year so that their salient feature, the arrangement of their branches, is still clearly recognizable. This is reminiscent of Alexander Cozens's set of tree drawings, published in 1771, which showed the 'Shape, Skeleton and Foliage' of thirty-two different kinds of tree: in these, too, the structural pattern of the skeleton remains visible beneath the garment of leaves, as a kind of abstract of visual observation. To this, Friedrich adds light and shadow, in clear gradations of drawing. Thus, the drawing of an oak is a precise reproduction of Nature, but also a structural analysis of a thing perceived, and so it provides the artist with knowledge that he can use freely in a painting while retaining truth to Nature.

However, there seem to be a few exceptions to the rule: in one short period, between 1820 and 1824, Friedrich painted a small number of oil studies that were not made with a view to inclusion in a pictorial composition and therefore lack a referential dimension. These would probably not have existed without the influence of Johan Christian Dahl. Dahl had come to Dresden in 1818 and had immediately become friendly with Friedrich, and we have Nature oil studies of his, made in the neighbourhood of Dresden in 1819. In the winter of 1820–21, while Dahl was away in Italy, Friedrich painted close-up views in oil of ice-floes and ice breaking on the Elbe, and these he used directly as sources for *Sea of Ice* in 1823–24 (colour plate p. 97); three of them were in Dahl's studio at his death and bear inscriptions in his hand. Friedrich no doubt considered that, for this rare phenomenon, mere drawings with indications of colour were not enough. He captured the shapes and gradations of colour of the ice-floes in oil studies, such as had long been customary in painting plants or rock formations for use in the foregrounds of composed landscapes.

Before he left for Italy, Dahl was prompted to make oil studies by Christopher Wilhelm Eckersberg (who had returned from Italy in 1816); while he was in Italy, his principal influences in this respect were Achille Etna Michallon and François Granet. It was certainly Michallon, pupil of Pierre-Henri Valenciennes and teacher of Corot, who played the more important intermediary role. His master, Valenciennes, not only painted

oil studies himself, with particular emphasis on changeable atmospheric states and their effect on objects, but was the leading advocate of the establishment of a Prix de Rome for landscape painting, for which the submission should consist both of a large finished landscape composition and of an oil sketch of a landscape. The first such prize, awarded in 1817, was won by Michallon. The result was a flood of French oil studies.

The first German artist to respond to this seems to have been Maximilian Johann Georg von Dillis, who was in Rome in 1818 with the Crown Prince of Bavaria and there painted oil studies of the view from Villa Malta. Dillis owed another debt to Valenciennes: in his *Eléments de perspective pratique* of 1799–1800 Valenciennes recommends a careful study of clouds, recorded in drawings with colour notations, with a view to capturing the shifting state of the weather. On his return from Italy between 1819 and 1824 Dillis made over 150 drawings of clouds, but in these other influences were probably at work too.

It was long supposed that Valenciennes's oil studies, now in the Louvre, and mostly dating from the 1780s, were invariably painted from nature. It was therefore taken for granted that this also applied to the hundreds of surviving oil sketches by Dahl. In both cases, however, some caution is in order. The format, the free handling and the material of the support – mostly cardboard or paper on cardboard – do not necessarily prove in themselves that these studies were done in the presence of Nature. In many cases it is quite conceivable that a summary, drawn notation underlies the work, and that this was almost immediately translated into a painted sketch in the studio. This would explain why many of Dahl's sketches reveal a degree of pictorial organization, as exemplified by the golden section and by formal and proportional analogies. It can even be assumed that without these the intrinsically worthless and evanescent motifs in question would have had no right to appear in art at all. Even for Dahl, however, oil studies were not an end in themselves: in his *Liber veritatis* they do not appear as paintings in their own right, and he subscribed all his life to the demand for classical perfection in official landscape painting, just as Valenciennes did.

Pure cloud studies became increasingly frequent in Dahl's work in 1823 after his visit to Italy. There were

Fig.1 Carl Blechen, *Cloud Study*, Staatliche Museen zu Berlin Preußischer Kulturbesitz, Kupferstichkabinett

probably two reasons for this. One was that in that year he moved within Dresden to a house on the banks of the Elbe which he shared with Friedrich; the cloud studies could have been painted from a window of the house. The other, and probably more important, was that Carl Gustav Carus would have drawn his attention to Goethe's work on Howard. Published in full in 1822 in the fourth instalment of Volume 1 of *Zur Naturwissenschaft überhaupt* ('On Natural Science in General'), this consisted of the essay '*Wolkengestalt nach Howard*' ('Cloud Form According to Howard'); an expanded version of the poem '*Howards Ehrengedächtnis*' ('In Honoured Memory of Howard'); and Goethe's own translation of Howard's autobiography. Carus read this at once, and its importance was crucial. He stopped work on his *Landschaftsbriefe* ('Letters on Landscape') for more than a year and a half, and resumed them only at the end of 1823 with Letter 6, in which – to cut a long story short – he renounced the Romantic Nature mysticism of Friedrich in favour of a more scientific, Goethean attitude.

Carus's paintings underwent a corresponding shift. He continued to agree with Schelling that art was capable of truly fulfilling the aspirations of science. However, this was no longer to be done in an intuitive, subjective leap but in familiarity with the observation of Nature; this was the scientific aesthetic to which Goethe – and with him, above all, Alexander von Humboldt – subscribed. In the seventh of his letters on landscape painting, written in 1824, Carus discussed Goethe's '*Howards Ehrengedächtnis*' in specific detail and coined the term *Erdlebenbildkunst*, 'pictorial art of earthly life' which was to dominate his own *Briefe über das Erdleben* ('Letters on Earthly Life') composed from 1826 onwards. In these he called for the Romantic mood landscape to be replaced by a conception of landscape based on natural law and indebted above all to geology (together with meteorology). The first traces of geological thinking, concerned above all with geological models of the origins of the earth, can be discerned in Carus's painting from 1820 onwards.

In the early 1820s, and especially from 1822 onwards, there were thus some members of Friedrich's circle who subscribed to an antisubjectivistic view of Nature, based on objective observation and insistent on natural laws

which could not have left Friedrich entirely unaffected. In 1824 he painted three oil sketches – including the celebrated *Evening* now in Mannheim – which limit themselves to the 'pure' rendering of Nature. Friedrich makes this absolutely plain: not only does he adopt the convention of the oil sketch by painting in oil on cardboard – as he rarely did elsewhere, even in small paintings – but he writes in the time of day and the date, 'October 1824', far too large and in the case of the Mannheim work scratched in the narrow dark strip of earth. This ensures that all three paintings remain studies. But in contrast to the Mannheim painting – which consists of nine-tenths sky and a narrow, violet-black, wholly undifferentiated strip of earth – the *Evening* study in a private collection shows two of the Dresden churches, with the Hofkirche sporting a Gothic helm roof instead of its onion dome, and both rising needle-like on the misty skyline. Even here Friedrich cannot resist including interpretative hints.

In 1823 yet another artist came under Dahl's influence: Carl Blechen, who visited Dahl and probably Friedrich in Dresden in that year. A series of pure cloud studies in oil on paper directly reflect the stimuli he received, but the influence did not last. For in 1824, on Karl Friedrich Schinkel's recommendation, Blechen was appointed set painter to the Königstädtisches Theater in Berlin. This work affected his painting; he came to favour a Romantic theatrical *frisson*, based on literary sources, with a clear popular appeal, yet tinged with his own instinctive gloom. Subliminally, even here, a realistic intention persisted, and this became dominant after he gave up his theatrical work, both before and during his visit to Italy in 1828–29. Blechen's Italian cloud studies (fig. 1), with their audacious use of colour and their free, fluent handling, outdo Dahl and often rest content with summary but remarkably telling hints. They often use against-the-light effects, and anticipate his official Italian landscapes. These now seem to us entirely conventional, both in staffage and in composition, but contemporary critics condemned their harsh colouring and sketchy handling as violations of all the rules of art. One reviewer wrote of Blechen's *Afternoon on Capri* (1832) that the sheer brilliance of the sunlight made the effect garish, as if it were the work of a crack-brained man; the whole thing looked 'like a lye contaminated with dull-red and bluish ingredients'.

Even before the experience of the Italian light, however, Blechen was quite capable of doing justice to natural phenomena. A study of rocks, clearly and proudly dated 1828, and known, probably wrongly, as *Chalk Cliffs on Rügen* (on the strength of a supposed visit to the island in that year) is utterly direct (colour plate, p. 236). It dispenses with any anecdotal or ennobling embellishments and limits itself to two ranges of tone, from brown to yellowish-white for the cliffs and from grey to weak blue for the section of sky. The chalk or limestone cliff is convincingly reproduced, both in its phenomenal appearance and in its geological structure.

Blechen was declaring his adherence to a tradition that had begun with the geologically exact illustrations to Humboldt's travels in which draughtsman, painter and engraver followed Humboldt's own designs in the endeavour to emphasize structural features and thereby show not only the characteristic form but, in accordance with the Romantic tradition, the essence of a landscape. Humboldt himself hoped that these works would lead to the emergence of a new art of landscape painting; only this would compensate aesthetically for the lost wholeness of Nature.

There is an evolutionary connection between these works and Carus's views of Fingal's Cave on the Hebridean island of Staffa which reflect not only mythological associations but also geological theories of the origins of the earth (cat. 35). After earning Goethe's approval in 1820 by painting the pillar-like basalt for-

mations near Zittau, Carus in his turn founded a tradition of what he himself called 'Geognostic Landscapes', which found successors in German art as late as 1850, as exemplified by Carl Rottmann. Romantic and scientific elements combined in the key term 'characteristic', the meaning of which Goethe and Friedrich Schiller had explored as far back as the 1790s.

Werner Busch

Translated from the German by David Britt

Elemental Forces

The leading proponents of the literary movement known as *Sturm und Drang* (Storm and Stress) which flourished in the 1770s and included Johann Gottfried Herder and the young Johann Wolfgang von Goethe, had no doubt which living painter most fully embodied their own emotional intensity and belief in the power of unbridled genius. This was Johann Heinrich Füssli, known in Britain as Henry Fuseli, who had grown up in an intensely literary milieu in Zurich. After deciding to become a professional painter he spent eight years in Rome beginning in 1770, and then settled in London for the rest of his life where he achieved great eminence as Professor of Painting at the Royal Academy. His connection with *Sturm und Drang* is expressed in a letter of 1773 in which Johann Caspar Lavater, the Swiss writer and physiognomist, gave the latest news of Fuseli to Herder with the understanding that it would be passed to Goethe: 'He is everything in extremes – always an original; ... He despises everything and everybody ... . His wit is unbounded. He seldom acts, except with pencil and brush but when he does, he must have a hundred yards of space, or else he would trample everything to pieces. He has devoured all the Greek, Latin, Italian and English poets. His look is lightning, his word a thunderstorm; his jest is death, his revenge hell ... . He cannot breathe a single common breath.'

This character-sketch is entirely borne out by the evidence of his art, his impact on his contemporaries, and his self-portrait (plate, p. 242). For the rest of his long life he cultivated an air of danger and unpredictability, yet none of this prevented him from mixing in the most cultivated circles in London or rising to high office, or left him short of wealthy and well-connected patrons. Even more remarkable is the fact that, despite his reputation among *Sturm und Drang* authors in his youth, he essentially deserted them in 1770 when he left for Rome and then settled in London. Though Goethe and others kept a keen interest in his doings, he seems to have shown no curiosity about them or overt allegiance to them after he finally settled in England.

Yet for Fuseli to have settled in England was a kind of fulfilment of his *Sturm und Drang* destiny, for it was the country not only of Shakespeare and Milton but of a contemporary literature sympathetic to the expression of feeling. Shakespeare and Milton remained the subject of his most serious paintings, and he interpreted Classical Antiquity always as an age of primitive energy and heroism and not, like his great contemporary Johann Joachim Winckelmann, as one that could achieve at its highest level social harmony and artistic perfection.

Fuseli, though he was never fully part of *Sturm und Drang*, in a sense never developed beyond it. In leaving the German context at a critical juncture in 1770 he did not confront the particular concerns with Antiquity and nature which subsequently dominated the minds of Goethe and those he influenced. Goethe himself showed some equivocation towards Fuseli's achievement and after his own visit to Italy he was more susceptible to Asmus Jakob Carstens and his grave and primitivistic drawings of ancient and primeval scenes. Yet neither Fuseli nor Carstens were interested in nature beyond the human body, and both really preceded the great flowering of landscape painting in Germany. It is an index of the breadth of Goethe's artistic sympathies that his own concerns as a draughtsman were mainly with landscape, though there are a few drawings which attempt to evoke the sublimity of his most ambitious writings.

It is not coincidental that Carstens's most devoted pupil, Joseph Anton Koch should find himself eventually as a landscape painter of an heroic and elemental kind, and in his work one can often sense not only the classical past but also a Northern landscape redolent of Ossian. For the *Sturm und Drang* authors German literature could only be revived through the retrieval of Northern origins as well as those of Greece and Rome, and especially in ancient myths like those of Ossian. Goethe makes Werther's reading of the wildness of the landscape in Ossian mirror his alienation and despair, and Fuseli's paintings and drawings of Germanic myth are perhaps not entirely serious. It is, however, in landscape painting that the wild setting of Ossian's Northern scenery is most fully realized in Germany (this is less true of Danish or Scottish artists like Nikolaj Abraham Abildgaard and Alexander Runciman who, under Fuseli's influence, retained a primary interest in the human figure), and it resounds through the work of the great Romantic painters like Philipp Otto Runge and Caspar David Friedrich.

The strange and intensely personal work of the etcher Carl Wilhelm Kolbe represents another and later derivation of the *Sturm und Drang* spirit. The imagery is consistently Arcadian or derived from Dutch landscape, but all sense of harmony and balance is thrown off by the distortions of scale which reduce shepherds and shepherdesses to elves and fairies among an undergrowth of gigantic plants, all etched with an obsessive concentration.

All these artists were known to a varying extent to the later Romantic painters. If Carstens foreshadowed the distinctive gravity of nineteenth-century German Classicism, Koch the mountain landscape of Friedrich, and Kolbe the minute and sacramental observation of the Olivier brothers, then Fuseli's bizarre imagination resonates through the imagery of E.T.A. Hoffmann's tales and drawings. Collectively the *Sturm-und-Drang*-influenced artists opened up many possibilities for new forms of art, above all for new forms of German art.

David Bindman

Solitude and Community

Definitions of the Romantic human image are as disparate as those of Romanticism itself. Nevertheless, the 'Romantic spirit', hedged about with such contrasting stylistic terms as Neoclassicism, Biedermeier and Realism, concentrates itself into a number of essential characteristics.

The German Early Romantics present themselves to us as youthful revolutionaries, with writers and poets in the vanguard. Wilhelm Heinrich Wackenroder, Ludwig Tieck, Friedrich and August Wilhelm Schlegel, Novalis and the painter Philipp Otto Runge were united by a new response to life, which only later became an aesthetic. It arose from the struggle to cast off the eighteenth-century burden of authority: courtly and bourgeois convention, rationalist philosophy, Neoclassical doctrine. Its roots lay in a new ethos of authentic feeling.

The youthful idealism of the Romantics derived its aesthetic dimension from their enthusiasm for medieval history, art and civilization – as far as Raphael and Albrecht Dürer – and also for a Catholic version of Christianity. These ideals were pursued, in particular, by the Nazarenes; the exponents of North German Romanticism – such as Runge, Caspar David Friedrich, Georg Friedrich Kersting and Carl Blechen – stood somewhat aloof from any such nostalgic response to history.

The Image of the Artist

The Romantic spirit appears in concentrated form, as it were, in the genre of the artist's portrait which is frequently also a self-portrait (fig. 1). It is a form that says a great deal about the self-image of a whole generation. It should, of course, be remembered that the great ideas and emotions of the age were confined to the work of a chosen few. Even in the first decades of the nineteenth century, the bulk of portraiture was still entirely conventional, devoted to the creation of a prosaic likeness.

What sets Romantic portraits apart is the profound sense of inwardness and shared humanity that they manifest in their dialogue with the viewer. It is an inwardness that embraces many psychic states, from brimming enthusiasm to solitary gloom. The portraits of the Romantics are direct and serious accounts of individuality. These concerns find distinctive expression in the portraits of the Nazarene circle from 1808 onwards; all emotional excesses and pretences to sensibility are avoided, all the attributes of status and dignity omitted. All that counts is the face, the mirror of the soul.

In Rome, in the years around 1810, Franz Pforr and his friends Friedrich Overbeck and Joseph Wintergerst, followed by Johann Philipp Veit, Peter von Cornelius, Julius Schnorr von Carolsfeld and Ferdinand Olivier, produced many drawings and small oil studies in which they elaborated a new portrait type, tightly concentrated on the head and neck but occasionally also showing chest and shoulders. It is probably no coincidence that these works echo the portrait drawings of Dürer, Grünewald and Hans Holbein.

Another form of Nazarene portrait shows the sitter in an interior or a garden bower, with a landscape beyond; historical costume and props are used to establish a link with an idealized past. Jens Christian Jensen has pointed to the origins of this type in Italian Quattrocento art, from Pietro Perugino to Raphael.[1] This is not eclectic imitativeness on the artists' part, but a deliberate commitment to a historical point of reference.

By contrast with the Roman art scene, where the emphasis was on cooperation, artists in northern and central Germany found themselves relatively isolated. Initially, their portraits were an unspectacular continuation of the eighteenth-century tradition of bourgeois portraiture, as perfected by Jens Juel in Copenhagen and Anton Graff in Dresden. Then, in his self-portraits of 1801–02, Runge achieved a new quality that was to influence not only his own period but the whole nineteenth century. This new manner combined intense clarity with depth of feeling and revelation of the individual soul; its supreme achievements were Runge's large, almost monumental group portraits of his family and closest friends.

Fig.1 Caspar David Friedrich, *Self-Portrait c.*1810, Staatliche Museen zu Berlin Preußischer Kulturbesitz, Kupferstichkabinett

Solitude

In the Romanticism of northern Germany, the portrait – and indeed all figure painting – constantly evokes the idea of solitude. Isolated and uncomprehended by society, the artist or thinker who has lapsed from the religious and social ties of Church and State appears as the exponent – and at the same time the product – of solitude. This isolation is the direct result of the sovereign autonomy of the Great Man.[2] Ludwig van Beethoven, Friedrich Hölderlin, Novalis, Heinrich von Kleist and Arthur Schopenhauer were among the great solitaries of the age; and Runge himself frequently complained of his isolation as an artist.[3] The true prototype of the solitary Romantic artist, however, was Friedrich: 'I must remain alone, and must know that I am alone, in order to see and feel Nature fully. I need solitude for the dialogue with Nature.'[4]

Solitude is simultaneously a painful destiny and a necessary precondition of Romantic creativity. In this sense, the figures in Friedrich's landscapes who stand with their backs to the viewer are symbolic of the artist himself. His art is an expression of the human condition bereft of God: 'the most appropriate psychic state ... is deep melancholy and grief unto death.'[5] Where solitude turns to bereftness, *Angst* and despair, it can lead to a cataclysm and end in madness or suicide.

A less tragic form of solitude is the self-imposed seclusion that is implicit in the artistic theme of the hermit or eccentric recluse. This conveys the desire for the simple, idyllic life, 'the state of non-separation from nature'[6] – but also the world-weary need to meditate undisturbed, far from civilization, and to find an alternative definition of self.

Brethren and Friends

Solitude, freedom from ties and emptiness brought a renewal of the need for community, friendship and brotherhood. New social ideals and artistic objectives induced young men to set up student fraternities (*Burschenschaften*) and artistic clubs. In the *Lukasbund*, German artists in Rome discovered the sense of community that the Church could no longer offer them. The initial bond between them lay in their shared convictions and objectives; this was later reinforced by participation in such collective tasks as the Casa Bartholdy and Casino Massimo murals. They were living in a foreign country, far from home, and this too had its effect. Initially austere and almost monastic, the Nazarene brotherhood later turned into a liberal band of comrades, a 'Republic of Artists', such as would have been unthinkable at home in Germany.

When Carl Philipp Fohr arrived in Rome, he brought with him not only the fashion for 'Old German' costume but some of the rituals of the very first Heidelberg *Burschenschaft*. Artists foregathered in cafés and wine bars or in the open air; and there was plenty of undergraduate high spirits at the annual spring festival of the German artistic community, the *Cervaro-Fest*. Franz Ludwig Catel, Franz Nadorp, Dietrich Wilhelm Lindau and Fohr's friend Hans Hübsch painted commemorative pictures of such occasions. The large engraving projected by Fohr himself for which he made a number of drawings, was intended rather as a collective portrait, showing his friends and fellow-artists assembled in the Caffé Greco. It was to be his memorial to the German artists of Rome.

One thing mattered even more to the Romantics than group solidarity: this was friendship, which they elevated into a kind of religion with highly exclusive, elitist implications. 'What are all earthly things, compared with friendship?' Pforr demanded.[7] This cult of friendship, with its roots in eighteenth-century sensibility, found expression not only in countless documents but also in the so-called *Freundschaftsbild* or friendship portrait which crystallized between 1810 and 1830 into one of the characteristic art-forms of the age.[8] This type of group portraiture was particularly current among German artists in Rome.

In the North things were different. For Runge, Friedrich and Kersting, blood-brotherhood counted for less than family ties. The loveliest expression of this is Runge's group portrait *We Three*, which shows the artist with his wife and brother. From time to time, even the reclusive Friedrich expressed his deep affection for his family in far-off Greifswald.[9] This is apparent from his letters and from one remarkable family portrait, set against the marketplace of his native city, which is exceptional among his works in creating a faithful image of a milieu.

With the transition to late Romanticism and Biedermeier, the form and meaning of the friendship portrait changed, and it ceased to be an ethical and religious confession of faith. Paintings of friends – artists in their studios, say – turned into anecdotal records of specific occasions. Where the early Romantic friendship portrait, with its austere linearity and abstract composition, had expressed the lofty spirituality of the relationship that was its theme, painters now produced scenes of great immediacy, realized in spatial depth, in which contact between the figures was maintained by some anecdotal or dramatic action.

Fig.2 Philipp Otto Runge, *The Artist's Parents* 1806, Hamburger Kunsthalle

In Praise of the Family

Family feeling – the love of parents, spouses and children – came into increasing prominence from the middle of the eighteenth century onwards, as part of the rising bourgeois ethic. It was the Romantics who found new and appropriate pictorial forms – untainted by conventions, whether Rococo, quasi-Dutch or sentimental – in which to treat such themes. In fact, even Runge's large drawing *Homecoming of the Sons* (1800), intended as the basis of a large painting, still betrays traces of all those traditions: it was not until 1805–06, when he painted his self-portrait with his wife and brother, *We Three*, and the portrait of his parents (fig. 2), that he achieved an entirely new sense of tranquil clarity.

Fig.3 Philipp Otto Runge, *The Hülsenbeck Children* 1805–06, Hamburger Kunsthalle

shows an affinity with the North German Romanticism that produced, in Runge's portraits of children (fig. 3), some of the supreme achievements of German portraiture. These works show children freed from all the constraints of a conventional pose, and true to their individuality and to their biological status, they reveal a debt to Jean-Jacques Rousseau, and to the new century of which he was the prophet.

Hans Joachim Neidhardt

Translated from the German by David Britt

1 Jens Christian Jensen, 'Die Bildniskunst der Nazarener', in exh. cat. *Die Nazarener in Rom: Ein deutscher Künstlerbund der Romantik* (Munich, 1982), 40.

2 Werner Hofmann, *Das Irdische Paradies: Motive und Ideen des 19. Jahrhunderts* (Munich, 1974), 131.

3 Klaus Lankheit, *Das Freundschaftsbild der Romantik* (Heidelberg, 1952), 94.

4 Caspar David Friedrich in a letter to V. A. Zhukovsky, quoted from Lankheit (as note 3), 95.

5 Hans Sedlmayr, *Verlust der Mitte: Die bildende Kunst des 19. und 20. Jahrhunderts als Symptom und Symbol der Zeit* (Salzburg, 1948), 176.

6 Hans Ost, *Einsiedler und Mönche in der deutschen Malerei des 19. Jahrhunderts* (Düsseldorf, 1971), 208.

7 Quoted from Lankheit (as note 3), 96.

8 See Lankheit (as note 3).

9 In a letter from Dresden, 2 October 1825: 'From time to time I feel the need to tell you, my brothers, how dearly I love you and how boundlessly I trust you, all the more so as bitter experience increasingly leads me to withdraw into myself.' *Caspar David Friedrich in Briefen und Bekenntnissen*, ed. Sigrid Hinz (Berlin, 1979), 55.

10 Christa Wolf has said in an interview: 'Early Romanticism was a social experiment on the part of a small, progressive group.' Wolf, 'Kultur ist, was gelebt wird', in exh. cat. *Traum und Wahrheit: Deutsche Romantik* (Berne, 1986), 30.

11 See Christa Murken, 'Die Romantik in der Kunst – gestern, heute – Widerspruch und Weltentwurf', in exh. cat. *Romantik in der Kunst der Gegenwart*, ed. Axel and Christa Murken (Cologne, 1993), 51.

The youthful brethren of the *Lukasbund* found themselves temporarily obliged to project their vaguely erotic fantasies of marriage and parenthood back into an idealized past. Examples include Overbeck's portrait of his friend Pforr (1810) and Pforr's own *Sulamith and Maria* (1811; colour plate, p. 98).

However, at the very moment when the Nazarenes were creating this fabulous, hieratic image of Christian womanhood, contemporary society had something very different to offer: the self-assured, cultivated, witty women who moved in Romantic literary circles in Jena and Berlin, and who were the very first representatives of the modern idea of emancipation. In the circle dominated by such liberal figures as the Schlegel brothers, Friedrich Schleiermacher, Johann Gottlieb Fichte, Dorothea Veit, Caroline Schlegel and Rahel Levin, the institution of the family was called into question in a number of different ways; and there were some experiments with multilateral households and lifestyles that verged on libertinism.[10]

By contrast, Overbeck's self-portrait with wife and child of 1820 looks like a declaration of allegiance to the bourgeois family.[11] Solid in its immediacy, and yet with an almost religious dignity, it presents an uncommonly pure example of the types and forms of the fully evolved Nazarene idiom. The figure of the child, in particular,

The Craving for Identity and Liberty

When the *Lukasbrüder* left Vienna in 1810, turning their back on a stultifying Academy to find both artistic freedom and personal fulfilment in Italy, they had already equipped themselves with a number of the achievements of contemporary social and political life. Founded in 1809, their *Lukasbund* or Brotherhood of St Luke had its own letters of incorporation, coat of arms and motto, and a code of ethics for the six members. It was a fraternity analogous to the various compatriot societies of students (known as *nationes*) that had existed at the universities since the Middle Ages.[1] Its choice of patron saint was intended as an allusion to the medieval fraternities of St Luke, which were erroneously thought to have been painters' guilds. This rough-and-ready treatment of medieval history was characteristic of the whole period, and should certainly not be regarded as unique to the artists who became known as the Nazarenes.

Their achievement was their programme which won respect even in their own lifetimes: it was no less than the renewal of art in a national and Christian spirit – or, to put it another way, the strengthening of a nation through a Christian and moral art that was to be schooled by the example of the Middle Ages. Their blend of religion and patriotism attracted support from the most varied quarters, including even Johann Heinrich Meyer and Johann Wolfgang von Goethe, who in their essay on *Neu-deutsche religiös-patriotische Kunst* (Latter-Day German Religious-Patriotic Art, 1817) denounced the German art of the past forty years both for its excessive dependence on the Middle Ages and for its intensive reliance on imitation.[2]

Imitation was indeed carried to enormous lengths, as in the *Knight Errant* (1817), on a gold ground, by Carl Philipp Fohr, or in Franz Pforr's *St George and the Dragon*, or in Friedrich Overbeck's posthumous portrait of his friend in the garb of a medieval burgher. This last was probably not very far from literal truth, for the artists did sometimes dress in 'Old German' style as a gesture of defiance to the oppressive French influence that made itself felt in fashion as elsewhere.

One valuable, though often exaggerated, concern of the *Lukasbrüder* was with sensibility. This was religious in its motivation, in conscious reaction against the Enlightenment, and led to a number of conversions to the Catholic Church. With it went a keen interest in the Articles of Faith – and, even more, in the stories and legends of the saints.[3] For Peter von Cornelius, for example, the quest for profounder sensibility, and for new artistic themes derived from time-honoured traditions, marked a decisive turning-point in his artistic career. To put his ideas into practice, all he needed was the support of such a patron as Crown Prince Ludwig of Bavaria, for whose Christian and patriotic purposes Cornelius revived the art of fresco painting.

Following Cornelius, in 1833 Johann Philipp Veit painted an extensive cycle of frescoes for the Städelschule in Frankfurt am Main. His principal thematic focus, in a programme that also embraced Greek mythology, lay in a vast triptych with figures of Germania and Italia on the wing panels and a central painting on the theme of *The Introduction of the Arts to Germany by Christianity*,[4] which included figures personifying Religion, the Conversion of the Teutons, Poetry, Music and Chivalry. The artist, a Catholic convert (and stepson to Friedrich Schlegel), here displayed the Romantic agenda for the arts in all its facets: the awareness of the nation's history and of its Teutonic origins; the history and legends of Christianity, transformed into myth; and the translation of all this into music and poetry. The figures of Italia and Germania stand for the friendship between two nations that had been simultaneously threatened by Napoleon and had conceived the same ideals of liberty. To the Nazarenes, Italy was a new fatherland, the goal of all their dreams of Art, Nature and Poetry. Together, the ideal *form* of the Italian Renaissance and the *content* of the German Middle Ages were to provide the models for a renewal of art. In this historical *mélange*, Greek classicism was not rejected but continued to be recognized as a model.

It was in Rome, from 1813 onwards, that Cornelius drew his illustrations for the *Nibelungenlied*; possibly intended as sketches for a future fresco, they were published only in 1821. This medieval poem (rediscovered in 1755) first came to the attention of the *Lukasbrüder* in 1811–12, when the physician Christian Schlosser, brother to the Romantic art patron Councillor Schlosser, gave readings of it in Rome. The *Nibelungenlied* was well on the way to acquiring its status as the ultimate in folk (or rather *Volk*) poetry, and as an ideal myth of 'the unity, the loyalty and the mission of the German people'.[5] It was ranked with the poems of Homer, and folk poetry as a whole was believed to contain a system of German mythology. One result of this was Jakob Grimm's *Deutsche Mythologie* of 1835,[6] an encyclopedic compilation of mythological concepts and characters. Alongside the ancient Germanic gods, it features such supernatural beings as dwarfs, giants, witches, Death and the Devil. As the first of many dictionaries of superstitions and folklore, Grimm's *Deutsche Mythologie* casts light on the origins of the Romantic enthusiasm for fairytales.

Cornelius's designs and drawings for the *Nibelungenlied* and his illustrations for Goethe's *Faust* (etched by Ruscheweyh and Thaeter and published in 1816) are telling examples of the connection between patriotic élan, medieval enthusiasm and poetry. The artist himself regarded the *Faust* frontispiece (c. 1817), 'in the style of a Dürer prayerbook', as one of his best works.[7] Cornelius was one of many artists for whom Dürer was the supreme exemplar of an autonomous German art – the ideal that was now to be attained once more.

This objective had already been formulated in the writings of Wilhelm Heinrich Wackenroder: 'Blessed be thy golden age, Nuremberg! – the only time when Germany could claim to have a fatherlandish art of its own.'[8] In his commemorative tribute to Dürer, Wackenroder thus touched on two central themes of the public response to German art in the nineteenth century: the 'golden age' of Nuremberg, and the idea of 'fatherlandish' art. At the end of the sixteenth century, the imperial free city of Nuremberg was at the peak of its economic power and in the thick of passionate religious conflicts that threatened to lead it into defiance of the (Catholic) faith of the Empire and consequent loss of the Emperor's protection. In all this it revealed itself as

something of an ideal city state, with proud, wealthy councillors, powerful guilds and a comparatively well-educated, free citizenry. In late eighteenth-century Germany – still afflicted with feudalism and a patchwork of surviving petty states, threatened by revolution and enmeshed in a succession of wars that lasted from 1789 to 1815 – this must have seemed like a fairytale of civic freedom. Once the Holy Roman Empire of the German Nation had been abolished (in 1806), it became possible to idealize the vanished – and notoriously superannuated – imperial constitution for the sake of its supposed original merits.

Although the ideas of the French Revolution had their votaries in the German states, and many had hero-worshipped Napoleon himself, the whole period was characterized by a succession of wars against France, waged by a shifting assortment of allies. Few works by Romantic artists relate directly to the political events of the day. One of the exceptions, *The Holy Alliance* (1815, cat. 86), by Heinrich Olivier – who, like his brother Friedrich, had fought in the Wars of Liberation – refers to the alliance of the great European powers that sealed Napoleon's fate at the Battle of Waterloo in 1815. The central figure is Emperor Francis I, flanked by Czar Alexander I of Russia and King Frederick William III of Prussia. They are standing in what is meant to be a Gothic chapel, an unambiguously national architectural form, symbolic of the edifice of Empire beneath whose coat of arms the allies meet. As laid down in the programme of the *Lukasbrüder*, this is the representation of an ideal conjunction of Nation and Religion in Art. Ferdinand Olivier's *Count Habsburg and the Priest*, in Berlin, is equally backward-looking and equally charged with ideology.

The notions of Liberty, Equality and Fraternity had taken root in the minds of the younger generation, and they wanted to fight for them. Full of martial enthusiasm, they enlisted in the new nationalist armies and went off to the war, which Bettina von Arnim had praised as the 'crown of music, which crowns all other arts'.[9]

'Join with us, valiant youth of the oppressed land of Saxony! Join with us, we who are stalwart men of the stalwart people! Prussia's Eagles and Russia's Bears fight at our side, and God helps us to victory. In our ranks there is no distinction of birth, degree, country: we are all free men!'[10] The man who uttered this fiery call to arms did not long survive it: he was the painter Theodor Körner, who in 1813 joined with Veit, Friedrich Olivier and Georg Friedrich Kersting as enthusiastic recruits to the Lützow Volunteer Regiment. Kersting has left us an artistic record of their exploits in his painting of his fallen comrades *Körner, Friesen and Hartmann on Outpost Duty* (1815, colour plate, p. 248), as well as numerous studies and also self-portraits in uniform.

Caspar David Friedrich found a more subtle expression for his patriotic convictions in such paintings as *Tumulus by the Sea* (1806–07), *Tomb of Ancient Heroes* (1812, Hamburger Kunsthalle) and *Arminius' Grave* (1813) – and also more directly in the *Chasseur in the Forest* (1814) and *Hutten's Grave* (1824, Weimar). These paintings paralleled the idea of erecting monuments to the Unknown Soldier which originated in France and did not actually reach German-speaking countries until the consecration of the Alte Wache in Berlin in 1816.

Patriotism set the resurgent romances of chivalry in a new light. Götz von Berlichingen appeared as a brave fighter for a just cause, and his concepts of virtue and honour inspired the young, who enlisted as volunteers, rejected the effete manners of court life and hailed a rustic form of domesticity. The revival of religious feeling was another aspect of this same idealized image of an archetypal, indigenous humanity, rooted in the soil of Germany and uncorrupted by the temptations and comforts of urban life.

This view of the Middle Ages, not an easy one for us to understand today, was largely the result of inadequate historical knowledge. Even the name given to the medieval period, 'Gothic', was still believed to indicate that its artefacts originated among the Goths. Only in the mid-eighteenth century had Antonio Muratori, in Italy begun to examine the sources. The historical consciousness of the age was still utterly confused: the image of the 'golden age' of Nuremberg was an amalgam of the city's Gothic townscape with the early Renaissance period in which Dürer lived. The rediscovery of the Middle Ages, both in literature and in art, brought with it the acknowledgement of the Gothic as a national style of architecture in its own right, and as a worthy aesthetic achievement that had been spurned by the Enlightenment – partly, no doubt, because of its Christian content – as repulsively ugly.

'Under the rubric of *Gothic*,' wrote Goethe, 'I assembled, like an article in a dictionary, all the synonymous misconceptions that had ever passed through my head: imprecision, inferiority, unnaturalness, heterogeneity, patchwork, excess. No wiser than a nation that calls the entire world outside its borders barbarian, I called everything Gothic that failed to fit into my system, from the ornate and gaudily coloured figures and images that adorn the houses of our aspiring bourgeoisie to the first remnants of Old German architecture – concerning which, on the pretext of a few outlandish curlicues, I joined in the general chorus: "Entirely swamped in ornament!" And so I shuddered as I passed, as at the sight of a misshapen, bristling monster.'[11]

Nevertheless, Goethe did not permit himself to be deterred from visiting Strasbourg cathedral; and the sight of it so firmly convinced him of the value of Gothic architecture that he devoted an enthusiastic hymn of praise to its legendary architect, Erwin von Steinbach. This grew into a work of controversy, a riposte to Abbé Marie-Antoine Laugier, who had praised the classical ideal in his *Essais sur l'architecture* in 1753.[12] It was no coincidence that the medieval university towns, like Strasbourg and Heidelberg, were the main objects of Romantic yearning: it was there that the idea of nationhood was represented by the student fraternities, who looked to the Middle Ages for the unity that they longed for – and sought to restore – in the present. Goethe's thinking anticipated these efforts. His enthusiastic essay turned into a manifesto of national awareness, and in 1773 he gave the piece to Johann Gottfried Herder for publication in the latter's compilation volume *Von deutscher Art und Kunst* (On German Character and Art).

Goethe himself, in later life, did not like to be reminded of the excesses of his youth; and in *Dichtung und Wahrheit* (1813), with the benefit of hindsight, he delivered the following verdict on his youthful discovery of the German character of a supposedly barbaric form of art:

'Since I found this building, founded on ancient German soil and in a truly German age, to be so highly evolved; and since the Master's name on his modest tombstone was also fatherlandish by sound and origin, the merit of the work emboldened me to change the hitherto ill-famed designation of 'Gothic style of building', and to justify it as the 'German Architecture' of our own nation; nor did I fail to give vent to my patriotic sentiments, first verbally and then in a little essay dedicated to the Divine Master Erwin von Steinbach.'[13]

By 1813, Goethe (together with Wackenroder, Friedrich Wilhelm Schelling, Friedrich Schlegel, Clemens Brentano and Joseph Görres) was supporting the brothers Melchior and Sulpiz Boisserée in their campaign to complete the unfinished Cologne cathedral; some of the original drawings for the west front had been found in 1814, and Görres had been the first to publish a manifesto. A leading figure in the campaign was Crown Prince Ludwig of Bavaria, whose sympathies were covertly anti-French, and who was particularly interested in an assertion of German national identity after the victorious Battle of Leipzig. When, in 1840, the markedly patriotic and anti-French Frederick William IV mounted the Prussian throne,[14] Cologne cathedral finally became an undertaking of national importance. The success of this backward-looking enterprise established the whole principle of the conservation of ancient monuments.

Architects began to take an interest in restoration and to study the Gothic cathedrals. Karl Friedrich Schinkel was among the first to paint the vision of Cologne cathedral complete, towering above everything else in the city. At the same time he was working on the planning of a 'national cathedral' for Berlin; never realized, this possibly influenced his paintings. His paintings *Gothic Cathedral by the Waterside* (1813) and *Medieval City by a River* (painted in 1815 as a pendant to *Greek City by the Sea*) show almost mystic, diaphanous monuments that loom like filigree apparitions above the urban skyline. The figures that make up the staffage emphasize the exaggeration of scale: in one case, an emperor walks in procession with his knights to the cathedral, while a rainbow hangs in the sky; in the other, the figures are working people who barely notice the apparition. To Schinkel, Gothic was an architectural vision; one which, as in the *Gothic Cathedral by the Water* (colour plate, p. 224), he pursued to a conclusion in conjunction with other and highly un-Gothic, 'Schinkelian' architectural notions that he was later to take up at Babelsberg.

The Gothic cathedral as a vision, divorced from the medieval townscape and seen purely as a phenomenal image of Christianity, is a frequent subject in the art of Friedrich. Examples include the *Cross in the Mountains*

Fig.1 Caspar David Friedrich, *Visionary Cathedral* c.1818, Schäfer Collection, Schweinfurt

(*c.* 1812, Kunstmuseum, Düsseldorf), the *Winter Landscapes* (1811, Dortmund and London, colour plate, p. 220), and most especially the *Vision of the Christian Church* (*c.* 1820) and the *Visionary Cathedral* (*c.* 1818, fig. 1),[15] which is hailed by a choir of angels as it looms above the clouds. When he showed a Gothic building in its real surroundings, Friedrich always made it a ruin – even where, as in the case of Meissen cathedral, the church in question was still intact. The effort of imagination necessary to visualize the building complete generated a more credible image of Christian truth than an intact cathedral would have done.

Meanwhile, the people of Cologne, and with them the Romantic poets and scholars, went on dreaming of the completion of Cologne cathedral. For the last birthday he ever celebrated, in 1861, Ernst F. Zwirner, architect to the cathedral, received from his friend and pupil Vincenz Statz a watercolour entitled *Vision of the Completed Towers of Cologne Cathedral*, with the subtitle *And It Will Be Completed*.[16] It shows an architect in medieval garb, in a cave, with the towers of the cathedral looming before him as phantoms. The drawing not only refers to architectural issues, such as the intended symmetry of the towers, or the acceptance of existing changes to the plan, but also plays with fairytale motifs. Seen against his vast building, the architect looks like a crooked dwarf – like one of those hard-working hobgoblins who finish the work of righteous human beings on earth, if only the latter will have faith. The motto of the drawing also seems to be an allusion to this.

No Romantic painter failed to discover at least one Gothic ruin that fascinated him with its atmospheric mood and its spiritual message. But none depicted the interior of a cathedral so impressively as Carl Blechen in his *Ruined Gothic Church* (1826) in Dresden. Other illustrators had invariably emphasized the overwhelming height of Gothic towers and other buildings. In Blechen's version the ruinous condition of the structure, with its attendant intimations of destruction, becomes evident only in the upper right-hand corner of the image. There is no paving, and grass grows in the interior, splitting the floor into cracks that have filled with water. The building becomes a vegetable growth in itself: the piers seem not only to grow upward but to have acquired roots of their own, gnarled and sturdy enough to bear a cathedral. A youthful pilgrim sleeps in the foreground, adding the motif of sylvan isolation that became one of the most popular Romantic themes.[17]

Moritz von Schwind, in an initial sketch of 1822, has Erwin von Steinbach, in a dream, floating through a cathedral interior full of plant forms.[18] This is a direct reference to Goethe's outburst of enthusiasm, with its metamorphic metaphors that Blechen would also have known:

'So be it! Did not the Spirit come to our aid, which gave this injunction to Erwin von Steinbach: multiply the vast wall that you are to carry up towards Heaven, that it may rise like a lofty, spreading Tree of God, with its thousand branches, its millions of twigs and its leaves like the sand of the sea, proclaiming across the surrounding landscape the glory of the Lord its Master.'[19]

The natural philosophers built plant analogies of this kind into a system of the connection between nature and art. Thus, Friedrich Schlegel gives us a mystic-hymnic comparison of a Gothic cathedral with natural forms. By way of minerals, he makes the leap from the stone used in art to the stone formed in nature, to the plant, and to the spiritual experience of infinity:

'From a distance, with all its countless towers and turrets, the whole looks not unlike a forest; but when one steps somewhat closer, the whole organism seems more like a monstrous crystallization. In a word, these miraculous works of art, in their organic infinity and inexhaustible profusion of form, resemble nothing so much as the works of nature itself. The impression, at least, is the same.'[20]

In this presentation of the Gothic, it is the 'impression' that counts. The spiritual uplift conveyed, and the mystical religious experience, count for more than the 'subject matter' that so enchanted Romantic poets, painters and philosophers in the *Nibelungenlied*. No tales need be told. The images of the cathedrals and of their parts, their ruins or their interiors stand for the longing for a union with nature and religion. The idealized perception of the Middle Ages that sprang from patriotism and the new ideal of ethnic identity and solidarity ultimately gave rise to magical, unreal images that served a mystical enthusiasm.

In the history of Romantic art Goethe is a pivotal figure – even though the stubbornly individualistic Prince of Poets was at pains to dissociate himself from all fanciful enthusiasm and from the sentimental excesses of Catholic feeling, and made a determined effort to hold art in check through the annual Weimar prize competitions that he inaugurated in 1799. He felt it to be his duty to resist the 'sentimental, theatrical way; naturalism, allegory, patriotism', as well as all religiosity and all undue emphasis on the moral as against the sensory;[21] and to this end he set the competitors strictly defined subjects from Homer, and pronounced Greek classicism to be the only valid exemplar.

However, he also tolerated and even praised thematic references to the Middle Ages; just as his own first sight of Strasbourg cathedral had inspired him to begin work on *Faust*, he gave his approval when artists illustrated that work in a decidedly 'Old German' vein. He complimented the youthful Cornelius on his exemplary illustrations, encouraged him to carry on in the same vein, and accepted the dedication of the published edition of *Faust* prints. All the same, he abominated patriotic thinking and sought to set 'universal humanity' in its place.[22]

The path from this to the Youth Uprising of 1832 – with its rally where twenty or thirty thousand people assembled in the castle ruins at Hambach in the cause of their national ideal – was chronologically brief but conceptually circuitous in the extreme.[23] In the intervening time, Romanticism made a new historical start. Marked by the experiences of the French Revolution, unsettled by European wars and reallocations of territory, the Romantic agenda became one of fervid nationalism without a concrete programme.

Among the first to hail the Middle Ages as a precedent for a lively and varied society beneath the unifying rule of an Emperor was Görres. A leading critic of the Prussian Restoration – who was driven into temporary exile in France as a 'Revolutionary' – Görres nevertheless lived in horror of a German Revolution:

'A German Revolution would inevitably end with the expulsion of all the ruling dynasties, the shattering of all ecclesiastical forms, the extirpation of the nobility, and the introduction of a republican constitution; then, since every revolutionary nation necessarily becomes a nation of conquerors, as soon as it had found its fortunate Wallenstein it would cross its frontiers and overthrow the whole rotten edifice of European states, as far as the borders of Asia; but it would pay for all these glories, as the Netherlands once did, with the blood of many millions, with the destruction of half of the rising generation, with the shattering of the whole prosperity of Germany, and with the laying waste of all its provinces by a long and wearisome war – and ultimately it would gain not much more than is now attainable at far less cost.'[24]

In the twentieth century, this vision was to come true.

Brigitte Buberl

Translated from the German by David Britt

1 Before the outbreak of the Wars of Liberation, the home of patriotism was among the bourgeoisie; and it was in bourgeois clubs and associations that nationalism evolved as a means to the acquisition of collective identity. See Bernhard Giesen and Kay Junge, 'Vom Patriotismus zum Nationalismus: Zur Evolution der "Deutschen Kulturnation"', in Bernhard Giesen, ed., *Nationale und kulturelle Identität: Studien zur Entwicklung des kollektiven Bewußtseins in der Neuzeit* (Frankfurt am Main, 1991), 255–303.

2 Werner Busch, ed., *Kunsttheorie und Kunstgeschichte des 19. Jahrhunderts in Deutschland, I. Kunsttheorie und Malerei, Texte und Dokumente*, vol. 1 (Stuttgart, 1982), 127–35 (text no. 21).

3 Frank Büttner, 'Subjektives Gefühl, künstlerisches Ideal und christliche Wahrheit: Das religiöse Bild im frühen Werk von Peter Cornelius', *Wallraf-Richartz-Jahrbuch* 52 (1991), 237–61, especially 239.

4 Willi Geismeier, *Die Malerei der deutschen Romantik* (Dresden, 1984), 217.

5 Sibylle Ohly, *Literaturgeschichte und politische Reaktion im 19. Jahrhundert:*

August Friedrich Christian Vilmars 'Geschichte der deutschen National Literatur' (1845) (Göppingen, 1982), 114–36.

6 *Deutsche Mythologie* appeared in the middle of the prolific career of Jacob Grimm, the founder of German philology and author of *Deutsche Sagen*, 2 vols. (1816–18), *Deutsche Reichsaltertümer* (1828), *Deutsche Grammatik* (1818–37), and *Geschichte der deutschen Sprache*, 2 vols. (1848). But *Deutsche Mythologie* is still not a truly scientific examination of myth. The first attempts at such studies were made by scholars in the Heidelberg Romantic circle; and works such as Friedrich Schlegel's *Über die Sprache und Weisheit der Inder* (1808) and Joseph Görres's *Mythengeschichte der asiatischen Welt* (1800) may have prompted Grimm to make his collection. The scholars Karl Otfried Müller (*Prolegomena zu einer wissenschaftlichen Mythologie*, 1825) and Philipp Buttmann (*Mythologus*, 1828) suggested that Greek mythology had a popular origin; and this inspired investigations into Teutonic or German equivalents. See Jacob Grimm, *Deutsche Mythologie* (Göttingen, 1835; reprint, with introduction by L. Kretzenbacher, 3 vols., Graz, 1968).

7 Andreas Blume, exh. cat. *Goethezeit und Romantik: Einhundert Meisterzeichnungen aus einer Privatsammlung* (Hanover, 1990), no. 51.

8 Wilhelm Heinrich Wackenroder, 'Ehrengedächtnis unseres ehrwürdigen Ahnherrn Albrecht Dürers, von einem kunstliebenden Klosterbruder', in Busch (as note 2), vol. 1, 47.

9 Dieter Strauss, *Deutsche Romantik: Geschichte einer Epoche* (Gütersloh, 1986), s.v. 'Kriege', 121–22.

10 Hannelore Gärtner, *Georg Friedrich Kersting* (Leipzig, 1988), 102.

11 Johann Wolfgang von Goethe, *Von deutscher Baukunst* (1773) (Camburg/Saale, 1945), 7.

12 Reinhard Liess, *Goethe vor dem Straßburger Münster: Zum Wissenschaftsbild der Kunst* (Leipzig, 1985). Includes a reprint of the original version of *Von deutscher Baukunst, Divis Manibus Erwini a Steinbach* (1772).

13 Liess (as note 12), 14.

14 See Harold James, *Deutsche Identität 1770–1990*, trans. Wolfdieter Müller (Frankfurt am Main and New York, 1991), 29. James emphasizes the part played by France, and particularly by Paris, as a place of exile for German radicals, revolutionaries and dissidents – such as Karl Marx, who was in Paris in 1830, and Heinrich Heine.

15 Werner Hofmann, ed., *Caspar David Friedrich; Kunst um 1800* (Munich, 1974), 62, fig. 215.

16 Exh. cat. *Meisterzeichnungen von Leonardo bis zu Rodin. Wallraf-Richartz-Museum Köln: Auswahl von Miniaturen, Handzeichnungen und Aquarellen aus der Graphischen Sammlung* (Cologne, 1986), 210, no. 98.

17 Brigitte Buberl, exh. cat. *Erlkönig und Alpenbraut: Dichtung, Märchen und Sage in Bildern der Schack-Galerie, Bayerische Staatsgemäldesammlungen* (Munich, 1989), 73ff.

18 Buberl (as note 17), 75, no. 26.

19 Liess (as note 12), 11.

20 Friedrich Schlegel, *Briefe auf einer Reise durch die Niederlande, Rheingegenden, die Schweiz und einen Teil von Frankreich* (1804–05), quoted from Regine Prange, 'Die kristalline Gotik: Friedrich Schlegel und Caspar David Friedrich', in Prange, *Das Kristalline als Kunstsymbol. Bruno Taut und Paul Klee: Zur Reflexion des Abstrakten in der Kunst und Kunsttheorie der Moderne* (Hildesheim, Zürich and New York, 1991), 9. See also Prange's essay in this volume.

21 Johann Wolfgang von Goethe, *Schriften zur Kunst*, part 1, quoted from Carla Schulz-Hoffmann, *Studien zur Rezeption der deutschen romantischen Malerei in Kunstliteratur und Kunstgeschichte* (Munich, 1974), 30.

22 'Perhaps the conviction will soon gain ground that there is no such thing as patriotic art or science. Both, like all good things, belong to the whole world, and can be promoted only through the general free interaction of all those alive at any one time, with constant reference to what survives and is known of the past.' Johann Wolfgang von Goethe, 'Flüchtige Übersicht über die Kunst in Deutschland, 1800', quoted from Werner Busch and Wolfgang Beyrodt, eds., *Kunsttheorie und Kunstgeschichte des 19. Jahrhunderts in Deutschland, I: Kunsttheorie und Malerei, Kunstwissenschaft* (Stuttgart, 1982), 92.

23 James (as note 14), 67.

24 Joseph Görres, *Teutschland und die Revolution* (1819), quoted from Klaus Peter, ed., *Die politische Romantik in Deutschland: Eine Textsammlung* (Stuttgart, 1985), 12–13 (introduction), 203–74 (text in full).

Tales into Pictures

The Fairytale King's Homecoming is a large drawing by Ferdinand Olivier, in the Kupferstichkabinett in Dresden.[1] Stiffly dignified, the aged, bearded King rides across a simple bridge. In the background are the stout towers and steep-gabled houses of a city built on a rock. A little dog enthusiastically welcomes the King's horse, but the townsfolk seem to know nothing of his impending arrival. The solitary figure of the King (a retinue is merely hinted at), the dialogue between the animals, the tranquil image of the city and its surrounding trees, rocks and waters: all form part of the Romantic vocabulary of an artistic imagination that loved to immerse itself in the past. The motif of the King's return derives from no known fairy tale, and yet it could occur in any. The drawing itself has been squared up, presumably for a painting. Its date coincides with Olivier's return to Vienna from Rome, when he found himself at the centre of a circle of Protestant Romantics who aimed – like their Catholic counterparts, the *Lukasbrüder* or Nazarenes – to revive art in a national, German vein. *The Fairytale King's Homecoming* was Olivier's ticket of admission to this group.

It is surprising to find so generalized a theme considered worthy of a painting in its own right, in the absence of a dramatic narrative or a moral message, and without any definable content or context. The viewer is expected to devise a story – evidently a fairytale – for himself or herself; and this casts a veil of mystery, magic and wonder over the scene. The viewer is being weaned away from the desire to see either the reproduction of nature or the Classical and academic ideal.

This drawing is a manifesto of a central concern of Romantic and especially Late Romantic art: the illustration and invention of fairytales. It was a trend that culminated in the work of Moritz von Schwind, a painter strongly influenced by Olivier, to whose Viennese circle he belonged. *Sir Kurt's Ride to His Wedding*,[2] painted by Schwind between 1835 and 1839, looks like a sequel to Olivier's scene. We now seem to have arrived within the fairytale city. However, fanciful though it is, this subject is not the artist's own invention: the painting illustrates Goethe's ballad *Ritter Kurts Brautfahrt* (1804). By the time Schwind painted it, fairytale themes were so much second nature to him that he did not keep strictly to the letter of Goethe's text but – as in medieval art – combined several episodes into a single image. The principal action takes place in the left-hand half of the painting. Pausing at the fair to buy finery for his bride, Sir Kurt is vigorously assailed by his creditors. The bride, who approaches on the arm of her portly father swoons away for sheer shame. A throng of retainers, children, old people and numerous pretty girls arranges itself around a fountain.

This important early work by Schwind contains much warm humour and lively characterization; among the figures are portraits of his friends. The theme of the confrontation between debtor and creditors, described by Schwind himself as the 'profound subject' of the work, emerges as a colourful fairground gallery of the most varied popular types. Despite the ostensible seriousness of his themes, Schwind's literary subjects always appeal to a contemporary audience through a degree of affectionate mockery. The friends portrayed in *Sir Kurt* become participants in the action or witnesses to it.

Similar humorous and often caustic touches, as well as contemporary allusions, are to be found in the work of Romantic writers from Johann Karl August Musäus and Heinrich von Kleist to Clemens Brentano. So close is the alliance between Romantic painting, literature and music that what applies to one tends to apply to all three. One of the most important maxims of Romantic art must be the saying of its greatest representative and – at times – its severest critic, Johann Wolfgang von Goethe: 'True art can spring only from the most intimate connection between Earnest and Play.'[3] To illustrate this, Goethe devised a playful-looking schematic formulation that reads a little like a magic spell (see p. 21)

Play and Earnest are thus elevated into leitmotifs of artistic creation. Only when they are held in equilibrium can there be a 'maturing into the general' that elevates them into a specific Style. If one ever outweighs the other, the work becomes too superficial, too minute, or too sketchy. These were entirely new criteria of thinking about art in which not only Play but Imagination came into its own.

The Enlightenment, the rise of rationalism and the political shifts and upheavals of the Napoleonic and post-Napoleonic period – which left behind them an array of more efficient administrative and educational institutions – were more than enough to elicit a powerful backlash; and this was true in art above all. Artists looked to archetypal origins – *das Ursprüngliche* – to find scope for the imagination and liberation from academic constraints. They seized on childhood as a time in which Logic and Imagination, Play and Earnest were still inseparable. There, they believed, the archetypes of human thought and poetic creation were to be found; in the naivety of childhood, primal images must have the same ready familiarity that they otherwise possess only in dreams.[4] Nor does childhood, in this context, refer only to biological childhood. It also applies to the childhood of the human race itself: 'Myth (as distinct from historical legend) can benefit poetry only if it is living myth: that is to say, if it has originated as myth – as the involuntary poetry through which childlike humankind seeks to humanize nature – and if it remains current in popular belief.'[5]

This statement rests on a philosophy in which dreams derive from an animate nature whose meaning lies far beyond the comprehension of the waking mind and seems to be bound up with myth and with the archaic 'childhood' of humanity. Such, at least, is the interpretation offered by Gotthilf Heinrich Schubert in his *Symbolik des Traumes* (Symbolism of Dreams, 1814). In writing of the 'language of dreams', Schubert may have been summarizing familiar ideas taken from Johann Gottfried Herder and Friedrich Schlegel, but his influence must not be underestimated. Schubert was a member of the same circle as Caspar David Friedrich, and the influence of his sometimes eccentric notions of dream hieroglyphs seems to have extended beyond the writers and poets of his time.[6]

The strong Romantic partiality for the dark or 'nocturnal' aspect of the human psyche, and for sleep as the effect and origin of dream images, was later to influence the theories of Sigmund Freud who knew – to take only one example – Schwind's work well.[7] It was common knowledge that the imagination influenced the evolution of the soul. The painter and physician Carl Gustav Carus who published *Psyche: Zur Entwicklungsgeschichte der menschlichen Seele* ('Psyche: On the Evolution of the Human Soul') in 1846, was giving lectures on this topic as early as 1829–30.[8]

Dreaming and creativity were so closely allied for Romantic theorists that there was a revival of interest in those poets of the past who had drawn on elements of tradition, superstition and myth. Schubert invoked the 'language of dreams' as something common to all peoples and all times; and writers in general were keen to acquire a multilingual and multicultural education and to make foreign writers available in translation. The eighteenth century saw a revival of publishing interest in Torquato Tasso and Ludovico Ariosto; and James Macpherson's Ossianic writings were much read in the translation by a Viennese Jesuit, Michael Denis, which was published in 1768, eight years after the original, as *Die Gedichte Ossians, eines alten celtischen Dichters* ('The Poems of Ossian, an Ancient Celtic Poet'). Macpherson had presented his own conflation of scraps of traditional epic as a rediscovered Gaelic tradition.

Christoph Martin Wieland, poet and collector of sagas, used the vocabulary of painting to describe the fascination that Shakespeare exerted on contemporaries: 'He is almost unique in painting men, customs, passions from nature; he has the precious talent of beautifying nature without violating her proportions.'[9] In 1760–62 Wieland translated the complete works of Shakespeare. Later Friedrich Schiller translated *Macbeth*, and in the early years of the nineteenth century August Wilhelm Schlegel and Dorothea and Ludwig Tieck produced another translation of the complete works.

Interest in the Italian poets of the sixteenth and seventeenth centuries was strongest among poets, including Wieland, Goethe and Gotthold Ephraim Lessing. Goethe's copy of Tasso was the translation by Johann Friedrich Koppe, *Versuch einer poetischen Übersetzung des Tassoschen Heldengedichtes oder das befreite*

Jerusalem (1744).[10] Other sixteenth- and seventeenth-century poets who were much read included John Milton; there were translations of both *Paradise Lost* and *Paradise Regained*.

These examples should suffice to indicate the availability of the great poets in German versions. Exceptionally active and well-educated, the eighteenth-century reading public valued them for their affinity to the writers of antiquity whom Dante had been the first to bring back to life. He, too, was among the poets whose epic creations, full of strong emotions and colourful scenes, inspired late eighteenth-century writers and artists to produce interpretations of their own.

Seekers after ancient traditions no longer rested content with the literature of antiquity or with the early medieval epics, and there was a revival of folk poetry which began to be published in – allegedly – unretouched transcriptions. This began with the poets of the *Sturm und Drang* period who collected songs and legends under Herder's influence in the 1770s;[11] and they were followed by Wieland, Musäus, Gottfried August Bürger, Johann Jacob Bodmer and the painter Philipp Otto Runge. Two members of an older generation, the brothers Grimm, Jacob (1785–1863) and Wilhelm (1786–1859), pursued their own collection with even greater energy, organization and concern for detail; its publication in 1812 and 1815 inaugurated the scholarly study of the fairy tale.

The immediate precursor of the Grimms' collection was the song anthology *Des Knaben Wunderhorn* ('The Boy's Magic Horn'),[12] published in three volumes in Heidelberg in 1806. Ludwig Achim von Arnim and Clemens Brentano were the prime movers, supported by the Grimms – including a younger brother, the illustrator Ludwig Emil Grimm (1790–1883). The second-hand experience enshrined in these two vast collections – that is, the record of oral tradition – served to bring literature into closer contact with the people and its traditions, and provided the *Wunderhorn* songs with an archaic-seeming past. As is now known, they mostly stemmed from written sources such as broadsheets, manuscript collections and periodicals; even where genuine oral tradition was involved, it came from educated lips and not from the mythical old wives seen in Ludwig Grimm's illustrations. By casting an aura of mystery over the genesis of their folk-tale collection, viewed as the maintenance of an ancient tradition of wisdom, the brothers Grimm presented it as – in a very Enlightenment sense – an 'educative book'.[13]

In his essay on Strasbourg cathedral and in his history play *Götz von Berlichingen*, Goethe was a pioneer of the Romantic movement; but he subsequently became, for a time, the adversary of any contemporary art that violated the maxims of his Weimar school of painting. His own narrative, *Märchen* (Fairy Tale, 1795), reveals a deep interest in the nature and structure of this narrative form. It combines all the elements and character types of the fairy tale, and reveals it as a kaleidoscopic vision of a complex world of human growth and development, full of unaccountable happenings and steeped in the longing for the infinite and the wondrous. Goethe's attempt in this story to delineate the wonders of the world through geological, topographical, atmospheric and mental phenomena may seem incomprehensible to us today, but it represented a new and confident handling of the nature of the genre, well before the advent of the general Romantic enthusiasm for tales and legends.

No contemporary artist ever ventured to illustrate *Märchen*, and the only contemporary work remotely comparable with it is Brentano's tale *Gockel, Hinkel und Gakeleia*, with its intricately fantastic illustrations by the author himself. These were inspired by the drawings of Runge whom Brentano knew. Runge was one of the first of many painters who were fascinated by fairy tales and derived motifs from them. The resulting works were by no means always straightforward essays in fairy-tale illustration; and indeed the genres of tale, saga and legend constantly overlapped, both in literature and in painting. Modern literary tales – and with them the paintings of the Romantic artists – drew simultaneously on the happy-ever-after metaphysics of the fairy tale, the everyday marvels of the sagas, and the time and space of legend.

One drawing by Runge provides a typical instance of the alliance between fairytale themes and the image of the poet: this is *The Spring and the Poet* (1805, fig. 1). It contains elements that remain typical of much later imagery based on fairytale and legend: a strong, emotive, active male figure; a delicate woman with softly rounded forms and flowing movements; gravity-defying

Fig.1 Philipp Otto Runge, *The Spring and the Poet* 1805, Hamburger Kunsthalle

putti; an idyllic but also melancholy sylvan scene, with many varieties of plants and grasses. The action is in the foreground, where it takes place on a relatively shallow stage, with the forest behind like a backdrop. The contrast between the man and the woman, associated with his yearning for her and the moment of mutual discovery, is among the most important fairytale archetypes. Its starting-point – and one possible explanatory model – often lies in the dawning sexual maturity of the protagonists. Their consequent anxiety and fear evoke spirit entities for which personifications become required.[14] Runge's drawing presents the 'wondrous' in terms of a rich, delightful and fruitful life in the wilderness.

In the fairy-tale imagery of the Romantics true enchantment lies in the feminine principle. Goethe's Erlking (*Erlkönig*) is escorted by seductive nymphs; and wherever an individual male figure appears – such as the mountain spirit Rübezahl – his interest is always enhanced by some connection with the female sex. Dreaming boys, pensive prisoners and sleeping knights earn their place in painting by dreaming of ideals of love, whether heavenly or earthly.

Knights in armour stand for the virtues of valour, faith, fortitude and adroitness; they embody both the medieval ideal of courtly love and the guile of the heroes of antiquity. More than human in his gleaming armour, the knight positively offers himself as a projection of the wondrous. In a work by Asmus Jakob Carstens, he does

battle with the spirit of Loda (from Ossian); Karl Philipp Fohr shows him as St George fighting the dragon, and Julius Schnorr von Carolsfeld as Ruggiero in Ariosto's *Orlando furioso*, freeing Angelica. Wonder is always founded in nature, and particularly in human nature.[15] The prime actors in all this – as in the medieval mystery plays – are 'Knight, Death and Devil'. They are accompanied by Woman, in all imaginable postures and with a variety of functions, from the seductive witch to the abducted, pure-as-the-driven-snow princess. She corresponds precisely to a host of characters in the literature of the time: faithful, brave, a virgin, and honour-bound to find the right husband.

These painters' literary interpretations are curious blends of (in Goethe's phrase) 'Poetry and Truth'. Observations of nature, with detailed depictions of plant life, coexist with fairytale events shown as imaginary theatrical performances, staged by actors who look too human to exist in a world of imagination. By contrast, Schwind, Runge, Koch, Schnorr von Carolsfeld, Ludwig Richter and Edward von Steinle manipulate their figures like marionettes and thereby contrive to retain the supernatural quality of the action. Sir Kurt faces his tormentors against the backdrop of a fairytale village; Ruggiero sets Angelica free in a landscape with no depth at all, and his winged horse might just as well be a dummy on strings.

Ultimately, the best actor for a fairytale is a puppet. The art of fairytale illustration and interpretation is the art of make-believe, the art of apparent reality, possible only in the theatre – and more particularly in the puppet theatre. The smoother and more natural the performances, the more plausible and graceful the tale becomes. The figures devised for these works can best be likened, perhaps, to the complex and enigmatic figures in Brentano's *Gockel, Hinkel und Gakeleia*. The little heroine, Gakeleia, stoutly insists that her toy is not a doll or puppet but 'a pretty automaton'; the riddle is solved when it proves to be a puppet, manipulated by none other than a mouse princess.

The figures in Romantic fairytale paintings are full of similar ambiguities; for when the artist paints them he is fully aware that he is inventing. They must not be drawn from nature; and in most cases they appear as idealized and invented figures, moving in obedience to aesthetic criteria alone. Schwind, in particular, worked away at the construction and composition of his figures until they froze into ornamental embodiments of a specifically Romantic moral-sensual mood. Making a drawing of his own painting *Sir Kurt's Ride to His Wedding* alone took him more than three months.[16] Other artists, too – Olivier, Schnorr von Carolsfeld and Peter von Cornelius among them – aimed at an extremely precise, premeditated line that would endow their figures and compositions with exceptional elegance and lightness. They were aware that too much deliberation might impair the forms, but it was their aim to attain a higher form of grace.

Kleist's reflections in his essay 'Über das Marionettentheater' ('On the Puppet Theatre', 1810) read like a declaration of Romantic doctrine: 'After awareness has – as it were – travelled through all infinity, grace returns; so that grace is at its most perfect in the human physique whose consciousness is either nil or infinite: that is, in a jointed manikin or in a God.'[17]

By contrast, the drawings and sketches for paintings of the 'painter-poets'[18] have an attractive freedom of line and design. The cramped look of the form in the final paintings is part of the method and reveals the artists' deliberate intention of reducing the image to two dimensions. The negation of spatial depth and volume and the liking for juxtapositions of primary colours – whether or not as a quotation from medieval art – led these artists to make the figures in their paintings look like ornaments.

A classic instance is Steinle's lithograph *Storyteller* (1841): here, in a clear, elegantly linear drawing, he shows an old woman in idealized garments, telling tales to a group of princely looking children. The arrangement of the children, the way their bodies nestle together, and their linear arrangement in two dimensions, combine with the drapery folds to create a two-dimensional composition with no real depth at all. The art of storytelling has its own visual counterpart in the tendrils of an arabesque, rooted in thin air, with the characters in the tale – dragon, knight, princess and sleepwalking boy – enmeshed in its foliage. The association between the ornamental form of the figures and the figurative ornament of the arabesque harmonizes with the subject of the image – the telling of a Christian fairy tale – and lends the print a sense of wonder.

The structural principle of the arabesque, its combination of disparate elements in varying combinations, not only holds good for writers such as Brentano but it also, and especially, serves as a compositional principle in the illustrations of such artists as Steinle, Eugen Napoleon Neureuther or Ludwig Emil Grimm. The arabesque is the form most closely allied to the imagination, and it was already used in this way in the Renaissance. With its combination of floral and personified elements, it establishes an ideal compromise between writing and image, and can therefore be used in areas traditionally regarded as marginal to art: literally marginal, in the drawings by Lucas Cranach and Albrecht Dürer in the borders of the *Prayerbook of Emperor Maximilian I*, published as lithographs by Johann Nepomuk Strixner in 1808 (cat. 91). Strixner proved the independent validity of the arabesque by publishing it separately from the text. On Goethe's recommendation and at the instance of Cornelius, Neureuther imitated these lithographs in his *Marginal Illustrations to Goethe's Ballads and Romances* (1829–30, cat. 85)). The colouring of the individual prints, each printed in a single hue, shows Neureuther's striving for the subtlest tonal values. The viewer is compelled to 'read' the illustrations as attentively as the poems.

The Romantic illustration of folk and fairytales was very much more than simple book-illustration. Artists selected their motifs with the greatest care. Like the poets, they too were on the track of the archetypes of human desires, and they used the available literary material as a means to that end. Very much in tune with their time – and in some respects ahead of it – they delved into the dreams and longings of the human soul in quest of a lost childhood in which all humanity, and also the human individual, seemed to have known more than in the present. However, these Romantics were so highly educated, at least in musical and literary matters, that any desire for the naïveté of childhood was a highly perverse one – in Brentano's phrase, a false desire – that never opened any doors into a lost paradise.[19] In word and image, the quest for naturalness and for archetypal origins resulted in graceful and exquisite artifice.

Brigitte Buberl

Translated from the German by David Britt

1 Ill. in Marianne Bernhard, ed., *Carl Blechen (1798–1840) bis Friedrich Olivier (1791–1859)*, vol. 2 of Bernhard, *Deutsche Romantik: Handzeichnungen* (Munich, 1973), 1003.

2 R. Theilmann and Edith Ammann, cat. *Die deutschen Zeichnungen des 19. Jahrhunderts* (Karlsruhe: Staatliche Kunsthalle Karlsruhe, Kupferstichkabinett, 1978), 602 (no. 3956), 84 (fig., drawn copy of painting for engraving); 578 (no. 3859), 81 (fig., preparatory drawing for the painting). An oil study of the whole composition is in the Staatliche Museen Preußischer Kulturbesitz, Nationalgalerie, Berlin, inv. no. NG 1412, oil on copper, 23 × 24 cm. The painting itself, executed between 1835 and 1839, was destroyed in the fire at the Glaspalast in Munich in 1931.

3 See Chr. Lenz, 'Goethe und die Nazarener', in exh. cat. *Die Nazarener* (Frankfurt, 1977), 306 n. 42.

4 The exemplary representative of the ideal of childhood, and of the *topos* of the poet as child, is Clemens Brentano, in whose work the felicity of childhood is a constantly recurring topic. For further discussion of Brentano's attitude to the dream and to dreaming in relation to poetic composition, see Gerhard Schaub, *Le Génie enfant: Die Kategorie des Kindlichen bei Clemens Brentano* (Berlin and New York, 1973), 109ff.

5 Friedrich Schlegel, 'Goethes Hermann und Dorothea', in *Taschenbuch für 1798* (Berlin, 1798), 128.

6 In his *Symbolik des Traumes* (1814), Gotthilf Heinrich Schubert described the language of symbolism as a product of Nature and sought to elucidate it: Alina Dobrezecki, *Die Bedeutung des Traumes für Caspar David Friedrich: Eine Untersuchung zu den Ideen der Frühromantik*, Beiträge zur deutschen Philologie, no. 55 (Giessen, 1982). Gotthilf Heinrich Schubert, *Symbolik des Traumes* (1814; reprint, with postface by Gerhard Sander, Heidelberg, 1968), iii ff.

7 Alexander Grinstein, 'A Psychoanalytic Study of Schwind's Dream of a Prisoner', *American Imago* 8, no. 1 (March, 1951): 3–29.

8 Carl Gustav Carus, *Psyche*, abridged and ed. Ludwig Klages (Jena, 1926); Carl Gustav Carus, *Vorlesungen über Psychologie 1829–30* (Darmstadt, 1958). The work of imagination was acknowledged, at precisely this time, by a projected – though not fully implemented – reform of the teaching of drawing in schools: Wolfgang Kemp, '. . . einen wahrhaft bildenden Zeichenunterricht überall einzuführen': *Zeichnen und Zeichenunterricht der Laien 1500–1870* (Frankfurt am Main, 1979), 149ff.

9 Christoph Martin Wieland, *Ausgewählte Briefe*, quoted from Leo Balet and E. Gerhard, *Die Verbürgerlichung der deutschen Kunst, Literatur und Musik im 19. Jahrhundert*, ed. Gert Mattenklott (Frankfurt am Main, 1979), 455.

10 Torquato Tasso, *Werke und Briefe*, ed. and trans. Emil Staiger (Munich, 1978), 13. Wilhelm Heinse's prose translation, *Das Befreite Jerusalem von Torquato Tasso* (1782), was superseded only in 1802 by the first complete and linguistically accurate – albeit wilful – translation, that of Dietrich Gries; Karl Streckfuss's correct but dry rendering dates from 1835.

11 Manfred Grätz, *Das Märchen in der deutschen Aufklärung; Vom Feenmärchen zum Volksmärchen*, Germanistische Abhandlungen, no. 63 (Stuttgart, 1988), 207–24.

12 Johann Wolfgang von Goethe, review of *Des Knaben Wunderhorn*, Part 1, in Goethe, *Schriften zur Kunst, Schriften zur Literatur, Maximen und Reflexionen*, vol. 12 of *Werke* (Hamburg, 1967), 270–84, 676–77.

13 Jacob and Wilhelm Grimm, *Kinder- und Hausmärchen*, 2 vols. (Berlin, 1812, 1815), 2, viii.

14 Max Lüthi, 'Psychologie und Pädagogik', in Lüthi, *Märchen* (Stuttgart, 1979), 106–11.

15 Max Lüthi, 'Das Wunder in der Dichtung', in Lüthi, *Es war einmal . . . : Vom Wesen des Volksmärchens* (Göttingen, 1962), 116–28. *Deutsches Wörterbuch*, founded by Jacob and Wilhelm Grimm, 14, col. 1782–1824, s.v. 'Wunder'.

16 Theilmann and Ammann (as note 2), 602.

17 Heinrich von Kleist, *Der Zweikampf, Die heilige Cäcilie, Sämtliche Anekdoten, Über das Marionettentheater und andere Prosa* (Stuttgart, 1993), 92.

18 The term 'Painter-Poets' (*Malerpoeten*) was coined by C. J. Wolf to describe the circle of south German painters who surrounded Schwind and Neureuther: C. J. Wolf, *Deutsche Malerpoeten* (Munich, 1919).

19 Wolfgang Frühwald, 'Das verlorene Paradies: Zur Deutung von Clemens Brentanos "Herzlicher Zueignung" des Märchens "Gockel, Hinkel und Gakeleia" (1838)', *Literaturwissenschaftliches Jahrbuch*, n.s., 3 (1962), 113–92.

Longing for the South

'Kennst du das Land, wo die Zitronen blühn?' sings Mignon in the celebrated song from Goethe's novel *Wilhelm Meisters Lehrjahre* ('Wilhelm Meister's Apprenticeship') (1794–6). Of course Germans knew that land, even if they had never been there. It was the land of their dreams, the earthly paradise.

Italy had been looked to for centuries by the rest of Europe as the seat of culture and learning the birthplace of the Renaissance and preserver of antiquity. It had been habitual for ambitious artists from all countries to travel to Italy (and Rome in particular) to drink from the source of classic art. But for Germans of the Romantic generation it became something different.

In one sence Italy became more distant. The revival of an interest in national culture encouraged German artists to look in other directions – to the depiction of their own natural world – as in the landscape paintings of Caspar David Friedrich – and to the rejection of classical 'academic' art in favour of the local tradition that could be traced back to Albrecht Dürer and other *altdeutsch* masters of the sixteenth century.

In another sense, however, Italy became more present, playing a new and even more alluring role. The interest in transience, the processes of time, encouraged the view of Italy as part of an ideal historical past. It was a land locked in that earlier state of being before the Fall. It was – to borrow the distinction used by Schiller in discussing poetry – the 'naïve' to be set against the 'sentimental' of the modern world.

Italy was seen as being in a more innocent and blessed state of being that contemporary Germany. It is no surprise that the Romantics should have taken Goethe's evocation of it in *Wilhelm Meister* so much to heart. The country appeared in similar guise in many other novels of the time – ranging from Ludwig Tieck's *Franz Sternbalds Wanderungen* ('Franz Sternbald's Walking Tours') of 1798 to Joseph Freiherr von Eichendorff's *Aus dem Leben eines Taugenichts* ('Memoirs of a Good for Nothing') of 1826. In the visual arts it soon became a focus for the medieval revivalists. This was particularly

the case with the *Brotherhood of St Luke* that was established by students at the Academy of Vienna in 1808. It was the aim of the Brotherhood to replace the 'corrupt' values of academic art with the honesty and spirituality evident in the art of the Middle Ages. They saw themselves as reviving a 'national' art by these means, but they soon thought of doing so in terms of submerging themselves in the culture of Italy. In 1810 the leading members of the group – including Friedrich Overbeck and Franz Pforr – left Vienna to settle in a deserted monastery in Rome. There they soon gained their better-known name of 'Nazarenes'. This was a nick-name given to them by the Italians on account of their appearance: by this time they had taken their medievalism to the point of growing their hair long and wearing long, flowing robes.

As was typical of the Romantic generation, the Nazarenes intertwined their love of Italy – its nature and its past – with their sense of their own personae. Soon after they arrived in Rome Overbeck and Pforr worked on producing a pair of 'friendship' pictures in which their views of each other's characters were expressed in terms of the relationship of Italy and Germany. They did this by illustrating a fable of two girls, 'Sulamith and Maria', which had been written by Pforr. Sulamith (the Hebrew name means 'Peace') stood for Overbeck's tranquil character, and for the 'peaceable' land of Italy. Maria was Pforr and the North; – a more passionate and melancholic figure who looked towards Sulamith and the South with longing. In Overbeck's design, Maria leans forward towards Sulamith (cat. 93). In Pforr's painting (colour plate, p. 98) Maria is in a darkened chamber with a lattice window that looks out onto the flower garden in which Sulamith can be found, seated calmly like a Raphael Madonna.

Pforr died in 1812, and after this the Nazarenes began to lose their intense obsession with the personal. It is a sign of this that they were soon joined by Peter von Cornelius (cat. 56), a Düsseldorf artist already committed to re-establishing a national German art on a monumental scale. Cornelius saw the experience of Italy as a necessary stage in this rebirth. He felt the need to study, as did the other Nazarenes, from the 'pure' source of the early Italians. But in doing so he was also intending to replace them. 'Their age is past, ours is to come,' he declared. In 1815 the Nazarenes received a commission that was of critical importance to their fortunes. This was to decorate the ante-room of the Prussian Consul in Rome with frescoes illustrating the biblical story of Joseph. Cornelius's main contribution was a fresco showing the point where Joseph makes himself known to his brethren and forgives them their crimes against him (colour plate, p. 264). It was an image of reconcilliation highly appropriate to the mood following the Napolonic Wars. These frescoes brought the Nazarenes international fame. When Crown Prince Ludwig of Bavaria came to Rome in 1819 he was deeply impressed by their work, and arranged for Cornelius to come to Munich, where the painter masterminded the transformation of that city into a major centre for contemporary German monumental art.

Ludwig's patronage gave the Nazarenes prominence in Germany. But they also remained a presence in Italy. Overbeck lived in Rome until his death in 1869, and continued to attract an international following. Other artists came to join them, such as Julius Schnorr von Carolsfeld. Schnorr joined Overbeck and other members of the group in the depiction of scenes from Dante, Tasso annd Ariosto in the garden Casino of the Italian aristocrat, the Marchese Carlo Massimo. Schnorr had already been drawn to Ariosto as a source for his art (cat. 96). He brought a lyrical line to his archaizing art, which seemed to emphasize the view of Italian painting as the relic of a lost poetic past. He also depicted scenes of the Italian countryside in a similar manner (colour plate, p. 266).

The Nazarenes brought a new dimension to the German interest in the art, culture and countryside of Italy. It was one that was to be continued by later generations, notably the *Deutsch-Römer* (German-Romans) Arnold Böcklin, Hans von Marées and Anselm Feuerbach (see section *Symbolist Fantasies*). In the case of these later artists, however, the idyllicism was overlaid by a more troubling mood.

While Italy remained the principle focus for the German interest in the South, there was at the same time a growing attraction towards Greece. Greece had, of course, always been admired for its classical culture since the Renaissance but it had been difficult to visit it on account of the Turkish occupation and the general danger of travel in the eastern Mediterranean. Even that great apostle of Greek art, Johann Joachim Winckelmann – the author of *Reflections on the Imitation of the Greeks in Painting and Sculpture* (1755), the book that exhorted modern artists to copy the art of ancient Athens – had never visited the country. In the Romantic period Greek art had an ambivalent position. On the one hand it was the fountainhead of ideal art – on the other it was the product of a pagan nation that lacked the spiritual insight to be found in the Christian art of the early Italians. Different artists took opposing views on the matter. Cornelius was a fervent admirer. Overbeck regarded it with disdain.

Attitudes towards Greece as a country changed dramatically as a result of the War of Independence. The heroic struggle of the Greeks to throw off the rule of the Turks attracted support throughout Europe. After the establishment of an independent Greek state in 1832 Prince Otto of Bavaria was chosen as king. This led to a strong German presence in Greece in the coming decades. The German artist Carl Rottmann travelled through Greece in 1834–5, producing a series of views of famous classical sites for King Ludwig of Bavaria (colour plate, p. 267). In contrast to the idyllic views of Italy by Schnorr and other Nazarene artists, these pictures have a brooding sense of tragedy that seems to prefigure the attitude toward the South found later in the works of the *Deutsch-Römer*.

William Vaughan

Walhalla:
The Temple of Fame on the Danube

The Walhalla (fig. 1) is the most important – and indeed the only – German national monument to have been completed in the first half of the nineteenth century. National monuments were set up in other countries: the Victor Emmanuel Monument in Rome (1885–1911) commemorates the unification of Italy; the unfinished 'Parthenon' on Calton Hill in Edinburgh (1822) commemorates the fallen of Waterloo. The Statue of Liberty in New York (1871–84) is another national monument – an embodiment of the American Idea – and the French have their Panthéon in Paris (1791). The roots of the concept lie partly in the Renaissance: as far back as the fifteenth century, the Duomo in Florence was decorated as a patriotic Hall of Fame.

The Walhalla was built by Leo von Klenze (1784–1864) on the Bräuberg, near Donaustauf, nine kilometres east of Regensburg, in 1830–42. Commissioned by Ludwig I (1786–1868), who reigned as King of Bavaria 1825–48, it was inaugurated on 18 October 1842, the anniversary of the Battle of Leipzig. This national monument soon attracted a cultivated public from all over Europe, and in 1836 the English travel writer Frances Trollope likened its fame to that of the Vatican. A number of nineteenth-century French authors wrote lengthy accounts of it, and a four-volume study in Spanish was published in Madrid in 1910. It now receives well over two hundred thousand visitors every year, from all over the world.

As Crown Prince of Bavaria, Ludwig was present on Napoleon's side when the French occupied Berlin in 1807. Profoundly mortified, the Romantic youth resolved that, just as soon as the 'days of Germany's deepest disgrace' were past, he would erect a monument to the 'Germans of greatest fame'. He made an immediate start by commissioning three marble busts from Johann Gottfried Schadow, who had designed the *Quadriga* on the Brandenburg Gate. In the same year, 1807, the name 'Walhalla' was suggested to the Crown Prince by Johannes von Müller, a Swiss historian in the Prussian service. Schadow carved a bust of him in 1808.

Walhalla or Valhalla is the paradise of Germanic myth, the blissful abode of fallen heroes. It is a Nordic Elysium, the place of immortality.

Ludwig's Doric temple of fame was built on the model of the Parthenon in Athens, but with significant variations. The stylobate lacks its curvature, which the archaeologists of Klenze's day had yet to discover. The sculptures in the tympana of the external pediments were carved by the Munich sculptor Ludwig Schwanthaler. The north pediment shows the Battle of the Teutoburg Forest, which took place in AD 9. The central figure is Arminius (Hermann), Prince of the Cheruscans, who defeated a Roman army in that battle. The vanquished general, Varus, falls upon his own sword.

The German Romantics liked to link this event with the struggle against Napoleon, as Heinrich von Kleist does in his drama *Die Hermannsschlacht* (1808). The most important allusion to it in painting is Caspar David Friedrich's *Graves of the Fallen Warriors of Liberty* (Hamburger Kunsthalle, 1812), in which a shattered gravestone in the foreground bears the name 'Arminius'; a snake in the French colours crawls across it as a symbol of national disunity. In 1838–75 Ernst von Bandel erected an immense commemorative column, the Hermannsdenkmal (fig. 3), in the Teutoburg Forest itself.

By contrast, the south pediment of the Walhalla presents a scene of peace and concord. Enthroned in the centre, Germania receives the homage of the victors in the Wars of Liberation: the German states and their federated strongholds.

The massive podium (cat. 102) is another feature not found in Greek temples. It is made up of an eclectic variety of components. From the great terrace, half-way up, a short flight of steps leads to the doorway of the Hall of Expectation. The doorway, with its 'Vitruvian opening', recalls the Etruscan tombs, though the pyramid-like façade looks more Egyptian. The lowest terrace, to which the main steps lead from below, is built of polygonal masonry, which Klenze called 'Pelasgic construction'.

Fig.1 Leo von Klenze, *The Walhalla* 1830–42, photograph

Fig.2 Leo von Klenze, *The Interior of the Walhalla* 1842

This technique is known from the temple of Apollo at Delphi and from the earliest perimeter wall of the Acropolis in Athens; the ancient writers spoke of *pelargiskon* or *pelasgikon*. Klenze supposed it to have been invented by the aboriginal Mediterranean population, the Pelasgians. Above the Egyptian pyramid level is a three-stepped pyramid crossed by a flight of steps. This looks rather like a Mesopotamian ziggurat, a traditional form long known in the West: it was the form in which artists visualized the Tower of Babel.

The curious, composite structure of the podium bears a cultural reference of its own. It points to Romantic ideas about the migration of myths, languages and peoples in the dawn of history. A number of thinkers, including Müller, Friedrich Schlegel and Joseph Görres, believed that the common ancestors of the Greeks, Italians and Germanic peoples had migrated from Central Asia by way of the Caucasus to the Near East, and thence into the various parts of Europe. According to this theory, the Germans made their way into Central Europe along the Danube. It is an idea that has left traces in the writings of Friedrich Hölderlin and Heinrich Heine, among others.

Classically educated and widely read, Klenze translated this theory of prehistoric migration into architecture. And this was his justification for his much criticized choice of a Greek temple to house the German national monument.

The interior of the Walhalla (fig. 2) differs from that of a Greek temple. With its three bays of wall piers, its clerestory and its 'choir' at the far end, it looks rather like a Christian church. Schwanthaler's *Valkyries* support the entablature that carries the iron roof structure. Martin von Wagner's continuous relief frieze depicts the early history of the Teutons, from their departure from the Caucasus and arrival in Central Europe to their conversion by St Boniface of Crediton, the 'Apostle of the Germans'.

Ludwig I personally selected the members of his marble congregation. Achievement was the criterion, and the common factor was 'the German tongue' (*die teutsche Zunge*), by which the King did not mean German alone but the whole Germanic family of languages: there are heroes from Switzerland, Sweden, the Baltic, the Low Countries and Britain. There was no political megalomania in all this: Ludwig had every intention of preserving his kingdom as a separate and independent state. All he wanted was to see Germany become a confederation of such states. To him, the word 'Fatherland' was an expression of cultural affinity.

Figures from the mists of antiquity, for whom no authenticated portrait exists, are commemorated by name alone, along the upper part of the walls. They include Arminius the Cheruscan, the unknown poet of the *Nibelungenlied*, St Hildegard von Bingen and the three who swore the Oath of the Rütli.

Ludwig I's book *Walhalla's Genossen* ('Walhalla's Comrades', cat. 104) includes the following sentence: 'No degree is excluded, nor is the female sex.' The idea of equality is the reason why all the marble heads are arranged in uniform rows, relieved only by Christian Daniel Rauch's beautiful *Victories*. The King justified this principle on the grounds that in death all human beings are equal and all earthly distinctions are removed. His collection of busts continues to be subject to some misinterpretation. Its true intellectual sources lie in the Enlightenment: the Walhalla is ruled by the egalitarian principle of historical merit. Viewed as a political statement, this is a clear echo of the ideal of equality proclaimed by the French Revolution. Ludwig I was pursuing a humanistic and educative agenda: the pilgrim was meant to leave the Walhalla purified and ennobled, with a sense of the sublimity of the past.

This idealistic intention was entirely in tune with contemporary thinking – as, for example, with Friedrich Schiller's idea of the theatre as a moral institution. Johann Wolfgang von Goethe, who met Ludwig I in Weimar in 1827, spoke of him as a man who had 'preserved his inborn humanity alongside the dignity of a king ... a rare phenomenon, and all the more welcome'.

Art could best realize such an ideal in the open air, in the midst of Nature, far from the constraints of politics. The gentle landscape in which the Walhalla stands reflects the liberal intentions that presided over its building. Klenze's model here was the English landscape garden, with its libertarian principles enriched by a new, Romantic imagery. The site, east of Regensburg, was carefully chosen. The Walhalla stands high above the Danube as it flows eastward to the Black Sea, towards Asia and therefore – in the Romantic view of things – towards the common origins of humanity. For this reason, the Walhalla is intended to be seen at its best in morning sunlight. The nearby castle ruin of Donaustauf

Fig.3 Ernst von Bandel, *Hermannsdenkmal* 1838–75

provides a picturesque, medieval contrast, further accentuated by Klenze's pilgrimage church of St Salvator (colour plate, p. 269, cat. 103). On the western, evening side, the Grecian temple of fame finds a far-off contrast in the Gothic cathedral of the former imperial free city of Regensburg: a representative of the old German nation that ended with the coming of Napoleon.

The man-made, cultural landscape of the Walhalla is thus dominated by the Romantic theme of the rhythmic alternation of evening and morning, as exemplified in Philipp Otto Runge's *The Times of Day* (colour plates, p. 212–13, cat. 9). Runge himself marked the same rhythm in 1805 in a pair of paintings, *The Rest on the Flight into Egypt* and *The Spring and the Poet*, which he interpreted in terms of the history of civilizations as 'Evening of the West' (*Abend des Abendlandes*) and 'Morning of the East' (*Morgen des Morgenlandes*). In 1809, Runge enlisted the same rhythm for a patriotic purpose. For the front cover of the magazine *Vaterländisches Museum* (cat. 108), he initially designed an image of a fallen warrior, couched beneath the sod over which his widow, with her child, drives the plough: Death becomes the fertile soil of a new life. Runge's second design for the front cover shows a winged genius striking the broken heart of the Fatherland with the rod of war, which is also symbolized by the spades and halberds at the side, entwined with the passionflower. On the back cover (cat. 109), the heart of the Fatherland is revived, and the genius warms it with the torch of love. From it grow lilies of the valley, and on either side tall lilies shoot up to the halo of the dove of peace.

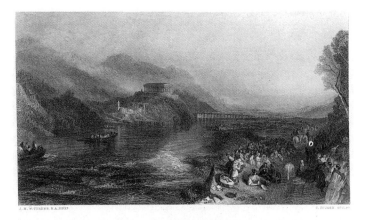

Fig.4 J.M.W. Turner, *The Opening of the Walhalla* 1843, steel engraving by Charles Cousen

Against the wide horizons of its quintessentially German, Danubian landscape, the Walhalla itself becomes a symbol of renewal and rebirth. J. M. W. Turner saw this with the sympathetic eye of a great painter, and in 1843 he exhibited his painting *The Opening of the Walhalla* (fig. 4) at the Royal Academy in London. He also wrote a poem on the subject, with the epigraph *L'honneur au roi de Bavière*.

Turner's painting shows the national monument in a wide-angle view across the Danube, with its old wooden bridge, the market at Donaustauf, and the foothills of the Bavarian Forest. It is early morning; on the near river-bank, a festive band of pilgrims sets off towards the light-filled temple on the heights. One is reminded of the pilgrim choruses of Richard Wagner. Turner sees the Walhalla as a *fata morgana*, a vision of a better world of peace and concord after the Napoleonic Wars.

In his poem, Turner speaks of Napoleon's gunshot wound at the siege of Regensburg in 1809, and of the celebrated spirits 'of German fatherland', in whom – as so often in the pictures that he painted on his travels – he reveres the genius of humanity. In the foreground a palette and brushes lie on the earth. The celebrated artist thus lays down his art, as it were, at the feet of the German temple of fame. Of all the tributes that the Walhalla has received over the years, this is the finest to date.

Jörg Traeger

Translated from the German by David Britt

The 'Official' Art of Romanticism as a Synthesis of the Arts

In Germany in the years around 1800 there was a wide-spread awareness of a deep crisis of European civilization. It was an awareness that left a lasting imprint on Romantic views of art. The sense that the French Revolution was the end of an era underlay, for instance, the impulse felt by Philipp Otto Runge to look for new forms in art, and his vision of 'landscape' as the art form of the future.[1] The Nazarenes – the artists who had formed the *Lukasbund* in Vienna, under the leadership of Friedrich Overbeck and Franz Pforr, and who were later joined in Rome by Peter von Cornelius, Julius Schnorr von Carolsfeld and others – analysed the art of their contemporaries and came to the conclusion that art had lost touch with the life of the people.[2]

Part of the blame for this, in their view, lay with those who had controlled art in the past, the German princes: 'Their hearts are not where the people's hearts are.'[3] But the true cause of the crisis in art, according to the Nazarenes, was its evolution towards autonomy. The history of art, which Friedrich Schlegel said was the best art theory, seemed to confirm that art always flourished best when it served religion and public life, as in the Gothic and Renaissance periods. There could be no new flowering of art, said the Nazarenes, until art returned to its former condition. Only by giving up its autonomy could art resume its true place in the life of the people and help to overcome the historical crisis.[4]

A second conclusion that the young Romantics drew from their study of the history of art was that art flourished best where it was promoted by great commissions. In Germany, however, great commissions were in short supply. During the Revolutionary and Napoleonic Wars, the German courts commissioned no major works of art. Secularization meant that the Church was no longer a patron. In these circumstances, many artists made their way to Rome, in the hope of finding takers for their work; for the Eternal City still, as ever, attracted art-loving tourists. In 1814, when it became known that the Chancellor of the Austrian Empire, Prince Metternich, planned to set up an Austrian Academy in Rome to compete with the Académie de France, the German artists composed a memorandum in which they argued that academies had never done anything but hinder the progress of art, and that the arts might be far more effectively promoted by direct patronage.[5]

In 1820 Johann David Passavant proposed, as an alternative to an academy, that a major monument should be projected and embarked on, on which 'work might continue for a century and more, until completion'.[6] The academy training was to be supplanted by the ideal of the medieval masons' lodge. Budding artists would learn by working on the monument under the direction of their masters. Such a monument would also bring artists together; and, united, they would wield more influence.[7] The source of this vision of a synthesis of the arts – a *Gesamtkunstwerk* – was the medieval cathedral. Karl Friedrich Schinkel had already produced designs for such a cathedral, which was simultaneously to be a monument. Passavant's projected national monument was to be a historical one, on the lines of the Walhalla that Crown Prince Ludwig of Bavaria was already planning. Passavant also made a number of other suggestions for buildings that might be set up for the promotion of all the arts. All these proposals reflect the general sense of German national pride – in which artists fully shared – after the victorious outcome of the Wars of Liberation. Another common factor was the high value that all the proposals attached to art as a means of (moral) education.[8]

The first of the Nazarenes to draw up a programme for a national revival of art was Cornelius. In 1814 he wrote a letter to Joseph Görres, the editor of the democratic and nationalist *Rheinischer Merkur*, calling for the revival of fresco painting as the most effective means of renewing art.[9] Cornelius saw the fresco, which was both inseparable from architecture and subordinated to it, as the perfect example of 'ministering' art, public by its very nature. It was also the best corrective against the decline of art, because it would educate popular taste and thus influence future commissions for the better.

Furthermore, for as long as fresco painting had been dominant in Italy, it had prevented the fragmentation of art into such individual genres as portrait, landscape, and the rest. In the form of a monumental decorative scheme, it would have an integrative effect, knitting art and architecture together. The classic instances cited by Cornelius were Raphael's Loggie and Stanze in the Vatican.

When Cornelius delivered this stirring appeal, his ideas were purely utopian. At the time of the Congress of Vienna, the German states were in no mood to start commissioning any national monuments, which might have been misinterpreted as a concession to the advocates of democracy. And yet Cornelius had caught the spirit of the age, and his proposal met with a growing degree of assent. The first opportunity to put it to the test came when Salomo Bartholdy, the Prussian Consul in Rome, commissioned Cornelius and his friends to decorate one room of his rented apartment in the Palazzo Zuccari with a fresco cycle on the Old Testament theme of the *Story of Joseph*. Then Marchese Massimi ordered frescoes illustrative of the poems of Dante Alighieri, Ludovico Ariosto and Torquato Tasso for three rooms in his Casino.

These two private commissions were mere curtain-raisers. The breakthrough came in 1818, when the Crown Prince of Bavaria (later King Ludwig I) commissioned Cornelius to paint frescoes in the Glyptothek in Munich. This was a museum of ancient sculpture, begun two years previously by the architect Leo von Klenze.[10] It was Cornelius's task to decorate the rooms in the rear part of the museum, the back vestibule and two adjoining halls intended for ceremonial occasions. His scheme was dominated by fresco painting, with relief carving and decorative plasterwork to ease the transition between painting and architecture.

Cornelius was given a free hand to devise his own programme. He set out to lead the visitor back into the mental world of ancient mythology, and thus to facilitate access to the works of art exhibited elsewhere in the building. For the first hall, Cornelius designed a mythological image of the world. The three wall lunettes show the three realms into which Zeus, Poseidon and Hades, the sons of Kronos, divided the world after their father's downfall. In the cells of the depressed cross vault, the four Times of Day are represented by the ancient deities Eos, Apollo, Diana and Nyx. The key to the whole is the depiction of the four elements, each represented by the bird or animal attribute of the corresponding deity: Jupiter's eagle for Fire; Juno's peacock for Air; Cerberus, the hound of Hades, for Earth; and Poseidon's dolphin for Water. Each creature is led by an Eros, as an indication that the principle of love rules even the elements. The power of love is one leitmotif in these frescoes; another is the power of art, which appears, for instance, in the representation of Orpheus in the 'underworld' and in that of Arion in the 'watery world'.

The so-called Hall of Heroes was originally intended to contain depictions of the myths of the Greek heroes. Cornelius reduced this programme to a cycle of the myths connected with the Trojan War. The most important leitmotif here is Eris, the personification of discord. In the crown of the vault, she is shown appearing at the wedding of Peleus and Thetis, where she unleashes the conflict by throwing the golden apple of discord among the guests. In the mythical world of these frescoes, everything turns on the opposing principles of Eros and Eris.

Cornelius made no attempt to devise a philologically accurate image of Greek mythology: myth, to him, was a language of the imagination, which he could use to express his own convictions in visual terms. This was an ideal world, intended – in accordance with prevailing ideas – to 'uplift' the viewer. In the world of art, something could be done that was impossible in the world of reality: namely, to overcome the contradiction between the ideal and the real. This idea of art's 'conciliatory' function – a product of German classicism – held a particular appeal for the practitioners of official art.[11]

In the organization of the work, which took a whole decade, Cornelius took his cue from Raphael. The process began with highly precise designs, which were transferred to full-size cartoons in a second phase of work. By the cartoon stage, Cornelius was already relying on the aid of his pupils, who also did a large part of the execution of the frescoes. This division of labour came in for some contemporary criticism. But Cornelius attached no particular value to the artist's personal handiwork. What really mattered to him was the invention and the drawing, which embodied the artistic idea. He regarded colour as an incidental, an optional ornament;

and in this he was deliberately holding out against prevalent tendencies in art. The more important the expressive power of the artist's personal touch came to seem – the higher the value attached to the 'original' work of art – the less popular Cornelius's works became.

In Cornelius and his successors, the suppression of individual character went hand in hand with the aim of universal validity. It was this aim, and the negation of subjectivity, that enabled their works to satisfy the nineteenth-century requirements of 'official' art.[12] When Ludwig I of Bavaria ordered his own and his Queen's apartments in the Residenz in Munich to be decorated with a fresco cycle commemorating the most celebrated German and ancient poets, he was not expressing a personal preference but finding a visual expression for the culture that he regarded as the foundation of the state. Ludwig did not regard these apartments as 'private' but opened them once a week for the edification of the public. He had adopted the Nazarenes' ideas of the public influence of art.

The example set by Ludwig I, in commissioning frescoes for his own palace and for his new museums and churches, was soon followed all over Europe. The decoration of the new Houses of Parliament in London, for which Cornelius was retained as a consultant, is perhaps the best known example of the continuing influence of the Romantic idea of 'official' art.[13]

In the course of the years known in Germany as the *Vormärz* – the period that led up to the revolution of March 1848 – such art began to lose something of its lustre. Its claim to 'popular' appeal became more and more questionable.[14] What the public liked was not official art at all, but such inferior genres as landscape and genre painting. In the first half of the century, conservative art critics gave 'official' art the highest rank among the arts; but they later relegated it to a lower status, as an art designed to educate the common people.[15] 'True' art must never submit to an ulterior motive. The evolution of art in the direction of autonomy, which the Nazarenes had tried to arrest, had ultimately prevailed after all.

Frank Büttner

Translated from the German by David Britt

1 Jörg Traeger, *Philipp Otto Runge und sein Werk: Monographie und kritischer Katalog* (Munich, 1975), 31ff.

2 The fullest contemporary account of the Nazarenes' views on art is provided by Johann David Passavant, *Ansichten über die bildenden Künste und Darstellung des Ganges derselben in der Toscana, zur Bestimmung des Gesichtspunktes, aus welchem die neudeutsche Malerschule zu betrachten ist* (Heidelberg and Speyer, 1820). See Keith Andrews, *The Nazarenes: A Brotherhood of German Painters in Rome* (Oxford, 1964).

3 Letter from Peter von Cornelius to Joseph Görres, November 1814, in Ernst Förster, *Peter von Cornelius*, vol. 1 (Berlin, 1874), 154.

4 On the Nazarene theory of art, see Jens Christian Jensen, 'I Nazareni, das Wort, der Stil', in exh. cat. *Klassizismus und Romantik in Deutschland: Gemälde und Zeichnungen aus der Sammlung Georg Schäfer* (Nuremberg: Germanisches Nationalmuseum 1966), 46ff.; Frank Büttner, *Peter Cornelius: Fresken und Freskenprojekte* (Wiesbaden, 1980), 1, 117ff.

5 K. Simon, 'Eine unbekannte Denkschrift der deutsch-römischen Künstlerschaft an Fürst Metternich', *Zeitschrift des Deutschen Vereins für Kunstwissenschaft* 3 (1936), 445ff.

6 Passavant (as note 2), 120–21.

7 Julius Schnorr von Carolsfeld, *Briefe aus Italien . . . geschrieben in den Jahren 1817–1827* (Gotha, 1886), 265.

8 Frank Büttner, 'Bildungsideen und bildende Kunst in Deutschland um 1800', in *Bildungsgüter und Bildungswissen*, part 2 of Reinhart Koselleck, ed., *Bildungsbürgertum im 19. Jahrhundert* (Stuttgart, 1990), 259ff.

9 Büttner (as note 4), 72ff.; see also note 3, above.

10 Büttner (as note 4), 125ff.; Klaus Vieneisel and Gottlieb Leinz, eds., exh. cat. *Glyptothek München 1830–1980* (Munich, 1980).

11 It was Friedrich Schiller, above all, who paved the way for these ideas in his theoretical works, notably 'Briefe zur ästhetischen Erziehung des Menschen' (1795) and 'Über naive und sentimentalische Dichtung' (1795–96).

12 See Magdalena Droste, *Das Fresko als Idee: Zur Geschichte öffentlicher Kunst im 19. Jahrhundert*, Kunstgeschichte: Form und Interesse, no. 2 (Münster, 1980), 127ff.

13 T. S. R. Boase, 'The Decoration of the New Palace of Westminster, 1841–1863', *Journal of the Warburg and Courtauld Institutes* 17 (1954), 319ff.; William Vaughan, *German Romanticism and English Art* (New Haven and London, 1979), 177ff.

14 Werner Busch, *Die notwendige Arabeske: Wirklichkeitsaneignung und Stilisierung in der deutschen Kunst des 19. Jahrhunderts* (Berlin, 1985), 235ff.

15 Büttner 1990 (as note 8), 268–69.

Symbolist Fantasies

Symbolist Fantasies

Echoes of Romantic art in painting were not always picked up in the latter half of the nineteenth century. Only individual threads from the Romantic fabric were woven into each piece of new material, and in contrast with literature and music the Romantic painting tradition was uneven. The main survivor on a broad scale was the Nazarene tendency, which had rapidly become ossified and academic. Peter von Cornelius, Friedrich Overbeck, Philipp Veit, Julius Schnorr von Carolsfeld and their pupils continued working well after the revolutions of 1848 and the preceding period; they were covered with decorations, but ultimately embittered because they were cut off from any relevance to the present. Their religious art was trivialized to the point of mass production, just as Moritz von Schwind's forest fairytale lyricism degenerated into superficial printed wall decoration. Ludwig Richter successfully consolidated the Romantic shift towards popular life and popular tales, and brought it back among the people through his book illustrations, though not without some constraints; this approach was continued, somewhat questionably, by Hans Thoma and his school. But the 'North German' Romantics were as good as forgotten, mainly because their activities faded out so soon. In the first wave of realist light-painting Romanticism inspired at best Luminism's special effects; these were still sublime in the work of Carl Rottmann, but decidedly superficial in the case of Oswald Achenbach. Caspar David Friedrich, Philipp Otto Runge and Carl Blechen were considered peripheral to the development of art and were only properly rediscovered at the turn of the century. Their ideas continued to be influential only 'underground', and were not even supported by local tradition: the deep impressions left by Friedrich, Carl Gustav Carus, Ernst Ferdinand Oehme and Johan Christian Clausen Dahl in Dresden were soon lost as well.

For decades the most popular and lively road for painting remained the exploration of sensually accessible reality – in terms of visual phenomena as well as representational work. But anyone who left that road, escaping from the materialism of the industrial and commercial world and looking for symbolic expression, inevitably took up Romantic ideas.

But the most powerful impetus to undertake that hike across the summits was unrepeatable. The North German Romantics, interacting closely with contemporary writers, had confronted the Industrial Revolution and its accompanying political and spiritual phenomena with complete designs for the world. The breadth and acuity of their approach, their systematic quality, the unity of their design and the way in which they explored the world remained forgotten and were replaced by more diffuse emotional values – right down to the melancholy landscapes of the Worpswede painters around Otto Modersohn und Heinrich Vogeler. Then a new commitment to the present emerged.

Despite Arnold Böcklin's Swiss origins, his contemporaries counted him as a German artist. Indeed, the famous polemic conducted by Julius Meier-Graefe in the name of victorious Impressionism against Böcklin's poeticized and archaic art reached its climax in the sentence: the 'Böcklin case' is a 'German case', because this painter 'represented all the sins committed by the Germans against the logic of art'.

His 'poeticized' art is derived from Romanticism. Even contemporaries were aware of his efforts 'to transfer subjective sensations to others'. Böcklin's pictorial worlds conceal subjective myths, and even when these are fundamentally old and familiar Böcklin still distances himself from his sources. He was in fact extremely well read, and so had to resort to a feigned naïveté; this is confirmed in notes by his confidant Gustav Floerke. Even the ruined castle in the picture of the same name (1847, Nationalgalerie Berlin), silhouetted against a gloomy sky, an early work by the twenty-year-old, has reminded more than one viewer of Caspar David Friedrich. The stormy, moody landscape is certainly derived from the Düsseldorf painter Carl Friedrich Lessing's late Romantic style. However, the skeletal ruin, set exactly parallel with the picture plane, and the

Fig.1 Arnold Böcklin *Vita Somnium Breve* 1888, Kunstmuseum Basle

light, flaring up magically behind the window openings, and only there, seem directly indebted to the painter of the *Abbey in the Oakwood*. And its former companion piece (now in the Kunstmuseum Basel) shows a tumulus, of all things! German paganism and the Christian Middle Ages, Ossian and Walter Scott confront each other, all fragments of a particular past (fig. 1).

Telling stories, making a myth out of a little piece of Nature – rather than taking Nature as a whole – links Böcklin with Schwind. But there is also an element of tough realism: grotesque, trivial details that cut against a pure, ideal image. Böcklin's friend Floerke spoke with obvious pleasure of 'kitchen Oceanids', 'marine Tyroleans', 'errand boys' of the sea. Is it just a 'homerically' sensual totality of life at work here? Or is

Romantic irony involved as well? The first does not exclude the second. In an age of railways and high finance, true mythical worlds can be imagined only by using this kind of refraction, refraction that can encompass everything. Thus in Böcklin's work rippling water, foaming waves, despite a close study of legs dangling in the water, seem as artificial as they do in the films of Federico Fellini (who deliberately used artificial foil to create such effects). Here too is an entirely 'ironic' attitude to Nature (unlike the brilliant water substitutes created with brazen skill by Anselm Feuerbach). As the years pass, light for Böcklin increasingly becomes a glow emanating from the colour of the image; this anticipates international Symbolism, but also refers back to Runge. The idea of workshop and apprentice communities is familiar from Runge and was practised by the fresco painters Cornelius and Schnorr. It also recurs in Böcklin ('but the most humble person is too proud for that', was what he felt about it), and Hans von Marées practised this Romantic mixture of idealism and pragmatism in his relationship with his pupils.

Marées's work is an attempt to justify the existence of creation at a time when it is endangered. His problematical, melancholy paradises can be made comprehensible only through form. The venture is Romantic in its approach. His entire oeuvre does not contain a single 'pure' landscape without figures, or even with small staffage figures, nor a single landscape study. This would not be surprising if his aim were Neoclassical art with figures, for which limited backgrounds would have been adequate. But Marées is seeking a harmony between figures and their surroundings, man and Nature. As in Böcklin's work, each is a comment upon the other – though using fundamentally different means, and totally rejecting Böcklin's narrative verve.

Max Klinger's work – Giorgio de Chirico recognized him as a 'Romantic-modern spirit' – and his rich graphic quality in particular, concentrates and focuses the different possibilities of European Romanticism. He presents dream visions much influenced by heavy melancholy. They always bring the artist's person into play in the role of confessor and simultaneously expound the problems of all life-forces in the name of inspiration. This approach takes up ideas of 'Black Romanticism' that have remained traditional in France (and Belgium) in

Fig.2 Max Klinger *To Beauty* 1898, (plate 12 from *Of Death*, Part Two, Opus XIII)

literature and graphics, and effortlessly flow into Symbolism. We have scant information on Klinger's direct sources. He read a great deal. Francisco de Goya's graphics must have had a profound influence on him. He follows Goya's technique in some of his work – by using aquatint – but also adopts his expressive fantasy and sense of the mystical. Klinger finds his own work anticipated in Goya the Romantic, whose sequence of *Proverbios* he owned: building a bridge from the naturalistic to the fantastic.

The young Klinger's gaze stiffens into a hallucinatory and excessive sharpness of focus when confronting the urban present – in the first work in the Glove cycle (cat. 127), for example. This is reminiscent of Erdmann Hummel's world, inhibited by the dictates of perspective and the constraints of eccentric reflections, easily misunderstood if one overlooks its close link with early Romantic scepticism. Klinger revives the gloomy wit of *Bonaventura's Night-watch* (1804, attributed to

Friedrich Gottlob Wetzel), where everything is unmasked as appearance and deception: 'And the bone-house echo cries out for the last time: "Nothing!"'. In Klinger's world 'God is dead', as Friedrich Nietzsche puts it, and no-one is crying out to him either. In the etching *To Beauty* (1893, from the cycle Of Death, Part Two, fig. 2) there is a lack of proportion between the momentary ecstasy of the kneeling figure – who first had to remove his clothes to attain a 'state of innocence' – and the timeless uproar of the wind in the trees. Klinger decided to do without the appearance he had planned in the sketch of Aphrodite above the water; thus the withdrawal of the gods (and God) from the human cycle of experience is repeated in the composition's origin. Klinger's sublime landscape-spaces are a sounding-board for human emotions.

All Klinger's main graphic works are arranged in cycles – usually by attaching subsidiary ideas to a main theme. This is the experience of a dreamer who is trying to stop the flight of his inner world, as opposed to the Romantic cycles, which follow a systematic order (the seasons, the days of the week). With their mixture of materials and rapid combination of different types of images, Klinger's works are arranged like so many *Gesamtkunstwerk* and, in this respect, have similarities to the Romantics' fresco programmes. But here too the system is subjective: the world's mythic system rests upon the artist's shoulder alone – hence the huge imaginative effort required to understand the artist at the turn of the century.

The later work of the Swiss painter Ferdinand Hodler provides a bridge between Romantic and Expressionist universal feeling. His background of powerful naturalism – like that of all major Symbolists – does not allow spiritual expression to become anaemic, even when heightened to the point of ecstasy. This is how the great (North German) Romantics pursue their spiritualized explorations: they are based on an attentive, vital sense of reality, and this is often not recognized. Hodler's final landscapes are empty pictures made up of a few horizontal strips of colour: a reduction of the kind Friedrich presented with unparalleled boldness and which is close (though hardly related) to modern abstraction.

Hodler's work is introduced by a large self-portrait *The Student* (1874, Kunsthaus Zürich), which has an almost disturbingly direct affinity with self-portraits by the young *Lukasbrüder* or Victor Emil Janssen's semi-nude self-portrait (cat. 63): the pose is upright and solemnly self-conscious, T-square and plumb-line in one hand, the other hand raised to swear an oath, the gaze directed uncertainly yet fixedly at the mirror in front of which the lonely ritual is taking place.

Even if one ignores thematic correspondences, a concern with the seasons – *Night* and *Day* are among the main works – and a preference for cyclical work, there are still some striking common features: a striving for 'real' allegory, two-dimensional, symmetrical composition, a general inclination towards formal systems (in Hodler's case the theory of 'parallelism', by which he understood 'any kind of repetition' and which he saw as 'a generally valid law of the world and Nature', that guarantees timeless, cosmic unity); rhythmically ornamental and balletic elements (the body as arabesque), the relationship of figure and universe, children, flowers. In addition to all this: the publicly commissioned historical wall paintings, scarcely recognizable but still indubitably successors of Nazarene frescos.

A transcendental interpretation of landscape is even more marked in the case of Edvard Munch, who often worked in Germany. In his work place always refers beyond itself. Ten years younger and more radical than Hodler, Munch restricts himself to the essentials of topography: horizon, smooth surfaces of earth or water, stars, patterns of light that can be perceived everywhere in the same way and at the same time. In this virtual infinity a place can be more closely defined only with figures. This emphasizes the contrast between their brooding quality and the vastness of the space in which they remain alien. But the expressive, infinite curves that fill the space in an Ossianic fashion prove to be echoes of inner processes. Outside is inside, and unlike Friedrich's orderly, God-filled cosmos no reality is valid outside man. In fact Munch could have come across Friedrich at a very early stage through his friend Andreas Aubert, who was the first critic to study Friedrich's work. More importantly: Munch is united with the North German Romantics by his view of the cycles of human life (*Dance of Life*, *Frieze of Life*), by the riddles of beginnings and the end, and by growth itself (*Madonna*, fig. 3), by the symbolism of the child, and in general by his

Fig.3 Edvard Munch *Madonna* 1895/1902, colour lithograph

replacement of traditional mythology with a new symbolism. Klinger's theme of the dying *Mother* (here cat. no. 132) with the elf-like new-born boy was also taken up by Munch on a number of occasions, but Munch is inwardly closer – though outwardly further away – from the Romantics when he raises the *Sick Girl* to the status of an icon. This link backwards to Romanticism also forms the basis of Modernism. In this gloomy logic the open-ended nature of Romantic art finds an echo.

Claude Keisch

Translated from the German by Michael Robinson

Anselm Feuerbach
Iphigenia, 1871
(cat. 120)

Arnold Böcklin
Self-Portrait with Death the Fiddler, 1872
(cat. 118)

Hans von Marées
Horseman Plucking Oranges, with Seated Woman, *c.*1870
(cat. 133)

Arnold Böcklin
Silence of the Forest, 1885–6
(cat. 119)

Ferdinand Hodler
Study for 'Day', c.1897
(cat. 121)

Ferdinand Hodler
Evening Rest I, c.1903–04
(cat. 122)

Ferdinand Hodler
Eiger, Mönch and Jungfrau Rising above a Sea of Mist, 1908
(cat. 123)

Ferdinand Hodler
The Niesen from Heustrich, 1909
(cat. 124)

Paula Modersohn-Becker
Seated Nude Girl with Flowers, 1907
(cat. 135)

Modernism

Erich Heckel
Two People in the Open Air, 1909
(cat. 137)

Otto Mueller
The Judgment of Paris, c.1910–11
(cat. 138)

Emil Nolde
Landscape with Young Horses, 1916
(cat. 143)

Emil Nolde
Tropical Sun, 1914
(cat. 142)

Erich Heckel
Self-Portrait, 1919
(cat. 145)

Ernst Ludwig Kirchner
Schlemihl in the Loneliness of His Room, 1915
(cat. 146)

Paul Klee
With the Rainbow, 1917
(cat. 152)

Wassily Kandinsky
Improvisation 21, 1911
(cat. 150)

Wassily Kandinsky
Design for the Cover of the 'Blue Rider' Almanac, 1911
(cat. 148)

Wassily Kandinsky
Design for the Cover of the 'Blue Rider' Almanac, 1911
(cat. 149)

Franz Marc
Red Horse and Yellow Cow, 1913
(cat. 155)

Franz Marc
The Small Yellow Horses, 1912
(cat. 153)

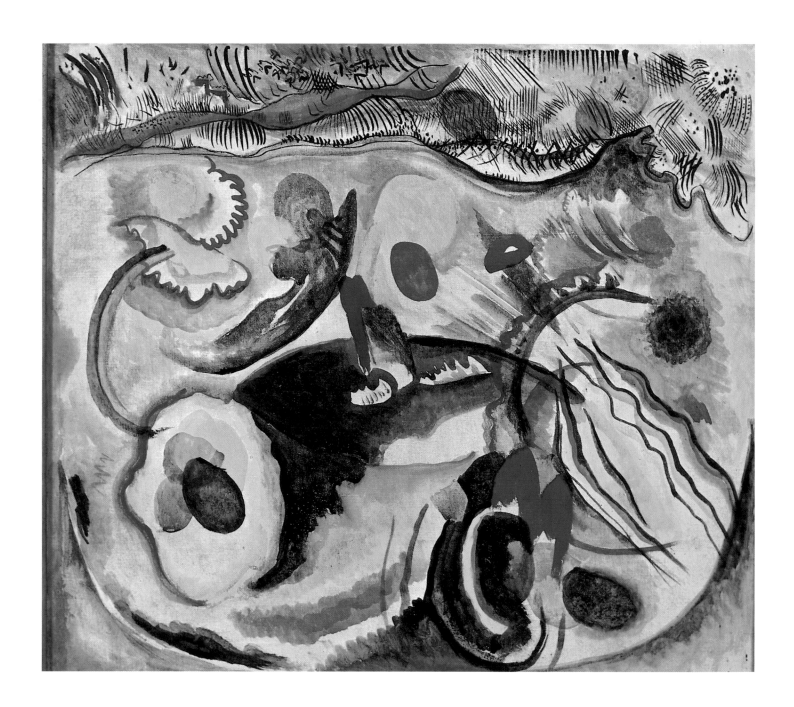

Wassily Kandinsky
On the Theme of the Last Judgment, 1913
(cat. 151)

Franz Marc
Fighting Forms (Abstract Forms I), 1914
(cat. 156)

Franz Marc
Arsenal for a Creation
Page 12 from the Sketchbook from the Field, 1915
(cat. 157)

Franz Marc
Untitled
Page 20 from the Sketchbook from the Field, 1915
(cat. 157)

Franz Marc
Magic Moment
Page 21 from the Sketchbook from the Field, 1915
(cat. 157)

Franz Marc
Fragment
Page 30 from the Sketchbook from the Field, 1915
(cat. 157)

Paul Klee
Mural from the Temple of Longing ↖ Thither ↗, 1922
(cat. 163)

Paul Klee
Departure of the Ships, 1927
(cat. 166)

Paul Klee
Threatening Snowstorm, 1927
(cat. 167)

Paul Klee
North Sea Picture, 1923
(cat. 164)

Oskar Schlemmer
General plan of the wall decorations in the Workshop Building
of the State Bauhaus in Weimar. Ground plan and perspective, 1923
(cat. 172)

Oskar Schlemmer
Design for the Cover of 'Utopia', 1921
(cat. 169)

Oskar Schlemmer
Bauhaus Stairway, 1932
The Museum of Modern Art, New York; Gift of Philip C. Johnson, 1942

Lyonel Feininger
Gelmeroda III, 1913
(cat. 158)

Wassily Kandinsky
Design for the left-hand wall of a music salon
for the 'Deutsche Bauausstellung' in Berlin, 1931
(cat. 160)

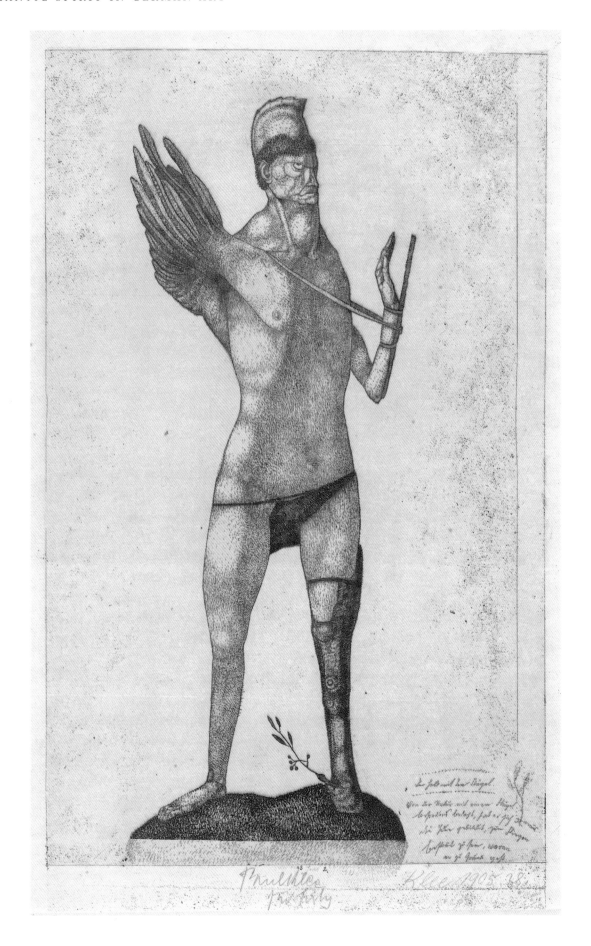

Paul Klee
Hero with the Wing (Invention 2), 1905
(cat. 181)

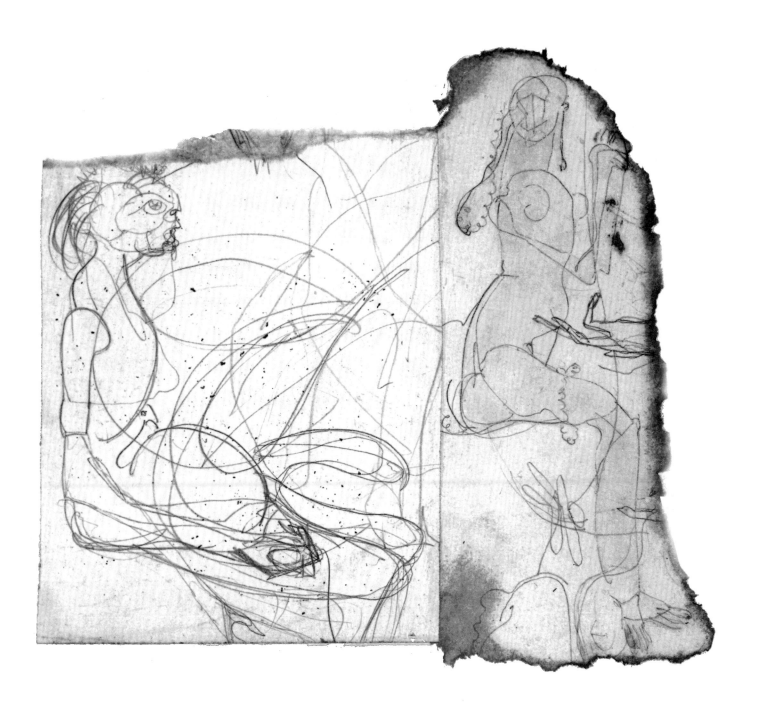

Paul Klee
Pregnant Girl, Seated); Female Nude with Suggestion of Leg Covering, 1905
(cat. 180a and 180b)

Hans Arp
Forest, c.1917
(cat. 182)

Kurt Schwitters
Untitled (Relief with Red Pyramid), c.1923–25
(cat. 186)

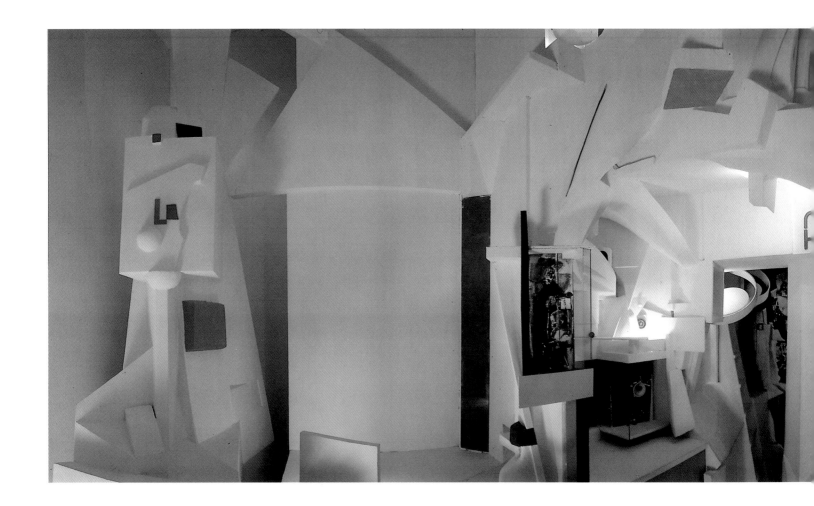

Kurt Schwitters
Reconstruction (by Peter Bissegger) of the Hanover MERZbau (original c.1923–36), 1980–83
(cat. 187)

Max Ernst
Max Ernst Showing a Girl the Head of His Father, 1927
(cat. 184)

Max Ernst
Sea and Sun, 1925
(cat. 183)

Max Ernst
La joie de vivre, 1936
(cat. 185)

Georg Scholz
Cacti and Signals, 1923
(cat. 190)

Otto Dix
Nelly with Toys, 1925
(cat. 188)

Georg Schrimpf
Three Children, 1926
(cat. 192)

Alexander Kanoldt
Olevano, 1927
(cat. 189)

Franz Radziwill
The Beach at Dangast with Flying Boat, 1929
(ex. cat.)

Nature and Primitivism: The Brücke

During the summer months of 1909 to 1911, Ernst Ludwig Kirchner and Erich Heckel, joined in 1910 by Max Pechstein, went to the Moritzburg Lakes near Dresden to 'paint nudes in a natural setting without being disturbed'.[1] In his memoirs Max Pechstein describes the search for models: 'we had to find two or three who were not professional models and could therefore be relied upon to move without studio dressage'.[2] Marzella and Fränzi, two young daughters of a circus family, were recruited and went with the artists to Moritzburg, sometimes accompanied by the latters' women friends.

The studies done in the summer of 1910 and the paintings that resulted from them are among the most important examples of the so-called *Brücke* style, the product of a close artistic interchange that continued at such a pitch of intensity for only a short time. This style was clearly influenced by familiarity with the work of artists such as Munch, Van Gogh, Gauguin and the *Fauves*, and by the adaptation of types of non-European art, which inspired not only the drawings and paintings of the Brücke artists, but also their wood sculptures. In works from supposedly primitive cultures they saw evidence of a natural, original way of life and a view of the world that paralleled their own endeavours[3], which were reflected in the themes of the works done at Moritzburg. The depiction of 'bathers' also linked up directly with contemporary artistic tradition and the examples of Cézanne. It is to be found in the work of both French and German Impressionists, as well as that of the Symbolists and the *Fauves*, who had a closer affinity to the *Brücke* artists. This complex of motifs was already anticipated in the works of German artists in Rome, whose themes were still strongly coloured by mythology. In particular one should mention the influence of Arnold Böcklin. Also important was the transformation of the theme in Gauguin's depiction of South-Sea-Islanders. A related approach can be seen in the work of Otto Mueller, who joined the *Brücke* community in 1910. The journeys to Moritzburg were not isolated; other *Brücke* artists set off alone or in pairs to Goppeln (near Dresden), Alsen, Dangast, Fehmarn or Nidden in search of the stimulus afforded by living and working in natural surroundings.

In his reminiscences Kirchner tries to clarify the artistic importance of the study of moving nudes in a natural setting, which was a logical development of the communal studio exercise of the 'fifteen-minute nude paintings': 'From 1912 to 1914 I spent the summer months on Fehmarn with Erna. Here I learned to create the ultimate unity of human being and nature and completed what I had begun at Moritzburg.'[4] He describes his preoccupation with new themes – 'birth and death, love and hate, sensuality and sickness' – as a turning away 'from the Arcadian lakes and woods of his nudes to real life'.[5] The experience of the paradisiac harmony between man and nature, which Kirchner describes, without any illusions, as a Sunday episode, becomes the starting point for a vision of 'originality' which the *Brücke* artists were dedicated to exploring in the course of repreated retreats into nature. One need only recall how Emil Nolde and Pechstein visited the South Seas in 1913–14 and how Kirchner periodically withdrew to Switzerland from 1917 onwards.

At the beginning of the century the quest for 'originality' had found a wide echo in youth movements and among nature-lovers. Parallels are to be found in the early attempts of contemporary psychology to investigate childhood and the subconscious. For the Expressionists it was closely linked with the idea of the nature and mission of the artist. They held that the creative imagination enabled the artist to penetrate beyond outward appearance to the spiritual heart of things, if he 'reproduces, directly and without falsification, what spurs him to create' (*Programme of the 'Brücke'.* 1906).[6] The proclamation of an 'inner necessity' as the starting-point of every true artistic creation, in which the whole of the Expressionist movement concurred,[7] was bound to be followed by a rebellion against the restriction of the search for form. It was directed also against the production of bravura pieces designed for effect, against the orientation towards Classical models favoured by academic tradition, and emphatically against the purely outward reproduction of nature in the manner of a superficial Impressionism devoid of content.

The question of the relations of the *Brücke* artists to German Romanticism can be related above all to their idealistic position, which found expression in the conception of nature just outlined.

A number of statements on the theory of art from both periods suggest a comparison: 'In order to reveal our spiritual life, painting must set out on paths other than those of the pure imitation of nature. The inward spiritual vision of an idea, of an experience, is the model that the painter tries to realize in his work, not the nature that presents itself to his eyes,' writes Kirchner in the introduction to an exhibition of his work in Davos.[8] In this piece, written in 1926, he draws up a kind of intellectual balance of his work. As Friedrich Wilhelm Schelling declared, in a speech about the relation between the arts and nature: 'The highest relation between art and Nature is achieved when the former makes the latter the medium through which the soul within it becomes visible'.[9]

In his seminal study *Primitivism in Modern Art* Robert Goldwater addressed the central points of comparison.[10] He identifies the development of the consciousness of history as an essential precondition for the status of 'unclassical' statements about art, in which such values as simplicity and honesty are seen to express an original, unspoilt creativity. With the analysis of binding and rationally comprehensible norms, the honest capturing of the subjective and the quest for the unfalsified and the original gain importance.

Caspar David Friedrich remarked that 'the painter should paint not merely what he sees in front of him, but also what he sees inside him. If he sees nothing inside him he should also refrain from painting what he sees in front of him.'[11] This demand, together with Philipp Otto Runge's wish 'to ensure if possible that faults in the execution are overlooked rather than faults in the ideas'[12], seem to point forward directly to the Expressionist principle of creation from 'inner necessity' and the consequent rejection of a superficially mimetic approach.[13] The ability to move creatively beyond the reproduction of external reality in order to illustrate

deeper feelings and cosmic connections gives rise to the idea of the artist's quasi-priestly status, which was familiar to Romantics and Expressionists alike.

In their orientation towards medieval religious works the Nazarenes saw a return to the sources of true art. They too described their models as 'primitive'. The artists of the early twentieth century found traces of creative originality in the supposedly less developed cultures of distant lands – which they thought closer to the 'beginnings' – and also in popular art, children's drawings, or art produced by the mentally sick. One can find interesting isolated correspondence between the *Brücke* and the Nazarenes in their choice of particular models – Albrecht Dürer, Lucas Cranach or the Italians of the early Renaissance. These might lead to further reflections – on the rediscovery of the woodcut technique, for instance, or the significance of the linking of surfaces in compositions that produce abstraction by linear contours. One might also consider the relevance of Jean Jacques Rousseau's ideas to the development of the idea of the 'natural' and its effect on Romanticism, or the incipient interest in the religions and cultures of non-European peoples in the early nineteenth century.

Yet from the views that have just been briefly referred to, it is difficult to derive more than a few concrete links between the *Brücke* and Romanticism.[14] Rather, we find analogies that point to correspondences on an abstract, conceptual plane. Individual artists of the *Blaue Reiter* can be shown to have been concerned with specific aspects of Romanticism. In the case of the *Brücke* artists it is mainly indirectly, on the basis of the incorporation of Romantic ideas in the work of Arnold Böcklin or, to a greater extent, in the literature of French Symbolism, that connections can be established.

If one thinks of the paintings done at Moritzburg, this finding is confirmed by the visually different character of the works. The longing they express for an original paradisiac state has often been thought to contain – in general terms – a similarity to Romanticism.[15] The pictorial tradition of the theme could be traced back through the 'Golden Age' of Ingres, by way of Poussin, to Cranach. Yet in this form it is not a central theme in early German Romantic painting, although it *is* a central theme in early German Romantic literature. (See Peter-Klaus Schuster's article in this same volume.)

At Moritzburg, Kirchner, Heckel and Pechstein attempted, by means of a rapid, spontaneous and often deliberately hasty representation, to reduce the natural form and so capture what was essential to it. This procedure differs from those of successive abstraction and sythesis based on detailed nature studies, such as we find in German Romanticism, above all because of the element of movement. Of interest in this connection is Kirchner's use of the term 'hieroglyph' – Runge used it in a different sense – to denote the artistic abbreviation that conveys the expression and so to indicate its semantic dimension. Above all, the dynamism and vividness of the Moritzburg paintings give an impression quite different from that produced by Romantic works. This becomes obvious when one compares them with the thematically related compositions of Otto Mueller, which convey a calmer, often melancholy expression and thus seem visually much closer to Romantic works. This aspect becomes clearer still if we compare the Moritzburg paintings with the wide northern or tropical landscapes of Emil Nolde, often devoid of human beings, his atmospheric seascapes and his sunsets. Linking up with the natural lyricism of the turn of the century, the works of the older painter, who had only a brief association with the *Brücke*, form part of the debate over the tradition of the nineteenth century, but in a quite different way. As far as we know, Nolde never expressed an opinion about Romanticism. Yet the composition, the choice of motifs and above all the contemplative character of many of his works suggest an affinity to the Romantic atmospheric landscape.[16]

Petra Kuhlmann-Hodick

Translated from the German by David McLintock

Avantgarde in Deutschland 1905–1920 (as note 3), 77.

7 See Wassily Kandinsky, *Über das Geistige in der Kunst* (3rd ed. Munich, 1912), 55 *et passim*.

8 Ernst Ludwig Kirchner, 'Die Kunst der Malerei: ein paar Worte zur Ausstellung meiner Bilder in Davos' (1926), reprinted in Lothar Grisebach (as note 5), 225.

9 Friedrich Wilhelm Schelling, 'Über das Verhältnis der bildenden Künste zu der Natur' (Munich, 1807), 46, quoted in exh. cat. *Caspar David Friedrich 1774–1840. Kunst um 1800* (Hamburger Kunsthalle, 1974), 23.

10 Robert Goldwater, *Primitivism in Modern Art* (New York, 1938, rev. ed. 1966) 51f, 251ff.

11 Sigrid Hinz (ed.), *Caspar David Friedrich in Briefen und Bekenntnissen* (Berlin, 1968), 128.

12 Philipp Otto Runge, *Hinterlassene Schriften, Zweyter Theil* (Hamburg, 1841), 90.

13 Emil Nolde's reservations regarding the overvaluation of technique point in the same direction. See exh. cat. *Emil Nolde. Eine Ausstellung des Württembergischen Kunstvereins Stuttgart und der Stiftung Seebüll Ada und Emil Nolde* (Stuttgart, 1988), 113.
On the relation between ideal conception, imitation of Nature and technique in Romanticism, see the summary given by Werner Busch, 'Zu Verständnis und Interpretation romantischer Kunst', *Arte Fakten. Kunsthistorische Schriften*, ed. Ludwig Fischer (Annweiler, 1987), 12–14.

14 Editor's note: In a letter to Gustav Schiefler (11 January, 1927) Kirchner acknowledged that in his youth his main artistic models had been Peter von Cornelius, Anselm Feuerbach and Arnold Böcklin. (Wolfgang Henze (ed), together with Annemarie Dube-Heynig and Magdalena Kraemer-Noble, *Ernst Ludwig Kirchner, Gustav Schiefler: Briefwechsel, 1910–1935/1938* (Stuttgart and Zurich, 1990), 451.) Kirchner's library also contained a number of books on Caspar David Friedrich, Philipp Otto Runge, Friedrich Schlegel, Friedrich Schleiermacher and other Romantic artists and writers, not to mention several books by Friedrich Nietzsche, whose anti-rationalist philosophy stemmed in part from the Romantic movement and inspired the young *Brücke* artists in Dresden. Erich Heckel is known to have read the works of the Romantic writer Jean Paul avidly by 1917 and his murals in the Angermuseum in Erfurt (1922–23) are replete with references to Caspar David Friedrich and Philipp Otto Runge.

15 See Manfred Schneckenburger, in exh. cat. *Weltkulturen und moderne Kunst* (Munich: Haus der Kunst, 1972), 456 and 457ff.; also Donald E. Gordon 'Primitivism in 20th Century Art. Affinity of the Tribal and the Modern' in exh. cat. (New York: The Museum of Modern Art, 1984), II, 399.

16 Annegret Rittmann, for instance, sees in Nolde a spiritual 'continuation of the Romantic tradition' in the context of both the natural lyricism of the Worpswede circle and the Expressionism of the *Brücke*. See exh. cat. *Emil Nolde. Aquarelle und figürliche Radierungen* (Münster: Westfälisches Landesmuseum, 1992), 39. Martin Urban compares Nolde's landscape art with that of Caspar David Friedrich. See Martin Urban, *Emil Nolde. Landschaften, Aquarelle und Zeichnungen* (Cologne, 1969), 7.

1 Max Pechstein, *Erinnerungen*, ed. Leopold Reidemeister (Wiesbaden, 1960), 42.

2 Ibid (as note 1), 42.

3 See Ernst Ludwig Kirchner, 'Chronik der Brücke' (1913), reprinted in *Expressionisten. Die Avantgarde in Deutschland 1905–1920* (Staatliche Museen zu Berlin, Nationalgalerie and Kupferstichkabinett, 1986), 122.

4 Eberhard W. Kornfeld, *Ernst Ludwig Kirchner. Nachzeichnung seines Lebens. Katalog der Sammlung von Werken von Ernst Ludwig Kirchner im Kirchner-Haus Davos* (Kunstmuseum Basel, 1979), 337.

5 Lothar Grisebach, *E.L. Kirchners Davoser Tagebuch. Eine Darstellung des Malers und eine Sammlung seiner Schriften* (Cologne, 1968), 85.

6 'Programme of the *Brücke*' (1906), reprinted in *Expressionisten. Die*

Der Blaue Reiter

'On the broad meadow there grew a flower.
The flower was blue.
It was only a flower on the meadow.
And yet, and yet, and yet. It was there'[1].

The *Blaue Reiter* (or Blue Rider) marked the convergence of a number of different influences and the distillation of ideas and beliefs which were common currency around the turn of the century. The name initially was given by Wassily Kandinsky and Franz Marc to the artists' almanac which they planned to produce on a regular basis and to the two international exhibitions which they organized in Munich of 43 paintings, from 18 December 1911 to 3 January 1912 (with a subsequent tour of Germany), and of 315 works on paper, from 12 February until April 1912. As Kandinsky was later to recall, the name was thought up over coffee at Franz and Maria Marc's house in Sindelsdorf and referred to both painters' predilection for the colour blue, to Marc's love of horses and Kandinsky's love of riders[2]. It is hard also not to be reminded of the mysterious blue flower which inspired the passionate longing of Novalis's fictional character, Heinrich von Ofterdingen. The editors' ambitious aim was no less than the renewal of all branches of artistic life and thought and, ultimately, of society through the involvement in their project of painters, sculptors, musicians, dancers, writers and theoreticians. Kandinsky and Marc were joined in this undertaking by Kandinsky's companion, Gabriele Münter and friends among the Russian artistic community in Munich, along with the composer, Arnold Schoenberg, who was taking lessons in painting from Kandinsky, Kandinsky's near neighbour, the Swiss artist Paul Klee, and Marc's Rhineland friend, the painter August Macke.

The two exhibitions of the *Blaue Reiter* emphasized the international nature of the enterprise, with the participation of the French, German and Russian avant-garde. Gauguin, Van Gogh, Cézanne, Matisse and the recently deceased Douanier Rousseau were included alongside Delaunay, Derain, Vlaminck, Picasso, Braque, Goncharova, Larionov, Malevich, the *Brücke* artists and members of the organizers' immediate circle. At a stroke the Munich avant-garde established its international credentials. As Franz Marc proclaimed in his prospectus for the publication[3]:

'Art today is following paths undreamt of by our forefathers; we stand, as if in a dream, in front of these new works and hear the apocalyptic riders in the air; we feel an artistic tension throughout Europe – new artists wave to each other, on all sides; a glance, a pressure of hands is enough to create an understanding'[4].

In relatively few pages, the almanac brought together up-to-the-minute illustrations of work by artists who had contributed to the group's two exhibitions, alongside examples of children's drawings, Bavarian behind-glass paintings, Russian popular prints (*lubki*), Old Master prints, and illustrations of a wide range of archaeological objects and artefacts from the Ancient Egyptians and the Greeks, through Byzantium to African and Polynesian sculpture and masks. The texts included contributions by Marc and David Burljuk on the German and Russian *Fauves* ('Wilden') respectively; Kandinsky's essay on form ('Über die Formfrage'); quotations from Goethe and Delacroix; an article on 'Masks' by August Macke; Kandinsky's composition for the stage, *Der gelbe Klang* ('Yellow Timbre'), preceded by a theoretical text; an essay by Erwin von Busse on Robert Delaunay's compositional methods; excerpts from compositions by Arnold Schoenberg and his pupils, Alban Berg and Anton von Webern; and essays by different authors on 'Anarchy in Music', 'Free Music' and Scriabin's 'Prometheus'.

Many of the ideas of the circle of artists, musicians and writers associated with the *Blaue Reiter* were common to the group of aristocrats and intellectuals who frequented the salon of the Russian painter, Marianne von Werefkin. Werefkin and her cousin, Alexei Jawlensky, who had come to Munich to study art and set up house together in 1897, had initially attempted, with a group of like-minded émigrés, to form an artistic community modelled on the idea of the Nazarenes' brotherhood of St Luke, whose aim it had been to cultivate a moral approach to art and the subordination of individual expression to a higher goal. Werefkin was steeped in the literature of the French Symbolists, had personal contacts with a number of them, including Huysmans and Maeterlinck, and had entertained two former Nabis, Paul Sérusier and Pater Willibord Verkade in her *salon* on a number of occasions, between 1906 and 1908. In addition, she was thoroughly versed in the literature of the German Romantics and had recorded in her diary her view that:

'Romanticism brought about a thorough renewal of art, in a way that was quite different from the Renaissance but no less comprehensive. The great merit of Romanticism was that it laid the foundations for the art of the future. That great genius, Wagner, understood this well. The art of the future is artistic emotion.'[5]

In 1909 Jawlensky and Werefkin set up the *Neue Künstlervereinigung München* (the New Artists' Association, Munich) which was the forerunner of the *Blaue Reiter*, with Kandinsky as its chairman. It was probably these Russian friends who, in 1908–1909, introduced Kandinsky to the teachings of the anthroposophist Rudolf Steiner and the writings of the early theosophists, such as Madame Blavatsky, Annie Besant and C.W. Leadbeater. Under the influence of these occult scientists and his own Russian orthodox background and mystical leanings, Kandinsky came to believe that the turn of the century marked the beginning of a revolt against western materialism and positivist philosophy, and the dawn of a new age. Writing in the third person he said: 'Kandinsky regards the end of the nineteenth century as the beginning of the greatest epoch in the spiritual life of humanity. He calls it the Epoch of Great Spirituality'[6].

This became the central theme of Kandinsky's theoretical writings and, notably, of his book, *On the Spiritual in Art* ('Über das Geistige in der Kunst'), completed in 1910 and published in late 1911, where, besides tracing the evolution of western painting and colour theory up to the Impressionists, Neo-Impressionists, Matisse and Picasso, he established the theoretical basis for an abstract art, whose emotions were directly communica-

ble to the viewer and corresponded to the hidden laws of the universe.

It is not certain to what extent Kandinsky was acquainted at first hand with the writings of the early German Romantics, though he wrote in a letter to Will Grohmann on 11 December 1925:

'There ought to be a New Romanticism just as nowadays there is a New Objectivity. I once wanted to write about this and intended to devote a chapter to Romanticism in the new edition of *On the Spiritual*'[7].

At all events, he was familiar with certain aspects of Goethe's scientific research, and it is likely that he was introduced to the latter's colour theory through Rudolf Steiner's editions of his scientific writings[8]. Spurred on by this and by Goethe's references to the 'sensuous, ethical effect of colour' (*sinnlich – sittliche Wirkung der Farbe*) he went on to dedicate a whole section of *On the Spiritual in Art* to the subject of synaesthesia, in which he recapitulated the theories of Delacroix, Baudelaire, Rimbaud and others.

Kandinsky dreamed of a harmonious new universal order, in which the barriers of distance and time and the traditional distinctions between organic and inorganic matter, and between the material and spiritual worlds, would be abolished – symbolized by the victory of St George over the dragon of materialism, in his initial conception for the cover design of the almanach. In this he would have felt reinforced, not only by the nature philosophy of the Romantics and occultism of the Rosicrucians and theosophists, but also by the latest scientific discoveries in areas such as relativity, radiology and quantum physics, and the technological advances in communications, celebrated by the Futurists. Like the Romantics, who had revolted against the excessive rationalism of the Enlightenment and the industrialization of the towns, he dreamed of an art which transcended reason and physical reality and expressed, through intuitive means, the underlying harmony of the universe. He sought to capture the 'inner sound' of the cosmos through the increasing reductiveness of his graphic style and the liberation of colour from its descriptive role, which led to his development of an autonomous abstract pictorial language in the years 1910–1914.

In his struggle to develop a visual language which corresponded to his spiritual vision and in his practical efforts to proselytize, publish and exhibit, Kandinsky found an ally and a capable organizer in his new friend, Franz Marc, whom he first met in January 1910. Marc had a direct, personal link to the Romantics through an ancestor, Julia Mark, whose unhappy relationship with E.T.A. Hoffmann provided the inspiration for the latter's *Musikalische Leiden des Kapellmeisters Kreisler* ('The Musical Sufferings of Johann Kreisler, the Kapellmeister'). He had inherited a part of Julia's library, including first editions of a number of Hoffmann's books, and was fond of quoting from the edition of Novalis's collected works that he owned. Marc is known to have admired the paintings of Philipp Otto Runge, Caspar David Friedrich, Wilhelm von Kobell, Carl Blechen, Alfred Rethel and Moritz von Schwind. As Klaus Lankheit has shown, he must have been familiar with Schelling's Nature philosophy and doctrine of the unity of Nature and the spirit. Like Kandinsky, he believed that he stood at the threshold of a new age, on the verge of collapse of the old, materialist order and he consciously emphasized the continuity of thought with the early Romantics, a century earlier:

'... we believed then that we were standing at the turning point between two long epochs; there was nothing new in this intuition; the call had been heard still louder, a hundred years before'[9].

In common with many others at the time – not least, the *Brücke* artists around 1910 – Marc had initially sought refuge in nature from the increasing mechanization and artificiality of urban life. His paintings of animals and the increasing extent to which he integrated their forms into the contours of the landscape expressed his yearning for a lost harmony and innocence. As he wrote in a letter to his publisher Reinhard Piper, 'I am trying to heighten my sensitivity to the organic rhythm of all things and trying to empathize pantheistically with the tremulous coursing of the blood in nature, the trees, the animals and the air ...'[10].

His striving to 'animalize art' (he called it 'Animalisierung der Kunst'[11]) was given fresh impetus through contact with the formal innovations of the Cubists and Futurists and, in particular, the 'Orphist' Robert Delaunay, whom he visited in Paris, in the company of August Macke, in October 1912. In much the same way as Kandinsky turned to theosophy and the new sciences to provide a theoretical justification for the increasing abstraction in his work, Marc found in the philosophy of the Romantics, Schopenhauer and Nietzsche, and in a personal form of religiosity, the means to transcend the physical world and 'create symbols to be placed on the altars of the coming spiritual religion'[12]. Following Runge and others, he developed a colour symbolism of his own, in which he sought the key to a deeper understanding of natural appearances. Thus, he identified blue as 'the male principle, astringent and spiritual', yellow as 'the female principle, gentle, cheerful and sensuous', and red as 'brute matter', in opposition to the other two colours[13]. The fractured style and increasing abstraction of Marc's work of 1913–1914 seemed already to predict the apocalyptic breakdown of the social and material order. He saw war, when it came, not merely as a calamity, but as 'hygiene' which would purge Europeans of their nationalist egotism and evolutionary positivism and lead to a moral and spiritual regeneration.

Paul Klee was deeply affected by his brief association with the *Blaue Reiter*, and his inclusion in the second exhibition, in May 1912, with seventeen drawings, marked the true beginning of his international career. Up until then, he had achieved distinction as a draughtsman and etcher, working in the Symbolist tradition and close in spirit to the older artist, writer and illustrator, Alfred Kubin (another exhibitor with the *Blaue Reiter*). The protagonist in Kubin's significantly titled novel, *Die andere Seite* ('The Other Side') of 1909 invented a kind of psychographic 'handwriting' – more like writing than drawing – which could be used, like a meteorological instrument, to record the slightest shifts in his vital disposition[14]. Inventions such as this were directly derived from the writings of the early Romantics (Novalis's '*Chiffernschrift*' or encoded script, for example) and encouraged Klee to develop an idiosyncratic linear style whose freedom far surpassed anything of which Kubin was capable. Klee was fascinated by the hidden aspects of life, but conscious of their ambiguous nature. His favourite Romantic writers were not so much the mystics, but the sceptics, ironists and humourists, from E.T.A. Hoffmann to Heinrich Heine, for whom the discrepancy between reality and the ideal was a source of pain, longing and disillusionment.

Klee's breakthrough to colour and stylistic maturity occurred in the course of his trip to Tunisia, in the company of August Macke and Louis Moilliet, in 1914. His subsequent move to a hard, crystalline abstraction, influenced by the ripening of his friendship with Marc, bore a superficial resemblance to Marc's own work, in its last phase, but instead of embodying the utopian synthesis of spiritual and physical reality to which Marc aspired, it amounted to a rejection of the harsh reality of the physical world, inflicted by the cruelty and suffering of the war.

The war brought with it the dispersal of the avant-garde, in Munich as elsewhere – the death in the trenches of Macke and Marc, in 1914 and 1916, respectively, and Kandinsky's eventual return to Russia, for a number of years, via Sweden. As a project for the artistic renewal of the world the *Blaue Reiter* enjoyed only a limited success. Personal differences, financial and other difficulties, then war, prevented the realization of a number of other important projects. Among these were a volume devoted to illustrations of the Bible, for which Marc was to tackle the story of the Creation from Genesis and Kandinsky, the Book of Revelations; a publication dedicated to the theatre, in which Kandinsky and Hugo Ball would have developed further some of the ideas and theories about the *Gesamtkunstwerk* embodied, for instance, in Kandinsky's stage compositions, *Der Gelbe Klang* and *Der Violette Vorhang* ('The Violet Curtain'); and Kandinsky's and Marc's plans for a publication effecting a reconciliation between the arts and sciences.

The *Blaue Reiter* may not have achieved the spiritual revolution that it intended, but at the very least it seemed to those who came after to offer a blueprint for a new world, which was seized upon, first by the artistic and political rebels of the *Novembergruppe* and then the humanitarian, social reformers of the Bauhaus. Klee and Kandinsky continued their association at the Bauhaus and found an outlet, through their teaching, for their shared philosophical and musical, as well as literary interests[15]. Lyonel Feininger, who had been invited by Marc to exhibit with the *Blaue Reiter* artists at Herwarth Walden's First German Autumn Salon in Berlin in 1913, was called upon by Walter Gropius to produce a woodcut cover design for the Bauhaus prospectus, which depicted a crystalline cathedral, as an evocation of the collaborative endeavour of the medieval masons' lodges and a symbol of the striving of artists and artisans, painters, sculptors and architects to construct a new world of the spirit and a new democratic society. Through Kandinsky, Klee, Feininger, Itten, Gropius, Schlemmer and their colleagues at the Bauhaus, the universalist ideals of the *Blaue Reiter* became absorbed into the mainstream of German and western culture.

Henry Meyric Hughes

1 Transl. from, Wassily Kandinsky 'Einiges' from *Klänge*, (Munich, 1913).
2 Wassily Kandinsky 'Der Blaue Reiter (Rückblick)' in *Das Kunstblatt* XIV, 57.
3 The word 'Almanach' was removed from the cover at the last minute, at the insistence of the publisher, Reinhard Piper.
4 Klaus Lankheit (ed.), *Der Blaue Reiter* (Munich 1965), 315.
5 Marianne von Werefkin, *Briefe an einen Unbekannten, 1901–1905.* ed. Clemens Weiler, (Cologne, 1958).
6 Transl. from Wassily Kandinsky in *Das Kunstblatt III*, (1919), 172 ff.
7 Transl. from a quotation in Otto Stelzer, *Die Vorgeschichte der abstrakten Kunst, Denkmodelle und Vor-Bilder* (Munich, 1964).
8 This question and the influence of Steiner's teachings on Kandinsky have been examined in some detail by Professor L.D. Ettlinger and Sixten Ringbom and most extensively in the latter's *The Sounding Cosmos. A Study in the Spiritualism of Kandinsky and the Genesis of Abstract Painting* (Helsingfors, 1970).
9 Transl. from Franz Marc, *Schriften*, Klaus Lankheit (ed.), 144, quoted in Carla Schulz-Hoffmann, 'Franz Marc und die Romantik' in *Franz Marc 1880–1916*, (Munich, 1980).
10 Transl. from Reinhard Piper, *Vormittag. Erinnerungen eines Verlegers* (Munich, 1947), 429.
11 Transl. from Franz Marc, *Schriften* Klaus Lankheit, ed. (Cologne, 1978), 98.
12 ibid. (as note 11), 143.
13 Transl. from letter to August Macke of 12 December 1910. Quoted in August Macke/Franz Marc *Briefwechsel* (Cologne, 1964), 28.
14 Will Grohmann, *Kandinsky* (New York, 1958), 179–80.
15 V. Hajo Düchting, *Franz Marc*, (Cologne, 1991), 130 ff.

The Bauhaus Utopia

The Bauhaus was created in 1918 (the year of the German Revolution) by the architect Walter Gropius and his friends from the *Arbeitsrat für Kunst* (Workers' Council for Art) and the *Novembergruppe* (November Group). The unity of conception and execution in this utopian project and in its successive metamorphoses as a centre of education and production over the fourteen years of the Weimar Republic, ranks among the supreme achievements of German cultural history.

Gropius was a catalyst. He succeeded in uniting a multiplicity of ideas, tendencies and personalities of widely differing origins, and brought them together in the service of a single objective. Initially, this central purpose looked like a revival of the medieval masons' lodge, which was the body of craftsmen engaged in the building of a cathedral. Such was the inspiration of the woodcut made early in 1919 by Lyonel Feininger as a headpiece for Gropius's programmatic statement, *Staatliches Bauhaus in Weimar* (ex. cat.), which begins: 'The ultimate end of all creative activity is building [*der Bau*]!'

The untranslatable neologism *Bauhaus* itself is a reference to the masons' lodge (*Bauhütte*), and thus a deliberate evocation of the unity of all the arts. With its radiant stars, reminiscent of the Soviet star, Feininger's woodcut gave rise to the catchphrase 'Cathedral of Socialism'. Its technique and style confirm the strong affinity between the Bauhaus idea and the Expressionist love of crystalline and vigorously simplified forms. As a school, the Bauhaus adopted the basic structure of the masons' lodge, with an emphasis on craft training in specific materials, such as wood, metal, weaving, glass and also mural painting. The terms 'apprentice', 'journeyman' and 'master' (in Weimar until 1924, there were separate masters for form and material) stem from traditional craft structures, as distinct from the academic practices imported from France.

The dominant artistic personality in this initial phase was the Swiss painter Johannes Itten. He liberated the students from the copying exercises of the academy tradition and devised the celebrated *Vorkurs*, the preliminary course that was eventually imitated all over the world. In this, the students were made to explore materials, emotions and bodily movements, of which they gave their own holistic interpretations. An integral part of the course was Itten's own *Farbenkugel in sieben Lichtstufen und zwölf Tönen* (Colour Sphere in Seven Gradations of Light and Twelve Tones; ex. cat.), which was inserted into the most important early Bauhaus publication, *Utopia – Dokumente der Wirklichkeit* ('Utopia – Documents of Reality', 1921; cat. 168).

Mystics of past centuries, such as Jacob Böhme ('regenerate Man, as God's image, is no longer an individual but a species') or Meister Eckhart, were as important in the utopian ideology of the early Bauhaus, as were the contemporary German youth movement, or the legacy of such workers as William Morris, or the 'Breath and Health Doctrines' of Mazdaznan – in 1922 Itten produced a leaflet, *Nach Jacob Böhme: Einatmen – Ausatmen* ('After Jacob Böhme: Inhalation – Exhalation') – or Buddhism or the Greek philosophy of Plotinus.

This first Bauhaus phase is as vividly represented by Feininger's programmatic woodcut as it is by the idiosyncratic typography, with almost every letter separated, of Itten's leaflet, a blend of medieval book illustration and contemporary Dada collage. The first Bauhaus logo, designed by the student Peter Röhl, showed a kind of runic matchstick man, like a medieval mason's mark.

The transition to the second phase of the history of the Bauhaus was marked by the adoption of a new logo, designed by Oskar Schlemmer in 1922 (and subsequently almost unaltered), in which a strictly rectilinear human profile fills a circle. The basic forms of square, circle and triangle, in association with the primary colours of red, blue and yellow, also governed the design of seating (Marcel Breuer's slatted chair), other furniture (Peter Keler's cradle), household utensils (Marianne Brandt's kettle) and houses (Georg Muche's Haus Am Horn). In a total break with crystalline Expressionism, this phase represented the utopia of the union of all

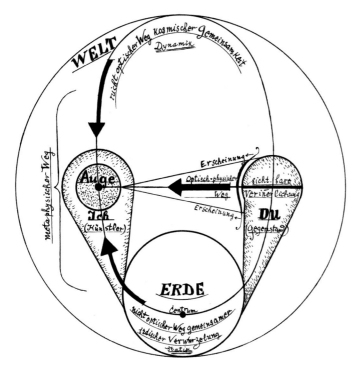

Fig.1 Paul Klee, *Eye, Centre, You*, illustration for the essay *Wege des Naturstudiums* (Ways of Nature Study), published Weimar 1923 (cat. 165)

forms, from the microcosm of everyday utensils to the macrocosm of town planning.

In the *Vorkurs* the students absorbed the basics of design through the colour theory of Wassily Kandinsky and the analytical studies of line and space ('Ways of Nature Study') made by Paul Klee (fig. 1). This emphasis on the formal aspects of design made possible not only a move away from individual expressivity but also a link with international movements such as De Stijl (Theo van Doesburg influenced the Bauhaus from late 1921 onwards), with Russian Constructivism and with the ideas of Le Corbusier.

In 1923, however, and even more so in the two years that followed, the demand for 'functional' design prevailed. 'Art and Technology – a New Unity' was the slogan of a major piece of self-advertisement that was forced on the Bauhaus by the exigencies of Thuringian politics: the great Bauhaus Exhibition of 1923. The first tubular steel chairs followed in 1925, along with a functional typography that incorporated elements of photography, and the conception of a psychologically based, functionally oriented, monochrome mural painting.

The move to new Bauhaus buildings in Dessau on 4 December 1926 signalled the beginning of the third

phase in the teaching of the school. The masters of form and of material in each subject workshop were now to be one and the same person, and that person would be a product of the Bauhaus's own work and teaching: Breuer, Josef Albers, Herbert Bayer, Hinnerk Scheper, Gunta Stölzl.

In this third phase the slogan (coined in America) was 'Form Follows Function', and the Bauhaus began to work directly with industry. There followed lamps, tubular steel furniture and other products, devised by students at the Bauhaus and developed to the production stage in industrial laboratories. The quintessential product of this phase is the tubular steel chair that Breuer designed from 1925 onwards in a number of variants, one of which – the sprung seat of 1927, made out of a single tube, without hind legs – became a classic and is still in production.

Also in 1927, painting classes were inaugurated. Thereafter Klee and Kandinsky no longer taught only in their own studios, in the Masters' houses along the Burgkühnerallee in Dessau, but also officially at the Bauhaus itself. Since the move from Weimar, Feininger had ceased to hold an official Bauhaus post, but he still had great influence as a unifying influence and as an artistic personality. At the Bauhaus all these differences and tensions were never glossed over but brought into the open and vigorously debated. At dazzling parties, stage galas and birthday celebrations, people danced the night away to the strains of the Bauhaus band; but there was a strong sense that this was a community under constant threat from outside.

The fourth phase, which began in 1928, is closely associated with the name of the new director, Hannes Meyer, an architect who had been called in from Switzerland only one year previously in order to focus the Bauhaus's work, at last, on the central theme of architecture. Meyer's strictly rational, analytical working methods were reflected in a practical syllabus. His maxims – 'building is a biological process and not an aesthetic operation'; 'building is not an individual emotive gesture but a collective action' (1930) – document the transformation of the Bauhaus and its new emphasis on Marxist principles. Production of household utensils made under Bauhaus licence was boosted to maximize the school's income.

The characteristic product of this phase is surely the Bauhaus wallpaper printed by the firm of Gebr. Rasch, at Bramsche, near Osnabrück. An internal Bauhaus competition was won by a Swiss student, Hans Fischli, who was later to work as a painter, sculptor and architect. His design was a simple, almost monochrome paper, with a design created with a decorator's comb; it could be hung without matching up the pattern repeats. As a mass-produced, economical replacement for painted wall surfaces, it allowed the architect to specify his colours precisely. The revolutionary impact of the Bauhaus globe lamps, tubular steel chairs and wall-papers is almost impossible to exaggerate; for these are objects that we have come to take for granted.

Other features of the fourth Bauhaus phase were the first exhibitions of 'Young Bauhaus Painters' and the inauguration of a photography class (under Walter Peterhans), with an emphasis on aesthetic fundamentals and precise craftsmanship rather than on the uses of photography as political weapon or documentary record.

Under Meyer, the playful experimental activities of Schlemmer's Bauhaus theatre came to an abrupt end. Meyer affronted Schlemmer – dancer, painter and perhaps the most versatile Bauhaus personality of all apart from László Moholy-Nagy – by asking him to include more political sketches in his shows. Schlemmer's *Gesamtplan* (Overall Design) for the mural decoration of the workshop building at the Weimar Bauhaus in 1923 proclaimed his faith that 'Man is the measure of all things.' He exploited the difficulties of the architectural setting designed by Henry van de Velde to create a complex and subtle artistic synthesis, or *Gesamtkunstwerk*, that took in all the surfaces of the hallways and staircases and ranged from reliefs against coloured surfaces to purely linear figures. His theme was the human figure as the vector of the ideal unity of body and spirit, as a source of architectural scale, and as a rhythmic pivot of spatial movement.

In all this he drew inspiration from Philipp Otto Runge, from Jean Paul and from Heinrich von Kleist's ideas in *Über das Marionettentheater* ('On the Puppet Theatre'). In his journal for July–August 1923, Schlemmer noted: 'It remains to be said that, in today's God-deprived world, an art that relies on great themes, as monumental painting and sculpture do, is in a particularly forlorn state . . . And yet one great theme remains immeasurably old, eternally new, the object and formative principle of art in every age: Man, the human figure. Of this it is said that it is the measure of all things . . . The elemental factor in figurative art is the type. Its creation is the ultimate, supreme task.'

The fifth and last phase of the existence of the Bauhaus was dominated by the architect Ludwig Mies van der Rohe, who became director in 1930. Mies found Bauhaus design dominated by Marxist principles and reduced to the analysis of function, and he made a start – but no more than a start – on reconciling this with the principles of simplicity and truth to materials. Expulsion from Dessau to Berlin, and final closure by the Nazis in 1933, marked the end of the work of the Bauhaus in Germany, and at the same time the beginning of the fruitful, worldwide activity of exiled Bauhaus people in Holland, England, Japan and above all the USA (at Black Mountain College, North Carolina, the New Bauhaus in Chicago and elsewhere).

To this day, the worldwide impact of the Bauhaus is symbolized by Schlemmer's painting *Bauhaus Staircase*, and by its present location. With financial support from Philip Johnson, Alfred H. Barr bought the work for The Museum of Modern Art in New York from the Schlemmer exhibition, closed down by the Nazis in Stuttgart in 1933; since then it has hung almost uninterruptedly in the stairwell of that temple of Modernism. It was painted three years after Schlemmer's own final exit from the Bauhaus, in nostalgic memory of that glorious time, and as an epitome of the work of the school. Schlemmer has filled the staircase with light by fronting it with glass (like the workshop front at Dessau). The stylized figures strive upwards, linked together only by colour and movement. They embody the individual in the common life; building as the supreme purpose; the new humanity as the measure and rhythmic base of the whole. This is painting as a microcosm of a new world that cries out to be given shape, an 'idea' (as Mies called the Bauhaus in his brief eulogy of Gropius) that is intrinsically utopian and yet is becoming reality, one little step at a time.

Wulf Herzogenrath

Translated from the German by David Britt

Irony and Grotesque
The Other Side

Die andere Seite (The other side) is the title of Alfred Kubin's famous fantasy novel published in Munich early in 1909. A grotesque quality – Kubin's narrative technique mixes greyness and the ridiculous – is the only element that makes the apocalyptic events of this novel tolerable to the reader; it is full of violence, murder and manslaughter, sexual perversion, bloody orgies and finally the terrible destruction of the dream city of 'Perle', heightened to a visionary level. This novel, which Kubin also illustrated, caused a considerable stir among contemporaries – writers like Franz Kafka, but also fine artists like Wassily Kandinsky, Franz Marc and Paul Klee. It was seen among other things as a metaphor for decline in their own period, as a vision of the destruction of the old world, which had become questionable. The illustrations for *Die andere Seite*, and the style of their graphic, linear, pen-and-ink drawing, represent Kubin's ultimate departure from the excessively clear and sculpturally contoured inventions of his early works dating from 1900 to 1904.

Kubin himself described the 'birth-hour' of this early work very impressively in a much-quoted passage in his autobiography. As a young art student, still feeling his way, he saw Max Klinger's *Paraphrase über den Fund eines Handschuhs* (Paraphrase on the finding of a glove) in the Staatliche Graphische Sammlung in Munich, 'saw and trembled with rapture', then roamed the streets of Munich in strange excitement. 'And then I was suddenly overwhelmed by a whole surge of visions in black and white – I simply cannot describe the thousandfold wealth my imagination conjured up.' It was as though a veil had been drawn back from a world of darkness, lurking in the depths of the consciousness, revealing the possibility of creating psychic hallucinations similar to those provided by Klinger's etchings. Images from distant spheres started to appear in Kubin's work, visions of superior strength, powerlessness, desire and ruin, in new symbols that seem to have been drawn from the subconscious of the 'modern soul'. After this initial experience, the young Kubin worked like a man pos-

sessed on the unusual images that make up his early work, which is still shocking today. Mercilessly he surprises us with the figments of our own anxiety, desires and obsessions. Even an early critic wrote of Kubin's art that it showed symbols of secret powers, 'whose proximity is revealed to us only in wild dreams and fantasies, in conditions of clairvoyant over-stimulation of the nerves.'

A number of these sensational drawings were published as copperplate prints in the so-called *Hans-von-Weber-Mappe*, a portfolio that included such works as *The Hour of Birth*, *The Best Doctor*, *Horror* and *Forgotten – Lost in Thought*. Thus they represent a dominant complex of ideas in Kubin's early work; they demonstrate control by the threatening, inescapable powers of fate, and circle in ever new forms around representations of ruin, death and dependence. Another important thematic group involves sexuality and eroticism, centred mainly on the myth of woman as destructive seductress, but also as someone condemned by her own sexuality and especially – a theme derived from Kubin's traumatic experience of being seduced as a child – by her pregnant body. A portfolio was also planned for this subject-complex, but the drawings remained unpublished, probably because of the anticipated scandal.

The mature drawings of Kubin's early period are dominated by striking symbolic figures set alone in front of a diffuse empty space with unclear borders. Some are monstrous imaginary forms, some grotesque figure-montages, raised to a gigantic scale. But these exactly worked, washed or spattered ink drawings, whose precisely drawn framing lines further underline the claim to pictorial completeness, were all too often subjected to accusations of dilettantism, technical weakness or even pathological incompetence from the daily press. But the unmistakable sensual quality of Kubin's visions, impinging directly upon the viewer, makes itself felt precisely because of the strange mixture of hard line and empty space, the colourless chiaroscuro of the indeterminate pictorial space and the oppressive physical presence of the apparitions. At the same time this makes it clear that

Kubin's 'sickly and evil products' – or as Hans Holzschuher writes in his introduction to the *Hans-von-Weber-Mappe*, the 'hurrying and heavy dream-figments, hallucinations of fleeting hours, nebulous images, slipping by like will-o'-the-wisps' – these snapshots from the darkroom of the consciousness, were definitely not drawn in the ecstatic heat of the moment. On the contrary, it is the tormenting tension between the drawing, the clear simplicity and lack of compromise of the form, that Kubin's drawings depend upon, for no small part of their effect.

The terminology of early psychoanalysis places Kubin's drawings in another context. Beyond subjective pathology, his work touches the nerve of a period whose mood of crisis and radical change was reflected in the catastrophic threat to existence in the soul of modern man. No other artist has so pitilessly treated the irruption of the unconscious, carrying with it, as it did, the stigma of social psychosis – despite the fact that at the time he did not know the early writings of Sigmund Freud, who, with the publication in 1900 of his *Interpretation of Dreams*, revolutionized the contemporary view of man. Flagrantly encoded constellations of consciousness, preconscious images, still below the zone of the feelings they trigger, are revealed in the palely-lit black and white of dream residues. This goes well beyond the piquant encodings of artists like Odilon Redon and the Symbolists, and also beyond the extremely personal statements of an artist like Edvard Munch, or the Expressionists. Christoph Brockhaus has plausibly described this creative process in terms of the four mechanisms of dream work identified by Freud; compression, dislocation, consideration of presentability and secondary processing. In so doing, Kubin drew upon spiritual and artistic models from his own time. A number of such stimuli, from Klinger's etchings for example, can be found in the *Hans-von-Weber-Mappe*. This makes him even more of a key figure for his epoch. With rare perceptiveness he reflects its traumas, from the demonization of woman down to fantasies of destruction. Kubin's contemporaries – such as the disciples of Friedrich Nietzsche – recognized in his pictorial inventions (often called 'literary' at the time) not only his origins in Symbolism (which he outgrew), but the influence of certain philosophers. Both the nihilism in Kubin's

works and their latent tendency to create heroes – the reverse side of his fantasies of excessive power and impotence – show him to be an heir of Schopenhauer's and Nietzsche's philosophy, which was at that time the common property of all intellectuals. The *Weber-Mappe* drawings in particular are dominated by hero-creation and its psychological counterpart, dependency and subjection to a superior force that is incomprehensible, uninterpretable, impersonal, and this produces symbols of atavistic anxiety. Today, over ninety years after this portfolio appeared, our social standards may have changed, and the material satisfaction of desire and desire substitutes may have largely suppressed such images; however, the immediate impact made by Kubin's drawings is a measure of their lasting power.

Kubin and Paul Klee had not met at the time of their first independent artistic expressions, the former's 'early work' in Munich and the latter's *Inventionen*, produced in Berne from 1903–05. It was not until January 1911 that the two artists got to know each other properly. Klee, like Kubin, had just arrived at a new stylistic stage, replacing the agonizing, dissecting pseudo-realism of his first major works, the sequence of etchings called *Inventionen*. We start to notice grotesques here, and more irony than is to be found in Kubin's horror fantasies, all executed with a hitherto rare precision. The first of these etchings, including *Woman and Animal* (cat. 176), *Virgin in Tree* (cat. 175) and *Woman, Sowing Weeds* were created by Klee in the seclusion of his parents' home in Berne in the summer of 1903. With a hard, finely chiselled line, in this sequence of eleven prints (fifteen including variations), he invented a new form of symbolic representation. It turns away from a comfortable symbolism in the extreme way in which it analyses and reveals the design, while turning its back on realism by making disturbing breaks between the picture plane and pictorial space. Like Kubin, Klee goes back to models provided by Félicien Rops or Max Klinger, but the epigrammatic riddles and exaggerated, strangely distorted figures introduce a new, very modern trait of alienation. Klee's formal devices have often been described in terms of a lack of foreshortening, the transformation of volume into highly developed relief and contradictions between plasticity and two-dimensional surface qualities. In addition the bodies and faces of his figures, partly grotesque hybrids like *Ancient Phoenix* and *Hero with the Wing* (cat. 181), that seem to have been constructed like sculptures, along classical line, are thrown into doubt by their obscene ugliness. Marcel Franciscono maintains that part of the satirical effect of the drawings is derived from this travesty of tradition: 'For the *Inventionen* Klee selected a consciously meticulous and demanding technique that forced him to reproduce individual forms with extreme precision and detail. It was an attempt to introduce into his work something of the monumentality and creative austerity that he had found in the art and architecture of Italy, without thereby striving for the classical ideal of beauty that he admired, but did not feel capable of realizing. His solution was a style that he was retrospectively to call gothic-classical.'

It is no coincidence that Klee's artistic origins are closely connected with satire. His first creative experiments, after his drawings as a child, were caricatures and satirical marginal drawings in his school exercise books. They show a pronounced interest in physiognomy but also a sharp and ironic wit; this occurs in Klee's early diary entries as well. In subsequent years he showed his admiration for leading *Simplicissimus* caricaturists like Thomas Theodor Heine and Bruno Paul, and for a time Klee himself seriously thought of working as a caricaturist for newspapers and pamphlets once he had finished his Munich course; he submitted a number of drawings to *Jugend* and *Simplicissimus*. He wrote to his friend Hans Bloesch from Munich in 1898: 'Do you know what I want to be for a bit: a painter? No, just a common or garden draughtsman. But a caustic one. I should like to make humanity look ridiculous, nothing less than that. And with the simplest possible means, e.g. black on white. At the same time, oh blasphemy, I should like to attack our Lord God quite vigorously.' Even in his early drawings the markedly individual form – the personal form which was what Klee was ultimately struggling for in these experiments – was a striking feature, and this made them unacceptable to popular satirical magazines; later, however, the early Klee's ironic distance becomes the 'hereafter' distance that is the hallmark of the independent creator-artist: the mature Klee liked to describe himself as master of a world of elemental phenomena. This idea is already present in a letter that Klee wrote to

Alfred Kubin while serving in the war in January 1918. He said that the difficult times had 'strongly affected' his output 'in the aesthetic sense. This has created a new conscious basis, in which I see possibilities that fill an outwardly fettered man with a great urge to show, quite calmly, that he belongs to the centre.'

By that time the period of most intensive contact between the two artists was over. In June 1912, during a visit to Zwickledt, Klee had shown Kubin his illustrations for Voltaire's *Candide*, which he had started in the previous year, and which were not to find a publisher until Kurt Wolff brought them out in Leipzig in 1920. These economical, black-and-white pen-and-ink drawings, with dematerialized, brittle, shadowy, excessively tall figures made a profound impression on Kubin. Their mimic style, driven almost to the point of caricature, can still be detected in many of Kubin's scenes with figures as late as 1915. But the crucial differences between Kubin's and Klee's drawings at this period has also been repeatedly pointed out. While Kubin, despite all the brittle dissolution and nervous torsion of his figures always remained the 'fantastic realist', attached to drawing corporeal objects in their concrete context, Klee's completely two-dimensional, transparent figures become abstract ciphers. As independent configurations they transcend traditional pictorial laws and act effortlessly as metaphors. Later this becomes the abstract sign language with figurative and emotional resonances, that was to be so typical of Klee's work. For Klee the *Candide* illustrations so admired by Kubin meant a breakthrough to new, expressive devices of his own, for which he had been looking so tirelessly in previous years.

Annegret Hoberg

Translated from the German by Michael Robinson

Max Ernst and Romanticism

Friedrich Hölderlin, Novalis, Achim von Arnim, and also Christian Dietrich Grabbe, Goethe and Heinrich Heine: these are the German Romantic writers named by Max Ernst in the magazine *View* in 1942, on a double page headed 'Max Ernst's Favorite Poets Painters of the Past'. The favourite painters do not include a single Romantic.[1] This is astonishing, given the fact that Ernst declared in a conversation with Eduard Roditi in 1960: 'The fact is that I've always had Friedrich's pictures and ideas more or less consciously in mind, almost from the day I started painting.'[2] Ernst could have seen originals by Caspar David Friedrich in the Berlin Nationalgalerie as early as 1916.[3]

Ernst often talked about Novalis and Achim von Arnim in the circle of literati around Paul Eluard, Louis Aragon and André Breton, to which he belonged from 1922. He passed their thoughts and poetry on to his friends. Breton's close bond with Romantic thought is confirmed by the key sentence in the First Surrealist Manifesto (1924): 'I believe in the future dissolution of these two entirely opposed conditions, dream and reality; they will become a kind of absolute, or – if you like – super-reality.'[4] The Surrealists also had a crucial effect on the reception of German Romanticism. For example, Madeleine Landsberg published the first monograph on Friedrich as 'Maler der romantischen Angst' ('Painter of Romantic *Angst*') as an article in the magazine *Minotaure*.[5]

Ernst was familiar with the art and ideas of German Romanticism. But how does this express itself in his paintings? 1925, the year in which he painted *Sea and Sun* (colour plate, p. 363), was a year of radical change. It was the year in which he systematically exploited frottage, his method for fixing finds from his expeditions into the depths of the subconscious and the sieve of natural forms. *Sea and Sun* is one of the works that demonstrate vividly that frottage is more than a new way of drawing, but that processes inspired by it can also be used in painting.

Nothing in *Sea and Sun* is familiar from our visual experience – except for the blue of the sky and the line of the horizon. We wonder, in some irritation: Is that a sea at the bottom? If so, it's red. Or isn't it more like a stratigraphic cross-section of the earth? What does the black disc at the bottom mean? Why does the giant star with the black disc on a red background have an eye? This irritation is comparable with the extreme disapproval with which Friedrich's anti-classically composed landscapes were met by many of his contemporaries. The concept *Erdlebenbild* (earth-life image),[6] coined by Carl Gustav Carus and used by the painter-doctor to describe his friend Friedrich's painting, suggests an approach that goes much deeper. But Ernst was not depicting landscape; in his case rubbing and drawing circles, imagination and geometry, produce an image of the life of the earth, a world-image.

Ernst, who came from the Rhineland, addressed the forest as a subject intensively between 1926 and 1927. The forest pictures dating from these years are close to the Romantic spirit. For Romantic poets the forest was a place of particular emotion. Ernst called it *Naturgefühl* (nature-feeling): nature's all-powerful quality is experienced in the forest, both her beauty and her terror. Ernst reports that even when he was a child he felt like this when he went into a forest.[7] This memory creates a link with the Romantic search for things original and natural.

Impressive forest pictures like those in the Kunstmuseum in Basel, for example, or the Kunsthalle in Karlsruhe, show the forest not as something boundless, but as though it were on an island, rampantly growing out of itself. It seems both dead and alive at the same time, as if burnt down, made up of charred boards, but alive. Behind and above it is a ring-shaped star, unseen but imaginable. The star in particular fills the forest pictures with magic power. It is this magic that forms the close link with Friedrich's painting, for example with the early *Cromlech in the Snow* (1807) in Dresden. In Friedrich's case there is no element of the super-real, every detail is depicted faithfully. And yet pictures of this kind are composed with such aloofness, often without any traditional mood-creating elements, that they seem unfamiliar, alien and strange, both close and at the same time far away, comprehensible and incomprehensible – and this makes them exude magic power.

There is only one forest picture that Ernst chooses to charge with tense drama by placing a horrific scene in the foreground, as if on a stage. It is called: *Max Ernst Showing a Girl the Head of his Father* (colour plate, p. 362). This act has caused the full-breasted, empty-faced young girl's hair to stand on end; the father's head with its formidable moustache seems to sit on the frame, and what we perceive as his brain hangs in front of a leaf whose stalk is being held in pointed fingers by the monstrous form that bears the artist's name. This hand is large and fleshy, and so is the other one. But otherwise the body of this figure that comes crashing into the picture seems to be merely a covering, empty shells, and instead of a head it has colourfully decorated horns. Love and patricide, the father's head as a tribute to the beautiful beloved – this is the burden of this scene, which turns the forest into a backdrop. But it is a backdrop that is by no means ineffective. Ernst is playing with horror here, although it is not possible to make out a definite story. It is Romantic literature, rather than painting, that might have inspired this scene, gruesomely reminiscent of E.T.A. Hoffmann's *Elixiere des Teufels* 'The Devils Elixir' of 1815/16 and Grabbe's exclamation: 'And so it is all-powerful malice that turns the circle of the world and then destroys it!'[8]

The Petrified City (Manchester City Art Gallery), painted in 1935, is an image of paralysed life. The tilted slabs piled on top of each other are reminiscent of Friedrich's Hamburg painting *Sea of Ice*. Although the mood of Friedrich's work is icy, and Ernst's is dominated by warm colours, there is an external and an internal link between them. Ernst applied the red, orange and yellow paint to the black with stencils; rhomboid and square pattern predominate. It is like looking through bars into a fire. Above the summit a giant moon floats in an overcast grey sky. Behind a mountain glowing with fire another one rises, pale blue and pink, its topmost slab touching the disc of the moon. Here and there life emerges between the slabs. They may be only vegetable, stencil-like ornaments, but they stand for teeming life that exists even in this scene of paralysis. Friedrich also

used such symbols of resistance, of new life, when he painted pictures of paralysis.

The forest pictures painted between 1936 and 1938 are pictures of the jungle, of luxuriant proliferation, of seeds and shoots. The title *La joie de vivre* is a manifesto but it is also directed against Catholic education's warnings about the pleasures of the flesh. When one remembers that *joie de vivre* is an everyday saying in French the title acquires an ironic aspect: this is the only life that leads to joy, my dear – *n'est-ce pas?* The heat of lurking lust is presented as normal.

Romantic literature must have nourished Ernst's delight in exuberant sensuality. As a polyglot reader he was just as aware of Edgar Allen Poe's stories and Victor Hugo's poems as he was of E.T.A. Hoffmann's tales. In *La joie de vivre* (colour plate, p. 364), when he changes leaves into an upright 'salamander' with human hands and arms, or a pair of copulating mantises, he was realizing the picture dreamed up by the violent knight Ludovico in Ludwig Tieck's novel *Franz Sternbalds Wanderungen* (1798). Ludovico imagines: 'Then I would paint extremely strange shapes, in confused, almost incomprehensible combinations, figures made up of all species of animals and ending as plants down below: insects and worms, which I wanted to make look strangely like human characters … .'[9]

In works like *Totem and Taboo*, produced between internment, escape and being recaptured, Ernst used the technique of decalcomania for painting the forest in a state of rottenness and decay. The abstract, dark-brown structures coagulated to form birds with long beaks, an eagle's head, a mask or a seductive woman. The Berlin etcher Carl Wilhelm Kolbe was working in a related spirit when he produced a sheet like *Dead Giant Oak Tree*. Hideous faces, shapes and demons appear in the split trunk, in the torn bark, in the splintered, withered branches, depicted with the same degree of reality as 'broken nature'. Even the park-like idyll in the background of Kolbe's etching has its counterpart in the little wood and pale moon in *Totem and Taboo*.

In his late work Ernst adopted a radical pictorial structure. This simple structuring of top and bottom by the line of the horizon, as in the Hamburg painting *A Beautiful Morning* (1965) is also to be found in Friedrich. But for the painter from Greifswald such determined artistic asceticism is rare: works that could be mentioned are the Berlin *Seashore by Moonlight*, the Dresden *Large Enclosure* or the late Hamburg sepia sheet *Moonrise by the Sea. A Beautiful Memory* is an earth-life image of the kind that Carus meant. The strip structure – horizontal at the bottom and zigzag at the top – probably produced by an underlay of hard objects when painting, enlivens the dual colour scheme: dark and light red at the bottom, cold and warm yellow on a red ground at the top. Shapes that can be read as fluttering ribbons float around an irregular blue rectangle. Jörg Traeger has related this picture to Philipp Otto Runge's *Morning*, in which the centre is taken up by the light of Aurora rising from the depths.[10]

In May 1971 Ernst travelled to the Rhineland, at the age of eighty. He met his friend Eduard Trier, professor of art history at the University of Bonn, when visiting the Cologne exhibition *Deutsche Malerei des 19. Jahrhunderts* (19th-century German painting). Trier drew his attention to Arnim and Brentano's fictitious dialogue between viewers 'Verschiedene Empfindungen vor einer Seelandschaft von Friedrich, worauf ein Kapuziner' ('Various emotions before a seascape by Friedrich, with Capuchin'). Heinrich von Kleist edited and completed the text for publication in the *Berliner Abendblätter*.[11] Ernst translated it with Kleist's additions (including the famous sentence: '. . . and because in its monotony and boundlessness it has nothing but the frame as foreground, one feels, when looking at it, as though one's eyelids had been cut off.') Kleist's work inspired Ernst to create a lithograph, which appeared in 1972, with six collages – ironic commentaries on the dialogue – and the text in German and French: *Caspar David Friedrich; Seascape with Monk*.

Both the lithograph and the book are proof of Ernst's affinity with Friedrich's art and the creative thinking of Romanticism. Ernst transformed the stretched horizontal format of the painting, which was produced between 1808 and 1810, and is now known as *Monk by the Sea* (colour plate, p. 96), into a slender vertical format and raised the low horizon. Patterns of found shapes – at the bottom straight lines at a variety of angles, variously twisting lines at the top – produce the basic structure of the bipartite composition, as in *A Beautiful Morning*. The 'limitless watery desert' at the sides (Arnim and Brentano)

becomes the unfathomable depths of the sea, the peaceful clouds in the sky become swirling circulation. The Capuchin, exposed to nature without protection, gives Friedrich's picture a historical dimension, but Ernst's lithograph a *Seascape without Monk*, as Werner Spies calls it in the afterword, is an image of prehistoric nature.

The painter Johan Christian Clausen Dahl, Friedrich's friend, said these landscapes had 'a profound poetry of their own as dream-images of an unknown world.'[12] Ernst found a statement in Friedrich's writings that he made his own maxim: 'Close your bodily eye, that you may see your picture first with the eye of the spirit. Then bring to light what you have seen in the darkness, that its effect may work back on others from without to within.'[13]

Helmut R. Leppien

Translated from the German by Michael Robinson

1 *View*, vol. 2, no. 1 (1942). Max Ernst, *Beyond Painting* (New York, 1948), 6, and Max Ernst, *Écritures* (Paris, 1970), 322ff.
2 Eduard Roditi, 'Ein Mittagessen mit Max Ernst', *Der Monat*, vol. 13, no. 1950 (March, 1960), 70.
3 Karin von Maur, 'Max Ernst und die Romantik', in exh. cat. *Max Ernst: Retrospektive zum 100. Geburtstag*, ed. and introd. Werner Spies (London and Stuttgart, 1991/92), 342.
4 André Breton, *Manifestes du Surréalisme* (Paris, no year).
5 Madeleine Landsberg, 'Caspar David Friedrich: Peintre de l'angoisse romantique', *Minotaure*, vol. 6, no. 12–13 (May 1939). 25–28. See also Karin von Maur (as note 3), 342 and note 15.
6 Carl Gustav Carus, *Briefe über Landschaftsmalerei* (2nd ed., Leipzig 1835), 118.
7 Max Ernst, 'Biographische Notizen (Wahrheitgewebe und Lügengewebe)', in exh. cat. *Max Ernst* (Cologne and Zurich, 1962/63), 20: 'Mixed feelings as he stepped in to the forest for the first time, delight and depression. And what the Romantics christened *Naturgefühl* (nature-feeling). The wonderful delight of breathing freely in the open air, but at the same time the oppressive feeling of being incarcerated by hostile trees on all sides. Outside and inside at the same time, free and a prisoner.'
8 Christian Dietrich Grabbe, *Herzog Theodor von Gothland* (Frankfurt am Main, 1827), concluding monologue.
9 Ludwig Tieck, *Schriften XVI* (Berlin, 1829), 331; Ludwig Tieck, *Frühe Erzählungen und Romane* 3 (Darmstadt, 1968), 927.
10 Jörg Traeger, *Philipp Otto Runge und sein Werk* (Munich, 1975), 199.
11 *Berliner Abendblätter* 12 (13 October, 1810), 47 ff.
12 Johan Christian Clausen Dahl: 'It is precisely this that gives Friedrich's landscapes … as dream images of an unknown world – a profound poetry of their own.' Quoted from Andreas Aubert, 'Caspar Friedrich', *Kunst und Künstler* 3 (1905), 198.
13 Sigrid Hinz, ed., Caspar David Friedrich, *Was die fühlende Seele sucht: Briefe und Bekenntnisse* (Berlin, 1991), 78.

Neo-Romanticism and Neue Sachlichkeit

Sachlichkeit – objectivity or matter-of-factness – represented a volte-face, a change in fundamental beliefs, a new style after the First World War, the November Revolution of 1918 and the declared bankruptcy of Expressionism in 1920. The generation of painters born around 1890 began to think again about contemporary problems, social matters, 'nature', and tangible objects. But from the very beginning, in the dubious light of the Weimar Republic, this new realistic art had a Janus face of commitment and scepticism, closeness to reality and flight from contemporary matters. Curt Glaser remarked upon the emergence of 'Neo-Romanticism' as early as 1920, 'the undeniable fact that after almost exactly a hundred years we are once more heading for a Romantic movement', and gave an urgent warning about the danger of 'woolly mysticism'.[1] In the same year Paul Ferdinand Schmidt argued for the present day's 'right to Romanticism': '… (we) bear the legacy of Romanticism to new glory, disinterred and unfaded: an art of all-loving yearning, of mystic revelation, of inwardness.'[2] His line of German tradition ran as follows: the Middle Ages, Jakob Asmus Carstens, Philipp Otto Runge, Peter von Cornelius, the Nazarenes, Wilhelm Heinrich Wackenroder, Ludwig Tieck, Caspar David Friedrich. Shortly afterwards Schmidt turned his attention to contemporary realism. As early as 1922 the Mannheim Museum director Gustav Friedrich Hartlaub distinguished between two opposing tendencies in figurative art after Expressionism: 'I see a right and a left wing, one conservative to the point of classicism, and rooted in timelessness … . The other, the left wing, is contemporary and shrill … .'[3] On the right are timeless Neoclassicists and Neo-Romantics like Alexander Kanoldt and Georg Schrimpf, on the left socially critical realists like Otto Dix and George Grosz. But Hartlaub's simplified scheme did not exclude overlapping and the possibility of a synthesis (Dix, Franz Radziwill) between the poles. In 1923 he coined the all-embracing phrase *Neue Sachlichkeit*[4] for both directions, and this was also used for the exhibition in the Städtische Kunsthalle in Mannheim in 1925. But it was not early German Romanticism that gave the move towards *Neue Sachlichkeit* its metaphysical impetus, it was the *Pittura Metafisica* of Carlo Carrà and Giorgio de Chirico, influenced by the *trecento* and *quattrocento* and disseminated from 1919 in Germany by the Munich gallery-owner Hans Goltz, through the magazine *Valori Plastici*. The so-called 'Munich Group',[5] including Heinrich Maria Davringhausen, Carlo Mense and Schrimpf, with the exception of Kanoldt, absorbed aspects of the object-magic of the Italian 'Metaphysicals' into their work. A longing for Italy pervades Kanoldt's deserted architectural landscapes depicting Olevano (colour plate, p. 368) and Subiaco (in which he continued the Romantic tradition of the German-Romans Joseph Anton Koch and Franz Horny), Mense's twilight pastorals and Schrimpf's naïve Madonnas: paradises of reverie far from the depression of the postwar years. The Neoclassicists[6] were beginning to move towards Neo-Romanticism in about 1920, when the Munich artists 'unconsciously started to establish a supranational canon influenced by the south'[7] (Franz Roh), and became part of the 'Italian myth'. The essentially static new style was defined by 'sharpening cleanness', 'meticulous articulation' and 'shinily polished substance'. Roh, writing in 1920, saw in it 'many affinities with the *quattrocento* and with 1800'.[8] German Neoclassicism was a prologue and transitional stage before a restorative Neo-Romantic art, which attempted to approach early German Romanticism in its sensibility and 'moods' during the 1920s. The Romantic iconography of portrait and interior, window-motif and landscapes filled with longing acquired a new topicality. This reception process was accompanied by numerous exhibitions.[9] One critic found that the exhibition *Romantik und Biedermeier in der deutschen Malerei und Zeichnung* (1924; Romanticism and Biedermeier in German Painting and Drawing) in the Kunsthandlung Gerstenberger in Chemnitz 'summed up an epoch that shows striking parallels to some of the ambitions of recent painting. In both cases we see a stand against empty formalism.'[10] Carl Georg Heise mounted the *Overbeck und sein Kreis* (Overbeck and his Circle) exhibition in Lübeck in 1926, and Schmidt's monograph *Philipp Otto Runge, Sein Leben und sein Werk* ('Philipp Otto Runge, his Life and Work') and Willi Wolfradt's on *Caspar David Friedrich und die Landschaft der Romantik* ('Caspar David Friedrich and the Romantic Landscape') appeared as early as 1923. Dialogues with Romantic iconography and the topos of the *Rückenfigur*, the figure turned away towards the landscape were conscious paraphrases of quotations, and quite frequently an act of unconscious memory as well. A direct link with Runge's monumental figure-style can be detected in Schrimpf's early pictures of children (colour plate, p. 367), but only episodically in Dix's work (colour plate, p. 366). Friedrich's *Frau am Fenster* (Woman at a Window; colour plate, p. 253) became an unequalled cult image for many people, and placed in harmony with the landscape of Lower Bavaria by Schrimpf (cat. 191). Karlsruhe artist Georg Scholz combined the crystalline structure of his cacti (colour plate, p. 365) with the icy object-definition of modern technique in his purist window pictures. The Neo-Romantics painted from the outside inwards; Schrimpf, close to Friedrich's maxim, spoke for like-minded colleagues as well: 'I do not paint before nature at all ... all the experiences are to be found only – within myself.' A Romanticism of arrested time, a touch of Arcadia on the horizon, and here and there a pin-prick of disquiet.

Radziwill, a North German, stands alone somewhere between Neo-Romanticism and a more realistic approach. His Dresden dialogue with the *Erdlebenkunst* (earth-life art of Carl Gustav Carus and Friedrich[11]) in 1927–28 was a key experience for his 'Magic Realism' (Roh) of endangered existence. His ghostly day and night pieces (colour plate, p. 369) are haunted by aircraft as 'tools of destruction'. The demon of modern technology destroys the Romantic idyll. Novalis sums it up: 'Death is the romanticizing principle in our lives.'

The Neo-Romantic painters, more loners with a sense of affinity than a 'group', regularly held joint exhibitions from the early '30s onwards: *Die deutsche Neuromantik in der Malerei der Gegenwart* (German Neo-Romanticism in Contemporary Painting) in the Frankfurt Kunstverein (1931) and *Die stille Landschaft*

(The Quiet Landscape) in the Anhaltinischer Kunstverein Dessau (1931), *Deutsche romantische Malerei der Gegenwart* (Contemporary German Romantic Painting) in Ulm (1931). Theo Champion, Adolf Dietrich, Hasso von Hugo, Kanoldt, Franz Lenk, Radziwill and Schrimpf were rashly hailed as a group, 'Die Sieben' (The Seven), on the occasion of an exhibition in Barmen in 1932. But Neo-Romantic painting, particularly in the landscapes of Kanoldt, and Schrimpf, Lenk (cat. 194) was showing clear signs of stylistic fatigue and of turning into the 'Quiet Garden' of the German provinces. Justus Bier put on a programmatic exhibition called *Neue Deutsche Romantik* (New German Romanticism) in the Kestner-Gesellschaft in Hanover in 1933. This included photographs by Albert Renger-Patzsch and reproductions of works by Friedrich and Runge as well as pictures by Kanoldt, Radziwill and Schrimpf. Bier emphasized the 'relationship of spiritual goals' in early Romanticism and Neo-Romanticism, but also pointed out 'that these modern Romantics have different foundations, they lived through Expressionism.'[12]

After the Nazis seized power in 1933, the Biedermeier branch of *Neue Sachlichkeit*, which laid a romanticizing emphasis on things German[13] and also on Friedrich's 'national art',[14] came perilously close to Nazi cultural phraseology like 'blood and soil' and 'German-Nordic spirit'. 'Party members' such as Kanoldt and Radziwill, Lenk and Schrimpf, temporarily took over the chairs of avant-garde artists who had been driven out of their teaching jobs in 1933, and occasional exhibitions and commissions by protégés of the Nazi regime followed. These painters tried to conform for a time, without abandoning their inner distance from the Nazis. As late as 1936 the Kunstverein Düsseldorf showed *Neue Romantische Kunst* (New Romantic art) which included Lenk, Mense and Schrimpf. With the exception of peripheral Neo-Romantic figures such as Werner Peiner, all the Nazis' attempts to integrate and subjugate once and for all this movement's leading representatives ultimately came to nothing. The 'cultural-Bolshevik' Dix lost his teaching post in Dresden as early as 1933; Radziwill lost his professorship in 1935 and was excluded from the Nazi Party in 1938; Lenk resigned his teaching post because colleagues were being persecuted and felt a sense of 'irreconcilability with the prevailing state art'; Schrimpf was driven out of his teaching post in 1937 and died in 1938; Kanoldt in 1939. While Dix (colour plate, p. 393) and Lenk were forced to return to nature in a 'kind of emigration' (Dix), the symbolic background of Friedrich's landscapes evaporated in the Kanoldt and Schrimpf mountain views. Only Radziwill managed to transform his art in the 1930s into a 'Symbolic Realism' (colour plate, p. 396) that adopted Friedrich's *vanitas* metaphors and concealed montage concept.

It became clear that a dramatically glorified national-socialist 'state' could not be built on a distanced view and cool formal purism, on the idylls and melancholy of Neo-Romanticism. When the Nazis started their notorious move against 'degenerate art' in 1937 the Neo-Romantic painters were ostracized in just the same way as their Expressionist opposites had been before them. The Nazis' misuse of Friedrich, of classical Romanticism and Neo-Romanticism turned out to be a failed attempt to corrupt the origin and meaning of all true Romanticism within the overblown, 'German-Nordic-National' concept of culture. The unspeakable results of the Nazis' hollow, stylistic eclecticism at the *Grosse Deutsche Kunstausstellungen* (Great German Art Exhibitions) in the *Haus der deutschen Kunst* (Munich House of German Art) demonstrated the provisional violent 'end of Romanticism'. The émigré Paul Westheim wrote the following sarcastic comments from Paris in 1937: 'Viking Romanticism', 'Drawing-room Tyrolean Romanticism or more correctly custom-dominated Tyrolean Romanticism', 'Teutonic Romanticism', 'Heroic Romanticism', 'Racial Romanticism' – 'a mendacious art'.[15]

Roland März

Translated from the German by David Britt

1 Curt Glaser, 'Neuromantik', in *Kunstchronik und Kunstmarkt*, no. 15 (1920), 301 ff.
2 Paul Ferdinand Schmidt, 'Das Recht auf Romantik', in *Das Kunstblatt*, vol. IV (1920), 324.
3 Gustav Friedrich Hartlaub in 'Ein neuer Naturalismus?', questionnaire in *Kunstblatt*, vol. VI (1922), 390.
4 For the concept see Fritz Schmalenbach, *Die Malerei der 'Neuen Sachlichkeit'* (Berlin 1973). For the exhibition see Helen Adkins in exh. cat. *Stationen der Moderne: Die bedeutendsten Kunstausstellungen des 20. Jahrhunderts in Deutschland*, Berlinische Galerie (1988), 217–35.
5 Cf. Michael Koch, 'Der Beitrag Münchens zur nachexpressionistischen Malerei und Graphik', in exh. cat. *Die zwanziger Jahre in München*, Stadtmuseum (Munich: 1979), 121–39.
6 Cf. Peter-Klaus Schuster, 'Neo-Neo-Klassizismus: Neusachliche Tendenzen im Vergelich Italien-Deutschland', in exh. cat. *Mythos Italien – Wintermärchen Deutschland*, (Munich: Haus der Kunst, 1988), 71–76.
7 Franz Roh, *Nach-Expressionismus, Magischer Realismus: Probleme der neuesten europäischen Malerei* (Leipzig, 1925), 79.
8 Franz Roh in *Das Kunstblatt*, vol. IV (1920), 286.
9 Cf. Carl-Wolfgang Schümann, in exh. cat. *Realismus zwischen Revolution und Machtergreifung 1919–1933*, (Stuttgart: Württembergischer Kunstverein, 1971), 21–24.
10 In *Das Kunstblatt*, vol. VIII (1924), unpag.
11 Cf. Roland März, 'Franz Radziwill und Caspar David Friedrich: Ein Dialog in romantischer Ikonographie', in *Forschungen und Berichte*, Staatliche Museen zu Berlin, vol. 15 (Berlin, 1973), 151–55. Bernd Küster, 'Radziwill und die Romantik oder Ist das Wunderbare noch die Wirklichkeit?', in exh. cat. *Franz Radziwill*, (Berlin: Neue Gesellschaft für bildende Kunst, 1982), 49–56.
12 Justus Bier, in exh. cat. *Neue Romantik* (Hanover, 1933), preface.
13 For the 'end of *Neue Sachlichkeit*' cf. Sergiusz Michalski, *Neue Sachlichkeit: Malerei, Graphik und Photographie in Deutschland 1919-1933* (Cologne, 1922), 195–99. On the specifics of painter and work cf. Gerd Presler, *Glanz und Elend der 20er Jahre: Die Malerei der neuen Sachlichkeit* (Cologne, 1992).
14 Cf. Peter Rautmann, 'Romantik im nationalen Korsett: Zur Friedrich-Rezeption am Ende der Weimarer Republik und zur Zeit des Faschismus', in exh. cat. *Caspar David Friedrich: Winterlandschaften*, Dortmund: Museum für Kunst und Kulturgeschichte der Stadt, 1990), 33–41.
15 Paul Westheim, 'Das "Haus der deutschen Kunst" ferngesehen', in Paul Westheim, *Karton mit Säulen: Antifaschistische Kunstkritik*, ed. Tanja Frank (Leipzig and Weimar, 1985), 112–17. Gunter Aust, 'Traditionalismus und Trivialität', in exh. cat. *Die Dreissiger Jahre. Schauplatz Deutschland*, (Munich: Haus der Kunst, 1977), 65–93. Adam C. Oellers, 'Zur Frage der Kontinuitat von Neuer Sachlichkeit und nationalsozialistischer Kunst', in *Kritische Berichte*, 6 (1978), 42–55.

Romantic Twilight:
Art in the Third Reich

Aspects of the Art of the Third Reich

The fires that consumed the works of artists and writers of the Weimar Republic are not forgotten. Nazi ideologists such as Alfred Rosenberg, Josef Goebbels and Adolf Hitler had initiated the auto-da-fé. This act of barbarity was reminiscent of the iconoclasm which followed the Protestant Reformation, the *Bildersturm*. The Nazi 'cultural revolution' (*Kulturkampf*) aimed at the complete liquidation of the liberal Modernist culture that had been developing in Germany, despite fierce opposition from an unenlightened prejudiced bourgeoisie and from the Emperor's militaristic coterie, since the beginning of the century.[1]

The unification of Germany in 1870–71 and the founding of the Second Empire had in many respects fulfilled the national aspirations of the Romantic generation, who had longed for it since the Wars of Liberation against Napoleon. Under the reign of Wilhelm II self-satisfaction, jingoism and triumphalism replaced the Romantic vision. National energies were not invested in the German renaissance that many had hoped for, but in an imperialistic dream of superiority and expansionism. This was the powerful tradition that the National Socialists sought to re-establish.

When Germany was defeated in 1918 and the Emperor fled to Holland, the Germans were left in a leaderless limbo, uprooted and disorientated. An unfocused authoritarianism was still active in large sections of the population and contributed to the undermining and destabilizing of the Weimar Republic and its democratic constitution throughout its fifteen years of existence. It was the failed painter Adolf Hitler and his messianic message of the restoration of the old order and the creation of a greater, more powerful Germany, that found popular consensus and support. A generation of depressed dreamers and irrationalists unleashed the Third Reich, the tyranny of the mediocre. In its eyes the new state was, one day, to be the reincarnation of the Holy Roman Empire.

This overstretched historical horizon provided the justification for ruthless measures within German society and its institutions. Long discredited and obsolete values began to be re-established. Individual freedom was replaced by the assumption of a collective will, that of the Nazi Party.

The arts had flourished throughout the Weimar years. Artists who had benefited from unprecedented freedoms had also been engaged in the development of a reformed society, whilst achieving extensive international acceptance. The destruction of so thriving a culture by the Nazis had a long-lasting cataclysmic effect on German art and excluded it from international cultural developments. Not surprisingly, the study of the art which was rejected by the regime as 'degenerate' (*entartet*) has been a central concern of art historians for the last forty years.[2] The ferocious energy with which the Nazi concept of art was pushed into the foreground became explicit in 1937, when Hitler opened the *Haus der deutschen Kunst* (House of German Art) and his creation, the Great German Art Exhibition (*Grosse Deutsche Kunstausstellung*) in Munich.

'I do not want anybody to have false illusions: National Socialism has made it its primary task to rid the German Reich, and thus the German people and its life, of all those influences which are fatal and ruinous to its existence. And although this purge cannot be accomplished in one day, I do not want to leave the shadow of a doubt as to the fact that sooner or later the hour of liquidation will strike for those phenomena which have participated in this corruption ... . From now on we will wage an unrelenting war of purification against the last element of putrefaction in our culture ... .'[3]

The Nazis had proclaimed their seizure of power in 1933 as a National Revolution (*Nationale Erhebung*). In fact it was no more than a radical backlash organized and supported by anti-left and anti-semitic forces largely recruited from an alienated petit-bourgeoisie. Within a short time the regime was able to secure control of every aspect of public life; all cultural and artistic activites were eroded. The restoration of 'traditional values' which harked back to old Germanic tribalism and

Fig.1 Georg Sluyterman von Langeweyde (1903–1978) From the portfolio *The Führer Speaks* 1938, woodcut ('No recovery is possible that does not grow out of the root of national, racial and economic life, the farmer'. Adolf Hitler)

Fig.2 Georg Sluyterman von Langeweyde (1903–1978) *German Oak* 1940, linocut ('Death for the Fatherland is worth eternal honour.' Ewald Christian von Kleist, fallen in battle, 1759)

pre-Christian pantheism dominated the development of the arts. The condition of the nation resembled a state of permanent euphoria. Politics and art lost their grounding in the real and knowable world. The *Führer*, in the centre of this new state, unlocked the cult of the irrational, promising great anti-materialistic revelations that would lead to the regaining of a lost paradise. National Socialism was a decadent flowering of Romantic nationalism, aimed at restoring Germany to the status it had had in medieval times, encouraging an aggressive expansionist drive, supported by notions of race and *Lebensraum*. This utopia claimed it would resolve the irreconcilable discrepancy of living in a medieval world using pre-industrial modes of production with the requirements of a highly industrialized society in the twentieth century. Such a contradiction caused substantial neurotic tension, a restlessness that could be relieved only by war. War became a psychological necessity and provided the practical solution for ideological discrepancies. All problems would be resolved when Germany became the industrial powerhouse of a future Europe. In the conquered territories a population of settlers and peasant farmers would breed and multiply, ready to expand the *Reich* in future wars.

The permanent presence of propaganda was required to sustain the dynamic, neurotic spiral. The art of this period formed part of this complex, and was also an expression of it, with the obligation to visualize and make manifest all aspects of Nazi *Weltanschauung*. Narrative representation, in a revival of nineteenth-century genre painting, was most suitable for this politically inspired function, yet the resulting art was bloodless and limp. The gap between pretence and reality was never closed; art had to be simplified in order to communicate at the level of the lowest common denominator. Most works selected for the annual *Grosse Deutsche Kunstausstellung* were unimpressive constructs of official thinking.

In one of his wartime broadcasts Thomas Mann defined National Socialism as 'German Idealism gone wrong'.[4] The relationship that the Nazis had to the old ideals remained purely exploitative. Lip-service was paid to Romantic idealism by sentimental teachers in schools and colleges and by Party bureaucrats. The examples of Karl Friedrich Schinkel in architecture and sculpture and of Caspar David Friedrich and Philipp Otto Runge in painting were cited incessantly by the regime as examples of pre-Nazi art, but their magic evaded the usurpers. Newly created myths replaced the old without changing the appearance and surface of painting.

Programmatic art prescribed by the Party and the state often took the form of monumentalism with allegorical pathos and theatricality. The central underlying themes were *Volksgemeinschaft*, community of people and nation, blood and soil, race and fatherland, war and heroic death. In these images farmers, workers, mothers and youth all engaged in the struggle for survival in a mythological battle. The aims of the 'New German Painting' were described in a pamphlet by the Party theoretician, F.A. Kauffmann:

'In the centre of our art stands the German people … . True to instinct, artists search for models particularly among members of the community (*Volksgemeinschaft*), who have a naturally healthy physique. They can be found in areas where there is a particularly strong attachment to the soil, and strong regional continuity, which has prevented their blood from being watered down, where the power of tradition and the blessings of dignified labour have preserved healthy bodies. And so again and again our paintings reveal peasant faces and figures of men with occupations close to nature (*naturnahe Urberufe*), like the hunter, fisherman, shepherd, woodcutter and men who are masters of basic crafts, which symbolize the nobility of skill and constructive honesty … . There is the farmer seen in his fields, ploughing, sowing, harvesting … . the farmer who lives close to earth and sky, the fertile soil under his heavy boots … .

'When there is so much sensibility related to the earth in which we are rooted, it is only natural for us to see our occupation with landscape as the purest of artistic endeavours … . For us today the landscape represents the territory of the Reich which demands our dutiful dedication … . German painting today attempts to emphasize healthy physical roots, the biological worth of the individual and the renewal of nation and spirit.'[5]

The fusion of art and politics succeeded only to a limited degree. Nevertheless, within the 'Blood and Soil' genre, one can find examples of sufficient intensity and conviction. This may have to do with the fact that there existed an unbroken link, particularly through the Munich School, with the nineteenth-century *Bauernmalerei*, an idealization of landscape and peasant life, a world filled with the metaphors of hard work and the changing seasons. The works of Franz von Defregger and Wilhelm Leibl, Albin Egger-Lienz, even Ferdinand Hodler, inspired artists like Sepp Hilz, Constantin Gerhardinger

and Oskar Martin-Amorbach. Reverberations of the 'Old German' based on Moritz von Schwind and Albrecht Dürer imitations surfaced in the graphic works of Georg Sluyterman von Langeweyde (figs. 1 and 2), Ernst Dombrowsky and Adolf Finsterer. An indebtedness to the Neo-Romantic tendencies of *Neue Sachlichkeit* is found in the works of Adolf Wissel, Hermann Tiebert, Willi Paupie and Werner Peiner.

With the outbreak of the Second World War in 1939 these artists invested their skills in the war effort. In images of battle and of soldiers at the Front one now could see the farmer and his son fighting and marching through foreign lands. War painting was the logical continuation of the Blood and Soil genre, marked by a remoteness and by unfulfilled idealizations.

National Socialism never acquired the strength to stimulate original artistic personalities, it only activated artists who would have been otherwise marginalized by the progress of modern art. What remains of the art of the Third Reich has up to now been kept in storage, only of historical importance, not as part of a proud cultural heritage. When Hitler laid the foundation stone for his House of German Art in 1933, the hammer broke.[6] Retrospectively this may now be recognized as an omen of the tragedy that would befall Germany under the Nazis' 'civilizing mission'.

Lutz Becker

1 Peter Paret, *Die Berliner Sezession* (Berlin, 1981), 91.
2 Stephanie Barron '1937 – Modern Art and Politics in Pre-war Germany', in *Degenerate Art – The Fate of the Avant-Garde in Nazi Germany* ed. Stephanie Barron (Los Angeles, 1991), 9–13.
3 Excerpt from Hitler's inaugural speech originally published under the title 'Der Führer eröffnet die Grosse Deutsche Kunstausstellung 1937' in *Die Kunst im Dritten Reich*, vol. 1: (Munich, 1937) 7–8, translated by Ilse Falk in *Theories of Modern Art* (California, 1968).
4 Thomas Mann, 'Culture and Politics', in *Order of the Day* (New York, 1942), 223–37.
5 Excerpt from F.A. Kauffmann, *Die neue Deutsche Malerei* in series *Schriftenreihe der Deutschen Informationsstelle, Das Deutschland der Gegenwart* no. 11, (Berlin, 1941), 26. The style of this pamphlet is so convoluted that my translation can only give a taste of the original.
6 This detail has long been forgotten. Hitler was so furious about the breaking of his hammer that this moment was edited out of newsreels. The documentary film, *Das Haus der Deutschen Kunst* (Bavaria 1933–34) still contains the scene, Bundesarchiv Koblenz Filmarchiv No. 1599.

The author is indebted in his wider study of the subject to Bertold Hinz, *Die Malerei im Deutschen Faschismus, Kunst und Konterrevolution* (Munich, 1974).

Otto Dix
Randegg in Snow with Ravens, 1935
(cat. 193)

Adolf Wissel
Farming Family from Kalenberg, 1939
(cat. 197)

Oskar Martin-Amorbach
The Sower, 1937
(cat. 195)

Franz Radziwill
Lost Earth (The U-Boat War; Total War), 1939–60
(cat. 196)

Art
after 1945

After 1945

The Dutch painter Armando writes: 'We never learnt this at school, but everybody knows that Romanticism was not a style. There was no Romantic sculpture or architecture, that was all more or less Neoclassical. Romanticism was a *Weltanschauung*, an attitude to life, a life-style, and it still seems to be around. Nature was perceived as a counter-world, a world like art with its own laws and battles, nature as a mirror of the soul. Romanticism is so German that I cannot handle it without German words ...' And elsewhere he says: 'Look at titles like *Waldeinsamkeit* (Forest solitude), or *Erscheinung im Wald* (Apparition in the forest), or *Waldesrauschen* (Forest murmurs), or *Waldgespräch* (Forest conversation), or *Waldesruhe* (Forest peace). It's tempting to pick up a title like that and create an appropriate work of art, but that takes skill. It's not all that simple. Something else you could paint is *Die Rückkehr der Mönche* (Return of the monks) or *Ein gestrandetes Schiff* (A stranded ship). You can do what you like.'[1]

So, in historical retrospect German Romanticism is surprisingly heterogeneous for an outsider. The Romantic spirit in the art of the last fifty years is even more confusing and chaotic. And indeed there is no system, no thread, no visual common ground to be detected in the work of recent artists we could call Romantic. There are few common features in the work of Joseph Beuys, Gerhard Richter, Gotthard Graubner, and Günther Uecker. But German art since the 1960s – broadly speaking – seems to tackle history differently, with greater awareness. This also derives from the specifically German situation. Artists who had significant influence on German art in the 1960s, 70s and 80s – let us take Georg Baselitz, Anselm Kiefer and Richter as examples, as Beuys is discussed in detail elsewhere in this catalogue – did not experience National Socialism and its terrors as responsible adults who were directly affected, unlike the generation of Fritz Winter, Willi Baumeister and Ernst Wilhelm Nay. They were able to interrogate tradition differently and did not have to place their hopes in the regenerative powers of nature,

even when painting beautiful landscapes. Elemental forces did not have to be invoked from nature's self-creating sources alone. Their subject was not the introspection, the inner necessity, found in Wassily Kandinsky and Franz Marc.

Their pictures – despite all the differences between them, which must be stressed – in fact show an arsenal of heroes whose ironic and historic ambivalence also relates to the nineteenth century. Baselitz himself provides concrete pointers with titles like *Bonjour Monsieur Courbet* and *Man in the Moon – Franz Pforr*. But unlike the Gustave Courbet picture, in which the proud painter enjoys the greeting deferentially, a quotation from Franz Pforr seems more fitting for Baselitz's homeless hero: 'The artist's way has no goal, he must move forward restlessly and without repose; if he once stands still, woe! he goes back, he can see what is behind him sinking back in a blue mist, and so there is no sign that the end of his way is dawning. And so he hurries on until death claims him.'[2] This feeling of homelessness and eternal searching may also be a nineteenth century theme, but Baselitz uses painting to describe a specific state of postwar Germany; this was recently explained by Lóránd Hegyi in an article on the hero-pictures. He interprets them as a 'painterly metaphor of the internalization of history by subjectivizing the landscape or the view of the human body and its spatial surroundings. The dark meadows with abandoned, apparently ruined objects, scarcely recognizable under the hopeless, gloomy sky, become landscapes of the soul, landscapes of spiritual conditions shaped by historical memories and eerie feelings. Even the human figure becomes a painterly part of the landscape of the soul in these pictures. The body in its broken quality, in its changed proportions, in its lostness is entirely integrated into the landscape, its flesh seems like earth and stone, its limbs are like trees, tombs, hills.'[3]

Art will Survive, Just is perhaps more than a random title for a watercolour by Kiefer. It could indicate an assumed certainty that the fight against pleasure in apocalyptic destruction might be won. No *oeuvre* has been so permanently preoccupied with the theme of destruction and the devastated world as his. His desolate, empty landscapes are reminiscent of Caspar David Friedrich, although the painting is quite different, gestural and suffused with relics of our civilization. These world landscapes are characterized not by the paralysis of death but by traces of a struggle that has taken place; their models can be traced back further, to Albrecht Altdorfer's *Battle of Arbela*. Kiefer's art tells us that this kind of disaster is part of German history – in all its facets. It does not matter whether we are talking about the gods and heroes of the Nibelung saga, the legendary Hermann (Arminius) the Cheruscan, who defeated and wiped out the Roman general Quintilius Varus and his troops in the Teutoburg Forest in AD 9 and liberated the Teutons, or the poets and thinkers who later sang of these heroes and captured their exploits in words, or not least the Second World War generals: all of them went down as heroes in our cruel history. They are incorporeal presences in Kiefer's large pictures, in a way that is meaningful but hardly compelling, in the form of their inscribed names (Varus) or as hallucinatory heads that appear to hover (*Ways of Worldly Wisdom*). As memory and invocation they are part of blood-stained nature, a kind of controlled purgatory, whose domesticated fires could blaze up into a total inferno at any time, an inferno to which the whole world would then fall sacrifice, with all its spiritual heroes. Kiefer's art gives an unambiguous reply to the question of whether such purifying fire would bring about ultimate destruction or a possible new beginning.

A few years earlier, in fact in 1972, for his presentation in the German pavilion at the Venice Biennale, Gerhard Richter produced his *Forty-eight Portraits*. Something that looks comparable at first is in fact based on a different perception of history. Without any sentimentality, Richter puts together a republic of scholars in these randomly chosen portraits. It is intended to be neither a historical picture of mankind nor a national Walhalla. By doing this he clearly distinguishes himself from all his possible nineteenth-century predecessors. The relatively small pictures, painted from photographs in encyclopaedias, show philosophers, poets, musicians, mathematicians, physicists and biologists. They lived and worked at the turn of the century or in the first half of our century. Thus, as Benjamin H.D. Buchloch says, they are part of an 'accessible memory-space' that can be reached through one's own memory.[4] They are all men of the Modern movement but not – with the exception of Albert Einstein and Franz Kafka – radical innovators and lonely geniuses. They can be interpreted as a tableau of possible, but interchangeable elective affinities. This fact is also supported by the uniform design, the cramped selection of detail and the grey shades of the colour scheme.

'The Great Man' finds his limitations in uniformity and anonymity. Scope for action is restricted or even fatal, as suggested by the cycle about the deaths in Stammheim prison, *18 October 1977*, created in 1988. The last 'Heroes', visionary fighters for a more humane and more just world, foundered on the reality of life. Richter's memorial statements leave the dead alone in a world without consolation, just as Jacques Louis David let his Marat die unprotected.

Angela Schneider

Translated from the German by David Britt

1 Armando, *Die Wärme der Abneigung* (Frankfurt, 1987), 46, 47.
2 Werner Hofmann, *Das Irdische Paradies* (Munich, 1974), 138.
3 Lóránd Hegyi, 'Bemerkungen zu den Heldenbildern', in exh. cat. *Georg Baselitz: Retrospektive 1964–1991* (Munich, 1992), 36.
4 Benjamin H.D. Buchloch, *Gerhard Richter*, vol. 2, *Texte* (1993), 38.

Fritz Winter
Motive Forces of the Earth, 1944
(cat. 203)

Fritz Winter
Motive Forces of the Earth (Autumn Mood), 1944
(cat. 205)

Wols
The Pink Ship, c.1949
(cat. 211)

Wols
Composition Champigny, 1951
(cat. 213)

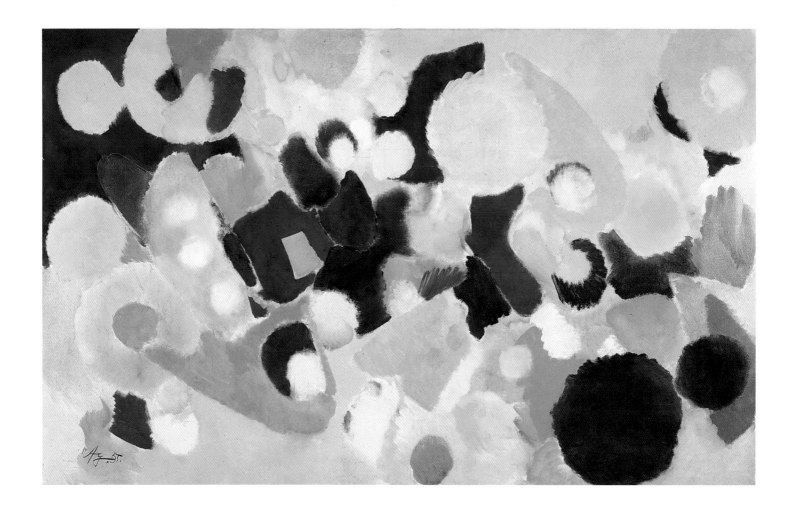

Ernst Wilhelm Nay
Pendulum in Balance, 1955
(cat. 200)

Willi Baumeister
Aru 5, 1955
(cat. 198)

Bernard Schultze
Hegitraf, 1957
(cat. 202)

Gotthard Graubner
colour-space-body I, 1973
(cat. 199)

Hermann Glöckner
Five Rays from the Upper Quarter, Thrice Reflected, on Blue, c.1933–35
(cat. 221)

Hermann Glöckner
Black and White Divided Square under Blue, c.1930–32
(cat. 220)

Hermann Glöckner
Circling Lines on Blue, 1959
(cat. 224)

Hermann Glöckner
Cross, between Red and Blue Sweeps, 1962
(cat. 225)

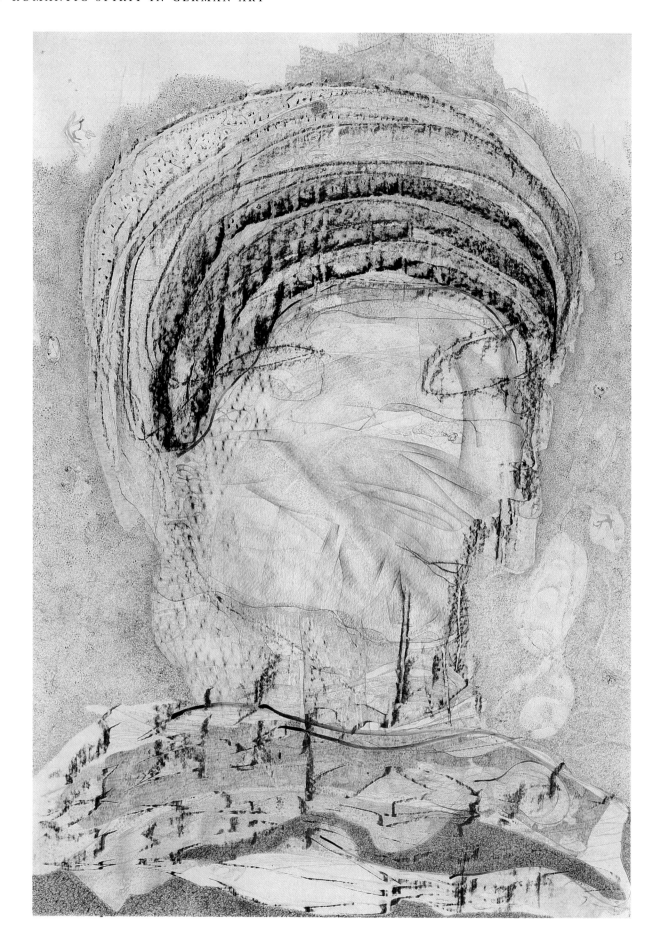

Gerhard Altenbourg
Undispelled, 1972
(cat. 218)

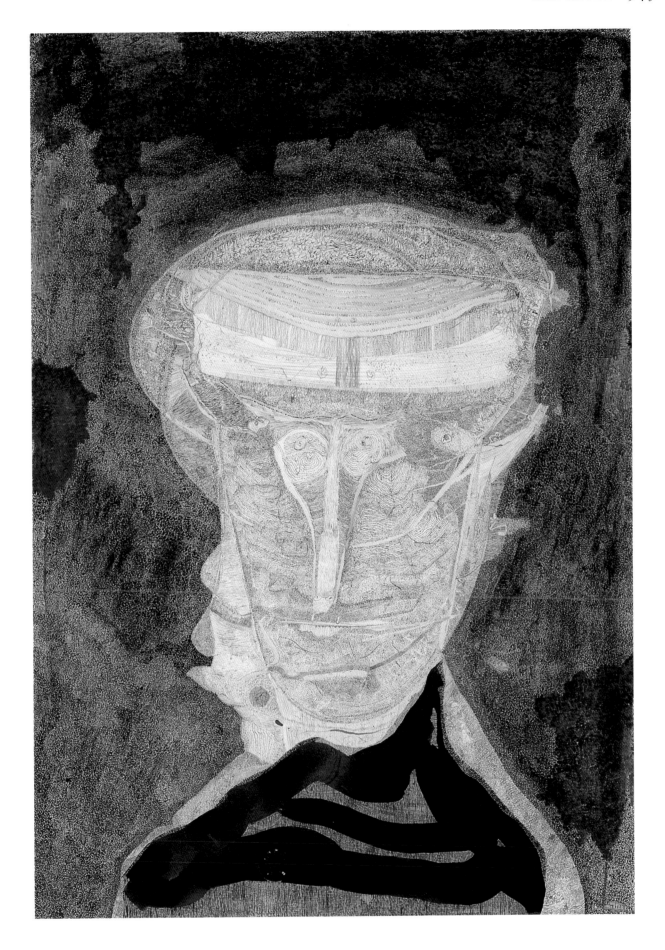

Gerhard Altenbourg
Sunk in the Ego Rock, 1966
(cat. 217)

Gerhard Altenbourg
Garten an der Spinnbahn, 1951
(cat. 214)

Gerhard Altenbourg
Dedicated to Caspar David, 1966
(cat. 216)

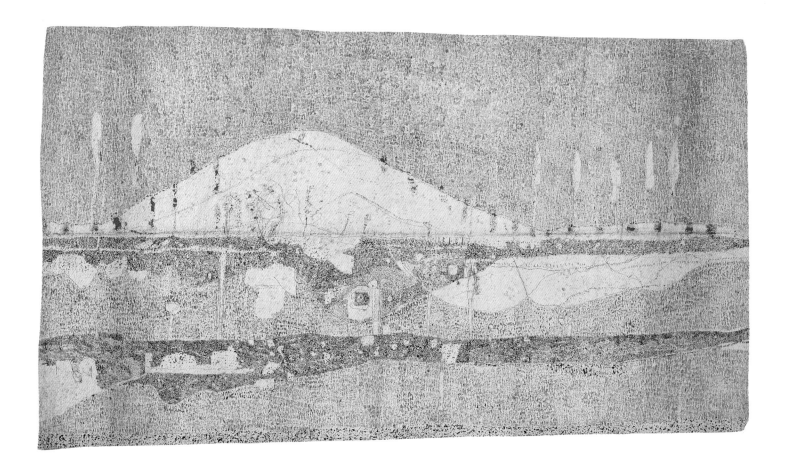

Gerhard Altenbourg
This is the Mountain, 1964
(cat. 215)

Gerhard Altenbourg
Tears of the Landscape, Unwept, 1973
(cat. 219)

Joseph Beuys
Mallee, 1947
(cat. 228)

Joseph Beuys
Prunus Laurocerasus, 1955
(cat. 235)

Joseph Beuys
Queen Bee, 1947
(cat. 227)

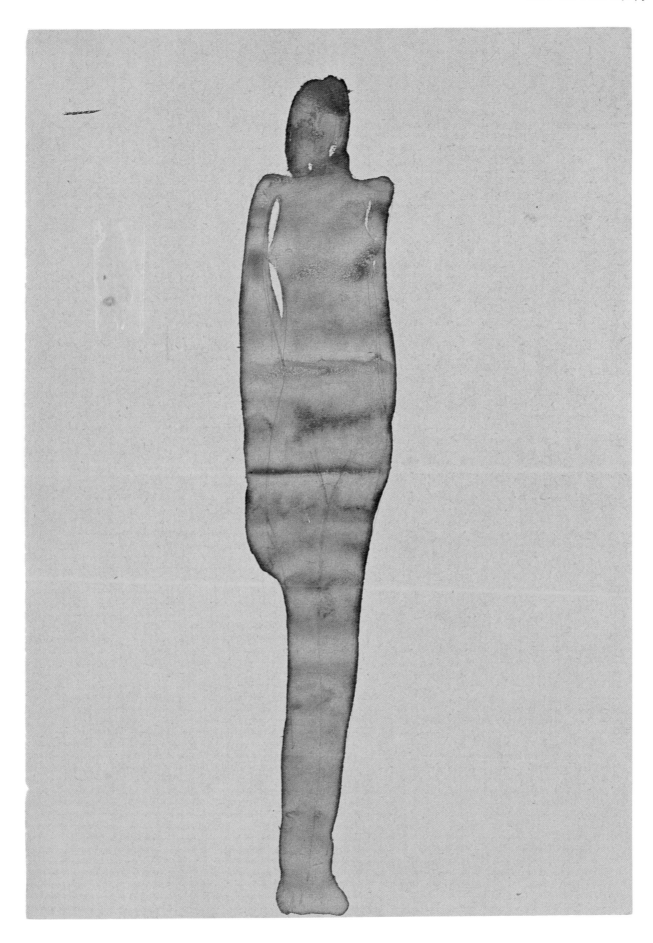

Joseph Beuys
Untitled, 1957–58
(cat. 243)

Joseph Beuys
Oblique Lightning Strikes Dead Arolla Pine, 1954
(cat. 231)

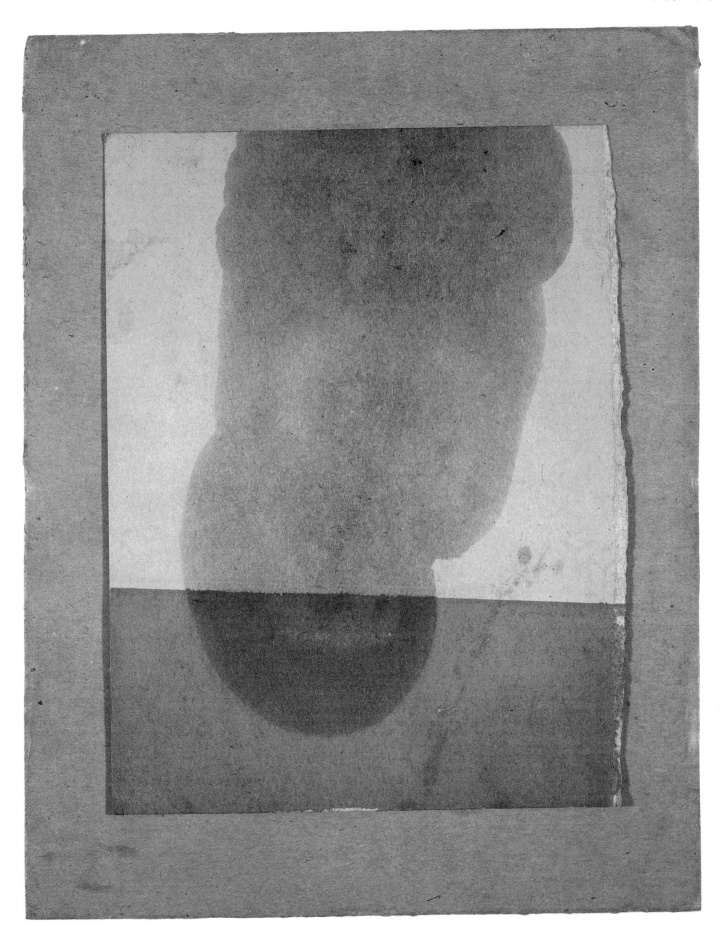

Joseph Beuys
fatty cloud detaches itself from the sea, 1959
(cat. 249)

Joseph Beuys
Ancient Sea with Pterosaur, 1956
(cat. 236)

Joseph Beuys
Drill of a Cave Dweller, 1957
(cat. 241)

Joseph Beuys
Cross, 1961
(cat. 251)

Joseph Beuys
2 Skulls Sea of Ice, 1982
(cat. 258)

Blinky Palermo
Untitled (By the Sea), 1965
(cat. 270)

Blinky Palermo
Hymn to the Night, 1967
(cat. 272)

Blinky Palermo
Untitled (Coloured Bows), 1971
(cat. 276)

Sigmar Polke
Front of one of the 13 panels of the Laterna Magica, 1990–93
(cat. 278) Back illustrated p. 432

Sigmar Polke
Back of one of the 13 panels of the Laterna Magica, 1990–93
(cat. 278) Front illustrated p. 431

Sigmar Polke
Front of one of the 13 panels of the Laterna Magica, 1990–93
(cat. 278) Back illustrated p. 434

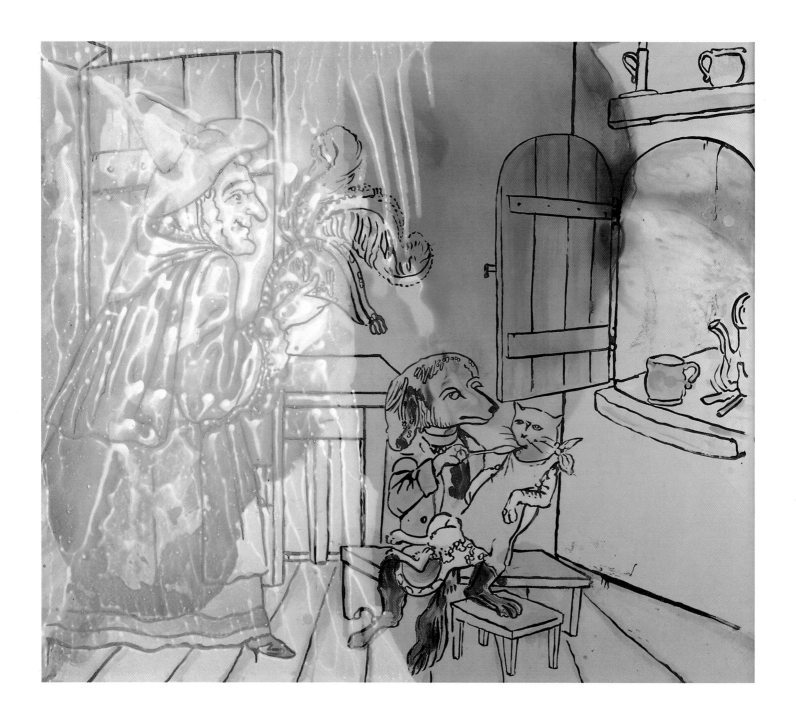

Sigmar Polke
Back of one of the 13 panels of the Laterna Magica, 1990–93
(cat. 278) Front illustrated p. 433

Sigmar Polke
Front of one of the 13 panels of the Laterna Magica, 1990–93
(cat. 278) Back illustrated p. 436

Sigmar Polke
Back of one of the 13 panels of the Laterna Magica, 1990–93
(cat. 278) Back illustrated p. 435

Sigmar Polke
Front of one of the 13 panels of the Laterna Magica, 1990–93
(cat. 278) Back illustrated p. 438

Sigmar Polke
Back of one of the 13 panels of the Laterna Magica, 1990–93
(cat. 278) Back illustrated p. 437

Gerhard Richter
Woman Reading, 1994
(cat. 279)

Gerhard Richter
Wall, 1994
(cat. 282)

Gerhard Richter
March, 1994
(cat. 281)

Georg Baselitz
The New Type, 1965
(cat. 262)

Georg Baselitz
A Modern Painter, 1966
(cat. 263)

Georg Baselitz
Partisan, 1965
(ex. cat.)

Georg Baselitz
Ludwig Richter on His Way to Work, 1965
(ex. cat.)

Anselm Kiefer
Sand of the Mark, 1980
(cat. 265)

Anselm Kiefer
Ways of Worldly Wisdom, 1976–77
(cat. 264)

Anselm Kiefer
Seraphim, 1984
(cat. 267)

Anselm Kiefer
The Stairs, 1982–83
(cat. 266)

Abstraction as a World Language:
Winter – Wols – Baumeister – Nay

'Abstraction as a World Language' – *Abstraktion als Weltsprache* – was the striking title of the central portion of the *Westkunst* exhibition held in Cologne in 1981. It was a variation on the title of a book published in the 1950s: *Abstrakte Kunst eine Weltsprache*.[1] Both undertakings, the exhibition (with its catalogue) and the book, describe broadly the same subject: the European and to some extent the American art of the 1940s and 1950s. In this, German – which in this context means exclusively West German – art plays no particularly distinctive role. Indeed, there can be no doubt that, whatever its separate identity, German art evolved under the influence of French art and in dialogue with it.

Nevertheless, the yearning for wholeness – *ein Weltganzes* (a world or universal whole) to cite a term used by Paul Klee – can be regarded as a specifically German phenomenon, just as much as Friedrich Schlegel's celebrated *Weltgeist* (world spirit). This yearning for wholeness and for the abolition of boundaries has been a characteristic of Northern Europe – here we cite Werner Hofmann – since the time of its conversion to Christianity, when the new spirituality was found to lack a contemplative basis in the world of the senses.[2] Ever since, German art has directed its interest towards art forms either more immediate or more remote than the limited easel painting, and has constantly been engaged in the quest for synthesis, for the total work of art, the *Gesamtkunstwerk*. Alongside art in 'public space' – from the late Gothic polyptych through the Baroque interiors to Kurt Schwitters's *MERZbau* – there have always been the small, portable formats of private watercolours, drawings and prints.

It may also, of course, have been conditions during the Second World War – when, particularly for 'degenerate' artists, there were virtually no painting materials to be had – that caused artists to make a start with small formats. In 1944, on convalescent leave from the Eastern Front, Fritz Winter made the forty-six drawings that he called *Motive Forces of the Earth*. With oil-saturated typing paper as a permeable first layer, he added two further layers of irregular, overlapping, lancet-like and near-semicircular forms, which concentrate themselves towards the centre and often also seem to force their way upwards. In the second layer he used some brown and grey – earth-coloured and wintry – colours; in the third he worked with tones of white, light grey, light blue, green, sometimes adding yellows or reds, which, as he wrote in his journal, 'belong to the lineages of earth. I am glad to be red and yellow, but I yearn for grey, the Infinite.'[3]

Participation in the whole, as the title of the works suggests, begins in the earth, to which we return in order to become nature ourselves once more. 'Nothing can be more moving,' wrote Winter in a letter home from the front, 'than when you possess nothing at all, you are no longer a human being in any civilian sense, and then you come across a flower or a leaf and become aware of the greatness of Creation.'[4] In a comparable situation, on the battlefields of France in the spring of 1915, Franz Marc had recorded his design for a new world, page by page, in his *Skizzenbuch aus dem Felde* ('Sketchbook from the Field').[5]

In all this there is a leitmotiv that pervades German art in the years after the Second World War: the search for origins, for beginnings uncontaminated by Nazi ideology. The great Nordic myths are excluded. What emerges is an ahistorical, nature-bound image of the world, with intermittent references to ancient Mediterranean and Near Eastern myths: Gilgamesh (Willi Baumeister), Hecate (Ernst Wilhelm Nay) or Orpheus (Werner Gilles). The world-view of postwar German art exists in the tension between myth and enlightenment.

In this context, Wols is an exception. He left Germany at the age of nineteen, in 1932, and moved to France; his work as a painter took shape – as has often been described – under the influence of Surrealism. Wols was fascinated by small and seemingly insignificant things. He explored their structures, and in tiny drawings and watercolours he transformed them into pictorial compositions that contained a whole world.[6] His poet friend Henri-Pierre Roché, with whom he spent the war in Haute-Provence, in the unoccupied sector of France, found words for this world very early on: 'Cobwebs, grasses, forests of waterweed, monsters, molluscs, city-mountains, building-ships, butcher-jewellery; show-pieces, chasms and assemblies of horror. All this and much more.'[7]

All these, said Wols himself in his 'Aphorisms', are ultimately metaphors of transience.[8] The reference is not only to the sources cited by Wols himself – among them Charles Baudelaire, Edgar Allan Poe, Arthur Rimbaud, Lautréamont, Vincent van Gogh, Antonin Artaud and Novalis – but also to German Romantic art, and to Caspar David Friedrich in particular, whose paintings Wols will have known from his childhood in Dresden.[9] Analogies of content might be drawn, for instance, between Friedrich's sailing ships and Wols's phantas-magorical cities; but the prime affinity seems to dwell in Friedrich's categorical demand that the artist see the world by looking inward: 'The painter must paint not merely what he sees before him but also what he sees within him.'[10]

To this Wols responded: 'Often I close my eyes to look at what I see. Everything is there; that is beautiful; that is exhaustive.'[11] Gréty Wols recalled: 'He said that what he was going to paint showed itself behind his right eyelid.'[12]

'Art remains inseparable from image-magic,' concludes Hofmann.[13] In a sense, Wols's watercolours, and his oil paintings above all, are impossible to analyse: they refuse to display what László Glozer called 'total intellectual receptibility'.[14] Reviewing Wols's second exhibition at the Galerie René Drouin in the spring of 1947, Georges Limbour put this more forcibly. According to him, Wols's paintings are conjurations of demons. At a given moment the demons appear on the canvas of their own accord, recalling the blot on Martin Luther's study wall that still marks the spot where the implacable Reformer hurled his inkwell at the devil. 'It is said,' Limbour concluded his review, 'that his painting is not abstract. So be it. And there really are demons, even if they are not directly visible. Let us say that this is abstract devilry.'[15]

Baumeister was another who acknowledged vision as the true motive force of his art, though not as its goal. It served him as a means to his true end of discovering the new, the never-before-seen, the unknown. This was the subject of his important theoretical treatise on *The Unknown in Art*,[16] written in 1943 and published in 1946, a direct result of the study of prehistoric painting techniques that he carried out in the enamel paint factory of Kurt Herberts, where he survived the Nazi years. The 'art forms of nature' fascinated him: 'It was the formative impulse within materials that primarily interested [him]; for every technique speaks a language of its own.'[17]

Baumeister subsequently painted pictures with titles such as *Perforation*, *Primal Forms*, *Bright Movement*, *Wind*, *Growth* and, in 1953–55, the *Montaru* and *Aru* series, which can be regarded as the summation of his work. These are images in which ever-larger masses of black paint displace the world of colour; and yet, despite the dominance of black, the effect is cheerful rather than gloomy. The black body looks potentially mobile and changeable, so that it seems to generate its own forms. In the quest for an ultimate, definitive form, it displaces and overlaps the forms that coexist with it. It constantly reaches out towards the edges of the painting, but never actually touches them. The *Aru* images seem to hover, to breathe, to be certain of their own existence. Baumeister realized that the ultimate form was unattainable precisely because of his own creative process, which carried his work towards unforeseeable shores.

Derived from formal qualities, such insights vividly capture the idea of content that Baumeister formulated in *The Unknown in Art*: 'What the artist extracts from the centre moves the world. It is more unexpected than all future events, for it is creation. This particularly applies to the art of today, which is an art that rises from the depths. Its great works are simple, self-evident, without pretence. They do not look as if they were made by someone but as if they spontaneously arose. Nature has expressed itself.'[18]

'Man a piece of nature, not lord of nature,' wrote Nay in 1935 to a recently dismissed museum director, Carl Georg Heise. 'The connection with the mythical primal entity allows us to know the true reality of nature. The picture not as a depiction of outward existence (appearances), or as a depiction of inner emotions: the picture as a form of being, more real than any realistic or naturalistic picture.'[19]

Later, in the 1950s and early 1960s, when Nay had risen to become the difficult but dazzling hero of postwar German painting, he went on writing theoretical pieces about his work, mainly discussions of the relationship between art and nature. In a letter to Eduard Trier he wrote:

'The constant manipulation of this or that immediately usable portion of the past cannot obscure the fact that in our day natural science has separated contemplation from concept: for us, object and nature are no longer identical – as they were, for example, in the idealist cosmogony of German Romanticism. Then, concept could become contemplation through the object. This prime requirement of all objective art no longer exists, and as a result objective art has lost its point.'[20]

Nay regarded his own work as an absolute art, resisting all attempts to impose a representational content on it – as when the *Disc Paintings* were interpreted as flowers, balloons, or cosmic emblems. He wanted them to be understood first and foremost as a purely artistic invention, which had emerged – automatically, as it were – from the activity of painting. The brush spontaneously falls into circular movements on the paper or canvas. He remained sceptical of all attempts to detect analogies in his work, as with his large painting for the Institute of Chemistry at Freiburg University: 'The red void in the centre of my painting – or so they [the Institute scientists] said – resembles the visualization of the genesis of a star: the centre empty, but hot, from which energy creates energetic mass. This is simultaneously the definition of potential energy.'[21]

Talking to Werner Haftmann, Nay recommended caution: 'With the Freiburg picture, please think twice before you bring in the cosmos and the universe. The Freiburg picture is contemporary because it is the first contemporary picture to manifest structure as colour, structure as colour! Colour as immanent spiritual value, and definitely not as impasto or line.'[22]

The fact is that the first postwar artist who had the youthful, utopian idealism to proclaim his allegiance to the cosmos and the immaterial was not a German but a Frenchman: Yves Klein. At eighteen, lying on his back on the beach, he signed the blue sky over Nice.

Angela Schneider

Translated from the German by David Britt

1 Georg Poensgen and Leopold Zahn, *Abstrakte Kunst eine Weltsprache* (Baden-Baden, 1958).
2 Werner Hofmann, 'Was ist deutsch an deutscher Kunst?' *art*, 10 (1985), 52–56, 120.
3 Exh. cat. *Fritz Winter* (Düsseldorf, 1966), n.p.
4 Exh. cat. *Fritz Winter* (St Gallen, 1962), 13.
5 Franz Marc, *Skizzenbuch aus dem Felde*, ed. Klaus Lankheit (Berlin, 1956), 19.
6 Wols, *Aufzeichnungen, Aquarelle, Aphorismen, Zeichnungen*, ed. Werner Haftmann (Cologne, 1963), 47.
7 Exh. cat. *Wols, Photograph* (Hanover, 1978), 113.
8 See Wols's aphorisms in Wols (as note 6), 50–55.
9 Elfriede Schultze-Battmann, 'Erinnerungen', in exh. cat. *Wols* (Zürich, Düsseldorf and Edinburgh, 1990), 385.
10 Quoted from Caspar David Friedrich, *Caspar David Friedrich in Briefen und Bekenntnissen*, ed. Sigrid Hinz (Berlin, 1984), 113.
11 Quoted from Wols (as note 6), 52.
12 Quoted from Wols (as note 6), 48.
13 Hofmann (as note 2), 56.
14 László Glozer, *Westkunst: Zeitgenössische Kunst seit 1939* (Cologne, 1981), 146.
15 Quoted from Glozer (as note 14), 152.
16 Willi Baumeister, *Das Unbekannte in der Kunst* (Cologne, 1988), Part 3.
17 Karin von Maur, 'Willi Baumeisters Spuren', in exh. cat. *Willi Baumeister* (Stuttgart, 1979), 16.
18 Baumeister (as note 16), 151.
19 Ernst Wilhelm Nay, *E. W. Nay 1902–1968: Bilder und Dokumente* (Munich, 1980), 62.
20 Nay (as note 19), 184–85.
21 Nay (as note 19), 156.
22 Nay (as note 19), 156.

Hermann Glöckner and Gerhard Altenbourg

Art produced in eastern Germany after 1945 was disrupted by politics on several occasions. Immediately after the war the territory was insufficiently defined. It was scarcely possible to tell which way Germany would go. At first, artists and intellectuals returning from exile in the West offered hope in the form of democratic socialism, but this was quickly shattered by the Cold War between the great powers and the dogmatism of the Stalinist state. German and international Modernism, and thus the link with the art-historical process that had been so ruthlessly broken by the Nazis, was rehabilitated only in West Germany. The 'formalism debate' imported from the Soviet Union made Modernism questionable again in the 1950s and 1960s and demanded a servile art subject to the dictates of Socialist Realism. Many artists who later became significant figures in West Germany left the German Democratic Republic, founded in 1949, before the Wall was built in 1961. Uncompromising art of the highest quality was an extremely valuable resource for this country's subversive culture, which also left its mark on officially tolerated art. There was an abundance of realistic images that provided nourishment, more or less metaphorically encoded, for the spiritual needs of a society living in concealed opposition, but several artists worked underground for a long period. They included Hermann Glöckner, born in 1889, of the same generation as Josef Albers, Willi Baumeister and Johannes Itten, whose constructive *Tafelwerk* (Panel-work) evolved between 1930 and 1937. Glöckner's path was made considerably more difficult as far as public recognition of his work was concerned by the tribulations of German history.

Glöckner's paintings and drawings were influenced by late Impressionism at first, before he discovered the art of the construction around 1930. His adoption of his own form of Constructivism was not entirely due to the ideas of the time. It was certainly based on encounters with work by great artists who contributed to the movement's high standing, but it remained fundamentally isolated. Glöckner drew on his own work, in which he now discovered a constructive grid that had established itself unconsciously, as a result of his early inclination towards geometry. 'This made me', Glöckner wrote later, 'examine the constructive, geometrical basis of my painting and find its elemental and complex coherence. I decided at that time to start again from the beginning, to cast aside everything that had happened before and to concentrate entirely on this question.'[1]

Glöckner's work over the next seven years, under the global title *Tafelwerk*, represented an important contribution to constructive painting. He submitted it only to a few exhibitions organized by the Künstlerbund, of which he had been a member since 1929. He was never shown in a group exhibition, and so little attention was paid to his work. In any case the Nazis' seizure of power in 1933, and their increasing persecution of Modernism, soon meant that he had no chance at all of comparing his work with that of other artists in public. Glöckner earned his living, both before and after the war, with pictorial or typographical *sgraffito* mural designs for the building industry. He often had to neglect his creative work in the difficult years during and after the war in order to earn a living.

The retrospectives in Dresden and Berlin, mounted after his death, provided impressive documentation of the extensive work that he produced despite his hardships. *Tafelwerk* grew to include over 150 works in the course of the years, and is at the heart of his *oeuvre*. The Dresden Kupferstich-Kabinett produced the first appreciation of his work in 1969, Glöckner's eightieth year. Glöckner's vast formal range is considerably greater than a first impression suggests. His work includes drawings, graphics and examples of other techniques, as well as paintings. He worked long and intensively with collage, using folded coloured paper, and also translated these shapes into three-dimensional form in metal. On close examination, his images designed according to geometrical rules are different from the austere structures of classical Constructivism. Compositions based on mathematical considerations include amorphous colour-fields as a lively counter-structure.

Glöckner, who took a studio in the turn-of-the-century castle-like house for artists designed by the Dresden architect Pietsch, was much influenced by the art-historical writings of Conrad Fiedler and Adolf Hildebrand. He was open to nineteenth century ideas despite all his inclination towards Modernism.

Glöckner's withdrawn life and late public presentation meant that his work and attitude were slow to affect younger East German artists.

Gerhard Ströch was born in Thüringen in 1926, and called himself Altenbourg after his birthplace (Altenburg). He did not meet Glöckner until 1969. This meeting confirmed his own artistic approach to life, which he had developed in similar seclusion in his parental home in Altenburg. Altenbourg started to study under Hans Hoffmann-Lederer at the Hochschule für Baukunst und bildende Künste in Weimar. He discovered German and international Modernism, which had been banished from public life by Nazism, and internalized its intentions. He produced only a few paintings in subsequent years, concentrating on drawings and prints. Altenbourg produced a highly sensitive and extensive body of drawings, stimulated by the work and ideas of Paul Klee, Wols and Henri Michaux. Drawing became a meditative working process. His extremely disciplined work at his tidy drawing table was like the ritualistic exercises performed by Christian or Buddhist monks. His style is highly subjective, and cannot be compared with East German stylistic trends current at the time. It involves submersion in the ramifications of nature's microcosm, whose interwoven latticework Altenbourg transforms into drawing imbued with spirituality. He saw 'drawings as tattooed signs, an entry into the hollows of physicality. Earth and moss simultaneously: a show of the inner shell, an attempt to spin the thread in the labyrinth that leads snail-like down into uncertainty, a distant, Janus-like quality, dissolution, somewhere between disembodied horror and ecstasy.'[2]

A concept that includes the various materials – pencils, inks, paper etc. – as fundamental aesthetic resources lies behind the tiny elements of the drawn structures. Dissolution of landscape and plant structures into lines, dots, paths and colour-fields to form a thickly woven, drawn carpet took Altenbourg's work close to abstraction, without its ever being abstract in the sense of non-figurative Western art. This superficially interpreted proximity led to long years of distance from official art, a case similar to Glöckner's. His first exhibitions and fame were in the West. Altenbourg's affinity with early German Romanticism can be seen in his closeness to nature, his distillation of spirituality, his choice of asceticism, his house and garden, stylized into a complete work of art, and his poetic vein, as well as other literary, philosophical and artistic sources. Altenbourg regularly studied nineteenth-century drawings in the National-galerie in Berlin. His own work suggests that he addressed that of Philipp Otto Runge, Caspar David Friedrich, Johann Heinrich Fuseli and William Blake, among others.

The 1966 drawing *Dedicated to Caspar David*, cat. 216 shows a portrait head woven into an imaginary landscape, a synthetic identification of Altenbourg the draughtsman with the important Romantic painter Caspar David Friedrich. The following autobiographical lines by Altenbourg could be a commentary on this elective affinity. 'I am worn through to the base, I once wrote in 1953. And now I say it at the beginning, as I intend to talk about the basis and the worn transparency of my existence, which is as if it were without a skin. And as this is the case I envy the plants, and as I spoke about the basis, I am talking about my roots. There has been forest in me, and forest-like things always around me, the land of Artemis. The floor of a forest gorge is present. I sit where the cloth is spun, and there the sylphs and then the gnomes are present, the ancient pastures are no longer far away. The poplar avenues are by the meadows and hills, and the hilly land is like the laps of women.'[3]

Eugen Blume

Translated from the German by Michael Robinson

1 Hermann Glöckner, 'Meine Arbeit ist mein Leben', in John Erpenbeck, ed., *Hermann Glöckner: Ein Patriarch der Moderne* (Berlin, 1983), 57.

2 Gerhard Altenbourg, 'Narbenrisse beim Durchstreifen jener Hügellandschaft: Autobiographische Notizen', in exh. cat. *Gerhard Altenbourg: Das einschauende Ausschauen: Köpfe und Szenen 1949 bis 1986*, Brusberg Dokumente 15 (Berlin, 1986), 5.

3 Gerhard Altenbourg, 'Klar dem Nächtlichen verschwistert', in *Altenbourg: Ich-Gestein* (Berlin, 1971), quoted from Eberhard Roters, 'Um ein Haar', in exh. cat. *Altenbourg* (as note 2), 96.

Joseph Beuys

There is no doubt that Joseph Beuys, born in 1921, was one of the most important and interesting artistic personalities of the postwar years.

Beuys served as a dive-bomber pilot after conscription in 1940. He was shot down in the Crimea in 1943; he was severely wounded, and was found and cared for by Tartars. This key existential experience subsequently strengthened his idea of an evolutionary change in social conditions and determined the character of his artistic statement as 'individual mythology' (Harald Szeemann). His first steps towards establishing theoretical foundations involved independent scientific study, accompanied by drawings from the early 1940s. In 1940, while working in Erfurt, he visited the Nietzsche-Archiv in Weimar and studied Rudolf Steiner's anthroposophical ideas. After the war Beuys opted for fine art, and studied sculpture at the Staatliche Kunstakademie in Düsseldorf from 1947; from 1949 he was under the sculptor Ewald Mataré, whose formal language clearly affected his early sculptural work. Beuys worked exclusively as a sculptor and graphic artist, and very quickly developed an original language in his drawings.

Beuys worked out his notions and a new work-concept that resulted from them in a long phase independent of contemporary art movements in the 1950s and 1960s. It was not until the early 1960s that he came into vigorous contact with Fluxus, an international art movement that emerged under the auspices of George Maciunas, Nam June Paik, Wolf Vostell and other artists. He saw its markedly 'actionist' approach and adoption of Marcel Duchamp's ready-made principle as parallel with his own ideas. Beuys was involved in key Fluxus events in Germany.[1] His actions involved unusual materials and consistently aimed to bring about a uniform process of social change perceived as evolutionary. This made him fundamentally different from other Fluxus artists, and caused him to distance himself from them critically. 'I wanted to address more profound dimensions and broader contexts, and so I could never understand why a large number of the Fluxus people, who also called themselves neo-Dadaists, appealed to Dada and used the concept very superficially as a shocking element.'[2] A programme for his ultimate aims is suggested by the action *The Silence of Marcel Duchamp is Overrated*, staged live in a television studio on 11 December 1964. Beuys's reference to the key figure of Marcel Duchamp signals the collapse of Modernism, which had not fulfilled its promise of uniform ideas for art and life. The concept of art that Beuys developed from his sculptural theory, even though parallels with the historic avant-garde can be discerned, is very largely based on nineteenth-century ideas, especially those of early Romanticism, but also on Nordic, Teutonic and Celtic mythology. 'I can connect only by going back as far as possible, radically. The other good starting-point would be the age of German idealism, in which the concept appeared in the same way that I see it. You find it in the Romantics, in Novalis, in the whole circle around Goethe, you find it in Carl Gustav Carus, in Caspar David Friedrich, you find it in Schelling, in Hegel etc.'[3] Beuys continued to have diverse points of contact. He constructed an eclectic edifice exploiting ideas that approach a concept of completeness. His sculptural theory, based on a dialectical dualism between chaotic, self-dissolving processes that are permanently evolving and firm formations that are the result of these, forms the basic conceptual structure of his totally committed approach. This generalized transformation of the traditional sculptural process makes it possible to define all movements in nature and society as sculptural processes. For Beuys this means that spiritual events in the broadest sense, but also processes that shape society, should be considered artistic. Steiner's idea of the three states of mind and matter is the essential basis for developing an alternative social structure.

Beuys became professor of monumental sculpture at the Staatliche Kunstakademie in Düsseldorf in 1961. He produced his most important actions after this date. As well as the Fluxus actions these include *How to Explain Pictures to the Dead Hare* in the Galerie Schmela in

Düsseldorf in 1965, *Manresa* in the same venue in 1966, *Eurasia-staff 82 min Fluxorum Organum* in the Galerie nächst St Stephan in Vienna in 1967, *I am Trying to Set (Make) You Free, Concert-Grandyom (Sphereyom)* in the Akademie der Künste in Berlin in 1969 and *Celtic (Kinloch Rannoch), Scottish Symphony* in Edinburgh in 1970, repeated in similar form in Basel in 1971. In 1967 Beuys started his attempt to affect political processes directly by founding the *Deutsche Studentenpartei als Metapher* (German Students' Party as metaphor). In 1970 this political work produced the *Organisation der Nichtwähler, Freie Volksabstimmung* (Non-voters' Organization, Free People's ballot). Beuys increasingly used his actions and participation in exhibitions, for example *documenta* in Kassel, to put his expanded concept of art aimed at social matters into practice. An attempt to break down the ossified structure of the Düsseldorf Academy ended in Beuys's dismissal in 1972, after occupation of the administrative offices. This led to the notion of the *Freie Internationale Universität*, the Free International University, intended to produce free, creative people independently of state constraints. The FIU first took concrete shape for a hundred days at *documenta 5*, in 1972. Beuys created a spiritual network for this active learning process in *Honey-pump at the Work-place*, an installation for *documenta 6*, in 1977.

Beuys was one of the active co-founders of the Green movement in Germany, and stood for parliament. He showed his first large ecological work, *7000 Oaks*, which won international acclaim, at *documenta 7*, Kassel in 1982. His planned continuation in a Hamburg cleansing bed polluted with poisonous substances failed, partly because of ignorance on the part of the politicians responsible.

Beuys had an astonishingly broad sphere of activity. His connections stretched throughout Europe to Ireland in particular, where he followed the tracks of James Joyce, for him the key figure of literary Modernism, to Scotland, France, southern Italy, and on to North America and Japan. The Guggenheim Museum in New York mounted the first major retrospective of his work in 1979. Despite international recognition Beuys remained a controversial artist in Germany right up to his death in 1986. The general recognition of his work that started after his death, mainly on the basis of

a material-aesthetic and iconographic interpretation, almost completely excludes his radical political ideas, which seem abstruse to many, but for Beuys represented an essential component of his work. Beuys saw art as the only way of reassembling a disintegrating world by a process of enlightenment. He felt that man could reach a position of freedom and thus a new, positive world approach by artistic activity detached from the élitist position of unique talent and made into a general creative process.

Eugen Blume

Translated from the German by Michael Robinson

1 *Festum Fluxorum. Fluxus* on 2 and 3 February 1963, Düsseldorf, Staatliche Kunstakademie; *Festival der neuen Kunst*, 20 July 1964 in Aachen; *Der Chef, Fluxus-Gesang* (The boss, Fluxus-hymn) on 1 December 1964 in Berlin; *24-Stunden Happening* (24-hour happening) on 5 June 1965, in the Galerie Parnass in Wuppertal, where Beuys was represented by the Fluxus action ... *in uns ... unter uns ... landunter* (... in us, among us, downland), and other items. Uwe M. Schneede, *Joseph Beuys. Die Aktionen* (Stuttgart, 1994)

2 Götz Adriani, Winfried Konnertz, Karin Thomas, *Joseph Beuys: Leben und Werk* (Cologne, 1963), 49.

3 'Wenn sich keiner meldet, zeichne ich nicht', conversation between Joseph Beuys, Heiner Bastian, Jeannot Simmen, Düsseldorf, 8 August 1979, in *Joseph Beuys: Zeichnungen*, exh. cat. , Nationalgalerie Berlin, Museum Boymans-van Beuningen (Rotterdam, 1979), 37.

'Hymn to the Night – for Novalis'
Thoughts on Blinky Palermo and Romanticism

Joseph Beuys repeatedly stressed the strong poetic element in the art of his pupil Blinky Palermo.[1] In spite – or because – of an almost total absence of concrete literary references or impulses, the achievement of Palermo's brief career is pervaded by an aura of lyricism.

Palermo's friends tell of his unusually keen interest in music, and in all the varied productions of the Underground Culture, as it flourished in America through the 1960s and early 1970s: it was the culture that reached its peak in the work of musicians such as Stevie Wonder and writers such as William Burroughs.[2] There are certainly no grounds for assuming that Palermo had any special feeling for the classic literature of the nineteenth and twentieth centuries – or, at any rate, that he made a close study of it. He was resistant to theories and highly sceptical of any limiting interpretation of his art. But in 1973, for the catalogue of an exhibition of his *Objects* at the Städtisches Museum, Mönchengladbach, he gave the then Director, Johannes Cladders, an extract from the text of James Joyce's *Ulysses* – a choice that presumably sprang from something more than sophisticated mischief.[3] Joyce's text reflects the same universal sense of Nature that seems to run through Palermo's work like a *cantus firmus*.

The only case of direct literary quotation in Palermo's work appears in a fragmentary work on paper with an inscription referring to one of the supreme works of Romantic poetry: 'Hymn to the Night / for Novalis / Ursula / Henning; from / Palermo / Copenhagen; Good Night'.[4] This undated scrap is closely related to one of the artist's major early two-part object works, the *Daydream II (Night Piece)* of 1966, which was preceded in 1965 by the formally very different *Daydream I*.[5] (The artist crossed out the original title, Night Piece, on the back of the panel and corrected it to *Daydream II*.) There is no divining the true inner connection between the Copenhagen work on paper, generally dated '*c.* 1967', and the object *Daydream II* (or, indeed, its change of title). It is clear, nevertheless, that between the life-size object and the delicate miniature there subsists a curious

poetic relationship that seems to reconcile structural ambition with purely painterly argument – two factors present, or at least latent, in the whole of Palermo's work.

Ten years later, shortly before the artist's death, there emerged a similar accumulation of related themes: the themes of humanity, time, space and the universe, reflected in such titles as *Cardinal Points*, *Times of Day* and *East-West*. With Palermo, sheer chance and spontaneous association are never to be underestimated as factors in the choice of titles; nevertheless, major phases in the inner development of his work are marked by the appearance of coherent groupings with titles that allude to 'landscape and 'cosmic' themes.

In *Daydream II* Palermo combines a precise, T-shaped construction of wooden laths with an amorphous two-dimensional element. These two components, covered in artificial silk and removed from direct contact with each other, appear formally separate and yet linked, as in a loose symbiosis. The colour, and the subtle painterly connection between the amorphous plane and the stiff T-shape, create a suspended dialogue in close proximity. The painterly handling of the cloud-like shape strongly suggests spatial, landscape-like depth. The framing of the whole causes the contrasting elements to centre themselves, as if in a burning-glass. The notched, opaque circle looms into the 'picture' out of the 'sky', like the face of the moon; the 'plain' beneath stretches out in restless horizontal bands. Involuntarily, our sensory perception of the painting seems to dissolve, as it were, into a Romantic vocabulary.

In the work on paper, *Hymn to the Night – for Novalis*, we notice at once that there has been a metamorphosis: the painterly area is directly joined to the T-shape, with which it shares its colour. It hangs like a droplet in the angle of the T, forming a cipher that seems to hover above the horizontal layers of space below. On purely formal grounds, it looks entirely plausible to suppose that the Copenhagen drawing was done *before* the object – as a first, swift notation of the pictorial idea. And yet the date of 1967 has to stand.[6] The

Fig.1 Blinky Palermo, *Daydream II (Night Piece)* 1966, Wittelsbacher Ausgleichsfonds, Collection of Prince Franz of Bavaria, Munich

drawing is therefore a paraphrase, an unusually lyrical, subjective interpretation, in which Palermo has succeeded in distilling a rapt inwardness out of the cool detachment of the original object.

The circumstances of its making are intensely private, as one of the dedicatees, the Danish composer Henning Christiansen, remembers.[7] Christiansen, a Fluxus artist and a close friend of Beuys, and his future wife, Ursula Reuter – a painter and a member of the inner circle of Beuys's pupils – had become friendly with Palermo in Düsseldorf. In the summer of 1967, Christiansen arranged a joint showing of work by Imi Knoebel, Imi Giese, Reiner Ruthenbeck and Palermo at the Academy of Art in Copenhagen. The artists set off for Copenhagen by truck, and Palermo stayed there for two weeks. Christiansen still vividly remembers the evening in his house when, aside from the usual 'fluid enjoyments of the spirit', the conversation centred on

the reading and discussion of Novalis, and of his *Hymnen an die Nacht* 'Hymns to the Night' in particular.

There is much that may seem fortuitous in the resulting fragment, which Palermo slipped under his hosts' bedroom door as a 'goodnight greeting'; but the obvious association with the shape of an eye, the a suggestion of a pupil and a contrasting oval iris, fits in with the implicit context of private life and personified emotions. It would be quite wrong to suppose that the work treats Novalis's volume of prose poems, published in 1800, simply as a source of content that the artist undertakes to express through imagery. However, as a creative artist, Palermo clearly felt a tacit, elective affinity with the associative richness and transcendental spatial imagination of Novalis's work.

The *Hymnen an die Nacht* were prompted by the untimely death of Novalis's fiancée. In the years that followed her loss, the poet's letters reveal an intensified interest in the natural sciences and in the writings of the mystic Jacob Böhme. Palermo's own unspoken rapport with philosophical and scientific modes of thought in the context of his own work is revealed not least by the fact that in 1975, instead of a statement for the catalogue of the São Paulo Biennale, he submitted an article on René Thom's catastrophe theory.[8] The combination of scientific clarity and poetry, in the search for a coherent metaphysics to reconcile this world with the world beyond – one of the central concerns of all Romanticism – will have presented an increasing challenge to an abstract artist like Palermo. His response was surely conditioned, in part, by his teacher Beuys, who was always fascinated both by Novalis and by the physicist Johann Wilhelm Ritter.

In Novalis's *Hymnen*, 'in a mystical withdrawal, Love, Dream and Death are hailed as the central experiences of an alternative, irrational world'.[9] In the fragmentary visual form of his *Hymn to the Night – for Novalis*, Palermo evokes a number of associations that are crucial to the texture of the poem. Without stretching the interpretation of Palermo's piece, we can detect in it those 'miraculous phenomena of expanded space', those 'countless transformations', those 'infinite eyes that Night has opened in us', of which Novalis speaks.[10] Again, it seems to capture the mysterious, metaphysical dream state in which 'the opposition of the realms of

Night and Light is annulled' – a state that is also implicit in Palermo's title *Daydream*.[11]

'Downward I turn', writes Novalis, 'to holy, inexpressible, mysterious Night ... I will sink into dewdrops and mingle with the ashes.'[12] Palermo's Novalis fragment suggests to us one of those 'disconnected thoughts'[13] in which an artist – inspired by great poetry – elevates the universal and the personal into one intricate, hermetic metaphor. As for the imaginative affinity between Palermo and Novalis – both died young, and with hindsight their legends have something in common – there is an evident 'alternation between emotion and calculation, between imagination and intellect'[14] that unites the two artists across the centuries. In Palermo's abstract work we find Novalis's 'art of "alienating" in a "pleasant" way, making an object alien and yet familiar and attractive'.[15] Novalis' ability 'to capture the meaning of Nature and to act in her spirit'[16] corresponds to Palermo's credo: 'to get close to Nature, to get further away from her, and to stand in the midst of her'.[17]

One sentence of Philipp Otto Runge's, which must have appealed to such artists as Otto Meyer-Amden, Oskar Schlemmer and Piet Mondrian, applies precisely to Palermo's world: 'Strict regularity is most important in just those works of art that spring from the imagination and the mysticism of our souls, without a outward historical theme.'[18] In Palermo, this 'strict regularity' is not disguised as a rationalistic pictorial vision but almost invariably takes the form of an open-ended and – as it were – contrapuntal parameter: a corrective within an *a priori* unorganized, unanchored, dialectical syntax. In most of his early, two-part objects, Palermo used a vertical staff or a T-form to complete the essential coordinates of zenithal axis and horizon.

We are immediately reminded of a series of drawings made by Mondrian, mostly in 1914, on the themes of Sea, Pier and Ocean. It has never been sufficiently stressed how strongly Mondrian's strict, landscape-based construction is present in Palermo's early work. In 1965 and 1966 he produced four works on paper under the title *By the Sea*:[19] their sober arrangement and radical reduction of form discreetly reflect the spirit of Mondrian. In the context of Palermo's 'Romantic' picture titles, *Daydream II (Night Piece)* and *Hymn to the Night – for Novalis*, it is revealing that Mondrian himself gave the drawing *The Sea* (now in New York) the title of *Sea and Starry Night on the Beach at Domburg*.[20]

Sea and cosmos are archetypal Romantic metaphors for the Infinite. Note that in Mondrian the sea makes its first appearance – perhaps in an echo of Pablo Picasso's and Georges Braque's Cubist paintings of 1910–11 – in the form of an oval: 'It is possible that this horizontal oval form is intended to represent the limits of the visual field, within the overwhelming expanse of the seascape, like a metaphor of seeing through the human eye'.[21]

In the catalogues of Palermo exhibitions, his engagement with Mondrian – and also with Kazimir Malevich – has tended to be dismissed as the casual and superficial adoption of an alien formal vocabulary. But there was more to it than this, as the works just discussed surely show. Within his own immensely sensitive pictorial idiom, Palermo surely reflects and transmutes Mondrian's lifelong dialectic between two dominant factors – the male or spiritual quality of line and the female or material quality of colour.[22] Palermo takes Mondrian's line/colour polarity, and – instead of interpreting it within the image – he liberates it through the object. His image-objects isolate the vertical or cruciform axis and set an 'amorphous' colour-form in an open relation to this given parameter, which itself recedes behind a 'painterly' veil.[23] This breathing contiguity – the 'porous' quality that Beuys discovered in Palermo – owes more to osmosis than to tight structural design. Where Mondrian devises an ingenious system of equilibrium between the opposites of line and colour, in which 'subject and object, encloser and enclosed, are of identical value',[24] Palermo seeks an open association and rapprochement of divergent parts in a spirit of lyrical dialogue.

In 1966–67, Ute Klophaus took a highly revealing series of photographs in the courtyard behind Sternstrasse in Düsseldorf; these cast much light on the idiosyncratic forms of Palermo's early two-part objects. Mostly, they show the artist posing, and sometimes tinkering, with his objects; but sometimes the objects are seen in isolation, naked and exposed against the dingy back walls of the buildings. One might almost believe that the recurrent form of one picturesquely ruinous building, with a 'cloud-shaped' hole in its façade, and its relation to the strict geometry of the staff, is more than a fortuitous piece of scene-setting.

One photograph shows only a large cruciform object with a piece of wood across its lower left angle. There is no telling whether the T-shape of Palermo's wall objects really derives from Beuys or can be deduced anthropomorphically from the cross shape: Dierk Stemmler, for one, rejects the idea.[25] A far more plausible conjecture is supplied by Franz Dahlem,[26] who says that Palermo took up found objects, including T-shapes that he extracted from stretchers.[27]

It may or may not be accidental, in our present context, that one of the prime classics of the Romantic artist's portrait, Georg Friedrich Kersting's painting *Caspar David Friedrich in his Studio*, displays – almost literally – the formal inventory of those early objects by Palermo: on the wall hang T-squares, stretchers and palettes, their respectively linear and amorphous forms practically identical with those of Palermo's objects. It would probably be going too far to interpret the striking analogy between the palette and T-square, on one hand, and the shapes in Palermo's objects, on the other, in iconographic terms as some kind of hidden allegory. But this is not the only remarkable coincidence involved. Not only does Kersting employ a repertoire of forms shared with Palermo's early objects: with cool, geometric clarity, he paints the cross formed by the glazing bars of a window, and beyond it in the sky is a diaphanous cloud formation. The whole 'poetic dualism' of heterogeneity – measure and cloud, T-square and palette – is captured in a nutshell just as Palermo, a century and a half later, was to translate it into the objectivized language of his own 'sensibilities'.

In this light, Palermo's art may legitimately be seen in the Romantic context of Novalis's poetry: 'stories, with no coherence, and yet with associations, like dreams … like so many fragments from the most disparate things …'[28] 'self-acting', 'connecting and creative', 'not as it is, but as it could be and must be'; the human mind and spirit as a 'substance of associations', a 'connection between things wholly unlike': 'it emerges from harmony – simultaneity in multiplicity – and maintains itself thereby', as 'a being that plays'.[29]

Michael Semff

Translated from the German by David Britt

1 László Glozer and Joseph Beuys, 'Über Blinky Palermo: Gespräch', in exh. cat. *Palermo – Werke 1963–1977'* (Winterthur, Bielefeld and Eindhoven, 1984–85), 99–105.
2 Franz Dahlem, 'Das Axiometer ist der Richtungsweiser für das Steuerruder von Schiffen', in exh. cat. *Blinky Palermo 1943–77* (New York, 1989), 24.
3 Johannes Cladders, 'Unzugänglich-zugänglich', in exh. cat. *Blinky Palermo* (Leipzig and Munich, 1993), 23.
4 Exh. cat. *Blinky Palermo 1964–1976* (Munich, 1980), 71.
5 *Blinky Palermo 1943–77* (as note 2), nos. 74, 75.
6 According to Henning Christiansen, Palermo's visit to Copenhagen probably took place in the summer of 1967.
7 Thanks are due to Henning Christiansen, for a lengthy and highly informative telephone conversation on 14 April 1994, and also to Bernd Klüser, of Munich, who established the contact with Denmark, for much valuable information.
8 See Evelyn Weiss in *Blinky Palermo 1943–77* (as note 2), 27.
9 Hans-Joachim Mähl, 'Friedrich von Hardenberg (Novalis)', in Novalis, *Werke in einem Band*, 3rd ed. (Munich, 1984), 654.
10 Novalis, *Hymnen an die Nacht*, in Novalis, *Werke* (as note 9), 149, 151.
11 Mähl (as note 9), 678.
12 Novalis, *Hymnen an die Nacht*, in Novalis, *Werke* (as note 9), 149.
13 Mähl (as note 9), 684.
14 Mähl (as note 9), 657.
15 Novalis, *Werke, Schriften und Briefe Friedrich von Hardenbergs*, ed. Hans-Joachim Mähl and Richard Samuel, 3 vols. (Munich, 1978–), 2:839.
16 Novalis (as note 15), 2:555.
17 Blinky Palermo (1978), in *Blinky Palermo* (as note 3), 29.
18 Quoted by Werner Haftmann, *Malerei im 20. Jahrhundert* (Munich, 1954), 342.
19 *Blinky Palermo 1964–1976* (as note 4), 74; see the oil painting in *Blinky Palermo* (as note 3), 64; exh. cat. Palermo (Bonn, 1981), nos. 15–17.
20 See exh. cat. *Mondrian; Zeichnungen, Aquarelle, New Yorker Bilder* (Stuttgart, The Hague, Baltimore, 1980–81), no. 95.
21 Mondrian (as note 20), no. 60.
22 To my knowledge, no one has ever pointed out the close relationship between Mondrian's late *New York City* paintings (1941–44) and Palermo's last, fifteen-part cycle of metal pictures *For the People of New York City* (1976–77).
23 Glozer and Beuys (as note 1), 101.
24 Haftmann (as note 18), 280.
25 Anne Rorimer, 'Blinky Palermo: Objects, 'Stoffbilder', Wall Paintings', *Artforum*, November 1978, 33–34.
26 Dierk Stemmler, in *Palermo* (Bonn; as note 19), 112.
27 Dahlem (as note 2).
28 Novalis (as note 15), 2:769.
29 Novalis (as note 15), 2:810, 698, 705.

The Un-Romantic Romanticism of Gerhard Richter

As a subject for art, Nature is inexhaustible: in taking it as a theme we are responding to our own need to make a statement about our relationship with Nature, and thus about ourselves. Since the 1960s, Nature in the form of landscape has been a recurrent motif in the work of Gerhard Richter. A number of art historians and critics have set these paintings within the tradition of German Romanticism, and have found in them an overt reference to the paintings of Caspar David Friedrich – without, however, arguing the case in detail.[1]

Richter has thus been incorporated into a national artistic tradition, although he has described his own landscapes, in this context, as 'cuckoo's eggs'.[2] Superficially, there may well seem to be formal and motivic parallels between Richter's and Friedrich's works, but it would be wrong to leap to the conclusion that these reflect equivalences in content. The relationship between Richter's landscapes and historical Romanticism is more complicated than it seems.

In an age when the religious consensus represented by the institutional Church was breaking down, Friedrich found sacred images and the associated, canonical Christian cultus to be outworn and unconvincing as forms of Divine worship. To replace them, he embarked on a 'sacralization of the profane';[3] and this he did by elevating landscape into a devotional subject. From a combination of minute Nature study, critical acumen and inner contemplation, Friedrich created works of great semantic and symbolic complexity that operated as specific vehicles of meaning.

His model achievement in this respect is the *Woman Against the Setting Sun*, painted in 1818 (see fig.1, page 29). The plain but solemn and – in spite of the small format – almost majestic structure evokes the impression of religious imagery. The elegantly dressed female figure, seen from behind, stands at the end of a path, in a rural landscape. Her dark, centrally placed figure masks the sun as it sets behind a mountain, so that figure and light-source, superimposed, together form the central focus of the composition. From the viewer's standpoint, the woman's figure is surrounded by an aureole of solar rays. Her pose is that of an *orans*: a figure in a traditional praying pose. By advancing to meet Nature in a posture of prayer, or at least of receptivity, she makes clear that Nature has become the object of subjective religious devotion and veneration. As her significant gesture simultaneously completes the circle of the sun beneath the horizon, she also unites the symbolic opposites of foreground and background, which can be interpreted as this world and the world beyond. In pictorial terms, at least, the human being in her finite nature is already at one with the still-unattainable Infinite.

Sunlight is the primal experience of God; it is therefore *the* manifestation of the Divine. And so Friedrich's sun, as contemplated or reflected upon by the *orans*, appears as a metaphysical symbol for the divine salvation for which she longs. The mountain dissolves in light, and its transparency and its height make it seem to embody a promise of salvation by uniting the planes of heaven and earth. The yearning to recover a supposedly lost identity between subject and object, finite and infinite, to which Walter Benjamin drew attention,[4] is fulfilled in Friedrich's painting through the way in which figure and Nature, dark and light, near and far, heaven and earth, melt into each other. Art thus becomes the true organ of a pantheistic-aesthetic religion.

Richter's practice of art is defined by its relationship to one specific factor of the social context. This is the ubiquitous and consciousness-defining presence of mass-produced imagery, and specifically of photography. With increasing force, media processes are shaping our perceptual reality; and Richter takes account of this by painting, not landscapes, but photographs of landscapes. For any claim to convey a direct experience of Nature by pictorial means – still a possibility in Friedrich's day – would now inevitably seem an anachronism. Richter's use of photographic originals in painting is the first and perhaps the most obvious difference between his art and that of Friedrich.

In Richter's painting, the specific response to a mediated reality – the picture itself – frequently looks seductive and atmospheric, in contrast to his photographic original, which is often deliberately banal and at times utterly uninteresting. Thus, the painting *Field Path*, of 1987, attracts us initially not so much through any interest we might have in the relatively insignificant motif as through the artistic treatment that elevates that motif into an object worthy to be painted. Richter commonly chooses to paint rather unprepossessing landscapes, most of them with the haphazard look typical of the amateur holiday snaps that the artist likes so much. His own photographs, in particular, often reveal a deliberate lack of self-sufficiency or compositional balance.

Friedrich broke with the classical, harmonious compositions of the eighteenth-century academic landscape painters, who set out to convey the impression of a spatial continuum with an organic unity of its own. By contrast, Friedrich's work, with its compositional *Pathosformeln* or 'emotive formulas', invariably reflects an artificial, highly structured formal approach, with an ideal quality that Richter deliberately avoids by the use of the camera eye: and this is the second fundamental difference between Richter's paintings and Friedrich's.

The most fundamental distinction, however, probably lies in the artistic intention. Richter's landscape paintings are not rooted in any religious interpretation of the world of Nature: he finds nothing transcendental there at all. In his paintings, no figures seen from behind invite the viewer to join them as they devoutly immerse themselves in a sublime natural spectacle. Friedrich's advice to the painter was this: 'Close your bodily eye, that you may see your picture first with the eye of the spirit.'[5] Richter, by contrast, opens up the 'eye' of his camera to find his motif, with the aid of a highly un-Romantic chemical and physical process. With him, the photographic medium is still an identifiable presence in the finished painting, negating the Romantic idea that the artist's God-given creativity is based in the introspection advocated by Friedrich. Touchingly atmospheric though it is, Richter's painting *Davos* is not a continuation or a revival of landscape painting in Friedrich's sense. The delicate technique, the misty atmosphere, the snow-covered mountains and the diffuse light may seduce us, but this sun is not a symbol of the metaphysical light, as is the sun in Friedrich's *Woman Against the Setting Sun*.

A critic who was Friedrich's contemporary, Friedrich Schiller, remarked that the yearning for communion with Nature and the loss of the immediate relation to Nature were two sides of the same coin: for it was only the loss of the original relationship that made human beings rediscover Nature with yearning and emotion.[6] Richter's painting is not filled with transcendental aspirations, but it is nevertheless defined – as the artist has made clear in an interview and in his own notes – by a nostalgic longing for a Nature intact and remote from civilization, and by a demand for the happiness of a private and undisturbed experience of Nature.[7]

In the practice of Richter's art, however, the imaginative conception of Nature as an extracultural *topos* does not go unchallenged. Knowing as he does that every piece of Nature that is depicted today has already been socially appropriated and domesticated by science, commerce, transport or tourism, Richter inserts into his landscapes occasional fragments of roads, traffic signs, fences, houses or bridges. In the last resort, the progressive alienation of humankind from Nature cannot be countered – even in aesthetic terms.

There is another and more conspicuous kind of yearning in Richter. In 1986 he said: 'I see myself as the heir to a vast, grand, rich culture of painting, and of art in general, which we have lost, but which still imposes obligations on us.'[8] If we reflect nevertheless that the depictive function of landscape painting, like that of portraiture, was taken over by photographic reproduction as far back as the nineteenth century – and that in the twentieth century the Romantic mission of conveying a cosmic sense of unity has mainly been assumed by abstract painting of various kinds – then has not Richter, in taking up landscape painting, chosen a more or less inaccessible or obsolete pictorial genre? In a seldom-cited interview given in 1974, he explains what particularly interests him about the landscape tradition: 'For me it's also a bit about recalling or probing a dream. Which always comes out very strangely, because, of course, we're not naive.'[9]

What informs Richter's work is not a naïve nostalgia for anachronistic pictorial genres and lost artistic positions, but a hopeful and also self-critical reassessment and revision of traditional paradigms. He practises an ambivalent blend of seduction and reflection, delicate sensuality and deliberate historicity. In discussing the context of history in Richter's work, Stefan Germer introduced Freud's concept of *Trauerarbeit*, the 'work of mourning'.[10] The work of mourning is memory, and at the same time it is the historical insight gained from that memory. Here, it signifies a discourse on the question of tradition and of the paintability of landscapes, portraits, history, etc. – in order to examine what practical possibilities still exist for painting. In this discourse, Richter's works prove that – despite all doubts – landscape painting as a historic genre remains possible even 170 years after Caspar David Friedrich.

Hubertus Butin

Translated from the German by David Britt

1 Robert Rosenblum, *Modern Painting and the Northern Romantic Tradition: From Friedrich to Rothko* (London, 1975), 129. Michael Danoff, 'Heterogeneity: An Introduction to the Work of Gerhard Richter', in exh. cat. *Gerhard Richter: Paintings* (Toronto: Art Gallery of Ontario; Chicago: Museum of Contemporary Art; Washington, DC: Hirshhorn Museum and Sculpture Garden; San Francisco: Museum of Modern Art, 1988), 12. Michael Edward Shapiro, 'Gerhard Richter: Paintings, Prints and Photographs in the Collection of the Saint Louis Art Museum', *The Saint Louis Art Museum Bulletin* 20, no. 2 (1992): 48. Jean-Pierre Criqui, 'Drei Impromptus über die Kunst Gerhard Richters', *Parkett*, no. 35 (March 1993), 35. Hervé Gauville, 'Richter peint tout', *Libération*, 15 October 1993. Werner Spies, '"Emotional und eisig", in der Hölle der Berührungsängste: Gerhard Richter im Modernen Museum der Stadt Paris', *Frankfurter Allgemeine Zeitung*, 20 October 1993.
2 Gerhard Richter, cited by Benjamin H. D. Buchloh, 'Interview with Gerhard Richter', trans. Stephen P. Duffy, in exh. cat. *Gerhard Richter: Paintings* (as note 1), 28.
3 Werner Hofmann, 'Zu Friedrichs geschichtliche Stellung', in exh. cat. *Caspar David Friedrich 1774–1840* (Hamburg: Hamburger Kunsthalle, 1974), 78.
4 Walter Benjamin, *Der Begriff der Kunstkritik in der deutschen Romantik* (1920; Frankfurt am Main, 1973), 52ff.
5 Caspar David Friedrich, *Caspar David Friedrich in Briefen und Bekenntnissen*, ed. Sigrid Hinz (Berlin, 1984), 92.
6 Friedrich von Schiller, 'Über naive und sentimentalische Dichtung', in Schiller, *Werke*, Nationalausgabe (Weimar, 1962), 2:430–31.
7 Gerhard Richter, cited by Dorothea Dietrich, 'Gerhard Richter: An Interview', *The Print Collector's Newsletter* 14, no. 4 (1985): 128. Gerhard Richter, 'Notizen 1981', in Richter, *Text*, ed. Hans-Ulrich Obrist (Frankfurt am Main and Leipzig, 1993), 89, 91.
8 Gerhard Richter, cited by Buchloh (as note 2), 21.
9 Gerhard Richter, cited by Gislind Nabakowski, 'Interview mit Gerhard Richter', *heute Kunst*, no. 7 (1974): 5.
10 Stefan Germer, 'Ungebetene Erinnerung', in exh. cat. *Gerhard Richter: 18 Oktober 1977* (Krefeld: Museum Haus Esters; Frankfurt am Main: Portikus, 1989), 52.

Georg Baselitz

It is hard for us to appreciate just how isolated was the position in which the young Georg Baselitz (still calling himself Georg Kern) found himself on his arrival in West Berlin in 1957. Born in Hitler's Reich, brought up, like a number of Germany's leading contemporary artists, in the G.D.R., Baselitz had rejected ideologically correct art – the heroic worker-and-soldier iconography of Socialist Realism – as much as he now questioned its capitalist alternative. The dominant style in West German art schools in the 1950s was *tachisme*, French abstract painting of an informal or lyrical kind that Baselitz came to regard as escapist and self-indulgent. In the 1960s, the creeping Americanisation of the Federal Republic affected even the visual arts, with extensive collections of American painting – Abstract Expressionism and later Pop art – being formed by West German museums or by industrialists like Peter Ludwig and Karl Ströher. The notion of an indigenous figurative tradition was suspect, if not unthinkable, given the moral and spiritual depths to which painting and sculpture had sunk under the Nazis.

Baselitz's achievement in the 1960s was to reintroduce the figure as well as a sense of its own history into Germany painting, but in a deeply sceptical and ambivalent way that seems to have led him, at the end of the decade, to doubt the very idea of painting as a vehicle for saying anything except perhaps to draw attention to the predicament of the artist. (This is in obvious contrast to Beuys, a public personality who believed that art had a didactic function.) In his work of the sixties, Baselitz knowingly recycles the Romantic concept of the artist as lonely hero at odds with society. Soft amorphous shapes, half vegetable, half human, gradually give way to harder forms defining heads and complete figures composed around a central focus and filling the height of the canvas or paper. The centrality of Baselitz's figurative imagery marks a radical break with the 'alloverness' of Abstract Expressionism and *informel* painting. Cruciform, or crucifixion, imagery is prominent. The connection with Romanticism is reinforced by Baselitz's

use of such devices as empathy and the pathetic fallacy, whereby, for example, trees are shown mutilated and bleeding or have other human characteristics.

Dressed in ragged battledress and struggling to remain upright in scorched and devastated landscapes, Baselitz's so-called 'new men' are occasionally given the names of nineteenth-century German painters such as Ludwig Richter or Franz Pforr. Richter's *Lake in the Riesengebirge* 1839 (Nationalgalerie, Berlin), with its clichéd Romantic image of the artist striding confidently through a wild and inhospitable landscape, carrying a knapsack and staff and accompanied by a small boy and a dog, was the source for a handful of Baselitz's anti-heroic figure pictures of the mid-sixties. These in turn were followed by a series of predominantly green paintings in which dismembered pieces of foresters and their dogs seem to spin around the picture plane, and the inclusion of an axe serves as a reminder of the artistic violence that has taken place.

None of these images is to be taken literally as a portrait or subject drawn from life; they are mental constructs or 'investions', to use Baselitz's word. Within individual pictures curious ruptures occur – unexplained disjunctions of scale and proportion; swollen, fragmented or dislocated forms – and in the green paintings colour plays an increasingly important role in blurring the outlines which separate figure from environment. Form and content are now independent of one another.

The origin of Baselitz's iconography of the sixties probably lies deep in the artist's unconscious. For him, as for so many, the childhood experience of war, occupation and displacement was indelible. When painting his woodcutters he may have had in mind the thousands of foresters and agricultural workers who fled from Germany's eastern territories following the defeat of Hitler. But more significant than their possible source in childhood memories is the ironical nature of these images. The broken, bleeding youths in torn combat uniform exposing their genitals suggest alienation and impotence; instead of a weapon they sometimes carry a paintbox, palette or brush – the attributes of the painter. The implication seems to be that the artist, far from offering hope of redemption, can only paint, faced by an absurd and hostile world.

The problem of creating a whole, integrated image of man or of making any kind of humanist statement after the atrocities of World War II was one which concerned not only German artists: we think of the fragile, emaciated figures of Giacometti or the agonised, contorted bodies in Francis Bacon's paintings. Baselitz turned for inspiration to an alternative tradition, of art by schizophrenics and social outcasts – an interest his Romantic forebears would have shared. For Baselitz this was a process of discovery and rehabilitation of suppressed material, since under the Nazis psychotic art had been classified as 'degenerate' and thousands of mentally ill or subnormal people murdered. But by 1969 Baselitz had painted personal and collective history out of his system. By deciding to paint the figurative motif or subject, not just fractured and displaced but on its head, he completed the process of undermining the relationship of painting to objects in the real world that he had begun a decade earlier. His subsequent work, in whatever medium, bears out his claim to be part of a German anti-classical tradition of disharmony and ugliness (*Häßlichkeit*) in art.

Richard Calvocoressi

Anselm Kiefer

If Baselitz in the 1960s may be said to have restored a limited sense of national identity to German art, Anselm Kiefer, beginning in the 1970s, delivered a severe shock to collective amnesia. The two artists exhibited together in the German pavilion at the 1980 Venice Biennale, where Kiefer's work in particular was attacked by German art critics for its alleged 'Teutonic' tendencies. Kiefer remained a controversial figure in Germany for much of the 1980s, although his work was enthusiastically received in the United States and Israel.

Following the example of Beuys, with whom he briefly studied, Kiefer has resuscitated as legitimate subject-matter the same discredited Romantic mythology which had been exploited by the Nazis for nationalistic reasons. Kiefer's intense preoccupation with the irrational side of the German psyche has perhaps led some critics to take his imagery too literally and to ignore the ironic devices and alienation techniques which he employs. His sensual approach to materials and his revival, with Baselitz, of traditional German mediums such as the woodcut have also tended to obscure his background in conceptual art. Kiefer's earliest works were in book form, containing photographic images, often of staged motifs, overpainted by the artist. He later evolved an eclectic and highly charged pictorial language, in which photography and the written word are frequently combined with paint, shellac, collage and found objects such as straw, sand and charcoal; the latter are introduced for their tactile qualities as much as for their symbolic associations.

Kiefer's art is redolent of German Romantic iconography. The solitary figure in the forest, symbol of introspection and the power of the unconcious, is a recurrent image in the early work. But it is in his sweeping historical landscapes and 'apocalyptic' architectural visions that Kiefer demonstrates most clearly his debt to Romanticism, and especially to the idea of the Sublime which they seem to parody. The series of paintings of the Mark Brandenburg, identified by the inscription of evocative place-names across the surface of the canvas, can be read as an allegory of loss and even nostalgia for an unspoiled pre-Nazi past. Similarly, the *Nuremberg* and *Meistersinger* pictures (also from the early 1980s), containing straw clogged with black paint, transform the festival grounds outside the city into a landscape of dirt and defilement. Nazism, inventor of the Nuremberg Race Laws and Nuremberg Rallies, has reduced the picturesque sixteenth-century town of German history and of Wagner's opera to a spiritual ruin. Similarly, by including the names of Prussian militarists and National Socialist martyrs in his mock-pantheon, *Ways of Worldly Wisdom*, Kiefer exposes the pretentiousness of Germany's claim, originating in the Romantic period, to be a land of poets and thinkers.

The paintings of deserted buildings were based on photographs of projects by Speer, Troost, Kreis and other architects to the Nazi regime. Here Kiefer exhibits a more equivocal attitude to recent history. Certainly his almost frenzied accumulation on the canvas of perishable materials, and the violent processes to which he subjects them, including burning and slashing, do suggest, as some writers have pointed out, a wish to undermine his imagery. The appearance of a palette in some of the paintings, mounted as if on a tomb or monument, and the use of titles and inscriptions referring to the 'unknown painter', further distance the artist from his subject. And yet the spectator cannot help experiencing a feeling of morbid fascination for this grandiose architecture, the doomed descendant of the Romantic Classicism of Schinkel and von Klenze. Kiefer would have been aware of the regret expressed by certain revisionist architects and historians in the early 1980s that many of the best examples of the style were blown up after the war. To asset the artist's right to allude to such politically emotive issues is an intrinsic part of Kiefer's art. It derives its peculiar force from the artist's ability to hold in balance contrary emotions, such as repulsion and attraction.

Richard Calvocoressi

Catalogue of Works in the Exhibition

Dimensions are in centimetres, height before width

*   Edinburgh only
**   London only

The initials in brackets after the commentaries refer to the respective authors. They are as follows:

JT   Jörg Traeger
HB-S   Helmut Börsch-Supan
WB   Werner Busch
DB   David Bindman
HJN   Hans Joachim Neidhardt
BB   Brigitte Buberl
CH   Christoph Heilmann
FB   Frank Büttner
CK   Claude Keisch
PK-H   Petra Kuhlmann-Hodick
KH   Keith Hartley
HMH   Henry Meyric Hughes
AH   Annegret Hoberg
RM   Roland März
EB   Eugen Blume
MS   Michael Semff
GH   Greg Hilty
RC   Richard Calvocoressi

ROMANTICISM

NATURE
PHILIP OTTO RUNGE: THE TIMES OF DAY

1
Philipp Otto Runge
Rose Sprig and Thornbush Sprig
Rosenzweig und Dornbuschzweig
Paper cut-out in white on blue paper
38 × 30.3 cm
Hamburger Kunsthalle

Runge's silhouettes are founded on an intensive study of Nature, and the plant species can often be precisely identified. Runge uses white instead of black paper, on mostly blue mounts. The plants thus stand out brightly, almost luminously, against the darker ground. The effect is not unlike that of Wedgwood blue jasper ware. *(JT)*

2
Philipp Otto Runge
Nasturtium
Kapuzinerkresse
Paper cut-out in white on violet-grey paper,
33.5 × 18.4 cm
Hamburger Kunsthalle

3
Philipp Otto Runge
Maple Leaves
Ahornblätter
Paper cut-out in white, foxed at edges, on blue-grey paper, 25.7 × 10 cm (silhouette, overall), 39.8 × 28.9 cm (paper mount)
Staatsgalerie Stuttgart, Graphische Sammlung

Cutting silhouettes out of paper was a popular pastime in German bourgeois society around 1800. Runge's silhouettes were much admired by Goethe, and Johanna Schopenhauer modelled her own finger-

exercises on them; they also inspired many other amateur artists. In 1843 Doris Lütkens published *Runge'sche Scherenschnitte zum Nachschneiden für Junge Mädchen* (Runge's Silhouettes as Patterns for Imitation by Young Girls). In 1894 Alfred Lichtwark – the first director of the Hamburger Kunsthalle, and the man who virtually rediscovered Runge – recommended them as models for the amateur art movement that he promoted: another link between Romanticism and turn-of-the-century *Jugendstil*. *(JT)*

4
Philipp Otto Runge
Primrose
Primel
Paper cut-out in white, foxed at edges, on blue-grey paper 10 × 24.5 cm (silhouette, overall), 20 × 31.5 cm (paper mount)
Staatsgalerie Stuttgart, Graphische Sammlung

This silhouette testifies to the virtuosity with which Runge achieves spatial effects in a two-dimensional medium. This applies above all to the relationship between the individual blooms. Runge said in 1797: ' ... the scissors have become the merest extension of my fingers, and it seems to me that this is just as much the case with a painter's brush or whatever; with this increment to his fingers, he need only recapture his emotion and his liveliest fancies ... ' *(JT)*

5;
Philipp Otto Runge
Spray of Leaves with Orange-Lily
Blattstaude mit Feuerlilie
Paper cut-out in white on black paper,
65 × 50 cm (silhouette, overall),
76.3 × 59 cm
(paper mount)
Hamburger Kunsthalle

Runge made silhouettes all his life, from childhood onwards, and his work in this medium is an important complement to his work as a draughtsman, painter and theorist. Its craft affinities are clear. The early silhouettes are mainly of animals and genre scenes, sometimes also of landscape motifs; later, Runge concentrated almost exclusively on plant subjects. This example is unusual in two respects: its large size, and the fact that it contains several species of plant, possibly orange-lily, hemlock and thistle. *(JT)*

6
Philipp Otto Runge
Mother Earth with Her Children 1803
Mutter Erde mit ihren Kindern
Oil on gold ground on cardboard, mounted on oak panel, 31.3 × 26.3 cm
Hamburger Kunsthalle

As early as August 1803, Runge was planning a coloured version of *The Times of Day*, which was to be painted on a gold ground –

an idea that may have emerged from his conversations with Ludwig Tieck in Dresden. By thus adopting a medieval practice, he was anticipating an important aspect of Nazarene art. However, the only part of the *Times* cycle ever executed in this form (probably in 1803) was the central group of *Day*. A precise preliminary drawing has also been preserved. From 1804 or 1805 onwards, Runge was systematically working out his theory of colour, and as a result he dropped the idea of a gold ground in favour of a more sensuous, Nature-bound conception. *(JT)*

7
Philipp Otto Runge
Morning 1803
Der Morgen
Pen and ink and pencil on paper,
74.3 × 49.5 cm
Hamburger Kunsthalle

This drawing forms part of the final phase of the development of Runge's designs, a process that began at Christmas 1802 and can be traced through a series of sketches. Some final small, but significant, changes of detail appear in the definitive version of *Morning*, completed on 17 May 1803. Its style owes something to John Flaxman's outline drawings for Homer (1795), which Runge had seen in 1800 as a student at the Academy of Art in Copenhagen. But Runge's line has a different artistic function. It is not archaically rigid, as Flaxman's is, but alive; it swells and contracts in a direct expression of the idea of organic growth in Nature. *(JT)*

8
Philipp Otto Runge
Evening 1803
Der Abend
Pen and ink on paper, 95.2 × 64 cm
Hamburger Kunsthalle

This design, like that for *Morning*, contains almost all the essential elements of the final drawing, which was completed on 16 June 1803. As to the colours that should accompany the rhythms of *Morning*, *Evening*, *Day* and *Night*, Runge had precise ideas, which were inseparable from the notion of vegetable growth. In *Morning*, the retreat of Night and the advent of Day were to be shown by a steady lightening of the sky, fading from dark blue at the top to merge with the mists at the bottom. An analogous transition is visible in *Evening*. By contrast with this dynamic two-way process, *Day* and *Night* represent the tranquillity of a perfect equilibrium. Products of Morning and Evening past, they contain the promise of an Evening and a Morning still to come. *(JT)*

9
Philipp Otto Runge
The Times of Day 1807
Die Tageszeiten
Etching, with engraving, on paper, second edition
Morning, 71.7 × 48.2 cm;
Day, 71.6 × 48 cm;
Evening, 71.9 × 48.3 cm;
Night, 71.3 × 48.1 cm
Hamburger Kunsthalle

Runge always referred to these four prints as 'etchings', but in fact they combine the techniques of etching and engraving. The engravers, in Dresden, were Johann Adolph Darnstedt, Ephraim Gottlieb Krüger and Johann Gottlieb Seyfert. The first edition of 25 sets appeared in 1805. On 26 April 1806 Runge sent a set to Johann Wolfgang von Goethe in Weimar, where Sulpiz Boisserée was to admire them in 1811. In 1807 Goethe's enthusiastic review in the *Jenaische Allgemeine Literaturzeitung* prompted Runge to bring out a second and considerably larger edition; these impressions are distinguished from the first by the inscriptions in the space between the central image and the border. Joseph Görres published his sympathetic literary interpretation of Runge's work in 1808. *(JT)*

10
Philipp Otto Runge
Construction of a Cornflower 1808–09
Konstruierte Kornblume
Pen and ink on paper, 25 × 19.4 cm
Hamburger Kunsthalle

This drawing relates to Runge's projected easel painting of *Day*. The top and side views of the flower correspond to the plan and elevation of a building. Goethe, in his 'Versuch, die Metamorphose der Pflanzen zu erklären' (Attempt to Explain the Metamorphosis of Plants, 1790) wrote of the 'assembling of different organs around a centre according to specific numbers and measures'. Runge stressed the necessity of a 'strict regularity' in 'those works of art that spring from ... our souls'. In 1808–10 he wanted to apply 'the art of measurement to the study of plants', and explore their 'architectural solidity and form'. This initiative was to bear fruit, much later, in *Jugendstil* and Art Nouveau. *(JT)*

11
Philipp Otto Runge
The Two Right-Hand Angels of Musika 1809
Die zwei rechten Engel der Musika
Sanguine, black and white chalk on brownish paper, 34.9 × 53.2 cm
Staatliche Museen zu Berlin Preußischer Kulturbesitz, Kupferstichkabinett

At the end of October 1808, after completing his *Morning* (small version), Runge began to plan the *Morning* (large version). He made numerous drawings, both for the central motif and for the border. The five lighting studies for the figure of Aurora, for the rose genii, and above all for the lily of light, are among the finest drawings in all German art. 'Musika' was Runge's name for the motif of the lily, with musical genii flying out of the buds. The figure composition represents the music of the cosmos, in delicately moulded forms, their tonal values graded with the utmost subtlety: life takes shape in the twilight realm between light and darkness. There is a close affinity with the idea of polarity that underlies Runge's essay *Die Farben-Kugel* (The Colour-Sphere), of 1810. *(JT)*

12
Philipp Otto Runge
Lily of Light and Morning Star 1809
Lichtlilie und Morgenstern

Pen and ink and pencil on paper,
60.9 × 44.5 cm
Hamburger Kunsthalle

This drawing forms part of the complex of work connected with the large version of *Morning*. The lily with the pairs of children corresponds to the version seen in the small version of *Morning*; but beneath the Morning Star, at the request of Runge's brother Daniel, three child figures have been brought back in place of the three heads of cherubs. The constructional lines marshal the group of three soaring figures into a pyramidal shape. The plane of their feet corresponds to the calyx of the lily. This drawing clearly shows how far Runge's outline style has grown away from John Flaxman's impassive line: plant and human forms alike seem to spring from the shared energy of natural growth. *(JT)*

13
Philipp Otto Runge
Farben-Kugel 1810
Colour Sphere

Published by Friedrich Perthes, Hamburg, 1810
Staats- und Universitätsbibliothek, Hamburg

As *The Times of Day* cycle evolved, so did Runge's interest in colour theory. On 3 July 1806 he wrote on the subject to Goethe, who printed the letter in his own *Farbenlehre* (Theory of Colour, 1810). Like Runge, Goethe saw colours as evolving between the extremes of light and darkness. In Runge's globe white and black are the poles, and the primaries – red, yellow and blue – and their mixtures are the equator. Every hue shades towards white or black as we trace it along a quadrant to the pole. Inside the globe, the grey scale forms the axis. Equally ahead of its time was Runge's listing of harmonious and inharmonious colours. His work was a turning-point in the long history of colour theories in art. In the next century his vision of all colours in one geometric solid notably influenced Paul Klee and Johannes Itten. *(JT)*

14
Philipp Otto Runge
Picture Supplement to the 'Colour-Sphere' 1810
Bildbeigabe zur 'Farben-Kugel'

Watercolour, etching and aquatint on paper, 22.5 × 18.9 cm
Städtische Kunsthalle, Mannheim

SYMBOLIC LANDSCAPES

15
Carl Blechen
Building the Devil's Bridge c.1833
Bau der Teufelsbrücke

Oil on canvas, 77.6 × 104.5 cm
Bayerische Staatsgemäldesammlungen, Munich (on permanent loan from the Federal Republic of Germany)

Crossing the Alps on his return from Italy in 1830, Blechen saw the old Devil's Bridge over the river Reuss being replaced by a new structure. In his imagination, the crossing of the ravine became a parable of death. Strikingly, the sleeping builders, who lie like dead men, are on the near side of the river only. The crane looks very like a gallows. (Blechen was later to paint a storm-lashed landscape with a gibbet.) On the far bank, the eye is drawn towards the blue triangle of sky. In this painting, Blechen presumably drew inspiration from Caspar David Friedrich's *High Mountain Landscape*, then in Berlin, where it had been exhibited in 1826 (it was destroyed in 1945). *(HB-S)***

16
Carl Blechen
Girls Bathing in the Park at Terni c.1836
Badende Mädchen im Park von Terni

Oil on canvas, 105 × 78.5 cm
Collection Georg Schäfer, Schweinfurt

This is a replica of a painting by Blechen himself, now in the Nationalgalerie, Berlin. It was one of the last pictorial ideas treated by the artist before he lost his mind. Along the deep valley of the Nera, which often overflows its banks and exposes the roots of the trees, two girls bathe in a pool in the midst of a cool, dark wood. The idyll is disturbed by something that startles the girls – a recurrent motif in Blechen, who often uses it in combination with a ravine, his central metaphor for the constraints of earthly life and the menace of death. This is not the cheerful genre scene that it seems: the girls might equally well be hunted animals. *(HB-S)*

17
Caspar David Friedrich
Landscape with Obelisk 1803
Landschaft mit Obelisk

Pencil, watercolour on paper, 12.9 × 20.2 cm
Ashmolean Museum, Oxford

In 1803, in a cycle embracing the four Times of Day as well as the four Ages of Man, Caspar David Friedrich achieved his first totally coherent symbolic landscapes. This drawing, which comes from a dismembered sketchbook and probably shows a scene in Saxony (at Stolpen?), offers signs of transience – the foreground obelisk, which is a milestone; a wayside cross further back; a village dominated by two massive ruined towers – but displays no compelling overall context of meaning. *(HB-S)*

18
Caspar David Friedrich
Coastal Landscape with Cross and Statue c. 1807
Küstenlandschaft mit Kreuz und Statue

Pencil and sepia on paper, 40.7 × 58 cm
Staatliche Museen zu Berlin Preußischer Kulturbesitz, Kupferstichkabinett

In the foreground, Friedrich's drawing (which has probably been heavily trimmed) shows a figure of a woman, veiled and evidently in mourning. This stands on high ground, from which the eye traverses a wooded gorge to a second hill, on which a cross points heavenward, flanked by two trees that converge to form a kind of gateway. The consolations of the Christian religion provide an answer to grief; the viewer is enabled to see in the landscape the promise that is invisible to the veiled, downcast gaze. Statues tend to have a negative significance in Friedrich's work; they show the human figure in a state of petrified rigidity. He regarded the Neoclassical veneration of sculpture as a pagan throwback, something to be transcended. *(HB-S)*

19
Caspar David Friedrich
View from a Window onto a Park c.1810–11
Fensterausblick mit Parkpartie

Sepia and pencil on paper, 39.8 × 30.5 cm
State Hermitage Museum, St Petersburg

20
Caspar David Friedrich
Winter Landscape 1811
Winterlandschaft

Oil on canvas, 33 × 45 cm
National Gallery, London

Discovered only in 1987, this painting is the pendant to another *Winter Landscape*, now in Schwerin, which shows a wayfarer leaning on a crutch in a wide, snowy expanse of landscape, flanked by tree stumps and a pair of dead oaks. The London painting is the answer to that image of deadlock and despair. In it the wayfarer, who seems to be Friedrich himself, has sunk down in the snow. He has thrown away his crutch and leans against a rock, the symbol of faith. He prays before a crucifix, against a background of spruce trees: as evergreens, these are emblems of Christian hope. In the background, beyond a wall, a Gothic church looms out of the mist, balancing the conifers and creating an equation. *(HB-S)*

21
Caspar David Friedrich
Two Men Contemplating the Moon 1819
Zwei Männer in Betrachtung des Mondes

Oil on canvas, 35 × 44 cm
Staatliche Kunstsammlungen Dresden, Gemäldegalerie Neue Meister

22
Caspar David Friedrich
Solitary Tree 1822
Einsamer Baum

Oil on canvas, 55 × 71 cm
Staatliche Museen zu Berlin Preußischer Kulturbesitz, Nationalgalerie

This painting is first mentioned in 1828 (as *Morning Light*), in the catalogue of the collection of Consul Joachim Heinrich Wilhelm Wagener. The space is unusually wide and invites the gaze to wander – a metaphor for the perspective of life as seen in youth, limited only by far-off mountains. The eye is kept occupied by a multitude of details – some of which, however, are reminders of transience. Two pools reflect the sky. The oak begins to die off at the very

point where it intersects the outline of the foreground mountain range. The shepherd in the foreground is part and parcel of the landscape. He watches his sheep, without surrendering to the enjoyment of the view. *(HB-S)*

23
Caspar David Friedrich
Moonrise on the Seashore 1822
Mondaufgang am Meer

Oil on canvas, 55 × 71 cm
Staatliche Museen zu Berlin Preußischer Kulturbesitz, Nationalgalerie

A companion piece to *Solitary Tree*, this work contrasts with it in composition, in colouring, in the hour that it depicts and in its expected mode of viewing. It shows few objects, which call for a concentrated, meditative gaze. The human figures come to the scene as strangers; they have reached a frontier where nothing remains but to look. The two ships on the left and the group of women with a man on the right are symmetrically placed on either side of the rising moon. The closer the ships come to the shore, which signifies the end of life's voyage, the higher the moon climbs, and the brighter its light becomes. The rock on which the people sit arches its back to meet the sky; the fringe of the clouds sags downward. *(HB-S)*

24
Caspar David Friedrich
Trees and Bushes in the Snow c.1828
Gebüsch im Schnee

Oil on canvas, 31 × 25.5 cm
Staatliche Kunstsammlungen Dresden, Gemäldegalerie Neue Meister

25
Caspar David Friedrich
Owl in Gothic Window 1836
Eule in gotischem Fenster

Sepia and pencil on paper, 37.8 × 25.6 cm
State Hermitage Museum, St Petersburg

The window is a motif from the *Ruin on the Oybin*. The owl as a bird of night and of death – but also as a symbol of divine wisdom, first appeared in Friedrich's work in a lost sepia drawing of 1806. It became a frequent motif in Friedrich's late period, beginning with an oil painting of c.1820 (also lost). He consistently associated it with the full moon, a symbol of Christ. Here, as the *Dreamer*, the window affords a prospect of redemption through a Christian death. This is conveyed by the thin, dead branch that intersects the full moon. *(HB-S)*

26
Caspar David Friedrich
Two Men at Moonrise by the Sea c.1835–37
Zwei Männer bei Mondaufgang am Meer

Sepia and pencil on paper, 24.5 × 34.5 cm
State Hermitage Museum, St Petersburg

Here Friedrich plays a variation on a motif first used in an oil painting of 1817 (Berlin, Nationalgalerie). Two wayfarers in Old German garb have reached the seashore, and with it the goal of their life's journey. They contemplate the revelation of Christ, as represented by the rising full moon, which stands exactly tangential to the horizon. Their heads are level with it, thus indicating their bond with Christ though faith. Here the act of seeing becomes a view out of the finite into infinity. *(HB-S)*

27
Caspar David Friedrich
Boat on Beach by Moonlight 1837–39
Boot am Strand bei Mondschein

Sepia and pencil on paper, 24.4 × 41.6 cm
State Hermitage Museum, St Petersburg

The motif of the large sepia drawing *View of Arkona with Rising Moon* has here been reduced to the contrast between the beached boat and the rising moon to which the oar points. As in the drawing *Two Men at Moonrise by the Sea*, the theme is that of faith in Christ in the face of death. *(HB-S)*

28
Carl Friedrich Lessing
The Castle on the Rock 1828
Das Felsenschloß

Oil on canvas, 138 × 194 cm
Staatliche Museen zu Berlin Preußischer Kulturbesitz, Nationalgalerie (on loan to Kunstmuseum Düsseldorf im Ehrenhof)

The format, unusual in the German landscape painting of the time, marks Lessing's intention of evoking an atmosphere of medieval chivalry. The avowed source is Sir Walter Scott's novel *The Abbot*, in which he tells of the escape of Mary, Queen of Scots, from Lochleven Castle. The reader's imagination takes wing, and this enables the painter to tell the story with a minimum of staffage. No path or road is visible, but the composition invites the eye to explore both architecture and landscape. The detailed evocation of the (imaginary) castle reveals the artist's architectural knowledge, acquired as a pupil of Karl Friedrich Schinkel. Lessing's propensity for gloom induced several contemporary critics to see him as a natural successor to Caspar David Friedrich; but there are no religious or patriotic messages in his landscapes. Their content is purely narrative. *(HB-S)*

29
Ferdinand Olivier
St Peter's Graveyard in Salzburg 1818
Der Petersfriedhof in Salzburg

Pen and ink on paper, 17.5 × 26.7 cm
Staatliche Kunstsammlungen Dresden, Kupferstichkabinett * *

30
Ferdinand Olivier
On the Frauensteinberg at Mödling 1823
Am Frauensteinberg in Mödling

Pen and ink, with white highlights, on grey-greenish paper, 56 × 44.3 cm
Staatliche Kunstsammlungen Dresden, Kupferstichkabinett

This drawing of a scene near Vienna maintains the contrast between left and right. To the left, beneath the luxuriant foliage of a large tree, a nun is devoutly reading her breviary; to the right, two daring boys are climbing a rock. One holds a crossbow and wears a military cap; the other has just spotted the nun and points her out to his friend. Feminine demureness is contrasted with masculine vigour. The late Gothic church of Mödling presides over this divided world. *(HB-S)* *

31
Karl Friedrich Schinkel
Gothic Cathedral by the Water, 1813
Gotischer Dom am Wasser

Oil on canvas, 80 × 106.5 cm
Staatliche Museen zu Berlin Preußischer Kulturbesitz, Nationalgalerie

Schinkel's fame today is as an architect, but until the end of the Wars of Liberation he worked mostly as a painter. This *Gothic Cathedral by the Water* is his architectural vision of a Gothic Revival cathedral – an original creation in which he uses some elements of English origin (as he was to do in practice, on a much smaller scale, in the Friedrich-Werdersche Kirche, Berlin). His main interest is in the transparent structure; the building looks like latticework against a dramatic sky that floods every arch and opening with light. The foreground figures are dwarfed by the 'celestial' building that is not only separated from them by the water but raised on a hilltop. The only access to it is across a tall bridge, an architectural masterpiece in its own right, that seems to mark the transition into the world beyond. *(BB)*

32
Karl Friedrich Schinkel (after)
Starry Hall of the Queen of the Night 1815
Sternenhalle der Königin der Nacht

Etching and colour aquatint, 32.5 × 47.5 cm
Hochschule der Künste Berlin, Hochschulbibliothek

Schinkel's first great achievement as a theatre designer was the set of twelve designs for a production of *Die Zauberflöte* (The Magic Flute), by Wolfgang Amadeus Mozart, performed at the Berlin Opera on 18 January 1816 as part of the Prussian peace and coronation celebrations. In true Romantic vein, he brought out the contrast between Day and Night while simultaneously seeking to reconcile them in a gesture to the defeated enemy, France. Hence this magnificent presentation of Night, with the starry sky as a domed vault: a reference, too, to the natural symbolism inherent in human architecture. The print, after Schinkel's gouache of 1815, is by Karl Friedrich Thiele. *(HB-S)*

EMPIRICAL STUDIES OF NATURE

33
Carl Blechen
Chalk Cliffs on Rügen 1828
Kreidefelsen auf Rügen

Oil on canvas, 27.5 × 34.3 cm
Niederlausitzer Landesmuseum, Cottbus

Helmut Börsch-Supan suggests that the painting known as *Chalk Cliffs on Rügen* really represents the limestone quarries at Rübersdorf, near Neustadt-Eberswalde. It was long believed to date from a hypothetical visit to Rügen, directly before Blechen's departure for Italy in 1828. As Blechen shows nothing but the rock formations and a tiny scrap of sky, it is hard to tell. As late as 1930, even so Romantic a work as Caspar David Friedrich's celebrated *Chalk Cliffs on Rügen* could still be interpreted primarily as a study of picturesque rock formations – and consequently attributed to Blechen. In the nineteenth century, geology and geogony could never be entirely isolated from their

mythological and, above all, Christian connotations. *(WB)*

34
Carl Gustav Carus
Misty Landscape c.1825
Nebellandschaft

Oil on paper, mounted on cardboard
19.5 × 26 cm
Staatliche Museen zu Berlin Preußischer Kulturbesitz, Nationalgalerie

Carus's landscape is sketchier in execution and (probably under the influence of Johan Christian Clausen Dahl) bolder in colour – from the yellow-violet of the sky through the startling blue band in the distance to the green-grey of the foreground – than Caspar David Friedrich's austere *Mist in the Elbe Valley*. But it concentrates more closely on the reproduction of natural phenomena; with its repoussoirs, it is also more conventional in design. In the Friedrich, we are challenged to take a view and thus induced to reflect on what is shown; here, nothing comes between us and the direct enjoyment of the natural phenomena that are on display. *(WB)*

35
Carl Gustav Carus
Staffa, Fingal's Cave 1844 or later
Staffa, Fingalshöhle

Pen and watercolour on paper,
27.8 × 31.1 cm
Kunstmuseum Basel, Kupferstichkabinett

Carus's early drawing of the same subject, now in Dresden, derives from the tradition of travel-book illustration founded by Thomas Pennant (1774, German edition 1779), who illustrated the geology of the straight drums of the basalt columns by regularizing them; the result looks like a stage set. By contrast, the Basel drawing is an eye-witness record. Carus visited Staffa in 1844 and there saw that the caves were irregular in structure, that the basalt columns stood oblique rather than straight, and that the roof of the cave was mostly not basalt but yellowish-black trap. In his travel memoir of 1844, Carus describes the geological phenomena with enthusiasm but also with great precision. The myth of Fingal is mentioned, but it is the geological interest that prevails. *(WB)*

36
Carl Gustav Carus
Evening Clouds over the Riesengebirge
c.1850
Abendwolken über dem Riesengebirge

Oil on cardboard, 13 × 18 cm
Städtische Kunstsammlungen, Görlitz

In 1820 Carus went on a walking tour of the Riesengebirge, on the Bohemian border, which led to his first scientific renderings of natural phenomena – and of rock structures in particular. From then on, under Goethe's influence, he put the subjective Nature mysticism of early German Romanticism behind him and sought to attain a holistic view of Nature through the study of natural law. This found artistic expression in his *Erdlebenbilder* or 'earth-life images'. The ninth and tenth of his *Zwölf Briefe über das Erdleben* (Twelve Letters on Earth Life) deal with atmospheric phenomena, and above all with the colouring of the atmosphere

through refraction of light. This late oil sketch records his observations in an uncommonly free manner that is reminiscent, once again, of Johan Christian Clausen Dahl. *(WB)*

37
Johan Christian Clausen Dahl
Cloud Study with Top of Vesuvius 1820
Wolkenstudie mit Gipfel des Vesuvs

Oil on canvas, 7 × 15 cm
Göteborgs Konstmuseum

Dahl's view of Vesuvius differs radically from the veduta tradition current in the eighteenth century. The traditional veduta shows Vesuvius at a distance, from the Bay of Naples, either by day or during a nocturnal eruption. A second type, found in the work of Jacob Philipp Hackert and Pierre Jacques Volaire, shows the track of the glowing lava from a closer vantage point on the Campi Flegrei but still almost invariably includes a view of the Bay of Naples. Dahl gives us no identifiable prospect at all: only the impression of a phenomenon, in which smoke blends with the clouds to mask the mountain almost entirely. Without the inscription on the reverse, it would be hard to tell that this is Vesuvius at all. There seems to be just one direct precedent for this close attention to the specific phenomenon: Pierre Henri de Valenciennes, who twice painted the very same rounded mountaintop under cloud. *(WB)*

38
Johan Christian Clausen Dahl
Study of Drifting Clouds 1835
Gewitterluft

Oil on paper, mounted on board,
18.5 × 23 cm
Nasjonalgalleriet, Oslo

It was probably not until his first visit to Italy, in 1820–21, that Dahl began to paint pure cloud studies in oils. Like his landscape sketches, these appeal to present-day taste and indeed seem to define Dahl's artistic individuality; but he himself regarded them as study material and nothing more. In Italy, he probably derived the idea of making sketches of this kind from the school of Pierre Henri de Valenciennes; back in Dresden, he was no doubt encouraged to persevere by Carl Gustav Carus, and by Goethe's treatise on Luke Howard's cloud terminology. Dahl uses no system of cloud classification as such, but comes freshly to the perceived phenomena. To what extent these sketches were done in the presence of Nature must remain an open question. *(WB)*

39
Johann Georg von Dillis
Cloud Study 1819–24
Wolkenstudie

White chalk, stumped, on blue handmade paper, 25.2 × 38.8 cm
Staatliche Graphische Sammlung, Munich

Returning to Munich from a visit to Italy in 1818, Dillis produced numerous pure cloud studies, mostly in white and black chalk on blue paper. He seems to have been reacting to three stimuli. First, there was the traditional advice derived from the sixteenth-century manuals known as

Illuminierbücher and perpetuated by such works as Willem Goeree's *Zeichenkunst* of 1670 (countless editions through the eighteenth century); in the late seventeenth century, as William Gilpin records, Willem van de Velde the Younger made cloud drawings on the Thames in black and white on blue paper. Second, there was the oil-sketch tradition of the French colony in Rome, which also produced pure cloud studies. Third, there were Goethe's treatises on Luke Howard's proposed classification of cloud structures. *(WB)*

40
Caspar David Friedrich
Old Oak Tree with Stork's Nest 1806
Alte Eiche mit Storchennest

Pencil on paper, 28.6 × 20.5 cm
Hamburger Kunsthalle

The precise date of 23 May 1806, written on the drawing, makes it clear that this is a direct study from Nature. Together with a series of other drawings, it was done near Neubrandenburg, shortly before Friedrich went to Rügen in 1806. He used this tree study for a finished sepia of the same year and also for the painting *Solitary Tree*, of 1822 (Nationalgalerie, Berlin) – in both cases omitting the stork's nest, presumably discarded as too anecdotal for the context. In all his tree studies, Friedrich was careful to make a precise record of the branching structure, to reproduce light and shade, and to distinguish the windward side of the tree. *(WB)*

41
Caspar David Friedrich
Mist in the Elbe Valley c.1821
Nebel im Elbtal

Oil on canvas, 33 × 42.5 cm
Staatliche Museen zu Berlin Preußischer Kulturbesitz, Nationalgalerie

Helmut Börsch-Supan has rightly pointed out that – if only because of the disproportion between the sizes of the objects shown – this landscape cannot be a pure study from Nature: it is a deliberately composed landscape. It is, however, impossible to extract from it any single, emblematic message in terms of institutional Christianity. The emphasis on the central vertical axis, and the absence of active figures, are invitations to meditate on the nature of perceived reality; but, just as the objects in the picture are veiled by smoke, mist and clouds, its meaning too is only hinted at, and individual viewers are left to piece it out for themselves. *(WB)*

42
Carl Wilhelm Kolbe
Dead Oak Tree c.1830
Toter Eichbaum

Etching on paper, 31.9 × 42.8 cm
Staatliche Graphische Sammlung, Munich

Late in life, Kolbe made two large etchings of dead oak trees. He seems to have charged them with metaphors related to old age. Beneath one oak, naked children play; beneath the other, an elderly wayfarer rests after his (life's) journey. One tree is home to a nestful of storks and still possesses a few growing shoots, the other is totally dead. The intensified realism of the graphic style is the salient characteristic of this isolated

artist, especially in his plant pieces (*Krautstücke*) of the 1790s. Like all hyper-realism, it has a disquieting, surreal effect. *(WB)*

43
Friedrich Olivier
Two Withered Leaves 1817
Zwei welke Blätter

Pen and brown ink, pencil and grey wash, heightened with white, on paper,
15.3 × 24.9 cm
Staatliche Museen zu Berlin Preußischer Kulturbesitz, Kupferstichkabinett

Together with Julius Schnorr von Carolsfeld, who influenced his use of line, Olivier was drawing withered maple leaves in Vienna in the winter of 1816–17. Olivier takes this inconsequential subject and not only measures it accurately but imposes a strict order by placing it in an axial arrangement on the paper. As a Nazarene, Olivier believed that the revival of Old German values opened the way not only to the long-choked wellsprings of art but to its primal origin: a Nature grounded in religion. This implied a reverent love of all microcosmic phenomena. Olivier's drawing is a faithful rendering of Nature; but it is also stylized, under the influence of Old German graphic ornament, into a positively metallic sharpness. *(WB)*

44
Johann Christian Reinhart
Three Large Broad-Leaved Trees 1803
Drei große Laubbäume

Chalk on brownish paper, 88.9 × 66.8 cm
Staatsgalerie Stuttgart, Graphische Sammlung

Unlike the drawings of Caspar David Friedrich or the Nazarenes, those of Reinhart are classically composed, like paintings. In themselves the large formats, often in mixed media, strive for the perfection of painting. The heir to a traditional conception of landscape, and to the tradition of Salomon Gessner, Reinhart used his drawings to develop a heroic landscape formula. In this he was encouraged by the theorist Carl Ludwig Fernow, who dedicated his *Aufsätze über die Landschaftsmalerei* ('Essays on Landscape Painting') to him in 1806. Fernow defined a type of ideal landscape that in Reinhart's case – for all his devoted study – made him incapable of the surrender to phenomenal Nature that was achieved by Romantics, Nazarenes and Realists alike. *(WB)*

45
Friedrich Wasmann
Head of a Dead Woman c.1842
Kopf einer toten Frau

Pencil on paper, 23.4 × 19.6 cm
Staatliche Graphische Sammlung, Munich

Wasmann had connections with Friedrich Overbeck and the Nazarenes, and this led him to convert to Catholicism in 1835. Especially in his portrait drawings, he espoused their sternly Old German style; he also believed in a direct rendering of Nature, free of conceptual baggage, that found its outlet in a large number of oil sketches of landscape. Early in his career he studied the sick, the dead and the insane in the Hamburg infirmary; later, at Meran (Merano) in South Tirol in the 1840s, he

produced a number of starkly dispassionate post-mortem portraits of the victims of a typhus epidemic. The crisp linearity of the style jars disconcertingly with the nature of the subject. *(WB)*

MAN
ELEMENTAL FORCES

46
Henry Fuseli
The Nightmare 1781

Oil on canvas, 101 × 127cm
The Detroit Institute of Arts, gift of Mr. and Mrs. Bert L. Smokler and Mr. and Mrs. Lawrence A. Fleischman

Fuseli's *Nightmare* was reproduced a number of times in the eighteenth century, and frequently adapted for caricature in the nineteenth century. The deliberate outlandishness of the image hints at private deeds and feelings, but made 'respectable' by learned and witty references to northern legend and ideas of the sublime. The woman's abandoned posture unmistakably suggests sexual desire, while the grimacing incubus on her chest and the wild head of the 'nightmare' itself, create a demonic atmosphere. *(DB)***

47
Henry Fuseli
The Artist in Despair over the Magnitude of Antique Fragments c.1778

Red chalk and sepia wash on paper,
42 × 35.2cm
Kunsthaus, Zurich

Probably done in Zurich on Fuseli's way back to London from his extended stay in Rome. The drawing is presumed to be of the artist reflecting on the awe-inspiring experience of Rome, exemplified by the fragments of the Colossus of Constantine in the Capitoline Museum. Its overtly emotional response to the Antique can be read as a gesture of defiance towards what Fuseli called the 'frigid reveries' on Antiquity by the highly influential German authors Johann Winckelmann and Anton Rafael Mengs. *(DB)*

48
Henry Fuseli
Self-Portrait c.1780–90

Black chalk heightened with white on paper,
27 × 20cm
The Board of Trustees of the Victoria and Albert Museum, London

This self-portrait, showing the artist in middle age, gives an idea of the intensity of his physical presence, so often remarked on by contemporaries. *(DB)*

49
Henry Fuseli
Thor Battering the Midgard Serpent 1790

Oil on canvas, 131 × 91cm
Royal Academy of Arts, London

This is Fuseli's Diploma painting given by him to the Royal Academy in 1790. The subject is a characteristically obscure one from northern mythology, reflecting his Sturm und Drang background, yet it also makes reference to contemporary political events. The subject is from the Edda of Soemondus, known in England from Mallet's Northern Antiquities, 1770. It tells

the fable of Thor who pursues the Great Serpent Midgard, finally catching him on a hook and destroying him after an heroic struggle. Siegmar Holsten sees the subject as an allegory of freedom represented by the young god Thor, the defender of mankind against the race of giants and the enslaving power of Midgard. Such an allegory of the triumph over tyranny painted around 1789–90 must reflect Fuseli's initial enthusiasm for the French Revolution, which he shared with others in his circle like Mary Wollstonecraft, the feminist writer. *(DB)*

50
Henry Fuseli
Silence c.1799–1802

Oil on canvas, 63.6 × 51.5cm
Kunsthaus, Zurich

The painting depicts an allegorical figure without any obvious literary source. The posture of despair is close to the expressive language of his friend, the artist and poet William Blake. *(DB)*

51
Henry Fuseli
Brunhild Watching Gunther Suspended from the Ceiling 1807

Pencil and grey and umber wash on paper,
47.8 × 31.6 cm
City of Nottingham Museums; Castle Museum and Art Gallery

The subject is taken from the Niebelun-genlied (X, 648–50), and it depicts the unhappy wedding night of Gunther and Brunhild. Gunther was about to make love to Brunhild when she managed to tie his hands and feet. She then hung him with an iron staple, leaving him suspended throughout the night. Brunhild remains a seductive figure on her bed, while Gunther is contorted and impotent. It is a particularly witty example of Fuseli's many obsessive drawings depicting male figures at the mercy of strong-minded women. *(DB)*

52
E. T. A. Hoffmann
A Midsummer Night's Dream, a Caricature c.1820
Karikatur 'Ein Sommernachstraum'

Pencil on paper, 9.2 × 16 cm
Kunstsammlungen, Weimar

53
Joseph Anton Koch
Hell 1825
Die Hölle

Watercolour, pen and grey and black inks and pencil on paper, 36.6 × 56.5 cm
Museum Boymans-van Beuningen, Rotterdam

54
Carl Wilhelm Kolbe
Girl Dreaming among Dense Vegetation c.1830–35
Träumendes Mädchen im Kraut

Etching on paper, 3rd state, 35 × 55 cm
Kunsthalle, Bremen

This is perhaps the most intense of Kolbe's highly-wrought etchings. In this late work the figure seems overwhelmed by the gigantic and slightly sinister forms of the vegetation. Perhaps there is an intimation of death in the pensive figure of the girl. *(DB)*

55
Philipp Otto Runge
Dream Images c.1798–99
Die Traumgesichter

Pen and ink on paper, 23 × 19 cm
Ashmolean Museum, Oxford

An early and untypical work by an artist better known for his great series of mystical images known as the *Zeiten* ('The Times of Day') of 1802–9. This drawing was done in the artist's early twenties, possibly in connection with a pleasure-trip with friends to Mecklenburg, and it shows an unexpected assimilation of the caricature tradition. *(DB)*

COMMUNITY AND SOLITUDE

56
Peter von Cornelius and Friedrich Overbeck
Double Portrait of Overbeck and Cornelius
1812
Doppelbildnis Overbeck und Cornelius

Pencil on paper, 42.4 × 37 cm
Private collection

This drawing is the most celebrated example of the Romantic friendship portrait. The occasion of its making was an entirely private one; its importance rests on its masterly execution, but also on the historical importance of the sitters. It bears a dedication to their mutual friend Johann Christian Schlosser (a nephew of Goethe's brother-in-law, Johann Georg Schlosser), who left Rome in 1815. As an expression of spiritual brotherhood, the two leaders of the Nazarene fellowship have drawn each other, on the same sheet of paper. The heads face the same way, to convey the harmony of their ideas and aims. The relief-like shallowness of the space and the bust-like form of the portraits suggests a drawing of a memorial. *(HJN)*

57
Caspar David Friedrich
Self-Portrait 1800
Selbstbildnis

Black chalk on paper, 42 × 27.6 cm
Department of Prints and Drawings, The Royal Museum of Fine Arts, Copenhagen

58
Caspar David Friedrich
Woman Seated on a Rock with Face Averted
1801
Auf einem Felsen sitzende Frau mit abgewandtem Gesicht

Pen, india ink, brush on paper,
18.6 × 11.8 cm
Städtische Kunsthalle Mannheim

Thematically, this image relates to the *Woman with Spider's Web* and to the associated drawing of 1801. As there, the juxtaposition of landscape and figure looks artificial and maladroit. This is presumably meant as a scene of mourning. Helmut Börsch-Supan considers the dead tree to be a symbol of impending death, the rock an emblem of the certainties of faith. It is doubtful whether this woman has anything to do with Dürer's *Melencholia*, or this rock with the rhomboid crystal in that engraving. It is equally speculative to suppose that the scythe (sketched on the lower part of the sheet, some four weeks later) is meant to relate, as a symbol of death, to the drawing above. *(HJN)*

59
Caspar David Friedrich (after)
Woman with Spider's Web 1803
Die Frau beim Spinnennetz

Woodcut on paper, 16.9 × 11.8 cm
Hamburger Kunsthalle

This woodcut was probably made in Greifswald by Christian Friedrich, from a lost drawing by his brother Caspar David. An early stage of the image appears on a leaf from the latter's dismembered *Mannheim Sketchbook*, dated 5 October 1801 (Dresden, Kupferstichkabinett). Commentators have often drawn a connection between this woodcut and Albrecht Dürer's engraving *Melencholia*. But Friedrich's image is not an allegory: it shows an individual who retreats into melancholy and grief. Thistles and bare trees are appropriate symbols. *(HJN)*

60
Caspar David Friedrich (after)
Woman with Raven on the Edge of a Chasm
c.1803
Die Frau mit dem Raben am Abgrund

Woodcut, 16.8 × 11.8 cm
Hamburger Kunsthalle

Like *Woman with Spider's Web*, this woodcut is probably by Christian Friedrich. On 19 December 1801, Caspar David drew a study in the (later dispersed) *Mannheim Sketchbook*, which shows the same figure leaning over a chest or trunk with the lid open. The image of the woman on the edge of a chasm is a moving symbol of the lonely and precarious nature of human life. This message is reinforced by such attributes as the crooked fir and the raven on the dead tree. The death symbolism of the foreground is, however, countered by emblems of life, faith and hope: the fir on the crag and the distant mountaintops. *(HJN)*

61
Caspar David Friedrich
Woman at a Window 1822
Frau am Fenster

Oil on canvas, 44 × 37 cm
Staatliche Museen zu Berlin Preußischer Kulturbesitz, Nationalgalerie

This painting 'would be very true and very pretty', wrote a contemporary in 1822, 'had Friedrich not succumbed, yet again, to his whimsical penchant … for depicting persons from the rear; his wife stands at the window, and both pose and light are highly unflattering'. The interior is that of his studio, at home in Dresden, overlooking the Elbe, and as so often in Friedrich's lifetime, the critic has missed the symbolic point. Erik Forssman supplied an apt interpretation in 1966: the woman at the window embodies 'the longing of the soul to escape from earthly captivity into the infinity of Nature … or, simply, all unquenchable longing'. The rectilinear structure of the dark room contrasts powerfully with the light-filled outer world that the woman faces. *(HJN)*

62
Heinrich Hübsch
Fohr and a Party of Artists in the Open Air
Fohr und eine Künstlergesellschaft im Freien

Pencil and watercolour on paper,
12.1 × 23 cm
Staatliche Kunstsammlungen Dresden, Kupferstichkabinett

When Carl Philipp Fohr arrived in Rome in 1816, he brought with him to the German artistic colony the patriotic ideals of the first student fraternity, the Heidelberg *Burschenschaft*. The idea of a student and graduate elite drew its strength from the unifying vision of a patriotic, democratic renewal of the state. Here Fohr is seen with his dog Grimsel, about to join a party of artists at their table beneath the verdant roof of an airy arbour. Fohr's companions wear Biedermeier dress; his own Old German costume is an outward sign of his libertarian views (also symbolized by the openness of the arbour). In this drawing, Hübsch, a friend and fellow student of Fohr's since Heidelberg days, pays posthumous tribute to an artist who died young. *(HJN)***

63
Victor Emil Janssen
Self-Portrait at the Easel 1828
Selbstbildnis vor der Staffelei

Oil on paper on canvas, 56.6 × 32.7 cm
Hamburger Kunsthalle

In this intensely private studio scene, intended purely as an instrument of self-knowledge, Janssen has turned a pitiless eye upon himself. With clinical acuteness, the young man shows himself as he feels: sickly and asthenic, with the hollow chest and rounded back of a man under threat of death from tuberculosis. As he stares out at us, wide-eyed, it is clear that the twenty-two-year-old Janssen has a premonition of his own death, echoed by the wilting flower-stem in the foreground. 'His life', wrote his friend Rudolf Friedrich Wasmann, 'was … perennial self-doubt.' Janssen's unsparing self-interrogation places him in a tradition that runs from Albrecht Dürer by way of Adolf von Menzel to Otto Dix. *(HJN)*

64
Georg Friedrich Kersting
Caspar David Friedrich in his Studio c.1812
Caspar David Friedrich in seinem Atelier

Oil on canvas, 53.5 × 41 cm
Staatliche Museen zu Berlin Preußischer Kulturbesitz, Nationalgalerie

65
Georg Friedrich Kersting
Theodor Körner, Friesen and Hartmann on Outpost Duty 1815
Theodor Körner, Friesen und Hartmann auf Vorposten

Oil on canvas, 46 × 35 cm
Staatliche Museen zu Berlin Preußischer Kulturbesitz, Nationalgalerie

In Dresden in April 1813, encouraged by his friend Theodor Körner, Kersting enlisted in the Lützow Volunteer Regiment to fight in the War of Liberation against Napoleon. In the victory year of 1815 he paid tribute to his fallen comrades in two paintings, *The Wreath Maker* and *Theodor Körner, Friesen and Hartmann on Outpost Duty*. It was a moment when 'personal friendship expanded

into national fellowship' (Klaus Lankheit). The warriors are sheltered by a dense forest of oak, a national symbol ever since the onset of the patriotic revival in the eighteenth century. The scene has a curious tranquillity. 'With the dreamy look of the Romantics,' the three men 'gaze into the Endless and the Unknown, which was so soon to engulf them' (Lankheit). *(HJN)*

66
Georg Friedrich Kersting
The Wreath Maker 1815
Die Kranzwinderin

Oil on canvas, 40 × 32 cm
Staatliche Museen zu Berlin Preußischer Kulturbesitz, Nationalgalerie

This unsentimental commemorative image conveys both mourning and veneration of the heroic dead. A fair-haired girl in a dress of bridal white sits on a grassy bank, lost in her thoughts of the fallen, for whom she fashions oaken wreaths. They are present in the oak trees in whose bark their names are carved. The flowing water of a foreground brook alludes to the transience of life; the ivy on the oak tree stands for immortality. Klaus Lankheit has discussed the affinity between this figure and the sentimental eighteenth-century allegory of 'Grieving Friendship'. *(HJN)*

67
Georg Friedrich Kersting
Before the Mirror 1827
Vor dem Spiegel

Oil on wood, 46 × 35 cm
Kunsthalle zu Kiel

68
Carl Julius Milde
Self-Portrait with Dresden Friends 1824
Selbstbildnis mit den Dresdener Freunden

Pencil on paper, 12.6 × 19 cm
Museum für Kunst und Kulturgeschichte der Hansestadt Lübeck

In 1824, the young Hamburg painter Milde moved to Dresden for a year to pursue his studies at the Kunstakademie. This group portrait shows him among his new student friends. He drew the six portraits, including his own, separately and then fitted them together to create his image of friendship. Three of the heads are in strict profile, two in semi-profile and one almost full-face. Crowded together in a row, they look as flat as playing-cards, with no interaction between them. The bodies are given no space and look like abstract signs. The artist himself is to be identified only by the coat of arms, and none of the friends is named either. *(HJN)*

69
Friedrich Overbeck
Portrait of his Wife Nina with their Son Alfons
c.1820
Bildnis von seiner Frau Nina mit dem Sohn Alfons

Pencil and chalk on brown paper,
34.2 × 26.8 cm (paper size)
Kunstmuseum Basel, Kupferstichkabinett

70
Johann Anton Ramboux
The Brothers Eberhard 1822
Die Brüder Eberhard

Oil on canvas, 33 × 33.5 cm
Wallraf-Richartz-Museum, Cologne

The sculptor and painter Konrad Eberhard and his brother and fellow artist Franz were sent to Rome by Crown Prince Ludwig of Bavaria; there, despite their ages – when Ramboux painted them, both were over fifty – they became pupils of Bertel Thorvaldsen and Antonio Canova. 'They lived and worked', wrote Ludwig Richter, 'in the closest harmony … Their strongly marked, earnest, ingenuous features bore the stamp of deep religious feeling, along with their native Swabian physical type.' The plain work-clothes echo the age of Dürer and reinforce the air of an Old German woodcut; the faces are cramped together, enhancing the sense of unity and harmony. In 1822, after their return to Munich, Johann Anton Selb issued a lithograph of this painting. *(HJN)*

71
Ferdinand von Rayski
Suicide of the Artist in His Studio 1837–40
Selbstmord des Künstlers im Atelier

Pencil on paper, 21.3 × 29.2 cm
Staatliche Kunstsammlungen Dresden, Kupferstichkabinett

This drawing serves to correct Rayski's popular image as a lightweight 'gentleman painter' and perennial joker. It bears witness to hours of unhappiness and self-doubt, despair and tragic loneliness. The suicide who dangles from his own easel is Rayski himself, a member of the Romantic generation. A ruined painting leans against the wall. Rayski's thoughts of death were prompted – or confirmed – by the suicide of his poet friend Gottfried August von Maltitz (1794–1835), whose portrait, pierced by a dagger, he (later?) included in this work. Maltitz's own verses, inscribed by Rayski on the back, go beyond anecdotal inspiration to the tragedy of every 'modern' artist: 'The life of a true artist is never long – bears within it the seeds of death – true artists are glad to die!' *(HJN)**

72
Alfred Rethel
Death as Assassin 1847–48
Der Tod als Erwürger

Pencil and wash with white highlights on paper, 38.8 × 33.5 cm
Staatliche Kunstsammlungen Dresden, Kupferstichkabinett

In 1831 there was a terrifying outbreak of cholera in Paris. The account written a few months later by Heinrich Heine for the *Augsburger Allgemeine Zeitung* inspired Rethel to make this drawing. Cholera appears at a masked ball as an outlandish figure in Oriental garb armed with a scourge. Her partner, Death, plays his song of mortality to the thoughtless revellers; the idea of Death as a fiddler stems from the medieval tradition of the Dance of Death. In this image, Rethel's serenely idealizing pursuit of beauty flips over into its opposite: stern asperity and a monumental rhetoric of the demonic and the macabre. A woodcut by Hugo Bürkner, based on this drawing, was published in Dresden in 1851. *(HJN)**

73
Alfred Rethel (after)
Another Dance of Death from the Year 1848 1849
Auch ein Totentanz aus dem Jahre 1848

Portfolio of 6 wood engravings on paper, each 22 × 32 cm:
1 *Death Rises from the Grave* (Der Tod steigt aus dem Grab)
2 *Death Rides to Town* (Der Tod reitet zur Stadt)
3 *Death at the Bar* (Der Tod vor der Schänke)
4 *Death Hands the Sword to the People* (Der Tod übergibt dem Volk das Schwert)
6 *Death as Victor* (Der Tod als Sieger)
The Board of Trustees of the Victoria and Albert Museum, London

The *Vormärz* or 'Pre-March' period, between the Napoleonic Wars and the revolutionary uprisings of March 1848, produced many Romantic groupings of like-minded artists and others, but also a number of political organizations, foremost among them the German student body, the *Burschenschaft*. In 1848, students and young intellectuals fought alongside oppressed artisans and industrial workers for the cause of human rights and German unity. Rethel was entirely sympathetic to the aims of the revolution, but his *Dance of Death* cycle amounts to an anti-revolutionary pamphlet, and conservatives used it as an instrument of reactionary propaganda. Unlike the medieval Dances of Death, it does not show Death as inexorable destiny: he strikes only those who, in their political blindness, allow 'demagogues' to lead them into murderous violence. Their goal of Liberty, Equality and Fraternity is achieved only in death. *(HJN)*

74
Alfred Rethel
Death as Assassin 1851
Der Tod als Erwürger

Wood engraving on paper, 39 × 34 cm
The Board of Trustees of the Victoria and Albert Museum, London

75
Alfred Rethel
Death as Friend 1851
Der Tod als Freund

Wood engraving on paper, 34 × 31 cm
The Board of Trustees of the Victoria and Albert Museum, London

76
Adrian Ludwig Richter
Wilhelm von Kügelgen Drawing in the Forest near Dettenhausen 1826
Wilhelm von Kügelgen im Wald bei Dettenhausen zeichnend, 1826

Pencil on paper, 16.6 × 19.6 cm
Staatliche Kunstsammlungen Dresden, Kupferstichkabinett

Tramping across the Rigi in Switzerland, on his way home from Rome, Richter chanced to meet Wilhelm von Kügelgen, son of the Dresden painter Gerhard von Kügelgen. The pair, who were of an age and had known each other as students in Dresden, went on their way together. Richter wrote in his memoirs: 'From Tuttlingen we passed through part of the Black Forest; when the July heat became too much to bear, we took up quarters in a lonely hamlet in the depths of the forest and there passed the day in the cool shade of immemorial beech trees, in friendly converse, reading and drawing.'

This portrait, drawn with a sharp, delicate point, illustrates Richter's words. His friendship with Kügelgen was a lifelong one. *(HJN)**

77
Philipp Otto Runge
Self-Portrait at the Drawing Board 1801
Selbstbildnis am Zeichentisch

Black and white chalk on brown paper, 55.2 × 43.3 cm
Hamburger Kunsthalle

During his first stay in Dresden, in 1801–02, Runge produced many self-portraits in close succession. This drawing marks the climax of a sequence indebted to the tradition of Baroque painting. Softly modelled in white chalk, body and face stand out effectively against the dark ground. The turn of the head to face the viewer, and the wide-eyed look, suggest an uninhibited self-revelation utterly foreign to the 'amiable, jovial remoteness favoured by the eighteenth century' (Jens Christian Jensen). In 1798 Runge had written to his brother: 'I feel that I am alone; and one is not self-sufficient, alone.' *(HJN)*

78
Philipp Otto Runge
Luise Perthes 1805
Oil on canvas, 143.5 × 95 cm
Kunstsammlungen, Weimar

79
Philipp Otto Runge
Portrait of Otto Sigismund in a Folding Chair 1805
Bildnis Otto Sigismund im Klappstuhl

Oil on canvas, 40 × 35.5 cm
Hamburger Kunsthalle, on loan from Dr Fritz Runge, Heidelberg

80
Karl Friedrich Schinkel
The Artist's Daughter Marie 1816
Bildnis der Tochter Marie

Black chalk on reddish prepared paper, 53.2 × 42.3 cm
Staatliche Museen zu Berlin Preußischer Kulturbesitz, Kupferstichkabinett

One of the finest portrait drawings of North German Romanticism, this stems from the artist's visit to the Netherlands in autumn 1816 with his wife and their eldest daughter Marie, then six years old. She is seen 'on the North Sea shore near Scheveningen, where she played in the sand and looked for shells with a fisherboy, whom she half understood' (Schinkel to Christian Daniel Rauch, 14 November 1816). Schinkel concludes his Romantic phase with one of his supreme achievements in portraiture. For all its graceful linear stylization, the drawing retains an enchanting spontaneity and sureness of observation. As sympathetically as the child portraits of Philipp Otto Runge, it captures the essence of childhood. *(HJN)*

81
Julius Schnorr von Carolsfeld
Female Nude
Weiblicher Akt

Black and red chalk on paper, 42.5 × 29.3 cm
Kunstmuseum Düsseldorf im Ehrenhof

82
Moritz von Schwind
Parting in the Early Dawn 1859
Abschied im Morgengrauen

Oil on cardboard, 36 × 24 cm
Staatliche Museen zu Berlin Preußischer Kulturbesitz, Nationalgalerie

This is one of a series of about forty small paintings that Schwind produced, mostly between 1857 and 1862, as 'occasional lyrics', with – in some cases – a confessional content. They are the swan-song of the Romantic age in Germany. This work is a last evocation of some of the favourite Romantic themes: parting, the wayfarer on foot, the longing for distant places – with possible echoes of the day when Schwind left his own family home in Vienna in the 1820s. Courtyard and house wear the stillness of early morning; outside the gate, above the forest trees, hangs the sickle of the waning moon. A companion piece, identical in size, *Wayfaring (Auf der Wanderschaft)*, was destroyed in the Glaspalast fire in Munich in 1931. *(HJN)*

UTOPIAS OF THE PAST
MEDIEVALISM

83
Heinrich Anton Dähling
Käthchen von Heilbronn and Count Wetter von Strahl c.1825
Käthchen von Heilbronn und der Graf Wetter von Strahl

Oil on canvas, 53.5 × 49.7 cm
Niedersächsisches Landesmuseum, Hanover

Painted while Dähling was a Professor at the Berlin Academy, this illustrates Act 4, Scene 2, of Heinrich von Kleist's *Käthchen von Heilbronn*. The Count, whom the girl Kate has obsessively pursued, hears her talking in her sleep of the prophecy that made her so determined to become his bride. The play and its main characters – the innocent girl, who has the courage of a sleepwalker; her brave and charismatic but fickle knight; their witch-like adversary – offered such a wealth of Romantic themes (as well as undertones of social criticism) that it was widely performed and attracted many reviews, adaptations and even parodies. This is among the most vivid illustrations of the dream scene; there is a near-contemporaneous version by Moritz von Schwind. *(BB)*

84
Ferdinand Theodor Hildebrandt
The Warrior and his Child 1832
Der Krieger und sein Kind

Oil on canvas, 105 × 93 cm
Staatliche Museen zu Berlin Preußischer Kulturbesitz, Nationalgalerie (on loan to Kunstmuseum Düsseldorf im Ehrenhof)

By the time this was painted, Hildebrandt had become a teacher at the Kunstakademie in Düsseldorf. It shows a marked tendency towards the emergent genre of historicist painting, with its Gothic (or, as was then supposed, Old German) elements and hyper-realistic technique. At the same time, behind the motif of the knight as a staunch, loving, God-fearing father and his innocent, cuddlesome child there lies a widespread Romantic literary ideal: one of its representatives is the eponymous hero of Goethe's *Götz von Berlichingen*. *(BB)*

85
Eugen Napoleon Neureuther
Marginal Illustrations to Goethe's Ballads and
Romances: The Erlking; The Fisherman
1829–30
Randzeichnungen zu Goethes Balladen und
Romanzen:
Der Erlkönig; Der Fischer

Two lithographs on paper
Each 33.3 × 20 cm
Staatliche Graphische Sammlung, Munich

Neureuther produced his *Marginal
Illustrations to Goethe's Ballads and
Romances* at the suggestion of Peter von
Cornelius, and they were intended for
publication from the start. In them,
Neureuther presented himself as the inventor
of a new form of arabesque that owed
nothing to classical antiquity: it was a
freehand invention, loosely based on the
writing-master flourishes devised by
Albrecht Dürer and Lucas Cranach. The
delicate colours of the prints bothered
Goethe, who would have preferred to see
them in a deep black. But then they would
have lost the extraordinary delicacy that
reveals them as the inspired and idealized
phantoms of the imagination. *(BB)*

86
Heinrich Olivier
The Holy Alliance 1815
Die heilige Allianz

Gouache on paper, 44 × 35 cm
Anhaltische Gemäldegalerie, Dessau

As volunteer warriors who survived the
Wars of Liberation, the brothers Heinrich
and Friedrich Olivier perhaps had their own
personal reasons to bring Restoration
politics into art – something that other
Romantics did covertly, if at all. Heinrich
Olivier celebrates the peace, Napoleon's
defeat and the Congress of Vienna by
showing the victorious allied monarchs –
Emperor Francis I of Austria (centre), Czar
Alexander I of Russia (left) and King
Frederick William III of Prussia – as knights
in shining armour in a lofty Gothic chapel.
Like St George (whose figure stands in a
niche behind them), they are Christian
warriors with a mission from above. The
Prussian King's gesture makes the scene into
a loyalty oath, invoking God as witness to
the fraternal bond. The Nazarenes' utopian
medievalism, and the dream of a universal
Christian monarchy, find their apotheosis in
the glittering, golden figure of Emperor
Francis. *(BB)*

87
Karl Friedrich Schinkel
Castle by a River c.1816
Schloß am Strom

Pen, ink and wash with white highlights on
paper, 52.6 × 64.4 cm
Staatliche Museen zu Berlin Preußischer
Kulturbesitz, Kupferstichkabinett

This drawing (which led to a painting with
the same title, completed in 1820) seems to
have emerged from a friendly dispute as to
the merits of the visual and verbal
presentation of a fairy tale by Clemens
Brentano, who – along with Achim von
Arnim – was a member of Schinkel's circle
of Romantic friends. This explains the rich
assortment of fairy-tale motifs, including the
serried battlements and turrets of the castle,

the distant view across the river, and the
tame deer on the terrace. The centralized
composition, with a central tree, is common
to a number of Romantic images; perhaps it
may be interpreted as a visual barrier
between the viewer and the dream
landscape, whose visionary unreality it
enhances. *(BB)*

88
Julius Schnorr von Carolsfeld
Kriemhild's Death 1849
Kriemhilds Tod

Watercolour on paper, 55.3 × 75.3 cm
Staatliche Museen zu Berlin Preußischer
Kulturbesitz, Kupferstichkabinett

In 1826 Schnorr von Carolsfeld moved to
Munich as a professor at the Academy. He
did so on the strength of an expected
commission for a cycle of frescoes on the
subject of the *Odyssey*, and was
disappointed when he found that his theme
was to be the *Nibelungenlied* instead. Work
on the frescoes dragged on, listlessly, for
forty years. In the end, Schnorr simply
submitted the cartoons and took up the offer
of a post in Dresden. Stiff, pedantic and
technically defective, the frescoes as executed
pleased no one, not even the artist. The
watercolour shows how the frescoes might
have been: lively, colourful, inventive. At the
same time, they reveal the unmistakable
influence of Peter von Cornelius's much-
praised illustrations to the *Nibelungenlied*.
(BB)

89
Moritz von Schwind
Rübezahl c.1845

Oil on canvas, 64.4 × 39.9 cm
Bayerische Staatsgemäldesammlungen,
Schack-Galerie, Munich

Rübezahl was a legendary forest spirit of
Silesia, who appeared in many guises and
played tricks on wayfarers, righting their
wrongs and occasionally falling victim to a
trick himself. Developed in numerous
drawings and paintings, Schwind's Rübezahl
is one of his most celebrated inventions and
one of the most sympathetic interpretations
of legendary characters in art. Schwind
makes him into a character study, isolated
from the other players, and stresses his
solitude by setting him against a theatrical-
looking forest – the detail of which seems
eerily full of life. Rübezahl's literary fame
dated only from the late eighteenth century,
when Johann Karl Musäus retold the legends
with unusual sensitivity in his *Volksmärchen
der Deutschen*. *(BB)*

90
Moritz von Schwind
The Captive Princess c.1860
Die gefangene Prinzessin

Oil on canvas, 106.3 × 60.5 cm
Bayerische Staatsgemäldesammlungen,
Schack-Galerie, Munich

The first sketch for this painting dates from
the artist's late teens, in 1822. He reverted to
the theme in the early 1860s, with a number
of studies and this painting. Its composition
owes much to a number of works by
Raphael, including the *Dream of Scipio* in
the National Gallery in London. The colours
of the Princess's garments belong to the
traditional iconography of the Madonna. In

the guise of an idealized royal saint, she
summons the knight in a dream to rescue her
from the monster. Here Schwind draws on
the popular Romantic notion of Christian
chivalry, and on the medieval ideal of
courtly love; but he also makes the picture
into a male fantasy, a *Liebestraum* based on
the fact of yearning for an unattainable
woman. *(BB)***

91
Johann Nepomuk Strixner
Albrecht Dürer's Christian-Mythological
Drawings (Prayerbook of Emperor
Maximilian) 1808
Albrecht Dürers christlich-mythologische
Handzeichnungen (Gebetbuch Kaiser
Maximilians)

Book of 43 pages, 3 title pages and 1
portrait, all in lithography, 39 × 30 cm
Staatliche Graphische Sammlung, Munich

Early in 1807 Strixner embarked on making
lithographic copies of Dürer's drawings in
the Prayerbook of Emperor Maximilian I for
the publishing firm of A. Senefelder, Fr.
Gleissner & Co., which issued them in seven
fascicles containing a total of 43 prints. One
of the most important reproductive projects
of the early nineteenth century, this
delicately coloured series went through a
number of editions between 1808 and 1845.
The meticulously faithful copies were made
at the peak of the German cult of Dürer and
influenced a number of subsequent
illustrative cycles, among them Eugen
Napoleon Neureuther's *Marginal
Illustrations to Goethe's Ballads and
Romances*. *(BB)*

LONGING FOR THE SOUTH

92
Peter von Cornelius
Joseph Reveals Himself to His Brothers 1817
Joseph gibt sich seinen Brüdern zu erkennen

Watercolour and pencil on paper,
16.6 × 23.1 cm
Staatliche Kunstsammlungen Dresden,
Kupferstichkabinett*

93
Friedrich Overbeck
Sulamith and Maria 1811–12
Sulamith and Maria

Black chalk and charcoal on paper,
91.7 × 102.2 cm
Museum für Kunst und Kulturgeschichte der
Hansestadt Lübeck

This cartoon derives from a sketch made by
Overbeck in October 1811 for a projected
painting intended as an exchange for Pforr's
small painting *Sulamith and Maria*. In both
works, the two friends undertook to express
their complementary artistic ideals through a
pair of youthful, allegorical female figures.
Overbeck identified with Sulamith (the
Shulamite) in the Song of Solomon; Maria
(right) personifies the 'Old German' artistic
ideals of Pforr. In the background on the
left, largely erased, can be seen the double
wedding of the two friends to their ideal
brides. It was not until 1815 that Overbeck,
commissioned by the Frankfurt bookseller
Johann Friedrich Wenner, began to turn the
cartoon into a painting. By the time this was
completed, in 1828, it bore a new title: *Italia
and Germania* (Neue Pinakothek, Munich).
(CH)

94
Friedrich Overbeck
Portrait of Nina 1825–30
Overbecks Frau Nina

Pencil on paper, 20.6 × 18.4 cm
Ashmolean Museum, Oxford

This drawing, probably one of Overbeck's
numerous studies for his portrait of his
family (Lübeck, Behnhaus; completed 1830),
must be dated after 1825 (the date of the
watermark on the Whatman paper). Anna
(Nina) Overbeck (née Hartl, from Vienna)
was then over thirty-five, but retained much
of her youthful charm. She found many
admirers among the Germans in Rome, one
of whom, Julius Schnorr von Carolsfeld,
described her as exceptionally beautiful and
witty into the bargain. She first met
Overbeck at the artists' party given for
Crown Prince Ludwig of Bavaria at the Villa
Schultheiß in 1818, and married him on 11
October of that year (the feast of St Luke,
patron saint of painters). *(CH)*

95
Carl Rottmann
Delos 1837–53

Oil on cardboard, 35.5 × 45.5 cm
Staatliche Kunsthalle Karlsruhe

Between 1838 and 1850, for King Ludwig I,
Rottmann painted a set of twenty-three
murals showing historic landscapes in
Greece. *Delos* (completed in 1840) was the
thirteenth in the series, and Rottmann
painted, to order, a number of variants in
oils, of which this is one. The whole cycle is
based on sketches made by Rottmann in
Greece in 1834–35. Parts of the island are
bathed in the light of the rising sun – an
allusion to its mythical significance as the
birthplace of the sun god, Apollo. Rottmann
brings the image down to earth by showing
two shepherds, one of whom is waking the
other to show him the new day. *(CH)*

96
Julius Schnorr von Carolsfeld
Fight of the Six Knights on the Island of
Lipadusa 1815
Sechskampf auf der Insel Lipadusa

Pen and ink on paper, 102 × 170 cm
Staatliche Museen zu Berlin Preußischer
Kulturbesitz, Kupferstichkabinett

97
Julius Schnorr von Carolsfeld
The Vine of the Archpriest in Olevano 1821
Vigna des Arciprete in Olevano

Pen and ink on paper, 22 × 30 cm
Staatliche Kunstsammlungen Dresden,
Kupferstichkabinett**

THE NATION AND THE PEOPLE:
THE WALHALLA

98
Carl von Fischer
Project I for the Walhalla, Elevation 1809–10
Projekt I zur Walhalla, Aufriß

Pen, ink and wash on paper
100 × 61.5 cm
Architekturmuseum, Technische Universität,
Munich

The planning of the Walhalla extended over
the period from 1807 to the laying of its
foundation stone on 18 October 1830.
Fischer's first project shows a cruciform

composition with a central, domed rotunda on the lines of the Roman Pantheon. Two flanking wings are to contain one hundred marble busts. The entrance is formed by a triple Doric portico. This major Neoclassical architect worked concurrently on an alternative project for the Walhalla, also Doric: this was a peripteral temple, based on the survey of the Parthenon published by James 'Athenian' Stuart and Nicholas Revett in *The Antiquities of Athens* (1787). In Fischer's architectural drawings there is an attractive, sculptural clarity in the use of light and shade. *(JT)*

99
Leo von Klenze
Principal Façade of the Walhalla: Competition Design 1816
Hauptfassade der Walhalla: Konkurrenzentwurf

Pen and ink on paper, 41.6 × 50.5 cm (image size)
Staatliche Graphische Sammlung, Munich

As early as 1814, Klenze had designed a European Peace Monument as a temple on a high podium. This, his earliest Walhalla project, closely followed the competition brief. The problem of harmonizing with the landscape could be set aside, since the location was only finally settled in 1826. Like the Parthenon, Klenze's Doric temple of 1816 had eight by seventeen columns. The cella, as in Quatremère de Quincy's reconstruction of the temple of Zeus at Olympia (published in France in 1815), was spanned by a coffered tunnel vault. Klenze clung to this formula for many years. It was not until 1836, after news of the achievements of iron construction had reached Germany from England, that he replaced the vault with iron roof trusses. *(JT)*

100
Leo von Klenze
Rotunda Project for the Walhalla with Four Doric Porticoes 1819
Rundbauprojekt für die Walhalla mit vier dorischen Portiken Aufriß Walhalla. Zentralbauentwurf

Pencil, pen and ink and wash on paper, 52 × 73.7 cm
Staatliche Graphische Sammlung, Munich**

101
Leo von Klenze
Elevation of the Walhalla: Design for a centrally planned building 1820
Aufriß Walhalla. Zentralbauentwurf

Pen, ink and wash on paper, 41.6 × 53.6 cm
Staatliche Graphische Sammlung, Munich

This project marks Klenze's attempt to break free of the Parthenon model. His argument was a symbolic one: only a circular building, he said, could outwardly manifest 'the idea of a centre' of German virtue. He nevertheless expressly retained the Doric order. Peter von Cornelius criticized the design on these grounds in 1820, asking why 'the greatest German and solely German monument must be so absolutely Grecian', and why it must ignore 'the great, magnificently, genuinely original German architectural style', namely the Gothic. Cornelius saw the choice of style as an issue of congruity; it was for this reason that he had designed his own illustrations to

Goethe's *Faust* in 1811, and to *Die Nibelungen* in 1818, in the so-called Old German manner. *(JT)*

102
Leo von Klenze
Walhalla with its Podium 1837
Walhalla mit Unterbau

Pencil and pen and ink on paper, 53 × 73.5 cm
Staatliche Graphische Sammlung, Munich**

103
Leo von Klenze
The Church of St. Salvator and the Walhalla 1839
Salvatorkirche und Walhalla

Oil on canvas, 84.3 × 126.5 cm
Museen der Stadt, Regensburg

104
Ludwig I, King of Bavaria (author)
Walhalla's Genossen, geschildert durch König Ludwig den Ersten von Bayern, den Gründer Walhalla's
Walhalla's Comrades Described by King Ludwig I of Bavaria, the Founder of Walhalla (1st ed. 1842)
2nd ed., Munich, 1847

Bayerische Staatsbibliothek, Munich

In his book, Ludwig supplies pen portraits of all the worthies who are commemorated by an inscription or bust in the Walhalla, with special emphasis on the values represented by each; the earliest is Arminius (Hermann) the Cheruscan. Ludwig's introduction reveals his didactic intentions. His peculiar literary style, with its numerous participial constructions, was much mocked by his contemporaries (Heinrich Heine foremost among them). It represents an attempt to bring German closer to Latin. First published to mark the inauguration of Ludwig's national monument in 1842, *Walhalla's Genossen* needs to be read in conjunction with Klenze's simultaneous publication, *Walhalla in artistischer und technischer Beziehung* (Munich, 1842). *(JT)*

105
Gustav Kraus
The Ceremonial Opening of the Walhalla on 18 October 1842 1842
Die Einweihung der Walhalla am 18. Oktober 1842

Pen and ink on paper, 28 × 45.8 cm
Museen der Stadt, Regensburg

106
Daniel Joseph Ohlmüller
Gothic Project for the Walhalla, Elevation 1814–16
Walhalla-Entwurf im gotischen Stil, Aufriß

Pen, ink and wash on paper, 52 × 36.5 cm
Architekturmuseum, Technische Universität, Munich

Like Karl Friedrich Schinkel's Walhalla competition entry, this 'Old German' project by Ohlmüller, a Neo-Gothic architect from southern Germany, is a riposte to the Crown Prince's stipulation that all entries must be Doric. Ohlmüller's exterior is rich in Gothic tracery, blind arcading, dwarf galleries and flying buttresses; the centrally planned building is entered through a rectangular, crenellated vestibule. The marble busts are

to be housed in canopied niches in seven chapels, with stained-glass windows above. Religious in origin, the rotunda motif later played a part in the planning of the Befreiungshalle, near Kelheim; it reappeared as the Temple of the Holy Grail in Richard Wagner's *Parsifal* (1882). *(JT)*

107
Friedrich Perthes (editor)
Vaterländisches Museum
Patriotic Museum

Vol. 1, Hamburg 1810
Hamburger Kunsthalle

A close friend of Philipp Otto Runge's, the Hamburg bookseller and publisher Friedrich Perthes started up his patriotic magazine early in 1810. Perthes saw the book trade as the sole bond that united the whole German nation. Among his contributors were Friedrich and August Wilhelm Schlegel, Friedrich Ernst Schleiermacher, Achim von Arnim, Clemens Brentano, Joseph Görres and Friedrich Karl von Savigny; Goethe proved elusive. In the first year there were six numbers, all with the cover design by Runge; only one more appeared, and in this Perthes replaced Runge's motif with an ornamental strip of patriotic oak leaves. *(JT)*

108
Philipp Otto Runge
Fall of the Fatherland 1809
Fall des Vaterlandes

Design for the front cover of *Vaterländisches Museum*
Pen and ink and pencil on paper, 19.3 × 13.4 cm
Hamburger Kunsthalle

Runge saw Germany's patriotic war as part of a cosmic process, in which the death of a human being fructifies the world and shines like a light in a dark place. The piled lances and helmets evoke the might of medieval Germany. The central concept of the design has parallels in literary Romanticism. Joseph Görres wrote in 1810: 'Time has driven its plough over Germany and has cut deep furrows, which are ready to receive any good seed.' According to Runge's brother Daniel, the design was 'too trenchantly explicit': it was consequently never used for the cover of the periodical. *(JT)*

109
Philipp Otto Runge
Fall of the Fatherland 1809
Fall des Vaterlandes

Design for the back cover of *Vaterländisches Museum*
Pen and ink and pencil on paper, 19.5 × 13.4 cm
Hamburger Kunsthalle

Runge drew this back cover design, like its fellow, for conversion into a woodcut. It shows an empty picture frame. The cavetto of the moulding is reeded, and round the reeding twines a passionflower. The two blooms in the centre correspond to the Janus-head on the front cover. In keeping with the Christian tone of his patriotism, Runge uses the passionflower as a symbol of suffering and resurrection. It has the same significance in *Day*, in the *The Times of Day* cycle, where it is combined with the motif of the Serpent of Eden. *(JT)*

110
Karl Friedrich Schinkel
Design for a Commemorative Hall in Gothic Style (Walhalla?) c.1814–15
Entwurf für eine Gedächtnishalle in gotischem Stil (Walhalla?)

Pencil on paper, approx. 40 × 60 cm
Staatliche Museen zu Berlin Preußischer Kulturbesitz, Schinkelmuseum

After the fall of Napoleon in 1814, Crown Prince Ludwig held an architectural competition for his Walhalla (also for the Munich Glyptothek and for an Invalidenhaus or old soldiers' home). The 'edifice in memory of great Germans' was to be 'in the purest antique taste' and in the 'archaic Doric order'. Schinkel, however, sent in a Gothic design (since lost) for a Campo Santo. Among his preliminary studies is this open, centrally planned Gothic structure, with twelve piers and pointed arches rising from a stepped podium. Schinkel's project was an implicit criticism of the stipulated Grecian temple. Ever since Goethe's essay on Strasbourg cathedral (1772), the Gothic had been (wrongly) supposed to be a specifically German architectural style. Schinkel also used it in his unexecuted design (1814—15) for a cathedral in Berlin to commemorate the Wars of Liberation. *(JT)*

THE 'OFFICIAL' ART OF ROMANTICISM AS A SYNTHESIS OF THE ARTS: THE GLYPTOTHEK FRESCOES

111
Peter von Cornelius
The Underworld 1818
Die Unterwelt

First project for a wall in the Göttersaal (Hall of Gods) in the Glyptothek in Munich
Pencil on paper, 40.2 × 74.4 cm
Staatliche Graphische Sammlung, Munich

The terms of Cornelius's commission laid down that he was to adorn the halls of the Glyptothek with 'arabesques'; in his first designs for the Hall of Gods, done while he was still in Rome, he accordingly stressed the ornamental. The lunette is divided into three by grotesques imitated from Raphael's Loggie in the Vatican. In the central scene, Hades and Persephone sit enthroned, as Orpheus takes up his lyre and sings to secure the release of Eurydice; his art melts even the heart of the monarch of the underworld. The scene on the left shows the Judges of the Dead; that on the right Odysseus's journey to Hades. In the completed fresco, Cornelius omitted the ornamental features, with the exception of the outer frame, executed in plaster relief. *(FB)*

112
Peter von Cornelius
Hyacinthus, Clytië and Leucothoë 1819
Hyakinthos, Klytië und Leukothoë

Cartoon for the vault of the Göttersaal (Hall of Gods) in the Glyptothek in Munich
Charcoal on paper laid down on canvas, 150 × 170 cm
Staatliche Museen zu Berlin Preußischer Kulturbesitz, Alte Nationalgalerie, Sammlung der Handzeichnungen

In the cartoon for the left-hand cell of the Apollo vault, Cornelius shows three individuals who suffered for love of the god. Where the Daphne scene conveys the Power of Poetry, this image emphasizes the other leitmotif of Cornelius's Hall of Gods, the Power of Love: for Eros, who is shown as the ruler of the elements in the crown of the vault, is also ruler of humankind. In these two leitmotifs, Cornelius has chosen to illustrate two of the key themes of German Romantic literature. *(FB)*

113
Peter von Cornelius
Apollo in his Chariot 1819
Apoll im Sonnenwagen

Cartoon for the vault of the Göttersaal (Hall of Gods) in the Glyptothek in Munich
Charcoal on paper laid down on canvas,
169 × 215 cm
Staatliche Museen zu Berlin Preußischer Kulturbesitz, Alte Nationalgalerie, Sammlung der Handzeichnungen

The ceiling of the Hall of Gods presents the four Times of Day through their mythological representatives. Apollo, the sun god, traditionally represents noon; in clear reference to antique precedents (mostly derived from gems), his car is shown in a direct frontal view. This is the sun as it rises from the sea, followed by the Horae as personifications of the hours of the day, and holding sway over the seasons (as indicated by the Zodiac that Apollo holds in his hand). The adjoining scene to the right (*Apollo and Daphne*) shows Apollo in his other capacity as god of poetry. *(FB)*

114
Peter von Cornelius
Apollo and Daphne 1819
Apollo und Daphne

Cartoon for the vault of the Göttersaal (Hall of Gods) in the Glyptothek in Munich
Charcoal on paper laid down on canvas,
150 × 170 cm
Staatliche Museen zu Berlin Preußischer Kulturbesitz, Alte Nationalgalerie, Sammlung der Handzeichnungen

The ceiling of the Hall of Gods consisted of four cross vaults; one cell of each showed one of the gods associated with the Times of Day. To the right of the day god, Apollo, Cornelius has placed the myth of Apollo and Daphne – but not the usual scene of pursuit. Daphne lies on the ground, supported by Apollo. The laurel shoots that sprout from her hands twine into a wreath around the head of the god. The union that she once spurned is now accomplished in perfect chastity. In a revival of the leitmotif of the power of poetry, the myth is transformed into a sentimental allegory of poetry, viewed as the ascent from pangs of love to eternal fame. *(FB)*

115
Peter von Cornelius
The Assembly of the Gods: The Admission of Heracles into Olympus. Cartoon for the Göttersaal (Hall of the Gods) in the Glyptothek in Munich 1819–20
Götterversammlung: Aufnahme des Herakles in den Olymp für den 'Göttersaal' in der Glyptothek, München

Pencil on paper, 42.5 × 78.6 cm
Staatliche Graphische Sammlung, Munich**

116
Peter von Cornelius
Initial Design for the Vault Decoration of the Heroensaal (Hall of Heroes) in the Glyptothek in Munich 1824–25
Erster Entwurf für die Gewölbedekoration des Heroensaals, Glyptothek München

Pencil on paper, 32 × 48.8 cm
Staatliche Graphische Sammlung, Munich

The frescoes in the second hall of the Glyptothek were originally intended to encompass all the Greek heroic myths. Cornelius, however, reduced this to the complex of myths associated with the Trojan War. His initial design reveals the extraordinary compositional gift that enabled him to fill even awkward formats without a sign of strain. The principal subjects are two of the exploits of Odysseus: left, the discovery of Achilles among the daughters of Lycomedes; right, the theft of the horses of King Rhesus of Thrace. In the compartment above is the Judgment of Paris. For Cornelius, the myths of the Trojan War are an image of the historical world, ruled by Eris, goddess of discord. *(FB)*

117
Peter Von Cornelius
Cupid with Cerberus. Fragment of the Original Decoration of the Vaults of the Göttersaal (Hall of the Gods) in the Glyptothek in Munich 1820
Eros mit dem Kerberos

Fresco on plaster, 63 × 31 cm
Staatliche Antikensammlungen und Glyptothek, Munich

SYMBOLIST FANTASIES

118
Arnold Böcklin
Self-Portrait with Death the Fiddler 1872
Selbstbildnis mit fiedelndem Tod

Oil on canvas, 75 × 61 cm
Staatliche Museen zu Berlin Preußischer Kulturbesitz, Alte Nationalgalerie

Böcklin evidently knew the histrionic Romantic self-portraits of Gustave Courbet; here he also relies on precedents from 'Old German' art, the Dance of Death and the *Vanitas* portrait, with particular reference to a painting then ascribed to Hans Holbein, which he saw in Munich. The ghostly figure of Death may possibly be a late addition, intended to motivate the painter's pose. Old German echoes are part of the Romantic legacy – as is the idea of the artist's daemonic destiny and supernatural inspiration. As he hears the music of grinning Death, the artist gazes into the mirror, which shows him the image he will paint. This work was to inspire others by Hans Thoma, Lovis Corinth and Edvard Munch. *(CK)*

119
Arnold Böcklin
Silence of the Forest 1885–86
Das Schweigen des Waldes

Oil on canvas, 60.5 × 51.5 cm
Private Collection, Switzerland

120
Anselm Feuerbach
Iphigenia 1871
Iphigenie

Oil on canvas, 192.5 × 126.5 cm
Staatsgalerie Stuttgart

Feuerbach's *Iphigenia* has become celebrated as an evocation of Teutonic yearning – *deutsche Sehnsucht* – and as a subliminal self-portrait. Feuerbach painted this version in Rome, nine years after his first attempt; another variant followed in 1875. The allusion to the first line of Goethe's play *Iphigenie* ('Das Land der Griechen mit der Seele suchend': Seeking the land of Greece with all my soul) stands for the riches of the past, the Classical ideal, and the soul's emancipation from social bonds. Eberhard Wächter's *Cornelia* (c. 1813) supplies one prototype; but the main symbolic source is Albrecht Dürer's *Melencholia*. Unlike Caspar David Friedrich's seashore figures, the richly garbed Iphigenia on her gaol-like crag dominates the image. In trying to blend Romantic feeling with monumental grandeur, Feuerbach betrays the impotence of his pursuit of an anachronistic ideal. *(CK)*

121
Ferdinand Hodler
Study for 'Day' c.1897
Studie zu 'Der Tag'

Pencil and watercolour on paper,
15.7 × 30.8 cm
Kunstmuseum, Berne

The four large paintings which the Kunstmuseum in Berne bought from Hodler in 1901 and which the young Paul Klee hailed as 'the most important productions of the present day' – included the first complete version of *Day*, finished early in 1900. (Hodler repeated the same composition on two later occasions.) The study exhibited here, one of many, is still far removed from the symmetry of Hodler's definitive solution, in which two flanking pairs of figures turn to face a fifth in the centre. The gestures of seeking refuge (from the incoming light) were later complemented by gestures of unfolding. Hodler's serial arrangement of variants on a single type or posture suggests a model of 'community' that – paradoxically – emphasizes both isolation and the euphoric experience of bonding. *(CK)*

122
Ferdinand Hodler
Evening Rest I c.1903–04
Abendruhe I

Oil on canvas, 100 × 80 cm
Kunstmuseum Winterthur

Despite its international fame, Hodler's art remained controversial even after the turn of the century; and when the Winterthur museum bought *Evening Rest I* in 1908 the result was a public row. Since painting *Dissolving into the Universe* (1892), Hodler had constantly explored the expressive value of large single figures in emotive movement, seen against bleak backgrounds. The landscapes often loom close to the upper frame; the lack of a horizon makes them cohere into a single plane, isolating the figure and stressing its symbolic character. Aureoled by the green hillside, rapt in a dream that cuts her off from everyday

concerns, the woman in *Evening Rest* walks down a path that itself acts as a strong countervailing form within the picture. Hodler called it the Symbolic Path: the path of life. *(CK)*

123
Ferdinand Hodler
Eiger, Mönch and Jungfrau Rising above a Sea of Mist 1908
Eiger, Mönch und Jungfrau über dem Nebelmeer

Oil on canvas, 67.5 × 91 cm
Musée Jenisch, Vevey

Hodler often painted this celebrated glacier group in the Bernese Oberland. His late work gradually becomes more monumental and rougher; it displays a radical simplification of motifs and forms and, most conspicuously, a rhythmic repetition of sweeping curves; this is the effect that Hodler liked to call 'eurhythmy'. The elements in the picture can be imagined as continuing beyond the frame, as if one basic formula could embrace the universe. In this, Hodler places himself in direct succession to Caspar David Friedrich. Besides this generalized affinity there is a specific analogy in the motif of a 'sea of mist': in Friedrich's early *Morning Mist in the Mountains* (c.1807–08), the peaks loom out of a milky greyness in the same way. *(CK)*

124
Ferdinand Hodler
The Niesen from Heustrich 1909
Der Niesen von Heustrich aus

Oil on canvas, 80 × 91 cm
Aargauer Kunsthaus, Aarau

A single, unarticulated form fills the picture plane: the close-up of a bare peak, without foreground and without contrast. In a sense, what is Romantic about the motif is its brusque – and, at first sight, 'unromantic' – expressive content. Something similar appears in Joseph Anton Koch's Dresden watercolour *The Jungfrau Massif* (1793–94), although there it depends on the pretext that the work is a study. The first artist to dispense altogether with the principle of 'multiplicity' was Caspar David Friedrich (as in the *Cross in the Mountains* and *Tetschen Altar* in Dresden); the same happens in Romantic cloud paintings, though there, again, it is often legitimized by the word *study*. Hodler makes the reduction of the motif into something monumental. *(CK)*

125
Max Klinger
Early Spring 1874–77 (published 1879)
Frühlingsanfang

No. 4 of the 8-part suite *Etched Sketches* (Radierte Skizzen), Opus I
Etching and aquatint on paper, fourth state,
41.5 × 16.8 cm (plate size)
Staatliche Museen zu Berlin Preußischer Kulturbesitz, Kupferstichkabinett

Most of the eight prints in the twenty-two-year-old Klinger's first suite have nothing sketchy about them. They are free fantasies, *capricci*. Only two are landscapes, both seen in early spring. The young woman in the meadow, radiant in a light-filled space, is looking at a flower. The idiosyncratic pictorial idea – a horizontal figure contrasted with the vertical tree trunks – recalls the baby in the meadow in Philipp Otto Runge's *Morning* compositions. But the woman's thoughts are introverted, and not at all receptive to the light and the space. Her figure contrasts with the texture of the grass but has neither shadow nor clearly defined location; the idyllic motif is thus undermined by the form. Far from Runge's idea of 'limitless' illumination, the mind remains trapped within its own subjective bounds. *(CK)*

126
Max Klinger
Painterly Dedication (Invocation) 1879
Malerische Zueignung (Anrufung)

No. 1 of the 13-part suite *Rescues of Ovid's Victims* (Rettungen Ovidischer Opfer), Opus II
Etching and aquatint on paper, third state, 41.3 × 26 cm (plate size)
Staatliche Museen zu Berlin Preußischer Kulturbesitz, Kupferstichkabinett

Klinger dedicated this cycle to the memory of Robert Schumann – a gesture of allegiance to a late Romantic tradition. The etchings revisit three tales from Ovid's *Metamorphoses* and give them happier endings. This playful work is prefixed by a dedicatory image, larger than the rest, in which the artist's studio is encapsulated in a still-life. The artist himself is represented only by his tightly clasped hands; an Italian landscape and a bust of the poet emerge from the guttering light. The genius-cult is taken entirely literally: the life of the mind is associated with black magic. The ensuing (narrative) compositions are thus turned into quotations – which makes Klinger's tampering with the original stories seem even more astringent and disrespectful. *(CK)*

127
Max Klinger
Paraphrase on the Finding of a Glove 1881
Paraphrase über den Fund eines Handschuhes

10-part suite, Opus VI; fifth edition, issued 1924:
1 *Place* (Ort), etching and aquatint on paper, 25.7 × 34.7 cm (plate size)
2 *Action* (Handlung), etching on paper, 29.9 × 21 cm (plate size)
3 *Desires* (Wünsche), etching and aquatint on paper, 31.6 × 13.8 cm (plate size)
4 *Rescue* (Rettung), etching and aquatint on paper, 23.6 × 18.1 cm (plate size)
5 *Triumph*, etching on paper, 14.4 × 26.8 cm (plate size)
6 *Homage* (Huldigung), etching on paper, 15.9 × 32.7 cm (plate size)
7 *Fears* (Ängste), etching on paper, 14.3 × 26.8 cm (plate size)
8 *Repose* (Ruhe), etching on paper, 14.3 × 26.7 cm (plate size)
9 *Abduction* (Entführung), etching and aquatint on paper, 11.9 × 26.9 cm (plate size)
10 *Cupid* (Amor), etching on paper, 14.2 × 26.5 cm (plate size)
Scottish National Gallery of Modern Art, Edinburgh

On a skating rink, in the winter of 1878, Klinger met a woman from Brazil ('Brasilianerin T'), whom he was never to forget. Frustrated love built up a store of vitality that found immediate outlet in a series of pen drawings; he converted them

into prints in 1881. The first few are essays in contemporary observation, with a disconcertingly hyperacute vision reminiscent of Charles Meryon, James Tissot or Ford Madox Brown. Then an image of the dreaming artist introduces a series of fantasies woven around the glove, which becomes a fetish representing the person desired. It appears empty and formless, errant like a will-o'-the-wisp, elusive, menacing, in peril, idolized; finally it lies limp and gigantic beneath pendent roses, while a yawning Cupid marks a sobering conclusion. *(CK)*

128
Max Klinger
Forsaken 1884
Verlassen

No. 5 of the 15-part suite *A Life* (Ein Leben), Opus VIII
Etching and aquatint on paper, second state, 31.5 × 44.9 cm (plate size)
Staatliche Museen zu Berlin Preußischer Kulturbesitz, Kupferstichkabinett

A Life is dedicated to the Norwegian writer and literary historian, Georg Brandes. Woman as victim – of man and of society – is a leitmotif of Klinger's early period. The story is told in a loose sequence of images in varied styles, naturalistic and symbolic. The subaqueous, erotic nightmare fantasy of *Seduction* is followed by *Forsaken*, one of Klinger's few landscapes; in the sky, a dimly visible giant fist, demanding redress, adds a literary touch. The woman who despairingly roams the seashore suggests a comparison with Caspar David Friedrich's *Monk by the Sea*; but the change in the relative proportions of figure, sea and sky reveals the changed meaning: the drama lies within the figure, who is incapable of relating to her surroundings. *(CK)*

129
Max Klinger
New Dreams of Happiness 1887
Neue Träume von Glück

No. 7 of the 10-part suite *A Love* (Eine Liebe), Opus X
Etching and engraving on paper, second state, 45.8 × 35.7 cm (plate size)
Staatliche Museen zu Berlin Preußischer Kulturbesitz, Kupferstichkabinett

Dedicated to Arnold Böcklin, this cycle tells of a secret love affair, which, once revealed, brings ostracism and death to the woman. It starts off with a bourgeois scandal decked in a welter of detail that anticipates the collage novels of Max Ernst. Agonies of conscience are followed by a delusive fantasy in which the couple ascend from the chaotic darkness; the woman seems rapt in contemplation of the man as he stares, blinded by infatuation, into the dark mirror presented to him by a genius (Phantasus?). This pessimistic allegory clothes its vital impulse in a sumptuous profusion of forms; it belongs to the pervasive nineteenth-century French tradition of 'black' Romanticism. *(CK)*

130
Max Klinger
Night 1889
Nacht

No. 1 of the 10-part suite *Of Death, Part One* (Vom Tode. Erster Teil), Opus XI
Etching and aquatint, third state, 31.5 × 31.6 cm
Staatliche Museen zu Berlin Preußischer Kulturbesitz, Kupferstichkabinett

The cycle is summed up by the motto with which it ends: 'We flee the form of death, not death itself. For the name of our heart's desire is Death.' Like the late medieval *Dance of Death* cycles, it is a catalogue of ways of dying. The initial, melancholy self-portrait with a moonlit sea is an emblematic image of 'The Artist'. Surprising in this context, the solitary lily around which the soul-butterfly flutters is a reminiscence of Philipp Otto Runge. Its buds and dying blooms allude to the cyclic nature of life. The emergence of metaphysical ideas from an everyday, contemporary scene – in this case an elegant seaside resort – echoes Caspar David Friedrich's groups of figures by the sea, as in *The Stages of Life*; but Klinger's meditative figure has a staring look that sets it apart from the rest of the scene. *(CK)*

131
Max Klinger
Beauty (Aphrodite) 1894
Die Schönheit (Aphrodite)

No. 31 of the 41-part suite Brahms Phantasy (Brahms-Phantasie), Opus XII
Engraving on paper, second state, 27.6 × 14.9 cm (plate size)
Staatliche Museen zu Berlin Preußischer Kulturbesitz, Kupferstichkabinett

132
Max Klinger
Dead Mother 1898
Tote Mutter

No. 10 of the 12-part suite *Of Death, Part Two* (Vom Tode. Zweiter Teil), Opus XIII
Etching on paper, fourth state, 45.5 × 34.7 cm (plate size)
Staatliche Museen zu Berlin Preußischer Kulturbesitz, Kupferstichkabinett

The suite *Of Death, Part Two* was decades in the making; its dense compositions draw their complex content from history, philosophy and religion. Klinger put a 'Darwinist' gloss on *Dead Mother*: 'The individual dies – the species lives.' He repeatedly reworked the plate to clarify the concept. Adult at first, the child's face became elderly and demoniacally malevolent: it embodied Ferdinand Avenarius's notion of 'the child as murderer' and evoked the nightmare motif. Later, the mother's face grew thin and wasted, and the child took on a radiant beauty; a pair of trees – young shaded by old – appeared in the background. The formal analogy between background architecture and trees resolves the dichotomy between Nature and history. Echoes of Klinger's composition appear on Paula Modersohn-Becker's tombstone at Worpswede (by Bernhard Hoetger) and in the work of Edvard Munch. *(CK)*

133
Hans von Marées
Horseman Plucking Oranges, with Seated Woman, c.1870
Orangenpflückender Reiter und Sitzende

Oil on canvas, 109 × 77 cm
Staatliche Galerie Moritzburg, Halle

The seated woman has been identified as Irene Koppel, the wife of a Dresden writer in whose house Marées lived for two long periods before he returned to Italy; his unfulfilled love for her is reflected in the tension between expectation and renunciation that pervades the work. Turning away from the woman, the horseman reaches up into the orange tree; rapt in contemplation, neither she nor the child seems to notice what he is doing. (Comparable distancing devices appear later in Arnold Böcklin's *Odysseus and Circe* and in several works by Edvard Munch.) The glowing, deep-hued evening landscape – its chiaroscuro derived from Eugène Delacroix – suggests the earthly paradise that Marées, in his later work, ever more clearly shows to be a paradise lost. *(CK)*

134
Hans von Marées
Study for 'The Abduction of Ganymede' 1887
Entführung des Ganymed, Entwurf

Sanguine on paper, 49 × 39.3 cm
Staatliche Museen zu Berlin Preußischer Kulturbesitz, Kupferstichkabinett

In the myth of the boy who was carried off to join the gods, Marées – in marked contrast to the celebrated, parodistic version by Rembrandt, which he knew from the Dresden gallery – emphasizes the idea of the spiritualization of an elect individual and his liberation from the confines of earthly life. Eagle and boy blend into a single motif; its resemblance to a heraldic emblem is accentuated by the oval format. Over two years, Marées tried out a variety of formulas for this (far from weightless) ascent: in all of them, the motif of death is represented by the howling dog, below left. In this rendering of an apotheosis of beauty – his last, unfinished painting – Marées undoubtedly had in mind both his own destiny and that of the artist in general. *(CK)*

135
Paula Modersohn-Becker
Seated Nude Girl with Flowers 1907
Sitzender Mädchenakt mit Blumen

Oil on canvas, 89 × 109 cm
Von-der-Heydt-Museum, Wuppertal

The model for this figure, with her bright necklaces and garland of flowers, was undoubtedly one of the Worpswede farm girls whom Modersohn-Becker so often painted; but the type and modelling make her look like an African or Oceanic sculpture. In glowing colours, with no spatial depth, though strongly modelled in three dimensions, the image is worlds away from peasant reality. With an expression of disquiet that recalls Edvard Munch's *Puberty*, she holds a single bloom. Like a cult figure or sacrificial offering, she is surrounded by four kinds of flowers in four individualized vessels. Tamed and reduced, Nature makes a solemn, ominous setting for the maturing human creature. The pose may stem from Pierre Puvis de Chavannes's *Hope* or from Rembrandt's *Bathsheba*, which Modersohn-Becker drew in the Louvre. *(CK)*

136
Hans Thoma
Self-Portrait 1880
Selbstbildnis

Oil on canvas, 70.5 × 51 cm
Staatliche Kunstsammlungen Dresden,
Gemäldegalerie Neue Meister

ex catalogue
Hans Thoma
Self-Portrait VI with Flower 1919
Selbstbildnis VI mit Blume

Etching on paper, 51 × 39 cm
Staatliche Kunsthalle Karlsruhe,
Kupferstichkabinett

ex. catalogue
Heinrich Vogeler
Spring 1896
Frühling

Etching on paper, 34 × 23.7 cm
Kunsthalle, Bremen

The first half of Vogeler's career reveals a Biedermeier-like, Neo-Romantic longing for harmony, a retreat into the 'primal' world of childhood, fairy tales, the peasantry. In this etching, inspired by Max Klinger's *Early Spring* (cat. 125), the border harks back both to Klinger and to Philipp Otto Runge. Vogeler's imagination and sensibility are rooted in literary Romanticism; here, he reinterprets the Romantic motif of the watcher. Rapt and naive, this image is not an experience of dualism but a dream of life in harmony with domesticated Nature. A house occupies the skyline; a birdcage hangs on a tree. Instead of the supreme sensation of 'Dissolving into the Universe' (*Aufgehen im All*, painting by Ferdinand Hodler, 1892), we contemplate 'Bliss in a Corner' (*Das Glück im Winkel*, play by Hermann Sudermann, 1896). *(CK)*

MODERNISM
NATURE AND PRIMITIVISM: THE BRÜCKE

137
Erich Heckel
Two People in the Open Air 1909
Zwei Menschen im Freien

Oil on canvas, 80 × 70 cm
Private Collection

ex catalogue
Ernst Ludwig Kirchner
Japanese Theatre c.1909
Japanisches Theater

(verso: *Interior with Female Nude and Man* c.1924)
Oil on canvas, 113.7 × 113.7 cm
Scottish National Gallery of Modern Art,
Edinburgh

ex catalogue
Ernst Ludwig Kirchner
Standing Woman 1912
Stehende

Wood, 98 × 23 × 12 cm
Staatliche Museen zu Berlin Preußischer
Kulturbesitz, Neue Nationalgalerie

138
Otto Mueller
The Judgment of Paris, c.1910–11
Das Urteil des Paris

Distemper on sackcloth, 179 × 124.5 cm
Staatliche Museen zu Berlin Preußischer
Kulturbesitz, Neue Nationalgalerie

The theme of the 'harmonious unity of Man and Nature' links the work of Otto Mueller with the Moritzburg studies of his *Brücke* colleagues; but his tender, subdued colour contrasts strongly with their tensions and contrasts. The stylization of these elongated, simplified figures serves to idealize and monumentalize them rather than to fuel an expressive dynamism. The figurative language, and the transformation of the mythological theme, recall Hans von Marées – except that the anecdotal element is suppressed: myth is subsumed into the more general theme of an erotic encounter amid Nature. Exuberance gives way to melancholic reflectiveness: the figures turn away from the viewer and exist 'for and by themselves' – a state diametrically opposed to the self-display demanded by the story. *(PK-H)*

139
Emil Nolde
Sunset over Gotteskoog
Abendhimmel überm Gotteskoog

Watercolour on paper, 35 × 46.7 cm
Scottish National Gallery of Modern Art,
Edinburgh

140
Emil Nolde
Light Sea Mood 1901
Lichte Meerstimmung

Oil on canvas, 65 × 83 cm
Stiftung Seebüll Ada und Emil Nolde

At Lildstrand, in Jutland, in 1901, Nolde painted a series of studies of changing light over the sea. He described this 'sea mood' two years later: 'Often I stood long at the window, gazing ruminatively out over the sea. There was nothing there but water and sky. If a bird flew past, it was an event.' Despite its muted colour, closely based on the study of natural effects of light, the painting anticipates Nolde's later work: the seascape becomes an occasion for subjective, quasi-religious contemplation, and as a result both painterly and compositional means are reduced to a minimum. *(PK-H)*

141
Emil Nolde
Young Men from Papua 1914
Papuajünglinge

Oil on canvas, 70 × 104 cm
Staatliche Museen zu Berlin Preußischer
Kulturbesitz, Neue Nationalgalerie

142
Emil Nolde
Tropical Sun 1914
Tropensonne

Oil on canvas, 71 × 104 cm
Stiftung Seebüll Ada und Emil Nolde

The sun over the sea, as an image of the primal elements of the cosmos, was a theme of Nolde's from early in his career. In *Tropical Sun*, painted in the South Seas, the impression of Nature is laden with symbolism through the intensity of the colours of sky, sea, clouds and surf. Nolde was affected both by the sheer power of the impact of natural phenomena and by his fear of the desecration of these 'earthly paradises'. 'Sometimes,' he wrote, 'we sat on the beach on the other side, silent in the face of that great, silent ocean, as vast as if eternity dwelt beyond it.' But the inhabitants 'had almost entirely lost their primal state; they were coiffured and clothed almost exactly like ourselves. For the painter, the truest delight was gone.' *(PK-H)*

143
Emil Nolde
Landscape with Young Horses 1916
Landschaft mit jungen Pferden

Oil on canvas, 73.5 × 101 cm
Stiftung Seebüll Ada und Emil Nolde**

144
Max Pechstein
Seated Female Nude 1910
Sitzender weiblicher Akt

Oil on canvas, 80 × 70 cm
Staatliche Museen zu Berlin Preußischer
Kulturbesitz, Neue Nationalgalerie

ART, ARTIST AND COMMUNITY: THE BRÜCKE

145
Erich Heckel
Self-Portrait 1919
Selbstbildnis

Tempera on canvas, 89.5 × 72 cm
Staatliche Museen zu Berlin Preußischer
Kulturbesitz, Neue Nationalgalerie

Note the 'blue flower' of Novalis's Romanticism in the background.

146
Ernst Ludwig Kirchner
Pictures from Adelbert von Chamisso's 'Peter Schlemihl' 1915
Bilder zu Adelbert von Chamissos Peter Schlemihl

Portfolio of 7 colour woodcuts and lithograph cover:
Cover, lithograph on blue paper,
26.7 × 21.4 cm (image size)
Title-Page, colour woodcut on paper,
29.3 × 26.2 cm (image size)

1 *Selling His Shadow* (Der Verkauf des Schattens), colour woodcut on paper, 29.3 × 26.2 cm
2 *His Lover* (Die Geliebte), colour woodcut on paper, 28.9 × 23.9 cm
3 *Conflict* (Kämpfe), colour woodcut on paper, 33.4 × 21.4 cm
4 *Schlemihl in the Loneliness of His Room* (Schlemihl in der Einsamkeit des Zimmers), colour woodcut on paper, 33.5 × 23.7 cm
5 *Schlemihl's Encounter with the Little Grey Man on the Highway* (Begegnung Schlemihls mit dem grauen Männlein auf der Landstraße), colour woodcut on paper, 29.9 × 31 cm
6 *Schlemihls Encounter with His Shadow* (Schlemihls Begegnung mit dem Schatten), colour woodcut, 30.9 × 29.2 cm

Kulturkreis der Deutschen Wirtschaft im Bundesverband der dt. Industrie e.V., Köln, currently on loan to the Kunsthalle zu Kiel

Adelbert von Chamisso's supernatural tale *Peter Schlemihls wundersame Geschichte* ('Peter Schlemihl's strange history') of 1814 is one of the most famous of German Romantic short stories, in which a man sells his shadow to the Devil in return for gold. But everyone turns away from him, afraid because he has no shadow. He finds solace alone in Nature.

In Kirchner's portfolio, perhaps his supreme achievement in printmaking, he considers the often agonizing existence of the artist, split down the middle between his inner life and his place in the world about him, like Schlemihl separated from his shadow.

Writing to Gustav Schiefler in 1919 Kirchner explains what he was trying to do in the work: 'If you take away all its Romantic embellishments, the history of Schlemihl is really the life-history of a man suffering from a persecution mania, that is, a man who, through some incident or other, is suddenly made aware of how infinitely tiny he is; but, at the same time, recognizes the means whereby the world in general conceals this knowledge.' Kirchner was soon to suffer a nervous breakdown partly as a result of his joining the army at the outbreak of the First World War. *(KH)*

THE UNITY OF THE COSMOS AND UTOPIA I: DER BLAUE REITER

147
Wassily Kandinsky
In the Forest 1904
Im Walde

Mixed media on wood, 26 × 19.8 cm
Städtische Galerie im Lenbachhaus, Munich

148
Wassily Kandinsky
Design for the Cover of the 'Blue Rider' Almanac 1911
Entwurf für den Umschlag des Almanachs 'Der blaue Reiter'

Watercolour and pencil on paper,
27.5 × 21.8 cm
Städtische Galerie im Lenbachhaus, Munich

149
Wassily Kandinsky
Design for the Cover of the 'Blue Rider' Almanac 1911
Entwurf für den Umschlag des Almanachs 'Der blaue Reiter'

Watercolour and pencil on paper,
27.7 × 21.8 cm
Städtische Galerie im Lenbachhaus, Munich

150
Wassily Kandinsky
Improvisation 21 1911

Oil on canvas, 108 × 108 cm
Private Collection

151
Wassily Kandinsky
On the Theme of the Last Judgement 1913
Zum Thema Jüngstes Gericht

Oil and mixed media on canvas,
47.3 × 52.3 cm
Fridart Foundation

152
Paul Klee
With the Rainbow 1917
Mit dem Regenbogen

Watercolour on chalk ground on paper,
18.6 × 22 cm
Private Collection

153
Franz Marc
The Small Yellow Horses 1912
Die kleinen gelben Pferde

Oil on canvas, 66 x 104.5 cm
Staatsgalerie Stuttgart

154
Franz Marc
Two Sheep 1913
Zwei Schafe

Watercolour and collage on paper (postcard
to Wassily Kandinsky), 9 x 14 cm
Städtische Galerie im Lenbachhaus, Munich

155
Franz Marc
Red Horse and Yellow Cow 1913
Rotes Pferd und Gelbes Rind

Watercolour and collage on paper (postcard
to Alfred Kubin), 14 x 9 cm
Städtische Galerie im Lenbachhaus, Munich

ex catalogue
Franz Marc
Two Horses Before A Blue Mountain 1913
Zwei Pferde vor blauem Berg

Mixed media and collage on paper (postcard
to Lily Klee), 14 x 9.2 cm
Private Collection, Switzerland

ex catalogue
Franz Marc
Ibex 1913
Steinbock

Mixed media and collage on paper (postcard
to Lily Klee), 14 x 9.2 cm
Private Collection, Switzerland

ex catalogue
Franz Marc
Deer at Rest 1913
Ruhendes Reh

Mixed media and collage on paper (postcard
to Lily Klee), 14 x 9.2 cm
Private Collection, Switzerland

156
Franz Marc
Fighting Forms (Abstract Forms I) 1914
Kämpfende Formen (Abstrakte Formen I)

Oil on canvas, 91 x 131.5 cm
Bayerische Staatsgemäldesammlungen,
Munich

This painting was completed in the late
spring/early summer of 1914, at a time when
there were increasing rumours of war
manoeuvres and mobilisation. It relates both
to the current political situation in Europe
and the conflict which Marc anticipated
between the forces of spiritual regeneration
and the dead hand of materialism. It
expresses Marc's forebodings about the
imminent collapse of the world order and
faith in the ultimate triumph of the human
spirit.

Almost the whole of this large canvas is
taken up with the violent collision between
two opposing forces – the swirling fiery red
mass, which sweeps in diagonally across the
surface, from the upper left hand corner and
the compact, recoiling black mass, which
retreats upon itself in the lower right hand
segment.

Frederick S Levine and others have argued
plausibly that the attacking red shape is the
celestial eagle and that the scene unleashed

by the conflict evokes the drama
accompanying the breaking of the seventh
seal, in the Book of Revelations. Fresh light
is cast on this by Peter-Klaus Schuster in his
essay for the present catalogue. (HMH)

157
Franz Marc
Sketchbook from the Field 1915
Skizzenbuch aus dem Felde

Pencil on paper; 36 sheets in total, each 16.9
x 9.8 cm, or 9.8 x 16.9 cm
The following individual sheets will be shown
in Edinburgh:

18 Untitled (Ohne Titel)
19 Easter (Ostern)
21 Magic Moment (Zauberiger Moment)
24 Conflict (Streit)
30 Fragment (Fragment)
31 Untitled (Ohne Titel)
32 Untitled (Ohne Titel)
34 Untitled (Ohne Titel)
36 Untitled (Ohne Titel)

The following sheets will be shown in London:

2 Creation Stopped Short 2 (Stehen
  gebliebene Schöpfung)
3 A Lot of Light Green with Red Tips, Plant
  Life Growing (Viel Hellgrün mit roten
  Spitzen, pflanzliches Leben im Werden)
8 From the Days of Creation (Aus den
  Schöpfungstagen)
9 Very Colourful (Sehr farbig)
12 Arsenal for a Creation (Arsenal für eine
  Schöpfung)
13 Untitled (Ohne Titel)
20 Untitled (Ohne Titel)
22 Fragment (Fragment)
25 Untitled (Ohne Titel)

Staatliche Graphische Sammlung, Munich

THE UNITY OF THE COSMOS AND UTOPIA II:
THE BAUHAUS

158
Lyonel Feininger
Gelmeroda III 1913

Oil on canvas, 100 x 80 cm
Scottish National Gallery of Modern Art,
Edinburgh

159
Lyonel Feininger
The Cathedral (small version) 1919
Die Kathedrale

Woodcut, 18 x 11.5 cm
William Hardie Gallery, Glasgow

ex catalogue
Lyonel Feininger
Ruin by the Sea 1930

Oil on canvas, 68 x 115.5 cm
The Museum of Modern Art, New York

ex catalogue
Walter Gropius
Manifesto and Programme of the State
Bauhaus in Weimar 1919
Manifesto und Programm des Staatlichen
Bauhauses in Weimar

Four-page printed prospectus, text by Walter
Gropius,
title woodcut by Lyonel Feininger,
32 x 19.7 cm
Bauhaus-Archiv, Berlin

ex catalogue
Johannes Itten
Colour Sphere in Seven Shades of Light and
Twelve Tones: Supplement to 'Utopia –
Documents of Reality' 1921
Farbenkugel in sieben Lichtstufen und zwölf
Tönen: Beilage zu 'Utopia-Dokumente der
Wirklichkeit'

Lithograph on paper, 47 x 32 cm
Bauhaus-Archiv, Berlin

160
Wassily Kandinsky
Design for the Left-Hand Wall of a Music
Salon for the Deutsche Bauausstellung in
Berlin 1931

Oil on cardboard, 45 x 75 cm
Collection Artcurial, Paris

161
Wassily Kandinsky
Design for the Centre Wall of a Music Salon
for the Deutsche Bauausstellung in Berlin
1931

Oil on cardboard, 45 x 99.5 cm
Collection Artcurial, Paris

162
Wassily Kandinsky
Design for the Right-Hand Wall of a Music
Salon for the Deutsche Bauausstellung in
Berlin 1931

Oil on cardboard, 45 x 75 cm
Collection Artcurial, Paris

163
Paul Klee
Mural from the Temple of Longing <Thither>
1922
Wandbild aus dem Tempel der Sehnsucht
<dorthin>

Watercolour and transfer drawing on gessoed
cloth, 26.7 x 37.5 cm
The Metropolitan Museum of Art, New York,
The Berggruen Klee Collection, 1984

164
Paul Klee
North Sea Picture 1923
Nordseebild

Watercolour on paper on cardboard,
25.4 x 31.3 cm
Paul-Klee-Stiftung, Kunstmuseum Berne

165
Paul Klee
Eye, Centre, You c.1923
Auge, Centrum, Du

Illustration for the essay 'Wege des
Naturstudiums' (Ways of Nature Study)
Pen and ink on paper, 21 x 33.7 cm
Paul-Klee-Stiftung, Kunstmuseum Berne

166
Paul Klee
Departure of the Ships 1927
Abfahrt der Schiffe

Oil on canvas, 51 x 65.5 cm
Staatliche Museen zu Berlin Preußischer
Kulturbesitz, Neue Nationalgalerie

167
Paul Klee
Threatening Snowstorm 1927
Drohender Schneesturm

Tempera and ink on paper, 48.9 x 31.4 cm
Scottish National Gallery of Modern Art,
Edinburgh

168
Utopia – Documents of Reality 1921
Utopia – Dokumente der Wirklichkeit

Portfolio (de luxe edition) with cover designed
by Oskar Schlemmer and issued by the State
Bauhaus, Weimar, 33 x 24.5 cm (cover)
Collection C. Raman Schlemmer

169
Oskar Schlemmer
Design for the Cover of 'Utopia' 1921
Entwurf für Umschlag von 'Utopia'

Body colour on transparent paper,
35.4 x 26.2 cm
Oskar Schlemmer Family Estate

170
Oskar Schlemmer
Mystical Composition with Figure in Gold
Bronze c.1922
Mystische Komposition mit Figur in
Goldbronze

Watercolour and gold bronze on transparent
paper, 22.5 x 23.1 cm
Oskar Schlemmer Family Estate, Collection U.
Jaina Schlemmer

171
Oskar Schlemmer
Design for Mural Fresco inside the Workshop
Building of the Weimar Bauhaus 1922–23

Watercolour on paper, 23.2 x 30.4 cm
Oskar Schlemmer Family Estate

172
Oskar Schlemmer
General plan of the wall decorations in the
Workshop Building of the State Bauhaus in
Weimar. Ground Plan and Perspective 1923

Watercolour and pencil on paper,
42.5 x 55 cm
Oskar Schlemmer Family Estate

173
Oskar Schlemmer
Figurations. Design for Mural Fresco inside
the Workshop Building of the Weimar
Bauhaus 1923

Pencil and watercolour on transparent paper,
laid on card, 31.9 x 24.3 cm
Oskar Schlemmer Family Estate

174
Oskar Schlemmer
Man in the Sphere of Ideas c.1928
Der Mensch im Ideenkreis

Pen, ink gouache & coloured crayon on paper
on wood, 74.5 x 48.9 cm
Oskar Schlemmer Family Estate

IRONY AND GROTESQUE I: THE OTHER SIDE
(KLEE AND KUBIN)

175
Paul Klee
Virgin in Tree (Invention 3) 1903
Jungfrau im Baum (Invention 3)

Etching on paper, 23.6 x 29.6 cm (plate size)
Städtische Galerie im Lenbachhaus, Munich

The similarity between this etching and Giovanni Segantini's *The Evil Mothers* was noticed in the earliest Klee monographs. 'Klee's *Virgin* may be interpreted as a satirical reversal of a familiar symbol of female lasciviousness and wantonness: the seductive, naked tree-nymph, dryad or elf, who allures and teases the beast in man' (Marcel Franciscono). Klee wrote in his journal: 'The beasts (the pair of birds) are natural and coupled. The lady thinks highly of herself just because she is a virgin, but she does not cut an impressive figure. Critique of bourgeois society' (*Tagebuch* 1903, 514). On 18 July 1903 he wrote to his fiancée, Lily, that the work presents 'the truth of the enforced but prized virginity that is good for nothing'. *(AH)*

176
Paul Klee
Woman and Animal 1904
Weib und Tier
Zinc etching on paper, 19.4 × 22.4 cm
Paul-Klee-Stiftung, Kunstmuseum Berne

177
Paul Klee
Two Nudes, a Grown Man (Fragmentary) Holding a Child Nude by the Hand 1904
Zwei Akte, ein Erwachsener (fragmentarisch) und an dessen Hand ein Kinderakt
Pencil on paper, irregularly cut, 18.5 × 10.8 cm
Mounted together with Female Nude and Nude with Ass's Head
Paul-Klee-Stiftung, Kunstmuseum Berne

178
Female Nude, Fragmentary Below 1904
Weiblicher Akt, unten fragmentarisch
Pencil on paper, 18.6 × 6.9 cm
Mounted together with Two Nudes and Nude with Ass's Head
Paul-Klee-Stiftung, Kunstmuseum Berne

As in many of Klee's early pencil drawings, the glassy transparency of all these figures evokes the 'dematerialization' that he achieved by other means in his later work, with its array of abstract signs. The woman's 'fragmentary' lower part dissolves into a vein-like network of lines, in a metamorphosis like that of *Female Nude Donning a Shift* (1904–05) and its related etching, *Pessimistic Symbolism (Allegory) of the Mountains*, in which the figure's feet take root in the rock. Jürgen Glaesemer emphasizes Klee's 'planned spontaneity': 'He defines the element of ugliness in his drawings as an ideal of negative beauty, and confidently asserts in his journal that dissertations might be written on the meaning of their ugliness.' *(AH)*

179
Paul Klee
Nude with Ass's Head 1904
Akt mit Eselskopf
Pencil on paper, irregularly trimmed, 18.6 × 7.2 cm
Mounted together with Two Nudes and Female Nude
Paul-Klee-Stiftung, Kunstmuseum Berne

Alongside the anatomical studies from cadaver material, to which Klee was especially attentive while in Berne in 1902–03, he produced freer nude drawings, each with a subversive quirk of its own, such

as the ass's head in the present case. The nude, seen from behind, with arms raised, looks like a fleeting materialization. The slender, diaphanous figure reveals superimpositions; the pentimenti in the structure of the lower part stress the importance attached by Klee to the principle of experimentation. *(AH)*

180a
Paul Klee
Pregnant Girl, Seated 1905
Schwangeres Mädchen, sitzend
Pencil on paper, 12 × 15.3 cm
Mounted together with Female Nude with Suggestion of Leg Covering
Paul-Klee-Stiftung, Kunstmuseum Berne

180b
Female Nude with Suggestion of Leg Covering 1905
Weiblicher Akt mit Andeutung des Beinkleides
Pencil and watercolour on paper, 15.5 × 17.1 cm
Mounted together with Pregnant Girl, Seated
Paul-Klee-Stiftung, Kunstmuseum Berne

These two images belong to a small group of pencil drawings done between 1904 and 1906, in which Klee uses seemingly primitive means to explore astonishingly modern modes of representation. With delicate and in some cases seemingly random lines, he encompasses not the immediate outward appearance of the human figure so much as its inner structural laws. He thus pioneers an analytical and at the same time sensitive form of drawing that Joseph Beuys pursues in his studies of the material quality of objects: 'Also new is the bold provocation. Defying all the customary demands of aesthetics, he sets down tangled lines and overlapping sketches on dirty or smudged paper; stains and corrections remain visible' (Jürgen Glaesemer). *(AH)*

181
Paul Klee
Hero with the Wing (Invention 2) 1905
Der Held mit dem Flügel (Invention 2)
Etching on paper, 25.7 × 16 cm (plate size), Städtische Galerie im Lenbachhaus, Munich

One of the last and most exquisitely crafted of the *Inventions* series, this etching is inscribed on the plate: 'The Hero with the Wing. Endowed by Nature with one wing, he supposed that it was his destiny to fly; and this was his downfall.' Klee noted in his journal: 'The Hero with the Wing, a tragicomic hero, perhaps a Don Quixote of antiquity ... It was important to capture the contrast between the monumental solemnity of his pose and his already ruinous condition, as an emblem of the tragicomedy' (*Tagebuch* 1905, 585). Marcel Franciscono, in his subtle analysis, points not only to these inherent contradictions within the iconography but also to the rendering of the figure below the waist, which is – despite the classical modelling – absurdly flat and foreshortened, as is the surface of the ground. *(AH)*

ex catalogue
Alfred Kubin
The Best Physician 1901
Der beste Arzt
Pen, ink, wash and spray on mapping paper, 27.3 × 38.8 cm
Leopold Collection, Vienna

The Best Physician and the drawings that follow (with the exception of *Man*) were included by Kubin in the *Hans-von-Weber-Mappe*, a portfolio of facsimiles published in 1903. Here the spare figure of Death, in a black jersey and with a victor's medal on his chest, lays his right hand roughly on the rigid, white face of a dead woman. Her defenceless, elongated body is stretched out on a creased, white bed. According to Christoph Brockhaus, this image of Death combines the traditional iconographical formulas of 'Physician and Death' and 'Madame Mors'. He further points to parallels in the work of Willi Geiger, as well as formal influences from Munich *Jugendstil* or Art Nouveau. *(AH)*

ex catalogue
Alfred Kubin
Past (Forgotten-Submerged) 1901
Vergangenheit (Vergessen-Versunken)
Pen, ink, wash and spray on mapping paper, 29.6 × 39.5 cm
Leopold Collection, Vienna

This drawing bears all the classic signs of Kubin's early mature style. A huge, menacing, symbolic figure of a new kind – fantastic, but with a feeling of gross, physical reality – looms above a low horizon in a dark, unbounded pictorial space (created with a spray or spatter technique). The figure, a mysterious man-bird hybrid, enthroned statue-like on a rough stone plinth, seems to gloat over the relics of human handiwork that sink from view behind. Its bird head arches back into the darkness, evoking lost civilizations and, notably, Assyrian or Egyptian sculpture. Origins and the end of time combine in one cataclysmic vision. Franz Düllberg wrote: 'The deity throws back its head with all the arrogance of eternity. "Egypt", people will say; but here new life has blossomed from something five thousand years old.' *(AH)*

ex catalogue
Alfred Kubin
Man c.1902
Der Mensch
Pen, ink, watercolour and spray on mapping paper, 26 × 27.8 cm
Leopold Collection, Vienna

A naked human figure, with arms bound to his sides and hair blowing in the wind, hurtles down a steep track into the void. This much-reproduced drawing caught the feeling of the age. The poet Ernst Jünger wrote: 'Dream, lighted through, turns Vision, Crystal / To be, prime question, Madness, Cataract / Upright man, hurled into the All, / Hurricane-haired, pallid, solitary, naked.' This symbol of human disorientation in a cosmic void – here curiously blended with the elegant swirl of the *Jugendstil* line – expresses Kubin's own deepest conviction, summed up in February 1904 in his so-called 'suicide note' to his sister Maria: 'Death, Nothingness, is the goal of the world, and thus of everything in it ... Everyone runs like

a machine, *unconditionally*, down the preordained track.' *(AH)*

ex catalogue
Alfred Kubin
The Hour of Birth 1901
Die Stunde der Geburt
Pen, ink, wash and spray on paper, 25.5 × 30.6 cm
Leopold Collection, Vienna

The Hour of Birth was the second sheet in the *Weber-Mappe* of 1903, following *The Fate of Man*. One critic wrote: 'From the Birth of Man, in which a gigantic crustacean hurls the tiny children into the grey void with its fearsome claws, to his last hour ... one single mood prevails.' No other drawing by Kubin is as close as this to a prototype by Max Klinger. In Klinger's *Siesta I* of 1879, two lobsters lie in a similar position, parallel to the picture plane, on a strip of rock; one of them reaches down with its claw to catch a fish by the tail. Kubin has intensified the slow, latent menace of Klinger's invention for his own expressive purposes. *(AH)*

ex catalogue
Alfred Kubin
Horror 1901
Das Grausen
Pen, ink, wash and spray on mapping paper, 32.5 × 30.8 cm
Leopold Collection, Vienna

In Kubin's first one-man show at the Galerie Cassirer, Berlin, in 1901–02, the drawing *Horror* attracted much attention. One critic, who called it 'superb', gave this description: 'A tiny, shattered craft, dismasted, drifts through heavy seas ... From a huge wave looms Horror, a grinning skull with hideous teeth on a long neck. One eye is sunk deep in its socket; the other bulges out, dominating the face, like a vast, malignant plague-sore.' This motif of the staring, bulging eye appears in a woodcut in Katsushika Hokusai's *Hyaku monogatari* (100 Tales, 1830), in which a murderer sees his victim's ghost; Kubin was also inspired by Edgar Allan Poe's story 'A Descent into the Maelström' (1841) – though none of this detracts from his imaginative achievement. *(AH)*

IRONY AND GROTESQUE II:
DADA AND SURREALISM

182
Hans Arp
Forest c.1917
Painted wood, 34.2 × 20 × 6 cm
National Gallery of Art, Washington

183
Max Ernst
Sea and Sun 1925
Mer et Soleil
Oil on canvas, 54 × 37 cm
Scottish National Gallery of Modern Art, Edinburgh

184
Max Ernst
Max Ernst Showing a Girl the Head of His Father 1927
Max Ernst montrant à une jeune fille la tête de son père
Oil on canvas, 111.7 × 144.8 cm
Private Collection (on loan to Scottish National Gallery of Modern Art, Edinburgh)

185
Max Ernst
La joie de vivre 1936
Oil on canvas, 72.7 × 91.5 cm
Private Collection (on loan to the Scottish
National Gallery of Modern Art, Edinburgh)

186
Kurt Schwitters
Untitled (Relief with Red Pyramid) c.1923–25
Oil on wood relief on plywood,
60 × 50.2 cm
Scottish National Gallery of Modern Art,
Edinburgh

187
Kurt Schwitters
Reconstruction (by Peter Bissegger) of the
Hanover MERZbau (original c.1923–36)
1980–83
Mixed media, 393 × 580 × 460 cm
Sprengel Museum, Hanover

Schwitters's *MERZbau* is collage on an
environmental scale: it gradually took over
his studio and part of his house in Hanover.
In its alternative title, 'The Cathedral of
Erotic Misery' (Kathedrale der erotischen
Elends), Schwitters recalls, however wryly,
the utopian ideal of the total, collaborative
work of art, exemplified supposedly by the
Gothic cathedral, which inspired the
Bauhaus.

The original *MERZbau* contained various
'grottoes' filled with found objects. Some of
these were devoted to the recent renewal of
interest in German national identity, which
expressed itself in such forms as the cult of
Barbarossa and the building of the
monument to him on the Kyffhäuser
mountain (a theme treated by Anslem Kiefer
later in the century). Dorothea Dietrich has
described the *MERZbau* as 'an all-
encompassing structure, in which each
successive part was integrated in an
evergrowing and complexly interwoven
whole and the many opposite components
finally subsumed under a dynamic, organic-
crystalline, cathedral-like shell, the new
architecture' (The Collages of Kurt
Schwitters: Tradition and Innovation,
Cambridge, 1993) *(RC)*

NEO-ROMANTICISM AND NEUE
SACHLICHKEIT

188
Otto Dix
Nelly with Toys 1925
Nelly mit Spielzeug
Oil and tempera on wood, 54 × 39.5 cm
Galerie der Stadt Stuttgart (on loan from Otto-
Dix-Stiftung, Vaduz)

189
Alexander Kanoldt
Olevano 1927
Oil on canvas, 91 × 71 cm
Staatliche Museen zu Berlin Preußischer
Kulturbesitz, Neue Nationalgalerie

Early in life, Kanoldt was impressed by the
idealized Italian landscapes of the early
nineteenth-century 'German-Romans',
Joseph Anton Koch and Friedrich Preller.
Before 1914 he visited the Tuscan hill-town
of San Gimignano, and in 1924 he went to
Olevano in the Sabine Hills, east of Rome.
Repeatedly painted, drawn and lithographed
between 1924 and 1927, Olevano became a

leitmotif. Kanoldt became the painter of
'silent houses, Latin in form; of houses
without windows; of nothing but mausolea'.
Fascinated by the aura of the seemingly
deserted village, and by the proto-Cubist
shapes of the houses, Kanoldt sought to
paint the 'soul of the town' in a timeless
moment, and to conjure up the spirit of its
past. *(RM)*

ex catalogue
Franz Radziwill
The Beach at Dangast with Flying Boat 1929
Der Strand von Dangast mit Flugboot
Oil on wood, 92.5 × 130 cm
Landesmuseum für Kunst und Kulturgeschichte,
Oldenburg

190
Georg Scholz
Cacti and Signals 1923
Kakteen und Semaphore
Oil on hardboard, 69 × 52.3 cm
Westfälisches Landesmuseum für Kunst und
Kulturgeschichte, Münster

In 1923–25, Scholz painted three still-lifes of
cacti in which he took up the topos of the
window-picture, which had been current
from the Romantics down to Hans Thoma.
He interpreted 'still-life with view from
window' as an emblem of time frozen,
caught in the polarity of inside and outside,
light and dark, near and far, silhouette and
solid, Nature and technology. The result is
total stasis: artificiality prevails, in both
manmade objects (railway signals, electric
lamps) and 'natural' elements (cacti, trees).
Adolf Wortmann wrote in 1925: 'Are not
the cacti vegetable crystals, living
architecture? Ball and roller, measure and
number? … We want law. To be human is
to be impelled to create form and cosmos;
and the symbol of this is the crystal. The
design of plants is crystalline.' *(RM)*

191
Georg Schrimpf
Girl at a Window 1923
Mädchen am Fenster
Oil on canvas, 52.5 × 37.5 cm
Museum Ludwig, Cologne

Barefoot, the housemaid sits pensively by her
garret window. As dawn breaks, she peeps
out at the world. Her simplified outline is
enlivened only by a red cloth on her knees.
'Even in the hour of greatest happiness,'
wrote Franz Roh, 'the human being is
harnessed to an enduringly "abstract"
framework, which encases and demarcates
him or her on every side.' Girl at a window,
woman at a window: in Caspar David
Friedrich, the longing to escape from
bourgeois constraints into the infinity of
Nature; in Schrimpf, the apotheosis of self-
containment and of the anonymous sense of
belonging within a peasant world.
Schrimpf's painting has more harmony than
duality, more Biedermeier than
Romanticism. *(RM)*

192
Georg Schrimpf
Three Children 1926
Drei Kinder
Oil on canvas, 80.4 × 65.5 cm
Private Collection, courtesy of Galerie
Gunzenhauser, Munich

Franz Roh wrote in 1924: 'Schrimpf once
more shows us healthy, vigorous volumes,
youthful bodies, remote from all decadence,
innocent as children and beasts … ' All this
he found in his own sons Marc and Peter –
and also in *The Hülsenbeck Children* by
Philipp Otto Runge (1805–06, Hamburger
Kunsthalle). Runge's composition was a
direct source for Schrimpf's *Three Children*.
Child's play in Runge is a statuesque
performance by well-fleshed bourgeois
children; Schrimpf captures the mute self-
absorption of poor children in the shadow of
bleak suburban tenements. In Runge the
fence reveals glimpses of a world beyond; in
Schrimpf it blocks the view. Like Runge,
Schrimpf captures childhood pure and
intact; his inspiration is Runge's call for
artists to see the world 'like children'.
(RM)

ROMANTIC-TWILIGHT: ART IN THE
THIRD REICH

193
Otto Dix
Randegg in Snow with Ravens 1935
Randegg im Schnee mit Raben
Mixed media on hardboard, 80 × 70 cm
Otto-Dix-Stiftung, Vaduz

The snowclad village of Randegg is painted
from Dix's temporary studio in a tower of
the castle. The bare 'tree of life' is remotely
reminiscent of Caspar David Friedrich's oak
trees in snow. The wintry landscape is a
metaphor of numbness and rigidity. Where
Dix's *Jewish Cemetery near Randegg in
Snow*, also of 1935, conveys a political
metaphor, *Randegg in Snow with Ravens* is
an atmospheric record of Dix's own state of
'inner emigration' and of his identification
with the landscape:
'I painted landscapes – and that was
emigration.' *(RM)*

194
Franz Lenk
Undergrowth 1932
Gebüsch
Oil and tempera on canvas mounted on
wood, 90 × 115 cm
Galerie von Abercron, Munich

At the closest possible range, *Undergrowth*
captures the annual dying of Nature. The
undergrowth with its dense network of
branches is a place of seclusion, a haven, out
of time; somewhere beyond, we sense
infinity and the void. With its axially placed
motif, its minute detail executed in the
studio, and the lamenting gestures of its
dying plant forms, the work recalls the
metaphorical plants that are associated with
hermits and cripples in the work of Caspar
David Friedrich. To Lenk, as to Friedrich,
dead wood is a parable of human transience.
In 1931, a Berlin critic wrote of Lenk: 'He is
a landscapist of sensibility, with a "reverence
for minuteness". His paintings are Romantic
and backward-looking in their formal
conception, tranquil and gentle in their
objectivity; they have a Biedermeier
transparency.' *(RM)*

195
Oskar Martin-Amorbach
The Sower 1937
Der Sämann
Oil on canvas, 253 × 163 cm
Property of the Federal Republic of Germany

ex catalogue
Richard Oelze
Expectation 1935–36
Erwartung
Oil on canvas, 81.6 × 100.6 cm
The Museum of Modern Art, New York,
Purchase, 1940

196
Franz Radziwill
Lost Earth (The U-Boat War; Total War)
1939–60
Verlorene Erde (Der U-Boot Krieg; Der totale
Krieg)
Oil on canvas on wood, 123 × 170 cm
Private collection (on loan to Städtische
Galerie im Lenbachhaus, Munich)

Originally painted in 1939 as *The U-Boat
War* (part of a projected *First World War*
triptych for the Marineschule at Mürwik,
near Flensburg), this work was overpainted
and retitled twice: as *Total War* in 1944,
and as *Lost Earth* in 1960. The first version
was largely reportage, featuring the
submarine as an engine of war, but no
figures; later, Radziwill added more
weaponry and intensified the apocalyptic
dimension of his 'symbolic realism' by
showing a white sail on the horizon and a
human silhouette, and by metamorphosing
the cloud into an angel. The shipwrecks,
rock fragments and graves with crosses are
allusions to the *Sea of Ice* (1823–24), by
Caspar David Friedrich; the diminutive
human figure is quoted directly from
Friedrich's *Monk by the Sea*. *(RM)*

197
Adolf Wissel
Farming Family from Kalenberg 1939
Kalenberger Bauernfamilie
Oil on canvas, 150 × 200 cm
Property of the Federal Republic of Germany

ART AFTER 1945
POSTWAR ABSTRACTION

198
Willi Baumeister
Aru 5 1955
Oil on canvas, 185 × 130 cm
Staatliche Museen zu Berlin Preußischer
Kulturbesitz, Neue Nationalgalerie

199
Gotthard Graubner
colour-space-body I 1973
farbraumkörper I
Oil on perlon over synthetic fleece on canvas,
201 × 131 cm
Kunstsammlung Nordrhein-Westfalen, Düsseldorf

ex catalogue
Heinz Mack
Dynamic Structure in White (White on White)
1959
Dynamische Struktur in Weiß (Weiß in Weiß)
Kunstharz auf Nessel, 140 × 120 cm
Staatliche Museen zu Berlin Preußischer
Kulturbesitz, Neue Nationalgalerie

200
Ernst Wilhelm Nay
Pendulum in Balance 1955
Pendelbalance

Oil on canvas, 125 × 200 cm
Private Collection (on loan to Scottish National
Gallery of Modern Art, Edinburgh)

201
Otto Piene
Soleuil 1958

Oil on canvas, 80 × 130 cm
Staatliche Museen zu Berlin Preußischer
Kulturbesitz, Neue Nationalgalerie

202
Bernard Schultze
Hegitraf 1957

Oil and mixed media on fibreboard, 105 ×
140 × 3 cm
Hamburger Kunsthalle

ex catalogue
Günther Uecker
White Field 1964
Weißes Feld

Nails on canvas on wood, painted white,
87 × 87 × 7.6 cm
Tate Gallery, London

203
Fritz Winter
Motive Forces of the Earth 1944
Triebkräfte der Erde

Mixed media on paper, 28.5 × 20.5 cm
Fritz-Winter-Haus, Ahlen, Westphalia

204
Fritz Winter
Motive Forces of the Earth 1944
Triebkräfte der Erde

Mixed media on paper, 30 × 20 cm
Fritz-Winter-Haus, Ahlen, Westphalia

205
Fritz Winter
Motive Forces of the Earth (Autumn Mood)
1944
Triebkräfte der Erde (Herbststimmung)

Mixed media on paper, 28 × 20 cm
Fritz-Winter-Haus, Ahlen, Westphalia

206
Fritz Winter
Motive Forces of the Earth 1944
Triebkräfte der Erde

Mixed media on paper, 28.5 × 20.5 cm
Fritz-Winter-Haus, Ahlen, Westphalia

207
Fritz Winter
Motive Forces of the Earth 1944
Triebkräfte der Erde

Oil and tempera on paper, 48.6 × 40 cm
Galerie der Stadt Stuttgart

208
Fritz Winter
Motive Forces of the Earth 1944
Triebkräfte der Erde

Oil and tempera on paper, 48.6 × 40 cm
Galerie der Stadt Stuttgart

209
Fritz Winter
Motive Forces of the Earth 1944
Triebkräfte der Erde

Oil and tempera on paper, 29 × 20.5 cm
Galerie der Stadt Stuttgart

210
Fritz Winter
Motive Forces of the Earth 1944
Triebkräfte der Erde

Oil and tempera on paper, 31.7 × 20 cm
Galerie der Stadt Stuttgart

211
Wols
The Pink Ship c.1949
Le bateau rose

Oil on canvas, 38 × 46 cm
Private Collection

212
Wols
Composition on Grey Ground c.1949
Composition sur fond gris

Oil on canvas, 46 × 38 cm
Private Collection

213
Wols
Composition Champigny 1951
Oil on canvas, 68 × 57 cm
Private Collection

GERHARD ALTENBOURG AND
HERMANN GLÖCKNER

214
Gerhard Altenbourg
Garten an der Spinnbahn 1951

Mixed media on paper, 61 × 86 cm
Anneliese Ströch, Altenbourg

The Garten an der Spinnbahn is a corner of
landscape not far from Altenbourg's home at
Altenburg. His walks in the immediate
environs of his native town, often by night,
were important sources of inspiration for
Altenbourg's drawings. He works the
impressions gained on these expeditions into
minutely detailed structures that reveal the
large-scale landscape form but also – and
equally – its microcosmic inner world.
(EB)

215
Gerhard Altenbourg
This is the Mountain 1964
Dies ist der Berg

Watercolour, india ink, lithographic crayon on
canvas, 37.5 × 65 cm
Annegret Janda, Berlin

On close inspection, this drawing in a
'landscape' format turns out to be a real
landscape, rising in successive planes and
dominated by a mountain in the
background. Altenbourg is depicting one of
the majestic hills of his native Saxon
landscape. The minute grid structure of the
drawing, supported by the weave of the
canvas, spiritualizes and holds in suspension
the emotional response to landscape. The
fragility of the structure evokes the
multiplicity of natural formations that are
indiscernible in a distant view. In his
drawings, Altenbourg combines ways of
seeing that are naturally separate. He takes
an overview of the landscape and cuts a

section across the teeming variety of natural
forms to create a synthesis, which he defines
– choosing his words carefully – as
'introspective outlook' (einschauendes
Ausschauen). (EB)

216
Gerhard Altenbourg
Dedicated to Caspar David 1966
Caspar David gewidmet

Tempera, india ink, chalk, pencil, pastel on
thick handmade paper, 61 × 55 cm
Private collection, Leipzig

Altenbourg is referring to Caspar David
Friedrich's famous black chalk self-portrait
of 1810, in the drawing collection of the
Kupferstichkabinett in Berlin (formerly
Nationalgalerie). Only a few attributes
render the connection still visible: the hair
combed forward, the side-whiskers and the
wide-eyed expression. Altenbourg has
extended Friedrich's background hatching
over the face, which thus recedes, mirage-
like, to blend with its surroundings into a
landscape-like form. He sees Friedrich's self-
portrait not as a record of outward
appearances but as something more
profound, an existential insight. (EB)

217
Gerhard Altenbourg
Sunk in the Ego-Rock 1966
Versunken im Ich-Gestein

India ink, watercolour, sanguine, bistre, pastel
on cardboard, 60.2 × 42.7 cm
Private collection

After landscapes, heads are the principal
motif in Altenbourg's work. The self-portrait
has been shaped into a precious, glowing
vessel, interwoven with a darkly blooming,
rocky landscape. The linear structure of the
rock, shimmering in brown, yellow, green
and blue, continues through the head form,
where it is marked out as a different state, a
spiritual existence, by the use of lighter
tones. At approximately the same time,
Joseph Beuys was drawing self-portraits that
showed heads in rock formations as an
emblem of the essence of the artist's work:
the mental and spiritual processes that
dissolve rigidity. (EB)

218
Gerhard Altenbourg
Undispelled 1972
Unverwehet

Graphite, india ink, pencil, tempera,
watercolour, pastel, chalk on Schoeller's
'Parole', smooth, 103 × 72 cm
Collection Dieter Brusberg, Berlin

This colossal landscape head was inspired by
some phrases from Friedrich Gottlob
Klopstock's epic poem Der Messias, which
the artist inscribed on the back: 'Undispelled
/ that for them the airs of the earth
dispersed, like dust that the messenger
shakes from his foot / He hung aloft like the
tempest, and lightnings were his sweeping
blows! / Before whom the shattered forest
steams / Dust his grave, and a plaything of
the airs / That overhanging rock, swept from
the face of the earth, as the victor lifts up his
head / But in the garment of his light, the
palm wafted before him' (reproduced in exh.
cat. Gerhard Altenbourg [Berlin, 1986], 48).
(EB)

219
Gerhard Altenbourg
Tears of the Landscape, Unwept 1973
Tränen der Landschaft, ungeweinte

India ink, pencil, chalk, watercolour, pastel on
Schoeller's 'Hammerkarton', rough,
72.8 × 101.7 cm
Berlin, private collection

220
Hermann Glöckner
Black and White Divided Square under Blue
c.1930–32
Schwarz und weiß geteiltes Quadrat unter
Blau

Tempera on paper, lightly varnished,
50 × 35 cm
Staatliche Museen zu Berlin Preußischer
Kulturbesitz, Kupferstichkabinett

This is one of a series of strictly geometric
works under the title of Tafelwerk (Panel
Work). The surface is divided into a square
and a rectangle, with the lower, square area
further divided diagonally into a black half
and a white half. The rectangle above is
blue. The colour planes are not strictly
monochrome but structurally amorphous, so
that the colour plane opens out into a colour
space that offsets, in a sense, the
constructional division of the surfaces.
(EB)

221
Hermann Glöckner
Five Rays from the Upper Quarter, Thrice
Reflected, on Blue c.1933–35
Fünf Strahlen vom oberen Viertel, dreimal
reflektiert, auf Blau

Paper, pen, ink on cardboard, 50 × 35 cm
Staatliche Museen zu Berlin Preußischer
Kulturbesitz, Kupferstichkabinett

In several works, Glöckner rings the changes
on a ray of light that is reflected and
refracted in two dimensions. The 'panel'
shown here experiments with a pencil of five
rays, reflected three times and thereby
creating a harmonious division of the
surface. (EB)

222
Hermann Glöckner
Coloured Strips on Black 1945 or later
Farbige Streifen auf Schwarz

Tempera, collage (strips of tissue paper) and
lacquer on cardboard, 25.2 × 34.7 cm
Staatliche Museen zu Berlin Preußischer
Kulturbesitz, Kupferstichkabinett

Glöckner's Oriental-looking folded paper
strips on a black ground are an early form of
his Foldings. The tissue strips, in various
colours, have a translucent quality, which is
enhanced by the coat of clear lacquer to give
them a glassy, floating look. (EB)

223
Hermann Glöckner
Construction with Eight Points on a Red
Ground 1948
Konstruktion mit acht Zacken auf rotem Grund

Tempera, paper, charcoal and lacquer on
cardboard, 49.4 × 34.8 cm
Staatliche Kunstsammlungen Dresden,
Kupferstichkabinett**

224
Hermann Glöckner
Circling Lines on Blue, 24 June 1959
Kreisende Linien auf Blau

Wax and tempera on cardboard, 45 × 62 cm
Staatliche Kunstsammlungen Dresden,
Kupferstichkabinett

Circling Lines on Blue exemplifies a different
and non-constructional mode of working.
Glöckner has drawn sweeping lines on the
support with a wax candle and makes them
visible by applying blue paint, which is
resisted by the wax.   (EB)**

225
Hermann Glöckner
Cross, Between Red and Blue Sweeps 20 July
1962
Kreuz zwischen roten und blauen Schwüngen

Tempera and transfer on paper on cardboard,
50 × 36 cm
Staatliche Kunstsammlungen Dresden,
Kupferstichkabinett

The spontaneous mode of working used in
Circling Lines on Blue is taken up with
renewed vigour in this work. The red and
blue sweeps here are dashed down in a single
action. The cross and the amorphous brown
forms have been added by using an offset or
transfer technique: Glöckner painted on a
second piece of cardboard in tempera,
placed it over the present work and printed
it off under gentle pressure. The cross is a
common sign in postwar art – as in the work
of Joseph Beuys or Antoni Tàpies.   (EB)*

JOSEPH BEUYS

226
Joseph Beuys
Syringa 1945

Pressed lilac leaf, matt black paper (foil-lined
envelope), 32 × 19 cm
Collection of Céline and Heiner Bastian

227
Joseph Beuys
Queen Bee 1947
Bienenkönigin

Watercolour, pencil, on light-yellow card,
creased top right, left and bottom edges torn,
25 × 16.3 cm
Collection of Céline and Heiner Bastian

228
Joseph Beuys
Mallee 1947

Pencil, ink, dried leaf, mounted on assorted
card, 24.6 × 22.8 cm
Collection of Céline and Heiner Bastian

229
Joseph Beuys
Mussel Beds of Norderney 1949
Muschelbänke von Norderney

Watercolour, pencil, on lightweight buff-
coloured paper, right edge irregularly torn,
6.5 × 11.3 cm
Collection of Céline and Heiner Bastian

230
Joseph Beuys
Mother and Child in the Presence of Nature
1950
Mutter und Kind vor der Natur

Pencil on heavy, slightly yellowed, white
watercolour paper, top and bottom edges
perforated, 28.7 × 21 cm
Collection of Céline and Heiner Bastian

231
Joseph Beuys
Oblique Lightning Strikes Dead Arolla Pine
1954
Querblitz in tote Zirbelkiefer

Watercolour, ink, on lightweight white writing
paper, 29.6 × 20.9 cm
Collection of Céline and Heiner Bastian

232
Joseph Beuys
From: Intelligence of Swans 1954
Aus: Intelligenz der Schwäne 1954

Pencil on white writing paper, mounted on
assorted card, 29 × 42 cm
Collection of Céline and Heiner Bastian

233
Joseph Beuys
Seeress 1955
Seherin

Pencil on two sheets of smooth, lightweight,
buff-coloured artist's board, upper sheet with
regular incisions in left edge
Each 25.4 × 26.1 cm
Collection of Céline and Heiner Bastian

234
Joseph Beuys
VASE D'ELECTION 1955

Ink, collage of dried flower, black, irregularly
cut linen, light-brown card (envelope), upper
left edge torn, 37.4 × 22.7 cm
Collection of Céline and Heiner Bastian

235
Joseph Beuys
Prunus laurocerasus 1955

Oil paint, collage of dried laurel leaf, waxed
paper, mounted on heavy black card,
45.1 × 34.3 cm
Collection of Céline and Heiner Bastian

236
Joseph Beuys
Ancient Sea with Pterosaur 1956
Altes Meer mit Flugechse

Watercolour on smooth, thin card,
29.8 × 21 cm
Collection of Céline and Heiner Bastian

237
Joseph Beuys
Large Gold Sculpture 1956
Große Goldskulptur

Gold bronze, pencil, on thin, white paper,
bottom edge irregularly torn, 22.8 × 21.6 cm
Collection of Céline and Heiner Bastian

238
Joseph Beuys
Unicorn 1956–57
Einhorn

Watercolour, ink, burn hole, on heavy, brown
card, all sides irregularly cut, 14.8 × 20.8 cm
Collection of Céline and Heiner Bastian

239
Joseph Beuys
Recumbent Elk 1957
Liegender Elch, 1957

Oil paint on matt drawing paper, mounted on
thin paper, top and bottom edges torn,
11 × 23.8 cm and 18.3 × 27.3 cm
Collection of Céline and Heiner Bastian

240
Joseph Beuys
Odysseus 1957

Watercolour on white artist's board
(two sheets), 15.9 × 16.4 cm (left),
16.1 × 16.3 cm (right)
Collection of Céline and Heiner Bastian

241
Joseph Beuys
Drill of a Cave-Dweller 1957
Bohrmaschine eines Höhlenbewohners

Watercolour on white artist's board, incision
on right edge, all sides irregularly trimmed,
17 × 24.5 cm
Collection of Céline and Heiner Bastian

242
Joseph Beuys
Circe's Bathroom 1954–58
Badezimmer der Circe

Watercolour, gold-bronze, on assorted paper,
mounted on thick, irregularly torn card,
21.1 × 30.4 cm
Collection of Céline and Heiner Bastian

243
Joseph Beuys
Untitled 1957–58
ohne Titel

Hare's blood, pencil, on thin, yellowed paper,
creased in centre, adhesive film top right,
20.9 × 14.7 cm
Collection of Céline and Heiner Bastian

244
Joseph Beuys
Slime Was Before the Bone, Before the Stone
1958
Schleim war vor dem Knochen, vor dem Stein

Watercolour (lime and water) on smooth,
fat-impregnated paper, 29.8 × 21.6 cm
Collection of Céline and Heiner Bastian

245
Joseph Beuys
The Female Crusoe on the Beach 1959
Der weibliche Robinson am Strand

Oil paint, indelible pencil, on light-brown
card, 35.3 × 23 cm
Collection of Céline and Heiner Bastian

246
Joseph Beuys
Woman with Falling Stone 1959
Frau mit fallendem Stein

Pencil on printed writing paper (account book),
29.6 × 20.7 cm
Collection of Céline and Heiner Bastian

247
Joseph Beuys
Unrepeatable Seconds of Excitement in
Horse's Grave 1959
Einmalige sekundenlange Erregung im
Pferdegrab

Pencil, traces of fat, on white writing paper,
27.6 × 21.5 cm
Collection of Céline and Heiner Bastian

248
Joseph Beuys
Love Arm with Love Ring 1959
Liebesarm mit Liebesring

Watercolour, pencil, on folded white paper
napkin, 16.5 × 16.4 cm
Collection of Céline and Heiner Bastian

249
Joseph Beuys
fatty Cloud detaches itself from the sea 1959
fettige Wolke löst sich aus dem meer

Watercolour, fat, on thick, light-brown card,
right edge irregularly torn, mounted on heavy,
brown card, 32.2 × 25.4 cm
Collection of Céline and Heiner Bastian

250
Joseph Beuys
Metal Sculptures with Electromagnetic Charge
and Telephone 1960
Metall-Skulpturen mit elektromagnetischer
Ladung und Telefon

Pencil on thin, white writing paper,
28 × 21.6 cm
Collection of Céline and Heiner Bastian

251
Joseph Beuys
Cross 1961
Kreuz

Thinned oil paint on strips of card, mounted on
white card, 43 × 36.5 cm
Collection of Céline and Heiner Bastian

252
Joseph Beuys
Untitled 1961–62
ohne Titel

Watercolour on packing cardboard, all sides
irregularly torn and cut, 13 × 23.3 cm
Collection of Céline and Heiner Bastian

253
Joseph Beuys
Untitled 1961–62
ohne Titel

Blood on grey-brown packing paper, brown
card, mounted on smooth, heavy,
buff-coloured, dirty card, 64.8 × 98.8 cm
Collection of Céline and Heiner Bastian

254
Joseph Beuys
Untitled 1964
ohne Titel

Pencil on smooth, white artist's board,
23 × 16.2 cm
Collection of Céline and Heiner Bastian

255
Joseph Beuys
Score (Celtic) 1970
Partitur (Celtic)

Pencil on smooth white artist's board, left edge
irregularly cut, 29.1 × 20.1 cm
Collection of Céline and Heiner Bastian

256
Joseph Beuys
Untitled 1972
ohne Titel

Pencil on lightweight, semitransparent, white
paper, 59.4 × 42 cm
Collection of Céline and Heiner Bastian

257
Joseph Beuys
Brain 1973
Brain (–)

Pencil on lightweight, white writing paper,
perforated on left side, 21.5 × 14 cm
Collection of Céline and Heiner Bastian

258
Joseph Beuys
2 Skulls Sea of Ice 1982
2 Schädel Eismeer

Oil paint, titanium white, shellac,
on newspaper, folded several times,
40 × 28.5 cm
Collection of Céline and Heiner Bastian

259
Joseph Beuys
Opossum Tree 1982

Pencil on lightweight, smooth, white artist's
board, left edge irregularly torn,
25.4 × 25.8 cm
Collection of Céline and Heiner Bastian

260
Joseph Beuys
Dreaming Gap (Sternklarer Himmel) 1982

Pencil on lightweight, white writing paper,
21 × 29.7 cm
Collection of Céline and Heiner Bastian

261
Joseph Beuys
The End of the Twentieth Century 1983–85
Das Ende des 20. Jahrhunderts

31 basalt stones with clay-filled cavity and
cone-shaped insert wrapped in felt, overall
size variable
Tate Gallery, London

Installed in varying numbers and
configurations on a number of occasions
under the title *The End of the Twentieth
Century*, Beuys's basalt rocks are linked with
the environmental sculpture *7000 Oaks*,
installed at *documenta 7* in Kassel in 1982.
Two-thirds of the way along each stone, a
cone shape has been machined out, wrapped
in felt and reinserted, padded out with clay;
this lends expressiveness to the inert mass of
rock. The stones represent the twentieth-
century historical process; at its end are the
open issues of utopia and altered
consciousness. In this work, Beuys sums up
his own efforts towards the
Gesamtkunstwerk of 'Social Sculpture', an
artistic synthesis whose long evolutionary
gestation is still in its earliest phase. *(EB)*

ASPECTS OF CONTEMPORARY ART

262
Georg Baselitz
The New Type 1965
Der neue Typ

Oil on canvas, 162 × 130 cm
Collection Froehlich, Stuttgart

Baselitz's figure paintings of the mid-1960s
are a paradoxical fusion of Romantic
prototype, Nietzsche, and the powerfully
expressive art of the mentally deranged. The
Romantic image of the artist as some kind of
lonely hero or prophet was given renewed
urgency at the close of the nineteenth
century by Nietzsche's concept of the
superman violently opposed to the liberal
and materialistic values of western society.
The extremist aspects of Nietzsche's
thought, his glorification of the 'will to
power' over reason and morality, were in
turn taken up by Nazi ideologists such as
Alfred Rosenberg, who in his *The Myth of
the Twentieth Century* (1930) extolled the
creation of 'a new type of man out of a new
myth of life'. Baselitz's 'new types', by
contrast, present a pathetic spectacle:
barefoot, ragged and weighed down by

disproportionately large limbs, they seem
scarcely to have the will to live. By
borrowing from the obsessive iconography
of the insane – for example, the interest in
bodily distortion and sado-masochistic
imagery – Baselitz further underlines the
irony of his approach, since this type of art
had been used by the Nazis to expose the
'degeneracy' of Modernism.

ex catalogue
Georg Baselitz
Partisan 1965

Oil on canvas, 162.6 × 130.1 cm
Courtesy Anthony d'Offay Gallery, London

ex catalogue
Georg Baselitz
Ludwig Richter on His Way to Work 1965
Ludwig Richter auf dem Weg zur Arbeit

Oil on canvas, 162 × 130 cm
Private Collection

263
Georg Baselitz
A Modern Painter 1966
Ein moderner Maler

Oil on canvas, 162 × 130 cm
Berlinische Galerie, Museum für Moderne
Kunst, Photographie und Architektur, Berlin

264
Anselm Kiefer
Ways of Worldly Wisdom 1976–77
Wege der Weltweisheit

Oil, acrylic and shellac on sackcloth aid down
on canvas, 305 × 500 cm
Collection Sanders (on loan to the Van
Abbemuseum, Eindhoven)

The paintings assembled here indicate
something of the range and ambition of
Kiefer's art. From ironical reflections on
Germanic myth and Germany's tragic
history (as here) to the Holocaust – a subject
which Beuys, in his more oblique fashion,
also addressed – Kiefer insists on the artist's
right to deal with any theme, no matter how
sensitive. The overwhelming sense of
despoliation and distress conveyed by
Kiefer's violent use of materials suggests an
inversion of the Romantic idea of the
Sublime. *(RC)*

265
Anselm Kiefer
Sand of the Mark 1980–82
Märkischer Sand

Emulsion paint, sand, painted paper collage
and oil on photograph laid down on canvas,
330 × 555 cm
Stedelijk Museum, Amsterdam

266
Anselm Kiefer
The Stairs 1982-83
Die Treppe

Emulsion paint, oil, straw and photograph on
document paper on canvas, 330 × 185 cm
Private Collection (on loan to the Kunstmuseum,
Bonn)

267
Anselm Kiefer
Seraphim 1984

Emulsion paint, oil, shellac and Aquatex on
canvas, 280 × 280 cm
Courtesy Anthony d'Offay Gallery, London

268
Blinky Palermo
Untitled (Landscape with Head) 1964
Ohne Titel (Landschaft mit Kopf)

Watercolour and pencil on squared paper,
19.5 × 11.3 cm
Deutsche Bank AG, Frankfurt am Main

269
Blinky Palermo
Untitled (Landscape) 1964
Ohne Titel (Landschaft)

Watercolour and pencil on squared paper,
19.5 × 11.3 cm
Deutsche Bank AG, Frankfurt am Main

270
Blinky Palermo
Untitled (By the Sea) 1965
Ohne Titel (Am Meer)

Oil paint, thinned with turpentine substitute, on
paper, 40 × 25.5 cm
Collection Klüser, Munich

The austere constructions of Piet Mondrian,
which are a product of the experience of
landscape, are strongly present in Palermo's
early work. In 1965 and 1966 he produced
four works on paper under the title *By the
Sea*, with a sober layout and radical
economy of form that recall the spirit of
Mondrian (and in particular his drawings of
1914, *Sea*, *Pier* and *Ocean*). It is revealing,
in the light of Palermo's use of 'Romantic'
titles, that Mondrian himself gave to a
drawn variant of *The Sea* a title full of
archetypal Romantic metaphors for the
Infinite: *Sea and Starry Night on the Beach
at Domburg*. *(MS)*

271
Blinky Palermo
Untitled 1966
Ohne Titel

Pencil and coloured pencil on paper,
28.5 × 18.9 cm
Deutsche Bank AG, Frankfurt am Main

272
Blinky Palermo
Hymn to the Night 1967
Hymne an die Nacht

Watercolour, silver bronze and pencil on
paper, 25 × 20 cm
Collection Klüser, Munich

This drawing probably represents the only
direct literary quotation in Palermo's entire
oeuvre. It is a paraphrase – an uncommonly
lyrical and subjective one – of his two-part
object of 1966, *Daydream II (Night Piece)*.
The circumstances of its making were
intensely private. The Danish composer
Henning Christiansen (a friend of Joseph
Beuys) arranged a showing of Palermo's
work in Copenhagen, and he went to stay at
the home of Christiansen and the painter
Ursula Reuter. They talked of Novalis's
Hymnen an die Nacht; and these prose
poems, with all their multiple levels of
interpretation, their wealth of association
and their power of spatial imagination, seem
to have struck a powerful chord with
Palermo. *(MS)*

273
Blinky Palermo
Untitled (Abstract Watercolour) (Eagle) 1970
Ohne Titel (Abstraktes Aquarell) (Adler)

Watercolour and copying pencil on squared
paper, 23.9 × 18.4 cm
Deutsche Bank AG, Frankfurt am Main

274
Blinky Palermo
Untitled 1971
Ohne Titel

Watercolour and pencil on torn paper,
mounted on paper, 70 × 50 cm
Private collection

The aesthetic – mediated by Beuys – of paper
and *objets trouvés*, mounted and assembled
to create a pictorial space of their own, is
shared by this and another *Untitled* work of
1971, identical in colouring (exh. cat. *Blinky
Palermo* [Leipzig and Munich, 1993], no.
67), which accentuates the collage principle
still further by incorporating a modified
book cover. *(MS)*

275
Blinky Palermo
Study for Silkscreen 1971 (?)
Entwurf für Siebdruck

Oil on paper, 50 × 51 cm
Private collection, London

Palermo's dating of the print (1970) and of
the sketch (1971) is perplexing, since it looks
as if the sketch was used in the preparation
of the print, which was not published until
1971. In his early, two-part objects, Palermo
used a vertical staff or a T-shape to establish
the basic coordinates of world-axis and
horizon. This almost square drawing is
dominated by the vertical that plunges from
above, rather than by the rising T-shape. It is
worth considering whether this might be a
response to a contemporaneous work by
Walter De Maria, his project for an *Olympic
Earth Sculpture*, designed for Munich and
ultimately realized as the *Vertical Earth
Kilometre* in Kassel; it is a symbolic
monument in counterpoint to Constantin
Brancusi's *Endless Column*. *(MS)*

276
Blinky Palermo
Untitled (Coloured Bows) 1971
Ohne Titel (Farbige Bögen)

Coloured crayons and pencil on paper,
14.3 × 10.4 cm
Private collection, London

This drawing was made in the hotel where
Palermo stayed when he was in Munich for
an exhibition at the Galerie Heiner Friedrich
in the spring of 1971. In delicate, floating
colours, the artist additively explores a motif
that remotely recalls a landscape. The serial
juxtaposition of similar motifs seems
comparable with that in the watercolour
Untitled, of 1965 (see exh. cat. *Blinky
Palermo*, Winterthur, 1984, no. 32). The
present work gave rise to a sequence of
seven watercolours, exhibited at Friedrich's
but unpublished to date. *(MS)*

277
Blinky Palermo
Untitled (Study for a Mural Drawing) 1971
Ohne Titel (Studie für Wandzeichnung)

Watercolour on paper, 25.5 × 15 cm
Private collection, London

This watercolour formerly belonged to
Gerhard Richter, who exchanged it for one
of his own works. By comparison with
Palermo's other studies and sketches for
murals, this has an unexpectedly
atmospheric softness that conveys a strong
sense of painterly openness. The light
yellow, surrounded by a darker frame, seems
to suggest the magic of a space of colour and
light, open to the sky (though not at all in
the Conceptual vein): something that
Palermo never realized in this form. (MS)

278
Sigmar Polke
Laterna magica 1990–93

Various lacquers on transparent polyester
fabric, 13 paintings, each 135 × 150cm
The artist

A series of connected wooden panels, each
framing polyester screens on which have
been painted - on both sides - a hectic array
of images, colours, and varnishes, was first
publicly exhibited in Sigmar Polke's
American retrospective in 1991. At the
Brooklyn Museum, the Laterna Magica was
shown to the side of the artist's main show,
in a low-ceilinged dark room reserved for
nineteenth-century American landscape
painting. The work acted both as a puzzling
interloper into the tidy categories of the
museum, and as a bridge between the art of
the past and Polke's own work spanning
thirty years.

The Laterna Magica, although comprising
paintings, is in a true sense an installation,
designed to involve the viewer in a magical,
transformative spectacle. Both the number of
panels and their configuration are variable,
the presentation always symmetrical and
maze-like, obliging viewers to circulate
around and through the work, equally aware
of the particular panel they are considering
and what lies behind and beyond it. This
transparent, unpretentious but structured
format avoids the magisterial aura of the
large canvases that Polke normally employs,
to powerful effect, and allows a more open
ground for the layering of radically different
images and meanings that has characterised
Polke's work at least since the early 1970s.

The imagery itself derives largely from
folk and fairy tales taken from popular
sources of the eighteenth and nineteenth
centuries; they speak of worlds turned
upside down, of alchemical experiments and
animal inversions, and follow on from the
artist's earlier use of the illustrations of
Grandville and Lewis Carroll. It seems that
Polke is directing the rationale of Pop Art
backwards into history. The images often
obscure and enhance each other, allowing
endless visual pranks and doubles-entendres.
These samplings of pre-existing motifs are
connected by gestural marks both accidental
and deliberate, their richness again enhanced
by being applied to both sides of the screen.
It can be no accident that Polke's use of
transparent material and manipulation of
historical popular imagery, both hinted at in
earlier works, became more prevalent at the
same time, around 1988, reaching their most

complete form in the Laterna Magica. He
has uncovered a means to study the past
without being bound by its forms. (GH)

279
Gerhard Richter
Woman Reading 1994

Oil on canvas, 72 × 102 cm
The artist

280
Gerhard Richter
Wall 1994

Oil on canvas, 240 × 240 cm
The artist

281
Gerhard Richter
March 1994

Oil on canvas, 250 × 200 cm
The artist

282
Gerhard Richter
Wall 1994

Oil on canvas, 250 × 200 cm
The artist

283
Gerhard Richter
Woman Reading 1994

Oil on canvas, 51 × 71 cm
The artist

Biographies

Gerhard Altenbourg
Rödichen-Schnepfenthal/Thüringen 1926 – 1989 Meißen

Real name: Gerhard Ströch. Pseudonyms: Ismael Lysa, Stephan Kambienna, Altenbourg. 1929 In Altenburg, lived here with brief interruptions from 1944 to 1959. 1944–45 war service and confinement to military hospitals. 1945–46 Worked as a journalist and writer under the pesudonym Ismael Lysa. 1946–48 Drawing lessons with Erich Dietz in Altenburg. 1948–50 Studied at the Weimar College of Architecture and Fine Art, under Hans Hoffmann-Lederer until 1952. Start of friendship with Thea and Fritz Henning. 1949 First lithographs; work with printers Arno Fehringer and Horst Arloth. Changed name to Stephan Kambienna. From 1955 used 'Altenbourg' as his *nom de guerre*. 1957 First hand-written book for Rudolf Springer 'dulce et decorum'; first sculpture. 1959 First woodcuts. 1961 Guest studio in the West Berlin Academy of Art. 1965 Started work with printer Werner Lorenz in Altenburg. 1970 Elected member of the West Berlin Academy of Arts. 1973 Started work with printer Tobias Lorenz in Altenburg. 1981 First dry-point engravings. 1989 Killed in a car accident.

Hans Arp
Strasbourg/Alsace 1886 – 1966 Basle/Switzerland

1900–01 Enrolled at the École des Arts et Métiers in Strasbourg. 1904 Trained in Ludwig von Hoffmann's studio in Weimar. 1906 In Weggis near Lucerne, Switzerland. 1908 In Paris at the Académie Julian. 1909 Return to Switzerland. 1911 Co-founder of the 'Modernes Bund' in Lucerne. 1912 Worked on the joint *Der Blaue Reiter* statement, took part in the exhibition of the same name. 1913 In Berlin; worked on Herwarth Walden's magazine *Der Sturm*. 1914 Interest in mysticism, read Jacob Böhme, Meister Eckhart, the pre-Socratics and investigated Oriental thought. First meeting with Max Ernst. Contact with the 'Rhineland Expressionists'. 1914–15 In Paris; met Amedeo Modigliani, Pablo Picasso, Max Jacob, Guillaume Apollinaire. 1915–19 In Zürich. Co-founder of the Zürich Dada movement (1916–19). 1918 Friendship with Kurt Schwitters. 1919 Link with Dada-Cologne, Max Ernst and Johann Theodor Baargeld. Member of 'Zentrale W/3' (the three stupid men of the West: Baargeld, Ernst, Arp). 1920 Took part in the 'First International Dada Fair' in Berlin. Returned to joined Dada-Paris. 1920 Trip to Rügen island with Schwitters and Hanna Höch. 1921–28 Lived in Zürich. 1922 Married Sophie Taeuber. 1925 Took part in the first Surrealist exhibition. 1926 French citizenship. First wooden sculptures. 1927 Worked on the magazine 'Les Documents Internationaux de l'Esprit Nouveau'. From 1929 studio in Meudon-Val-Fleury near Paris, lived there from 1934. 1930 First collages. Took part in the *Cercle et Carré* group exhibition. 1932–43 Member of the committee for the magazine *Abstraction-Création*. 1936 Took part in the 'Cubism and Abstract Art' and 'Fantastic Art, Dada and Surrealism' exhibitions in New York. 1937 Member of the 'Allianz' group. From 1939 also known as Jean Arp. 1942–45 In Switzerland. 1943 Death of Sophie Taeuber-Arp. 1945 Return to Meudon-Val-Fleury. 1946 First complete edition of his poems (1915–45) in French. 1947–49 Member of the 'Salon des Réalités Nouvelles' committee. 1949, 1950 and 1958 travelled to America. 1959 Married Marguerite Hagenbach. Settled in Locarno-Solduna. 1960 Visited Egypt, Jordan and Israel.

Georg Baselitz
Deutschbaselitz, Saxony 1938 – lives and works in Derneburg near Hildesheim, Lower Saxony and in Imperia, Italy.

Born Hans-Georg Kern. 1956–57 Studied at the Academy of Fine and Applied Arts in East Berlin. Expelled from Academy for socio-political immaturity. 1957–62 Continued studies in West Berlin. Began friendship with Eugen Schönebeck and Benjamin Katz. 1960 Preoccupation with the art of the mentally ill (collection Prinzhorn). 1961 Changed name to 'Baselitz'. '1. Pandämonium' Exhibition and manifesto with Eugen Schönebeck in Berlin. 1962 '2. Pandämonium' Manifesto with Eugen Schönebeck. Exhibition in Berlin. Confiscation by authorities of two paintings on display; Letter and manifesto 'Dear Mr W.' 1964 First etchings. '1. Orthodox Salon (Oberon)' Exhibition in Berlin. Began friendship with Johannes Gachnang. 1965 Florence. 1966 'Why the painting "The great friends" is a good painting' Manifesto and exhibition in Berlin. Move to Osthofen near Worms. First wood engravings. 1973 Studio in Musbach on the Weinstrasse. 1975 Move to Derneburg near Hildesheim. 1978–83 Professorship at the Karlsruhe Academy. 1979 'Four walls and light from above or better no painting on the wall' speech and manifesto during the conference on architecture in Dortmund. First sculptures. 1981 Additional studio in Castiglion Fiorentino near Arezzo. 1983–88 Professorship at the Berlin Academy of Arts. 1985 'The painter's utensils': Manifesto and speech, held in Amsterdam 1987 and London as well as in Paris 1991. Since 1987 additional studio in Imperia, Italy. 1990 Editor of the journal *Krater & Wolke Nr. 7*.

Willi Baumeister
Stuttgart 1889 – 1955 Stuttgart

1905–07 Apprenticeship as a painter-decorator. 1906 Met Oskar Schlemmer and Otto Meyer-Amden. 1907–08 Military service. 1909–22 studied at the Stuttgart Academy for Fine Arts under Gustav Igler, Adolf Hölzel and Heinrich Altherr. His first stay in Paris. 1912–1913 Stay in Amden near St Gallen/Switzerland. 1914–18 Military service. 1919 Stuttgart. Began murals. Founding of the Üecht- group. 1922–24 Beginning of the *Chessplayer* and machine paintings. 1924 Paris. Met Amédée Ozenfant, Le Corbusier and Fernand Léger; 1925 Beginning of sports paintings. 1926 Met Piet Mondrian; 1927 Hans Arp, Kasimir Malewitsch, Theo van Doesburg and Albert Gleizes. Co-founder of the 'Ring Neuer Werbegestalter' with Kurt Schwitters and others. 1928–33 Professorship at the Städelsche Academy in Frankfurt am Main. 1930 Member of the Parisian group *Cercle et Carré*. 1931 Member of the *Abstraction-Création* group. 1933 Dismissed from teaching post in Frankfurt; return to Stuttgart. *Sandbilder Valltorta*. 1935 Line figures. 1937 *Ideogramme*. 1938 *Eidospictures*. 1938–43 Wuppertal and Stuttgart. 1941 Exhibition ban. 1942 *African Paintings* and *Gilgamesch* series. 1943 Drawings and illustration cycles to *Esther*, *Saul*, *Gilgamesch* and to Shakespeare's *Tempest*. 1946 Publication of his book *Das Unbekannte in der Kunst*. 1946–55 Professorship at the Stuttgart Academy. Took part in the 'Darmstädter Gespräche', defence of modern art. 1952–55 *Safer*, *Kessaua*, *Montaru* paintings. *Aru* series, *Monturi* paintings, *Bluxao* paintings, *Laterne* and *Han-i*.

Joseph Beuys
Krefeld 1921 – 1986 Düsseldorf

Youth and adolescence in Kleve. 1941–45 Military service as stuka pilot. 1945–46 Prisoner of war. 1946 Return to Kleve. 1947–51 Studied sculpture, Düsseldorf, under Joseph Enseling and Ewald Mataré. 1952–54 Studio in Düsseldorf. 1959 Marriage to Eva Wurmbach. 1961 Professorship for monumental sculpture at Düsseldorf Academy. 1962 First contacts with Fluxus movement. 1963 First participation in Fluxus actions. 1964 Actions: *Marcel Duchamp's Silence is Overrated* and *Der Chef* in Düsseldorf. In Düsseldorf 1965 action *How to Explain Pictures to a Dead Hare*. 1966 *Eurasia* action; *34th Movement of the Siberian Symphony* in Copenhagen and *Manresa* in Düsseldorf. 1967 Founding of the 'German Students' Party as Metaparty' in Düsseldorf; Beginning of political activities. *Eurasienstab 82 min fluxorum organum* action in Vienna. 1968 Academy expresses no confidence in Beuys's action *I'm trying to set you free, grand pianojam* in Berlin. 1970 Founding of the 'Organisation of Non-voters, Free Referendum'. Performance *Celtic (Kinloch Rannoch)* in Edinburgh. 1971 Founding of the 'Organization for Direct Democracy through Referendum'. Founding of the 'Committee for a Free Academy'. 1972 After occupying secretariat of the Academy by students, dismissed without notice from his teaching post in Düsseldorf. 1973 Co-founder of 'Club to promote a Free International Academy for Creativity and Interdisciplinary Research'. 1974 Together with Heinrich Böll founding of the Free Academy in Düsseldorf. Guest professorship at the Hamburg Academy of Fine Arts. 1975 Kenya with Charles Wilp. 1976 Parliamentary candidate. 1977 Establishment of Free International Academy for Creativity and Interdisciplinary Research. 1978 Industrial tribunal declares dismissal from Academy in Düsseldorf illegal. 1979 met Andy Warhol. Parliamentary candidate for Greens in European Parliament. Performance *yes, now we're going to break off the shit* in Berlin. 1982 Took part in the 'documenta 7' in Kassel with the performance *7000 Oak Trees*. Journey to Australia. Met Dalai Lama in Bonn. Took part in the party convention of the Greens in Hagen. 1984 Japan.

Carl Eduard Ferdinand Heinrich Blechen
Cottbus 1798 – 1840 Berlin

1815–1817 Apprenticeship at a bank in Berlin. 1820–22 Bank clerk in Berlin. 1822–24 Studied at Berlin Academy. 1823 Student under Peter Ludwig Lütke. Visited Sächsische Schweiz and Dresden, met Dahl. Presumably met Friedrich. First graphic works. 1824–27 With the help of Karl Friedrich Schinkel he became scenery painter at the Königstädtische Theatre in Berlin. 1826 Accepted into the Berlinische Künstlerverein. 1828 Trip to the Baltic Sea and to the island of Rügen. 1828–29 Study trip to Italy with his student Leopold Schlösser. In Rome shared house with Koch and Johann Christian Reinhart. Excursions to Tivoli, Subiaco, Ostia, to Colli Albani and the Campagna. Visited Bertel Thorvaldsen. Return to Berlin via Terni, Assisi, Florence, Milan, Basel, Freiburg, Karlsruhe. 1831 Professorship for landscape painting at the Berlin Academy. With the art dealer Louis Friedrich Sachse to Paris. Died of mental illness.

Arnold Böcklin
Basle 1827 – 1901 San Domenico near Fiesole, Italy

1845–47 Studied at the Düsseldorf Academy under Schirmer, Theodor Hildebrand, Wiegmann. Influenced by Carl Friedrich Lessing. 1847 Went to Belgium with Rudolf Koller; impressed by the works of Peter Paul Rubens and the Old Dutch school. His paintings show the influence of the late Romantic school of Carl Friedrich Lessing. 1948 Paris, studied at the Louvre. 1850–57 Rome with interruptions. Stayed in Olevano, Subiaco and Tivoli. Friendship with Ludwig Thiersche. 1857 Moved to Basle. 1858 Went to Hanover and later to Munich. 1860–62 Taught at the art school in Weimar. 1861 Friendship with Reinhold Begas and Franz von Lenbach. 1862–66 Rome, friendship with Anselm Feuerbach, Hans von Marées; after 1865 with Rudolf Schick. 1863 Trip to Pompeii. 1866 Moved to Kleinbasel. 1869 Trip to Northern Italy to study the frescoes of Antonio Allegri and Correggio. 1871–74 Munich, friendship with Hans Thoma, contact with the Leibl circle. 1872 Vienna. 1874–85 Florence. Friendship with Hans von Marées and Adolf von Hildebrand. 1879 Trip to Naples and Ischia. 1880 Met Richard Wagner. 1883 Berlin. 1885–93 Zurich. Met Gottfried Keller. 1892 Florence.

Carl Gustav Carus
Leipzig 1789 – 1869 Dresden

1804–10 Studied natural sciences, philosophy and medicine at University of Leipzig. 1811–12 First landscape paintings. 1811–14 Assistant doctor at maternity hospital, Leipzig. 1814 Professor of obstetrics and director of the maternity hospital in Dresden. 1816 First exhibition. 1818 Friendship with Friedrich. First exchange of letters with Goethe. Trip to the island of Rügen. 1820 Journey to the Riesengebirge. 1821 Visited Goethe in Weimar. First trip to Switzerland and to Italy. 1822 Co-founder of the Society of German Nature Researchers and Doctors. 1827 Became personal physician to king of Saxony. 1828 Trip to Switzerland and to Italy. 1831 Publication of his *Nine Letters about Landscape Painting, written 1815–1824*. In later life published books on Friedrich and Goethe, and 4 volumes of memoirs.

Peter von Cornelius
Düsseldorf 1783 – 1867 Berlin

First taught by his father, Düsseldorf gallery inspector Aloys Cornelius. From 1795 studied at the Düsseldorf Academy under Johann Peter von Langer. First artistic success with his drawings for 'Faust I'. 1809–11 With his friend Christian Xeller and copperplate engraver Carl Barth in Frankfurt. 1811–19 In Rome, contact with the Nazarenes. Friendship with Johann Friedrich Overbeck. 1817–18 Preparatory work for the Dante room in the Casa Bartholdy. 1818–30 Fresco work in the Munich Glyptothek. 1819–24 Summer in Munich, winter in Düsseldorf. 1821 Director of the Düsseldorf Academy. 1925–41 Lived in Munich; director of the Munich Academy. 1825 Raised to the peerage. 1830–31, 1833–35 Visits to Rome. 1828–36 Preliminary drawings for paintings in the loggias of the Alte Pinakothek. 1839–40 Frescoes in the Ludwigskirche in Munich. 1838 Visited Paris. 1840 Rift with Ludwig I of Bavaria and rivalry with Leo von Klenze. Called to Berlin by Friedrich Wilhelm I of Prussia. 1841 Moved to Berlin. 1843–44, 1845–46 and 1853–61 Visited Rome. 1843–67 Cartoons for the planned Campo Santo of the Prussian kings.

Johan Christian Clausen Dahl
Bergen/Norway 1788 – 1857 Dresden

1803–09 Apprenticeship in decorative painting, Bergen. 1811–17 Studied at Copenhagen Art Academy under Carl Adolf Lorentzen, Nicolaj Dajon and Georg Haas. Interest in atmospheric phenomena. 1814 and 1816 Stayed on island of Engelholm. 1817 Trip to southern Sweden with Christian Jürgensen Thomsen, founder of nordic archaeology. 1818 In Dresden; first meeting with Caspar David Friedrich who was to become a close friend. 1820 Member of the Academy in Dresden. Move to Naples, painted there with Franz Ludwig Catel among others. 1821 Rome, in circle

around Bertel Thorvaldsen. Return to Dresden. Pure cloud studies. From 1824 Professor at Dresden Academy. 1826, 1834, 1839, 1844 and 1850 Trips to Norway. 1847 Paris and Brussels.

Heinrich Anton Dähling
Hanover 1773 – 1850 Potsdam

Pupil at the Berlin Academy from 1793. 1811 Member of the Berlin Academy. Founder member of the Berlin Artists' Association, professor there 1814. Produced mainly drawings from 1839.

Maximilian Johann Georg von Dillis
Grüngiebing near Wasserburg, Upper Bavaria 1759 – 1841 Munich

1777–1781 Studied philosophy and theology at the University of Ingolstadt and in the Collegium Albertinum. 1782 Ordination to priesthood. Education at Munich Academy of Drawing under Franz Ignaz Oefele and Johann Jakob Dorner, the elder. For a short time freemason. 1786 Dispensation from his spiritual commitments. Drawing instructor to nobility, Munich. 1790 Inspector of the Electoral Art gallery at Hofgarten in Munich. 1792 Trip to Dresden, Prague and Vienna. 1794/95 Italy: Livorno, Corsica, Rome, Naples and Vienna at invitation of Sir Gilbert Elliot, viceroy of Corsica. 1796–97 Saves paintings from the French. 1800–1801 Moves Electoral painting to Ansbach for safety. 1805/06 Italy, with Anton Koch, Angelika Kauffman and Bertel Thorvaldsen. Tivoli, Subiaco, Naples, Pompeii and Rome. 1806 Return to Munich via Paris, meets Crown Prince Ludwig. Detailed studies in the Louvre and of the collections in the Palais Luxembourg. 1808 Ennobled. 1804–10 Professor of landscape painting at Munich Academy. 1812, 1816 and 1817–18 Trips to Italy. Close contacts with circle of artists around Thorvaldsen. 1820 Restructuring of the galleries in Nuremberg, Bamberg, Würzburg and Aschaffenburg. 1822 Gallery post. 1827 Concludes purchase of the Boisserée collection.

Otto Dix
Untermhaus near Gera/Thüringen 1891 – 1969 Siegen/Hohentwiel

1905–09 Trained as an interior decorator in Gera. 1910–14 Attended the Dresden School of Arts and Crafts. 1913 Study visit to Austria and Italy. 1914–18 Army service. 1919–22 Attended the Dresden Academy of Art, master-classes with Max Feldbauer and Otto Gußmann. Co-founder of the Dresden 'Secession Gruppe 1919'. 1920 Took part in the 'First International Dada Fair' in Berlin. 1922–25 Continued his studies at the Düsseldorf Academy of Art under Heinrich Nauen and Wilhelm Herbertholz. Member of the circle around Johanna Ey and the 'Young Rhineland' group. His scenes depicting brothels and sexual murders led to charges of disseminating obscene pictures by the Hessen state prosecution service in Darmstadt and a trial by the Berlin district court; acquitted. 1923 Married Martha Koch. Birth of his daughter Nelly; painted numerous pictures of children. 1924–1925 Study visits to Italy and Paris. 1925 Took part in the 'Neue Sachlichkeit' exhibition in Mannheim. Moved to Berlin. Friendship with Georg Grosz and Heinrich George.

1927 Son Ursus born. Moved to Dresden. 1927–33 Professor at the Dresden Academy of Art. 1928 Son Jan born. 1931 Full member of the Prussian Academy of Arts in Berlin. 1933 Relieved of office. Resigned from the Prussian Academy. Member of the Reichskulturkammer. Moved to Randegg on Lake Constance in the summer. 1934 Forbidden to exhibit. 1935 Exhibition with Franz Lenk in the Galerie Nierendorf in Berlin. 1936 Moved to Hemmenhofen on Lake Constance. 1945–46 Member of the Volkssturm, prisoner of war. 1946 Returned to Hemmenhofen. 1947–66 Annual working visits to Dresden. From 1953 several study visits to the south of France, southern Italy and Alsace.

Max Ernst
Brühl near Cologne 1891 – 1976 Paris

1910–14 Studied classical philology at University of Bonn. 1910–11 Began friendship with August Macke. 1913 in Paris. Worked on *Der Sturm*. 1914 Met Hans Arp in Cologne. 1914–18 Active service. 1916 Met George Grosz and Wieland Herzfelde in Berlin. 1918 Moved to Cologne. 1919 Visited Paul Klee in Munich. Founded the Dada group in Cologne: 'W/3 (W=West Stupidland)'. First Dada exhibition in Cologne. Co-editor of several short-lived magazines *Ventilator*, *Bulletin D*, *Der Strom*. 1920 Co-editor of the single issue of the magazine *Die Schammade*. Second and last Dada exhibition in Cologne. Participated in the 'First International Dada Show' in Berlin. Together with Baargeld, created *Fatagagas*. 1921 Tarrenz, Tirol with Sophie Taeuber-Arp, Arp and Tristan Tzara. First exhibition in Paris at invitation of André Breton. Manifesto 'Dada Au Grand Air: Der Sängerkrieg in Tirol'. Met Paul and Gala Eluard. From 1922 in Paris. Worked on magazine *Littérature*. 1924 Co-founder of Surrealist movement. 1925 Participated in the first Surrealist exhibition in Paris. First frottages. 1926 Publication of the series of frottages *Histoire naturelle*. 1927 Used frottage technique in painting (*grattage*). 1929 Publication of the collage novel *La femme 100 têtes*. 1930 Worked on film *L'Age d'Or*. 1931 First exhibition in New York. 1943 Visited Alberto Giacometti in Maloja, Switzerland. 1936 Took part in 'Fantastic Art, Dada, Surrealism' exhibition in New York. Applied decalcomania in his works. 1938 Broke with Surrealists. Moved to Saint-Martin d'Ardèche in South of France. 1941–51 USA with interruptions. Trip to Arizona, New Mexico and California. 1942 Co-editor of the periodical *VVV*. 1948 Took American citizenship. Wrote the treatise *Beyond Painting*. 1949 Wrote *Paramyths*. 1949–50 Trip to Europe. 1952 At University of Hawaii. 1953 Return to Paris. 1954 Exclusion from Surrealists. 1955 Settled in Huismes in the Touraine. 1958 Took French citizenship. 1960 Trip to Germany with Patrick Waldberg. 1963 Moved to Seillans, South of France. 1964 Publication of his book *Maximiliana*.

Lyonel Feininger
New York 1871 – 1956 New York

Born Léonell Charles Feininger of German parents. 1887 Studied at the general trades school in Hamburg. 1889 First cartoons. 1889–92 Student at Berlin Academy and 1891–92 in Adolf Schablitz's studio in

Berlin. 1892 Rügen. 1892/93 Paris, worked in Filippo Colarossi's studio. 1893–1906 Berlin. Illustrator and cartoonist for German magazines and journals and *Chicago Sunday Tribune*. 1901–1904 Rügen. 1906–08 Paris, met Robert Delaunay. 1907 First paintings. 1908–17 in Berlin. 1909 Member of Berlin Secession. 1911 Paris. First encounter with Cubism. 1912 Friendship with Alfred Kubin. Met Erich Heckel and Karl Schmidt-Rottluff. First architectural compositions. 1913 First painting of Gelmeroda. 1918 Joined the *Novembergruppe*. 1919 Woodcut *Cathedral* for Bauhaus manifesto. 1919–25 Director of design in print workshop at Bauhaus in Weimar. 1921 Composed his first fugue. 1922 Met Wassily Kandinsky and Franz Marc. 1924 With Kandinsky, Paul Klee and Alexej von Jawlensky founded group *Die Blauen Vier*. 1926–32 Responsible position at Bauhaus in Dessau. 1937 Settled in New York. 1944 Friendship with Mark Tobey. First major solo exhibition in America at the Museum of Modern Art, New York. 1945 taught at Black Mountain College.

Anselm Feuerbach
Speyer 1829 – 1880 Venice

1845–48 Studied at Düsseldorf Academy under Schadow, Schirmer and Lessing. 1848–50 Munich. 1849 Joined Karl Rahl's studio. 1850/51 Studied at Antwerp Academy under Wappers. 1851–54 Paris. 1852–53 In Thomas Couture's studio. Met Gustave Courbet. 1855 With Joseph Victor von Scheffels to Venice. 1856–1873 Active mostly in Rome; numerous trips to Germany, Heidelberg and Baden-Baden. 1857 Member of the German Club of Artists in Rome. Friendship with Reinhold Begas, Ludwig Passini and Arnold Böcklin. Excursions into the Campagna, Colle Albani and Sabine Hills. 1860 First meeting with Anna Risi. 1865 Met Hermann Levi, Johannes Brahms and Conrad Fiedler in Baden-Baden. 1866 Study trip to Naples and Pompeii. 1872–77 Professors at Vienna Academy. Afterwards mostly in Venice.

Carl (Karl) von Fischer
Mannheim 1782 – 1820 Munich

1796–99 Trained under the Elector's court architect Maximilian von Verschaffelt in Munich. 1799–1806 Studied at the Vienna Academy. 1803–06 Commissioned by Pierre de Salabert to build the Prinz-Karl-Palais by the English Garden in Munich. 1808–09 In Rome, studied Renaissance architecture and the work of Palladio. 1809 Returned to Munich, professor of architecture at the Academy there, later senior building councillor. Key involvement in the general plan for Munich as a member of the building commission. 1811–18 Built the National Theatre. From 1816 he was ousted from building in Munich by Leo von Klenze. His designs for the Glyptothek and the Regensburg Walhalla were rejected in favour of Klenze's.

Caspar David Friedrich
Greifswald 1774 – 1840 Dresden

1790 Student of Johann Gottfried Quistorp, the drawing master at the University of Greifswald. 1794–98 Studied under Nicolai Abraham Abildgaard and Jens Juël at the Copenhagen Academy. Lived in Dresden after 1798. 1801 Met Philipp Otto Runge. 1801–02 Lived in Neubrandenburg, Greifswald and on the island of Rügen. 1802 Return to Dresden with Friedrich August von Klinkowström. 1806 Another trip to Neubrandenburg, Greifswald and to the island of Rügen. Acquaintance with Gotthilf Heinrich Schubert. 1807 and 1808 Trips to Northern Bohemia. 1808 Quarrel about his *Cross in the Mountains*. 1809 Trip to Greifswald and Neubrandenburg. 1810 Walking tour in the Riesengebirge with Friedrich Georg Kersting. External member of the Berlin Academy. Heinrich von Kleist's essay on his *Monk by the Sea*. 1811 Walking tour through the Harz with the sculptor Gottlieb Christian Kühn. Visited Goethe in Jena. 1815 Trip to Greifswald. 1824 Associate Professor at Dresden Academy. 1817 Met Carl Gustav Carus. 1818 Trip to Greifswald, Wolgast, Stralsund and to the island of Rügen. Met Johan Christian Clausen Dahl. 1824 Stay in Meißen.

Henry Fuseli
Zurich 1741 – 1825 Putney Hill near London

Also known as Johann Heinrich Füssli. While studying theology, influenced by Johann Jakob Bodmer, who introduced him to Homer, the *Nibelungen*, Dante, Shakespeare and Milton. Acquaintance with Klopstock, Pestalozzi and Wieland. 1761 Ordination as reformed protestant pastor. 1763 Berlin at house of the Swiss mathematician and art historian Johann Georg Sulzer. With Lavater and Hess to Swedish Pomerania to the protestant moral philosopher Johann Joachim Spalding. 1764 Move to London. 1765 Publication of his translation into English of Johann Joachim Winckelmann's *Reflections on the Painting and Sculpture of the Greeks*. 1766 Trip to Paris, met Jean-Jacques Rousseau and David Hume. 1768 Met Sir Joshua Reynolds. 1770–78 Rome. Trips to Venice. 1775 To Naples, Pompeii and Herculaneum. 1779 Return to London. 1787 Friendship with William Blake. 1801–05 and again from 1810 till his death, professor of painting at the Royal Academy, whose 'keeper' he was in 1804. 1802 Trip to Paris, where he visited the Louvre and Jacques Louis David's studio in his absence.

Hermann Glöckner
Cotta near Dresden 1889 – 1987 West Berlin

1904–07 Apprenticeship as pattern designer, Dresden. 1907–10 and 1913–20 Worked as pattern designer. 1909 Studied under Carl Rade. 1915–18 Military service. 1919 In Dresden-Neustadt. 1919/20 First abstract compositions. 1923 Studied at the Dresden Academy. 1926 Methodical experiments in the constructive structure of drawings and paintings. 1932 Joined the 'Dresden Secession'. 1935 First spatial folding of a rectangle as sculpture. 1937 Work on roll-paintings and numerous material studies done. Worked in construction and specialized in *sgraffito*. Commissions for script and decorative design. 1945 Contributed to the exhibition 'Der Ruf, Befreite Kunst', Dresden. 1951 Beginning of cooperation with Hans Hopp from the Berlin School of Architecture. 1952–54 Emphasis on activities in architecture. 1954 Trip to the Baltic Sea. 1955 Contacts with Max Bill in Ulm. After 1956 Emergence of

large-format collages and stencilled work and a concentration on sculpture. 1967 Preoccupation with colour theories of Goethe and Itten. 1977 Met Georg Muche, Lake Constance. 1979–87 Lived in West Berlin.

Johann Wolfgang von Goethe
Frankfurt 1749 – 1832 Weimar

1765–68 Studied law in Leipzig. Drawing lessons and instruction in copperplate engraving, woodcuts and etching. Studied Paracelsus's mystical essays on the philosophy of nature and carried out chemical experiments. 1770–71 Continued studies in Strasbourg. Attended lectures in medicine and surgery. 1771 *Geschichte Gottfriedens von Berlichingen mit der eisernen Hand, dramatisiert* (first version of *Götz*). 1772 *Von deutscher Baukunst* completed. 1771 *Götz von Berlichingen* (second version). First work on 'Faust'. 1774 Epistolary novel *Die Leiden des jungen Werther*; play *Clavigo*; poem 'Ganymed'. 1775 Visited Switzerland and Weimar. Produced landscape drawings and nocturnal moonlit scenes. 1776 Geological and mineralogical studies associated with his supervision of the mines in Ilmenau. 1777, 1783 and 1784 Visits to the Harz mountains. 1779 Took over the Weimar war commission and direction of road building. Appointed full privy councillor. First (prose) version of *Iphigenie*. 1782 Ennobled by Joseph II. President of the chamber of finance. 1784 Treatise on granite. 1785 First botanical studies. Finished many years of work on *Wilhelm Meisters Theatralische Sendung*. 1786–88 Italian journey. Contact with Johann Heinrich Meyer, Johann Heinrich Wilhelm Tischbein, Angelica Kauffmann, Karl Philipp Moritz. Completed verse version of *Iphigenie*. 1787 Landscape drawings. Completed *Egmont*. 1788 First meeting with Friedrich Schiller. Essay *Nachahmung der Natur, Manier, Stil*. Contact with Wilhelm von Humboldt. 1790 *Faust. Ein Fragment*. Completed *Torquato Tasso*. *Versuch, die Metamorphose der Pflanzen zu erklären*. 'Römische Elegien'. Visited Venice. 1791 Took over direction of the Weimar court theatre. Work on colour theory. 1793 Essays on colour theory; studied Isaac Newton. 1794 Visited Schiller, discussions on the primal plant. Amicable, extremely fruitful work with Schiller on his magazine *Die Horen*. 1796 Completed *Wilhelm Meisters Lehrjahre*; 'Der Sammler und die Seinigen'. 1797 Completed the epic *Hermann und Dorothea*. Contact with Friedrich Schlegel. 1798 *Die Metamorphose der Pflanzen*. Met Novalis, Johann Gottlob Fichte, Friedrich Wilhelm Joseph Schelling and Jean Paul. 1798–1800 Edited the art magazine *Die Propyläen*. 1800–05 Annual competition on a particular artistic subject, participants included Philipp Otto Runge and Peter von Cornelius. 1801 Met Georg Wilhelm Friedrich Hegel and Achim von Arnim. 1803 Founded the *Jenaische Allgemeine Literaturzeitung*. Director of the Jena library and the university's scientific institutes. 1804 Became working privy councillor, addressed as Excellency. Stage version of *Götz von Berlichingen*. 1805 Completed essay and anthology *Winckelmann und sein Jahrhundert*. From 1806 Contact with Runge about colour theory investigations. 1809 Completed *Die*

Wahlverwandtschaften and the *Farblehre*. 1810 Visited Caspar David Friedrich. Stayed with Boisserée in Heidelberg. 1815 Essay 'Kunst und Altertum am Rhein, Main und Neckar'. Met Joseph Görres. 1820 Essay 'Wolkengestalt nach Howard'. 1825 Attempt at a weather theory. 1831 Completed *Dichtung und Wahrheit* and *Faust II*.

Gotthard Graubner
Erlbach, Vogtland 1930 – lives in Düsseldorf and in Berlin, teaches in Düsseldorf and in Hamburg.

1947–48 Studied at Academy of Fine Arts in West Berlin; 1948–49 and 1951 at the Dresden Academy. 1954–59 Student at Düsseldorf Academy. 1958 Took part in the seventh evening performance of Group 'Zero'. From 1962 pillow-paintings. 1962–65 Took part in numerous exhibitions of Group 'Zero'. 1964–65 Art teacher in Düsseldorf. 1965 Gave lectures at Hamburg Academy of Fine Arts. 1968–71 Environments *Nebelräume*. After 1969 Professor of painting at Hamburg Academy. 1971 Study trips to Brazil, Columbia, Peru, and Mexico. 1973 India, Nepal, and Bhutan. Since 1976 Professor at Düsseldorf Academy.

Walter Gropius
Berlin 1883 – 1969 Boston/USA

1908–10 Worked with Peter Behrens in Berlin. 1909 Ideas on prefabricated buildings. 1910 Opened his own architect's office with Adolf Meyer in Berlin. Took over direction of the Works Council for Art. 1919–28 Director of the Academy of Art and the Schools of Applied Art, which he amalgamated to form the Staatliches Bauhaus in Weimar. 1923 Mass-produced prefabricated buildings, with Meyer. 1925–26 Designed the new Bauhaus building for Dessau. 1929–58 Vice-president of Congrès Internationaux d'Architecture Moderne (CIAM) in Zurich. 1934 Moved to London. 1934–39 Worked as private architect in England, in partnership with E. Maxwell Fry. 1937 to America. 1937–52 Professor of architecture at Harvard. 1937–41 Worked as private architect in partnership with Marcel Breuer. 1944 American citizenship. 1949–69 Partner in The Architects' Collaborative (TAC) in Cambridge, Mass.

Erich Heckel
Döbeln, Saxony 1883 – 1970 Radolfzell, Baden

1901 Friendship with Karl Schmidt-Rottluff. 1904–05 Studied architecture at Dresden Institute of Technology under Fritz Schumacher. Friendship with Ernst Ludwig Kirchner and Fritz Bleyl. 1905 Co-founder of *Die Brücke* in Dresden. Impressed by the works of Vincent van Gogh, Paul Gauguin and the Neo-Impressionists, also by Theodor Fontane, Hofmannsthal, Holz, Meyer and Friedrich Nietzsche. 1905–07 Worked in Wilhelm Kreis's architect's office in Dresden. 1906 First etchings. 1907 Dangast marshland; Schmidt-Rottluff. Series of woodcuts on *Ballad of Reading Gaol* by Oscar Wilde and his first lithograph. Return to Berlin by way of Dresden, visited Max Pechstein in Berlin. 1909 Trip to Italy. Spent summer at Moritzburg Lakes near Dresden

with Kirchner. Stayed with Schmidt-Rottluff in Dangast in autumn. 1910 Trip to Berlin; friendship with Otto Mueller. Stayed in Dangast with Schmidt-Rottluff and Max Pechstein. Spent the summer at the Moritzburg Lakes with Kirchner and Pechstein. Visited Gustav Shiefler, art collector, in Hamburg together with Kirchner. 1911 Moved to Berlin. Summer in Prerow, Pomerania and then in Moritzburg with Kirchner. 1912 Became acquainted with Christian Rohlfs and Lyonel Feininger. In the summer in Stralsund on the Hiddensee and with Kirchner on Fehmarn. Studied Fyodor Dostoevsky's works. 1913 Dissolution of *Die Brücke*. 1915–18 Medical orderly in Flanders. Met Max Beckmann and James Ensor. 1918 Return to Berlin. Co-founder of the 'Works Council on Art' with Emil Nolde, Pechstein among others. Member of 'Novembergruppe' for a short time. Trips to Germany, France and Italy. 1919 Friendship with Paul Klee. 1937 Prohibition of his exhibitions. Confiscation of his works in German museums. 1944 His Berlin studio was destroyed by fire; moved to Hemmenhofen on Lake Constance. 1949–55 Taught at Karlsruhe Academy.

Ferdinand Theodor Hildebrandt
1804 Stettin – 1874 Düsseldorf

First studied at the Berlin Academy in Friedrich Wilhelm Schadow's master class. 1826 Accompanied his teacher to Düsseldorf. 1830–31 Visited Rome with painter friends. 1831 Assistant teacher at the Düsseldorf Academy. 1844 Visited St. Petersburg. 1849 Visited Antwerp. From 1836 Heinrich Christoph Kolbe's successor as professor at the Düsseldorf Academy. 1854 Resigned as a result of emotional problems.

Ferdinand Hodler
Bern 1853 – 1918 Geneva

1867 Apprenticeship with veduta painter Ferdinand Sommer-Collier in Thun. 1871 In Geneva, produced studies after Alpine painters Alexandre Calame and François Diday. 1872 Pupil of Barthélemy Menn at the École des Beaux Arts in Geneva; attended Carl Vogt's philosophy lectures. c. 1885 Became interested in French symbolism. Shook off the influence of Corot in order to achieve the linear parallelism that became his trademark. 1891 Showed his painting *Night* in Paris. 1892 Showed his picture *Disappointed Souls*. From 1895 turned to history painting. 1897 Wall painting *Retreat of the Swiss Troops at Marignano*, intended for the armoury of the Schweizerische Landesmuseum in Zürich. 1900 Member of the Berlin Secession, and of the Munich Secession from 1903. 1904 Took part in the 'Secession' exhibition in Vienna. 1909 Completed the wall painting *Departure of the Jena students during the Wars of Liberation* for Jena university. 1914 Excluded from all German art associations because he signed a manifesto against the bombardment of Reims cathedral by German artillery.

E.T.A. Hoffmann
Königsberg 1776 – 1822 Berlin

Actually Ernst Theodor Wilhelm Hoffmann. 1792–95 Studied law in Königsberg. 1807–08 Worked in Berlin as a musician, draughtsman and literary figure. 1813 Director of music in Leipzig and Dresden. 1814 Visited Berlin, in Prussian state service again. Contact with Friedrich de la Motte-Fouqué, Adelbert von Chamisso, Ludwig Tieck. 1815 Dispatch clerk in the Ministry of Justice. Contact with Clemens von Brentano. 1816–16 Published *Die Elixire des Teufels*. 1816 Appointed councillor in the supreme court. Première of opera *Undine*. Double life as councillor and artist satirized in the uncompleted double novel *Lebensansichten des Katers Murr nebst fragmentarischer Biographie des Kapellmeisters Johannes Kreisler in zufälligen Makulaturblättern* and in the Knarrpanti episode in *Meister Floh*.

Gottlieb Heinrich Christian Hübsch
Weinhein/Bergstraße 1795 – 1863 Karlsruhe

1815–18 Studied architecture under Friedrich Weinbrenner in Karlsruhe. 1822 Publication of his essays 'Athen mit seinen Denkmalen' (Athens with its monuments) and 'Über griechische Architektur' (On Greek architecture), a polemic against Aloys Ludwig Hirt. 1823 Publication of this treatise *Architektonische Verzierungen für Künstler und Handwerker* (Artistic decorations for artists and craftsmen). 1824 Appointed teacher in the School of Architecture at the Städel Institute in Frankfurt am Main. 1827 Residence architect in Karlsruhe. 1828 Published his essay 'In welchem Style sollen wir bauen?' (In what style should we build?), a plea for the use of round arches and vaults. 1832–53 Director of the School of Building in the Polytechnic Institute. 1837 Visited Italy via Munich. 1847 Publication of his essay 'Die Architektur und ihr Verhältnis zur heutigen Malerei und Skulptur' (Architecture and its relationship to contemporary painting and sculpture). His works include numerous churches, the Ministry of Finance in Karlsruhe, the Trinkhalle in Baden-Baden (1837–40), the first council chamber in Karlsruhe (1839–41, with pictures by Moritz von Schwind), the Academy in Karlsruhe (1840–49), the theatre in Karlsruhe (1851–53), renovation of the west façade of Speyer cathedral (1854–58), refurbishment and extension of the Minster in Constance (1846–52).

Johannes Itten
Südern-Linden/Bernese Oberland 1888 – 1967 Zurich

1906–1910 Trained as primary school teacher and art teacher. 1910–12 Studied mathematics and science at Bern university. 1913–16 Studied at Stuttgart Academy of Art under Adolf Hölzel. Start of friendship with Willi Baumeister, Oskar Schlemmer. 1916–19 Vienna, own art school there. 1917 Friendship with Alma Mahler and contacts with Alban Berg, Arnold Schoenberg. Studied Indian and far-eastern philosophy of religion, and theosophy from 1918. 1919–22 Director of the foundation course at the Bauhaus in Weimar. 1923–26 Founded the Ontos workshops for weaving in Zurich. 1926–34 Own art school in Berlin. 1928 Discovery of 'subjective colours'. From 1931 Director of Textile Art in Krefeld, and Zurich 1943–60. 1952–56 Director of the Rietberg Museum in Zurich. 1955 Taught at the Hochschule für Gestaltung in Ulm.

1960 Took part in the 'Concrete Art' Exhibition in Zurich. 1961 Publication of his *Kunst der Farbe* and in 1963 *Mein Vorkurs am Bauhaus, Gestaltungs- und Formlehre*.

Victor Emil Janssen
Hamburg 1807 – 1845 Hamburg

Originally a pupil of Siegfried Detlev Benixen in Hamburg. 1827–33 Studied at the Munich Academy under Peter von Cornelius. 1833–35 In Rome as a scholarship holder, close contact with Friedrich Wasmann. 1835 Back to Munich. Assisted Heinrich Heß on the frescoes in St. Bonifatius. 1843 Returned to Hamburg for health reasons.

Wassily Wassilewitsch Kandinsky
Moscow 1866 – 1944 Neuilly-sur-Seine near Paris

1886–93 Studied law and economics at the University of Moscow. 1893 Research assistant, University of Moscow. 1896–98 Attended Anton Azbè's School of Painting in Munich. 1897 Met Alexej von Jawlensky, Marianne von Werefkin, Dimitri Kardovsky and Igor Grabar. 1900 Studied at the Art Academy, Munich, under Franz Stuck. 1901 Co-founder and president of 'Phalanx' group. 1902 Met Gabriele Münter. 1903–06 Trips to Holland, Tunisia, Italy, France and Odessa. 1906 Moved to Sèvres near Paris. 1907–08 Berlin. 1908 Munich. Met composer Thomas von Hartmann. In Murnau with Jawlensky, Werefkin and Münter. 1909 Co-founder and president of 'New Association of Artists, Munich'. 1910 Met Franz Marc. Participated in 'Karo-Bube' (Jack of Diamonds) exhibition in Moscow. The first *Composition* created. 1911 Beginning of his friendship with Arnold Schoenberg and Paul Klee. Left 'New Association of Artists' with Marc, Münter and Alfred Kubin. First exhibition of *Der Blaue Reiter*: Publication of *On the Spiritual in Art*. 1912 Second *Blaue Reiter* exhibition in Munich and the publication of almanac. 1913 Participated in the 'International Exhibition of Modern Art' in New York, Chicago and Boston and in the 'Erster Deutscher Herbstsalon' (First German Autumn Salon) in Berlin. 1914 Return to Russia. 1915–16 In Sweden. 1918 Member of People's Commissariat for Cultural Education, director of Free State-Run Art Workshops, honorary professor at University of Moscow. 1920 Taught in Moscow. 1921 Co-founder and vice-president of the Russian Academy of Art. Return to Berlin. 1922–33 at Bauhaus in Weimar, Dessau and Berlin. 1924 Member of *Die blauen Vier* group with Feininger, Jawlensky and Paul Klee. 1926 Publication of *Point and Line to Plane*. 1928 German citizenship. 1930 The beginning of his connection with *Cercle et Carré* group. 1933 Move to Neuilly-sur-Seine. 1934 Met Joan Miró, Piet Modrian, Alberto Magnelli and the renewal of his friendship with Hans Arp. Participated in the events of *Abstraction-Création* group. 1939 French citizenship.

Alexander Kanoldt
Karlsruhe 1881 – 1939 Berlin

1899–1901 Studied at Karlsruhe School for Arts and Crafts. 1901–06 Karlsruhe Art Academy. 1903–04 Military service. 1908

First contact with circle of artists around Wassily Kandinsky and Alexej von Jawlensky. 1909 Munich. Joined 'New Artists' Association Munich'. 1911–12 Trips to Dalmatia, Southern Tyrol, London. 1913 Founding member of the 'New Munich Secession'. 1914–18 Active service. 1918–21 Munich. 1921–31 Pasing. 1924 Longer stays in Olevano/Italy. 1925 Took part in the 'Neue Sachlichkeit' exhibition in Mannheim. 1925–31 Professorship at the Breslau Academy of Arts and Crafts. 1927 Founding member of 'Baden Secession' in Freiburg/Breisgau. 1931 Move to Garmisch. Opening of his own private painting school. 1932 Membership in the NSDAP. Participation in the 'Die Sieben' (The Seven) exhibition in Barmen and other places with Franz Lenk, Georg Schrimpf, Franz Radziwill, Hasso von Hugo, Adolf Dietrich and Theo Campion. 1933 Took part in the 'Neue Deutsche Romantik' exhibition in Hanover. 1933–36 Director of the Academy of Fine Arts in Berlin-Schöneberg.

Georg Friedrich Kersting
Güstrow 1785 – 1847 Meißen

1805–08 At Copenhagen Academy under Jens Juël, Nicolai Abraham Abildgaard and Carl Adolf Lorentzen. 1808 Dresden. Friendship with Friedrich, Dahl, Carus and Kügelgen. 1810 Hike through the Riesengebirge with Friedrich. Teaches drawing at Dresden Academy. 1811 Trip to the Harz. 1813–15 Rifleman in Liberation Wars. 1816–18 Taught drawing to Princess Sapieha, Warsaw. 1818 Director of painters at Meißen factory. 1822 In Berlin. 1824 In Weimar with Goethe and Nuremberg. 1844 back in Berlin.

Anselm Kiefer
Donaueschingen 1945 – lives and works in Barjac, Southern France

1963–66 Trips to France, Italy, Sweden and the Netherlands. 1965 Studied law and Romance languages and literature in Freiburg/Breisgau. 1966–68 Studied painting under Peter Dreher in Freiburg. 1969 Continued his studies in Karlsruhe under Horst Antes and 1970–72 under Joseph Beuys, Düsseldorf. 1971 Move to Buchen in the Odenwald. From 1976 Complete secrecy of private life. 1984 Trip to Israel. 1992 Moved to New York. Since 1993 lives in Barjac, South of France.

Ernst Ludwig Kirchner
Aschaffenburg 1880 – 1938 Frauenkirch-Wildboden near Davos, Switzerland

Pseudonym: Louis de Marsalle. 1901–05 Studied architecture in Dresden with diploma in engineering. Friendship with Fritz Bleyl and Erich Heckel. 1903 Impressed by beam carvings of Palau islanders in the Ethnological Museum in Dresden. In October study trip to Nuremberg, there impressed by Albrecht Dürer's wood engravings. 1903–04 Munich, continues studies under Anton Hess and Paul Pfann, and under Wilhelm von Debschitz, Hermann Obrist and Hugo Steiner-Prag. 1905 Founded *Brücke* group with Heckel, Bleyl and Karl Schmidt-Rottluff in Dresden. 1906 Wrote group's programme. 1908 Summer on Fehmarn. 1909 Summer with Heckel at Moritzburg Lakes. 1910 Moritzburg Lakes with Max

Pechstein, Heckel and his favourite models Fränzi and Marzella. Met art collector, Gustav Schiefler, and founder of Folkwang Museum in Essen, Ernst Osthaus, also Otto Mueller. 1911 With Mueller in Mnischek/Bohemia; with Heckel at Moritzburg lakes. Move to Berlin. Foundation of the 'MUIM-Institute' (modern teaching in painting) with Max Pechstein in Berlin. 1912 Took part in the exhibitions of the *Blaue Reiter* in Munich and Berlin. 1912–14 Summer stays on Fehmarn. 1913 Break-up of *Die Brücke*. Break with Pechstein and closing of the 'MUIM-Institute'. 1915 Military service. Autumn, *Self-portrait as a Soldier*; woodcuts for Adelbert von Chamisso's *Peter Schlemihls wundersame Geschichte*. 1916 Sanatoriums in Königstein/ Taunus and Berlin with nervous breakdown worsened by alcohol and narcotics. 1917 Move to Davos. Acquaintance with Henry van de Velde. 1917–18 In sanatorium in Kreuzlingen, Switzerland. 1920 Began writing about his own art under pseudonym 'Louis de Marsalle'. 1923–38 Frauenkirch-Wildboden. 1934 Visits Oskar Schlemmer. Acquaintance with Paul Klee. 1938 Suicide.

Paul Klee
Münchenbuchsee near Berne, Switzerland 1879 – 1940 Muralto-Locarno

1808–1901 Attended Heinrich Knirr's School of Drawing, Munich. 1899 Etching lessons from Walter Ziegler in Burghausen. 1900–01 Studied at art academy there under Franz Stuck. 1901–02 Italy with sculptor Hermann Haller; Naples and trips to Pompeii, Sorrento and Amalfi. 1902–06 Berne. Trips to Munich, Berlin and Paris. Engagements as a violinist and music critic. 1903–05 Made the series of etchings called *Inventions*. 1904 Studied illustrations by Aubrey Beardsley, William Blake and Goya at the Staatliche Graphische Sammlung in Munich. 1906 Moved to Munich. 1908 Member of the Association of Swiss Graphic Artists 'Die Walze' (The Roller). Participated in exhibition of 'Munich Secession' and 'Berlin Secession'. 1911 Beginning of his friendship with Alfred Kubin. Met August Macke, Wassily Kandinsky. Charter member of 'Sema' group, which Alfred Kubin also belonged to. 1912 Met Alexej von Jawlensky and Marianne von Werefkin. Member of *Der Blaue Reiter* and participated in its second exhibition in Munich. Trip to Paris, visited Robert Delaunay. Began friendship with Franz Marc. 1914 Went to Tunis with August Macke and Louis Moilliet. Charter member of the 'New Secession' in Munich and its chairman from 1918–20. 1916–18 Military service. 1919 Member of the Council of Artists in Munich and of the 'Committee of Revolutionary Artists' in Munich. In Zurich, contacts with Dada group: Hans Arp, Hans Richter and Tristan Tzara. 1920 Publication of his essays *Creative Confession* and *Colour as Science*. 1920–31 Teacher at Bauhaus in Weimar and Dessau. 1921 Beginning of his *Contributions to Sculptural Form*. 1923 Publication of his essay 'Ways of Nature Study.' 1924 Foundation of *Die Blauen Vier* with Kandinsky, Jawlensky and Lionel Feininger. 1925 Published his *Pedagogical Sketchbook*. Participated in first Surrealist exhibition in Paris. 1928 Published his essay 'Exact Experiments in the Field of Art'. In Berlin.

Met Emil Nolde. Trips to Egypt and Italy. 1931 Professorship at the Düsseldorf Art Academy and 1933 dismissal. Moved to Switzerland. Visited Ernst Ludwig Kirchner.

Leo von Klenze
Schladen in the Harz Mountains 1784 – 1864 Munich

1800 Studied law, Berlin. Met architect Friedrich Gilly. 1800–03 Studied architecture in Berlin under Adolf Hirt. Friendship with Karl Friedrich Schinkel. 1803 Further education in Paris. Trip to southern France and Genoa. 1804–13 Court master-builder of King Jérôme in Kassel. 1806/07 Rome, Naples and Venice. 1812–15 Building of the theatre in the Palace of Wilhelmshöhe. 1813/14 Paris. 1814 Vienna and Munich, meets Crown Prince Ludwig of Bavaria. 1816 Munich. First plans for the Sculpture Gallery. 1818 Rome with Crown Prince Ludwig, met Deutsch-Römer. 1820–25 Director of court construction in Munich. 1823–24 Sicily and Paestum to study Antique architecture. 1823–31 Munich. The gate to the Hofgarten, Ministry of War, Odeon, the arcades to the Hofgarten, Sculpture Gallery. 1825 Royal Building Counsellor. 1834 Trip to Greece on the behalf of King Ludwig I to save the Greek antiquities. 1836 Munich. Finishing of the Residence, Pinakothek and Court Church. 1838 Design for Museum of Fine Arts and antiquities wing in Hermitage, Petersburg. In Bavaria; building of Maximilian Straße. 1839–1852 Numerous trips to Russia, Greece, Italy and to Switzerland. 1846–60 Building of the Propyläen. 1853 Partially relieved of official duties. 1959 Retirement. Klenze was also active as a landscape and veduta painter.

Max Klinger
Leipzig 1857 – 1920 Großjena near Naumburg

1874 Studies under Ludwig Coudres and Karl Gussow at the Karlsruhe Academy. 1875–77 Continued under Gussow at Berlin Academy of Arts. 1876–77 Military service. 1879 Studied in Brussels, under Emile Charles Wauters. 1881 Studio in Berlin. Friendship with Karl Stauffer-Bern, who interested him in engraving. 1882 Member of the Club of Berlin Artists. 1883–86 Studio in Paris. 1883–1907 Trips to Italy, France, Greece, Spain and Netherlands. 1887 Berlin, acquaintance with Arnold Böcklin. 1888–1890 Member of Munich Academy. 1891 Publication of his treatise Painting and Drawing. 1892 Co-founder of 'Eleven' in Berlin. 1893 Settled in Leipzig. 1894 Member of Berlin Academy. Visited Johannes Brahms in Vienna. 1897 Professorship in Leipzig. Acquaintance with Gustav Mahler and Alma Mahler-Werfel. 1903 Second home in Großjena. Vice-president of the newly founded German Association for Artists in Weimar. 1906 Chairman of the Villa-Romana-Club, in Leipzig.

Joseph Anton Koch
Obergibeln, Tirol 1768 – 1839 Rome

1792–83 Trained under sculptor Martin Ignaz Ingerl in Augsburg. 1785 Student of Philipp Friedrich Haper at Hohe Karlsschule in Stuttgart, went to Strasbourg, then Basle and Switzerland, where he was impressed by the Alpine scenery. 1795–1839 Lived in Rome. In contact with Jacob Asmus Carstens, friends with Bertel Thorwaldsen, Christian Gottlieb Schick and Johann Christian Reinhart, later worked with Nazarenes. 1796–98 Took lessons from Reinhart. 1812–15 in Vienna. 1825–28 Frescoes in Dante Room of Casino Massimo. Most important illustrator of Dante in nineteenth century.

Carl Wilhelm Kolbe the Elder
Berlin 1759 – 1835 Dessau

From 1789 contact with his relation and benefactor Daniel Chodowiecki. From 1793 turned exclusively to drawing. His subjects were the oak forests around Dessau, hence his later nickname 'Eiche (oak) Kolbe'. 1790–95 Studied at the Berlin Academy under Jakob Asmus Carstens and Johann Wilhelm Meil the Younger. 1792 Return to Dessau. Full member of the Berlin Academy. 1796–1828 Teacher of drawing in Dessau. 1798 Court copperplate engraver to Duke Leopold Friedrich of Anhalt-Dessau. 1805–07 in Zürich, to engrave Geßner's legacy of gouaches. 1808–35 Lived in Dessau.

Gustav Friedrich Kraus
Passau 1804 – 1852 Munich

From 1824 in Munich; studied at the Academy there under Wilhelm von Kobell until 1826. 1836 Bought a property in Munich and founded a publishing house; became a citizen of Munich. Produced lithograph for the great procession to celebrate the 25th wedding anniversary of King Ludwig I and Queen Therese. 1838 Pictorial reporter at the Augsburg military encampment. 1840 Drawings and lithographs of scenes from the two great military encampments at Nuremberg and Heilbronn. 1848 Member of the artists' voluntary corps. Pictures of revolutionary unrest.

Alfred Leopold Isidor Kubin
Leitmeritz/northern Bohemia 1877 – 1959 Zwickledt/Upper Austria

1887 Mother died. 1891–92 Apprenticeship at the State Craft School in Salzburg.1892–96 Apprentice photographer in Klagenfurt. 1896 Attempted suicide at his mother's grave. 1897 Military service, cut short by a severe nervous disorder. 1892 Brief attendance at Nikolaus Gysis's 'nature class' at the Munich Academy of Art. Impressed by Max Klinger's cycle of etchings Paraphrase über den Fund eines Handschuhs. 1903 Contact with Edvard Munch in Berlin. 1904 Participated in the exhibition by the Phalanx association of artists in Munich. Met Klinger in Leipzig. 1906 To Paris, visited Odilon Redon. Contact with Alexej von Jawlensky and Marianne von Werefkin. 1907 Death of his father. 1907/08 Severe depression. 1908 Illustrations for Edgar Allen Poe story. Wrote novel Die andere Seite. 1909 Work on second volume of Poe illustrations. 1909–11 with the Neue Künstlervereinigung München. Close contact with Wassily Kandinsky. 1919 Illustrations for Wilhem Hauff's Fairy Tales. Contact with Paul Klee. 1911 Contact with Lyonel Feininger. 1912 Took part in the second Blaue Reiter exhibition in Munich, 'Schwarz-Weiß'.

Started work for magazine Simplicissimus. Friendly contact with Franz Marc. 1913 Took part in the Erster Deutscher Herbstsalon, Berlin. Appearance of his illustrations for E.T.A. Hoffmann's Nachtstücke and Fyodor Dostoevsky's 'The Double'. 1916 Buddhist crisis, brought about by Marc's death in the war and the suicide of Ernst Sonderegger's wife. 1922 Visited the Prinzhorn collection in Heidelberg, which inspired the essay 'Die Kunst des Irren'. 1924 Essay on art theory 'Rhythmus und Konstruktion' appears. 1932 Completed illustrations for Strindberg's 'Tschandala'. 1933 Publication of his essays 'Dämmerungswelten' and 'Malerei des Übersinnlichen'. 1936 Took part in the Fantastic Art, Dada and Surrealism exhibition in New York.

Franz Lenk
Langenbernsdorf, Vogtland 1898 – 1968 Schwäbisch Hall

1912 Training as interior decorator. 1912–15 Apprenticeship as lithographer. 1915–24 Studied at the Dresden Academy under Richard Müller, Ludwig von Hofmann. 1922 Studied under Ferdinand Dorsch and Robert Sterl. 1916–18 Military service. 1925 Took part in the last exhibition of the 'Secession Group 1919' in Dresden. 1925–31 Studio in Lausa. 1926 Move to Berlin. Teaching position at Berlin Academy. Trips to Amrum, to the Vogtland, Rothschönberg and 1928 to Thuringia. 1930 To the Neckarbergland, Danube valley, Hegau, and Lake Constance. 1932 Took part in touring exhibition of 'The Seven' with Alexander Kanoldt, Georg Schrimpf, Franz Radziwill, Hasso von Hugo, Adolf Dietrich and Theo Champion. Studio in Berlin-Charlottenburg. 1933–37 Professorship at Berling-Schöneberg art school. Friendship with Georg Schrimpf. 1936 Member of board of Berlin Secession. 1937 Admitted to Prussian Academy of Arts. 1938 Gave up teaching post in protest against the persecution of colleagues by the Third Reich. Move to Orlamünde in Thuringia. 1944 more moves to Wilhelmsdorf near Ravensburg and then to Fellbach near Stuttgart. 1959 Move to Schwäbisch Hall where he is put in charge of cultural affairs for the city.

Carl Friedrich Lessing
Breslau 1808 – 1880 Karlsruhe

Great-nephew of Gotthold Ephraim Lessing. 1882 Joined the Berlin School of Architecture, directed by Karl Friedrich Schinkel; drawing lessons under Ferdinand Collmann, Heinrich Anton Dähling and Johann Gottlob Samuel Rösel at Berlin Academy. Broke off his studies at School of Architecture after a trip to Rügen. 1826 Met Wilhelm von Schadow through Carl Ferdinand Sohn. Studied under Schadow. 1827 Founding of Landschaftlicher Componirverein with Johann Wilhelm Schirmer. 1832 Trip to Eifel. 1833 Moved into his own studio in Düsseldorf Academy. 1836 Trip to Harz Mountains. 1846 Refusal of a professorship for historical and landscape painting in Frankfurt. 1848 Founding member of Malkasten (painting box) club, Düsseldorf. 1858 Gallery appointment, Karlsruhe. 1863–66 Artistic director of Karlsruhe Art School. 1878 Trip to Harz Mountains. Although not a member of the staff of the Düsseldorf Academy he had lasting influence on students there.

Ludwig I of Bavaria
Strasbourg 1786 – 1868 Nice

King of Bavaria 1825–48. Son and successor of Maximilian I. 1806–09 Fought for Napoleon I. 1810 Married Princess Thérès of Sachsen-Hilburghausen. 1813 Commander-in-chief in charge of armaments. Repeated journeys to Rome, close contact there with Johann Friedrich Overbeck, Peter von Cornelius, Julius Schnorr von Carolsfeld etc. 1818 Encouraged implementation of liberal constitution; enthusiastic supporter of the Greek War of Liberation (his second son Otto became King of Greece in 1832). 1825 Accession to throne. Summoned scholars and artists to Munich. 1825 Moved the state university from Landshut to Munich. Reorganized the Academy of Art. Built a great deal: Odeon, Royal Residence, Basilika, All Saints' church, the Ludwigskirche and the Marienkirche in the suburb of Au, Hall of Fame, Feldherrnhalle, Siegestor, library, university, Glyptothek, art exhibition buildings, Propyläum, Walhalla near Regensburg, Hall of Fame and Hall of Liberation on the Michaelsberg near Kelheim, improvements to the cathedrals of Bamberg, Regensburg and Speyer. Increasingly reactionary trends in his politics after 1830.

Heinz Mack
Lollar, Hessen 1931 – lives and works in Mönchengladbach and Ibiza.

1950–53 Trained as art teacher at Düsseldorf Academy. 1956–58 Met Georges Mathieu, Jean Tinguely and Yves Klein in Paris. Development of 'Dynamic Structures' in painting and drawing. 1956–64 Art teacher in Düsseldorf. 1957–60 Together with Otto Piene organized evening exhibitions, the origin of the 'Zero' Group. 1958 First 'Light-Reliefs' and 'Light cubes'. Publisher of the Zero-catalogue-journal, Volume I and Vol. II. 1958–59 Emergence of the Sahara project from the idea of a vibrating light column in the desert. 1959 Together with Piene organized exhibition 'Dynamo I' in Wiesbaden. Met Günther Uecker. Through Piero Manzoni met Lucio Fontana. Took part in the exhibition 'Vision in Motion – Motion in Vision' in Antwerp organized by Tinguely, Daniel Spoerri and others. From 1961 on with Piene and Günther Uecker numerous Zero-performances. 1962–63 Morocco and Algeria. First light experiments in desert. 1963 Last painting 'painted' on canvas. 1964 Trip to Djourbel in Senegal, where he created two 'Waterwalls'. 1964–65 Studio in New York. Met Barnett Newmann. 1966 Last joint 'Zero' exhibition with Piene and Uecker in Bonn. Organized 'Zero' festival in Rolandseck station for the end of the 'Zero' era. 1967 Moved to Huppertzhof in Mönchengladbach. Edited Mackazins. 1968 Member of Berlin Academy. Stage sets for Opera House, Düsseldorf. 1974 Took part in the first North–South expedition through the Tenere desert in Africa. 1977 Publication of das Silber meine Farbe ist. Numerous trips: Tunisian Desert 1968, New York 1969, Japan 1970, Africa 1974, Egypt, Greenland 1976, Aegean Islands 1977, Morocco, Greece, East India 1979, Egypt 1982. From 1990 on studio on Ibiza.

Franz Moriz Wilhelm Marc
Munich 1880 – 1916 killed in action, Verdun

1900–03 Training at the Munich Academy of Arts under Gabriel Hackl and Wilhelm von Dietz. 1901 Trip to Venice, Padua and Verona. 1903 Paris with Friedrich Lauer. 1905 Met animal painter Jean Bloé Niestlé. 1907 Again in Paris, impressed by the works of Vincent van Gogh and Paul Gauguin. 1910 Friendship with August Macke. Move to Sindelsdorf/Upper Bavaria. Joined the 'New Association of Artists, Munich'. 1911 Met Alexej von Jawlensky and Marianne von Werefkin. Co-initiator of treatise *Fighting for Art*. Founded *Der Blaue Reiter* with Wassily Kandinsky and organized first exhibition with this name. 1912 In Berlin, contacts with the painters of the *Brücke*. Publication of the *Der Blaue Reiter* almanac with Kandinsky. With Macke to Paris, met Robert Delaunay. 1913 Trip to Southern Tyrol. Helped organize First German Autumn Salon in Berlin. 1914 Move to Ried near Benediktbeuren. Military Service.

Johann Hans Reinhard von Marées
Elberfeld (near Wuppertal) 1837 – 1887 Rome

1883 Attended Eduard Holbein's preparatory class for the Berlin Academy. 1854–55 Trained in Atelier Steffeck in Berlin. 1855–56 Military service. 1857 Moved to Munich. Acquaintance with Karl Raup, Wilhelm Bode, Franz von Lenbach, Heinrich Lang etc. 1864 Acquaintance with Graf Schack, who sent him to Florence and Rome. Met Arnold Böcklin. 1865 Visited Florence, then Adolf von Hildebrand there. 1866 In Rome, contact with Conrad Fiedler. 1867 Friendship with Adolf von Hildebrand. 1869 with Fiedler to Spain, France, Belgium and Holland. 1870 Military service. Moved to Berlin, then to Dresden in 1972. 1873 Travelled to Naples via Vienna, frescoes there with Hildebrand for Anton Dohrn's Stazione Zoologica. 1874–75 Stayed with Hildebrand in the S. Francesco di Paola monastery in Florence. 1875 Rift with Hildebrand. Moved to Rome. 1878 Programmatic picture *Die Lebensalter* (*Orangenbild*) (Ages of Man; Orange picture), 1879 Started the *Die Hesperiden* (The Garden of the Hesperides) triptych, the right-hand panel led to the *Goldenes Zeitalter I* (Golden Age I). 1882 First sculpture. 1887 Completed the 'Entführung des Ganymed' (Abduction of Ganymede).

Oskar Martin-Amorbach
Amorbach/Odenwald 1907 – 1987 Roßholzen/Allgäu

Real name: Oskar Martin. 1924 Studied at Munich School of Arts and Crafts. Turned to church painting. Member of the *Die Welle* artists' association. 1929 Paintings in the Jesuit church in Pullach and the Redemptorist church in Munich. 1939 Professorship. 1943 Appointed to Berlin Academy of Fine Art to teach history painting. After 1945 returned to Franconia. Restored frescoes destroyed in the war. Designed façades for industrial buildings and private houses in sgraffito, plasterwork, stone mosaic and stucco relief. From 1960 painted mainly portraits and landscapes.

Karl Julius Milde
Hamburg 1803 – 1875 Lübeck

1824 Attended Dresden Academy. 1825 With Erwin Speckter to Munich, attended the Academy there. 1826 and 1830–32 in Rome. Subsequently settled in Hamburg as a portrait painter. Worked as a painter, glass-painter and etcher in Lübeck from 1838.

Paula Modersohn-Becker, née Becker
Dresden 1876 – 1907 Worpswede

1892 Drawing lessons with Bernhard Wiegandt in Bremen and at a private art school in London. 1893–95 Trained as teacher in Bremen. 1896–98 Studied with 'Society of Women Artists in Berlin'. 1897 Visited Fritz Mackensen in Worpswede; lived there since 1898. Friendship with Clara Westhoff. Trip to Leipzig and visited Max Klinger; also trips to Vienna, Copenhagen and Oslo. 1900 First trip to Paris. Studied at the Académie Colarossi. Met Emil Nolde and became friends with Rainer Maria Rilke. 1901 Married Otto Modersohn. 1903 in Paris, again drawing courses at the Académie Colarossi. Visited Auguste Rodin. Returned to Worpswede. 1904 Met Louis Moilliet. 1905 Back in Paris. Studied at the Académie Julian. Visited Edouard Vuillard and Maurice Denis. Visited Carl Hauptmann in Schreiberhau. Met Otto Mueller. 1906–07 Last stay in Paris; took courses at the Ecole des Beaux-Arts. Impressed by the works of Paul Cézanne and Paul Gauguin.

Otto Mueller
Liebau, Riesengebirge 1874 – 1930 Obernigk near Breslau

1890 Apprenticeship as a lithographer in Görlitz. 1894–96 Attended Dresden Academy of Arts. 1896–97 In Liebau. Trips to Switzerland and to Italy with Gerhart Hauptman. 1898–99 Studied in Munich, under Franz von Stuck; return to Dresden. 1903–04 Met Paula Modersohn-Becker. 1908 Berlin. Met Wilhelm Lehmbruck and Rainer Maria Rilke. Summer sojourn on Fehrmarn. 1910 Co-founder of New Secession in Berlin. Member of *Brücke*. 1911 Bohemia with Ernst Ludwig Kirchner and together with Erich Heckel to the Moritzburg Lakes. 1912 Several exhibitions with the *Blaue Reiter* in Berlin. Left 'New Secession' in Berlin. 1913 Disbandment of the *Brücke*. Summer sojourn with Kirchner on Fehrmarn. 1916–18 Military Service and hospitalization. 1919–20 Professorship at Breslau Academy of Arts. From 1924 trips to the Balkans.

Ernst Wilhelm Nay
Berlin 1902 – 1968 Cologne

1925–28 Studied at Berlin Academy of Fine Arts under Carl Hofer. 1928 Trip to Paris; enthusiastic about the works of Nicolas Poussin. 1930 On the Danish island of Bornholm. 1931–32 Rome. Surrealist-abstract paintings. 1934–36 Summers in Pomerania. 1937 Guest of Edvard Munch in Norway and on the Lofoten Islands. 1938 Back on Lofoten Islands and trip to Romsdalen, Norway. 1939 Bulgaria. 1940–45 Military service. 1945 Studio destroyed. Move to Hofheim, Taunus. Until 1948 mythical-magical 'Hecate' paintings; from 1949–51 'Abstract-figurative' paintings. 1951–68 Lived in Cologne. 1952 Beginning of the 'Rhythmic paintings'. 1953

Visiting lecturer at the State Art School in Hamburg. 1954 Summer in Denmark. 1955 Beginning of the *Scheibenbilder* period. First one-man exhibition in USA. Publication of his theoretical treatise *Vom Gestaltwert der Farbe*. 1956 Member of Berlin Academy of Arts. 1957–58 Paris. 1959, 1963 and 1966 Trips to USA. 1963 Beginning of the *Augenbilder* (Eye paintings); 1965 The period of the late paintings.

Eugen Napoleon Neureuther
Munich 1806 – 1882 Munich

First training with his father, the painter Ludwig Neureuther, then under Wilhelm von Kobell in Munich. 1825–30 In Peter Cornelius's team of assistants for the frescoes in the Munich Glyptothek, worked on the arabesque framing. From 1826 illustrated Goethe's poems; start of a correspondence with Goethe. 1829–32 Lithographic marginal drawings for Goethe's *Balladen und Romanzen*. 1830 To Paris, studies for his illustrations of the July Revolution. 1836–37 In Rome. 1841 Founded the 'Münchner Radierklub' (Munich etching club) 1847–56 Artistic director of the Nymphenburg porcelain factory. 1868–76 Professor of decorative painting at the Munich School of Arts and Crafts.

Emil Nolde
Nolde, Northern Schleswig 1867 – 1956 Seebüll, Northern Schleswig

Born Emil Hansen. 1884–88 Apprenticeship as a furniture designer and carver in the Sauermann Woodcarving School in Flensburg. 1888–91 Designer and carver in several furniture factories in Munich, Karlsruhe and Berlin. 1889 Attended the Karlsruhe College of Commercial Art. 1892–97 Taught at Industrial and Commercial Museum in St Gallen. Trips to Milan, Vienna and Munich. 1898–99 Studied under Friedrich Fehr in Munich and Adolf Hölzel in Dachau. 1899–1900 Studied at the Académie Julian in Paris, many visits to the Louvre. 1900–01 in Copenhagen. 1902 Artist's name 'Emil Nolde'. Studio in Berlin. 1903–16 Moved to island of Alsen; spent the winter months in Berlin. 1904–05 in Italy. Met art collector, Gustav Schiefler. 1906–07 Member of *Die Brücke*. On island of Alsen with Karl Schmidt-Rottluff. Met Edvard Munch. 1908 Member of 'Berlin Secession'. 1909 Moved to Ruttebühl. 1910 First religious paintings. Exclusion from the Berlin Secession. Co-founder of the 'New Secession'. 1911 Visited James Ensor in Ostend. Studied at the Ethnological Museum in Berlin. 1912 Participated in the exhibition of *Der Blaue Reiter* in Munich. 1913–14 Trip to New Guinea as member of an expedition. 1916 Moved to Utenwarf. 1918 Co-founder of the 'Works Council on Art' with Max Pechstein, Erich Heckel among others. 1920 Danish citizenship. 1921 Trips to England, Spain and France. 1925 Went to Italy. 1927 Moved to Northern Schleswig; winter stays in Berlin. 1931 Publication of first volume *My Life*. Member of the Art Academy in Berlin. 1934 Publication of second volume of autobiography *Years of Struggle*. 1937 Visited Paul Klee in Bern. 1941 Banned from painting and exhibiting. 1956 Establishment of the 'Seebüll Ada and Emil Nolde' Foundation. His former residence is now a museum.

Richard Oelze
Magdeburg 1900 – 1980 Posteholz/Weserbergland

1914–18 Trained as lithographer. Studied life drawing at the Magdeburg School of Arts and Crafts. 1921–25 Student at the Bauhaus in Weimar; studied under Johannes Itten, worked for a time in Paul Klee's studio, in the stage workshop and on photography. 1926 Dresden Academy of Art under Otto Dix and Richard Müller. Friendship with Will Grohmann and Gret Palucca. Briefly at the Bauhaus in Dessau, subsequently taught at Johannes Itten's Moderne Kunstschule Berlin. Worked with Walter Peterhans and Hans Richter on photography and film. 1929–30 Ascona. 1930–33 Berlin. 1933–36 Paris. Friendship with Max Ernst, René Crevel, Tristan Tzara, Thea Sternheim and Mina Loy. Took part in the international Surrealist exhibition in London and New York. 1936–38 Ascona and Positano. 1938 Returned to Germany. 1939 Settled in Worpswede. 1940–45 War service, prisoner of war. 1945–62 Worpswede. 1962 Moved to Posteholz.

Daniel Joseph Ohlmüller
Bamberg 1791 – 1839 Munich

1815 Competition design for the Valhalla (monumental centrally-planned building). 1815–19 Study visit to Italy, Florence, Rome and Naples. 1819–30 Supervised the building of the Glyptothek under Leo von Klenze.

Johann Heinrich Ferdinand Olivier
Dessau 1785 – 1841 Munich

Brother of Friedrich and Heinrich. Came to art through Carl Wilhelm Kolbe. 1804–07 With brother Heinrich in Dresden. 1807–10 Started with the diplomatic mission in Paris. Studies of work by Raphael in the Musée Napoléon, with Heinrich. First picture in the Nazarene style for the church in Wörlitz. 1810 Returned to Dessau. Travelled in the Harz mountains with his brother Friedrich. 1811 With Friedrich to Vienna, met Joseph Anton Koch there. Friendship with Julius Schnorr von Carolsfeld. 1812 Deeper devotion to Protestantism, but remained friendly with the circle around Schlegel and the Catholic Nazarenes. 1816 Accepted as member of the Lukasgilde. 1823 Lithographs *Seven areas from Salzburg and Berchtesgaden after the seven days of the week, connected by two allegorical sheets*. 1825 First ideal landscapes. 1830 Moved to Munich. From 1833 general secretary of the Munich Academy and professor of art history.

Woldemar Friedrich Olivier
Dessau 1791 – 1859 Dessau

Brother of Ferdinand and Heinrich. Turned to painting after training under Dessau court sculptor Friedemann Hunold. 1817 Visited Salzburg and district with his brother Ferdinand and Julius Schnorr von Carolsfeld. 1818 With Schnorr to Rome, links with Johann David Passavant, Friedrich Overbeck, Gottfried von Schadow, Peter von Cornelius and Johannes Veith. 1823 Returned to Vienna. From 1829 in Munich. Assisted Schnorr in painting the *Nibelung* Rooms and the Hall of Homeric hymns in the Munich Residence. 1850 Settled in Dessau.

Heinrich Olivier
Dessau 1783 – 1848 Berlin

Brother of Ferdinand and Friedrich. First art training under Carl Wilhelm Kolbe. 1801 Studied philology at Leipzig university. 1804–06 With his brother Ferdinand in Dresden, contact with Caspar David Friedrich there. 1807–10 with Ferdinand in Paris, studied Raphael's works in the Musée Naploéon. 1810 Return to Dessau. 1810–10 First picture in the Nazarene style, *The Last Supper*. 1813 Officer in the German Legion. 1814–15 Stayed with Ferdinand in Vienna. Illustrations for the magazine *Friedensblätter*. Friendship with Dorothea Schlegel. 1815 Produced the gouache *The Sacred Alliance*.

Johann Friedrich Overbeck
Lübeck 1789 – 1869 Rome

1804 First instruction with Joseph Nicolaus Peroux. 1806 Went to Hamburg. Visited Tischbein and Runge. 1806–10 Began studying at Vienna Academy. Friendship with Franz Pforr and acquaintance with Eberhard Wächter, who supported his growing opposition to academic teaching. 1808 Regular meetings with Pforr, Johann Hottinger, Joseph Sutter, Ludwig Vogel and Joseph Wintergerst. 1809 Co-founder of the *Lukasbund*, the seed of the Nazarene movement. 1810 Went to Rome by way of Venice, Bologna and Urbino (Raphael's birthplace) with Pforr and Vogel. 1811 Friendship with Peter von Cornelius. 1813 Conversion. 1816 Frescoes for the Prussian consul Jakob Salomo Bartholdy. 1816–17 Worked with others on the frescoes in the Casa Bartholdy. 1819–27 Frescoes for the Tasso Room in the Casino Massimo. 1827 Paintings with mostly Christian content. 1831, 1855 and 1865 Trips to southern Germany and to Rhineland.

Blinky Palermo
Leipzig 1943 – 1977 Karumba/Maldives

Real name: Peter Schwarze; adoptive surname: Heisterkamp. 1952 Moved to Münster/Westfalen with his adoptive family. 1962 Attended the Werkkunstschule in Münster. 1962–67 Studied at the Düsseldorf Academy of Art under Bruno Goller and Joseph Beuys. Adopted the *nom de guerre* 'Blinky Palermo'. Friendship with Sigmar Polke, Gerhard Richter and Imi Knoebel. Master pupil under Beuys from 1966. 1969 Moved to Mönchengladbach, studio with Ulrich Rückriem. 1970 Visited America with Gerhard Richter. 1972 Studio with Imi Knoebel. 1973 Moved to New York. 1976 Returned to Düsseldorf. Worked in Gerhard Richter's former studio. 1977 Died during a visit to the Maldives.

Hermann Max Pechstein
Eckersbach near Zwickau 1881 – 1955 Berlin

1896–1900 Apprenticeship as painter and decorator in Zwickau. 1900–03 Studied commercial art in Dresden. 1901–02 Worked for Wilhelm Kreis and Otto Gußmann in Dresden. 1902–06 Studied at Dresden Academy. 1903 Studied under Otto Gußmann. 1906 Member of *Die Brücke*. 1907 Spent the summer in Goppeln near Dresden with Ernst Ludwig Kirchner. 1907–08 Went to Italy, studied Classical and Renaissance art there. Returned by way of

Paris, was impressed by Fauvist paintings. Moved to Berlin. 1908 Series of graphic portraits of his friends in *Die Brücke*. 1909 in Moritzburg with Kirchner and Erich Heckel. Member of Berlin Secession. 1910 One of the founders of the Berlin 'New Secession'. Visited Heckel and Schmidt-Rottluff in Dangast. Stayed with Heckel and Kirchner at Moritzburg. Lithographs *Franz and Carneval*. Contact with artists of *Der Blaue Reiter*. 1911 Trip to Italy. Spent the summer in Nidden. Founded the MUIM Institute in Berlin with Kirchner. Series of woodcuts of *Bathers*. 1912 Took part in the exhibition of graphics of *Der Blaue Reiter*. Expelled from the *Brücke*. MUIM Institute closed. 1914 Trip to Palau Islands in the Pacific. 1915–17 Active service. 1917–18 Series of Palau paintings and lithographs. 1918 One of the founders of the 'Works Council on Art' with Emil Nolde, Erich Heckel among others. Organizer of the 'Novembergruppe'. 1921–44 regular stays in Pomerania; trips to Switzerland, Italy (Monterosso, Positano) and to South of France. 1922–37 Taught at Berlin Academy. 1933 Paintings and exhibitions banned. 1944–45 Labour Service in Pomerania and prison. 1945 Return to Berlin. 1945–55 Professorship at Berlin Academy of Fine Arts. 1947 Speech 'Fight against Kitsch' on Berlin radio.

Otto Piene
Laasphe/Westphalia 1928 – lives and works in Groton, Mass./USA

1944–46 Active service, taken prisoner. 1948–49 Attended Blocherer School, Munich. 1949–50 Studied at Academy of Fine Arts, Munich. 1950–53 at Art Academy, Düsseldorf. 1951–64 Teacher at the School of Fashion, Düsseldorf. 1953–57 Studied philosophy at University of Cologne. 1957 First frames from which emerge the light ballet. 1957–60 First evening exhibitions in his studio, from which 'Zero' Group emerges. Friendship with Yves Klein and Piero Manzoni. 1958–61 Publication of 'Zero' catalogue and magazine with Mack. 1959 Took part in 'Vision in Motion–Motion in Vision' exhibition with Jean Tinguely, Daniel Spoerri among others in Antwerp. 1960 First mechanical and programmed sculptures of light-environments, fire paintings. 1961–66 Organization of 'Zero' exhibitions, projects and their production with Mack and Günther Uecker. Met Lucio Fontana. 1964 Lectures at University of Pennsylvania. 1964–65 Light sculptures for the City Opera House in Bonn, since then many commissions for institutions. 1965 Move to New York. 1966 Last cooperative 'Zero' exhibition with Mack and Uecker in Bonn. Dissolution of Group 'Zero'. 1968–71 Resident Fellow at the Center for Advanced Visual Studies at M.I.T. Since then several air projects of large dimensions. 1972 Visiting Professor for Environmental Art at the Department of Architecture of M.I.T. 1974 Director of the Center for Advanced Visual Studies at M.I.T. Since then many group projects with artists, scientists and engineers at M.I.T. 1981, 1982, 1983 and 1986 Director of the SKY ART Conference.

Sigmar Polke
Oels/Silesia 1941 – lives and works in Cologne

1959–60 Apprenticeship as glass painter in Düsseldorf. 1961–67 Studied at Düsseldorf Academy of Art under Gerhard Hoehme and Karl-Otto Götz. 1963 Postulate of 'Capitalistic Realism'. 1970–71 Guest professor at Hamburg Academy of Fine Arts. 1972 Moved to Gaspelhof in Willich/Lower Rhine. 1974 Trip to Pakistan and Afghanistan. 1977 Lecturer at Hamburg Academy of Fine Arts. 1978 Move to Cologne. 1989 Professorship at Hamburg Academy of Fine Arts.

Franz Radziwill
Strohausen near Rodenkirchen/Weser Marshlands 1895 – 1983 Wilhelmshaven

1909–13 Apprenticeship as a mason. 1913–15 Studied architecture in Bremen. Met Otto Modersohn, Heinrich Vogeler, Clara Westhoff-Rilke among others. 1915–19 Soldier and prisoner of war. 1919 Resumed commercial art studies in Bremen. Co-founder of the 'Grüner Regenbogen' group. 1920–23 Berlin, met with Karl Schmidt-Rottluff, Erich Heckel, Max Pechstein, Otto Dix, George Grosz, Franz Lenk, Rudolf Schlichter. 1920 Member of 'Free Secession' in Berlin. 1923 Dangast. 1925 Trip to Holland. 1927 in Otto Dix's studio in Dresden. Impressed by the works of Caspar David Friedrich. 1929 Participation in the 'Neue Sachlichkeit' exhibition in Amsterdam. 1931 member of 'Novembergruppe' in Berlin. 1932 In touring exhibition of 'Die Sieben' in Barmen etc. with Alexander Kanoldt, Franz Lenk, Georg Schrimpf, Hasso von Hugo, Adolf Dietrich and Theo Champion. 1933 Took part in 'Neue deutsche Romantik' exhibition in Hanover. 1933–35 Professorship at the Art Academy in Düsseldorf. 1935 Dismissed from teaching post in Düsseldorf; return to Dangast. 1936–39 Trips to the Canary Islands, Brazil, Northern Africa, Spain, Great Britain and Scandinavia. 1938 Expulsion from the NSDAP. Banning of his exhibitions. 1939–42 and 1944–45 Active service. 1963 Rome. 1972 Gave up painting because of poor eyesight.

Johann Anton Alban Ramboux
Trier 1790 – 1866 Cologne

First artistic training under the Trier drawing teacher Hawich (first name unknown), from 1803 under the painter-monk Jean Henri Gilson (monastic name Abraham) in Florenville. 1807–12 In Paris, in Jacques Louis David's studio. 1813–15 In Trier. 1815 Studied at the Munich Academy of Art, contact with the sculptor brothers Franz and Konrad Eberhard. 1816–22 In Rome, contact with the Nazarenes. Impressed by the work of Joseph Anton Koch, Carl Fohr and Friedrich Overbeck. Started to collect water-colour copies, particularly of 14th to 16th century wall paintings. 1832–42 Second period in Rome, continued collecting. 1822–32 in Trier, where numerous water-colours were produced. From 1830 worked exclusively as a copyist. From 1840 curator of the Wallraf Collection, later the Wallraf-Richartz-Museum. Moved to Cologne, where he worked as a conservator and water-colour copyist. 1854 Pilgrimage to Jerusalem.

Louis Ferdinand von Rayski
Pegau, Saxony 1806 – 1890 Dresden

First instruction in drawing from Traugott Faber. 1821–25 Member of the royal cadet corps in Dresden. Trips to Weimar. 1823–25 Studied at Dresden Academy. 1825–29 Guards officer in Ballenstedt. 1830–31 on estates in Hanover and Silesia. 1831–34 Studied again at the Dresden Academy of Art. 1835 in Paris. 1835–39 Return to Dresden stopping at Trier, Frankfurt, Würzburg, Mainsondheim, Franconia, Munich among other places. 1848–50 in Bieberstein. 1855 Trip to Berlin. 1857 Went to Prague and Marienbad. 1862 Went to the French-speaking part of Switzerland and to England. From 1887 in Dresden.

Johann Christian Reinhart
Hof/Upper Franconia 1761 – 1847 Rome

1779–83 Studied at Leipzig Academy and in Dresden. 1784 Returned to Leipzig. 1785 Start of friendship with Friedrich Schiller. 1786–89 At court of Duke Georg of Sachsen-Meiningen. From 1789 in Rome. Friendship with Asmus Jakob Carstens and Joseph Anton Koch. In the circle around Wilhelm von Humboldt and friendship with art writer Carl Ludwig Fernow. 1800 Painted *Storm Landscape with Two Riders*. Contact with Crown Prince Ludwig of Bavaria, who stayed in Rome on a number of occasions after 1805. 1812 First German Artist's Spring Festival at the Cervara caves under his direction. 1813 Membership of the Accademia di San Luca. Allowance from Ludwig I of Bavaria from 1825.

Alfred Rethel
Diepenbend near Aachen 1816 – 1859 Düsseldorf

Pupil of Johann Baptist Joseph Bastiné in Aachen. 1829–36 Studied at Düsseldorf Academy under Kolbe and Schadow. Influenced by Lessing. 1834 Illustrated the *Rheinischer Sagenkreis*. 1836–47 Continued his education under Philipp Veit in Frankfurt at the Städelsches Kunstinstitut. 1840 Woodcuts for Marbach's edition of the *Nibelungs*. 1844–45 and 1852–53 Trips to Italy. 1847–53 A cycle of frescoes in Town Hall, Aachen. Worked in Düsseldorf or Dresden during winters. 1848 Series of woodcuts *Another Dance of Death* (6 drawings), *Death as Assassin*, *Death as Friend*, Bible illustrations (4 drawings). From 1853 mentally disturbed.

Gerhard Richter
Waltersdorf/Oberlausitz 1932 – lives and works in Cologne, teaches in Düsseldorf.

1949–53 Worked as a commerical and stage painter and in a photographic laboratory. 1951–56 Studied at the Dresden Academy of Art. 1957–60 Freelance artist in Dresden. 1960 Moved to Düsseldorf. 1960–63 Studied at the Düsseldorf Academy of Art under K.O. Götz. 1963 Publication of his 'Bericht über eine Demonstration' (Report on a demonstration). 1967 Visiting professor at the Hamburg College of Fine Art. 1969–69 Worked as art teacher in a grammar school in Geresheim, Düsseldorf. 1971 Visited America with Blinky Palermo. From 1971 professor at the Düsseldorf Academy. 1972 Took part in 'documenta 5' in Kassel. 1974 Publication of his essay

'Farben in 4 Permutationen' (Colours in 4 permutations) and in 1975 'About eight years ago', and a 'statement' in 1976. 1977 Took part in 'documenta 6' in Kassel. 1978 Visiting professor at the Nova Scotia College of Art in Halifax/Canada. 'Statements' appeared in 1980, 1982 and 1989. 1982 Took part in 'documenta 7' in Kassel. 1983 Moved to Cologne. 1987 Exhibited in 'documenta 8' in Kassel, 'documenta 9' in 1993.

Ludwig Richter
Dresden 1803 – 1884 Loschwitz near Dresden

First taught by his father, the draughtsman and engraver Carl August Richter. 1820–21 Visited the south of France. 1823–26 In Rome, where Joseph Anton Koch introduced him to landscape painting. Friendship with Julius Schnorr von Carolsfeld and Heinrich Reinhold. After returning to Dresden taught drawing at the Meißen School of Drawing under Georg Friedrich Kersting. From 1836 professor at the Dresden Academy of Art. From 1840 very active as an illustrator and centre of a circle of illustrators and young artists.

Carl Rottmann
Handschuhsheim near Heidelberg 1797 – 1850 Munich

First instruction from father, the engraver and graphic artist, Friedrich Rottmann, and Johann Christian Xeller. Influenced by Carl Philipp Fohr and Georg August Wallis. 1818 Trip to the Rhine and Mosel with Joseph Wintergerst among others. 1822 Studied at the Munich Academy of Art. Influenced by Joseph Anton Koch's landscape paintings. Trip to the Salzburg region. 1823 Trip to the Inn Valley and to the Ammersee. 1826–27 Trip to Italy; came in contact with the artists gathered around Ludwig I. 1829–30 in Italy and Sicily. 1830–33 Frescoes of 28 views of Italy in the Hofgarten cloisters in Munich. 1834–35 in Greece to prepare a series of Greek landscapes for King Ludwig I. From 1841 royal court painter.

Philipp Otto Runge
Wolgast/Pommern 1777 – 1810 Hamburg

1789 Attended Wolgast school. The headmaster was the theologian and poet Gotthard Ludwig Kosegarten. 1797–98 First lesson with painters Heinrich Joachim Herterich and Gerdt Hardorff the Elder in Hamburg. Studied Ludwig Tieck's novel about an artist 'Franz Sternbald's Wanderungen' and the early Romantic poems of Heinrich Wilhelm Wackenroder. 1799–1801 Studied at the Copenhagen Academy of Art under Jens Juël. 1801 Acquaintance with Caspar David Friedrich and Johann Gottfried Quistorp. 1801–03 Studied at the Dresden Academy of Art; contact with Anton Graff, Ferdinand Hartmann and Tieck who introduced him to Jacob Böhme's mysticism and Novalis's views; visited Goethe in Weimar. Conception of fundamental pictorial ideas, particularly for the 'seasons'. 1802 Acquaintance with Friedrich Schlegel. First meeting with Friedrich August von Klinkowström. Unsuccessful entry for Goethe's Weimar prize. First designs for the *Tageszeiten* (The Times of Day) cycle. 1803 To Ziebingen with Maria Alberti zu Tieck.

Visited Berlin, where he visited August Wilhelm von Schlegel in August. Met Johann Gottlob Fichte and Wilhelm Tischbein. Moved to Hamburg in the winter. 1804 Painting lessons with Hofrat Eich in Hamburg. Studied old German painting. 1805 Group portrait *Wir Drei* (We three) and drawings for 'Ossian'. 1806 Start of correspondence with Goethe on problems of colour theory. In Wolgast and on Rügen island. Wrote the fairy-tales 'Von dem Machandelboom' (About the juniper tree) and 'Von dem Fischer un syner Fru' (About the fisherman and his wife) in Plattdeutsch for the Grimm Brothers' collection. 1807 Moved to Hamburg. 1808 Joseph Görres's commentary on his *Zeiten* (Times) etchings appears. First version of *Morgen* (Morning) produced. 1809 On foot to see Wilhelm Tischbein in Eutin. 1810 Publication of his essay *Farben-Kugel* (Colour-sphere). Outbreak of tuberculosis.

Karl Friedrich Schinkel
Neuruppin 1781 – 1841 Berlin

1798–1800 Trained in Berlin architect Friedrich Gilly's workshop, then at the Building Instruction Establishment in Berlin. First designs and buildings. 1803–05 Visited Italy. Lived in Berlin from 1805. 1807 First architectural paintings and banner pictures. 1811 Member of the Berlin Academy. Visited Dresden, Moscow, Prague, Salzburg. 1815 Appointed Privy Building Councillor. Started his work as a theatrical set-painter (until 1832). Buildings: Palais Prinz August, Neue Wache, Schauspielhaus. 1816 Visited Johann Wolfgang von Goethe in Weimar. 1817 First town plan for Berlin. 1820 Appointed professor of architecture. Member of the Academy of Art senate. Visited Goethe in Jena with sculptors Christian Daniel Rauch and Christian Friedrich Tieck. Buildings: Schloß Tegel, Scharnhorst tomb, St. Nikolai in Magdeburg, Altes Museum. 1824 Second visit to Italy. 1826 Visited France, England and Scotland. 1830 Appointed Privy Senior Building Director. 1838 Appointed Senior Land Building Director. Buildings include: Friedrichs-Werdersche church in Berlin, Arkona/Rügen lighthouse, Kolberg town hall, Palais Prinz Albrecht in Kamenz, Grafschaft Glatz, Glienike bridge.

Oskar Schlemmer
Stuttgart 1888 – 1943 Baden-Baden

1903–05 Apprenticeship in marquetry, Stuttgart. 1906–10 Studied at the Stuttgart Art Academy. Friendship with Willi Baumeister among others and from 1916 with Johannes Itten. 1911 Became acquainted with the art of Paul Cézanne, Cubism and Futurism. Studied Wassily Kandinsky's publication *On the Spiritual in Art*. 1911–12 in Berlin. 1912 Returned to Stuttgart Art Academy. 1914 Met Ernst Ludwig Kirchner. Trip to Amsterdam, London and Paris. 1914–18 Active service. 1918–20 Continued studies at Stuttgart Art Academy. 1920–28 at the Bauhaus in Weimar and Dresden, artistic director of stone sculpture (until 1925); director of mural painting and theatre design. 1925 Moved to Dessau. 1922 Première of *Triadic Ballet* in Stuttgart. 1924 'Man and Figure' is written. 1929–32 Professorship at Breslau. 1930 Met Piet Mondrian and Hans Arp. 1932 *Stairway Scene, Bauhaus Stairway*,

Banister Scene and numerous watercolours. Moved to Berlin. 1933 Dismissal from teaching post. 1934 in Switzerland; visited Ernst Ludwig Kirchner. 1934–37 in Eichberg near Stein am Rhein, South Baden. 1935 Beginning of his friendship with Julius Bissier. Overpainted earlier paintings. 1936 Stayed at Schloß La Sarraz near Lausanne, met Max Ernst and Herbert Read among others. *Heroic Scenes*, *Arabesques* and compositions in oil crayon. 1938 Participated in the Bauhaus exhibition at the Museum of Modern Art and in Read's London exhibition 'Twentieth Century German Art'. Worked in a Stuttgart painter's workshop and from 1940–43 in Dr Herbert's paint laboratory in Wuppertal. 1942 Series of 'Window Paintings' and painted plaster reliefs.

Julius Schnorr von Carolsfeld
Leipzig 1794 – 1872 Dresden

First instruction from his father, the painter Hans Veit Schnorr von Carolsfeld. 1811–17 Studied at the Vienna Academy. Influenced by Joseph Anton Koch, friendship with Friedrich and Ferdinand Olivier and with Friedrich Schlegel, who drew his attention to Old German and Old Dutch painting. 1817 Went to Salzburg with Friedrich Olivier. 1818–27 in Rome, came into contact with the Nazarenes. 1820–26 Painted the Ariosto Room at the Casino Massimo. 1825 Summoned to Munich by Ludwig I. 1826 Trip to Sicily. 1827–46 in Munich, painted the *Nibelung* Rooms in royal residence (until 1867). 1846 Moved to Dresden. Professorship at academy there and director of painting gallery (until 1871).

Walter Hans Georg Scholz
Wolfenbüttel 1890 – 1945 Waldkirch

1908–14 Studied at the Karlsruhe Art Academy under Carl Langhein, Ernst Schurth, Caspar Ritter, Ludwig Dill and Hans Thoma. 1912–14 Pupil of Wilhelm Trübner. Studied with Lovis Corinth in Berlin. 1914 free-lance artist. 1915–18 Military service and stay in a military hospital. 1919 Settled in Grötzingen near Karlsruhe. Member of the KPD (Communist Party of Germany). Co-founder of the 'Gruppe Rih', which was connected with the 'Novembergruppe'. Contacts with George Grosz, John Heartfield and Rudolf Schlichter in Berlin. 1920 Illustrations for *Robinson Crusoe*. Took part in the 'First International Dada Show' in Berlin. 1921 One of the signers of the 'Open Letter to the November Group,' which appeared in *Der Gegner* also signed by Otto Dix, Grosz, Raoul Hausmann and Schlichter. 1923 Teaching assistant under Ernst Würtenberger in the lithography class of the Baden School of Art in Karlsruhe. 1925 Took part in the 'Neue Sachlichkeit' exhibition in Mannheim. 1926–33 Professor at Baden School of Art. 1926 Worked on *Simplicissimus*. 1927 Member of the 'Baden Secession'. 1929 Friendship with sculptor Christoph Voll. 1933 Studio in Haßmersheim. 1935 Moved to Waldkirch. Conversion. 1937 Painted St Urban in Freiburg-Herdern. 1939 Prohibition to practise his profession. 1945 Mayor of Waldkirch.

Georg Franz Xaver Schrimpf
Munich 1889 – 1938 Berlin

1902–12 Apprenticeship and work as pastry-cook in Passau and Munich. 1905–06 Trips to Belgium, France and Holland. 1910 Member of Social Democratic Party. 1913 Several months in Ascona. 1914 Military service, discharged due to illness. 1915 Began to work on magazine *Freie Straße*; woodcuts for *Die Aktion* and *Der Sturm*. 1915–17 Stay in Berlin. Worked as free-lance artist. 1916 Exhibition in *Der Sturm* gallery in Berlin. 1917 Married Maria Uhden. 1918 Moved to Munich. Arrested for stealing Lichnowsky diary. 1919 Four-month membership of Communist Party. Member of the 'Committee of Revolutionary Artists' in Munich. 1920 Member of the Munich 'Der Morgen' group. 1921 Member of the Berlin 'New Secession'. 1922 Italy, contacts with *Valori plastici*, especially Carlo Carrà. 1923 Visited Alexander Kanoldt. 1924–25 Trip to Sicily and Italy. 1925 Trip to Switzerland. Began teaching in Haubinda, Thuringia. Took part in 'Neue Sachlichkeit' exhibition in Mannheim. 1925–26 Member of 'Rote Hilfe'. 1927–32 Taught in Munich. 1929 Lived Lochhausen. Took part in 'Neue Sachlichkeit' exhibition in Amsterdam, and 1929–33, touring exhibition 'Die Neue Romantik'. 1929–38 Taught in Berlin. 1933 in Rome 1933–37 in Berlin-Schöneberg. Moved to Berlin. 1936 Took part in 'Neue romantische Kunst' exhibition in Düsseldorf.

Bernard Schultze
Schneidemühl (Pila)/Poland 1915 – lives and works in Cologne

1934–39 Studied at the Berlin College of Art Education and the Düsseldorf Academy of Art. 1947–68 Frankfurt. 1951 *informel* pictures. Regular stays in Paris. 1952 Co-founder of the Quadriga group of artists. 1954 Three-dimensional elements stuck and melted into the pictorial ground. 1955 Took part in the 'Zen 49' exhibition in Munich. 1956 First relief pictures. 1957 *Tabuskris* and free three-dimensional pictures. Took part in the Gruppe 53 exhibition in Düsseldorf. 1959 and 1964 Took part in 'documenta 2' and '3' in Kassel. 1961 First *Migofs* and tongue collages. 1965 Use of window-display mannequins for free-standing coloured sculptures. 1960 Produced *The big Migof Labyrinth*. Has lived in Cologne since 1968. 1977 Took part in 'documenta 6' in Kassel and the 'Westkunst' (Western art) exhibition in Cologne in 1981.

Moritz von Schwind
Vienna 1804 – 1871 Niederpöcking on the Starnberger See

1818–21 Studied philosophy at University of Vienna. 1821–23 Attended Vienna Academy. Came into contact with Ludwig Schnorr von Carolsfeld and Peter Krafft. Mostly self-educated. Friendship with Olivier brothers, Franz Schubert, Eduard von Bauernfeld, Franz Grillparzer. 1827 Met Peter von Cornelius. 1828–40 in Munich. Trained under Cornelius for a short time. 1832–34 Frescoes in the Tieck Room of Munich royal residence. 1835 Trip to Italy, where he worked on the painting *The Ceremonious Reception of the Bride by Kurt the Knight* based on a ballad by Goethe.

Cartoons for frescoes of scenes from the *Wilkina* saga, the *Lohengrin* saga and Tasso for the Hohenschwangau Castle. 1836 Cartoon for the children's frieze for the Habsburg Room in the festival hall building of the Munich royal residence. 1840–44 in Karlsruhe, where he worked on decorative schemes in the House of Parliament and the Kunsthalle. 1844–47 in Frankfurt; painted *The Contest of Minnesingers in the Wartburg* for the Städelsches Kunstinstitut. From 1847 Professorship at Munich Academy. Woodcuts for *Fliegende Blätter*, and *Münchener Bilderbogen*. Friendship with Carl Spitzweg. 1849 Trip to Thuringia, met archduke of Weimar. 1854–56 Two series of frescoes in the Wartburg. 1857 Trip to England. 1866–67 Mural paintings in the Vienna Opera house.

Kurt Schwitters
Hanover 1887 – 1948 Kirkby/Kendal, England

1908 Studied at Hanover School of Commercial Art. 1909–14 Studied at the Dresden Academy under Carl Bantzer, Gotthard Kühl and Emmanuel Hegenbarth. 1915 Returned to Hanover. 1917–18 technical draughtsman in ironworks. Wrote first poems. 1918 Exhibition in *Der Sturm*, Berlin. 1918–19 Studied architecture at Hanover Institute of Technology. Met Hans Arp and Raoul Hausmann. 1919 Created the first MERZ painting. Publication of *Anna Blume*. 1920 Began working on the first *MERZbau*. 1921 Lecture tour to Prague with Raoul Hausmann, Hannah Höch and Helma Schwitters. 1922 Took part in the 'Dada' convention in Weimar. 1922–23 Participated in 'Holland-Dada Campaign' with Theo and Nelly van Doesburg and Vilmos Huszár. Since 1923 editor of the *MERZ* journal. Publication of *August Bolte*. 1934 *The Fairy Tales of Paradise* are created with Käte Steinitz; *Nasci* with El Lissitzky (*MERZ 8/9*). 1927 Co-founder of the group 'die abstrakten hannover' and of 'the circle of new advertising designers'. 1928 Trip to Italy. 1929 Participated in 'Abstract and Surrealist Painting and Sculpture' exhibition in Zurich. Spitzbergen, Norway. 1930 Lengthy stays in Norway. Worked on journal *Cercle et Carré* and took part in the exhibition of the same name in Paris. 1931 Trip to Mediterranean. 1932 Member of the group *Abstraction-Creation, art non-figuratif* in Paris. *Original Sonata* appears as the last *MERZ* publication. 1933 and 1934 Lengthy stays in Norway. 1936 Participated in 'Cubism and Abstract Art' and 'Fantastic Art, Dada, Surrealism' exhibitions in New York. 1937 Emigrated to Lysaker near Oslo, Norway. Began working on the second *MERZbau*. 1940 Fled to England. 1941 Internment camp. 1941–45 in London. 1945 Moved to Little Langdale near Ambleside in the Lake District. 1947 worked on the third *MERZbau*.

Johann Nepomuk Strixner
Altötting 1782 – 1855 Munich

First instruction in drawing from sculptor Eichhorn. 1799 Pupil of Jakob Dorner for copperplate work, then of Christian von Mannlich. 1804 Commissioned by Mannlich to engrave the former's copies of Raphael for book on works of Raphael. 1807–08 Pen lithographs for Alois Senefelder's (q.v.)

Emperor Maximilian's prayer book with Dürer's marginal drawings. 1810–16 With Ferdinand Piloty the Elder, edition of *Les Oeuvres Lithographiques* with reproductions of old master drawings from the royal collection. 1815–17 Co-editor of *Königliche Baierische Gemälde-Saals zu München und Schleißheim.* 1820 Invited to Stuttgart by Sulpiz Boisserée, copied the collection *Galeriewerk altdeutscher Gemälde* for him. From 1836 in Munich to complete his work for Boisserée. Subsequent co-edition of the publication *Pinakothek in München*, published by Cotta.

Hans Thoma
Bernau 1839 – 1924 Karlsruhe

1853–54 Apprenticeship as lithographer and painter in Basel. 1855 Trained as clockmaker. 1855 Return to Bernau. 1859–66 Studied at the Karlsruhe Academy of Art under Ludwig des Coudres, Wilhelm Schirmer and Hans Canon. 1867 Düsseldorf; contacts at Art Academy. Friendship with Otto Scholderer. 1868 Trip to Paris, met Gustave Courbet there; afterwards in Bernau, Säckingen and Karlsruhe. 1870–73 and 1875/76 in Munich. Met Arnold Böcklin, Wilhelm Leibl, Carl Schuch and Wilhelm Trübner. 1874 Trip to Italy with Albert Lang. Met Hans von Marées and Adolf von Hildebrand; in Rome with Emil Lugo. 1874–99 Frankfurt. 1879–82 Trips to England, Italy and Bayreuth. 1884 Met Conrad Fiedler, Florence. 1887 Visited Hildebrand and Marées. 1892 Venice. 1897 Trip to Italy and 1898 Trip to Holland. 1899 Director of the Karlsruhe Kunsthalle (until 1919) and professor at the Art Academy there. 1899–1924 Lived in Karlsruhe. 1901 Founded the Majolica factory in Karlsruhe. 1904 and 1905 Trips to Switzerland.

Günther Uecker
Wendorf/Mecklenburg 1930 – lives, teaches and works in Düsseldorf

1949 Apprenticeship as a painter and advertising designer. 1949–53 Studied at the Professional School for Applied Art in Wismar and then at the Academy in Berlin-Weißensee. 1952 Took an interest in Zen-Buddhism. 1955–58 Studied at the Art Academy in Düsseldorf under Otto Pankok. 1955–57 structural paintings, adoption of plastic elements, first nail paintings. 1957 Friendship with Yves Klein, Heinz Mack, Otto Piene and Jean Tinguely. 1958 Participation in 'Das rote Bild' exhibitions from which 'Group Zero' emerged. 1958–59 Research into optical phenomena. 1960 The first revolving structural disks. Participation in 'Monochrome Malerei' exhibitions in Morsbroich and 'Konkrete Kunst' in Zurich. 1961 First light plantation; first light film. Joined 'Group Zero'. Participation in 'Nul' exhibition in Amsterdam. 1963 Publication of book *weißstrukturen*. 1966 Studio in New York; cooperation with Willoughby Sharp. Last 'Zero' exhibition with Mack and Piene in Bonn. Dissolution of 'Group Zero'. 1968–82 Publication of the Zero issue of the *Uecker-Zeitung*. 1972 Video project *Schwarzraum-Weißraum*. Since 1976 Professorship at Art Academy, Düsseldorf. Designs for stage sets and sketches for costumes for *Parsifal* together with Götz Friedrich; 1979 costumes for Richard Wagner's *Lohengrin* in Bayreuth with

Friedrich. Publication of his writings. 1983 Manifesto 'Art cannot save man …' 1986 Series *The Endangerment of Man by Man* and *Paintings after Chernobyl*. 1987 Sit-in with students at the Centre for Nuclear Research at Max Planck Institute in Frankfurt. 1992 Sit-in with students at Finnish-Russian border Loma Kitsi. Since 1971 Numerous trips to Latin America to study Indian cultures (1971), Africa (1973), Asia (1974), the Sahara (1981), the Navajo reservations in the USA and Russia, Siberia, Mongolia and China as well as Japan (1984), and Cambodia to study the Khmer culture (1993).

Heinrich Vogeler
Bremen 1872 – 1942 near Karaganda/Kazakhstan

1890–93 Studied at the Düsseldorf Academy of Art. 1892 Visisted Holland, Belgium and Italy. 1893 Paris. 1894 Moved to Worpswede. 1895 Bought the Barkenhoff. 1897 Dresden. 1898 Visited Florence, where he met Rainer Maria Rilke. 1899 Munich for an extended period, worked on the *Insel* magazine. 1901 Visited Bruges, Amsterdam, Paris, Italy and Ceylon. 1909 Founded the Worpswede Workshop for interior design and furniture. 1909 Visited England to study workers' housing estates. 1911–1913 Several visits to Paris, Switzerland and Berlin. 1914–18 War service. 1918 Member of the first Bremen workers' and soldiers' council. People's commissars met at Barkenhoff. 1919 Period under arrest. Agitprop writing and lectures for the Communist society. Foundation of the Barkenhoff workers' commune. 1923. After the collapse of the commune, handed the Barkenhoff over to the *Rote Hilfe* movement. Visited Moscow. 1926–27 Second visit to the Soviet Union. 1928 Founder-member of the Association of German Revoluntionary Fine Artists. 1929 Draughtsman in an architect's office. 1930–31 Final stay in Worpswede, then permanently in the Soviet Union. Worked on rural building projects.

Rudolf Friedrich Wasmann
Hamburg 1805 – 1886 Merano

First training under Hermann Wilhelm Soltau in Hamburg. 1824–28 Studied at the Dresden Academy of Art under Gustav Heinrich Naeke. 1829 Continued his studies at the Munich Academy of Art under Peter von Cornelius, Joseph Schlottauer and Heinrich Hess. Friendship with Victor Emil Janssen and Julius Oldach. 1830 Moved to Obermais near Merano. 1832–35 In Rome, contact with Friedrich Overbeck and the Nazarenes, and with Joseph Anton Koch and Bertel Thorvaldsen. 1835 Conversion. 1835–39 Back in Munich. 1839–43 In Merano and Bolzano. 1843–46 In Hamburg. Lived in Merano from 1846.

Fritz Winter
Altenbögge near Unna 1905 – 1976 Herrsching/Ammersee

1919 Apprenticeship as electrician. 1926 Worked in mine as fitter. Took an interest in the works of Vincent van Gogh and Paula Modersohn-Becker. 1927–30 Studied at the Bauhaus in Dessau under Josef Albers, Wassily Kandinsky, Oskar Schlemmer and Paul Klee. 1929–32 Stayed with Ernst Ludwig Kirchner in Wildboden near Davos,

Switzerland. 1930 Worked as a free-lance artist in Berlin with Franz Ehrlich and Heinz Loew as the 'Studio Z Group'. Worked in Naum Gabo's studio. 1931 Taught in Halle. 1933–35 in Allach near Munich. 1939–49 Active service and prison camp. 1949 Co-founder of the 'ZEN 49 Group'. 1953 Guest professor, Hamburg. 1955–70 Professor at Kassel Academy of Fine Arts. 1974/75 Established the Fritz Winter House in Ahlen/Westphalia.

Adolf Wissel
Velber near Hanover 1894 – 1973 Velber near Hanover

1911–14 Studied at Hanover School of Arts and Crafts. 1919–22 Trained as scene-painter. 1922–24 Continued to study at the Kassel Academy of Art. Free-lance artist from 1924. Hanover. Produced rural genre scenes and portraits. 1935 Took part in the 'Heroische Kunst' (Heroic art) exhibition in Berlin. 1937–44 Regular showings at the 'Great German Art Exhibitions' in Munich. Hitler bought his picture *Farming Family from Kalenberg*. 1938 Refused offer of professorship as 'artist in war service'.

WOLS
Berlin 1913 – 1951 Champigny-sur-Marne near Paris

Born Alfred Otto Wolfgang Schulze. Training as a violinist. 1931–32 Apprenticeship as a photographer in Genja Jonas's studio in Dresden. 1932 in Berlin; encounter with Laszlo Moholy-Nagy; in Paris in the same year, probably student of Fernand Léger. 1933 First watercolours and drawings based on Paul Klee's art. Contacts with Surrealists. 1933–35 Barcelona. Conscientious objector. Went from Mallorca to Ibiza. Drawings, watercolours and photographs. 1935 In prison in Barcelona for three months. 1936 Paris. 1937 Changed name to WOLS. 1938 Met Max Ernst and Alberto Giacometti. 1939–40 in internment camps in South of France. 1940–42 At Cassis near Marseille. 1942 Fled from Gestapo by going to Dieulefit near Montélimar. Interested in Tao. 1945–51 Return to Paris. Became interested in existentialist philosophy, met Jean-Paul Sartre and Simone de Beauvoir. Oil paintings, watercolours, pen-and-ink drawings and dry-points. 1951 Treatment for alcoholism.

Compiled by Marion Keiner

Chronology

<table>
<tr><td>

POLITICAL HISTORY

1789 Beginning of French Revolution

1792 France declares war on Austria, and Prussia declares war on France
1792–97 First Coalition War
1793 Louis XVI executed
1793–94 Reign of Terror in France
1794 Abolition of slavery in French colonies
1795–99 French Directory
1795 Peace of Basle between France and Prussia, Prussia grants Rhine frontier
1796–97 Napoleon in Northern Italy
1798–99 Napoleon in Egypt
1799–1802 Second Coalition War

1801 Peace of Lunéville between France and Austria, France obtains left bank of Rhine
1803 'Reichsdeputationshauptschluß': Diet of Ratisbon reconstructs Germany; abolition of most ecclesiastical princedoms and imperial cities
1804 Bonaparte crowned as Emperor Napoleon I
1805 Third Coalition War
1805 Battle of Austerlitz; Battle of Trafalgar: Nelson destroys Franco-Spanish fleet off Trafalgar
1806 Rhenish Confederation formed, Napoleon defeats Prussia at Jena and Auerstädt; End of the Holy Roman Empire
1806–7 Fourth Coalition War
1807 Peace of Tilsit; Abolition of slave trade in British Empire; Stein reforms Prussian administration
1809 Fifth Coalition War

1810 Hardenberg continues Stein's reforms in Prussia
1812 Napoleon in Russia
1812–1814 Second War of Independence in USA
1813–15 Alliance Wars against Napoleon
1813 Confederation of the Rhine dissolved
1814 Napoleon abdicates; First Treaty of Paris
1814–15 Congress of Vienna
1815 Napoleon returns to Paris: 'Hundred Days'; Louis XVIII flees; Battle of Waterloo; Napoleon exiled to St Helena
1816 Diet of German Confederation in Frankfurt
1817 Wartburg Festival of German students
1818 Constitutions in Bavaria and Baden
1819 Constitution of Hanover and Württemberg, Acts of Karlsbad

</td><td>

CULTURAL HISTORY

1789 Goethe: 'Torquato Tasso', Blake: 'Songs of Innocence'

1790 Kant: 'Critique of Judgment'
1793 Schiller: 'On the Sublime'
1796 Senefelder invents lithography
1797 Wackenroder: 'Outpourings of the Heart of an Art-Loving Monk'
1798 Tieck: 'Franz Sternbalds Wanderungen' (Franz Sternbald's Travels); Schlegel brothers start publishing the periodical 'Athenäum'
1799 Schleiermacher: 'Sermons, Concerning Religion'; Novalis: 'Die Christenheit oder Europa' (Christianity or Europe); Haydn: 'The Creation'

1800 Schelling: 'Transcendental Idealism'
1803–1805 F. Schlegel: 'Gemäldebeschreibungen aus Paris und den Niederlanden' (Descriptions of paintings from Paris and the Netherlands, published in the periodical 'Europe')
1804 Jean Paul: 'Flegeljahre'
1805 Beethoven: 'Symphony No.3 in E-flat major, op.55 ('Eroica')'
1806–8 Arnim und Brentano: 'Des Knaben Wunderhorn' (Old German Songs)
1807 Fichte: 'Sermons, Adressed to the German Nation'; Hegel: 'Phenomenology of Spirit'; Von der Hagen publishes 'Nibelungenlied'
1808 Goethe: 'Faust', Part I.
1809 Goethe: 'The Elective Affinities'

1810 Goethe: 'Theory of Colours'; Runge: 'Farben-Kugel'; Madame de Staël: 'On Germany'
1811 Goethe: 'Poetry and Truth'; Fichte: 'The Science of Knowledge'; Motte-Fouqué: 'Undine'
1812 Brothers Grimm: 'Kinder- und Hausmärchen' (fairy tales)
1813 Chamisso: 'Peter Schlemihl'
1814 E.T.A. Hoffmann: 'Phantasiestücke in Callots Manier' (Tales of Hoffmann); Beethoven: 'Fidelio'
1816 Goethe: 'Journey to Italy'; Hegel: 'Science of Logic'; Clausewitz: 'Vom Kriege' (On War)
1817 H. Meyer/Goethe: 'Über neudeutsche, religiös-patriotische Kunst' (On new German religious and patriotic art)
1819 Schopenhauer: 'The World as Will and Idea'; Goethe: 'West-Easterly Divan'
1819–1834 J.Grimm: 'Deutsche Grammatik' (German Grammar)

</td><td>

THE VISUAL ARTS

1789 David: 'Lictors Returning to Brutus the Bodies of his Sons'

1792 Hoban: White House, Washington
1793 David: 'Death of Marat'; Canova: 'Cupid and Psyche'
1794 (c.) Abildgaard: 'The Ghost of Culmin appearing to his Mother'
1795–1827 Soane: Bank of England, London
1797 Gérard: 'Cupid and Psyche'
1798 Goya: 'Caprichos'
1799 David: 'Sabine Women'

1800 David: 'Madame Récamier', 'Napoleon Crossing the Alps'
1801 Goya: 'The Naked Maja', 'The Clothed Maja'
1802 Canova: Bust of Napoleon; Gérard: 'Madame Récamier'
1804–1818 Blake: 'Jerusalem', 'Milton'
1807 Canova: 'Pauline Bonaparte as Venus'; David: 'Napoleon Crowning the Empress Josephine'
1808 Ingres: 'Bathing Woman' (The Bather of Valpinçon), Goya: 'Panic'; Gros: 'Napoleon at Eylau'
1808–1816 Goya: 'The Disasters of War'
1809 Constable: 'Malvern Hall'

1811–1817 Rennie: Waterloo Bridge, London
1812 Turner: 'Snowstorm: Hannibal and his Army Crossing the Alps'
1813 Turner: 'Frosty Morning'
1814 Goya: 'Third of May 1808'
1815 Goya: 'Witches' Sabbath'; Canova: 'Three Graces'
1816 Thorvaldsen: 'Hebe'
1817 Constable: 'Flatford Mill'
1818 Eckersberg: 'The Natanson Family'
1819 Ingres: 'Roger Rescuing Angelica'; Géricault: 'The Raft of the Medusa'

</td><td>

GERMAN ART

1790–1 Fuseli: 'The Nightmare'
1793 Hackert: 'View of the English Garden at Caserta'; Dannecker: Bust of Schiller
1794 von Hetsch: 'Cornelia, Mother of the Gracchi'
1795 (c.) Carstens: 'Night with her Children Sleep and Death'
1797 Schadow: 'The Princesses Louise and Friederike' (sculpture)
1798 Carstens: 'The Golden Age' (Cartoon); W.A.W. von Kobell: 'The Ford'

1800 Reinhart: 'Stormy Landscape with Two Men on Horseback'
1804 Koch: 'Heroic Landscape with Rainbow'; Runge: 'Self-Portrait with Wife and Brother' ('We Three'); The brothers Boisserée begin their collection of early German art
1806 Runge: 'The Artist's Parents', 'The Hülsenbeck Children', 'The Times of Day' (engravings, 2nd ed.); the brothers Riepenhausen: illustrations for Tieck's 'Genoveva'
1808 Foundation of the Brotherhood of St Luke ('Nazarenes'); Friedrich: 'The Cross in the Mountains'; Runge: 'Morning' (small version)
1809 Friedrich: 'Landscape with a Rainbow', 'Monk by the Sea', 'Abbey in the Oakwoods'; Overbeck: 'Franz Pforr', 'Self-Portrait'; Pforr: 'The Entry of Emperor Rudolf of Habsburg into Basle'

1810 Emigration of the Brotherhood of St Luke to Rome
1811 Koch: 'Schmadribach Falls'
1812 Kersting: 'Caspar David Friedrich in his Studio'
1815 Schinkel: 'Cathedral on a Hill by the Water', 'A Medieval City on a River'
1816 Städel founds museum and art school in Frankfurt; Schnorr von Carolsfeld: 'The Battle of Lipadusa'; Cornelius, Overbeck, Ph. Veit, W. Schadow begin the frescoes in the Casa Bartholdy in Rome; Klenze: Glyptothek, Munich (until 1830)
1817 Fohr: 'Group-Portrait of the German Artists in the Caffè Greco'; the Nazarenes begin the frescoes in the Casino Massimo (until 1829)
1818 Friedrich: 'Chalk Cliffs on Rügen'
1819 Friedrich: 'Two Men Contemplating the Moon'; Schnorr: 'The Marriage at Cana'

</td></tr>
</table>

POLITICAL HISTORY

1820 'Final Act' of Vienna
1821 Greeks rise against Turks
1822 Greece declares itself independent of Turkey
1825–1848 Ludwig I, King of Bavaria
1825–1855 Nicolas I, Tsar of Russia
1825 Revolt in Russian army

1830 Greece declares independence under protectorate of England, Russia and France; Revolution in France; Charles X abdicates; Belgian independence
1830–1848 Louis Philippe in France
1832 Greek National Assembly elects Prince Otto of Bavaria King; 'Hambach Festival' of South German Democrats
1834 Foundation of German 'Zollverein'; Foundation of 'Junges Deutschland' movement by Wienbarg
1835 Censorship of books by 'Junges Deutschland'
1837–1901 Queen Victoria

1842 Festival for the building of Cologne cathedral ('Dombaufest')
1844 Weavers riots in Silesia
1846 'Intellectual Diet of the German People'
1848 Revolution in France: Louis Napoleon comes to power as president of the French Republic; Revolution in Germany: German National Assembly proclaims Fundamental Rights in Frankfurt; Revolution in Italy
1849 German National Assembly passes Constitution but it fails to be granted; Prussia suppresses revolts in Baden and Saxony; German National Assembly dispersed by troops; Emigration of German intellectuals to Switzerland and USA

CULTURAL HISTORY

1821 Weber: 'Der Freischütz'
1824 Beethoven: 'Symphony No.9 in D-Major'
1826 Eichendorff: 'Memoirs of a Good-for-Nothing'
1827 Grabbe: 'Scherz, Satire, Ironie und tiefere Bedeutung' (Joke, satire, irony and deeper meaning); Schubert: 'Winterreise'
1829 Grimm: 'Die deutschen Heldensagen' (German Heroic legends); Goethe: 'Wilhelm Meister's travels'

1831 Carus: 'Vorlesungen über die Psychologie' (Lectures on psychology)
1832 Goethe: 'Faust', Part 2; Boisserée: 'Geschichte und Beschreibung des Kölner Doms' (A history and description of Cologne cathedral)
1835 Büchner: 'Danton's Death'
1838 Schumann: 'Kinderszenen' (piano pieces); Schwab: 'Gods and Heroes. Myths and epics of ancient Greece'
1839 Invention of daguerreotype; B.v. Arnim: 'Die Günderode – Correspondence of Fräulein Günderrode and Bettine von Arnim'
1839–1847 Ranke: 'Deutsche Geschichte' (German History)

1841 Hoffmann von Fallersleben: 'Deutschlandlied' (German National Anthem)
1843 Kierkegaard: 'Either-Or'; Wagner: 'The Flying Dutchman' (opera)
1844 Heine: 'Deutschland, ein Wintermärchen' (Germany, A Winter's Tale)
1845 Wagner: 'Tannhäuser' (opera); Poe: 'The Raven'
1847 Berlioz: 'La Damnation de Faust'; Hoffmann: 'Struwwelpeter'; Eichendorff: 'Über die ethische und religiöse Bedeutung der neueren romantischen Poesie in Deutschland' (On the ethical and religious meaning of the new romantic poetry in Germany)
1848 Marx and Engels: 'Communist Manifesto'; Grimm: 'Geschichte der deutschen Sprache' (History of the German language)
1849 Richard Wagner: 'Art and Revolution'

THE VISUAL ARTS

1820 Ingres: 'Christ Giving the Keys of Heaven to Peter'
1821 Constable: 'Haywain'
1822 Delacroix: 'Dante and Virgil in Hell'; Blake: illustrations for Dante's 'Divine Comedy'
1823 Delacroix: 'The Massacre at Chios'
1823–1847 Smirke: British Museum, London
1824 Gérard: 'Daphnis and Chloe'
1825 Nash: Buckingham Palace; Marble Arch, London
1826 Corot: Views of Rome, 'The Bridge of Narni'; Constable: 'The Cornfield'
1827 Ingres: 'Apotheosis of Homer'
1828 Delacroix: lithographs for the French translation of Goethe's 'Faust', 'The Death of Sardanapalus'; Corot: 'The Fountain of the French Academy, Rome'
1829 Turner: 'Ulysses Deriding Polyphemus'; Delaroche: 'The Sons of Edward IV'

1831 Thorvaldsen: 'Adonis'; Delacroix: 'Liberty on the Barricades'; Constable: 'Waterloo Bridge'
1832–1838 Wilkins: National Gallery, London
1834 Ingres: 'The Martyrdom of St. Symphorian', Delacroix: 'Women of Algiers'; Købke: 'The North Gate of the Citadel'
1835 Wappers: 'Episode from the Belgian Revolution of 1830'; Turner: 'The Burning of the Houses of Lords and Commons, October 16, 1834'
1838 Turner: 'The Fighting Téméraire'; Delacroix: 'Medea about to Kill her Children'

1840–1852 Barry Pugin: Houses of Parliament, London
1841 Mussini: 'La Musica Sacra'; Gallait: 'The Abdication of Charles V'
1842 Turner: 'Snow Storm – Steam-Boat off a Harbour's Mouth'
1844 Turner: '"Rain, Steam and Speed, The Great Western Railway'
1845 Ford Madox Brown: 'Chaucer at the Court of Edward III'
1848 Foundation of the Pre-Raphaelite Brotherhood in London
1849 Courbet: 'Burial at Ornans', 'The Stonebreakers'

GERMAN ART

1820 Schnorr: 'Annunciation'; Schinkel: 'Castle by a River'; Overbeck: 'Family Portrait'; Cornelius is appointed director of the Düsseldorf Academy
1821 Friedrich: 'Mist in the Elbe valley'
1822 Friedrich: 'Moonrise over the Sea', 'The Lonely Tree', 'Woman at the Window'
1823 Waldmüller: 'Beethoven'
1824 Friedrich: 'Ruin at Eldena', 'Man and Woman Contemplating the Moon'; Catel: 'Schinkel in Naples'
1824–28 Schinkel: Altes Museum, Berlin
1825 Blechen: 'Mountain Gorge in Winter'; Cornelius is appointed director of the Munich Academy
1827 The collection of the Boisserée brothers is bought for the Alte Pinakothek in Munich
1829 Blechen in Italy: 'Italian Monastery Buildings by the Water'

1830 Friedrich: 'Riesengebirge'; dissolution of the Brotherhood of St Luke ('Nazarenes') in Rome; Blechen: 'Waterfalls near Tivoli'; Ph. Veit is appointed director of the Städelsches Kunstinstitut in Frankfurt
1831–42 von Klenze: Walhalla
1832 Friedrich: 'The Great Enclosure near Dresden'
1833 Gärtner: 'The Neue Wache, Unter den Linden'; Preller: 'Odyssey' (murals); Olivier appointed professor of the History of Art at the Munich Academy
1834 Koch: 'Apollo among the Shepherds'; Blechen: 'Iron Rolling Mill, Neustadt-Eberswalde'
1835 Richter: 'Crossing by the Schreckenstein'; Blechen: 'View over Roofs and Gardens'
1839 Spitzweg: 'The Poor Poet'

1840 Overbeck: 'The Triumph of Religion in the Arts'; Menzel: Illustrations for Kugler's 'History of Frederick the Great'
1841 Richter: 'Sainte Geneviève in the Forest'
1842 Achenbach: 'Wreck of the Steam Ship "Präsident"'
1843 Schnorr von Carolsfeld: illustrations for the 'Nibelungenlied'
1845 Menzel: 'The Balcony Room'
1846 Menzel: 'View over the Gardens of Prince Albert's Palace'; von Kaulbach: 'The Destruction of Jerusalem'
1847 Menzel: 'The Berlin-Potsdam Railway'
1848 Menzel: 'The Honouring of the Insurgents Killed in March 1848'
1849 Rethel: 'Another Dance of Death' (woodcuts); Böcklin: 'High Mountains in Thunderstorm'

POLITICAL HISTORY	CULTURAL HISTORY	THE VISUAL ARTS	GERMAN ART
1850 Three-class suffrage in Prussia	1850 Wagner: 'Lohengrin', 'The Artwork of the Future'	1850 Delacroix: 'Lion Hunt'; Millais: 'Christ in the House of His Parents'; Daumier: 'Ratapoil'	1850 Waldmüller: 'Prater Landscape'; Menzel: 'Round Table' at Sanssouci'
1852 Napoleon III proclaimed Emperor	1851 Melville: 'Moby Dick'; Storm: 'Immensee'; J. Grimm: 'Über den Ursprung der Sprache' (On the origin of language); Great Exhibition in London	1851 Paxton: Crystal Palace, London	1851 Rauch: equesterian monument to Frederick the Great
1853–1856 Crimean War		1852 Martin: 'The Great Day of His Wrath'; Millais: 'Ophelia'; Brown: 'Work' (until 1865)	1852 Menzel: 'The Flute Concert'; foundation of the Römisch-Germanisches Nationalmuseum in Mainz and the Germanisches Nationalmuseum in Nuremberg
1854 Constitution of Orange Free State	1851–1853 Ruskin: 'Stones of Venice'		
1855 Crimean War: Sebastopol capitulates to Allies; Turkey surrenders to Russians	1852 Comte: 'The Catechism of Positive Religion'	1854 Hunt: 'The Awakening Conscience', 'The Light of the World'; Courbet: 'The Meeting or "Good Day, Monsieur Courbet"': Rousseau: 'The Edge of the Woods'	1854 Overbeck: 'Assumption' (Altarpiece for Cologne Cathedral); Schwind: 'Singing Contest on the Wartburg'
1856 Peace Congress of Paris: end of Crimean War	1853 Foundation of the 'Gartenlaube' in Leipzig		
1857 British and French occupation of Canton; Irish Republican Brotherhood (Fenians) founded; First world economic crisis	1854 Keller: 'Der Grüne Heinrich'	1855 Courbet: 'The Painter's Studio'; Daumier: 'Battle of the Schools – Idealism and Realism'	1855 Piloty: 'Seni and Wallenstein's Corpse'
	1855 Burkhardt: 'Cicerone'		
	1857 Baudelaire: 'Les Fleurs du Mal'	1856 von Ferstel: Votivkirche in Vienna (until 1879); Wallis: 'The Death of Chatterton'	1856 Menzel: 'Memories of the Théâtre du Gymnase'
1859 Italian War of Independence	1858 Busch: 'Max and Moritz'	1857 Millet: 'The Gleaners'	1858 Richter: 'For the Home' (woodcuts)
	1859 Darwin: 'The Origin of Species by Means of Natural Selection'; Wagner: 'Tristan and Isolde'	1858 Whistler: 'At the Piano'	1859 Menzel: 'Student Torchlight Procession'; Böcklin: 'Pan in the Reeds'; von Steinle: 'The Watchman'
1860 England and France occupy Peking	1860 Burkhardt: 'Civilisation of the Renaissance in Italy'	1860 Ingres: 'The Turkish Bath'	1860 Schwind: 'The Morning Hour'; Lenbach: 'Shepherd Boy'; Thoma: 'Black Forest Stream'
1861 Emancipation of Russian serfs; Foundation of German Progressive Party	1861 Dostojevsky: 'The House of the Dead'	1862 Millet: 'The Man with the Hoe'; Daumier: 'The Third-Class Carriage'	1861 Feuerbach: 'Nana'
1861–1865 Civil War in USA	1862 Hebbel: 'The Nibelungs'	1863 Doré: illustrations for Cervantes's 'Don Quixote'; Manet: 'Le Déjeuner sur l'Herbe', Whistler: 'Symphony in White'	1863 Thoma: 'Waterfall at St. Blasien'; Marées: 'Self-Portrait with the painter Lenbach'
1863 Foundation of German Workers' Association	1864 Bruckner: 'Mass No.1 in D-Minor'		
1864 International Workers' Association founded in London by Karl Marx	1864–1869 Tolstoi: 'War and Peace'	1864 Corot: 'Memory of Mortefontaine'; Rossetti: 'Beata Beatrix'	1864 Böcklin: 'Villa by the Sea'
1864 Prussian-Danish War	1865 Carroll: 'Alice in Wonderland'		
1865 Abolition of slavery in USA; Foundation of Ku-Klux-Klan in USA	1866 Haeckel: 'Generelle Morphologie der Organismen' (General Morphology); Dostojevsky: 'Crime and Punishment'; Smetana: 'The Bartered Bride'	1865 Doré: illustrations for the Bible; Manet: 'Olympia'	1866 Feuerbach: 'Medea'; Richter: 'Our Daily Bread' (woodcuts)
1866 Prussian-German Confederation War; Peace treaty in Prague; North German Confederation formed with Bismarck as first Chancellor	1867 Marx: 'Capital'; Gautier, Verlaine, Baudelaire found 'Les Parnassiens' ('L'art pour l'art'); Ibsen: 'Peer Gynt'	1866 Courbet: 'Covert of Roe-Deer by the Stream of Plaisir-Fontaine, Doubs'; Manet: 'The Piper'; Monet: 'St Germain l'Auxerrois'	1868 Lenbach: 'The Alhambra in Granada'
1867 British North America Act establishes Dominion of Canada	1868 Dostojevsky: 'The Idiot'	1868 Manet: 'Portrait of Zola'; Moreau: 'Prometheus'; Daumier: 'Don Quixote'	
1869 German Social Democratic Party founded		1869 Courbet: 'The Lady from Munich"	
1870 Franco-Prussian War; Abdication of Napoleon III; Proclamation of Third Republic in France	1870 Wagner: 'The Valkyrie'; Schliemann begins to excavate Troy	1870 Rossetti: 'Dante's Dream"; Degas: 'Musicians in the Orchestra"	1870 Thoma: 'Laufenburg'
1871 William I proclaimed German Emperor; Paris Commune	1871 Darwin: 'The Descent of Man'; Nietzsche: 'The Birth of Tragedy'; Dostojevsky: 'The Demons'; Verdi: 'Aida'	1871–81 Waterhouse: Natural History Museum, London	1871 Feuerbach: 'Iphigenia'; Menzel: 'Departure of King Wilhelm I for the Army on July 31, 1870'
1873 Alliance of three Empires of Germany, Russia and Austria-Hungary; World economic crisis in Europe, America and Australia	1871–2 Eliot: 'Middlemarch'	1873 Degas: 'Portraits in an Office – Cotton Exchange in New Orleans'; Monet: 'Wild Poppies'; Repin: 'Barge-Haulers on the Volga'	1872 Böcklin: 'Self-Portrait with Death the Fiddler'
	1872 Tchaikovsky: 'Symphony No.2'		1873 Marées: 'The Oarsmen'; Spitzweg: 'Village Parson with Pomeranian Dog'; Böcklin: 'The Battle of the Centaurs'
1875 Foundation of German Socialist Workers' Party	1873 Bakunin: 'State and Anarchy'; Brahms: 'Deutsches Requiem' (German Requiem)	1874 First exhibition of Impressionist painting in Paris	
1875–1878 Balkan Crisis	1874 Mussorgsky: 'Pictures of an Exhibition'; Wagner: 'Götterdämmerung'; Verdi: 'Requiem'	1875 (c.) Whistler: 'Nocturne in Blue and Gold: Old Battersea Bridge'	1875 Menzel: 'The Iron Rolling Mill'; Böcklin: 'Triton and Nereid'
1876 Foundation of German Conservative Party	1875 Bizet: 'Carmen'	1876 Renoir: 'Moulin de la Galette'; Moreau: 'The Apparition'; Degas: 'Absinthe', 'Beach Scene'	1877 Leibl: 'The Village Politicians'
1877–1878 Russian-Turkish War	1876 Bayreuth Festspielhaus opened with 'Ring of the Nibelung'	1877 Rodin: 'The Age of Bronze'; Monet: 'Gare Saint-Lazare'	1878 Marées: 'The Ages'
1878 Congress of Berlin with independence of Rumania, Serbia and Montenegro	1877 First tennis tournament in Wimbledon; Ibsen: 'Pillars of Society'; Tchaikovsky: 'Swan Lake'	1878 Renoir: 'Madame Charpentier and her Children'	
1878 German Socialists outlawed	1879 Dostojevsky; 'The Brothers Karamasov'; Tchaikovsky: 'Eugene Onegin' (opera)	1879 Manet: 'The Execution of the Emperor Maximilian'; Puvis de Chavannes: 'Young Girls by the Sea'	
1879 Austro-German Dual Alliance			

POLITICAL HISTORY

1880 Foundation of Socialist Party in France; Boer riots in South Africa
1881 Alexander II of Russia murdered; Persecution of Russian Jews; Renewal of Alliance of the Three Emperors
1885–1887 Bulgarian Crisis with Ferdinand, Prince of Coburg, as Prince of Bulgaria
1887 Reinsurance Treaty between Germany and Russia; Triple Alliance between Britain, Austria and Italy to maintain status quo in Near East
1889 New Japanese constitution

1890 Bismarck dismissed; Cancellation of Reinsurance Treaty between Germany and Russia
1891 Triple Alliance between Germany, Austria-Hungary and Italy renewed for 12 years
1892–1896 Economic crisis in USA
1893 Foundation of Independent Labour Party in Great Britain
1893 Military convention between France and Russia; Franco-Russian commercial treaty; Customs war between Germany and Russia
1894 Trial of Dreyfus in Paris; Commercial treaty between Russia and Germany
1895 Russian-Japanese Commercial Treaty
1898 Foundation of 'Action française'
1898 War between Spain and USA
1899–1902 Boer War in South Africa
1899 First Peace Conference at The Hague

1900–1903 Industrial crisis in Russia
1900 Boxer uprising in China; Proclamation of Commonwealth of Australia
1902 Anglo-Japanese Alliance against Russia
1904–1905 Russian-Japanese War
1904 Entente cordiale between France and Britain; Foundation of the 'Imperial Association against Social Democracy' in Germany
1905 Anglo-Japanese Alliance renewed; Military treaty between Germany and Russia; revolt in St Petersburg; Tsar issues reform programme
1905–1906 First Moroccan crisis
1907 Commonwealth of New Zealand and New Foundland; Second Peace Conference in The Hague
1908 Alliance between Germany, Denmark, Sweden and Russia; Austria annexes Bosnia and Herzegovina

CULTURAL HISTORY

1880 Ibsen: 'Ghosts'
1882 Wagner: 'Parsifal'; Nietzsche: 'The Gay Science'
1883 Dvořák: 'Stabat Mater'; Huysmans: 'L'Art Moderne'; Nietzsche: 'Thus Spoke Zarathustra'
1884 Mahler: 'Songs of a Wayfarer'; Bruckner: 'Symphony No.7'; Invention of linotype by Mergenthaler
1886 Fénéon: 'The Impressionists'; Nietzsche: 'Beyond Good and Evil'

1890 Exhibition of Japanese art in Paris; Foundation of the Société des Beaux-Arts; Wilde: 'The Picture of Dorian Gray'
1891 The Natanson brothers found 'La Revue Blanche'; Strauss: 'Tod und Verklärung'; Wedekind: 'Awakening of Spring'
1892 Hauptmann: 'The Weavers'; Maeterlinck: 'Pelléas and Mélisande'
1894 Beardsley illustrates 'The Yellow Book'; Debussy: 'L'Après-Midi d'un Faune'
1895 Fontane: 'Effi Briest'; Röntgen discovers x-rays
1896 Becquerel discovers radioactivity
1897 Establishment of the Vienna Secession
1898 Discovery of radium and polonium by Curie; Tolstoy: 'What is Art?'

1900 Freud: 'The Interpretation of Dreams'; Simmel: 'Philosophy of Money'; Sibelius: 'Finlandia'
1901 Thomas Mann: 'Buddenbrooks'; Husserl: 'Logical Investigations'; Strindberg: 'The Dance of Death'
1902 Debussy: 'Pelléas and Mélisande'; Schoenberg: 'Verklärte Nacht' (Transfigured Night); Strindberg: 'A Dream Play'
1903 Rilke: 'August Rodin'
1905 Weber: 'The Protestant Ethic and the Spirit of Capitalism'; Einstein: 'Theory of Relativity'; Strauss: 'Salome'
1906 Musil: 'Young Törless'; Reinhardt opens the Kammerspiele in Berlin with Ibsen's 'Ghosts' (stage set by Munch)
1907 Gorky: 'Mother'; Strindberg: 'The Ghost Sonata'
1907–1908 Mahler: 'Song of the Earth'
1908 Kautsky: 'Der Ursprung des Christentums' (The Origin of Christianity); Lasker-Schüler: 'Die Wupper'
1909 Schoenberg: 'George-Lieder' (song cycle); Marinetti: 'Futurist Manifesto'; Rilke: 'Requiem'

THE VISUAL ARTS

1880 Rodin: 'The Thinker'
1882 Manet: 'The Bar at the Folies-Bergère'
1883 Gaudí: Sagrada Familia, Barcelona (until 1926)
1884 Burne-Jones: 'King Cophetua and the Beggar Maid'
1885 van Gogh: 'The Potato Eaters'
1886 Munch: 'The Sick Child'; Rodin: 'The Burghers of Calais'; Seurat: 'A Sunday Afternoon at the Island of La Grande Jatte'
1888 Gauguin: 'Vision after the Sermon – Jacob Wrestling with the Angel'; van Gogh: 'Sunflowers'; Leighton: 'Captive Andromache'; Ensor: 'The Entry of Christ into Brussels in 1889'
1889 Gauguin: 'Self-Portrait with the "Yellow Christ"'; Eiffel Tower completed; Khnopff: 'Memories'

1891 Gauguin: 'Ia Orana Maria (Hail Mary)'; Monet: 'Two Haystacks'; Khnopff: 'I Lock my Door upon Myself'
1892 Gauguin: 'Two Tahitian Women'; Crane: 'The Horses of Neptune'; Sickert: 'Minnie Cunningham at the Old Bedford'
1893 Monet: 'Rouen Cathedral'; Munch: 'The Cry' (first version)
1894–98 Guimard: Castel Béranger, No. 16 Rue La Fontaine, Passy, Paris
1895 Munch: 'Madonna'; Cézanne: 'Still Life with Plaster Cupid'
1896 Sickert: 'Interior of St. Mark's, Venice'
1897 Pissarro: 'Place du Théâtre Français'; Gauguin: 'Where Do We Come From? What Are We? Where Are We Going?'
1897–99 Mackintosh: Glasgow School of Art
1899 Krøyer: 'Summer Evening at the Beach of Skagen'; Ensor: 'Self-Portrait with Masks'
1899–1905 Monet: 'Thames' series

1900 Munch: 'The Dance of Life'; Gwen John: 'Self-Portrait'
1900–01 Horta: 'L'Innovation' department store, Brussels
1902 Munch: 'Ibsen in the Grand Café'
1904 Mackintosh: The Willow Tea-Rooms, Glasgow; Cézanne: 'Montagne Sainte-Victoire' (one of many views)
1905 Picasso: 'Family of Saltimbanques'
1905–7 Gaudí: Casa Battló, Barcelona
1906 Matisse: 'Joie de vivre'
1907 Picasso: 'Les Demoiselles d'Avignon'

GERMAN ART

1880 Cologne Cathedral completed; Böcklin: 'The Island of the Dead'
1881 Thoma: 'Taunus Landscape'; Klinger: 'Paraphrase on the Finding of a Glove' (prints)
1882 Leibl: 'Three Women in Church'
1883 Böcklin: 'The Play of the Waves'
1884–85 Marées: 'The Hesperides II'
1885–87 Klinger: 'The Judgment of Paris'
1887 Thoma: 'Recollection of Orta'

1890 Hodler: 'Night'
1892 Foundation of the 'Münchner Secession'
1893 Stuck: 'Sin'
1896 Corinth: 'Self-Portrait with Skeleton'
1898 Foundation of the 'Berliner Secession'

1901 Kandinsky founds 'Phalanx' in Munich
1902 Opening of the Folkwang-Museum in Hagen; Klinger: 'Beethoven' (sculpture), Slevogt: 'The Singer d'Andrade as Don Juan'; Liebermann: 'The Parrot Keeper'
1904 First exhibition of the 'Deutscher Künstlerbund' in Weimar
1905 Foundation of 'Die Brücke' in Dresden; Kandinsky: 'Riding Couple'
1906 'Jahrhundertausstellung 1775–1875' in the Nationalgalerie in Berlin; first exhibition of 'Die Brücke' in Berlin
1907 Foundation of the 'Deutscher Werkbund' in Munich; Kandinsky: 'Motley Life'; Modersohn-Becker: 'Self-Portrait with Camellia Branch'; Olbrich: Exhibition building and Hochzeitsturm on the Mathildenhöhe, Darmstadt
1908 Foundation of 'Sonderbund'
1909 Foundation of the 'Neue Künstlervereinigung München'; Behrens: AEG Turbine factory, Berlin

POLITICAL HISTORY	CULTURAL HISTORY	THE VISUAL ARTS	GERMAN ART
1911 Second Moroccan crisis	1910 Rilke: 'The Notebook of Malte Lauridis Brigge'; Halley's comet observed	1910 Matisse: 'La Danse'; Vlaminck: 'Still Life – Cubist Forms'; Picasso: 'Girl with a Mandolin "Fanny Tellier"'	1910 Kirchner: 'Self-Portrait with Model'; Nolde: 'Dance around the Golden Calf'; Walden edits the art periodical 'Der Sturm'
1912 First Balkan War; Triple Alliance between Italy, Germany and Austria-Hungary renewed till 1918	1911 Hofmannsthal: 'Everyman'; Heym: 'Der ewige Tag' (The Eternal Day); Schoenberg's 'Harmonielehre';	1910 Boccioni: 'The City Rises'	1911 first exhibition of the 'Blaue Reiter' in Munich; Marc: 'The Large Blue Horses'; 'Blue Horse I'; Kandinsky:
1913 Second Balkan War with Treaty of Bucharest	1911–32 Franz Pfemfert edits periodical 'Die Aktion'	1910–20 Saarinen: Railway Station, Helsinki	'Composition IV'; Barlach: 'The Solitary One' (sculpture)
1914 Assassination of Franz Ferdinand at Sarajevo; Start of World War I.	1912 Weber: 'Religion und Kultur' (Religion and Culture); Sinking of the 'Titanic'; Jung: 'Psychology of the Unconscious. A Study of Transformations and Symbolisms of the Libido'; Strauss: 'Ariadne on Naxos'; Schoenberg: 'Pierrot Lunaire'	1911 Matisse: 'The Red Studio'	1912 Almanac 'Der Blaue Reiter' published in Munich; Marc: 'Tiger'; Dix: 'Self-Portrait with Carnation'; exhibition of Cologne Sonderbund
1915 Conference of Chantilly; First Battle of Ypres; Germans' first use of poison gas		1912 Redon: 'The Birth of Venus'; Picasso: 'Violin and Sheet-Music'; Bonnard: 'The Tuileries Gardens'; De Chirico: 'Place d'Italie'	1913 Dissolution of 'Die Brücke'; foundation of 'Das junge Rheinland' in Bonn; Kandinsky: 'Composition VII';
1916 Battle of Verdun; foundation of 'Spartacus Group' in Berlin		1913 Duchamp: 'Bicycle Wheel'; Picabia: 'Udnie'	Kirchner: 'Five Women on the Street'; first German 'Herbstsalon' (Autumn Salon) in Berlin
1917 Declaration of war on Germany and Austria-Hungary by USA; German Independent Labour Party (USDP) founded; Bolshevik Revolution in Russia	1913 Husserl: 'Phenomenology'; Kafka: 'The Judgment'; Wedekind: 'Lulu'; Thomas Mann: 'Death in Venice'	1914 Severini: 'The Collapse'	1914 Klee, Macke und Moilliet travel to Tunis; Kokoschka: 'The Bride of the Wind'
1918 Treaty of Brest-Litovsk and Bucharest; End of World War I; German Weimar Republic proclaimed	1914 Heinrich Mann: 'Man of Straw'; Trakl: 'Traum und Umnachtung' (poems); Kafka: 'The Trial'; Galeen/Wegener: 'The Golem' (film)	1915 Duchamp: 'Bottlerack', 'Fountain'; Malevich: 'Suprematist Composition'	1915 Grosz: 'The Street'
1919 Versailles Peace Treaty; Foundation of German Communist Party (KPD); Spartacus riots; Karl Liebknecht and Rosa Luxemburg murdered	1915 Benn: 'Gehirne' (Brains)	1916 De Chirico: 'Regret'	1916 first Dada-proclamation in Zürich
	1916 Kafka: 'Metamorphosis'; Becher: 'An Europa' (To Europe)	1917 Carrà: 'The Metaphysical Muse'	1917 'Dada' magazine published in Zürich; Westheim founds 'Das Kunstblatt'; Pechstein: 'Palau-Triptych'; Arp: 'Collage with Squares Arranged According to the Laws of Chance'
	1917 Goll: 'Requiem. Für die Gefallenen Europas' (Requiem. For Europe's Fallen); Foundation of the Malik-Verlag (publishing house); Freud: 'Introductory Lectures on Psychoanalysis'	1918 van Doesburg: 'Composition'; Picabia: 'Bring Me There'	1918 first Dada-evenings in Berlin; foundation of the 'Novembergruppe'
	1918 Bloch: 'Spirit of Utopia'; Spengler: 'Der Untergang des Abendlandes' (The Decline of the West); Thomas Mann: 'Reflections of an Unpolitical Man'		1919 Gropius founds the Bauhaus in Weimar; Schwitters: 'MERZbild 9b. The great I Picture'
	1919 Kafka: 'In the Penal Settlement'; Werfel: 'Der Gerichtstag' (Judgment Day)		
1920 League of Nations founded; Foundation of German National Social Labour Party (NSDAP)	1920 Toller: 'Masse Mensch' (Mass Man); Pinthus, ed.: 'Menschheitsdämmerung' (Twilight of Mankind); Kraus: 'The Last Days of Mankind'; Wiene: 'The Cabinet of Dr. Caligari' (film)	1920 Modigliani: 'Reclining Nude'; Hausmann: 'Evening Toilet'	1920 'First International Dada-Fair' in Berlin; Hausmann: 'Evening Toilet'; Dix: 'The Match Vendor I'; Heartfield: 'Dada Photomontage'; Schlemmer: 'Abstract Figure' (sculpture); Feininger: 'Eichelborn'; Höch: 'Mechanical Garden'
1921 Foundation of Partito Nazionale Fascista (PNF) in Italy	1921 Dingler: 'Physik und Hypothese' (Physics and Hypothesis); Hindemith/ Kokoschka: 'Mörder, Hoffnung der Frauen' (Murderer, Hope of Women); Wittgenstein: 'Tractatus Logico-Philosophicus'; Murnau: 'Nosferatu' (film)	1921 Picasso: 'The Three Musicians'; Mondrian: 'Tableau I'	1922 International Congress of the Constructivists and the Dadaists in Weimar; Ernst: 'The Rendez-vous of Friends'
1922 Mussolini's march on Rome		1922 Picasso: 'Figurative Forms'; Wright: Imperial Hotel, Tokyo; Bourgeois: Rue du Cubisme, Brussels	
1923 Attempted coup by Hitler in Munich; NSDAP and KPD are banned	1922 Joyce: 'Ulysses'; Eliot: 'The Waste Land'; Brecht: 'Drums in the Night', 'Baal'	1923 Monet: 'Water Lilies'; Marie Laurencin: 'Mademoiselle Coco Chanel'	1923 Grosz: 'Ecce Homo' (prints); first issue of 'MERZ'; first issue of 'G-Zeitschrift für elementare Gestaltung'; Corinth: 'Tree by the Walchensee'
1923–1925 French occupy Ruhr district	1923 Lukács: 'History and Class Consciousness'; Rilke: 'Sonnets to Orpheus'	1924 Wright: Freeman House, Los Angeles; Le Corbusier: Studios at Boulogne-sur-Seine; de Koninck: House in Uccle	1924 Bauhaus in Weimar closed; Nolde: 'Mill', 'Sea Woman'; Dix: 'War' (etchings)
1925 Locarno Conference and Treaties	1923–4 Lang: 'The Nibelungs' (film)	1924–27 Spencer: 'The Resurrection, Cookham'	1925 Exhibition 'Neue Sachlichkeit' in Mannheim; Bauhaus reopens in Dessau; Grosz: 'Portrait of the Poet Max Hermann-Neisse', Klee: 'Fish Magic'; Dix: 'Three Prostitutes on the Street'
1926 Foundation of 'Hitler-Youth'	1924 Thomas Mann: 'The Magic Mountain'	1925 Braque: 'Still-Life with Red Tablecloth'; Miró: 'The Harlequin's Carnival'	
1929 World economic crisis ('Black Friday'); Reichstag repeals Protection of Republic Act	1925 Pabst: 'The Joyless Street' (film); Eisenstein: 'Battleship Potemkin' (film); Berg: 'Wozzeck'	1926 O'Keefe: 'Street, New York, No.1'	1926 'Internationale Kunstausstellung' in Dresden; Grosz: 'Pillars of Society'; Dix: 'Portrait of Sylvia von Harden'
	1925–1927 Hitler: 'Mein Kampf'	1927 Davis: 'Egg-Beater No.2'; Aalto: Library in Viipuri, Finland; Hopper: 'Automat'	1927 El Lissitzky completes 'Abstract Cabinet', Beckmann: 'Self-Portrait in Tuxedo'; Schad: 'Self-Portrait with Model'
	1926 Lang: 'Metropolis' (film); Murnau: 'Faust' (film)	1928 Horta: Palais des Beaux-Arts, Brussels; De Chirico: 'Le Bal' (stage set); Demuth: 'Love, Love, Love: Homage to Gertrude Stein'	1928 Foundation of the 'Assoziation revolutionärer, bildender Künstler'; Dix: 'City-Tryptich'
	1927 Heidegger: 'Being and Time'; Hesse: 'Steppenwolf'; Brecht/Weill: 'Rise and Fall of the City of Mahagonny'	1929 Moore: 'Reclining Figure'; Aalto: 'Stool 60'; Dufy: 'The Harvest'	1929 van der Rohe: German Pavilion at the International Exhibition, Barcelona
	1928 Benjamin: 'One-Way Street'; Brecht/ Weill: 'Three-Penny Opera'	1929–1942 Vigeland: 'Monolith', Oslo	
	1929 Cassirer: 'Philosophy of Symbolic Forms'; Remarque: 'All Quiet on the		

POLITICAL HISTORY

1930 End of German Weimar Republic
1933 Hitler assumes dictatorial power in Germany
1934 German-Polish non-aggression pact for ten years
1935 Anglo-German Naval Agreement; Nuremberg laws; reintroduction of conscription in Germany
1936–1993 Spanish Civil War
1937 'Hoßbach' Act
1938 German occupation of Austria; violent pogroms in Germany ('Reichskristallnacht')
1939 German invasion of Poland; German alliance with USSR to partition Poland; USSR invades Finland; Outbreak of World War II

1940 Alliance between Germany, Italy and Japan; Finland signs armistice with USSR; Germany occupies Norway and Denmark; Battle of Britain; London Blitz; Raid on Coventry
1941 Germany and Italy declare war on USA; Japanese attack on Pearl Harbour
1942–1943 Battle of Stalingrad
1944 Unsuccessful attempt to assassinate Hitler in 'Wolfsschanze' (Wolf's Lair)
1945 German armed forces surrender; Hitler's suicide; Atomic bomb on Hiroshima and Nagasaki; Japan surrenders; Three-power conference at Potsdam with division of Germany into four occupation zones
1946 Nazi war criminals sentenced at Nuremberg
1947 'Marshall Plan' as European Recovery Programme; Indian Independence Act
1948 German currency reform in Western Occupation Zones; Soviet blockade of West Berlin; Israel proclaimed independent state
1949 Basic Law of Federal German Republic comes into force; German Democratic Republic established; Chinese People's Republic proclaimed

CULTURAL HISTORY

Western Front'; Döblin: 'Alexanderplatz. The Story of Franz Biberkopf'
1930 Fallada: 'Bauern, Bonzen, Bomben' (Peasants, Bosses, Bombs); von Sternberg: 'The Blue Angel' (film)
1930–1943 Musil: 'The Man without Qualities'
1931 Planck: 'Positivismus und die reale Außenwelt' (Positivism and the Real Outside World); Zuckmayer: 'Der Hauptmann von Köpenick' (The Captain of Köpenick)
1932 Popper: 'Logic of Scientific Discovery'; Fallada: 'Little Man, What Now?'; Brecht: 'Saint Joan of the Stockyards'
1938 Jaspers: 'Philosophy of Existence'; Brecht: 'Fear and Misery of the Third Reich'

1940 Chaplin: 'The Great Dictator' (film); Wells: 'Citizen Kane' (film)
1941 Marcuse: 'Reason and Revolution'; Hegel and the Rise of Social Theory'; Brecht: 'Mother Courage and Her Children'
1942 Andres: 'We are Utopia'; Seghers: 'The Seventh Cross'; Eliot: 'Four Quartets'; Camus: 'The Stranger'
1943 Hesse: 'The Glass Bead Game'; Brecht: 'Galileo Galilei'
1944 Seghers: 'Transit'
1945 Broch: 'Death of Virgil'; Popper: 'The Open Society and its Enemies'; Rossellini: 'Rome-Open City' (film)
1945–1949 Sartre: 'Les Chemins de la Liberté: The Age of Reason, The Reprieve, Iron in the Soul'
1947 Adorno/Horkheimer: 'Dialectic of Enlightenment'; Borchert: 'The Man Outside'; foundation of 'Gruppe 47'; Sartre: 'Existentialism and Humanism'; Camus: 'The Plague'; Cage: 'Music for Marcel Duchamp'; Auden: 'The Age of Anxiety'; Tennessee Williams: 'A Streetcar Named Desire'; Publication of the diary of Anne Frank
1949 de Beauvoir: 'The Second Sex'; Reed: 'The Third Man' (film); Orwell: '1984'

THE VISUAL ARTS

1931 Dalí: 'The Persistence of Memory'
1932 Marin: 'Brooklyn Bridge'; Hopper: 'Room in New York'
1933 Magritte: 'The Human Condition'
1934 Magritte: 'The Rape'; Lewis: 'Roman Actors'
1935 Dalí: 'Burning Giraffe'; Dufy: 'The Sea at Deauville'
1937 Picasso: 'Guernica'; Nash: 'Event on the Downs'
1938 Magritte: 'Time Transfixed'

1940 Delvaux: 'Entrance to the City'
1941 Picasso: 'Dora Maar'
1942 Morandi: 'Still-Life'; Nicholson: 'White Relief'; Grant: 'Portrait of Vanessa Bell'
1943 Pollock: 'Guardians of the Secret'; Mondrian: 'Broadway Boogie-Woogie'; Wright: Guggenheim Museum; New York (also 1956–59)
1944 Bacon: 'Three Studies for Figures at the Base of a Crucifixion'; Delvaux: 'Venus Asleep'
1945 Pollock: 'Totem II'; Dubuffet: 'Mother Goddess'
1945–50 van der Rohe: Farnsworth House, Illinois
1946 Laurens: 'The Siren'; Dalí: 'The Temptation of St. Anthony'
1947–1952 Le Corbusier: 'Unité d'habitation', Marseilles
1948 Rivera: 'A Sunday in Alameda Park' (mural)
1949 Le Corbusier: House for Dr Curuchet, La Plata; Rivera: 'Self-Portrait'; Giacometti: 'Three Figures' Miró: 'Women and Birds in the Moonlight'
1949–1951 Martin/Matthew: Royal Festival Hall, London

GERMAN ART

1931 Schlemmer: 'Group at Banister I'
1932 Bauhaus in Dessau closed down; teaching staff at Folkwang-Schule sacked; Breslau Academy closed down
1933 Artists, whose works are labelled as 'degenerate', begin to emigrate to Spain, France, England, Holland, the USA, the USSR and Switzerland
1936 Ernst: 'The Entire City'
1937 'Degenerate "Art"' exhibition in Munich (and tour)
1937/38 Kollwitz: 'Pietà'
1938 '20th-Century German Art' exhibition in London (and, later, Glasgow)
1939 Baumeister: 'Eidos VI'

1940 Klee: 'To the Neighbour's House'
1941 Beckmann: 'Perseus-Triptych'
1944–5 Wols: 'Painting'
1946 'Allgemeine Deutsche Kunstausstellung' (General German art exhibition) in Dresden
1947 'Meister des Bauhauses' (Masters of the Bauhaus) exhibition at the Hochschule der Künste, Berlin
1948 Nay: 'Moroccan Girls'; Ernst: 'Capricorn' (sculpture)
1949 Foundation of the artists' group 'ZEN'; Beckmann: 'The Prodigal Son'

POLITICAL HISTORY	CULTURAL HISTORY	THE VISUAL ARTS	GERMAN ART
1950 India proclaimed republic	1950 Buber: 'Paths to Utopia'; Cocteau: 'Orpheus' (film)	1950 Léger: 'The Constructors'; Pollock: 'Seven'; Calder: 'Performing Seal'; Newman: 'Eve'; Magritte: 'The Survivor'	1950 'Das Menschenbild in unserer Zeit' (The Image of Man in Our Time) exhibition in Darmstadt
1950–53 Korean War	1951 Adorno: 'Minima Moralia'; Salinger: 'The Catcher in the Rye'; Schoenberg: 'Moses and Aron' (first performance)	1950–53 Le Corbusier: Notre-Dame-du Haut, Ronchamp	1951 Foundation of the Hochschule für Gestaltung in Ulm
1951 Revision of occupation status of Federal Republic of Germany; European Coal and Steel Treaty signed	1952 Andersch: 'Die Kirschen der Freiheit' (The Cherries of Freedom); Hemingway: 'The Old Man and the Sea'; Steinbeck: 'East of Eden'; Henze: 'Boulevard Solitude' (opera); Cage: '4'33'	1951 Picasso: 'Massacre in Korea'; Wright: Price House, Phoenix, Arizona	1952 'Quadriga' exhibition in Frankfurt; Heldt: 'Sunday Afternoon'
1953 Anti-Communist riots in German Democratic Republic; Constitution of Federal People's Republic of Yugoslavia	1953 Böll: 'And Never Said a Word'; Miller: 'The Crucible'	1952 Picasso: 'War and Peace'; Pollock: 'Blue Poles'; Hopper: 'Hotel by a Railroad'; Freud: 'Portrait of Francis Bacon'	1953 'Gruppe 53' in Düsseldorf
1954 Paris agreements establish Western European Union and terminate occupation of Western Germany; Algerian crisis; USSR recognizes German Democratic Republic	1954 Frisch: 'I'm not Stiller'; Golding: 'Lord of the Flies'; Sagan: 'Bonjour Tristesse'; Fellini: 'La Strada' (film); Beckett: 'Waiting for Godot'; Tennessee Williams: 'Cat on a Hot Tin Roof'	1953 Bacon: 'Study after Velasquez's Portrait of Pope Innocent X.'; Nicholson: 'Abstract Composition'; Pollock: 'Portrait and a Dream'	1955 'Documenta I' in Cassel
1955 East-European Defence Treaty signed in Warsaw; Sovereignty of Federal Republic of Germany	1955 Marcuse: 'Eros and Civilisation'; Böll: 'The Bread of Those Early Years'; Nabokov: 'Lolita'	1954 Chagall: 'Bridges over the Seine'; Giacometti: 'Woman on a Chair'; Rothko: 'Untitled (Yellow, Orange, Red on Orange)'; Tàpies: 'Yellow Painting'	1956 'A Century of German Art' exhibition at the Tate Gallery, London
1956 Suez Crisis; Anti-Stalinist revolution in Hungary	1956 Bloch: 'Principle of Hope'; Osborne: 'Look Back in Anger'; Dürrenmatt: 'The Visit'; Bergman: 'The Seventh Seal' (film)	1955 Wright: Price Tower, Bartlesville; Rauschenberg: 'The Bed'; Calder: 'All Red'; Twombly: 'Free Wheeler'	1957 'German Art of the 20th Century' exhibition at the Museum of Modern Art, New York; 'Verkannte Kunst' (Unrecognised Art) exhibition in Recklinghausen; the artists' group 'Spur' in Munich
1958 Establishment of the European Economic Community (EEC)	1957 Frisch: 'Homo Faber'; Enzensberger: 'Verteidigung der Wölfe' (Defence of the Wolves); Stockhausen: 'Klavierstück XI' (Piano Piece XI); Beckett: 'Endgame'; Bergman: 'Wild Strawberries' (film); Barthes: 'Mythologies'	1956 Aalto: Vuoksenniska (Church) near Imatra; van der Rohe: Seagram House, New York; Picasso: 'Nude in a Rocking-Chair'	1958 'Dada – Dokumente einer Bewegung' (Dada – Documents of a Movement) exhibition in Düsseldorf; first 'Zero' magazine; Eiermann and Ruf: German Pavilion at the Expo' Brussels; Uhlmann: 'Large Fetish' (sculpture)
1959 European Monetary Union	1958 Hauser: 'Philosophy of Art'; Capote: 'Breakfast at Tiffany's'; Pasternak: 'Doctor Zhivago'	1957 Giacometti: 'Annette Seated'; Le Corbusier: Monastery La Tourette; Bacon: 'Study for Portrait of Van Gogh II'; Hamilton: 'Just What Is It That Makes Today's Homes so Different, so Appealing?'	1959 'German Art of Today' exhibition at the Smithsonian Institute, Washington; 'Documenta II'
	1959 Grass: 'The Tin Drum'; Sartre: 'No Exit'; Fellini: 'La Dolce Vita' (film)	1958 Chagall: Stained-glass windows for Metz Cathedral; Saarinen: John-F.-Kennedy Airport, New York; Johns: 'Target'	
		1959 Hrdlicka: 'Crucified Torso'; Kaprow: '18 Happenings in 6 Parts'; Rauschenberg: 'Canyon'; Rothko: 'Untitled'	
1961 German Democratic Republic seals off Berlin border: Berlin Wall; Establishment of Organization for Economic Co-operation and Development	1960 Gadamer: 'Truth and Method'; Resnais: 'Last Year in Marienbad' (film)	1960 Klein: 'Sponge-Relief, RE 39 (Blue)'; de Kooning: 'Door to the River'	1960 Exhibition of 'German Art after 1945' in Rio de Janeiro; Klapheck: 'The Ancestors'
1962 Cuban crisis	1961 Frisch: 'Andorra'	1961 Blake: 'Elvis-Wall'; Hockney: 'The Cha-Cha that was Danced in the Early Hours of 24th March'; Stella: 'New Madrid'	1961 Bauhaus Archive opened in Darmstadt
1963 President Kennedy assassinated	1962 Habermas: 'The Structural Transformation of the Public Sphere'; Dürrenmatt: 'The Physicists'; Esslin: 'Theatre of the Absurd'; Albee: 'Who's Afraid of Virginia Woolf?'	1962 Lichtenstein: 'Blam!'; Hepworth: 'Memorial'; Warhol: 'Twenty-Five Colored Marilyns', 'Big Torn Campbell's Soup Can'; Venturi/Rauch: Venturi-House, Pennsylvania; Caro: 'Early One Morning'	1962 Uecker: 'Breathing Volume'
1964 Treaty between German Democratic Republic and USSR; Formation of German National Democratic Party (NPD)	1963 Böll: 'The Clown'; Grass: 'Dog Years'; Hochhuth: 'The Deputy'; Development of the contraceptive pill; Stoppard: 'Rosencrantz and Guildenstern are Dead'	1963 Lichtenstein: 'O.K. Hot Shot'; Warhol: 'Black and White'; Calder: 'Temanor'; Hilton: 'Oi, yoi, yoi'	1963 'Fluxus Fluxorum Fluxus' in Düsseldorf; Albers: 'Homage to the Square: Green Scent'
1965 Middle East crisis	1964 Marcuse: 'The One-Dimensional Man'; Weiss: 'Marat'; Kipphardt: 'In the Matter of J. Robert Oppenheimer'; Kubrick: 'Dr Strangelove' (film)	1964 Rauschenberg: 'Axle'; Bacon: 'Studies for a Self-Portrait'; Moore: 'Atom Piece'; Rauschenberg: 'Quote'; de Kooning: 'Two Women'; Bacon: 'Three Figures in a Room'	1964 Opening of the Lehmbruck Museum in Duisburg; 'Documenta III'
1966 Economic crisis in Federal Republic of Germany; Cultural Revolution in China; Federal German government supports US policy in Vietnam	1966 Jaspers: 'The Future of Germany'; Capote: 'In Cold Blood'; Handke: 'Publikumsbeschimpfung' (Offending the Audience); Foucault: 'The Order of Things'	1965 Dorazio: 'Shock'; Lichtenstein: 'M-Maybe (A Girl's Picture)'; Dubuffet: 'Nunc Stans'	1965 Baselitz: 'Man in the Moon – Franz Pforr', 'The Great Friends'; Klapheck: 'The Logic of Women'; Beuys: 'How to Explain Pictures to a Dead Hare'
1967 Students' unrest in Federal Republic of Germany on state visit of the Shah of Iran; War between Israel, Syria and Jordan	1967 M. and A. Mitscherlich: 'The Inability to Grieve'; Adorno: 'Negative Dialectics'; Derrida: 'Of Grammatology'	1966 Warhol: 'Cow Wallpaper'; Lichtenstein: 'Yellow Sky'; Kosuth: 'Art as Idea'	1966 Bill: 'Black Columns with Triangular Octagonal Sections'
1968 Foundation of an 'Extra-Parliamentary Opposition' (APO) in Federal Republic of Germany; Assassination of Martin Luther King in USA; Prague Spring	1968 Lenz: 'The German Lesson'; Kubrik: '2001: A Space Odyssey' (film); Wolf: 'The Quest for Christa T.'	1967 Warhol: 'Marilyn'; Held: 'Mao'; Hockney: 'A Bigger Splash'; Warhol: 'Big Electric Chair'; Newman: 'Who's Afraid of Red, Yellow and Blue III'	1967 Opening of the Brücke Museum in Berlin
	1969 First manned landing on the moon (USA); Henze: 'Sixth Symphony'; Tarkovsky: 'Andrei Rubljov' (film)		1968 'Documenta IV'
			1969 Baselitz: 'The Forest on its Head'

POLITICAL HISTORY

1973 Soviet-US treaty for the prevention of a nuclear war; military coup in Uruguay
1973–1976 Military coup in Chile by General Perón and Isobel Perón
1973–1974 Watergate Scandal in USA
1974 President Nixon resigns; World Oil crisis; Turkish invasion of Cyprus
1975 Establishment of SELA in Latin America (23 countries); Trial of the Baader-Meinhof Gang begins in Federal Republic of Germany; End of Vietnam War
1978 Anti-nuclear power demonstrations in Federal Republic of Germany; Camp David Agreement with Sadat (Egypt), Begin (Israel) and Carter (USA)
1979 Sandinista government in Nicaragua; Ayatollah Khomeini returns from exile to Iran; Islamic constitution ratified in Iran; Soviet invasion of Afghanistan; SALT II treaty between USA and USSR; first direct elections for European parliament

1980 Military coup in Iran; Establishment of 'The Greens' as a political party in the Federal Republic of Germany; Anti-nuclear power demonstrations in Federal Republic of Germany; Foundation of 'Solidarity' in Poland
1981 Demonstrations against the western runway at Frankfurt airport; Peace movement demonstrations in Bonn; Occupation of Golan Heights by Israel
1982 People's Republic of China ratifies new constitution; Falklands War between Argentina and Great Britain
1986 USSR withdraws troops from Afghanistan; Reactor accident in Chernobyl, USSR
1987 New constitution in Nicaragua
1988 Proclamation of the state of Palestine by PLO with Jerusalem as capital; Independence movements in Baltic states; Constitutional reforms in USSR
1989 Civil riots in Georgia; Ban on Polish 'Solidarity' is lifted; Economic independence of Baltic states with political independence of Lithuania; Independence movements in Slovenia and Serbia; Students' riots in Beijing (Tiananmen Square); Declaration of state of emergency in Beijing; Mass emigration from German Democratic Republic to the West; Fall of Berlin Wall; Overthrow of Rumanian President Ceaucescu; 'The Velvet Revolution' in Czechoslovakia

1990 German Reunification

CULTURAL HISTORY

1971 Adorno: 'Aesthetic Theory'; Weiss: 'Hölderlin'
1972 Plenzdorf: 'Die neuen Leiden des jungen W.' (The New Sufferings of Young W.); Derrida: 'Positions'; Foucault: 'Madness and Society'; Buñuel: 'The Discreet Charm of the Bourgeoisie' (film); Fassbinder: 'The Bitter Tears of Petra von Kant'(film)
1973 Böll: 'The Lost Honour of Katharina Blum'; Struck: 'Klassenliebe' (Classroom Love)
1974 Lyotard: 'Libidinal Economy'; Kristeva: 'Revolution in Poetic Language'; Solzhenitsyn: 'The Gulag Archipelago'; Wenders: 'Alice in the Cities' (film)
1975 Weiss: 'The Aesthetics of Resistance'; Foucault: 'Discipline and Punish'
1976 Handke: 'The Left-Handed Woman'; Wenders: 'Kings of the Road' (film); Wolf: 'A Model Childhood'; Glass: 'Einstein on the Beach' (opera)
1977 Kant: 'Der Aufenthalt' (The Stay)
1978 Biermann: 'Preußischer Ikarus' (Prussian Icarus); Lenz: 'Heimatmuseum' (Museum of Local History); Kluge/Schlöndorff et al.: 'Deutschland im Herbst' (Germany in Autumn) (film); Bausch: 'Kontakthof' (dance theatre); Walser: 'A Fugitive Horse'
1979 Wolf: 'No Place on Earth'; Derrida: 'The Postcard'; Lyotard: 'The Postmodern Condition'

1980 Härtling: 'Grudging Love'; Bausch: 'Bandoneon' (dance theatre); Meinhof: 'Die Würde des Menschen ist antastbar' (The Dignity of Man can be Offended)
1981 Hildesheimer: 'Marbot'; Strauß: 'Couples. Passers-by'; Fassbinder: 'Lili Marleen' (film); Herzog: 'Fitzcarraldo' (film); Stockhausen: 'Donnerstag aus Licht' (Oper)
1982 Schneider; 'The Wall Vaulter'; Wenders: 'Hammett' (film)
1983 Jelinek: 'The Piano Player'; Scandal of the 'Hitler diaries' forgery; Wolf: 'Kassandra'
1984 Allende: 'The House of Spirits'
1985 Süskind: 'Perfume'; Bausch: 'Two Cigarettes in the Dark' (dance theatre)
1986 Biermann: 'Affenfels und Barrikade'; Jamusch: 'Down by Law' (film); Birtwistle: 'The Mask of Orpheus'
1987 Handke: 'Nachmittag eines Schriftstellers' (Afternoon of a Writer); Strauß: 'Niemand anderes' (No one else); Adlon: 'Baghdad Café' (film); Wenders: 'Wings of Desire' (film)
1988 Lyotard: 'The Inhuman, Reflections on Time'; Ransmayer: 'Last World'; Reich: 'Different Trains'
1989 Jelinek: 'Lust'; Handke: 'Versuch über die Müdigkeit' (Essay on Tiredness); Hein: 'The Tango Player'; Hürlimann: 'The Couple'; Kaurismäki: 'The Match Factory Girl' (film)

1990 Wolf: 'What Remains'; Bertolucci:

THE VISUAL ARTS

1968 Moore: 'Three Piece Sculpture: Vertebrae'; Chagall: 'The Large Circus'
1970 Venturi/Rauch: Trubeck and Wislocki Houses, Nantucket, Massachussetts; Rosenquist: 'Horizon Home Sweet Home'
1970–72 Christo: 'Valley Curtain'
1971 Lindner: 'And Eve'
1971–77 Piano/Rogers: Centre Georges Pompidou, Paris
1973 Segal: 'Picasso's Chair'; Reinhardt: 'Black Painting'
1977–1984 Stirling: Staatsgalerie, Stuttgart
1978 Stella: 'Harewa'
1979 Chicago: 'The Dinner Party'

1980 Stella: 'Brazilian Merganser'
1981–86 Koons: 'New Hoover Quadraflex, New Hoover Convertible, New Hoover Dimension 1000'
1982 Basquiat: 'Man from Naples', 'K'
1982–85 Meier: Museum für Kunsthandwerk (Museum of Applied Arts), Frankfurt
1983–86 Naumann: 'Human Nature/Knows Doesn't Know'
1985 James Lee Byars: 'The Book of the 100 Perfects'; Koons: 'Total Equilibrium Ball'
1986 Haring: 'Crack is Wack'
1987 Graham: 'Triangular Solid: Right Angles'
1989 Holzer: 'Truism: Inflammatory Essays, The Living Series, The Survival Series, Under a Rock, Laments'
1989–90 Sherman: 'Memories of Art History' Portraits

GERMAN ART

1970 'Jetzt – Künste in Deutschland' (Now – arts in Germany) exhibition in Cologne
1972 'Documenta V'
1973 'Kunst im politischen Kampf' (Art in the political struggle) exhibition in Hanover; 'Kunst in Deutschland' (Art in Germany) exhibition in Hamburg; Kiefer: 'Parsifal I, II, III, IV'
1974 Caspar David Friedrich exhibition in Hamburg; Kiefer: 'March Heath'
1976 Beuys: 'Tram Stop'
1977 'Tendenzen der zwanziger Jahre' (Tendencies of the 1920s) exhibition in Berlin; 'Documenta VI'
1978 'Deutsche Malerei 1890 – 1918' (German Painting 1890–1918) exhibition in Frankfurt; 'Neue Sachlichkeit' exhibition in London
1979 Beuys exhibition at the Guggenheim Museum, New York; Kirchner retrospective in Berlin (and tour); Max Ernst retrospective in Munich and Berlin

1980 'Die Neuen Wilden' (The New Savages) exhibition in Aachen; 'Heftige Malerei' (Wild Painting) exhibition in Berlin; 'Rundschau Deutschland' (Panorama Germany) exhibition in Munich
1981 'Mühlheimer Freiheit' exhibition in Köln; 'A New Spirit in Painting' exhibition in London; 'Westkunst' exhibition in Cologne; 'Art allemagne aujourd'hui' exhibition in Paris; 'Bildwechsel' exhibition in Berlin
1981–84 Ungers: Deutsches Architekturmuseum, Frankfurt
1982 'Documenta VII'; '12 Künstler aus Deutschland' (12 artists from Germany) exhibition in Basel; Beckmann retrospectives: Frankfurt 1983, Munich, Berlin, St. Louis, Los Angeles 1984/85; Beuys: 'Monuments to the Stag'
1983 Beuys: 'The End of the 20th Century'; Baselitz: 'Supper in Dresden'
1984 'Ursprung und Vision' (Origin and Vision) exhibition of modern German painting in Spain and Mexico; Penck: 'Quo vadis Germania'; Lüpertz: 'Pierrot Lunaire' (sculpture)
1985 Otto Dix exhibition in Brussels; Kurt Schwitters exhibition in New York, London and Hanover; 'German Art in the 20th Century, Painting and Sculpture 1905–1985' exhibition at the Royal Academy in London
1987 'Documenta VIII'
1987-90 Hollein: Museum of Modern Art, Frankfurt

1990 Richter: 'Forest'

Compiled by Michaela Giebelhausen and Nicole Pohl

List of Lenders

Denmark
Department of Prints and Drawings, The
Royal Museum of Fine Arts, Copenhagen

France
Collection Artcurial, Paris

Germany
Fritz-Winter-Haus, Ahlen, Westphalia
Anneliese Ströch, Altenburg
Annegret Janda, Berlin
Céline and Heiner Bastian
Bauhaus-Archiv, Berlin
Berlinische Galerie, Museum für Moderne
Kunst, Photographie und Architektur, Berlin
Hochschule der Künste Berlin,
Hochschulbibliothek
Dieter Brusberg, Berlin
Staatliche Museen zu Berlin Preußischer
Kulturbesitz, Alte Nationalgalerie
Staatliche Museen zu Berlin Preußischer
Kulturbesitz, Kupferstichkabinett
Staatliche Museen zu Berlin Preußischer
Kulturbesitz, Nationalgalerie
Staatliche Museen zu Berlin Preußischer
Kulturbesitz, Neue Nationalgalerie
Staatliche Museen zu Berlin Preußischer
Kulturbesitz, Schinkelmuseum
Kunsthalle, Bremen
Kulturkreis der Deutschen Wirtschaft im
Bundesverband der dt. Industrie e.V., Cologne
Museum Ludwig, Cologne
Sigmar Polke, Cologne
Gerhard Richter, Cologne
Wallraf-Richartz Museum, Cologne
Niederlausitzer Landesmuseum, Cottbus
Anhaltische Gemäldegalerie, Dessau
Staatliche Kunstsammlungen Dresden,
Gemäldegalerie Neue Meister
Staatliche Kunstsammlungen Dresden,
Kupferstichkabinett
Kunstmuseum Düsseldorf im Ehrenhof
Kunstsammlung Nordrhein-Westfalen,
Düsseldorf
Deutsche Bank AG, Frankfurt am Main
Städelsches Kunstinstitut und Städtische
Galerie, Frankfurt am Main
The Federal Republic of Germany
Städtische Kunstsammlungen, Görlitz
Staatliche Galerie Moritzburg, Halle
Hamburger Kunsthalle
Staats-und Universitätsbibliothek, Hamburg
Niedersächsisches Landesmuseum, Hanover
Sprengel Museum, Hanover
Staatliche Kunsthalle Karlsruhe,
Kupferstichkabinett
Staatliche Kunsthalle, Karlsruhe
Kunsthalle zu Kiel
Museum für Kunst und Kulturgeschichte der
Hansestadt, Lübeck
Collection H. Magold
Städtische Kunsthalle, Mannheim
Architekturmuseum, Technische Universität,
Munich
Bayerische Staatsbibliothek, Munich
Bayerische Staatsgemäldesammlungen,
Munich

Bayerische Staatsgemäldesammlungen,
Schack Galerie, Munich
Collection Klüser, Munich
Galerie von Abercron, Munich
Collection, courtesy of Galerie
Gunzenhauser, Munich
Staatliche Antikensammlungen und
Glyptothek, Munich
Staatliche Graphische Sammlung, Munich
Städtische Galerie im Lenbachhaus, Munich
Westfälisches Landesmuseum, Münster
Stiftung Seebüll Ada und Emil Nolde
Museen der Stadt, Regensburg
Collection Froehlich, Stuttgart
Galerie der Stadt Stuttgart
Staatsgalerie Stuttgart
Sammlung Georg Schäfer, Schweinfurt
Kunstsammlungen, Weimar
Von der Heydt-Museum, Wuppertal

Holland
Stedelijk Museum, Amsterdam
Sanders Collection (on loan to the Van
Abbemuseum, Eindhoven)
Museum Boymans-van Beuningen,
Rotterdam

Norway
Nasjonalgalleriet, Oslo

Russia
State Hermitage Museum, St Petersburg

Sweden
Göteborgs Konstmuseum

Switzerland
Aargauer Kunsthaus, Aarau
Kunstmuseum Basel, Kupferstichkabinett
Kunstmuseum Berne
Paul-Klee-Stiftung, Kunstmuseum Berne
Otto-Dix-Stiftung, Vaduz
Musée Jenisch, Vevey
Kunstmuseum Winterthur
Kunsthaus, Zurich

United Kingdom
Scottish National Gallery of Modern Art,
Edinburgh
William Hardie Gallery, Glasgow
Courtesy Anthony d'Offay Gallery, London
Fridart Foundation
National Gallery, London
Royal Academy, London
Tate Gallery, London
Victoria and Albert Museum, London
City of Nottingham Museums; Castle
Museum and Art Gallery
Ashmolean Museum, Oxford

USA
The Detroit Institute of Arts
The Metropolitan Museum of Art, New
York
The Museum of Modern Art, New York
National Gallery of Art, Washington

Family Estate of Oskar Schlemmer

Private Collections

Photographic Credits

Catalogue illustrations

Aargauer Kunsthaus, Aarau, 323 (cat. 124)
Fritz Winter-Haus, Ahlen, 401 (cat. 205)
Stedelijk Museum, Amsterdam, 446
(cat. 265)
Jörg P Anders, Berlin, 96, 222, 223, 224,
227, 230, 231, 248, 249, 253, 317, 327, 345,
405, 408, 409 (cat. 22, 23, 31, 16, 34, 41,
65, 66, 61, 118, 138, 166, 198, 221, 220)
Artcurial, Centre d'Art Plastique
Contemporain, Paris, 352, 353, 354 (cat.
160, 161, 162)
Bauer-Röhl, Ratekau, 98
Hochschule der Künste Berlin, 225 (cat. 32)
Staatliche Museen zu Berlin Preußischer
Kulturbesitz, Berlin, 100, 103, 215, 260,
271 (cat. 11, 84, 113)
Kunstmuseum Bern, 320, 357 (cat. 121,
180)
Joachim Blauel, Artothek München, 99,
101, 104, 226, 262, 263, 339 (cat. 15, 90,
89, 156)
Herbert Boswank, Dresden, 228, 229, 258,
259, 264, 266, 411 (cat 29, 30, 71, 72, 92,
97, 225)
Galerie Brusberg, Berlin, 412 (cat. 218)
Ebbe Carlsson, Göteborg, 234 (cat. 37)
Bernd Choritz, Eichow, 236 (cat. 33)
Wallraf-Richartz Museum, Cologne, 247
(cat.70)
Detroit Institute of Arts, 238 (cat. 46)
Gemäldegalerie Neue Meister, Staatliche
Kunstsammlungen Dresden, 221 (cat 21)
Kuperstichkabinett, Staatliche
Kunstsammlungen Dresden, 410 (cat. 224)
Kunstsammlung Nordrhein-Westfalen,
Düsseldorf, 407 (cat. 199)
Stedelijk Van Abbe Museum, Eindhoven,
447 (cat. 264)
Andrea Felske, Ahlen, 400 (cat. 203)
Mario Gastinger, Munich, 429 (cat. 272)
Städtische Kunstsammlungen, Görlitz, 232
(cat. 36)
Galerie Gunzenhauser, Munich, 367
(cat. 192)
Klaus Göken, Berlin, 270, 272, 330, 368
(cat. 112, 114, 145, 189)
Guignard, CH-Vevet, 322 (cat. 123)
Galerie Henze & Ketterer, Berlin 326,
(cat.137)
Rienhard Hentze, Halle, 318 (cat. 133)
Hamburger Kunsthalle, 245, 406
(cat 77, 202)
Sprengel Museum, Hannover, 360, 361 (cat.
187)
Staatliche Kunsthalle, Karlsruhe, 267
(cat. 95)
Kunsthalle zu Kiel, 331 (cat. 146)
Hermann Kiessling, 443 (cat. 263)
Lauri, Bern, 347 (cat. 164)
National Gallery, London, 220 (cat. 20)
Royal Academy, London, 239 (cat. 49)
Victoria and Albert Museum, London 242
(cat. 48)
Städtische Kusthalle, Mannheim, 216
(cat. 14)

Bayerische Staatgemäldesammlungen,
Munich, 240, 245 (cat. 51)
Städtische Galerie im Lenbachhaus, Munich,
102, 334, 335, 336, 356, 396 (cat. 148, 149,
155, 181, 196)
Staatliche Graphische Sammlung, Munich,
235, 268, 340, 341, 342, 343 (cat. 39, 101,
157)
Stiftung Seebüll Ada und Emil Nolde,
Neukirchen, 329, 328 (cat. 142, 143)
Metropolitan Museum of Art, New York,
344 (cat. 163), 350
Anthony d'Offay Gallery, London, 448
(cat. 267)
Landesmuseum für Kunst und
Kulturgeschichte, Oldenburg, 369 (ex. cat)
J Lathion, Oslo, 233 (cat. 38)
Hans Peterson, Copenhagen, 243 (cat. 57)
Wolfgang Pulfer, Munich, 394, 395
(cat. 197, 195)
Antonia Reeve, Edinburgh, 351, 363, 364,
404 (cat. 158, 183, 185, 200)
Renard, Kiel, 255 (cat. 67)
Dietmar Riemann, Berlin, 416 (cat 215)
Philip Schönborn, Munich, 428 (cat. 270)
Raman Schlemmer, Oggebbio, 348, 349
(cat. 172, 169)
Collection Froehlich, Stuttgart, 442
(cat. 262)
Galerie der Stadt Stuttgart, 366 (cat. 188)
Staatsgalerie Stuttgart, 316, 337 (cat. 120,
153)
Wilkin Spitta, Zeitlarn, 269 (cat. 103)
Otto-Dix-Stiftung, Vaduz, 393 (cat. 193)
R Wakonigg, Münster, 365 (cat. 190)
Elke Walford, Hamburg, 18, 94, 95, 96,
212, 213, 214, 216, 217, 218, 219, 237,
244, 250, 251, 257 (cat 10, 9, 12, 14, 6, 1,
5, 40, 63, 60, 59, 79)
John Webb, London, 362 (cat. 184)
Angelika Weidling, Berlin, 413 (cat. 217)
National Gallery of Art, Washington, 358
(cat. 182)
Kunstsammlungen zu Weimar, 254, 256
(cat. 78)
Kunstmuseum Winterthur, 321 (cat. 122)
Antje Zeis-Loi, Wuppertal, 324 (cat. 135)
Kunsthaus Zurich, 241 (cat. 50)

Text illustrations
Figure references given in italics
Fritz Winter-Haus, Ahlen, 205/10 & 11
Jörg P Anders, Berlin, 117/2, 172/3, 186/1,
189/3 (cat. 16)
Kunstmuseum, Basel, 313/1
Akademie der Künste, Berlin, 159/4
Staatliche Museen zu Berlin Preußischer
Kulturbesitz, Nationalgalerie, Berlin, 78/21,
79/22, 118/3, 141/4, 281/1
Kunstmuseum Bern, 119/4, 134/3, 135/4,
152/6
Musée des Beaux-Arts, Bordeaux, 29/2
Städtisches Museum, Braunschweig, 152/5
Brunzel, Kassel, 172/2
Bruno and E Büher, Schaffhausen, 162/8
Museum Ludwig, Cologne, 112/3
Staatliche Kunstsammlungen Dresden,

Contributors to the Catalogue

Gemäldegalerie Neue Meister, 43/1, 141/3
(cat. 21), 192/1 (cat. 21)

DT. Fotothek Kramer, Dresden, 188/2

Angermuseum, Erfurt, 111/2

Museum Folkswang, Essen, 29/1, 110/1,
176/6

Städelsches Kunstinstitut, Frankfurt, 26/8

Vladimir Fyman, 158/2

Staatliche Galerie Moritzburg, Halle, 175/4

George Platt Lynes, 182/4

Collection of Prince Franz of Bavaria,
Munich, 83/1

Staatsgalerie Moderner Kunst, Munich,
160/5

Hamburger Kunsthalle, 23/4 (cat. 9), 23/5
(cat. 9), 116/1, 140/2, 193/3, 287/2, 288/3,
298/1

Sprengel Museum, Hannover, 199/2

Louis Held, Weimar, 32/3

Museum der Bildenden Künste, Leipzig,
139/1

Hensmanns, Kassel, 172/1

Tate Gallery, London, 59/6

Victoria & Albert Museum, London, 56/3
(cat. 73)

Los Angeles County Museum of Art, 142/5

Roman März, 165/1 & 2, 166/3 & 4, 167/5
& 6, 168/7 & 8

Museum Schloß Moyland, 76/18

Alte Pinokothek, Munich, 67/8

Bayerische Staatsgemäldesammlungen,
Munich, 47/1, 49/3, 51/5

Staatliche Graphische Sammlung, Munich,
58/4 (cat. 42), 55/2 (cat. 91)

Staatsgalerie Moderner Kunst, Munich,
71/14, 73/16, 89/6, 90/8, 204/9

Städtische Galerie im Lenbachhaus, Munich,
113/4

Museum of Modern Art, New York, 203/8

Nottingham City Art Gallery, 22/3 (cat. 51)

Germanisches Nationalmuseum, Nurenberg,
201/5

Allen Memorial Art Museum, Oberlin
College, Ohio, 202/7

Hans Peterson, Copenhagen, 286/1 (cat. 57)

Musée national d'art moderne, Paris, 128/5,
146/8

Paulmann-Jungeblut, 161/6

Staatliche Museen Schloß Heidecksburg,
Rudolstadt, 192/2

Hallen für neue Kunst, Schaffhausen, 161/7

Schäfer Collection, Schweinfurt, 125/3,
292/1

Staatsgalerie Stuttgart, 69/10 (cat. 120)

Etta and Otto Stangl, Munich, 88/5

Österreichische Galerie, Vienna, 133/2

Elke Walford, Hamburg, 59/5, 63/1, 63/2,
63/3, 64/5, 65/6, 66/7, 68/9, 69/11, 70/12,
70/13, 72/15, 74/17, 77/20, 124/2, 157/1,
195/4 (cat. 64), 275/1

Kunstsammlungen, Weimar, 24/6, 24/7

Stiftung Weimarer Klassik, 20/1, 21/2

Galerie Michael Werner, Cologne, 90/7

Von der Heydt-Museum, Wuppertal, 201/6

*All uncredited illustrations are taken from
the publisher's and the authors' archives*

Becker, Dr Lutz, Painter and freelance
curator, lives in London.

Bindman, Professor David, Professor of the
History of Art at University College,
University of London.

Blume, Dr Eugen, Curator at the
Kupferstichkabinett of the Staatliche Museen
zu Berlin.

Butin, Dr Hubertus, Writer and freelance
curator, lives in Bonn.

Börsch-Supan, Professor Dr Helmut,
Curator at the Staatliche Schlösser und
Gärten in Berlin.

Boyd Whyte, Dr Iain, Director of the Centre
for Architectural History and Theory,
University of Edinburgh

Buberl, Dr Brigitte, Curator at the Museum
für Kunst und Kulturgeschichte in
Dortmund.

Busch, Professor Dr Werner, Professor of the
History of Art at the Freie Universität in
Berlin.

Büttner, Professor Dr Frank, Professor of the
History of Art at the University of Kiel.

Calvocoressi, Richard, Keeper at the Scottish
National Gallery of Modern Art in
Edinburgh.

Cardinal, Professor Roger, Professor of
Literary and Visual Studies at Keynes
College, University of Kent.

Feilchenfeldt, Professor Dr Konrad,
Professor of German Philosophy at the
University of Munich.

Frank, Dr Hilmar, Writer, lives in Berlin

Gage, Dr John, Head of the Department of
History of Art at the University of
Cambridge.

Hartley, Keith, Assistant Keeper at the
Scottish National Gallery of Modern Art in
Edinburgh.

Heilmann, Dr Christoph, Chief Curator at
the Neue Pinaktothek, Bayerische
Staatsgemäldesammlungen in Munich.

Herzogenrath, Dr Wulf, Chief Curator at the
Neue Nationalgalerie in Berlin.

Hoberg, Dr Annegret, Curator in charge of
the *Blaue Reiter*, Graphic and Kubin-
Archive Collections at the Städtische Galerie
im Lenbachhaus in Munich.

Hofmann, Professor Dr Werner, formerly
Director of the Hamburger Kunsthalle.

Keisch, Dr Claude, Curator at the Alte
Nationalgalerie in Berlin.

Kuhlmann-Hodick, Dr Petra, Assistant
Curator, Kupferstichkabinett, Staatliche
Kunstsammlungen in Dresden.

Leppien, Dr Helmut, Chief Curator at the
Hamburger Kunsthalle.

März, Dr Roland, Curator at the Alte
Nationalgalerie in Berlin.

Metken, Dr Günter, Freelance writer, lives in
Paris.

Meyric Hughes, Henry, Director of
Exhibitions at the South Bank Centre in
London.

Neidhardt, Dr Hans Joachim, former Chief
Curator of the Gemäldegalerie Neue Meister
in Dresden.

Prange, Dr Regine, Assistant at the
Eberhard-Karl-Universität in Tübingen.

Schmied, Professor Dr Wieland, Director of
the Akademie der Bildenden Künste in
Munich.

Schneider, Dr Angela, Chief Curator at the
Neue Nationalgalerie in Berlin.

Schulz-Hoffmann, Dr Carla, Chief Curator
at the Staatsgalerie Moderner Kunst,
Bayerische Staatsgemäldesammlungen in
Munich.

Schuster, Professor Dr Peter-Klaus, Director
of the Alte Nationalgalerie in Berlin.

Semff, Dr Michael, Curator at the Staatliche
Graphische Sammlung in Munich.

Traeger, Professor Dr Jörg, Professor of the
History of Art at the Institut für
Kunstgeschichte, at the University of
Regensburg.

Vaughan, Professor William, Professor of
the History of Art at Birkbeck College,
University of London.

Vergo, Professor Peter, Professor of the
History of Art at the University of Essex.

Verwiebe, Dr Birgit, Assistant at the Alte
Nationalgalerie in Berlin.

Wesenberg, Dr Angelika, Curator at the Alte
Nationalgalerie in Berlin.

Bibliographical Note:

The literature on German Romanticism, not
to mention that on Symbolism, Modernism
and postwar art, is too large to list even the
most important works. Those readers
interested in further reading are urged to
refer to the works mentioned in the
footnotes of the essays in this volume.